Cisco®
Networking
ALL-IN-ONE

FOR
DUMMIES®

by Edward Tetz

WILEY

John Wiley & Sons, Inc.

Cisco® Networking All-in-One For Dummies®

Published by
John Wiley & Sons, Inc.
111 River Street
Hoboken, NJ 07030-5774

www.wiley.com

Library of Congress Control Number is available from the Publisher.

ISBN 978-0-470-94558-2 (pbk); ISBN 978-1-118-13783-3 (ebk); ISBN 978-1-118-13784-0 (ebk); ISBN 978-1-118-13785-7 (ebk)

Manufactured in the United States of America

10 9 8 7 6 5 4 3 2

WILEY

About the Author

Edward Tetz graduated in 1990 from Saint Lawrence College in Cornwall, Ontario with a degree in business administration. He spent a short time in computer sales and support. In 1994, he added training to his repertoire. Since 2002, Edward has been a computer consultant for a value-added reseller, specializing in enterprise infrastructure in Halifax, Nova Scotia. Ed has continued to increase and improve his knowledge and skills through industry recognized certifications.

Some of the certifications Edward holds include Cisco Certified Network Associate (CCNA), VMware Certified Professional (VCP), A+, ITIL (IT Infrastructure Library) Foundation certificate in IT service management, Microsoft Certified Trainer (MCT), Microsoft Certified Systems Engineer (MCSE), Microsoft Certified Database Administrator (MCDBA), and the Chauncey Group Certified Technical Trainer (CTT). During his work experience, he has supported Apple Macintosh, IBM OS/2, Linux, Novell NetWare, and all Microsoft operating systems from MS-DOS to Windows 2008, as well as hardware from most of the major vendors.

Ed has designed and coauthored with Glen E. Clarke the award nominated *CompTIA A+ Certification All-In-One For Dummies* and has worked on certification titles involving topics, such as Windows and Cisco.

Ed welcomes comments from his readers and can be contacted at ed_tetz@hotmail.com.

Dedication

I want to dedicate this book, with love, to my wife Sharon and my daughters Emily and Mackenzie. They have always shown support in all my endeavors, at a cost of time with them. If I owe anyone my gratitude for having written this book, it is them.

Author's Acknowledgments

I want to thank Katie Mohr, my acquisitions editor, for inviting me to take on this project, and to Katie Feltman for letting her know about me. A great thanks to Katie Mohr and Jean Nelson, project editor, for keeping this book on track, which I am sure was an effort for them. I cannot forget James Russell, development editor; Jennifer Riggs, Teresa Artman, Melba Hopper, Brian Walls, and Virginia Sanders, copy editors; and Dan DiNiccolo, technical editor, for making sense of my words, providing accuracy, and in many cases, making my words sound better then when I originally wrote them.

In addition to the editors, I want to thank the rest of the staff at Wiley Publishing who worked behind the scenes taking care of many of the details that are required to get this book into print, and I am sure that because of their hard work, this book will be a success.

Publisher's Acknowledgments

We're proud of this book; please send us your comments at http://dummies.custhelp.com. For other comments, please contact our Customer Care Department within the U.S. at 877-762-2974, outside the U.S. at 317-572-3993, or fax 317-572-4002.

Some of the people who helped bring this book to market include the following:

Acquisitions and Editorial

Project Editors: Jean Nelson, James H. Russell

Senior Acquisitions Editor: Katie Mohr

Copy Editors: Teresa Artman, Melba Hopper, Jennifer Riggs, Virginia Sanders

Technical Editor: Dan DiNiccolo

Editorial Manager: Kevin Kirschner

Vertical Websites Project Manager: Laura Moss-Hollister

Vertical Websites Project Manager: Jenny Swisher

Supervising Producer: Rich Graves

Vertical Websites Associate Producers: Josh Frank, Marilyn Hummel, Douglas Kuhn, Shawn Patrick

Editorial Assistant: Amanda Graham

Sr. Editorial Assistant: Cherie Case

Cover Photo: © iStockphoto.com / braverabbit

Cartoons: Rich Tennant (www.the5thwave.com)

Composition Services

Project Coordinator: Patrick Redmond

Layout and Graphics: Nikki Gately, Corrie Socolovitch

Proofreader: Evelyn Wellborn

Indexer: Rebecca R. Plunkett

Special Help: Brian Walls, Becky Whitney

Publishing and Editorial for Technology Dummies

    Richard Swadley, Vice President and Executive Group Publisher

    Andy Cummings, Vice President and Publisher

    Mary Bednarek, Executive Acquisitions Director

    Mary C. Corder, Editorial Director

Publishing for Consumer Dummies

    Kathy Nebenhaus, Vice President and Executive Publisher

Composition Services

    Debbie Stailey, Director of Composition Services

Contents at a Glance

Table of Contents

Introduction

Cisco networking devices fill the needs in just about every area of your network. Although many books can help you get your Cisco certification, such as *CCENT Certification All-in-One For Dummies* by Glen E. Clarke, this book is not geared to getting you to pass a Cisco Certification exam. Instead, this book gives you the key information that you need to manage your network of Cisco devices.

About This Book

Cisco Networking All-in-One For Dummies is a practical, hands-on guide to managing your Cisco network devices. Although you can read this entire book from front to back, you do not have to. This book is a reference guide. Each minibook is divided into chapters, and each chapter into sections, each of which contains information about a specific task or feature that you may want to investigate or implement.

Although you can take fastidious notes, create flash cards, and memorize everything in this book, do not feel that you need to. Just keep the book handy as a reference. That way, if you are unsure about a particular topic, you can quickly review this book and get your answer.

Conventions Used in This Book

Conventions make your life easier by making things work in an expected manner. As far as conventions go, I make use of several in this book:

- ✦ *Italics* identifies new terms that I define or to add emphasis.

- ✦ **Bold** highlights keywords in a list, steps in numbered lists, or commands or text that you type.

- ✦ Monofont sets off URLs (such as www.dummies.com) or indicates a command within regular text. Code lines use a similar font, such as the following example:

```
Switch1>enable
Switch1#configure terminal
...
Switch1(config)#end
```

Foolish Assumptions

In writing this book, I had to make a few assumptions about you as a reader:

✦ You are familiar with the operation of a computer and specifically the installing and execution of a terminal emulator program such as `putty`. (Do not worry — if you can launch the program, I will show you how to use it.)

✦ You have Cisco equipment to work with. While you can follow along with the examples I have given in the book, to really get a feel for how things work, it is best to do them yourself.

How This Book Is Organized

As with all the *All-in-One For Dummies* books, chapters are organized into minibooks. The chapters in each minibook are related by a specific theme or topic. For example, Book V contains all wireless-related content needed to work with wireless devices on your network.

The following sections outline what you can find in each minibook.

Book 1: Overview

In this minibook, I cover a mixed bag of information that I think you need to know if you are going to get into working with networks and managing your network. Much of what I discuss here is not specific to Cisco networks, but rather all networks regardless of whose logo is on the front of the hardware. This minibook includes a bit of networking design principles, a bit of number systems, and a bit about the Cisco Internetwork Operating System (IOS).

Book II: Internet Protocols

In Book II, I focus on the most widely used networking protocol in the world, the Transmission Control Protocol/Internet Protocol (TCP/IP) suite. Because this may be the only protocol you ever need to use, I devote an entire mini-book to it. This knowledge helps you when working on any network.

Book III: Switching

Switching and Cisco switches are the focus of Book III. You see the configuration process from powering up the first time out of the box. I then show you how to use the main switching technologies, such as user isolation with virtual local area networks (VLANs) and redundancy with EtherChannel.

Book IV: Routing

Routing data with Cisco routers occupies your time as you work your way through Book IV. In this minibook, you get a view from the initial setup, through basic configuration, static routing, and dynamic routing protocols. By the time you read through this minibook, you can navigate the network routing waters.

Book V: Wireless

Book V gives you all the information you need to know about how to lay out your wireless network. I cover the main wireless technologies in the market and show you how to secure a wireless network. I also introduce the major classes of Cisco wireless devices.

Book VI: Security

The security information in Book VI lets you into "the know" on several Cisco-related security items that cross the different hardware platforms in the Cisco product line. After reading this minibook, you are aware of what risks you may face on your network and the common ways you can reduce them.

Icons Used in This Book

To make your experience with the book easier, I use various icons in the margins of the book to indicate particular points of interest.

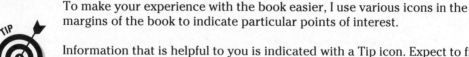

Information that is helpful to you is indicated with a Tip icon. Expect to find shortcuts and timesavers here.

The Remember icon is a friendly reminder for something that you want to make sure to keep in mind. This icon features information that may be useful to remember on the job.

Information that could cause problems to you or to the network is indicated with a Warning icon. If you see a Warning icon, make sure you read it. The network you save may be your own.

Sometimes I feel obligated to give you some technical information that may be above and beyond what you really need to know. I have included it because some people may feel that the background or in-depth point may crystallize an idea.

Where to Go from Here

Look over the Table of Contents or the index, and find something that catches your attention or a topic that you think can help you solve a problem. You can also just keep turning pages and start reading at Book I, Chapter 1.

After you spend some time using your fancy Cisco knowledge, you may be interested in certification. You may be interested in pursuing one of several Cisco certifications; if so, this book gives you a good start. However, to get certified, you need to take an exam. The certifications that you may be interested in include

✦ **Cisco Certified Entry Networking Technician (CCENT):** Validates your skills to manage — from installation to troubleshooting — a small branch network in all aspects. CCENT is the type of position that would be occupied by someone who is new to the world of networking and is the first step toward getting the CCNA certification. Many books can help you pass your exam, including *CCENT Certification All-in-One For Dummies* by Glen E. Clarke.

✦ **Cisco Certified Network Associate (CCNA):** Validates your ability to manage most aspects of an Enterprise network, including features like Wide Area Network (WAN) connections, routing protocols, security, and advanced troubleshooting. If you are interested in pursuing this topic, a good place to start is *CCNA Certification All-in-One For Dummies* by Silviu Angelescu.

✦ **Cisco Certified Design Associate (CCDA):** Validates your knowledge surrounding Cisco Enterprise networks and your ability to plan a converged network including routing and switching infrastructures; WAN and broadband access for organizations; and design around security, voice, and wireless networks.

Book I

Overview

The 5th Wave — By Rich Tennant

"I didn't know they made skins for mainframes."

Contents at a Glance

Chapter 1: Looking at the Cisco Network World

In This Chapter

✔ Meeting the OSI model (it does not bite . . . hard)

✔ Working with switches, routers, and firewalls

✔ Going wireless

✔ Getting your network voice

✔ Checking out the Cisco product lines

*I*f you are reading this book, you likely either have a network that is made up of Cisco networking products or you want to introduce the Cisco network products into your network. Although this book focuses its attention on Cisco products, you do not have to have Cisco network devices on your network to receive a benefit from reading this book. Although you examine many features that are specific to Cisco products, you also gain a wide range of networking knowledge that applies to all networking hardware, regardless of the vendor.

This chapter performs a quick overview of all the devices that exist on your network, allowing your computers, servers, and other user-related network devices to communicate with each other. I start with the network devices that your computer connects to and move further into the depths of the network from there, through routers and firewalls, then through wireless and network-connected phone hardware. After you read about these general hardware devices, you overview the classes of Cisco networking devices, such as enterprise, small business, and home devices.

After you read this chapter, you will have a rough grasp of network devices and how they all fit together on the network and an idea of the type of products that Cisco networking involves.

The rest of this book looks at most of these products and shows you how to configure, manage, and support them. Although some Home products are in this mix, I spend most of the time showing you the products you use on your small or large office network.

Although I do cover the whole network model, I do not go very deep on many of these topics. If you want detailed knowledge of the ins and outs of these devices, you may want to review Book I, Chapter 4.

Glazing Over the OSI Network Layer Model

Well, much as I hate to do this to you so early *(mwa ha ha ha)*, before I discuss the actual devices, you need to understand how the standards-setter in the networking industry, the International Organization for Standardization (ISO), defines how network devices should be designed to communicate with each other. The ISO has proposed a network model that allows for this communication to take place, and although this is good from a theoretical level, it is not always followed, especially since it was published after many networking protocols and methods had been created.

The network model that I describe is the *Open System Interconnection (OSI) model,* which has seven layers and defines what types of activities should be conducted at each layer. Figure 1-1 shows the seven layers graphically.

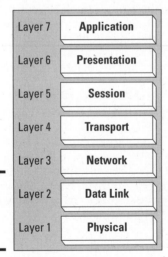

Layer 7	Application
Layer 6	Presentation
Layer 5	Session
Layer 4	Transport
Layer 3	Network
Layer 2	Data Link
Layer 1	Physical

Figure 1-1:
The OSI network model.

The order of the layers, as they are defined, go from the physical components at the lowest layer (which are used to attach a computer to the network) up to applications at the highest layer that are used on that computer. Some people find that it makes sense to be introduced to the layers in this *bottom-up* order; while others find the reverse or *top-down* order is easier to follow. I introduce the layers in the top-down order (highest to lowest as you follow Figure 1-1 from top to bottom), so if you find it confusing, read them from the bottom to the top. The seven layers are

✦ **Layer 7 — Application:** The role of the application layer in the OSI model is to interface with you on your computer or data on a server. For example, if you wish to load a page of data from a website, your web browser uses the *Hypertext Transport Protocol (HTTP)* application layer protocol. To develop a new web browser or web server software, you need only to understand that one application layer protocol. Your HTTP data request travels down through the layers on your computer, over the data network, and up through the network layers on the server, which retrieves the *Hypertext Markup Language (HTML)* file and returns it in the same manner.

✦ **Layer 6 — Presentation:** The presentation layer is responsible for data formatting. This may be character formatting, such as ASCII or Unicode data formats, or compression and data encryption. Think of the presentation layer as the formatting layer in the OSI model. For example, many web servers can compress data that is sent to the web browsers. This compression is the presentation layer component, and it needs to be understood by the presentation layer on the receiving computers.

✦ **Layer 5 — Session:** The session layer establishes a communication dialogue between the two participants in the communication process; that is, two computers over a network. After you have a piece of data that is formatted properly, the session layer ensures that it is ready to be sent over the network.

For example, if the OSI model was used by the post office, the application layer identifies the data on a sheet of paper, the presentation layer defines that the paper must be in an envelope, and the session layer defines that the envelope must have a properly formatted address on it — including a name, street number, street name, city, state, and zip code — and preferably, a return address as well.

✦ **Layer 4 — Transport:** The transport layer defines what type of checks may be performed to validate the data's delivery as either reliable or unreliable. *Reliable* delivery ensures that the data packets get to where they are supposed to go and that they arrive in the same order they were sent. *Unreliable* delivery does not guarantee that the data packets arrive in any specific order, and in fact, does not even ensure that the data packets arrives where it is supposed to go, at all.

Staying with the post office example, reliable delivery allows you to request a signature of the recipient and get a tracking number, whereas unreliable delivery just gives you a stamp and a post office box. Although most unreliable delivery does arrive where it is supposed to, you are never really sure whether it has, until you somehow confirm with the other party.

On your data network, some data is sent unreliably, such as a request for an Internet Protocol (IP) address from a network server. Other data is sent reliably, such as saving a file to a server.

✦ **Layer 3 — Network:** The network layer uses logical address and routing. *Logical address* applies an address that means something to the communication protocol that you are using, such as an Internet Protocol (IP) address, but may not mean anything to the physical delivery process, which makes use of a Layer 2 address. *Routing* the data delivers it to the required destination, which may be nearby or very far away. The network layer also splits large pieces of data into smaller pieces for delivery.

To continue the post office example from the Layer 5 discussion, you had to provide a properly formatted address to get your letter to a building or office for delivery by the postal service. Each part of the address has a zone (or place) where it is used, such as the zip code used by the postal sorting and routing department, the street address used by the mail carrier, and the name by people at the destination address. Depending on how mail delivery starts in your organization, some of this required information for the address may have originally been missing from the envelope. The mail delivery process may have started by dropping a letter addressed to John Smith, New York Office in your desk's outbox. That letter is picked up by your mail clerk who appended John's office number and the street address of the New York office. He then delivered (or *routed*) it to the postal service or courier company.

On your data network, this logical address is likely your *IP address*, which is used as a unique identifier on the Internet to determine the endpoint for communication. IP routing moves the data through a series of interconnected networks until the data arrives at the targeted computer or device.

✦ **Layer 2 — Data Link:** The data link layer assigns or makes use of physical addressing as well as controlling access to the physical medium. If you are dealing with standard Ethernet network cards, the manufacturer assigns a globally unique address to each card. This address is the *Media Access Control (MAC) address,* and it is used at that data link layer to establish communication between two locally attached devices.

The data link layer also controls how the data is interchanged between these two locally attached devices or network cards. Think of this layer as a physical language or a set of communication processes. When dealing with your network, two of the main communication processes would be either Carrier Sense Multiple Access with Collision Detection (CSMA/CD) or carrier Sense Multiple Access with Collision Avoidance (CSMA/CA). In the case of standard Ethernet networks, CSMA/CD is used, while CSMA/CA is used for AppleTalk and some 802.11 wireless networks. With this defined, the data link layer formats a stream of zeros and ones that are converted to electrical or visual signals that are sent over the network.

✦ **Layer 1 — Physical:** The physical layer is to perform management and transfer of the actual electrical or visual signals that are placed on to the physical networking media. On your network, this layer consists of the cables and connectors used to send the data signal from point to point.

You can use two mnemonic phases to remember the order of these layers. From Layer 1 up, it would be Please Do Not Throw Sausage Pizza Away; from Layer 7 down, it would be All People Seem To Need Data Processing.

When thinking about the OSI model, picture it on both the sending and receiving computers. Imagine that a piece of data moves through the process from one computer to another, and as that data passes each layer, a *header,* or a modification, is performed on the information at each layer. As the data moves through the system, only the application layer needs to know anything about the data's actual content, but each layer needs to know how to deal with the layer before and after it (for example, the session layer needs to know how to communicate with the presentation and transport layers). ISO figured that if a group wanted to write a new session interface, they could substitute it at the session layer, without knowing anything about layers any further away than directly before or after it.

Figure 1-2 illustrates the process of data movement by showing the flow of a piece of data — in this case, a *get* request from a web browser — through the layers and traveling between two computers. The first thing that happens is that the application layer applies a header to the data with relevant information related to the application that is used with this data. This application layer header is used by both the presentation layer to identify where the data came from as well as by the application layer on the receiving computer to send the data to the correct application. The application layer hands off the data — with its application header — to the presentation layer, which considers everything that it has received from the application layer as its data. The presentation layer also applies a header, possibly identifying the character formatting (ASCII or Unicode) and hands off the data — now data and two headers — to the session layer. This process continues with each layer applying a header with relevant information for the receiving computer to use to move the data to the correct application, with layers like the session layer identifying the session as http; the transport layer header identifying reliable transport being required; the network layer identifying the source and destination IP addresses; the datalink layer identifying the local network source and destination MAC addresses; and finally, the physical layer converting this to a sequence of signals to send out across the physical wire or media.

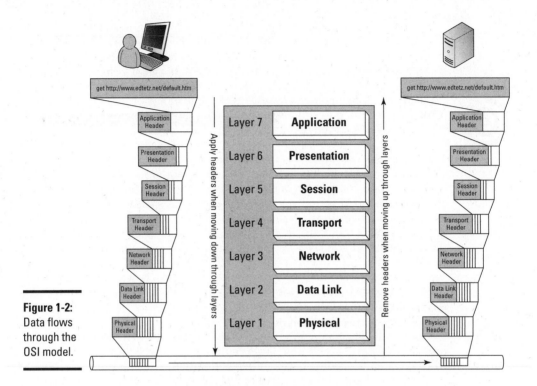

Figure 1-2:
Data flows
through the
OSI model.

When the data arrives at the destination computer or device, the physical
layer receives the series of signals and converts into a format the computer
can understand. It then reads the header on that data, which would be the
data link header, and passes all of the data it received — minus the physical header — to the data link component identified in the data link header.
The data link components would examine the data link header on the data,
which identifies any processing that needs to be done at the data link layer,
to ensure that they were supposed to receive the data, remove the data link
header from the data, process the data, and read the network layer header.
The data link layer would use the information in the network header to identify which network layer component was supposed to receive the data and
pass it onto those components. In this manner, the data will make its way up
through the layers on the receiving computer, with each layer removing its
own header, performing any necessary actions on the remaining data, and
using the next header to identify where to send the data. As the information
makes its way to the application layer, the application layer will read the
application layer header, perform any final changes to the data based on
instructions in the header, and pass the data to the computers destination
application — which, in this case, would be a web server application.

After the web server has retrieved the requested data — the contents of `default.htm` — the data would have an application header attached to it, and the whole process of sending the information back to the other computer would proceed down through the layers, over the network, and back up through the layers on the receiving computer. The final result would be that the web page, `default.htm`, would be displayed in the computer's web browser.

Connecting with Switches

With that introduction to the networking model out of the way, you can deal with the basic classification that the networking community performs with networking devices. This classification is based on the OSI network model layers at which the devices operate, specifically with switches (data link layer or layer 2 devices) and routers (network layer or layer 3 devices). While you could always refer to switches as data link layer device, IT professionals tend to prefer shorter options if available — as noted by the proliferation of acronyms — and will usually refer to them as layer 2 devices. So if you hear people discussing layer 2 and layer 3 devices, think switches and routers. If you are confused by this concept, I clear that up in this section. (Oddly enough, referring to a web server software as a layer 7 device has never really caught on. Thankfully.)

A *switch* is the main device that connects network devices. Prior to switches being used on data networks, repeaters, hubs, and bridges were used. Repeaters and hubs — also known as *multiport repeaters* — amplify the physical signal on the network cable, often amplifying noise as well, leading to degenerated data signal in the physical layer or layer 1. Bridges, on the other hand, work at the data link layer or layer 2, where they read the data provided to them from the physical layer, recompose the entire data structure, and send it back to the physical layer to retransmit cleanly over the network media. Switches act as multiport bridges, so they look like hubs with a large number of RJ-45 or other data jacks, but operate on the network in the same way as bridges, at the data link layer.

Hubs simply amplify the physical signals on the wire, whereas bridges and switches operate a layer higher, actually reading the data represented by those physical signals and retransmitting a perfect copy of the original piece of data. Switches work at the data link layer and can read and filter data based on the data link or MAC addresses.

Unlike a bridge that separated a larger network into pieces, a switch expects each port to have one computer connected to it, but it can deal with having another switch or hub connected to its ports.

Because a switch makes the connection to a computer, most networks have more switches than any other device. Each switch port typically has a number of lights associated with it to identify that something is connected to that port, as well as activity on that port, link speed, or duplex settings. You can find the core discussion about switches — how they work, how they fit into the overall network, and what duplex means — in Book III, Chapters 1 and 2.

Moving On Up with Routers

Switches connect multiple computers together on a network, and *routers* connect these networks together. Routers operate at a higher layer in the OSI model than switches do: switches are layer 2 or data link-layer devices that work with data link addresses, whereas routers are layer 3 or network layer devices that work with network protocol addresses. The actual network protocols used depends on the protocols that router is designed to work with.

These days, the network protocols typically work using Transmission Control Protocol/Internet Protocol (TCP/IP); in the past, they may have also worked with Internet Packet Exchange (IPX), AppleTalk, Systems Network Architecture (SNA), Xerox Network Systems (XNS), or Digital Equipment Company Network (DECnet).

Although the definition of network can vary widely from one person to another, for a router, a *network* is what is connected to each of the router's ports or interfaces. People often refer to their entire internal network infrastructure as the *network,* and the pieces that are connected to the router are *sub-networks, subnets, segments,* or *network segments.*

Through this book, I usually use the term *network* to describe an internal corporate network, and use *network segments* when talking about portions of that network or any network sections separated by a router.

The main purpose of the router is to pass, or route, data from one network segment to another network segment. Each network segment is identified by a network identifier (ID), and the only decision that a basic router makes is to pass the required data to the appropriate network or network segment. This decision to forward the data is based on known remote network segments in the router's routing table and directly connected network segments. In addition to forwarding the data, when the destination network segment is not directly attached to the router, the router needs to choose which router it will use to get the data one step closer to the destination network segment. Because routers only need to determine if they know about the destination network segment and what other router will be used to get the data to its destination, they can move data very quickly and efficiently.

Many network devices combine functionality, and one basic mixture is to combine switching and routing into one device. When routing functionality is added to a switch, the switch is referred to as a *layer 3 (network layer) switch,* differentiating it from a normal switch, which operates at layer 2 (the data link layer).

You can find out a lot more about routers in Book IV.

Taking the Network Wireless

Although networking allows for the transfer of information between devices on a network, wired networking has its limitations — most notably, the length of the wire. For a very long time, people have been working on solutions to break the tether of wires. Over the last decade, wireless technologies have grown in leaps and bounds to the degree that they are commonplace.

Although the world has been going wireless, there have always been people concerned about security, and rightly so. Wireless networks have a security implication, even if it is only not being able to precisely identify where the users of your network physically are. As such, some organizations still isolate some of their key systems to protect them.

When users are not concerned about security, or feel that they have mitigated their security risks, having wireless networking can be a great boon. Wireless networks allow for far greater mobility for the users, can simplify your network administration, and reduce wiring costs when adding, moving, and changing equipment.

When dealing with wireless network, you have likely dealt with residential wireless routers. You may think that a wireless router would be a layer 3 device in the OSI model, but this is not exactly true. Remember that multiple devices can be combined into a single physical unit, like the layer 3 switch, which supports routing. In the case of a wireless router, the two devices that are combined are a wireless access point (AP) and a router. On an enterprise or corporate network, the wireless access point is a separate device, allowing network devices with wireless network cards to connect and access the rest of the network. The AP actually functions as a bridge between wireless network devices and wired network devices, filtering traffic based on device MAC addresses.

If this introduction has piqued your interest in wireless networking, you can read a great deal more about it in Book V.

Securing Data with Firewalls

Firewalls in buildings and automobiles are designed to contain a fire in a specific area, leaving you safe on the other side of the wall. When dealing with *network firewalls,* the same is true, expect instead of a fire, the firewall keeps you safe from the scary people who want to get to your information.

Ever since computers have been connected together, users have been concerned with security. If you have been following along so far, you know that I just mentioned security on wireless networks; firewalls, however, are concerned about security on *all* networks, be they wireless or wired.

Firewalls can be implemented as software or hardware:

+ **Software firewalls:** In actuality, all firewalls are software. Software firewalls are often installed on the computers that they are supposed to protect.

+ **Hardware firewalls:** When the software runs on single-purposed hardware device, it is dubbed a hardware firewall. Hardware firewalls are often placed at access points to your network, such as between your network and the Internet.

Just as switches are sometimes built with routing features, as mentioned earlier, routers are often built with firewall features. As is often the case, when you combine feature sets like this, you end up with a product that solves two problems but often does not do the secondary job as well as a stand-alone product would in that role. This is true of the security features that are built into routers. Routers can filter traffic between two locations based on a specific set of rules that can be applied at the network layer (layer 3), but advanced firewalls can perform deep-packet inspection and filter data based on attributes at any level of the OSI model.

Deep packet inspection allow the firewall to read data in the network packet anywhere from layer 3 through layers 4, 5, 6, 7, or even in the actual data (like in the *get* request illustrated in Figure 1-2). This allows the firewall to allow or block traffic based on any information found in the network data packet.

In addition to firewall features, many firewalls support virtual private network (VPN) feature sets, allowing for site-to-site VPN connections as well as remote access VPN connections for remote network users. This VPN feature set makes sense when combined with a firewall because both functions are related to security filtering between computers on and off your network. Some devices act as single-purpose VPN devices, which is separate from core firewall services, while most VPN solutions are integrated into other network devices. Cisco tends to integrate VPN services into other network devices, primarily sticking to firewalls. The closest product in Cisco's product line that would be single purpose VPN is the Cisco Catalyst 6500 Series/7600 Series WebVPN Services Module, which is a VPN device on an expansion card, which can be added to 6500 series switches or 7600 series routers.

A VPN is a secured and encrypted network connection between two points over an unsecured network. This is typically done over the Internet (unsecured network), and can be set up between firewalls at two offices or from a remote user's laptop and a firewall at the office. When running between two offices, it allows the offices to be treated as directly connected for routing purposes; when used by a remote user's computer, it virtually puts that computer on the corporate network at the office. The important parts of the term VPN are *virtual* (these networks are not actually directly connected) and *private* (information sent over this connection is secured and encrypted).

You can read more about firewalls in Book VI.

Adding a Network Voice (Over IP, That Is)

So far in this chapter, I walk you through the connections from a computer to the networking interconnection, to the edge of your network. Voice services run over that entire infrastructure. Network voice devices, or what I refer to as *telephones,* are like small single-focus computers that boot up and connect to a central call-processing server. The call-processing server identifies what telephone holds what extension data, sets up sessions between remote telephone lines and telephones, sets up sessions among multiple local telephones, and closes or tears down sessions.

While the main voice devices most people think of are telephones, a common Voice over IP (VoIP) protocol is Session Initiation Protocol (SIP). As long as a device or piece of software supports SIP as a protocol, the actual voice device can be any device with a speaker and microphone attached to your network. Software like Cisco Communicator is a SIP client; VoIP phones from most vendors are SIP clients; and Skype and Vonage offer call processor services with SIP integration.

When looking at the Voice over Internet Protocol (VoIP) solution, identify several components, such as:

✦ **Call Manager:** A network device that identifies the device, which represents a phone extension. Call Manager is a Cisco-specific term for their call processor technology.

✦ **Phones:** Physical phone devices, which are single-purposed network computer devices that boot up, connect to a call processor, and allow placing of phone calls. These computers look like and operate like traditional phones.

✦ **Soft phones:** Software applications for your computer, which use your computer's processor and network card to connect to a call processor, and allow you to place phone calls. This software sometimes emulates a phone on your computer screen, but may appear like a chat application (like Windows Live Messenger).

✦ **Voicemail storage:** A network device with a hard drive that is used to store audio files containing voice mail messages. This is often integrated into the Call Manager device.

A company receives several benefits from switching to a VoIP system, including savings on long-distance calls between remote offices. The call data still has to traverse the distance between the two offices, but with VoIP, the traffic is now being monitored as and charged as data rather than as a voice call. When long-distance rates were high and data rates were low, this could yield substantial savings to heavy voice users. While cost of long distance may no longer be a large benefit, other financial savings come from administration of phones and extensions. Many phone providers make a large portion of their money by managing adds, moves, and changes (A/M/C) for users. For instance, when a user joins a network, you need to call your phone provider to set her up and attach her phone to a specific wall jack, which is attached to a port on a central call management system or Private Branch eXchange (PBX) — this is considered to be an *add*. The wall jack then becomes that extension, regardless of what phone actually gets plugged into that jack. If the user wants to move to another desk, you have to make another call to your phone provider to physically move the wires on the PBX to a different port to allow that extension to operate at a different desk — this is a *move* or *change*. With a traditional phone system, over the course of a year, you can spend a great deal of money to keep phones and extensions moving around with the users. If you do not spend that money, then users will have to keep telling people that their extensions changed when they moved to a new cubicle or office.

VoIP solutions typically save you from making these repeated calls to your phone provider because the phone keeps the extension information, regardless of where it is plugged in. Some of these phones work over a remote access connection, which is also a solution for teleworkers who are then able to have an office phone and extension, regardless as to where they happen to be in world.

Focusing on Small Business Networks

If you have worked with Cisco products in a large business environment, you have likely been working with Cisco Enterprise products. While Cisco has spent many decades delivering quality products to large enterprise customers, they have expanded into lower level markets with unique mixes of products to acquire clients in smaller businesses and even home users. With Cisco's acquisition of Linksys, the main categories of products are:

✦ **Enterprise products:** Powerful high-end devices supporting large companies. These products have advanced features and reliability, which are desired or demanded by large companies who do not have a problem paying a premium price for these premium products. This category of products can be broken down into smaller categories — Carrier, WAN, and Branch.

✦ **Cisco Small Medium Business (SMB) products:** Cisco developed products that are available at a lower cost and offering a reduced feature set when compared to the Enterprise product line. The reduced feature set does not cause an issue for SMB clients who tend not to use the high-end features that are removed from these products and would prefer not to have to pay the premium prices for the Enterprise products. As an added benefit, these products tend to come with easier to use management interfaces, causing less confusion for the SMB users who manage the devices.

✦ **Linksys SMB products:** Linksys SMB products typically come in at a lower price than the Cisco SMB products. Prior to the acquisition by Cisco, Linksys was attempting to break out of the home market into the SMB market and had developed a line of SMB products. This has left Cisco temporarily with two lines of SMB products, which they are in the process of integrating under a single Cisco brand. Typically, you will find the Linksys branded items will be a less expensive option to the Cisco branded items, but that reduced price tends to come with a reduced quality or feature set.

✦ **Home products:** Lower quality and reduced feature products make up the home market, where users tend to need even easier to use management interfaces to configure and manage their devices. Cisco bought their way into the Home market by purchasing Linksys — one of the leaders in the Home market. They are currently in the process of rebranding and introducing new products under the Cisco brand. While they are not giving up the Linksys brand name in this market segment, they have recently reduced a new line of home wireless routers under the Linksys (by Cisco) brand.

Cisco is working at integrating the Linksys SMB line into the Cisco SMB brand completely, so you can expect to see features of both of these product lines showing up in the newly branded Cisco SMB products.

Most of the SMB products have limitations (or rather, reduced features) when compared to the Enterprise product line, but products at the SMB level try to provide breadth of product features integrated into one device, rather than requiring an SMB company to purchase several single-purpose products. To get this breadth of product features into one unit, the sacrifice is in the depth of the features. So, while Enterprise products may offer access points with multiple radios and support for multiple virtual networks, the access point integrated into an SMB firewall would only support a single radio and not have virtual network support. This is not to say that the SMB products do not have powerful features; for example, both Cisco SMB routers and Linksys SMB routers support several features that would exist in much more expensive Enterprise devices, such as load-balanced dual Internet service provider (ISP) connections as well as advanced remote access and VPN features.

Taking Cisco Products Home

Cisco has never had much penetration into the home market, even though it owns the high-end enterprise market and has huge inroads into the price-conscious SMB market.

With the purchase of the Linksys product line, Cisco quickly made its way into the home market. Before Cisco acquired Linksys, Linksys was almost exclusively a home brand that had been trying to break in to the business market.

As a home-based product, Linksys products have attractive prices and a heavy integration of features to differentiate it from the competition. The Home products have been integrated into the Cisco support website. Previously, during the migration phase, the Linksys website provided information and support for the Linksys product line, but all support is not performed through the Cisco website.

At the entry level of their home-targeted product line, Cisco has done away with the Linksys logo and name, instead introducing the Valet brand. At the higher performance level of the home-targeted line, they have kept the well respected Linksys name. The higher performance Linksys devices have features that attract the home power user, such as better support for streaming video and Internet gaming, more concurrent users, and higher wireless bandwidth. All the new products support the management interface Cisco Connect, which is designed to simplify managing the home devices.

The integration of Linksys and Cisco has only been positive for home users, as it has allowed some Cisco standard features to be merged into the Home product line, for example, the Cisco Valet wireless router has a password-based guest access feature, which you would have previously seen only in Cisco SMB and Enterprise products.

The main focus of the Home product line is in integrated firewall/router/gateway combination devices. Cisco is also marketing home-grade *tele-presence,* or video conferencing, umi (pronounced *YouMe*) products. With Enterprise products, Cisco made a name for itself in the video-conferencing market, so it is bringing that technology to the home user. You can expect Cisco to find other Enterprise-type products that can be geared toward home users coming to you through the home market.

Chapter 2: Exploring Cisco Network Design

In This Chapter

✔ Checking out Cisco's three networking methodologies

✔ Wading through the layers of Cisco's networking model

✔ Reviewing the benefits of these methodologies

Networking devices can be a complex task to get just right. Although anyone can plug two devices together, doing so randomly without thinking through the connection's affect on the whole can produce a network with a less than desirable performance — or bring the entire network to a grinding, screeching halt.

This chapter identifies the methodologies that help you create stable and reliable networks, including how Cisco designs networks and the building blocks that Cisco uses to divide networks. Rather than designing the network as a single entity, Cisco breaks the overall network down into components, and designs each component separately, which makes up the network building blocks or modules. Because reviewing many of these topics in detail would involve several volumes of text, I focus on the most important principles that are necessary to make informed decisions about your network design.

By modularizing the network, you simplify how you work with and identify the components that make up your network. To start using this methodology, you may need only to make a few changes to your network, but it usually takes a shift in the way you think of your network and its devices. By looking at each section of specialization in network components, you can work in each section to identify issues, modularly grow or scale the network size, and simplify troubleshooting network problems by limiting the scope of the problem domain.

Embracing Methodologies

Cisco networking relies on three main design methods when dealing with network design or network layout. The first two methods in the following list relate to the goal of the network, whereas the third is an overall deployment method. Here are the three methods:

♦ **Intelligent Information Network (IIN):** The IIN framework can help add intelligence to your network. This intelligence spans layers of the network and links it to the rest of your IT infrastructure. If you consider that the network is simply a conduit that allows information from business applications to move from one application or location process to another, the design of the network ensures that the business processes that require this information will have it available when needed.

♦ **Service-Oriented Network Architecture (SONA):** The SONA framework takes a traditional network structure and helps it to evolve into an IIN. SONA assumes that your network will be unified, and that all data will traverse a single network architecture.

♦ **Prepare, Plan, Design, Implement, Operate, and Optimize (PPDIOO):** PPDIOO is a lifecycle method that Cisco uses for network management. Following this lifecycle management process assists in lessening the total cost of ownership for the network, increasing network availability, and improving agility to make changes to the network structure.

Each method has a place in the implementation of your networking solution. SONA gives you a structure to follow, allowing you to implement the IIN framework, while PPDIOO is a deployment model to follow when implementing any network changes, regardless of what the driving forces were for those changes.

Intelligent Information Network (IIN)

Your IT infrastructure includes not only your network, but also applications, servers, and services. The concept behind IIN is that network design should make information available when it is needed by business processes. To illustrate this concept, try drawing your network diagram, but rather than starting with something like a firewall, router, or switch, start the diagram with a business process, such as *purchase a widget*. The diagram needs to include the business logic and procedures that are involved in the process, as illustrated in Figure 2-1. The diagram then may branch out into the pieces of IT infrastructure that are used for this process, ending with how these IT components actually communicate.

Figure 2-1:
Widget
purchase
process.

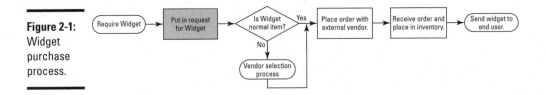

Taking this inclusive design approach allows you to see which IT components may need to be connected with higher-speed links or implemented with additional redundancies (such as backup systems or connections), rather than concentrating solely on the network as a separate entity. The three main points are

✦ The network as an integrated system

✦ Active participation of the network in service delivery

✦ Enforcing business processes through network rules

Here are the three points of integration, or the points on your network where you can add IIN components:

✦ **Integrated transport:** Involves the integration of network data, such as voice, data, and video. These components make up the Cisco Unified Network, which places these three main traffic types (voice, data, and video) on it, while allowing each to be optimized for usage through traffic management features.

✦ **Integrated service:** Takes common network elements, such as storage and servers, into account and allows for the function of business services in case of a local network failure. The ability to provide backup (or redundant) services is due in part to virtualization technology for servers as well as storage and network components, which allow for these services to be maintained in multiple physical locations at the same time.

✦ **Integrated application:** Allows the network to be aware of the applications that are running on it. When the network is application-aware, it can integrate network features to optimize data movement, implement security, and provide redundancy.

Service-Oriented Network Architecture (SONA)

The SONA network architecture contains three basic layers, as shown in Figure 2-2:

✦ **Network infrastructure layer:** Contains the enterprise network architecture, which includes switches, routers, communication links, and so on. This layer has redundancy built into it and contains network layer security to enforce business policies as needed. The components at this layer are discussed later in this chapter, and represent the components that map directly to the OSI model discussed in Book I, Chapter 1.

✦ **Integrated service layer:** *Virtualizes* services (or unties them from specific pieces of hardware) to allow them to be provided over a dispersed or centralized network environment. The following services are provided at this layer:

- *Identity:* Authentication services for user or device credentials, which can play a role for network or application access.

- *Mobility:* Allowing access to network resources from any location. This may rely on wireless technologies or a Virtual Private Network (VPN).

- *Storage:* Storage of important network data and replication or duplication of that data, over the network, to remote locations for disaster recovery.

- *Computing or processing:* Servers represent the main element of this component, while virtual servers allow for scaling and betting utilization of server processing power.

- *Security:* Security for your business is crucial, and the security level makes use of security features at the network level, such as intrusion detection and prevention systems (IDS and IPS).

- *Voice and collaboration:* Voice services now run over the main corporate data network, and have allowed for more options for users to communicate. These communication methods include the traditional telephone, but also include instant messaging and collaboration through websites, such as Microsoft's SharePoint.

✦ **Application layer:** Carries the responsibility for providing the applications that users rely on. These applications include the following product areas:

- *Customer relationship management (CRM):* Communication with clients, as well as all of their pertinent data, can be found in CRM applications.

- *Enterprise resource planning (ERP):* Business data for your organization is found in your ERP system. This is everything that would have been in a traditional accounting system, plus information on business processes and business logic, thereby allowing you to derive more planning and statistical information from the accounting system.

- *Procurement:* Purchasing can sometimes be tracked as part of the overall corporate ERP system, or can be a standalone system to manage purchasing from the request for a quote through to the deployment of the purchased product to the end user.

- *Supply chain management (SCM):* Procurement systems can purchase items, but SCM systems tell procurement what parts need to be purchased and when. In manufacturing and service organizations, good SCM systems will provide you with "just in time" inventory items right before you need those items.

- *Instant messaging (IM):* Instant messaging has come into businesses who now expect to be able to instantly communicate within their network infrastructure. This assists in users on your network in their collaboration goals.

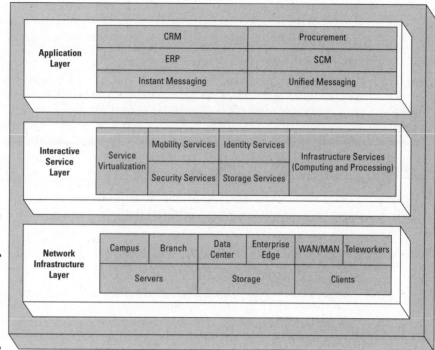

Figure 2-2:
The
composition
of the SONA
framework.

- *Unified messaging (UM):* Unified messaging talks all of the forms in which users can communicate and ties them together, allowing for unique situations, such as where an e-mail can be relayed to office voicemail, and then forwarded to a cell phone as a text message. Unified messaging takes control and integrates all communication and messaging formats within an organization, either partially or completely.

With each layer separate, you can focus on the applications that need to be supported in your organization, because not all applications on your network may be classified as critical to business operations. What the critical applications are will vary from company to company based on their specific business needs for those applications, so the business requirement for the application is used to determine the requirements for the supporting network components. In most cases, the application does not care specifically how things work. Instead, the application has a requirement for a specific feature, such as identity services. That feature can then be provided by something like Remote Authentication Dial In User Service (RADIUS) authentication against a user account database, which is stored in the Microsoft Active Directory (AD). The application does not care where the user information is stored, just that it can request authentication. At the same time, the RADIUS server does not care that the network link between itself and the AD server has to go over Wide Area Network (WAN) on two load-balanced connections.

I find it surprising how many companies have IT departments that implement technology for the sake of technology, and lose sight of the fact that they are in the business of providing support for the company by supporting their applications. So the application and its requirements should be the driving force for network changes, and not the fact that new and cool technologies are available.

The SONA framework provides scalability because it is modular, availability because of its redundancies, manageability through deployed tools, and efficiency by maximizing resource utilization.

Prepare, Plan, Design, Implement, Operate, and Optimize (PPDIOO)

You can step into the system described in the following sections at any point for your own network. In this instance, I start with deciding whether to implement a new network or to upgrade an existing network. When looking at Figure 2-3, you will notice that these elements form a never-ending circle, because the optimize step will typically identify changes, which can lead to better performance on your network, which then initiates a new prepare step.

In the following sections, I take a closer look at each phase.

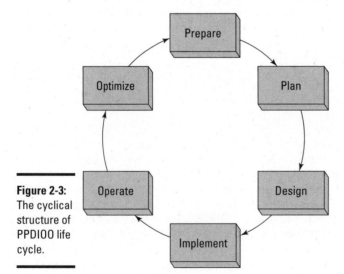

Figure 2-3: The cyclical structure of PPDIOO life cycle.

Prepare

During the Prepare phase of the process, examine the overall business requirements and develop a strategy for the network. You may also examine the technologies required to support the network environment you envision. The end goal in this phase is to create a business case to justify the cost of deploying the network changes.

When identifying the customer requirements, determine and document the following key items:

✦ **Network applications and services:** Knowing what network related applications and services are currently being offered to users of the network is critical in planning the design of the network, because you will need to know what the offerings are and where users of these offerings are to be located. In addition to the applications and services that are currently on the network, you will need to know what new applications and services will be implemented over the life of the current network design. Your network design life will often be the life of the networking components, so if your organization replaces all technology in a three to five year cycle, then you will want to plan for expected changes in that time frame. With that timeframe in mind, will the network be supporting streaming video, Voice over IP (VoIP), or video conferencing? This will influence your overall network design.

✦ **Organizational goals:** Design of the network will be in support of the overall organizational goals. These goals will vary from organization to organization, but may include goals such as reduce costs, improve customer interaction, add new services for customers, and improve competitive position in the market. With these goals in mind, you may choose to focus effort and money on certain areas of the network and network design.

✦ **Organizational constraints:** Every organization has constraints on what they can or cannot do. The one constraint that almost every organization has is money, so if there are no other constraints on you as the network designer, there is likely a budget that you need to operate within. Other constraints may be placed on an organization due to schedules, internal policies, or government regulations. These may all play a role in the overall network design, and knowing about them at the start of the design process prevents the need to redesign after the fact.

✦ **Technical goals:** Unlike the organization's goals, the technical goals tend to focus on technology, whereas the organization goals focus on business operations. However, these two sets of goals are not mutually exclusive. When examining the organizational goal of improving customer interaction, technical goals that would align with the organizational goal may be to improve website access and reliability, implement VoIP infrastructure, or reduce network response time. Other technology goals may be related specifically to the technology, such as modernize antiquated technologies, simplify management of technology, or reduce equipment failures.

✦ **Technical constraints:** Technology within the organization may also put limitations on what you can accomplish within your network design. Some examples of technology constraints include existing wiring limit network throughput and support for legacy networking equipment.

Plan

The Plan phase allows you to examine the network requirements needed to deploy the business services or applications defined in the Prepare phase. This may require using network management tools to examine the current network and classify its current level of services, resiliency, and performance.

The goal at this phase is defined by the organizational and technical goals, and an analysis of the gaps in that list (or *gap analysis*)— and how to fill those gaps— is the intended results. After you complete the Plan phase, you know the current state of the network as well as any identified shortcomings that you need to resolve.

Gathering Information

The information gathered in the Plan phase is critical in knowing how your network devices currently perform.

When you gather information about the network in the Plan phases, consider the following as sources of information:

✦ Current sources for documentation of your current network structure and configuration

✦ Results of a new network audit using exiting documentation and auditing or network performance tools

✦ Results of a new traffic analysis study using live data captured from an existing network

Cisco data gathering command-line tools

If you currently have Cisco devices, you can gather a plethora of data using commands, such as the following:

✔ `show tech-support`

✔ `show processes cpu`

✔ `show version`

✔ `show processes memory`

✔ `show running-config`

Although these commands may not mean anything right now, as you progress through this book, I show you how to run these commands and many others, starting in Book I, Chapter 5. As a brief example, the `show version` command run on a router named Router-1 yields the following output with the software version, system uptime, system software filename, processor type, the number of network interfaces, additional expansion modules installed, the amount of RAM, and the amount of flash memory:

```
Router-1#show version
Cisco IOS Software, C2600 Software (C2600-ADVIPSERVICESK9-M), Version 12.3(4)T4,
        RELEASE SOFTWARE (fc2)
Technical Support: http://www.cisco.com/techsupport
Copyright (c) 1986-2004 by Cisco Systems, Inc.
Compiled Thu 11-Mar-04 19:57 by eaarmas

ROM: System Bootstrap, Version 12.2(8r) [cmong 8r], RELEASE SOFTWARE (fc1)

Router-1 uptime is 7 minutes
System returned to ROM by power-on
System image file is "flash:c2600-advipservicesk9-mz.123-4.T4.bin"


This product contains cryptographic features and is subject to United
States and local country laws governing import, export, transfer and
use. Delivery of Cisco cryptographic products does not imply
third-party authority to import, export, distribute or use encryption.
Importers, exporters, distributors and users are responsible for
compliance with U.S. and local country laws. By using this product you
agree to comply with applicable laws and regulations. If you are unable
to comply with U.S. and local laws, return this product immediately.

A summary of U.S. laws governing Cisco cryptographic products may be found at:
http://www.cisco.com/wwl/export/crypto/tool/stqrg.html

If you require further assistance please contact us by sending email to
export@cisco.com.

Cisco 2621XM (MPC860P) processor (revision 0x300) with 125952K/5120K bytes of memory.
Processor board ID JAE081160XR (3618058385)
M860 processor: part number 5, mask 2
2 FastEthernet interfaces
1 Virtual Private Network (VPN) Module
32K bytes of NVRAM.
32768K bytes of processor board System flash (Read/Write)

Configuration register is 0x2102
```

Gather tools to get more information

The information found in the Cisco network devices can be comprehensive regarding configuration information and can provide some level of performance data. However, these devices can be lacking in many areas, such as historical trending, outage history, and traffic patterns. To deal with this, you need to use other tools to give you this other information. The following are just some of the tools you might want to use:

✦ **CiscoWorks:** Cisco's configuration and auditing toolset allows you to create and apply configuration changes to all your network devices, plus it provides you with a monitoring toolset to see the status of your network devices. More information can be found about CiscoWorks from www.cisco.com/en/US/products/ps11200/index.html. CiscoWorks is priced depending on the size of your network, with the smallest network size (50 or fewer devices) has a cost of approximately $2,000, but if you want to kick the tires on CiscoWorks, then head to the Cisco website and download an evaluation copy.

✦ **WhatsUp Gold:** Ipswith's network-device monitoring tool, which is capable of discovering network devices, tracking system health, and receiving Simple Network Management Protocol (SNMP) trap and Syslog data. Ipswitch provides a 30-day evaluation of the product, whose price starts around $1,500 for the ability to manage 25 devices. Check out their website at www.whatsupgold.com.

✦ **Multi Router Traffic Grapher (MRTG):** Open source *Round Robin Database* (RRD)–based network monitoring and graphing tool used to show current and historical information about network devices, specifically router and switch interface statistics. This tool is freely available from oss.oetiker.ch/mrtg/index.en.html.

✦ **Cacti:** Open source RRD–based network monitoring and graphing tool. If you have used MRTG but wanted something a little flashier or geared towards other types of devices, then Cacti may be for you. Cacti makes it easier to add devices such as servers to your monitored devices list. As with MRTG, this tool is freely available, and you can find it for download on their website, www.cacti.net.

✦ **Xymon Monitor (formerly Hobbit Monitor):** Open source–device monitoring and alerting tool, as shown in Figure 2-4, that displays current status information for network devices. Like Cacti and MRTG, Xymon is capable of gathering a wide range of information about your devices and offers historical information on those devices in the form of RRD–based charts. One difference with Xymon lies in its ability to send out alerts to configured users in the event that certain conditions have been met, such as a device has gone offline for more than 5 minutes or free disk space on a server has dropped below 100 MB. You will find Xymon on its Sourceforge page at xymon.sourceforge.net.

✦ **Wireshark:** Open source packet capture and analysis tool that is capable of collecting complete network data information from your network, allowing it to be reviewed in great detail. The data Wireshark collects are the data packets that pass by the computer performing the capture. After capturing this data, Wireshark can provide you with statistical data such as the most talkative network devices. This tool is freely available from their homepage at `www.wireshark.org`.

✦ **NetFlow:** A Cisco Internetwork Operating System (IOS) component (the Cisco IOS operating environment is discussed in Book I, Chapter 5) that collects and measures data as it flows through switch and router interfaces. While NetFlow on a switch or router collects data, it does not provide any of the analytical functions. For analytics, you will require a NetFlow collector.

✦ **Cisco NetFlow Collection Engine:** Cisco's NetFlow gathering and analysis tool that collects NetFlow data from network devices and allows for centralized analysis of the data. This data can be analyzed across the network to ensure that application data is passing over the network in a manner that is appropriate to the application. For example, you could use this tool to ensure that a business-critical accounting system is not being impacted by users watching YouTube videos. You can get more information about the NetFlow Collector Engine from `www.cisco.com/en/US/products/sw/netmgtsw/ps1964/index.html`, but be prepared — this product comes with a price tag in excess of $16,000. Other products such as WhatsUp Gold are capable of performing less exhaustive NetFlow analysis.

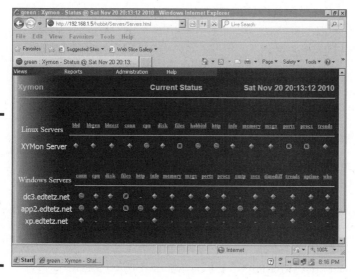

Figure 2-4:
Xymon
provides
up-to-the-
minute
statuses on
any of your
network
resources.

Using tools to monitor the health of your network

When using these tools, review the health of your network based on some of these criteria:

+ Ethernet segments must be less than 40 percent sustained utilization.

+ All segments that are added to the network should be switched (using switches) rather than shared (using hubs). Switches and switching are covered in Book III, Chapter 2.

+ WAN links must be less than 70 percent sustained utilization.

+ Response time between local systems must be quicker than 100 milliseconds (ms).

+ Less than 20 percent of traffic per segment should be broadcast (sent to all network devices) or multicast (sent to large groups of network devices).

+ Cyclic redundancy check (CRC) errors must be less than one per million bytes of data.

+ The rate of packet collisions on Ethernet segments should be less than 0.1 percent.

+ Device CPU utilization should be less than 75 percent for sustained intervals.

+ Queues should be less than 100 for output and 50 for input.

Design

After you complete the Plan phase, you know where you currently stand on the network and where you need to be. The Design phase defines what needs to be changed, removed, or added to the existing network. This includes creating network diagrams, building devices lists, and determining which high-level configuration options (such as the routing protocol, router placement, and main protocol options) will be implemented or required for the devices.

After completing this phase for many clients, it no longer surprises me the level of documentation that my clients maintain. This documentation ranges from nothing (or next to nothing) to very complete (with fully documented diagrams).

In a perfect world, everyone would have complete documentation about all aspects of their network, but in most cases, even the most complete documentation has some aspects that are either out of date or missing. You can usually expect to need some level of information gathering during other phases that you then review during the Design phase.

Network destination addresses

When sending data over the network, the data is marked with a destination data link or Layer 2 address. The destination address will fall into one of three categories:

- **Unicast:** Unique address that will match the data link or MAC address of one network card on the network. The only network device that will read or process this network frame will be the device with that matches the data link address.

- **Multicast:** Group address that does not match any data link or MAC address on your network. Any network devices on your network that belong to a data link address group will read or process this network frame.

- **Broadcast:** Special group address that automatically includes all member devices on the current data link or network segment. Any network frames that are sent to the broadcast address will be read or processed by every device on that network segment.

Implement

Following the Design phase is the Implement phase, which puts the design into action. This phase is where you remove, add, or reconfigure devices on the network. Because this phase impacts data moving on the network (for example, if you unplug a server from the network, people cannot communicate with it), you must plan the changes, determine outage times, communicate outage or migration issues, plan rollback steps, and manage the network changes. As a change is implemented, you must test it to ensure proper operation; after a system that has been changed has passed the test, it is ready to be moved into the Operate phase.

Before performing the full implementation of your new design, first perform a pilot or prototype in a smaller, controlled environment so that you can test the new design on a few computers before rolling it out to the whole network and waiting for the IT help desk requests to shoot through the roof. If new equipment is being implemented in the core of the network, this equipment needs to be configured to the deployment specification, and a simulated network traffic load needs to be placed on the test network to identify potential real-world issues prior to the live deployment. This test may take place in a prototype test bed or with a small pilot deployment that affects only a subset of all the users on the network.

Pilot versus prototype

The two main methods of testing a network design prior to rolling out a full deployment across your network are to use a pilot or a prototype.

✔ **When conducting a pilot test,** you choose a small section of your network to perform the upgrade or change. The choice of location will depend on the type of network changes you are conducting, as well as the structure of your network. In some cases, the pilot area may be a branch office or a floor of your building. With the pilot, you have limited the size of the deployment, thereby limiting the number of users affected by the deployment. If things go badly, then you have a smaller impact, and possibly more time to resolve the issue before reversing the changes. A benefit of this network testing method is that it allows you to test the network with real traffic and under a normal network traffic load; the drawback is that you may affect production users on your network during the pilot.

✔ **When conducting a prototype test,** you build a mock network that follows your new design. With the mock network, you must have more hardware available, which may be fine if this is being done in conjunction with a hardware replacement. The benefit of this testing method is that you can test a number of scenarios with no impact to the users; the drawback is that you need to mock up systems to communicate off the network, may miss unanticipated traffic, and will have trouble simulating high network traffic load scenarios.

If you replace or update core network components on any network, issues will likely affect all users on the network. Therefore, if you encounter issues, be prepared to roll back the implementation to an earlier point in time using a backup. No matter how much testing you have completed and how sure you are that your configurations and device selections are correct, unexpected things can result when implementing.

Operate

In the Operate phase, the network functions in its day-to-day role. The network does what it was designed to do, and data is moved from device to device. In a perfect world, your job would now be done; but wait, there is more.

Monitoring network resources is critical in this phase because monitoring can identify issues before they impact the users of the network. A great day is when you can identify a major network issue and resolve it without the network users ever being aware of it. As I mention earlier, in the Plan phase, you can run many tools on your network that capture performance counters and identify resources that are not responding on your network.

These tools are critical to use during the Operate phase to assist in quickly identifying network performance and configuration issues. By saving historical data from the monitoring process, you can chart an overview of the general health of the network and take corrective actions when thresholds are reached.

Optimize

After the Operate phase comes the Optimize phase because data regarding the health of the network that you continue to collect leads to identifying

✦ Chronic or recurring issues with the network

✦ Areas where performance is not what was expected

✦ Areas where performance has reduced over time because of excessive network load

During the Optimize phase you review your collected network data and based on that data identify items that need additional changes. At this point, you may go back to the Prepare phase and start over to incorporate those changes into your overall plan.

In some cases, these network changes just need to go through a change management process, whereas larger changes may require business cases and justification before implementation.

One advantage of the PPDIOO process is that the Design phase yields a complete set of documentation related to the configuration and structure of the network. As the pilot/prototype, and implementation changes the actual deployment plan, these changes are rolled in the documentation. If this documentation process proceeds after the fact, with changes being implemented through a change management process that updates or appends to the documentation, you continue to have a fully documented network.

Full network documentation makes continued troubleshooting easier and gives new employees a running start when learning the network structure or troubleshooting issues.

Examining the Layered Network Model

Cisco recommends implementing a hierarchical network model to

✦ **Save money:** Costs savings come from using appropriate technologies at each layer, rather than attempting to solve all problems with one routing or switching platform.

✦ **Simplify understanding:** The network can be identified by larger blocks, rather than attempting to visualize everything that takes place in a black box.

✦ **Allow for modular growth:** Because you have separated components to jobs at different layers, it is easier to upgrade or grow devices at a single layer.

✦ **Improve problem isolation times:** When troubleshooting issues, it is much easier to identify where the issue has occurred, reducing the time resolution.

By following this hierarchical model, you can treat each layer of the network as a discreet component. This allows you to focus on upgrades to separate areas rather than treating the network as a whole. With this model, you need to be concerned with four distinct areas, as shown in Figure 2-5:

✦ **Core:** The traffic flow center of the network whose main purpose is to pass data packets to and from the other layers as quickly as possible. On smaller networks, you would find your servers connected to the core, but on larger networks, your servers will exist on their own distribution and access layers.

✦ **Distribution:** Aggregates or collects data from the access layer and passes it to the core layer.

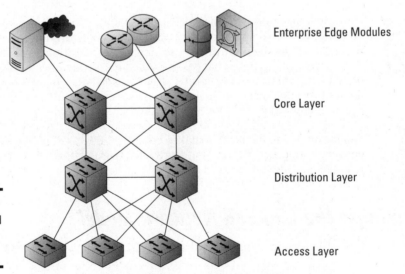

Figure 2-5:
Hierarchical
network
model.

Enterprise Edge Modules

Core Layer

Distribution Layer

Access Layer

✦ **Access:** Provides connection services for end-user systems or servers (when they have their own access layer). Devices on this layer will send their data to the distribution layer in order to be processed and passed onto the core networking layer.

✦ **Enterprise Edge:** Interfaces with systems that reside outside of the main enterprise campus. The remote systems need a pathway to get onto the network, and these edge components provide that link. This may be a connection to the Internet or VPN server components granting inbound access. Unlike the rest of the network, which is under complete control of your corporation's IT department and falls within their building, the edge components make use of external resources provided by a telco or Internet Service Provider (ISP) and grant access to systems that are not housed in the corporation's building.

Figure 2-5 shows the network model as a switched network; however, this same design may be implemented using a routed network.

Core layer

The core layer of the network is the data movement key of the data structure and focuses on the following components:

✦ **Fast transport:** The fastest interfaces available should be used for the core layer; in addition, all devices come with an internal data movement speed that can be found in the product specifications. This is as important as the speed of the external facing interfaces.

✦ **High reliability:** Due to the volume of traffic that is handled by this layer, it must be able to pass that data with very few errors. Some errors are normal on a data network. However, within the core, errors generated from this layer should be much lower than the network average.

✦ **Redundancy and fault tolerance:** In the event that there is a failure in any single device, redundancy in the design will provide you alternative paths that will allow the core of your network to continue to operate, though possibly at a reduced speed. Having redundant systems or components within a system (like backup power supplies) makes your network design fault tolerant.

✦ **Low latency:** As a network device handles data that it is moving, it introduces small delays; in the core of your network, these delays should be kept to a minimum and products or configuration options to reduce the processing time should be used.

✦ **Avoidance of slow packet manipulation caused by filters:** This is a continuation of the low latency point, in that filters on traffic, such as applying or evaluating Access Control Lists (ACLs) should be avoided because it will have an impact on the overall speed of data movement.

✦ **Limited and consistent diameter:** The *diameter* of your network is how many devices data must travel through to go from one point on your network to another, while travelling through the core. This should be kept as small as is reasonable and consistent across your network. In practical terms, this would mean that each computer would send data through the same number of devices to get to the servers with which the computer needs to communicate.

✦ **Quality of Service (QoS):** QoS allows the network core to send some data more quickly than other data. The core should not be classifying or marking data with priority levels, but if classified (marked) data arrives in the core, it should be passed according to the indicated QoS levels.

Although you may be tempted to build additional features, such as security through Access Control Lists (ACLs), resist the temptation because they reduce the speed of processing data packets, and speed and reliability are the two main considerations in the core. You examine many of these items as you progress through this book.

Distribution layer

The distribution layer acts as division between the core and the access layers.

The main responsibility of the distribution layer is to collect and organize data streams from the access layer that are then passed on to the core layer. Think of the distribution layer as a personal assistant for the core layer so that the core layer has to worry only about passing data to and from other distribution layer components.

The key networking features that you implement at the distribution layer include

✦ **Redundancy and load balancing:** I mention redundancy when talking about the core, and it is equally important here. At the distribution layer, you should also consider *load balancing,* which is having additional connections between devices, sharing the traffic between connections. You can read more about the differences between load balancing and redundancy in Book III, Chapters 6 and 7.

✦ **QoS classification:** If you have implemented QoS on your network, then you can have the distribution layer perform two roles related to QoS:

  • It can examine data and classify the network data with a priority tag based on criteria such as destination network address or traffic type.

  • It can honor existing QoS tags and process higher priority traffic faster than other traffic.

✦ **Security filtering:** In addition to examining data for QoS classification, your network devices can filter data to prevent certain devices from communicating with other devices over your network. This may be a case where you have high security servers that are only allowed to be accessed from certain workstations.

✦ **Aggregation and summarization:** Allows you to consolidate traffic data from slower connections, from workstations to slower network devices, and pass it to the higher speed core devices. If you had built this structure as a routed network, then this layer would also perform the task of consolidating routing table entries, which is called summarization. You can discover more about routing and switching in Books III and IV.

✦ **Intervirtual local area network (VLAN) routing:** If your network has made use of VLANs, then the distribution layer can provide routing services for devices from different VLANs that exist on the same side of the core network. For instance, two workstations that are attempting to communicate with each other would not need their traffic to travel to the core for routing between VLANs, and could have that routing performed at the distribution layer. This would be considered if it was a common traffic pattern and you wanted to take the network load off of the core layer.

✦ **Media translation:** Devices at the access layer may have different types of connections that they are making into the distribution layer and thereby the core layer. You may have a mixture of Ethernet, Asynchronous Transfer Mode (ATM), and Token ring clients on your network, the distribution layer has the responsibility for changing these connection and data formats into the type of data that will be used by the rest of the network.

This layer does the heavy lifting for these components, allowing the traffic sent to the core layer to be moved through the network.

The distribution layer, like the core layer, is blind to any aspect of the content of the data that moves — it could care less if it moves a signal to release nuclear weapons, the text of a love poem, or an MP3 file. Only the access layer cares about data's content.

When working in small network environments, where the entire network is composed of four or five network devices, you will likely combine the functionality of your core and distribution layers into a single device, rather than spend money on a device that will not be utilized to its full potential. With the smallest network, composed solely of one network device, you combine the functionality of all three levels into a single device due to necessity. In these cases, even though you are combining multiple roles into a single hardware device, keep the roles separate in your mind.

Access layer

The access layer is where all the user equipment, such as computers and printers, are connected. Therefore, this layer is where your users and their devices reside, and it can be the easiest location for to you implement security features, such as QoS classifications and ACLs. Features like QoS and ACLs should be implemented as close to the network equipment for which they are controlling data flow. There are many features that should be implemented at the access layer including

✦ **High availability:** Devices in the access layer should have high availability features, such as dual power supplies, because the equipment that is connected to these switches only supports a single network interface. This is different from the other layers, where multiple connections may exist between devices. You may be able to have spare switches or routers onsite, but if a switch fails, you will end up with a network outage for the connected users as you install a spare switch or router.

✦ **Port security:** Network devices have several security features, like only allowing a single MAC address to be connected to a port, or that the MAC address needs to be valid against a database of authorized network cards. These features are aimed at securing the network data jacks that exist around corporate offices.

✦ **Broadcast suppression:** There are times when one device on a network will start sending out broadcasts at an alarmingly high rate. This is not typical behavior and is usually a result of a hardware malfunction on a network card. These broadcasts are enough to cripple a network by overloading the network. The broadcast suppression feature watches the device connections and can disable ports where broadcast traffic accounts for more than your configured percentage of traffic.

✦ **QoS classification:** Although I placed QoS classification at the distribution layer, QoS classification will occur at the closest point possible to the sending device, which means you should apply it at the access layer. There will be times where it makes more sense to classify the data at the distribution layer because traffic from several devices is aggregated at that point. One such case may be when the access layer device does not support QoS. The drawback of classifying data at the distribution layer is that your traffic has crossed a portion of your network without the benefit of QoS priority routing.

✦ **Access Control Lists (ACLs):** Similar to QoS, in that ACLs typically are best applied close to the source or destination devices on your network, which means that the best place to apply these controls is in the access layer.

✦ **Spanning tree:** While spanning tree is often enabled across an entire network, it greatly benefits the access layer. It is the access layer where tech-savvy users may attempt to connect their own hubs and switches, potentially causing network loops that in the absence of spanning tree, can bring your network throughput to a screeching halt.

+ **Power over Ethernet (PoE):** Devices that require power, such as IP-based phones and wireless access points, almost exclusively exist at the access layer, which means that PoE will only be deployed at the access layer in support of these devices.

Because the access layer directly connects user equipment, and combines their data together as it goes to the distribution layer, your network design should plan to support this combined data as it moves to the distribution layer. Additionally, as each access layer switch is connected to the distribution layer, you should attempt to place an equal number of users on each access layer switch as this will reduce the chance of overwhelming the ports on your distribution layer device. For example, if you have two 48-port switches at that access layer, and 50 devices to connect, you should split them so that approximately 25 are placed on each switch, rather than using all of the ports on the first switch and only a couple on the second. In the latter scenario, one port at the distribution layer will need to process a substantially higher amount of traffic than the other port. Ideally you would split these client devices by the amount of traffic they will be generating, trying to keep the traffic balanced on the distribution layer ports (but who is to say that Sally will be generating more traffic than Phil?).

Thus far I have really been talking about user equipment being connected to the access layer and aggregated at the distribution layer. However, in large networks with dozens or hundreds of servers, you actually have two distribution and access layers: one access layer and one distribution would support the user devices, such as computers and printers; the other access layer and distribution layer would support the servers. Typically a server room (or data center) is a large room with raised floors (so all of your cabling can be managed under the floor), redundant power, air conditioning, and hundreds of servers. This room may be located in your main building, or could be housed in another building, dedicated to supporting this computer equipment.

Suggesting that your enterprise class network has many servers, Cisco uses the term *data center* when referring to the access and distribution layers that are to be used for your servers and server room devices. The other Cisco term that I introduce in this section is *campus*. In this case, campus refers to your office or internal corporate network. This may be a portion of a floor in a building, several floors of an office tower, or a private network that spans many buildings, such as a college campus; in all cases, it represents a network where you own all of the wires from the user computer through the network to your servers. Figure 2-6 illustrates these two additional layers in the network model. When working with this five layer version of network design, you can see that network core is actually in the middle of the path from the user computers and the servers.

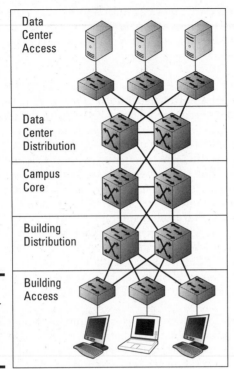

Figure 2-6:
Data center access and distribution layers.

Enterprise modules

Finally, in addition to the three layers in the network (see the previous sections in this chapter), you can include additional enterprise-level modules. The modularization of the network aids in identifying problem domains, and the enterprise modules keep these components in separate areas. I discuss the four main functional areas of your network, of which three areas will contain enterprise modules. Start with the network diagram shown in Figure 2-6, which depicts your internal corporate network. This is now labeled Enterprise Campus in Figure 2-7. It has this new name because you are now looking at the whole network from a slightly higher altitude. Figure 2-7 also shows you the three areas in which you will find the enterprise modules:

✦ **Enterprise Campus:** The main part of your network infrastructure that is directly connected to each other and where you own all of the wiring, which I discuss in the earlier section, "Access layer." This is the entire network if you have no remote connectivity, including Internet access.

✦ **Enterprise Edge modules:** As *edge* suggests, this is the edge of the corporate network as it relates to the Enterprise Campus components.

✦ **Service Provider (SP) Edge modules:** Facing the Enterprise Edge is the SP Edge, representing the edge of the Service provider network.

✦ **Remote modules:** Any enterprise resources that are away from the Enterprise Campus are part of the remote modules.

The full layout of the enterprise model is shown in Figure 2-7.

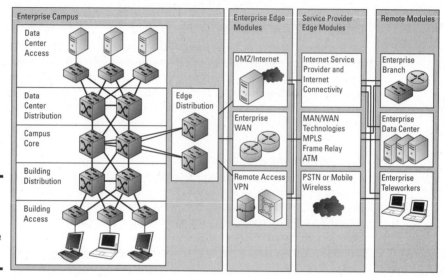

Figure 2-7: The enterprise architecture model.

Enterprise Campus

The three main network layers (core, distribution, and access) can still be identified in the Enterprise Campus, which is so named because it represents the entirety of your network's directly connected infrastructure, where you are in ownership of all infrastructure wiring, and thereby in control of the network infrastructure. Above the campus core, I included the server distribution and access layers that I introduce in the earlier section, "Access layer."

These are the server farm, or data center distribution and access layers. They play a similar role to the main access and distribution layers, but in this case, for traffic to and from your servers and other core network devices. The requirement for these additional layers is dependent on the number of devices that are in use in the server farm or data center.

Also connected to the core of the Enterprise Campus is the *edge distribution*. This distribution layer acts as the interface to all Enterprise Edge modules, which include all components that allow traffic to flow to or from the Enterprise Campus network, such as to a remote office, a remote user, or the Internet. This distribution layer acts like the other distribution layers you have seen in the "Distribution layer" and "Access layer" sections of this chapter: It aggregates data coming from the edge and remote modules as it moves to the campus core.

Enterprise Edge modules

All the components in Enterprise Edge Modules are enterprise-owned resources that connect to outside components, those that belong to other parties, such as a telephone company. All these devices connect to outside resources, such as Internet firewalls, Demilitarized Zone (DMZ) firewalls, Wide Area Network (WAN) routers, remote access servers, or virtual private network (VPN) devices.

Service Provider Edge modules

The main difference between Enterprise Edge modules and the Service Provider Edge modules is that Enterprise hardware is used in the Enterprise Edge modules, whereas with the Server Provider Edge modules, you deal with infrastructure that does not belong to Enterprise but rather is owned and operated by the service provider or telephone company. The telephone company hardware may specifically be hosted at your site, but management and ownership of the hardware is the telephone company or the third-party company. This may include any Internet access technologies, such as cable modems, Asynchronous Digital Subscriber Line (ADSL) modems, satellite links, fiber termination points, phone lines, or other hardware devices.

Remote modules

Remote modules represent any piece of the remote infrastructure that needs to use technology at the Service Provider Edge to communicate with the core network. This represents any devices that do not reside at the Enterprise Campus network location. These remote components may be remote data centers that are used as disaster recovery sites, branch offices, or remote teleworkers using any type of technologies to access data. Your BlackBerry device or smartphone represents a device that fits into this module.

Chapter 3: Knowing as Little as Possible about Math

In This Chapter

✔ Getting to know other number systems

✔ Figuring out the differences between bits and bytes

✔ Converting values between number systems

You might be wondering, "Why do I need to read about numbers? I learned them from zero to ten in kindergarten, so what more do I need to know?" Well, mathematicians might just disagree with you. But in this case, you encounter many types of numbers while working with computers and network devices. In this chapter, I give you a primer on those numbers.

You are probably used to the *Base 10* (decimal) number system, which has the ten numerals you are familiar with in it (0–9). This chapter introduces you to the limited Base 2 (binary), the Base 8 (octal), and the larger Base 16 (hexadecimal). With the familiar Base 10 number system having 10 numerals, you may already be thinking that the Base 2 number system only has two numerals; if that is the case, then you are correct. The two numerals in the Base 2 system are zero and one; while the eight numerals in the Base 8 system are zero to seven and the Base 16 number system has sixteen numerals. Wait, how do you get sixteen numerals? With the Base 16 number system, the first ten are your familiar zero to nine, and then you use A, B, C, D, E, and F.

After you complete this chapter, you will have a firm grasp of converting numbers between the different number systems (Base 2, Base 8, Base 10, and Base 16) that are commonly used with computing devices (in fact, those values in the Windows Registry might even make a little more sense). With this knowledge, you will not be quite so confused when you get deeper into routing, switching, and firewall security rules, or subnetting and the device configuration register as you read through this book.

Why These Number Systems Are Important

The main number system in our world is Base 10. I often wonder if we had six fingers whether society would have adopted a Base 6 number system. Although the Base 10 system works great with our body construction and we have become very used to working with it, it does not work equally well with all other things in our environment. Therefore, I discuss the other number systems that you encounter in your work with digital equipment. If you continue to look around computing devices, you start to notice how these values and number systems keep popping up.

Bit is short for *binary digit. Binary* is another name for the Base 2 number system. Binary, with its two digit values, nicely matches the two electrical states that exist — on and off, or current or no current. All electrical devices, including routers and switches, rely heavily on these two states. All core decisions that a computing device makes come down to `true` or `false` decisions, which means these decisions can be manipulated with electrical current.

When you look at the logic decision making process, some basic structures are used. These structures are *logic gates,* which include the following and are shown in Figure 3-1:

✦ **AND:** Bits are allowed through the output if both inputs are present. In Figure 3-1, two ones on the two input streams on the left of the gate resulted in a one on the right. The following two sets of digits were both composed of a one and a zero also both resulted in a zero on the right side of the gate for each pair of numbers. With the final set of input values, when there were two zeros in the input streams, the result on the right side of the gate was also a zero.

✦ **OR:** Bits are allowed through the output if either input is present. In Figure 3-1, two ones on the two input streams on the left of the gate resulted in a one on the right. The following two sets of digits were both composed of a one and a zero also both resulted in a one on the right side of the gate for each pair of numbers. Only when there were two zeros in the input streams did the result on the right have a zero.

✦ **NAND:** Standing for *NOT AND,* bit results are reversed of the AND. The initial processing of these calculations is identical to the AND processing, but prior to sending the value out of the gate, the value is reversed. So to examine each bit being processed in Figure 3-1, the two ones at the start of the input stream would AND to a result of one; but because this a NOT AND, the value is reversed to a zero in the resultant stream on the right of the gate. Similarly, the next three sets of input values all have at least one zero, which would AND to zero; but because this is a NOT AND, the result is reversed and the resultant stream ends up with three zeros.

✦ **NOR:** Standing for *NOT OR,* bit results are reversed of the OR. To visit Figure 3-1 one last time, this is similar to the NOT AND, in the case that all of the normal results will be reversed. So for the first three pairs of numbers from the two source data streams, there is a one in each pair, so the normal OR process would result in a stream of three ones. Because this is a NOT OR, each of these values is reverse before exiting the gate, resulting in a stream of three zeros. The final pair of values in the input streams are two zeros, which would result in an OR of one zero; but because this is a NOT OR, the final result would be a one.

These logic gates are used in computer programming decision-making, but they have been used for basic electrical systems for generations. Writing an entire computer program with just manipulating electrical states to on and off would be confusing and long. Picture Bart Simpson writing lines of ones and zeroes on the chalkboard and then multiply that by a million, and you have some idea how ridiculous that would be.

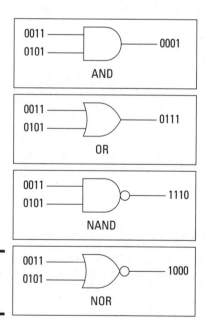

Figure 3-1:
Basic logic
gates.

To complicate things further, all programmers use high-level languages that take away from the zeros and ones so they can work with word length values to tell the computer what to do. A *word* is a group of bits that are moved as a unit; typically they would be from 8 to 64 bits in length, depending on the operating system. For example, you will often see DWords in the Microsoft Windows registry, which are 32 bit numbers, representing a Double Word length value. This can mean that you are now dealing with a lot more bits. To deal with numbers that take a long time to write, you can convert to different numbering systems. For example, eight binary digits could look like 11111111, but you could convert that into the following number systems:

✦ Base 8: 377

✦ Base 10: 255

✦ Base 16: FF

So using other number formats can save your hand from cramping, especially when writing a 128-bit IPv6 address such as 10010100101001001100111101010 00001111111100101010011000111000000011101010100111100001111000011110 0000000111110110100011110110111. I show you how to convert these numbers in the later sections of this chapter using the base 10 number 215.

You may notice from the previous example that Base 16 looks kind of easy to deal with — you have to write only two characters. For example, 00111111 in Base 2 is 77 in Base 8, or 63 in Base 10. Eight ones give a nice, easy to write and remember Base 16 number FF (two digits with the highest digit values in the Base 16 number system), and six ones gives a nice, easy to write and remember Base 8 number 77 (two digits with the highest digit values in the Base 8 number system). In either case though, the Base 10 number is nothing particularly graceful or spectacular, being 255 in the first example and 63 in the second example. After you get beyond one in Base 10, a lot of numbers are simultaneously memorable in both the Base 2 and Base 10 number systems.

Working with Bits and Bytes

While I said earlier that a binary digit (or *bit*) is the smallest unit you can work with, it is by far not the most the common. In Table 3-1, I detail the number of binary digits, the number of combinations from that digit, and the value of the last highest-order digit.

Table 3-1	Comparing Multi-Digit Binary Numbers		
Number of Digits	Total Combinations	Value of High Digit	Base 2 Notation
1	2	1	2^1
2	4	2	2^2
3	8	4	2^3
4	16	8	2^4
5	32	16	2^5
6	64	32	2^6
7	128	64	2^7
8	256	128	2^8
9	512	256	2^9
10	1024	512	2^10
11	2048	1024	2^11
12	4096	2048	2^12
13	8192	4096	2^13
14	16384	8192	2^14
15	32768	16384	2^15
16	65536	32768	2^16

Grouping together eight of these bits, which creates a *byte,* is very common. When converting from binary to decimal, a byte gives you up to 256 possible values ranging from 0 to 255.

If you have been working with computers or Cisco devices, you may notice that many of these numbers seem familiar because many appear as limitations, such as storage limitations based on bit or byte values, within electronic devices. For example, if you create a database, you need to define a storage space that holds a numeral value and is eight bits large, allowing you to store a number from 0 to 255. You see these limitations again and again when working with electronic devices. When working with computers and other electronic devices, you regularly encounter the same numbers as limitations. I dub these numbers *naturally occurring binary numbers.* Well, they are not truly naturally occurring because a programmer somewhere decided to use that value. Typically, limitations are based on conserving space or memory. As the amounts of memory in devices increases as quickly as it does today, though, memory becomes less of a concern.

Typically when storing data in a computing device, every attempt is made to store data in uniform-sized blocks. Because memory is a binary storage media, you start with a large block, such as 1KB or 1,024 bytes (in computers, you always use binary based numbers, so 1MB is a million or actually 1,048,576 bytes). If you break that 1KB block into even chunks by dividing it by another binary number, then you always end up with another binary number. In some cases, when this does not seem to match, you have some overhead, such as storing delimiter characters, which means a 16-byte storage space may allow you to store a 14–15 character word. That means that the 15-character word still makes sense in a binary storage world.

Take a bit of time and look at your electronics and Table 3-1. You may be surprised how many times these numbers appear.

Pondering the Significance of the Significant Bit

If you have followed along so far, you have read about bits and the maximum number of combinations from a binary number of a certain number of digits. In this section, I take that just a bit further and discuss the *significant bit*. If you see a binary number, such as 10010011, and you are asked which digit has the greatest value, you would likely say that it is the leftmost digit because people tend to read from left to right. However, in the computing devices world, two systems are in use: The most-used system for networking protocols is *big-endian,* which treats the leftmost digit as the most significant digit or high-ordered bit; most computer operating systems running x86 and x64 processors use little-endian, which treats the rightmost digit as the high-order bit.

For the purposes of this book, when I discuss the *high-order bit* or *most significant digit,* I mean the leftmost digit. When I discuss the *low-order bit* or *least significant digit,* I mean the rightmost digit.

Making Conversions

In the "Working with Bits and Bytes" section, earlier in this chapter, I discuss the difference between bits and bytes. Within standard computing systems, a byte is often enough to store data, which is less than eight bits. In cases where the data is greater than a byte, then multiple bytes are required to be used. When working with multi-byte values, in the computing world, the term *word* is used. As you move from one operating system (OS) to another OS, you will learn that the length of a word is not the same for all operating systems but words are typically 16-bits (2 bytes), 32-bits (4 bytes), or 64-bits (8 bytes) in length. This simply makes defined storage blocks easier to deal with in those operating systems. So in addition to bytes, words also define standard units of binary storage.

You may be wondering what you can store in these binary storage structures (bits, bytes, and words). A byte is 8 bits in length and can store up to 256 combinations or numbers from 0 to 255. To match this, the American Standard Code for Information Interchange (ASCII) defines a *character set,* which represents the standard characters or letters that you could type on a keyboard. The ASCII character set has only 256 unique characters or letters, numbered from 0 to 255. Therefore, with a byte being a standard unit of data, it can also represent a single character from the ASCII character set. If you attempt to store a different type of data, you use different amounts of storage. For example, to store a Boolean value, you need only one bit, which would be a zero or a one; whereas to store an integer, you need more space (see Table 3-2).

Table 3-2		Integer Storage	
Bits	*Name*	*Signed Range*	*Unsigned Range*
8	byte	−128 to 127	0 to 255
16	short int (integer)	−32,768 to 32,767	0 to 65,535
32	int (integer)	−2,147,483,648 to 2,147,483,647	0 to 4,294,967,295
64	long int (integer)	−9,223,372,036,854,775,808 to 9,223,372,036,854,775,807	0 to 18,446,744,073,709,551,615

Converting Base 2 (binary) to Base 10 (decimal)

Even though you might not think so, binary to decimal conversions are quite easy. Because many of the binary numbers you work with are in byte (8 bit) length, I work those in the example. A binary number like 10010011 is just like the Base 10 number system, except that each number represents a different column, not 1, 10, 100, 1,000, and so on. These binary numbers represent 1, 2, 4, 8, 16, 32, 64, and 128. Unlike the decimal system in which you have values from zero to nine in each column, with binary, you have only a zero or one in each column. If I start with a one in binary, it will be in first column; if I add another one to that value, I would add one to the first column. Because that exceeds the highest value for the one's column, I put a zero in the one's column and carry a one over to the second column (or the two's column). So in binary, 1+1=10, just like the joke, "There are 10 types of people in the world, those that understand binary and those that do not."

In Table 3-3, I show you the conversions. If you look at the decimal values, you simply need to total them to get the decimal value of 11010011, or 128 + 64 + 16 + 2 + 1, or 211. See, I told you it was going to be simple. You may become good enough to do that in your head.

Table 3-3 — Binary to Decimal Conversion

Column Value	Binary	Decimal
128	1	128
64	1	64
32	0	0
16	1	16
8	0	0
4	0	0
2	1	2
1	1	1

The tough part (for me, at least) is going the other way. As a decimal, 215, think of the binary conversion this way: Table 3-4 shows how to convert a base 10 number to a binary number; for simplicity, I have chosen a number that will result in an answer of eight bits or less.

Table 3-4 — Converting Decimal to Binary

Column Value	Decimal	Compared to Column Value	Resulting Action	Binary
128	215	Less than 256 but more than 128	Mark 1 for the 128 column and then subtract 128 from 215	1
64	87	More than 64	Mark 1 for the 64 column then subtract 64 from 87	1
32	23	Less than 32	Mark a 0 for the 32 column	0
16	23	More than 16	Mark a 1 for the 16 column and then subtract 16 from 23	1
8	7	Less than 8	Mark a 0 for the 8 column	0
4	7	More than 4	Mark a 1 for the 4 column and then subtract 4 from 7	1
2	3	More than 2	Mark a 1 for the 2 column and then subtract 2 from 3	1
1	1	Equal to 1	Mark a 1 for the 1 column	1

By going through the zeros and ones from top to bottom, the final binary number is 11010111. A zero is given to any position where that number is not present. Not quite as easy as the other way, but still not terribly complicated. If you work through a few numbers, you may find that it does not take long to figure out.

If you want some practice doing binary/decimal conversions quickly and in your head, give some of the Cisco training games a shot, which are available at `https://learningnetwork.cisco.com/community/connections/games`. One game that is good for binary to decimal conversion (and vice versa) is the Binary Game. This game is a Tetris-like game, as shown in Figure 3-2, in which you need to fill in the missing numbers to clear a row off-screen. When the screen is full, you lose, so work quickly.

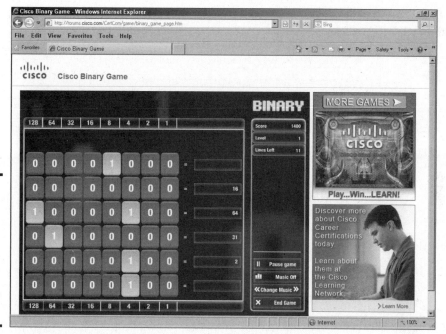

Figure 3-2: Cisco's Binary Game can make practicing binary conversions fun.

Converting binary to Base 8 (octal)

After you get the hang of binary to decimal conversions (see the preceding section), try converting from binary to octal. Binary to octal conversions are actually even easier. This is due to the fact that octal numbers can be managed by simply grouping your binary numbers in sets of three. For example, start with the binary number, 11010011, from the preceding section, which resulted from the conversion from the decimal number of 215. Because 11010111 is only eight digits, add a leading zero to make this easier:

011010111. By breaking this number into groups of three bits, you get 011, 010, and 111. Each of these three-bit binary numbers can now be converted into a number between zero and seven depending on the positions of the bits (see Table 3-5). After you convert these three groups of bits, your results should be 3 (from 011), 2 (from 010), and 7 (from 111), so the octal number is 327.

If you have been trying the binary to decimal conversions, converting binary numbers to octal, which are only three bits long, is easier.

Table 3-5	Binary to Octal Conversions
Binary Value	*Octal Value*
000	0
001	1
010	2
011	3
100	4
101	5
110	6
111	7

Converting from octal to binary is not really any more difficult because each octal digit simply expands to three binary digits. For example, if you are given an octal number like 247, break it apart to 2, 4, and 7. Then convert each digit to 010, 100, and 111, giving you a total of 010100111. (Again, I added the leading zero to make life easier.) The byte length value (minus the zero, that is) would be 10100111.

You may be thinking that this was fairly easy; however, it was easy only because binary matches up nicely with octal (Base 8) and hexadecimal (Base 16), as you will see in the next section, but not decimal (Base 10). Remember, 10 works well for humans (maybe because we have ten fingers and toes?), but 10 is not a natural binary number, whereas 4, 8, 16, and 32 are.

Converting binary to Base 16 (hexadecimal)

No sense in putting off the last conversion in this chapter — binary to Base 16 (hexadecimal). This conversion is easier than the binary to decimal conversion. The strangest thing about hexadecimal is that there are more than just ten numbers (zero to nine), so you need to use the following extra characters: A (10), B (11), C (12), D (13), E (14), and F (15) with each sequentially representing the extra values.

The easiest way to do the conversion is to again break the binary number in groups. Use the same binary number from earlier sections, 11010011; however, this time, break it into groups of four digits: 1001 and 0011. Each group easily converts into a hexadecimal number between 0 and 15, or 0 and F. Your results should be 13 (from 1001) and 3 (from 0011), so the hexadecimal number is D3. Table 3-6 helps you with these hexadecimal conversions.

Table 3-6	Binary to Hexadecimal Conversions
Binary Value	*Hexadecimal Value*
0000	0
0001	1
0010	2
0011	3
0100	4
0101	5
0110	6
0111	7
1000	8
1001	9
1010	A
1011	B
1100	C
1101	D
1110	E
1111	F

Hexadecimal to binary migration is fairly simple. Convert each digit to binary and then concatenate (or join then sequentially end-to-end) the numbers (remember to include all leading zeros). For example, break 9C into 9 and C, and then convert each to binary, yielding 1001 and 1100. The binary number is then 10011100.

The Windows Calculator is capable of making all these conversions for you. To launch the Windows Calculator in Scientific view:

1. **Choose Start⇨All Programs⇨Accessories⇨Calculator.**

   The Calculator opens.

2. **Choose View⇨Scientific (or View⇨Programmer if you are using Windows 7).**

You can also enable Digit Grouping from the View menu to make reading values easier. Figure 3-3 shows a conversion from hexadecimal to binary.

3. **To convert from one number system to another, select the Hex, Dec, Oct, or Bin radio button.**

   For example, to enter a hexadecimal number and convert it to binary, select the Hex radio button. The hexadecimal keys at the bottom of the keyboard are enabled.

4. **Type a number and select the Hex, Dec, Oct, or Bin radio button to see the equivalent value.**

Figure 3-3:
The Windows Calculator performs a conversion in Scientific mode.

Leading zeros and number systems

In most cases, placing leading zeros on any number looks odd or creates more writing. So that newspaper costs $2.50 or $000,000,002.50. These extra zeros do nothing to affect the numeric value of the cost of the paper. When dealing with binary, I discuss byte length values in the "Working with Bits and Bytes" section, and word length values in the "Making Conversions" section.

Because bytes and words represent a fixed length of data, eight bits for a byte, it can get confusing when you write out multiple bytes in sequence: For example, 101 followed by 10010 could look like 10110010 if you failed to leave a space. So now these two byte values look like a single byte value. By including the leading zeros, you can avoid confusion, especially if you are working in bytes. With the leading zeros, two bytes would look like 00000101 00010010, which does not change the numeric value of the bytes. At any time you feel you need to add a few leading zeros to make numbers easier to work with, go for it, because it only adds to the number of zeros you need to write out.

Chapter 4: Testing Your Core Networking Knowledge

In This Chapter

✔ Examining the OSI network model

✔ Troubleshooting the OSI layers

✔ Checking out the Ethernet packet frame structure

✔ Sharing network media with low- and high-level addressing

✔ Getting a handle on CSMA/CD and CSMA/CA

✔ Analyzing network data with Wireshark

In Chapter 1 of this minibook, you review some of the major components that make up a network, such as switches and routers. In this chapter, you get a little deeper into each of these components. You run up and down through the Open System Interconnection (OSI) model, pausing to examine components that exist at many of the layers. You are also introduced in more depth to the major networking protocols that are used on data networks, such as Transmission Control Protocol/Internet Protocol (TCP/IP). I go into detail right down to seeing how the signaling for the physical network works.

Whatever physical media you deal with, from the networking perspective, there are only two states: on and off, or 1 and 0.

Before you begin this chapter, you need to know your goals. By the end of this chapter you

✦ Have some comfort with the OSI model, such as why it was created and how it is used in networking today

✦ Have a basic understanding of *network frames,* which are the containers that hold data on the physical network, and the Internet Protocol (IP) packets that are contained in the frames

✦ Know the basic structure of a Media Access Control (MAC) address and how it is used to communicate on the network

+ Have some knowledge of some of the dominate protocols that have been used for networking

+ Can distinguish collision-detection mechanisms from collision-avoidance mechanisms

+ Have a rough working knowledge of the packet capture program *Wireshark,* which captures and analyzes network traffic

Layering the OSI Model

Working with the OSI networking model or other networking models aids in the understanding of how your network works and how components are separated but able to communicate with each other. This section focuses on the OSI model in detail and how to use this information to troubleshoot networking problems. For example, when you are informed that a computer cannot communicate with a server, very often the problem is described as "the network is down." (I personally love hearing this when discussing the Internet, because if the Internet was truly down, I am sure I would have heard about it on the radio. Rather, the connection to the network may be down.) With your knowledge of the OSI model, you can start your troubleshooting, working through the layers, until you locate the cause of the problem; validating that each layer is working as you move through the layers.

In Chapter 1, I introduce you to the OSI model by the International Organization for Standardization (ISO), but in this chapter you will dig a little deeper, but not so deep that I put you to sleep. Although the ISO has come up with the network model, most of the specifications for how devices actually communicate (such as Ethernet — 10 Mbps, Fast Ethernet — 100 Mbps, Gigabit Ethernet — 1Gbps, or any of the 802.11 wireless specifications) have been created, defined, or managed by another organization, the Institute of Electrical and Electronics Engineers (IEEE). The OSI model is a seven-layer model that includes the following layers:

+ Application

+ Presentation

+ Session

+ Transport

+ Network

+ Data link

+ Physical

You may find it helpful to remember the order of these layers from top to bottom with this mnemonic device, *All People Seem To Need Data Processing.* If you prefer the bottom-to-top approach, try *Please Do Not Throw Sausage Pizza Away.*

Regardless of how you approach the OSI model, you need to remember what each layer is responsible for. You also need to remember that the model represents a logical ideal of networking and not a real world requirement. The following sections review this model from the bottom to the top. I prefer this manner of reviewing the layers because if I am troubleshooting a network problem, I typically start with the physical layer (is the computer even plugged in?) and work up through the layers until the problem has been resolved. When troubleshooting from the application layer down, you will likely get a bunch of layers not working until you find the problem.

Layer 1: The physical layer

The physical layer represents the physical media, such as Category 5e cables and the Ethernet frame type (which you will see in the "Framing Data" section, later in this chapter) that is used to move the binary data across the network. Because the data is binary, it is composed of two states that represent zeros and ones: Zero is electrically off, and one is electrically on. With the OSI model, the application layer is not concerned with the physical media of the network; think of it this way, people are not typically concerned with the underlying technology used by their cellphone carriers, such as analog, digital, 1x, Edge, 3G, or 4G, as long as they can make calls. (If you are a geek, you probably want 4G or are already on it.)

So in the cellphone example, you could think of the call dialing and processing features of the cellphone as the application layer, the cellphone's Electronic Serial Number (ESN) or its Subscriber Identity Module (SIM) as being on the datalink layer (you see that in the next section), and the service type (3G or 4G) as the physical layer. The datalink layer cares about the underlying physical service type (a SIM-based phone does not work with ESN-based networks); while at the application layer, it only cares that information it sends down the network layers crosses the network and is able to communicate with the call processing application components at the cellphone carriers' offices.

The physical networking layer could use any or all the variants (a/b/g/n) of 802.11 wireless technologies, fiber, twisted pairs of copper wire (Cat4, Cat5, Cat6), cable (also copper wire, but different), satellite, or microwave. Again, typically the user of the device does not care what the technology is as long as it moves the data bits at a rate that is sufficient for their needs; for many users, this does not need to be very fast.

Layer 2: The data link layer

The data link layer is adjacent to the physical layer, so they are associated pretty closely together. Whereas the physical layer deals with the actual physical media (the cables and so forth that the data move over), the data link layer deals with signaling or the method used to send data across that media. Part of sending signals across the network's media is coming up with a way to identify the sending and receiving devices. To solve this issue, networks use numeric identifiers such as a MAC address associated with a network interface card (NIC). Every network card manufactured in the world has a globally unique MAC address associated with the card. To make identifying the MAC address easier for the end user, it is usually printed on the outside of the product box, written on the card as shown in Figure 4-1 (where 3Com decided to identify it as the EA number), or on the outside of the computer that it is installed in (if you have a laptop, turn it over and there is a good chance that you will see the MAC address).

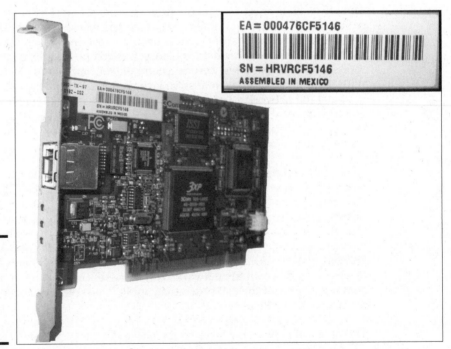

Figure 4-1:
An NIC
with its
identifying
hardware
address.

When looking for your MAC address, it will always be a 12-digit hexadecimal number, which was clearly identifiable from the serial number (SN) which includes non-hexadecimal characters.

The type of addressing or options that would be used at this layer depends to a degree on what physical layer is being used, so data link addresses for serial connections are different than Ethernet connections. Although in all cases, this includes some type of addressing that is compatible with the physical layer so that devices connected to that layer can identify themselves and other devices connected to the media. This is important, because when a computer sends data to a network file server, you would like that data to get to the server. The key thing to remember about the data link layer is that it contains those devices that communicate with the physical layer and a method of identifying physical parts of the network.

Layer 3: The network layer

The network layer routes the data from one location to another, or across several defined networks. A *network* is a series of devices that are connected to a single physical medium, or broadcast domain (discussed in Book III, Chapter 2). Some people might challenge this notion and say that a network is a collision domain, but I discuss the fine differences between these in Book II. For now, just know that if a network represents interconnected devices moving signals between one another, the network layer moves data between these networks of interconnected devices, dubbed an *internetwork*. This can be done on a small scale (separating data on a network of a dozen computers) or on a large scale (separating data for an international corporation across the globe).

The global Internet represents doing this on a very large scale, and its name is a contraction of the word *internetwork*.

Because data needs to move between networks, there must be an underlying protocol to support network identification and a manner of identifying paths between networks, which can be done manually or automatically using a compatible protocol.

A *protocol* is a set of standards or rules that all participants must adhere to. When dignitaries from different countries meet, they follow mutually agreed upon protocols for dealing with each other. In the case of the network, the participants are the networking devices (such as computers, routers, and switches), while the protocols are the rules which have been agreed upon to communicate with each other. Most of the hardware level protocols (like Ethernet standards) are managed by IEEE, while the Internet Engineering Task Force (IETF) manages the TCP/IP suite of protocols.

The network layer does not care much about the type of data it is moving, the path it takes, or the different media that it moves over. Typically, you are allowed to change physical media types at this layer. To connect different network types, you need an interconnection device that supports data links for different network types. Such a device includes different media connections on either side and, like the router in Figure 4-2, can connect gigabit Ethernet on one side of the device to something foreign, such as Token Ring, on the other side.

Just as the data link layer has addresses that it uses to identify other devices with which your computer communicates, these are hard to understand addresses and they are only valid for the current network segments (the area between two routers). This area between routers is also referred to as a *data link* because it is the only place where the local devices can communicate with each other, using MAC addresses (or data link layer addresses). The network layer of the OSI model also uses addresses, but these are network layer addresses and their specific format is based on the network layer protocol being used. Internet Protocol (IP) represents a common network layer protocol.

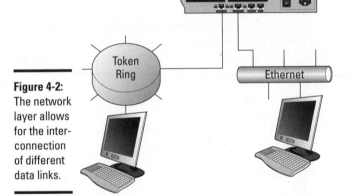

Figure 4-2:
The network layer allows for the inter-connection of different data links.

At the network layer, IP uses IP addresses to determine which two devices are communicating. The relationship between the network layer and the data link layer is that all communication over a data link will always be performed using data link (MAC) addresses, so as the network layer sends data down to the data link layer, it must also tell the data link layer what the destination MAC address is for this data. To accomplish this, IP makes use of the Address Resolution Protocol (ARP) to resolve the required MAC addresses for the IP address targets with which it wants to communicate. (You can find out more about ARP in Book II, Chapter 3.)

Layer 4: The transport layer

The transport layer is closely related to the network layer, but adds functionality to it. You can think of this layer as a traffic cop or a supervisor for the mindless mob of packets that is the network layer. As discussed in Chapter 1 of this minibook, the transport layer takes responsibility for verifying data delivery. The network layer may have a high success rate in getting data to the destination, but the transport layer is specifically told to ensure delivery of data. Either way, you are going to use transport layer delivery mechanisms, but you (or the application you are using) will need to make a decision as to whether you will be using verified data delivery or unverified data delivery. In both cases, you are still using a transport layer component or protocol.

The actual mechanisms that are used to guarantee data delivery are dependent on the networking protocol that is in use, whereas the concept of delivery reliability is more universal. When working with the TCP/IP protocol suite, verified delivery is performed using the Transmission Control Protocol (TCP), while unverified delivery is performed using User Datagram Protocol (UDP).

For example, compare a text message to a phone conversation. Even though a large number of text messages get through, there is no guarantee that any given message to a person has been received (something my wife occasionally needs to be reminded of), whereas an answered phone call and the ensuing interchange with the other person gives you the immediate feedback that the words are received by the recipient. (I will not say that the message got through, because that conveys the idea that the message was actually understood.) Similarly, voicemail is equally as useless as a text message in terms of feedback.

Now you may wonder why you would want to use unverified delivery. Well, in the case of person-to-person interaction, my wife often prefers text messages to voice calls, because she can get her message to someone without getting into a lengthy conversation, which involves exchanging pleasantries. She will know if the message got through when she receives a reply, or if that reply does not occur within a reasonable time frame, she can resend her message. The same is true of network communications, where the cost of verified delivery is additional overhead in establishing a delivery channel, verifying the data is received after you have sent the message, and closing down the delivery channel. If the data you plan to send is small or not very important, then this overhead can be tedious and slow the communication process down; but if you eliminate the overhead, you also eliminate the verification. This is not a problem that is of concern to the transport layer, the request to send that data came from the session layer.

If the session layer has marked the data as no verification required, then the session layer is responsible for performing its own check or verification of delivery. Based on the data, the session layer may choose not to worry about delivery or the session layer may have its own rules of delivery verification, such as it expects a response from the destination computer within five seconds, after which the session layer will resend the data.

Layer 5: The session layer

The session layer defines how the data is formatted between the devices on either side of the link. This is effectively the manner in which they maintain an open channel between the two devices. However, at lower levels of the OSI model, there is no permanent connection but rather a series of short bursts of data being sent back and forth. The session layer maintains a conversation over many of these bursts of data; in fact, it can take several bursts of data going back and forth just to establish the structure that will be followed for that session.

A real-world example of the session layer might be a pair of spies exchanging messages. They would have to establish an order of operations (a standard process that would be followed every time communications are established) that would be used to pass encoded messages back and forth. This process for passing the messages could be considered a session layer operation and may include steps such as using an agreed upon cipher to encode the message, placing a message in a predetermined location, and placing a marker someplace else to indicate that there is a message waiting. In the computing world, Windows file sharing has a session layer component when establishing sessions, as shown in Figure 4-3. The goal of the client computer in the Figure 4-3 is to get a list of shares on the server, but it must follow a session setup process in order to get the data that the client computer is after. The server in this process is in a constant state of listening for connection requests; as the client starts the process off, the session setup process runs like this:

1. The client sends a session request to the server.

2. The server acknowledges the request and includes in the acknowledgement a list of all session protocol that it is willing to support.

   In the case of the Windows server, the list includes older, less secure options such as LANMAN, as well as the newer and more secure NT LANMAN version 2 (NT LM 2).

3. The client reviews the list of supported protocols and chooses the most secure session protocol that it also supports.

   At this point, it sends the server the chosen session protocol that they will be using and requests to conduct an authentication. In this case, the authentication will verify a username and password from the server's user account database.

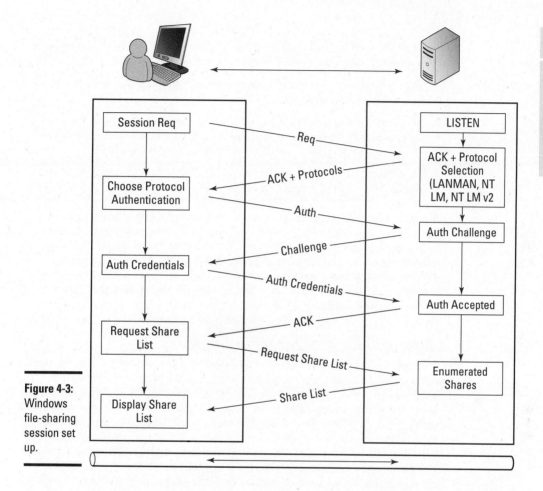

Figure 4-3:
Windows
file-sharing
session set
up.

4. The server creates a random string of characters that is included in the password challenge. This challenge is sent to the client.

5. The client takes the string from the password challenge and uses its own password as an encryption key to encrypt the random string.

6. The now encrypted string is then sent back to the server in an authentication credentials package that also includes the user's username.

7. The server retrieves the user's password from its user account database, and uses the password as the encryption key to encrypt the random character string that it sent to the client in the challenge step (Step 4).

8. The server compares the result it calculated to the result listed in the authentication credential package.

9. If the results match, as they do in Figure 4-3, then an acknowledgement (ACK) is sent to the client and the session is now active; but if they do not match, then the server sends a negative acknowledgement (NACK).

   If the client receives a NACK, then it would go back to Step 3 and issue a new authentication request.

10. At this point the session is set up, and the client can perform the request for the list of shares that are on the server, which would likely lead into a request of a list of files, and then the contents of a specific file.

   All of these future operations would be conducted though this single session that has just been created.

Step 10 in the preceding list shows the change from the session layer and the presentation layer. At the session layer, the communication channel to the Windows server components was established, but as the actual request was submitted for the list of shares available on the server, the request used the session layer communication channel, but was actually delivered through to the presentation layer and ultimately the application layer Windows Server service.

Layer 6: The presentation layer

Although the session layer opened an ongoing communication session, the presentation layer is responsible for how that data looks or is *formatted*. Consider the preceding spy example in which spies exchange encoded messages. The manner of passing the messages back and forth is defined by the session layer, but how the messages are encoded (or the cipher the spies used to obscure the message) is the responsibility of the presentation layer. Naturally, this has to be negotiated between the participants because it would be useless for one spy to encode a message that the other spy did not know how to decode. So with the presentation layer, all participants need to agree with the methods of encoding that are used at this layer. The same is true in the computer world — all participants, such as the servers and clients, need to agree with how the data will be formatted in order to exchange it. This is why standards for items like the HTML and XML languages allow servers to present data to clients and the clients to display this data to the users.

Differences among browsers make the actual display of the data slightly different on each browser, partially due to how they honor or interpret the data formatting presented by the web page. This formatting variance is why so many people have multiple web browsers installed on their computers. I personally alternate between Microsoft Internet Explorer, Mozilla Firefox, and Google Chrome with a fair amount of regularity; in fact, it is typical for me to have all three open at the same time. (Do not get me started on the mobile browsers for my iPod Touch or BlackBerry.)

Encryption is one of the key translations that takes place at the presentation layer. On outbound traffic from the server, the presentation layer encrypts data that is sent, and on the other end of the connection, it decrypts the data that is sent to the application layer. Figure 4-4 illustrates the flow of the data between a network client and the server. If the client computer is running an e-mail program and the server is the user's e-mail server, then on either end of the connection (both the client and the server sides), they are likely using the Simple Mail Transfer Protocol (SMTP) application layer protocol, or rather the encrypted version, SMTPS. The data flow would be as follows:

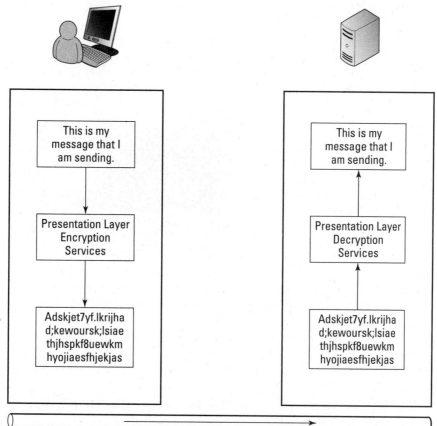

Figure 4-4:
Encryption
routines are
part of the
presentation
layer.

1. Using SMTPS, the client side of the application passes the text to the presentation layer services and requests encryption.

2. A Transport Layer Security (TLS) component at the presentation layer receives the unencrypted message and proceeds to encrypt the message using standard TLS processes.

3. The encrypted message flows down through the remaining OSI layers, over the physical network to the server.

4. At the server, the message is sent up through all of the layers until it arrives at the presentation layer.

   Now, the servers TLS processes will take over and decrypt the message so that it is clearly readable.

5. The clear text message is then delivered to the SMTP application layer protocol for processing.

   In this case, the next step would be to deliver the message to the recipient's mailbox.

Layer 7: The application layer

The application layer is the highest level in the OSI model and is the level that is closest to you — or furthest away from you if you are at the other end of the connection. The application layer effectively moves data between your computer and the server, and it is comprised of the server application that reads and writes files, such as the Apache Web Server or Microsoft's Internet Information Services (IIS), as well as the application you use at the client computer to write or read that data (such as an e-mail program).

Following the flow of data in Figure 4-5, the communication process between the application layer on a client computer and server is illustrated.

1. The process starts at the application layer with someone retrieving and opening an e-mail in an e-mail program, such as Microsoft Outlook.

   Outlook is the client program which operates the OSI model's application layer. Outlook communicates with application layer processes or programs being used on a server. In this example, when you start Outlook, it starts the process to request all e-mail from that server for the user.

   Any program may perform functions for other layers, such as the presentation layer by formatting the data in ASCII, Unicode, or Multipurpose Internet Mail Extensions (MIME), which is where things get muddy in comparing reality to ideals.

2. The server's Post Office Protocol version 3 (POP3) service responds to the request for the user's e-mail.

   The POP3 service runs at the application layer, and will retrieve the e-mail from the hard drive and prepares the e-mail message to be sent to the user's computer.

3. The data passes through the presentation, session, transport, network, data link, and physical layers, across the physical media, and backs up through all those layers on the client side of the connection.

4. The data arrives at the application layer on the destination computer, and is then displayed using a program such as Outlook.

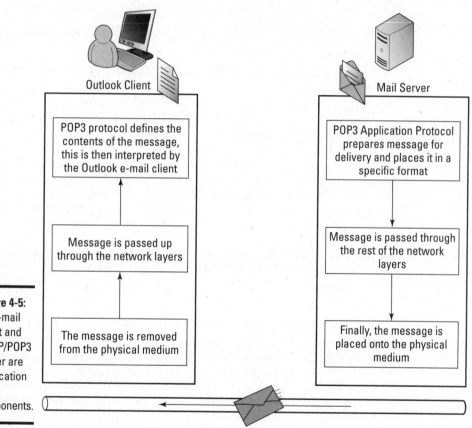

Figure 4-5:
An e-mail
client and
SMTP/POP3
server are
application
layer
components.

For most of the components on the Internet you deal with, you likely already refer to the application-level components:

✦ **Hypertext Transfer Protocol (HTTP):** Protocol for transferring data from web servers to web browser applications like Microsoft Internet Explorer.

✦ **Simple Mail Transfer Protocol (SMTP):** Protocol for sending mail from one computer to another. This could be from an e-mail client, like Microsoft Outlook, to an e-mail server, or from one e-mail server to another.

✦ **Post Office Protocol version 3 (POP3):** Protocol for e-mail client application, like Microsoft Outlook, to retrieve e-mail from an e-mail server.

✦ **Network Time Protocol (NTP):** Standard protocol for synchronizing time between computers and devices over the Internet.

✦ **Secure Shell (SSH):** Remote terminal access protocol that encrypts all data sent over the network.

✦ **File Transfer Protocol (FTP):** Transfers files to and from servers over the Internet.

Troubleshooting by Layers

When troubleshooting, unless you have seen the particular item or very similar symptoms, you may not have a particular spot to start looking for a solution. This is where the layered approach to troubleshooting comes in. You could start at one end of the layered model and work your way through to the other end, or you can use the symptom to determine where the best place to start is. What type of issue are you having? What are some primary items to check? The fact is that when you lack any other description for the user (other than "It is broken!"), you can usually start at the first layer and work your way up.

Troubleshooting the physical layer

Do not overlook the physical layer when you troubleshoot. Yes, troubleshooting the physical layer is not as sexy as say, troubleshooting on a Cisco Adaptive Security Appliance (ASA), but it is just as useful. For a user having connectivity issues, look around her system. If the problems are wireless, look for sources of interference that may be nearby. If the user is wired, look at the network cable.

Networking devices are often put in substandard locations because they do not usually beep if they get hot. I have seen switches well above their rated operating temperature, jammed into the tops of closets during a hot summer. In another type of hardware abuse, a user had his data cable looped around his desk with the cable acting as a speed bump for his chair. I was surprised that the cable was even in one piece, much less still passing data.

Rather than spending hours looking for the problem where it does not exist, check the physical items close to the network devices and between locations. I once had a coil of thin coaxial cable in a ceiling that was cut out and stolen, which left my network users without connectivity. This physical problem would not have been found without tracing the physical connection from end to end.

Troubleshooting the data link layer

In the OSI model, the data link layer is just above the physical layer. At this layer, check the following items:

- ✦ **Link status:** Most operating systems provide some sort of tools to check on the link status. Microsoft Windows always seems to tell you when you have connected or disconnected a network card. Make sure the network card is enabled in the operating system, if it is, then move on to the next steps.

- ✦ **Check the status lights:** Most network cards have one or two lights. These lights will identify link status and speed, as well as activity over the link. What information is displayed is based on the manufacturer settings, so you may need to check your documentation if they are not labeled. If you look at the switch your computer is connected to, you will also see status lights. These lights will show you link status, speed, duplex settings, and activity. (Switch lights and settings are covered in Book III, Chapter 2.) If you only have lights on one side of the connection, then you likely have a physical issue, like a break in some of the wires inside of the cable. If you have connection lights that agree at either end of the connection, such as both reporting gigabit connection speed, then you are partway to verifying data link connectivity. If there are no status lights, then check your physical connections again.

- ✦ **Attempt using Address Resolution Protocol (ARP):** Test to see if other computers on the network are visible at all. ARP is a command line tool that will display the MAC addresses of all devices with which you have recently communicated. This means that you can attempt to communicate with another device, and then check your ARP cache. (This is all explained in Book II, Chapter 3.) If you can see other computers, then your connection at the data link layer is likely working correctly.

Troubleshooting network and transport layers

Moving up in the OSI model, you arrive at the network and transport layers, and the issues you could deal with really open up. A myriad of problems can occur at these layers:

✦ **Check your protocol address:** If you use an incorrect protocol address for your network, you cannot communicate with any devices on your network. As a networking consultant, I regularly configure my laptop for a static IP address on my client networks when they may not have a Dynamic Host Configuration Protocol (DHCP) server running on that portion of their network, or when I need to configure a new network device. This often has me returning to my network with an improper IP address for my network, so I end up troubleshooting and saying, "D'oh, of course!"

✦ **Attempt to communicate with your router:** If you use a routable protocol, such as IP, then you should attempt to communicate with your router, or a device on the other side of your router (such as a server on the Internet). Ping (which you see in Book II, Chapter 3) is a great tool for testing this connectivity. It will give you instant feedback if you can communicate with the other device.

✦ **Attempt to communicate with other devices on your network segment or data link:** Your router from the previous item is a device on your data link that should always be up and running. If you could not communicate with the router, try another device, such as another computer, because it could be that your router is not working properly.

Most of the issues that occur at these layers are typically resolved with the configuration of the network protocol on your device or another device on the network.

If you use IP as your network protocol, something as simple as entering the incorrect subnet mask on a device can cause you to not be able to communicate with a large number of other network devices, either on your data link or on the other side of a router.

Other issues that occur at these layers revolve around name resolution. For example, you may be able to get to the destination server by IP, but if the name you are resolving is wrong, you cannot connect. Alternatively, you could be resolving the correct name but are getting the wrong address in your resolution.

Troubleshooting the application layer

You can have an issue at the application layer, but most issues you encounter happen at the other layers. However, some issues in the application layer or in other layers (depending on how you look at them) include items such as the following:

✦ **Software bugs, such as an application that crashes when sending data too quickly.** When things like this happen, all you can do is diagnose the issue, contact the software manufacturer, reduce the occurrence of the issues by adjusting other configuration elements, or change to an equivalent application if one is available.

✦ **Incorrect settings, such as host names or addresses, that may have changed and have not been documented.** Find out what the correct settings should be, even if it means double-checking client and server configurations. I regularly have clients who refer to ancient documents when I ask them for current network information.

✦ **Services are bound to an incorrect port, such as one running Remote Desktop Protocol (RDP) services or HTTP services on non-standard ports.** You may be able to get to the remote host, for example, but if you try to talk to the wrong port, you cannot connect. It is not uncommon for internal use servers to have multiple websites installed on them, with only one of them being allowed to run on the standard HTTP port of 80. Also, some IT administrators choose to run the RDP service on a non-standard port to keep unauthorized users from attempting to connect to the RDP service.

✦ **The client or server components that you use do not follow the published standards for the protocol.** I have had issues working with some client and server components, such as an FTP client and FTP server. After hours of troubleshooting connectivity issues, it turns out that the custom written FTP client did not honor all of the session control commands that were being issued by the FTP server. If it had, the issues would not have existed. This problem was only identified by reading published standards and capturing network traffic with the Wireshark network capture tool. (For more about Wireshark, see the "Sharking the Network Data" section, later in this chapter.)

Some companies that implement devices have taken liberties with implementing protocols and the features they support. This makes achieving compatibility with other devices from other vendors difficult and can be considered an application problem that is often resolved only after you change the client or server software that you use.

Framing Data

If you followed along so far, you know how all the layers work together. Here I focus on the lowest layers again: the physical and data link layers. Data travels over the physical media of the Ethernet network in small containers, or *frames*. There are different methods of framing Ethernet data, but the two that you are likely to see are Ethernet II and IEEE 802.3. The structure of these frames is similar, and the following explains each:

+ **Ethernet II:** Is a revision of the original Ethernet frame format. It is the standard framing type and is used to support required headers used by IP. I focus on this frame in this chapter because you are more likely to see it than any other frame type.

+ **IEEE 802.3:** Although I do not focus on this frame, you should know it was an expanded frame type that Novell chose to use to support its proprietary Internetwork Packet Exchange/Sequenced Packet Exchange (IPX/SPX) protocol. In fact, when Novell started to convert over to IP as its default protocol, it also changed the default Ethernet frame type back to Ethernet II. So unless you are on a 1990s Novell network, you are not likely going to encounter the 802.3 Ethernet frame type.

As shown in Figure 4-6, the standard Ethernet II frame has the following parts:

Field Length in Bytes

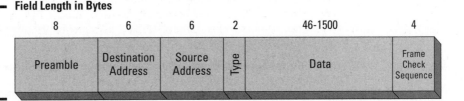

Figure 4-6: The Ethernet II frame structure.

8	6	6	2	46-1500	4
Preamble	Destination Address	Source Address	Type	Data	Frame Check Sequence

+ **Preamble:** The *preamble* is a unique sequence of alternating zeros and ones followed by two ones that is eight bytes in length and sets the start of the Ethernet frame. This series of pulses is picked up by the network card in your computer and, by design, this sequence will never occur in the middle of the frame. After the preamble sequence is seen on the network, the network card does not expect to see this again until at least 64 bytes of data has followed the preamble. (There is one of those binary based numbers again — 1, 2, 4, 8, 16, 32, 64).

+ **Ethernet header:** Although I refer to this as the *Ethernet* header, it could be the header for any type of physical network. The Ethernet header is made up of the following pieces:

  • *Destination address:* Six bytes that contain the MAC address of the NIC that is the target for the network frame.

  • *Source address:* Six bytes that contain the MAC address of the NIC that sends the data on physical media.

  • *Type:* Two bytes that denote the frame type. The type field identifies the higher layer protocol, which typically is IP.

✦ **Data:** Between 46–1500 bytes of data. If the data is fewer than 46 bytes, padding is added to bring the frame to the minimum 64 byte frame size. Remember the preamble description; there must be at least 64 bytes of data between preamble sequences.

✦ **Frame check sequence (FCS):** Four bytes of FCS data is stored at the end of the frame. Prior to sending the frame, the source computer generates a result from the data found in the frame and stores the result in the last four bytes of the frame. To generate this FCS value, the entire frame is broken into blocks. All those blocks are then added together, and FCS is a sum of all these blocks of data. The receiving computer calculates its own result from the data in the frame and compares the number it calculates to the FCS data. If the results do not match, the frame is considered to be damaged or inaccurate so the frame is discarded. Some people will also refer to this as cyclic redundancy check (CRC) data or a CRC sum. The purpose of the CRC and FCS is the same, which is to verify that the data that was received was not altered or damaged during transmission.

All network frames have the same basic structure as the Ethernet II frame, regardless of the type of data that they contain.

Even though the frame exists at the physical level, it is often referred to at the data link layer, because the only difference between the data link data and the physical layer structure is the preamble and FCS data, which is data that is not passed from the physical layer to the data link layer. If you refer to Book I, Chapter 1, you see that each layer applies a header to the data that will eventually be sent across the network. So if you consider that the information that the data link layer sends down to the physical layer is everything from the start of the Ethernet header to the end of the data, then the header (and trailer or footer) that the physical layer applies to data link data is the preamble and the FCS data. This means that most of the information could technically be considered data link information.

The reason I have given you both the data link and physical layer information together is that almost everyone will describe this data structure as the Ethernet frame, and will place it at the physical layer. For the purpose of moving you through the OSI model, you can consider both the physical and data link layers to have been covered.

Figuring Out Packets

In the network layer, you look only at the section of the frame that was referred to as data in the Ethernet frame (refer to Figure 4-6). As the Ethernet frame moves up from the data link layer to the network layer, the data link header is removed. Removing the data link information removes destination and source address fields (which store the MAC addresses of the network devices), and the type field. Because the preamble and FCS information was removed when the Ethernet frame was sent from the physical layer to the data link layer, this now leaves just the data. The data is not just a blob though. At the network layer, this information is referred to as a *packet,* and it has its own address data and fields; but when you look at it from the Ethernet frame level, you do not care what that data is.

Data containers are dubbed *frames* in the data link layer (Layer 2) and *packets* in the network layer (Layer 3).

Looking at packets

After you strip off the Ethernet or data link layer structures, you look at what the data link layer considered to be data, which is a packet. The packet's structure will be based on the network layer protocol. Because IP is the dominant protocol in the world, the most common type of packet data you will see is IP data. Because the network layer data structure is named a packet, and because my example uses IP as the network layer protocol, it is reasonable to call the packet an IP packet. Just like the Ethernet frame had an Ethernet header and a data section, the IP packet has an IP header and a data section. Figure 4-7 shows the contents of an IP packet contained within the Ethernet frame. Notice that the entire IP packet is found in the data field.

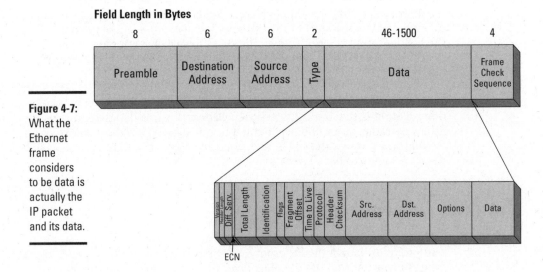

Figure 4-7:
What the Ethernet frame considers to be data is actually the IP packet and its data.

Field Length in Bytes

8	6	6	2	46-1500	4
Preamble	Destination Address	Source Address	Type	Data	Frame Check Sequence

IP packet fields: Version, Header Length, Diff. Serv., ECN, Total Length, Identification, Flags, Fragment Offset, Time to Live, Protocol, Header Checksum, Src. Address, Dst. Address, Options, Data

Viewing packet structure

The IP packet is defined by its header, and that header contains many fields. I discuss these fields in more detail in Book II, Chapter 2. However, the key elements that are in the header are

✦ **Version:** This is used to identify the IP version being used. There are really only two choices, either version 4 (the first production version of IP that was implemented), or version 6 (which is currently in the process of being implemented over the Internet). Because the headers between IP version 4 (IPv4) and IP version 6 (IPv6) are quite different, and in an effort not to overwhelm and confuse you, I only show the IPv4 header here because it is likely the one you will encounter most over the next decade.

✦ **Time to Live (TTL):** The length of time this packet can remain on the network. Each router that handles this packet decrements (reduces) this counter by at least one. You can read more about the purpose of the TTL in Book IV, Chapter 4.

✦ **Protocol:** The transport layer protocol where the data portion of the IP packet is to be delivered. This will be either Transmission Control Protocol (TCP) or User Datagram Protocol (UDP).

✦ **Header checksum:** In the earlier section "Framing Data," you read about the frame check sequence (FCS) and cyclic redundancy check (CRC) that are calculations based on the data found in the Ethernet frame and are used to validate the contents of the entire frame. The header checksum is a similar item, but in this case, the data that the calculation is based on is only the header data, and the result of that calculation is stored in the header checksum field. If the header is intact, IP considers the packet good. The higher-level protocols, such as TCP at the transport layer or FTP at the application layer, verify the contents of the data they receive, which they will do with their own checksum mechanism.

✦ **Source address:** The IP address of the device that sends the packet onto the network. This is also where any network-level error messages are sent, including Internet Control Message Protocol (ICMP) delivery failures or control messages (discussed in Book II, Chapter 3).

✦ **Destination address:** The address the packet is sent to.

✦ **Data:** As with the Ethernet frame, the data portion is sent to the transport layer, to either the TCP or UDP. IP does not care what is found here; it is merely the delivery means.

Getting the Lowdown on Low-Level and High-Level Addressing

You encounter addresses at various layers of the OSI model, but the most common are the data link and networking layers. If you examine the addressing for just these two layers, you have a hardware address (MAC) and a protocol address (IP address).

Taking control of MAC addresses

The MAC address is taken by default from the hardware address of the network card. The MAC address is a 12-digit hexadecimal number or 48 bits in length. This address is assigned by the hardware manufacturer and is globally unique, so you should not have duplicate addresses on your network (although cards with duplicate addresses have been manufactured by production errors in the past). Typically, the problem of duplicate MAC addresses arises because people choose not to use the vendor-assigned hardware address, but instead use a self-assigned address (also called a locally administered address). This is a technique used by hackers to circumvent MAC-based security restrictions. This is more common when using main frame systems that communicate via MAC addresses rather than protocol addresses (such as IP addresses). In the later case, if a computer or its network card is replaced due to a hardware failure, you would have to reconfigure several systems to work with the new MAC address, so it is far easier to assign the new network card the same MAC address as the failed card. Unless you are in the small minority of people with a system such as this, or are a big time hacker, you can safely ignore the ability to manage your own MAC address.

IEEE operates an online database where you can look up MAC addresses at `http://standards.ieee.org/develop/regauth/oui/public.html`. The first half of the twelve digit hexadecimal MAC address is used to register hardware vendors, and the second half of the address is assigned by the hardware vendor. Table 4-1 shows a list of the first 20 companies that have addresses registered.

Table 4-1   Hardware Vendors and Registered MAC Address IDs

Company	Hex Address
Xerox Corporation, USA	00-00-00 – 00-00-09
Omron Tateisi Electronics Co., Japan	00-00-0A
Matrix Corporation, USA	00-00-0B

Company	Hex Address
Cisco Systems, Inc., USA	00-00-0C
Fibronics LTD., Israel	00-00-0D
Fujitsu Limited, Japan	00-00-0E
Next, Inc., USA	00-00-0F
Sytek Inc., USA	00-00-10
Normerel Systemes, France	00-00-11
Information Technology Limited, United Kingdom	00-00-12
Camex, USA	00-00-13
Netronix, USA	00-00-14
Datapoint Corporation, USA	00-00-15
Du Pont Pixel Systems, United Kingdom	00-00-16
Tekelec, USA	00-00-17
Webster Computer Corporation, USA	00-00-18
Applied Dynamics International, USA	00-00-19
Advanced Micro Devices, USA	00-00-1A
Novell Inc., USA	00-00-1B
Bell Technologies, USA	00-00-1C

The companies that were first to register IDs on this list were some of the first companies in the networking field. Reviewing even the first few entries on the table, you notice some of those names as incumbent or early starters in the networking and computing world, including Xerox (which actually has the first ten registered numbers), Cisco, Fujitsu, and so on. By using the company registration as half of the MAC address length, there can be almost 17 million registered network card manufacturers, and each registered company can manufacture almost 17 million network cards.

If you are unlucky enough to get duplicated MAC addresses on your network, either by hardware vendor error or by using locally assigned MAC addresses, you are in for some network troubleshooting joy. A duplicated MAC address means you have multiple devices responding to data requests as if they are the only device with that address on the network, or you have a switch that keeps changing the port assignment for that address because the switch keeps seeing the device's MAC address moving from port to port. This causes any number of issues with network connectivity, as you can probably guess. I have only seen this happen once, and when I finally identified the issue as a duplicate MAC address I just had to say, "Wow, I would have never expected that to happen." Hopefully, knowing that duplicate MAC addresses might happen, you may not dismiss it as an impossibility, which will allow you to identify the problem more quickly.

Structuring the IP address

Unlike the 48-bit MAC address, the IPv4 address is only 32 bits in length. Therefore, far fewer possible IPv4 addresses are in the world than possible MAC addresses. The IPv4 address is broken into four groups of eight bits, or an *octet*. IP addresses are normally written in dotted decimal notation (decimal numbers with dots in between them). A typical IPv4 address looks like 192.0.2.245.

I cover the structure of IPv4 addresses in full detail in Book II, Chapter 1. Book II, Chapter 4 tells you what you need to know about IPv6.

One of the key things you need to know about IP is that it is *routable* — the entire network can be broken into smaller segments with data being routed back and forth through routers. Because of this, the size of a network has very few limits, such as the worldwide IP adoption as the standard Internet network protocol.

Reviewing Internetwork Packet Exchange

Unlike IP, which was developed as open protocol with no direct ownership of its technologies, Internetwork Package Exchange (IPX) was developed and is owned by Novell. IPX is also a routable protocol that became popular with Novell's NetWare server infrastructure.

Implementing IPX was much easier than implementing IP. Whereas IP needs to have addresses assigned manually or by a special server, IPX uses a far simpler technique. When a system starts, IPX creates a local link (or network) address that is primarily made up from the MAC address on its network card. IPX then appends a network ID to the beginning of the address to identify the network segment it belongs to. It identifies its network ID by listening to the traffic on the network, and using whatever network ID everyone else uses or by having the network ID manually set in your computer's network configuration. IPX assumes that typically you manually set the network ID on your servers and because they are always running, and the clients use the same network ID as the servers.

To route IPX, you need an IPX router, such as the Novell NetWare server, or a hardware router that supports IPX, such as Cisco 3900 series router.

Getting the basics with NetBIOS Extended User Interface

The use of Network Basic Input/Output System (NetBIOS) occurs at the session layer — not the network layer. This has caused a lot of confusion for many people because NetBIOS is sometimes used — incorrectly — as a synonym for *NetBIOS Extended User Interface (NetBEUI)*, which is a distinct network protocol that is built heavily around NetBIOS.

Microsoft uses NetBIOS heavily as a session layer protocol. As such, Microsoft also adopted NetBEUI as its default protocol for its operating systems.

Compared to IPX and IP, one of the major shortcomings of NetBEUI is that it is not a routable protocol. You cannot create a large multisite network using NetBEUI because you cannot route traffic between locations. You could set up a multisite bridged network, but even that causes a lot of unneeded traffic to cross the links between your offices or locations. This is not desirable. The address that is used to identify stations on a NetBEUI-based network is the MAC address of each station on the network. Your network devices will not have a network portion of their address like IPX and IP included with their addresses.

Watching the Traffic Go By

If you read Book I, Chapter 2, you read about traffic being sent out over the network. Now I discuss exactly how this task is performed. Here are the two main methods used to release traffic onto the network:

✦ **CSMA/CD:** Carrier Sense, Multiple Access with Collision Detection

✦ **CSMA/CA:** Carrier Sense, Multiple Access with Collision Avoidance

In this section, I tell you what you really need to know about both methods. The impact of either of these methods is reduced greatly when working on switched networks without shared access devices, such as hubs or wireless access points (WAPs).

CSMA/CD

CSMA/CD is the main frame-control process on wired Ethernet networks. Here is a breakdown of the name:

✦ **Carrier sense** is built into the network card. The network device can detect the carrier wave that is on the network. That goes along with the green light you get when the network is properly attached to the network.

✦ **Multiple access** allows for multiple devices to share the networking medium through some process, communication standards, or protocol. Because only one node on the wire can really transmit data at a time, you need a sharing method that everyone or every host on the network agrees to.

✦ **Collision detection** means that in addition to the multiple access sharing, you specifically use two factors to help determine whether a collision occurs:

- *Ethernet round trip time:* The time it takes for a frame to reach every possible node in your collision domain.

- *Interframe gap:* The minimum safe distance between frames on the network that allows time for the receive buffer (a small amount of memory on a network card used to store incoming data that needs to be processed) on the receiving stations to process all frames.

If a receiving station sees frames coming too quickly (that is, without a sufficient gap between them), it can send a jam signal to notify others of a collision. If a station sends a frame and sees more traffic before the round trip time has expired, it can send a jam signal as well. When a jam signal or collision is sent on the network, all systems wait for a random period of time before attempting to send their data again. This random wait reduces the chance of another collision on a network.

To reduce the chance of collision from occurring at all, prior to sending data frames on the network, the system will listen on the network to see if there is anyone currently sending a frame. If there is current activity on the network, the system will wait for a break and then send its frames out on the network. This process is illustrated in Figure 4-8.

CSMA/CA

CSMA/CA is a similar system to CSMA/CD but instead of dealing with collisions when they happen, the goal is to have them not occur at all. I know when I deal with my car, I prefer to avoid collisions rather than deal with them after they occur. The negative impact of network collisions is that you have to wait and retransmit data (unlike real-world collisions). The network cost of collisions is a mandatory waiting period, which takes longer to transmit your data. *Collision avoidance* is the process used on the Macintosh AppleTalk network and is still used on 802.11 wireless networks.

So how does collision avoidance differ from collision detection? Well, it is that whole *avoidance* bit in the name. To avoid collisions:

First attempt

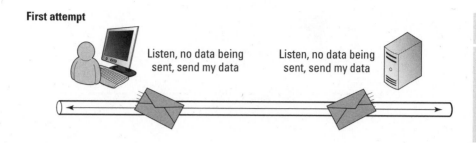

Listen, no data being
sent, send my data

Listen, no data being
sent, send my data

Failure

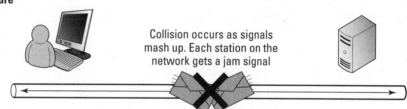

Collision occurs as signals
mash up. Each station on the
network gets a jam signal

Second attempt

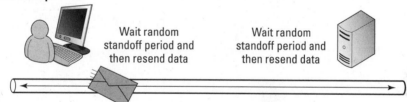

Wait random
standoff period and
then resend data

Wait random
standoff period and
then resend data

Figure 4-8:
The CSMA/
CD process.

1. Each station that wants to send data listens to the network to see whether the network is in use.

2. If the network is not in use, the station sends a Ready to Send (RTS) signal, hoping for a Clear to Send (CTS) signal back from the other stations.

3. After the other stations give the CTS signal, they are required to not send any data for a short length of time (milliseconds).

   This leaves the network free for the sending station to use, which ensures that you have a near zero chance of having a collision when you send your data. (You can see this process in Figure 4-9.) It is actually more likely that a collision would occur when the RTS request is sent out on the network.

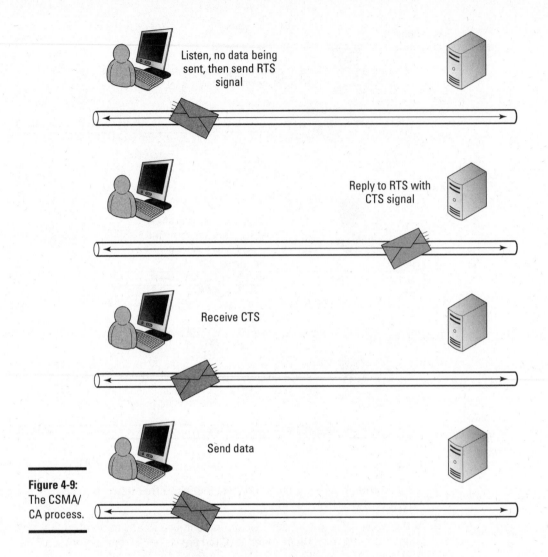

Listen, no data being sent, then send RTS signal

Reply to RTS with CTS signal

Receive CTS

Send data

Figure 4-9:
The CSMA/
CA process.

Choosing CSMA/CD or CSMA/CA

The drawback of the CSMA/CA system is that you may still have periods
of waiting. If you do not get a CTS signal, you have to wait a short random
period of time and send the RTS again and (possibly) again. Because the
RTS and CTS is actually data you send on the network, you still run the risk
of collisions, although this risk is greatly reduced due to the length of the
data. Ethernet was built using CSMA/CD. The developers of Ethernet rea-
soned that if you send small bits of data (in the form of RTS and CTS frames)
anyway, you may as well just send the full data, which speeds up the whole
process if the data gets through on the first attempt. Most speed tests that
have been conducted comparing the two systems support the Ethernet
case. When operating on a network, collision detections elimination of the

wait states and the collision resolution process allows for more overall data throughput on the network than the collision avoidance system allows. If a network is heavily congested, you have slower data transfers when using either method.

Moving to a switch-based network reduces collisions and wait states because each switch port becomes its own collision domain, typically with only one host on that network segment. This greatly reduces speed issues caused by excessive collisions, making CSMA/CD an even better choice.

Sharking the Network Data

Formerly Ethereal, *Wireshark* is network protocol analyzer, which is a tool that can view the details of network traffic. Before the prevalence of network switching, a tool like this could view all traffic that is flowing on your network. In switched environments, you see only the traffic destined for your computer or broadcast traffic on the network unless you have enabled a monitoring port on the network switch, allowing you to see all traffic on that switch.

Many products are in this category — some that you can purchase, and some that are free. As free products go, Wireshark is a fairly full-featured product and can be downloaded from www.wireshark.org. Wireshark is free under the GNU General Public License (GPL) and is available for Windows, Mac OS X, and Linux. Linux users typically find this application in their distribution by default.

Other products that you may also consider include:

✦ Microsoft Network Monitor from www.microsoft.com

✦ TCPDump from www.tcpdump.org

✦ Capsa Network Analyzer from www.colasoft.com

✦ ClearSight Analyzer from www.flukenetworks.com

Network protocol analyzers are also called *network sniffers.* While this book is aimed at Cisco networking, any of these tools will capture any data off of your network, regardless of the manufacturer of your routers or switches. Of course, they work great with Cisco network equipment as well.

Wireshark allows you to capture and analyze network traffic on your network, which can be critical to network troubleshooting efforts. One example involves Dynamic Host Configuration Protocol (DHCP) servers on your network. Typically, you will only have one DHCP server, but sometimes a network user will install a rogue (unauthorized and unknown) DHCP server on your network. This rogue DHCP server may then start to issue Negative Acknowledgments (NACKs) — a refusal — to all DHCP requests on your network. You could spend hours troubleshooting this issue, but within a few seconds of starting a network capture (to collect and view traffic on your network), you have easily identified the problem and the IP address of the offending system (the rogue DHCP server).

Although you could use the captured data for other purposes, such as viewing telnet sessions or other clear text traffic, Wireshark is great at viewing which systems are talking, who is sending the most traffic, and how to diagnose network issues from a very low level.

When you install Wireshark, you are prompted during the installation to install WinPcap, which is the actual capture driver that does the heavy lifting for Wireshark. Wireshark takes care of data display and analysis, while WinPcap is the capture driver that captures the live network traffic from the network. You can choose all the defaults for the installation; the only real question you may have is whether you want WinPcap to start with the operating system. If you choose to have WinPcap start with the operating system, then it will always be consuming some of your computer's resources, even when Wireshark does not need WinPcap.

Normally, WinPcap starts as needed when running Wireshark. If you are running Windows 7 though, the default Windows 7 security features will prevent the WinPcap driver from starting when running Wireshark. In that case, you want WinPcap to start with the operating system.

To set up a basic capture of data, follow these steps:

1. **Select the network card that you want to use to perform the capturing by choosing Capture⇨Interfaces.**

   The Capture Interfaces window shown in Figure 4-10 appears, showing you not only the listed interfaces but also the data received and sent on the interfaces on your computer. You could also select a capture interface by choosing Capture⇨Options, but I prefer using the Capture Interfaces window because seeing the data being sent and received on your computer's interfaces lets you identify the active network card. This is a benefit to you when you have more than one network card in a computer.

2. **Click the Start button next to your active network interface to kick off a capture session.**

Figure 4-10:
Preparing
to capture
data with
Wireshark
by viewing
interfaces.

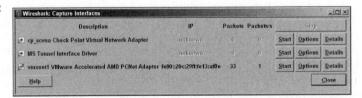

Formatting a MAC address

While IP addresses are typically displayed using the familiar dotted decimal notation (192.0.2.75), the same cannot be said about MAC addresses. You typically see four common formats for MAC addresses:

✔ 001D7EF823D6

✔ 001D7E-F823D6

✔ 00:1D:7E:F8:23:D6

✔ 00-1D-7E-F8-23-D6

There is not a functional difference between these formats; it is simply a choice by various application programmers to require MAC addresses to be typed a certain way, or to display a certain way.

On the screen that appears, data scrolls past. You see the following three basic panes, as shown in Figure 4-11:

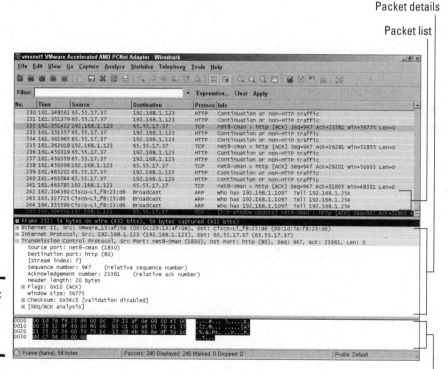

Packet details

Packet list

Packet bytes

Figure 4-11:
Capturing
data with
Wireshark.

✦ **Packet List:** The pane toward the top of the screen. This pane shows all the network frames that have been seen by your network card. If your network card is connected to a hub, then this will be all the traffic on the network; but if the card is attached to a switch, it will only broadcast frames and the network frames addressed to the card's MAC address. The information that you see here includes the frame number, as well as the following:

- *Time:* The number of milliseconds that has elapsed since the start of the network capture.

- *Source Address:* The address of the device that sent the network frame on to the network. This may be an IP address such as 192.168.1.123, or a MAC address such as 00:1D:7E:F8:23:D6. The display of either of these addresses depends on if a higher layer address (such as the network layer address) is present in the network frame; if it is not, then the MAC address is shown. Notice that the MAC address is displayed as Cisco-Li_f8:23:d6. This is because the default option of Enable Mac Name Resolution is enabled; this option shows a portion of the network card manufacturer in the manufacturer ID portion of the MAC address. This can be helpful, because you know that the address in the captured frame belongs to a Cisco device.

- *Destination Addresses:* The address where the network frame is being sent. The values and options are the same as the source address.

- *Protocol:* The highest layer protocol that is present in the frame. In Figure 4-10, you can see ARP, TCP, and HTTP.

- *Info:* This column displays summary information about the frame. This is a WireShark interpretation of what data is in the frame. The intention is to make it easier for you to understand what type of data is in the network frame.

✦ **Packet Details:** The pane related to the currently selected packet in the middle frame, with an expanding hierarchy. This allows you to drill into the sections of this data — like moving through the OSI layers. If you expand the Ethernet II section, you can compare the data to the Ethernet frame structure (described in the earlier section, "Framing Data"). If you expand the Internet Protocol section, you can compare the data to the packet structure (see the earlier section, "Viewing packet structure").

✦ **Packet Bytes:** This pane shows ASCII and hex data that is in the frame. Remember, all data sent in the network frame is binary, and that you can convert this binary data into hexadecimal, as described in Book I, Chapter 3. Finally, every eight bits or one byte can be represented by an ASCII character. This pane shows you all of the binary data in Ethernet frame in both its hexadecimal and ASCII equivalent. This can sometimes be helpful when looking for ASCII strings in the data. This data is seen in a neater format in the Packet Details pane.

By selecting different sections of the frame in the Packet Details pane the matching section of the Packet Bytes pane becomes highlighted. This can be helpful if you are attempting to locate a hexadecimal or ASCII equivalent for what you see in the Packet Details pane. If you are following along with Wireshark, try selecting different parts of the frame in the Packet Details pane.

Wireshark is a powerful data capture tool with a great deal of power and a huge amount of potential. While I attempt to cover some of the basic operation and options, this program could have an entire book devoted to it. There are many guides available for Wireshark, but if you are interested in unlocking more power that I show you, start by choosing Help➪Contents.

Capture options

If you want to explore the options available in Wireshark, you can get into the Capture Options dialog box by choosing Capture➪Options. In the Capture Options dialog box (see Figure 4-12), you have several, well, options. Some main options include

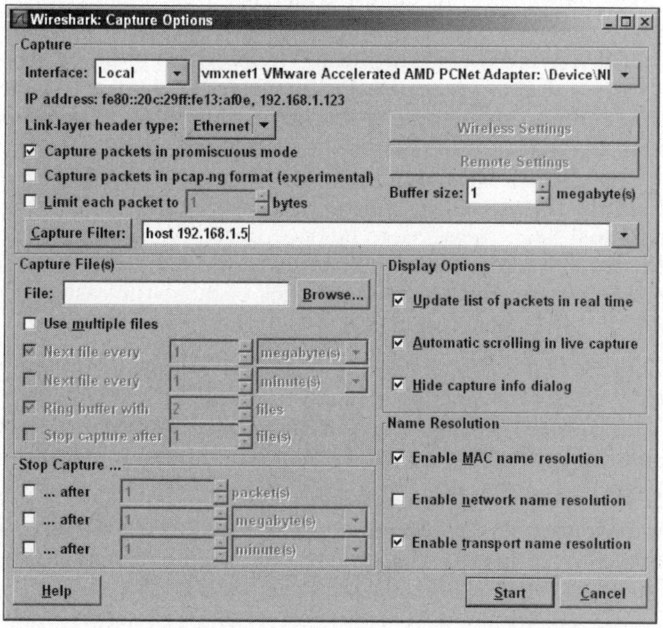

Figure 4-12:
Options available for capturing data.

(Screenshot of the Wireshark: Capture Options dialog box showing the following options)

Capture
Interface: Local ▾ | vmxnet1 VMware Accelerated AMD PCNet Adapter: \Device\NI ▾
IP address: fe80::20c:29ff:fe13:af0e, 192.168.1.123
Link-layer header type: Ethernet ▾
☑ Capture packets in promiscuous mode
☐ Capture packets in pcap-ng format (experimental)
☐ Limit each packet to 1 bytes
Buffer size: 1 megabyte(s)
Wireless Settings
Remote Settings
Capture Filter: host 192.168.1.5

Capture File(s)
File: [ ] Browse...
☐ Use multiple files
☑ Next file every 1 megabyte(s)
☐ Next file every 1 minute(s)
☑ Ring buffer with 2 files
☐ Stop capture after 1 file(s)

Stop Capture ...
☐ ... after 1 packet(s)
☐ ... after 1 megabyte(s)
☐ ... after 1 minute(s)

Display Options
☑ Update list of packets in real time
☑ Automatic scrolling in live capture
☑ Hide capture info dialog

Name Resolution
☑ Enable MAC name resolution
☐ Enable network name resolution
☑ Enable transport name resolution

Help | Start | Cancel

✦ **Capture Packets in Promiscuous Mode:** Allows you to see data destined for other devices on the network, assuming that traffic touches your network card.

✦ **Update List of Packets in Real Time:** Allows you to see data when it comes in to Wireshark.

✦ **Automatic Scrolling in Live Capture:** Scrolls the capture window's packet list, allowing you to see the most recent capture data. This can roll through data very quickly on a busy network.

✦ **Enable MAC Name Resolution:** Displays information on network card vendors when available.

✦ **Enable Network Name Resolution:** Resolves host names when possible.

✦ **Enable Transport Name Resolution:** Shows you the name of the protocol that is in use, which is not always the protocol in use because many client side ports are chosen randomly.

Filtering captured data

Wireshark will capture everything it sees (except what it discards when not capturing in promiscuous mode), which in either case can be a huge amount of data. You have a couple of options for filtering data. You can filter the data packets while you are capturing them, which reduces the amount of data you capture; or you can filter the displayed data, which cuts down what you see on the screen. You can set the capture filter on the Capture Options dialog box (see Figure 4-13). Options include

✦ **Capture Filter:** Using standard tcpdump options, such as `tcp port 80` and host `192.168.1.5`, to filter captured data, you can greatly reduce the amount of data that you capture. This is a great option if you want to capture data over a day or a week because the resulting capture file is much more manageable.

✦ **Capture File(s):** If you want to be able to review your capture data at a later date, you can choose to capture the data into one or more files. The Capture Files(s) section of the Capture Options dialog box allows you to specify your file options.

✦ **File:** In the File field, simply specify the file path and name where you want to save your capture data. You can also use the Browse button to browse to it directly and specify a filename to use. Capture files should be saved with the extension of `.cap`.

✦ **Use Multiple Files:** To keep file sizes down, you can specify to use multiple files by selecting this check box. After you have done that, you can then choose to create new files based on the size of the file or a period of time.

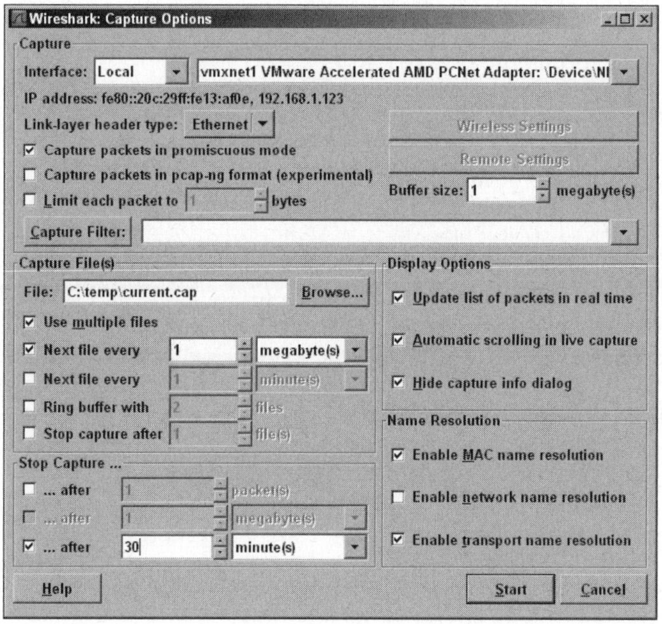

Figure 4-13:
Capturing
data to a
file.

✦ **Ring Buffer:** Although there are options to automatically stop
Wireshark capturing data, you may want Wireshark to capture data
constantly and to stop it after you have an incident on your network.
For example, if you have a recurring incident that you are troubleshooting, and the problem will likely occur over the next 24 hours,
then you can make use of the ring buffer. You would still set your multiple files option and specify to use a new file after an amount of data is
captured or when a period of time has passed. After you have set the
multiple files option, you can then set the number of files to use as the
ring buffer. Wireshark will then save the files until it has filled the specified number of files. When all files are full, it will loop back to the first
file and start overwriting the saved capture files. The benefit of this is
that when your random network incident happens, you can stop the
capture process, and you will have the most current network capture
leading up to the incident. This is helpful when troubleshooting this
type of intermittent problem. This option allows you to review the data
that occurred in the most recent period of time and have a predictable
size for the files.

✦ **Stop Capture:** Have the capture automatically stop after:

- A certain number of packets have been captured.

- A certain amount of data has been received, or when the capture file has reached a specified size.

- A period of time has passed.

If you have captured all your data and then decide that you need to reduce that amount of data you see in the Packet List pane, you can use the Filter box just above the Packet List pane (refer to Figure 4-11). This field uses similar options to the Capture Filter field in Capture Options dialog box, but to make your life interesting (and confusing), they are not identical in their format. (Do not blame me, I did not write the program!) To filter data, you could use options such as

✦ `arp`: Used to only show ARP network frames.

✦ `http`: Used to only show IP packets that have the http application layer protocol.

✦ `ip.addr==192.168.1.5`: Used to only show IP packets that have 192.168.1.5 as a source or destination IP address.

✦ `http and ip.addr==192.168.1.5`: Used to only show IP packets that contain http application layer protocol information and have 192.168.1.5 as a source or destination IP address.

In addition to the graphical Wireshark capture program to view and manipulate your captured data, the program `tshark.exe` is included with the installation of Wireshark on your computer. This is a command-line tool that can capture, view, and manage your network data. Quite a few options can be used with this program, and a huge online community can explain what some of the more advanced features do. Running `tshark.exe -h` from the Wireshark installation directory gives you a summary of the options that are available.

Chapter 5: Getting into the Cisco Internetwork Operating System

In This Chapter

✔ Navigating the operational modes like a pro

✔ Connecting your devices

✔ Managing the IOS image and the boot process

Although each type of Cisco product (such as switches, routers, or firewalls) has its own way of doing things, you see some common features or functions across much of the product line, such as assigning an Internet Protocol (IP) address to the device. Even within a product line, you may see a difference between specific devices, such as configuration commands between high-end and low-end switches.

Although several differences exist between some products, this chapter focuses on the items that are common across most of the enterprise-level devices. Here I show you the core features of the Internetwork Operating System (IOS) and how to make management connections to most Cisco devices.

As you move through the rest of this book (specifically Book III onward), you put this information to work in managing your Cisco devices.

This chapter starts pretty easily, but as with most work in the networking world, it gets a little heavy near the end. By the end though, you have a good understanding as to what the Cisco IOS is and how to navigate within it. I end this chapter with a few items, such as choosing a boot image and upgrading the IOS, that you need only to deal with periodically. However, this information aids in your understanding of the startup and operating process.

Working with the Internetwork Operating System

The Cisco IOS is often imitated, but thanks to a very strong legal department, not yet duplicated. The *Internetwork Operating System* is the core engine on Cisco routers, switches, and firewalls. The IOS is small, fast, and efficient; it carries out all tasks on these devices — just like the operating system on your computer makes the computing hardware perform your required actions.

All enterprise-level devices — routers, switches, and firewalls — share a similar IOS. The IOS software runs the different Cisco hardware platforms and provides different services or functions depending on the version of the software used. For instance, the Network Address Translation (NAT) was introduced into the Cisco IOS in version 11.3, so to make use of specific features, you will often require a specific version of the Cisco IOS.

Checking out the show command

Although routers, switches, and firewalls all have unique functions and the IOS will have different commands to support these functions, the IOS uses several core commands on all these devices.

At the start of this chapter, I really want you to review what I am doing, but not follow along with your own equipment just yet. In the later section, "Tinkering with Device Connections," I show you how to get a management connection established to your Cisco network device, but it helps to be familiar with some of the management interface operations before you get that connection. After you make the management connection to your own device, you may want to review this section. You also find information about connecting the management interface of switches and routers in Book III and Book IV, respectively. If you are planning to work through some of the examples in this chapter with a Cisco switch, then read Book III, Chapter 3 to learn how to get a management connection to the console port on the switch. If you are planning to use a router, then read Book IV, Chapter 3.

In this section, you examine the `show version` command. The `show version` command displays slightly different information depending on the type of device you use it on, whether that is a switch, router, or firewall. You look at the output of the `show version` command on all three of these device types. The goal of this section is to enforce the point that commands you use may not be exactly the same on each type of device.

Although I have said the command is `show version`, technically it is the `show` command and `version` is an option.

Flash memory

Your Cisco device does not have a hard drive on which it can store information in a permanent manner. Hard drives were not used due to their size, power consumption, and life span. Rather than using hard drives, Cisco uses flash memory, the same type you would find on a Secure Digital (SD) card or USB thumb drive. As this memory has come down in price, Cisco has increased the amount of memory built into devices.

Examining show version on a switch

As I mention earlier, in order to type the `show version` command yourself, you need to have a connection to the management interface of your switch. You can skip ahead to the "Tinkering with Device Connections" section to find out how to do this. Here, I want to show the difference in command operations between device types.

Look at the output of the `show version` command on a *switch* and take note of the following information:

✦ IOS version

✦ System uptime

✦ Image filename

✦ Type of processor

✦ Amount of RAM

✦ Number of ports on the switch

✦ Amount of flash memory

✦ MAC address

✦ Serial number

The management interface that you use is the console connection. This connection is made through the Console port on the device using the blue rollover cable that came with your device. After making the connection, you use a terminal emulator program (such as PuTTY) to see what is going on with the device. I cover this later in the chapter in the section, "Connecting directly via a Cisco rollover cable."

Through this book, you see code examples like the following one. In this example, you see that some of the text is bold. The full example shows what is taking place in a console screen using the Cisco CLI, while the bold text shows what was typed.

Here is a copy of what the `show version` command shows for my switch:

```
Switch>show version
Cisco Internetwork Operating System Software
IOS (tm) C2950 Software (C2950-I6Q4L2-M), Version 12.1(22)EA13, RELEASE SOFTWARE
    (fc2)
Technical Support: http://www.cisco.com/techsupport
Copyright (c) 1986-2009 by cisco Systems, Inc.
Compiled Fri 27-Feb-09 22:20 by amvarma
Image text-base: 0x80010000, data-base: 0x80570000

ROM: Bootstrap program is C2950 boot loader
```

```
Switch uptime is 0 minutes
System returned to ROM by power-on
System image file is "flash:c2950-i6q412-mz.121-22.EA13.bin"

cisco WS-C2950-12 (RC32300) processor (revision B0) with 20957K bytes of memory.
Processor board ID FAB0535Q22L
Last reset from system-reset
Running Standard Image
12 FastEthernet/IEEE 802.3 interface(s)

32K bytes of flash-simulated non-volatile configuration memory.
Base ethernet MAC Address: 00:06:D6:AB:A0:40
Motherboard assembly number: 73-5782-08
Motherboard serial number: FAB0535BC1K
Model revision number: B0
Model number: WS-C2950-12
System serial number: FAB0535Q22L
Configuration register is 0xF
```

Examining show version on a router

Review the output of the show version command on a *router* and try to locate the following information. The output gives you insight into the router's capabilities, and overall gives you practice reading the output of many Cisco commands:

- ✦ IOS version

- ✦ System uptime

- ✦ Image filename

- ✦ Type of processor

- ✦ Amount of RAM

- ✦ Number of ports on the switch

- ✦ Amount of flash memory

- ✦ Current configuration register

Here is what the show version command displays for one of my routers:

```
Router1#show version
Cisco IOS Software, C2600 Software (C2600-ADVIPSERVICESK9-M), Version 12.3(4)T4,
    RELEASE SOFTWARE (fc2)
Technical Support: http://www.cisco.com/techsupport
Copyright (c) 1986-2004 by Cisco Systems, Inc.
Compiled Thu 11-Mar-04 19:57 by eaarmas

ROM: System Bootstrap, Version 12.2(8r) [cmong 8r], RELEASE SOFTWARE (fc1)

Router1 uptime is 20 minutes
System returned to ROM by power-on
System image file is "flash:c2600-advipservicesk9-mz.123-4.T4.bin"
```

```
This product contains cryptographic features and is subject to United
States and local country laws governing import, export, transfer and
use. Delivery of Cisco cryptographic products does not imply
third-party authority to import, export, distribute or use encryption.
Importers, exporters, distributors and users are responsible for
compliance with U.S. and local country laws. By using this product you
agree to comply with applicable laws and regulations. If you are unable
to comply with U.S. and local laws, return this product immediately.

A summary of U.S. laws governing Cisco cryptographic products may be found at:
http://www.cisco.com/wwl/export/crypto/tool/stqrg.html

If you require further assistance please contact us by sending email to
export@cisco.com.

Cisco 2621XM (MPC860P) processor (revision 0x300) with 125952K/5120K bytes of
    memory.
Processor board ID JAE081160XR (3618058385)
M860 processor: part number 5, mask 2
2 FastEthernet interfaces
1 Virtual Private Network (VPN) Module
32K bytes of NVRAM.
32768K bytes of processor board System flash (Read/Write)

Configuration register is 0x2102
```

Examining show version on the Cisco ASA firewall

Look at the output of the `show version` command on an Adaptive Security
Appliance (ASA) and take note of the following information, as you have with
the previous devices:

- ✦ IOS version
- ✦ Name of the image file
- ✦ System uptime
- ✦ Type of processor and hardware platform
- ✦ Amount of RAM
- ✦ Amount of flash memory
- ✦ MAC address
- ✦ Number of ports on the switch
- ✦ Licensed features
- ✦ Serial number
- ✦ Current configuration register

Here is what the `show version` command displays for my ASA:

```
ciscoasa> show version

Cisco Adaptive Security Appliance Software Version 8.2(1)11
Device Manager Version 6.2(3)

Compiled on Mon 21-Sep-09 17:47 by builders
System image file is "disk0:/asa821-11-k8.bin"
Config file at boot was "startup-config"

ciscoasa up 28 mins 4 secs

Hardware:   ASA5505, 256 MB RAM, CPU Geode 500 MHz
Internal ATA Compact Flash, 128MB
BIOS Flash M50FW080 @ 0xffe00000, 1024KB

Encryption hardware device : Cisco ASA-5505 on-board accelerator (revision 0x0)
                             Boot microcode    : CN1000-MC-BOOT-2.00
                             SSL/IKE microcode: CNLite-MC-SSLm-PLUS-2.03
                             IPSec microcode  : CNlite-MC-IPSECm-MAIN-2.04
 0: Int: Internal-Data0/0   : address is 001f.ca8c.93da, irq 11
 1: Ext: Ethernet0/0        : address is 001f.ca8c.93d2, irq 255
 2: Ext: Ethernet0/1        : address is 001f.ca8c.93d3, irq 255
 3: Ext: Ethernet0/2        : address is 001f.ca8c.93d4, irq 255
 4: Ext: Ethernet0/3        : address is 001f.ca8c.93d5, irq 255
 5: Ext: Ethernet0/4        : address is 001f.ca8c.93d6, irq 255
 6: Ext: Ethernet0/5        : address is 001f.ca8c.93d7, irq 255
 7: Ext: Ethernet0/6        : address is 001f.ca8c.93d8, irq 255
 8: Ext: Ethernet0/7        : address is 001f.ca8c.93d9, irq 255
 9: Int: Internal-Data0/1   : address is 0000.0003.0002, irq 255
10: Int: Not used           : irq 255
11: Int: Not used           : irq 255

Licensed features for this platform:
Maximum Physical Interfaces   : 8
VLANs                         : 20, DMZ Unrestricted
Inside Hosts                  : Unlimited
Failover                      : Active/Standby
VPN-DES                       : Enabled
VPN-3DES-AES                  : Enabled
SSL VPN Peers                 : 2
Total VPN Peers               : 25
Dual ISPs                     : Enabled
VLAN Trunk Ports              : 8
Shared License                : Disabled
AnyConnect for Mobile         : Disabled
AnyConnect for Cisco VPN Phone : Disabled
AnyConnect Essentials         : Disabled
Advanced Endpoint Assessment  : Disabled
UC Phone Proxy Sessions       : 2
Total UC Proxy Sessions       : 2
Botnet Traffic Filter         : Disabled

This platform has an ASA 5505 Security Plus license.

Serial Number: JMX1214Z0LF
Running Activation Key: 0xe6135258 0xe84c9b0d 0x6c501544 0x90d4f8d0 0x400ab69d
Configuration register is 0x1
Configuration has not been modified since last system restart.
```

The base IOS feature set is the same across these three device platforms (switches, routers, and ASA firewalls), so in addition to a core block of information, each product line has some unique information that is returned by the `show version` command. For example, the firewall returned licensing information regarding the number of SSL VPN Peers that are supported. This number represents the number of client Virtual Private Network (VPN) connections that the ASA is licensed for when using secure HTTP over Secure Sockets Layer (SSL).

Understanding operating modes

Regardless of the device that you are configuring, there are a few standard but distinct modes or styles of the command prompt. You get to those command prompts using a cable, Secure Shell (SSH), or Telnet connection. Each prompt serves a purpose, so you need to become familiar with them and understand what you can do at the prompts. The prompt itself is the indicator of the operating system mode, and it is the operating system mode that determines what commands you are allowed to use.

The Cisco IOS has an escalating set of permissions as you move through the prompts or operating modes. When you first connect to a device you will be in User EXEC mode; then by issuing the `enable` command you are brought to Privileged EXEC mode; by issuing the `configure terminal` command you will be brought to Global Configuration mode; finally, by issuing one of any number of other commands you will be brought to an interface or subconfiguration mode. I point out when these other modes show up, but they would be too lengthy and boring to list them all here. Figure 5-1 graphically shows the escalation among these commands.

User EXEC mode

When you first connect to a router, switch, or firewall, you see an initial prompt that looks like the following (but bear in mind that it could say *switch* or *firewall* as well):

```
Router>
```

The text in the prompt represents the hostname of the device, which by default is the device type; but you may have already renamed your devices, in which case it could now be anything. The greater-than (>) sign denotes that you are in User EXEC mode, or User EXECute mode. This mode has only a few commands that you can execute, including the following, and these are commands that you should find in all devices, be they routers, switches, or firewalls:

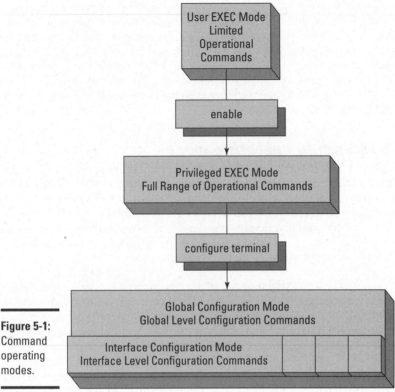

Figure 5-1:
Command
operating
modes.

* ✦ `connect`: Opens a terminal session to another switch or router.

* ✦ `disconnect`: Closes a session that was opened from a remote switch or router.

* ✦ `enable`: Enters Privileged EXEC mode or enables privileged commands.

* ✦ `ping`: Sends `ping` or Internet Control Message Protocol (ICMP) echo request packets to a remote IP host, which could be a switch or router. You read more on this command in Book II, Chapter 3.

* ✦ `show`: Displays configuration information. The information that can be viewed at this level is very limited.

* ✦ `systat`: Displays information regarding management connections.

* ✦ `telnet`: Opens a Telnet connection to a remote device, which could be a router or switch.

* ✦ `traceroute`: Traces a route to a destination displaying connectivity results along the path. You read more on this command in Book II, Chapter 3.

This limited command set does not allow you to do very much on the system itself, which is good because you can get to this mode without a password. To get to the real command set, enter Privileged EXEC mode, which by default has a password restricting access.

Privileged EXEC mode

User EXEC mode allows you to do only some very basic commands, whereas if you want to really have access to the system, you need to use Privileged EXEC mode. To enter this mode, run the `enable` command, which prompts you for a password, if configured. As the mode name suggests, this mode has extra privileges to allow you to make major changes to the system or to enter Configuration mode. When you are in Privileged EXEC mode, your command prompt resembles the following (this is the hostname, which by default is the name of the device, but could be anything else):

```
Router#
```

The hash/pound sign (#) denotes that you are in the Privileged EXEC mode. Some of the commands that are available include these commands that you should find in all devices, be they routers, switches, or firewalls

✦ `cd`: Change the current directory. Routers and switches have several file systems, including flash, nvram, system, and null.

✦ `clear`: Resets functions operating on the device. There are many values that are totaled for reporting that can be reset this way. You can also reset many system-wide configuration values.

✦ `clock`: Allows you to change the system clock.

✦ `copy`: Copy a file from one location to another. The location could be another local file system or a remote file system, such as a Trivial File Transfer Protocol (TFTP) server.

✦ `debug`: Turn on debug logging. This can be done for a specific interface or software component, or for all functions. This places a load on the device if the debugging level is too high and generates an incredible level of messaging on the console screen.

✦ `delete`: Removes a file from a file system.

✦ `dir`: Displays the list of files in the current directory.

✦ `disable`: Reverts the current session back to User EXEC mode and disables the privileged commands.

✦ `erase`: Removes all files in a file system. This is similar to an OS-level format command.

✦ `exit`: Exits from Privileged EXEC mode.

✦ no: Reverses a previously issued command. For example, debug all turns on all possible debugging, whereas no debug all turns off all possible debugging. Just about every command that can be issued can be reversed with the no command.

✦ ping: Sends ping or ICMP echo request packets to a remote IP host, such as a switch or router.

✦ pwd: Displays what the current file system directory is.

✦ reload: Restarts the device. This restart can be immediate or scheduled for the future. The reload command can also be used to cancel a scheduled reload.

✦ send: Sends a message to specific or all connected users. This is useful if you are about to perform certain maintenance tasks, such as rebooting the device.

✦ show: Displays configuration information. This is typically configuration information that is running, but it could also be used to view the startup configuration.

✦ systat: Displays information regarding management connections to this device.

✦ telnet: Opens a Telnet connection to a remote device, such as a router or switch.

✦ test: Tests subsystems, memory, and interfaces as part of your diagnostic or troubleshooting process.

✦ traceroute: Traces a route to a destination displaying connectivity results along the path.

✦ undebug: Disables debug commands that were set. This is an alternative to using the no command to perform these functions.

✦ write: Copies information in the running-config buffer to another location, such as memory, a TFTP server, or to the virtual terminal (vty) or console connection.

Global Configuration mode

When you type the configure command, you need to specify how you will make configuration changes. The most common manner of configuring devices is by using the terminal, so you use the configure terminal or conf t (for *configure terminal*) commands. The Global Configuration mode appears, and your command prompt will look something like this:

```
Router(config)#
```

This prompt is identified by the `(config)`, which is in the prompt. You also have a different list of commands that you can type. Here is just a sample of the commands at this level:

+ `access-list`: Manage Access Control Lists (ACLs) to restrict network connections to, from, or through the device you are connected to.

+ `arp`: Manage the Address Resolution Protocol (ARP) cache on the device you are connected to.

+ `banner`: Set a logon banner to issue a security warning to users connecting to the device you are connected to.

+ `boot`: Configure or modify the system boot parameters, such as the IOS version that will be used.

+ `cdp`: Cisco Discovery Protocol (CDP) tells you what is connected to you on network interfaces. CDP allows you to view this information.

+ `clock`: Allows you to change the system clock.

+ `config-register` (router only): Set the *configuration register,* which is the location in memory that stores a pointer to the system configuration information.

+ `enable`: Sets or changes `enable` passwords.

+ `exit`: Exits Global Configuration mode.

+ `hostname`: Sets the device hostname.

+ `ip`: Enters the IP configuration subcommands.

+ `interface`: Selects an interface for configuration.

+ `no`: Negates another command that has been issued.

+ `prompt`: Sets the devices command prompt.

Interface Configuration Mode

In many cases when you are working with Global Configuration mode, you enter an interface for configuration or any number of subconfiguration modes. At that point in time, any commands you type apply only to the interface. When you are in Interface Configuration mode, your prompt looks something like this, while other configuration prompts will vary slightly in the displayed text:

```
Router(configure-if)#
```

Each interface or subconfiguration mode has its own list of configuration commands. Here are some of the commands that you see on a network interface:

- ✦ arp: Sets an interface ARP type or timeout.

- ✦ cdp: Configures CDP for a specific interface.

- ✦ delay: Specifies the delay on interface throughput. This is useful for limiting throughput or for simulating slower connections in a lab.

- ✦ description: Sets a descriptive name for the interface.

- ✦ exit: Exits Interface mode and returns to Configuration mode.

- ✦ ip: Configures IP protocol on the interface.

- ✦ logging: Configures logging for the interface.

- ✦ media-type: Chooses a media type for interfaces that have the option.

- ✦ mtu: Sets the interface *maximum transmission unit (MTU),* which limits the size of the Ethernet frame.

- ✦ no: Negates other commands that have been issued.

- ✦ shutdown: Disables or shuts down the interface.

Type the exit command to leave a mode and move to the next higher mode. You need to do that if the commands you want to use do not work at that level. For example, to view the current configuration that is in use, use the show running-configuration command. That command can be used only in Privileged EXEC mode, so if you are in Global Configuration mode, you need to move one level up to use that command. If after viewing the running configuration, you decide that you need to change the IP address of the Fast/Ethernet0/0 interface of a router, you need to use a sequence like this (do not worry about the actual commands at this point, I only want you to see and understand how to move between the command modes):

```
Router#configure terminal
Enter configuration commands, one per line.  End with CNTL/Z.
Router(config)#interface FastEthernet 0/0
Router(config-if)#ip address 192.168.1.2 255.255.255.0
Router(config-if)#exit
Router(config)#exit
Router#
```

Saving your work

After you are happy with your configuration, you can save it. Your configuration is stored in two main locations: One is in RAM, and the other is in the configuration that is in use, or the *running configuration.* When you type commands, those commands are activated immediately and are stored in the running configuration, which is stored in RAM. Therefore, when the power is turned off, the configuration is lost. To save that configuration, copy it to the startup configuration, which means it is stored in non-volatile RAM (NVRAM), so that the configuration is retained when you turn off the power.

Dealing with old commands

Deprecated commands are commands which are still found in the Cisco IOS, but that Cisco plans to remove it from the system in the future. Cisco leaves the deprecated commands around to allow people to transition to the new commands, so during a future IOS upgrade, you should not be surprised if those commands are gone.

You can use two commands to save your configuration, the `write` command or the `copy` command. The `write` command is deprecated, but would look like this

```
Router#write memory
Building configuration...
[OK]
```

The newer version of the command is the copy command, which looks like

```
Router#copy running-config startup-config
Destination filename [startup-config]?
Building configuration...
[OK]
```

The deprecated command is short and single-purposed, not flexible with full options like the newer command.

For any command you only have to type as many letters as the IOS requires to uniquely identify the command. So you will find that a lot of old-timers use the following command as a reflex after they complete changes and when they exit Global Configuration mode to copy their current `running-config` to the `startup-config`:

```
wri mem
```

The `copy` command offers more flexibility and options. Not only can you copy the running configuration data to the startup configuration file, but you could copy it to a file on flash or to a TFTP server on your network. The `copy` command is only a little more to type:

```
copy run sta
```

Getting going with the command line

If you have followed along so far in this chapter, you are connected to the Cisco device and have a console connection open. You are now staring at this friendly command prompt, or something similar:

```
Router>
```

So now what? Well, you can ask the IOS for help. Type a question mark after `Router>`, and the IOS displays a list of commands that are possible at that level.

```
Router>?
EXEC commands:
  access-enable    Create a temporary Access-List entry
  access-profile   Apply user-profile to interface
  clear            Reset functions
  connect          Open a terminal connection
  crypto           Crypto
  disable          Turn off privileged commands
  disconnect       Disconnect an existing network connection
  enable           Turn on privileged commands
  exit             Exit from the EXEC
  help             Description of the interactive help system
  lock             Lock the terminal
  login            Log in as a particular user
  logout           Exit from the EXEC
  modemui          Start a modem-like user interface
  mrinfo           Request neighbor and version information from a multicast
                   router
  mstat            Show statistics after multiple multicast traceroutes
  mtrace           Trace reverse multicast path from destination to source
  name-connection  Name an existing network connection
  pad              Open a X.29 PAD connection
  ping             Send echo messages
 --More-
```

When the `--More-` text is displayed at the bottom of a page (see the preceding code), you can press Enter to advance the list by one line or press the spacebar to advance by one screen. If you prefer to start typing one of the commands, you can hit just about any key to exit from the `--More-` listing and type your command.

Other times you may start typing the letters of a command but you cannot remember what the actual command is. Anytime you type the command, you can add a question mark to the end of it to see what commands could be completed. Here is an example in Privileged EXEC mode:

```
Router#c?
call   ccm-manager  cd         clear
clock  cns          configure  connect
copy   crypto
```

Getting a command's options

The Cisco IOS has a great context-sensitive Help function, which means the IOS can help you find the specific item you are currently working with. To start using Help, you need to type a command in the CLI. After you type one command, you can ask the IOS for help with possible options for that command. After you type your selected command, type a space and a question mark to get a list of options for that command. For example, running the copy command with the question mark results in the following:

```
Router#copy ?
  /erase           Erase destination file system.
  /noverify        Don't verify image signature before reload.
  /verify          Verify image signature before reload.
  cns:             Copy from cns: file system
  flash:           Copy from flash: file system
  ftp:             Copy from ftp: file system
  http:            Copy from http: file system
  https:           Copy from https: file system
  null:            Copy from null: file system
  nvram:           Copy from nvram: file system
  pram:            Copy from pram: file system
  rcp:             Copy from rcp: file system
  running-config   Copy from current system configuration
  scp:             Copy from scp: file system
  startup-config   Copy from startup configuration
  system:          Copy from system: file system
  tftp:            Copy from tftp: file system
```

In fact, if you have not typed anything on the CLI, you can still type the question mark to get a list of all the available commands that you can use from your current mode. This is a very long list, so if you start with the first few letters of the command, you will greatly reduce the size of the list.

Autocomplete

If you would rather not type the complete command, use the command completion option. If you have to type enough letters of the command that the IOS knows it is unique, you do not have to type anything else; or you can press the Tab key to complete the word you are typing. I prefer pressing the Tab key because it saves me from making a typo. If you are not sure what options you can choose, add a question mark to the end.

In this example, I pressed Tab at the end of each line prior to typing the question mark, which completed each word of the command. Finally, I typed the question mark to see the options with my final command, the only option available is *carriage return* (<cr>), which means just pressing the Enter key on your keyboard.

```
Router#cop
Router#copy run
Router#copy running-config sta
Router#copy running-config startup-config ?
  <cr>
```

Using the command buffer

If you type the same commands again and again, you can make use of the command buffer, or terminal history. By default the command buffer holds ten lines, but it can be reconfigured with the Privileged EXEC mode `terminal history size 10` command. To see the contents of the buffer, use the following command:

```
Router(config)#do show history
  hostname Router
  int fastEthernet 0/0
  ip address 192.168.1.2 255.255.255.0
  exit
  int fastEthernet 0/1
  ip address 10.0.0.1 255.0.0.0
  exit
  do show history
```

The Privileged EXEC mode and Global Configuration mode each have their own command buffers, so if you make configuration changes and want to see them, use the do command. Remember, show is not an available command in Global Configuration mode. Instead, use the do command to tell the IOS to run the show command from Privileged EXEC mode rather than Global Configuration mode. There are only a few Privileged EXEC mode commands that you can run with the do command.

If you see a command in the command buffer that you want to run again, you can copy and paste it back into your terminal application. This process varies depending on the application you use. Later in this chapter, I review the PuTTY application, which is available for both Windows and Linux.

You can quickly review what commands are in the terminal buffer by using the up- or down-arrow key on your keyboard. Use the up-arrow key to scroll through your last commands; if you go too far, use the down-arrow key to go back.

Tinkering with Device Connections

Before you can make your configuration changes, you need to get a connection to your router or switch. The two basic methods of connecting to your device are either directly via a Cisco rollover cable or remotely via a Telnet or SSH connection. The following sections take a closer look at both methods.

Connecting directly via a Cisco rollover cable

You most likely make your initial configuration of your Cisco device through a direct serial cable connection via a *Cisco rollover cable* — the strange blue cable you get with each of your managed devices, as shown in Figure 5-2. (You can purchase unmanaged switches, which do not include the cable or the ability to perform any configuration management. I do not discuss unmanaged switches in this book because there is you do not configure them.) Some of the Cisco Small Business lines have only web configuration options, which I discuss later in this chapter in the "Graphical Configuration Interfaces" section.

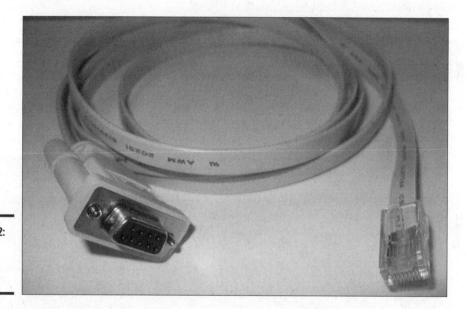

Figure 5-2:
A Cisco
rollover
cable.

To use this cable, you need to have a 9-pin serial port on your computer; otherwise, you need to use an adapter. These days, many laptops and desktop computers are *legacy-free;* they do not have any legacy computer ports. This includes PS/2 keyboard and mouse ports, parallel ports, or serial ports. This can slow you down a bit when trying to configure your Cisco device. Luckily, a large market for manufacturers of USB adapters, such as the serial adapter shown in Figure 5-3, exists.

Not all adapters are created equally, and I have had adapters that have not worked with some devices. Get a good price, but do not go cheap. To some degree, you do get what you pay for.

Figure 5-3:
An aftermarket USB/serial port adapter.

After you have a place on your computer to connect the cable, look on the device for the console port. On most Cisco devices, this is blue and labeled RJ-45 connector, as shown in Figure 5-4. If this is a 9-pin serial connector, you are dealing with a very old device.

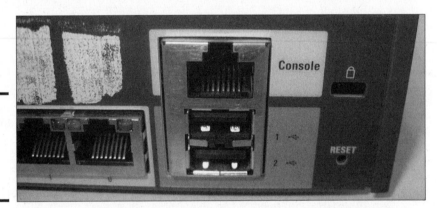

Figure 5-4:
Console/serial port on your Cisco device.

Connect your computer to the console port on your Cisco device, which may even already be running. The next, and last, piece of the puzzle is a terminal emulator application.

Some people use Microsoft HyperTerminal. However, I have always found this application confusing. To get a simple terminal connection, you need to create a dialup connection. HyperTerminal has been removed from the latest versions of Windows anyway, so you would still need to look for an alternative. As an alternative, therefore, I suggest either Tera Term (http://hp.vector.co.jp/authors/VA002416/teraterm.html) or

PuTTy (www.chiark.greenend.org.uk/~sgtatham/PuTTY). Both are free applications, but PuTTY is still actively supported and developed (well, the last update was 2007, but that is better than 1998).

If you choose to download PuTTY, you have many programs to choose from on the download page, such as

+ **PuTTY:** The Telnet and SSH client itself
+ **PSCP:** A Secure Copy Protocol (SCP) client, such as command-line secure file copy
+ **PSFTP:** A Secure File Transfer Protocol (SFTP) client, such as general file transfer sessions like FTP
+ **PuTTYtel:** A Telnet-only client
+ **Plink:** A command-line interface to the PuTTY back ends
+ **Pageant:** An SSH authentication agent for PuTTY, PSCP, and Plink
+ **PuTTYgen:** An RSA (Rivest, Shamir, and Adleman) and DSA (Digital Signature Algorithm) key generation utility

If you want to use PuTTY to make a terminal connection to your Cisco device, choose the full version of PuTTY, which is the first item on the list.

To make life easy, copy the PuTTY.exe file and paste it directly to your Windows folder (C:\Windows). This allows you to launch PuTTY by choosing the Windows Start menu⇨Run, as shown in Figure 5-5. In addition to making PuTTY easy to launch, after you have configured and saved a session, you can launch PuTTY and load a session automatically by using the PuTTY.exe -load COM command, which I discuss shortly.

Depending on the security settings on your version of Windows, you may be asked for confirmation to launch the application. For instance, Windows XP wants permission but you can change the setting so that you are not prompted in the future, as shown in Figure 5-6. As with all programs you download from the Internet, perform a virus scan to ensure that there are not any known issues with the application.

After PuTTY opens, the standard PuTTY Configuration dialog box appears. You can fill in your configuration settings and then click the Open button to make the connection, which opens a command window. If you regularly make connections to that device, save your settings by providing a session name and clicking the Save button. Figure 5-7 shows the session being saved for a serial connection through COM1 running at 9600 bps. After you save this connection, you can launch it automatically, as I mention earlier, by using PuTTY.exe -load COM from the Run dialog box. In most cases, you want to save sessions for your most used connections.

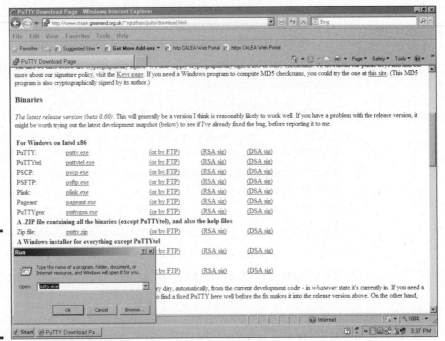

Figure 5-5:
Launching
PuTTY.exe
from the
Windows
Start menu.

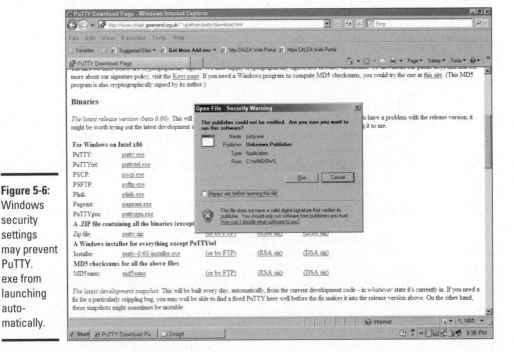

Figure 5-6:
Windows
security
settings
may prevent
PuTTY.
exe from
launching
auto-
matically.

Figure 5-7:
Saving
a PuTTY
connection
session.

The settings you just saved work for most Cisco devices, but the actual rec-ommended settings include a small adjustment in the PuTTY Configuration dialog box, as shown in Figure 5-8. These settings are a little slower than the default settings in PuTTY, so if your command window does not show the console data correctly, use these settings. Choose Connection⇨Serial in the left navigation pane, and put in matching configurations for

✦ **Connection Speed:** 9600 bps

✦ **Data Bits:** 8

✦ **Stop Bits:** 1

✦ **Parity:** None

✦ **Flow Control:** None

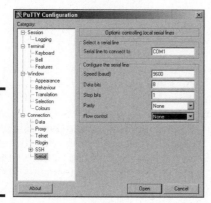

Figure 5-8:
Specific
recom-
mended
Cisco COM
settings.

The last locally attached way to configure your Cisco router is with a modem. By using your Cisco rollover cable and a modem adapter, you can attach a modem directly to the console port. This configuration allows you to dial in to the Cisco device through the modem to make configuration changes. This is very old school in the Internet age, but it does allow you to either have a back door into the configuration in case your service provider or other link is down, or to provide enhanced security by disabling Telnet, SSH, and HTTPS connections directly into the firewall, router, or switch (although this would be more common with the first two devices).

Connecting remotely via Telnet or SSH

A console cable is fine for managing a couple of devices if you are physically close to them or if you have a console server that can be connected directly to all the devices that you have; but this is not normally the case. Typically, you configure your devices, and then deploy them to different locations in your organization or you may move to a location where you are not physically close to the devices. What then? Well, you need a remote method of connecting to your devices.

Telnet

For years, Telnet has been the industry standard. Telnet gives you terminal access to your devices over an IP network. This functionality has been built into every router and managed switch that have been sold for decades; but Telnet has one little problem: It is not all that secure. Telnet passes all its traffic over the network in clear text, so anyone between you and the device on the network can use a packet-capture program to capture the entire conversation. This includes all the passwords and logon credentials you use during the session. With just a few lines of configuration, which I discuss in Book VI, you can secure your remote access by using Secure Shell (SSH) to connect to your devices.

Secure Shell (SSH)

SSH has been around for more than 15 years and has been widely used in Unix and Linux operating systems since 2000. SSH has seen its share of deficiencies and has been improved from version 1 to version 2. Even with these issues, it is a far better choice for remote access than Telnet because all communication is encrypted using a public/private key pair (standard for encrypting data such as SSL data). This security processing is not limited to terminal access because SSH can provide encryption for port forwarding, SFTP (Secure File Transfer Protocol), and Secure Copy Protocol (SCP).

Making an SSH connection is similar to making a Telnet connection from an end-user standpoint. PuTTY (which I discuss earlier in this chapter in the "Connecting directly via a Cisco rollover cable" section) handles both types of connections. Use the instruction in that section of the chapter to download and launch PuTTY, if you have not already done so.

Book I
Chapter 5

Getting into the
Cisco Internetwork
Operating System

The following steps explain how to make an SSH connection, which starts by launching PuTTY. Fill in the PuTTY Configuration dialog as shown in Figure 5-9:

1. **Fill in the IP address of the Cisco device you are connecting to in the Host Name (or IP address) field.**

2. **Select SSH to use SSH to make the connection.**

3. **Fill in a name to save the connection settings as in the Saved Sessions text box, and then click the Save button.**

4. **Click the Open button to establish the initial connection.**

This closes the PuTTY Configuration window and opens a command window with your connection to the Cisco device.

SSH version 2 allows you to perform interactive keyboard authentication or to use certificate-based authentication. To keep things simple, I explain how to perform user-based keyboard authentication.

Figure 5-9:
SSH
connection
settings
with PuTTY.

When you make your initial connection to any SSH device, you are asked to verify its public security key, as shown in Figure 5-10. This key is used as a safety device, and with PuTTY, if that key ever changes, you are prompted and you should question if it should have changed or if someone is trying to break into your Cisco device.

WARNING!

If your key ever changes but you did not authorize it, you may want to cancel the connection and find out why the key is different. For instance, someone could have tried to capture data on your network or spoof your Cisco device's IP address.

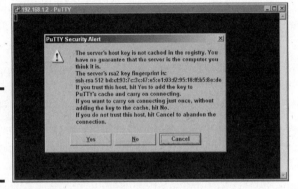

Figure 5-10:
SSH
initial key
verification
dialog box.

Graphical configuration interfaces

To make life easier for you, rather than making all your configuration changes from the command line, Cisco gives you some graphical options depending on the class of product you are using, which varies from Home to Enterprise products.

Small Business devices

To start with, many of the Small Business devices, such as the Security Appliance (SA) 520 firewall, do not have a standard IOS command line but instead offer a web interface for configuration. This web interface greatly reduces the complexity of configuration for Small Business users, who often perform much of their own configuration. Figure 5-11 shows the basic web interface of the SA 520, which places all configuration options in easy-to-navigate menus.

Home devices

Most Home users also perform their own configuration, or get a friend to do it for them. In the Home product line, streamlining configuration options in a few menus is critical for making the home experience easy and painless for users. Figure 5-12 gives you a small example of this with a Cisco WRT54G2 wireless router. By making these devices easy to configure, they often have limited functionality compared with their larger cousins. However, most Home users have no need for most of the functionality that is removed from these Home devices.

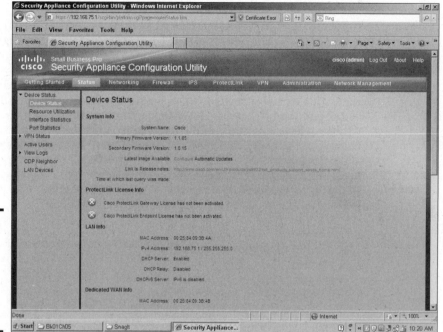

Figure 5-11:
Web
interface
from a
Cisco Small
Business
device.

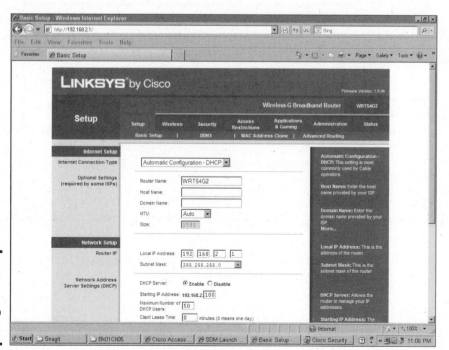

Figure 5-12:
Web
interface
from a Cisco
ome device.

Enterprise devices

Almost all Enterprise devices have an IOS command line for configuration, which for the most part varies little from platform to platform, other than functionality that exists only in a single platform. For example, the same basic commands are used to apply an IP address to a network interface, whether you work on an Adaptive Security Appliance (ASA) firewall, a router, or a switch. To make things simpler for some administrative users who do not want to get into the weeds learning how to do things, many of these devices now have web interfaces to make the configuration tasks easier. The Cisco switches have a web interface that applies basic port setup and monitoring configuration; however, detailed configuration still requires that you get into the command line. Many Cisco routers, especially the Branch Integrated Services routers have a Java-based graphical program, Security Device Manager (SDM), as shown in Figure 5-13.

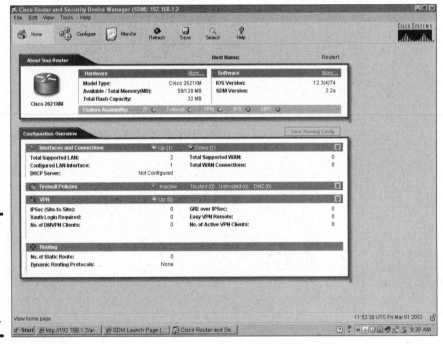

Figure 5-13:
The SDM interface makes Enterprise routers less intimidating.

You might note in the figure that the top menu has three main options: Home, Configure, and Monitor:

✦ The **Home page** gives you a basic snapshot of the device status.

✦ The **Configure page** has a navigation pane down the left of the screen that allows you to configure the main components of the system, such as network interfaces, firewall policies, virtual private networks (VPNs), and routing, to name a few.

✦ The **Monitor page** allows you to see more detailed information on the status of your device that you see on the Home page.

The Cisco ASA Security Device Manager (ASDM), as shown in Figure 5-14, is similar to the SDM in appearance, down to the three main menu items on the main toolbar. The ASDM is also similar to the SDM in operation, with the configuration performed on the Configure page. ASDM is a Java-based application that is stored on the device and launched from a web interface. Almost all functionality of the security device can be configured through the web interface, so a user rarely needs to venture into the depths of the command line.

Book I
Chapter 5

Getting into the
Cisco Internetwork
Operating System

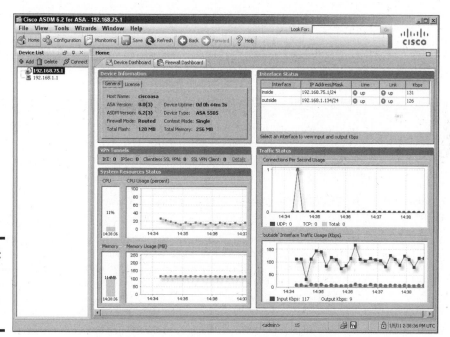

Figure 5-14:
The ASDM interface on the ASA Firewall.

In the case of both the SDM and ASDM, all configuration is performed through the command line. When the interface loads, it reads the `running-config` from the device and then displays it graphically. As you make changes, the software parses new commands to change the running configuration and applies that configuration to the device effectively at the IOS command line.

Although many of the network devices from Cisco have a graphical configuration interface, they are not all equal. In some cases, they are the only option for configuration, whereas in other cases, they augment the very powerful command line.

Upgrading Firmware and Booting an IOS Image

In this section, I show you how the basic boot process works for Cisco devices as well as how to update the *IOS image,* or the *firmware.*

Upgrading the IOS image

So how do you get the IOS file to the device in the first place? Some of the graphical management tools allow you to upload the image using your web browser and HTTP, but you can also use the USB port on some devices or a removable Flash card (the latter two require that you have physical access to the device). The most common way to get the IOS to your devices is through a TFTP server. Cisco used to provide a free TFTP server that you could download to load the image via the server, but Cisco has discontinued this because there are many inexpensive or free alternatives. Cisco puts its development efforts elsewhere. The following are a couple good (and free!) choices to use as your TFTP server:

✦ **Tftpd32:** Open source TFTP server software. (`http://tftpd32. jounin.net`)

✦ **The SolarWinds TFTP Server:** SolarWinds' TFTP server is available for download from its FTP site. When running their server software, SolarWinds is a bit chatty about telling you about great products for purchase, but submitting to their advertising is the price you pay for their "free" software. (`www.solarwinds.com/products/freetools/ free_tftp_server.aspx`)

Both of these user interfaces are shown in Figure 5-15.

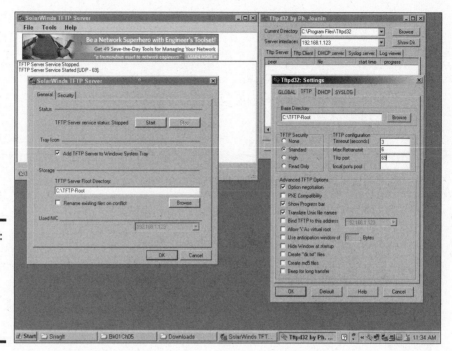

Figure 5-15:
Most TFTP
servers do
not require
much
configur-
ation.

With most TFTP servers, you

1. **Specify a directory to share or serve up via TFTP with the main screen showing you server activity.**

   You get a list of the IP addresses and what files they have uploaded or downloaded from the directory.

2. **Download your IOS image files from Cisco.**

   You need a support agreement to be able to download the IOS image files for your device. You can find this software at the Cisco support portal (www.cisco.com/cisco/web/support/index.html), following the Download Software link on that page, and then following the navigation tool on the page to locate the IOS image for your Cisco device. After you have them, you can move to Step 3.

3. **Place them in the C:\TFTP-Root directory (or whatever directory you have set as your root TFTP directory).**

With the files there, move over to your Cisco device to retrieve the files as you will see

```
Router1>enable
Password:
Router1#copy  tftp: flash:
Address or name of remote host []? 192.168.1.3
Source filename []? c2600-advipservicesk9-mz.123-4.T4.bin
Destination filename [c2600-advipservicesk9-mz.123-4.T4.bin]?
Accessing tftp://192.168.1.3/c2600-advipservicesk9-mz.123-4.T4.bin...
Loading c2600-advipservicesk9-mz.123-4.T4.bin from 192.168.1.3 (via FastEtherne
t0/0): !!!!!!!!!!!!!!!!!!!!!!!!!!!!!!!!!!!!!!!!!!!!!!!!!!!!!!!!!!!!!!!!!!!!!!!!!!!!
!!!!!!!!!!!!!!!!!!!!!!!!!!!!!!!!!!!!!!!!!!!!!!!!!!!!!!!!!!!!!!!!!!!!!!!!!!!!!!!!!!!!
!!!!!!!!!!!!!!!!!!!!!!!!!!!!!!!!!!!!!!!!!!!!!!!!
[OK - 23134968 bytes]

23134968 bytes copied in 102.648 secs (225382 bytes/sec)
```

After you copied the image to your Cisco device, use the same process you see later in this chapter in the "Choosing a boot image" section, to select a boot image. With the new IOS file set as the boot image, you can continue the boot process with the new IOS file. *Voilá!* System upgraded.

If you have enough storage space on your device, you can also do this process with the router running, and using the ROM Monitor mode, which is a small OS that is used to load the IOS image. This process is detailed in the "Recovering a Cisco device" later in this chapter.

After you have completed the upgrade and are sure that everything is working correctly, you can delete any old IOS images that you no longer need. This frees up space on Flash memory for future upgrades.

It is often a good idea to keep your last image around for a while until you are sure there are no major issues with the new IOS. You can also use this image for troubleshooting or diagnostics. Do not forget, before you delete the image, you can copy it to your TFTP server so that you can reload it later.

Managing the boot process

To get started, here is an overview of the Cisco boot process (see Figure 5-16):

1. The Boot ROM initializes all hardware and performs a Power-On Self Test (POST) to ensure that the hardware is functional.

Any errors are reported to the console as part of the POST process.

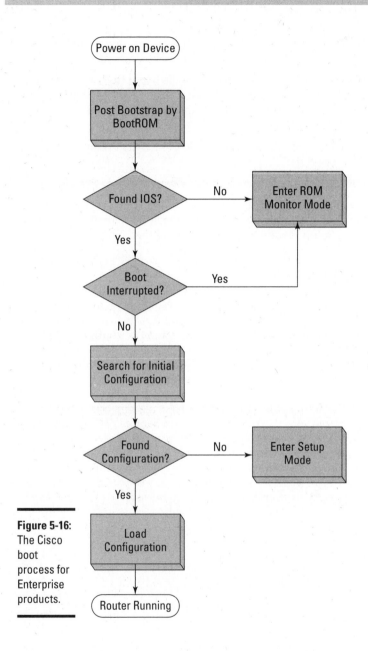

Figure 5-16:
The Cisco
boot
process for
Enterprise
products.

2. The Boot ROM locates and loads a valid Cisco IOS image and loads the first valid image it finds unless a boot value has been set.

   The Boot ROM looks for an image first in Flash and then if a Boot-Helper image is available, attempts to load an IOS from a TFTP server (tftp-dnld). If none is found, the Boot ROM loads the rxboot IOS image, or the ROM Monitor mode (ROMmon).

3. When a valid image is found, the IOS is loaded into system memory, or RAM.

4. The IOS checks the configuration register value stored in NVRAM.

   This is normally set to boot the `startup-config` file. If the `startup-config` is missing or if the configuration register value dictates, the device enters Setup mode rather than loading the configuration.

Recovering a Cisco device

If you need to change boot configuration options, you can interrupt the boot process. Within 60 seconds of starting or restarting the device, you need to press the Break key or Ctrl+C, depending on your hardware. Doing so brings you to the ROM Monitor mode (ROMmon). ROMmon is a small OS that allows you to do a few basic tasks, such as copy a file to your device so that it can be used as the boot image. In the worst-case scenario, you can get into ROMmon and bring yourself back from the brink.

After you are in ROMmon, you can use a few basic commands to load an image from a TFTP server (192.168.1.3). Here is a sample of the process to load an IOS via ROMmon when you do not have an IOS loaded on the router, or you have loaded the wrong file and the system will not boot. In the following example, the system is bootable, so this is just for illustration. Pay close attention to the question the ROMmon asks because it will erase all the contents of Flash, so any other files that you do not want to lose need to be backed up.

```
System Bootstrap, Version 12.2(8r) [cmong 8r], RELEASE SOFTWARE (fc1)
Copyright (c) 2003 by cisco Systems, Inc.
PC = 0xfff0ac3c, Vector = 0x500, SP = 0x680127d0
PC = 0xfff0ac3c, Vector = 0x500, SP = 0x680127c0
C2600 platform with 131072 Kbytes of main memory

PC = 0xfff0ac3c, Vector = 0x500, SP = 0x80004884

monitor: command "boot" aborted due to user interrupt
rommon 1 > dev
Devices in device table:
       id  name
    flash:  flash
```

```
rommon 2 > dir flash:
         File size               Checksum   File name
  23134968 bytes (0x16102f8)     0x9978     c2600-advipservicesk9-mz.123-4.T4.bin
      1885 bytes (0x75d)         0x454c     sdmconfig-26xx.cfg (deleted)
     16264 bytes (0x3f88)        0x1c9e     sdm.shtml
   3176448 bytes (0x307800)      0x1c34     sdm.tar (deleted)
      1462 bytes (0x5b6)         0x8c5e     home.html (deleted)
    216064 bytes (0x34c00)       0xf287     home.tar (deleted)
      1038 bytes (0x40e)         0xddd8     home.shtml
      1652 bytes (0x674)         0x6b5a     sdmconfig-26xx.cfg
    113152 bytes (0x1ba00)       0xac3e     home.tar
    234040 bytes (0x39238)       0x965b     attack-drop.sdf
   1007616 bytes (0xf6000)       0x1f57     common.tar
   4049920 bytes (0x3dcc00)      0xb4ce     sdm.tar
rommon 3 > IP_ADDRESS=192.168.1.1
rommon 4 > IP_SUBNET_MASK=255.255.255.0
rommon 5 > DEFAULT_GATEWAY=192.168.1.254
rommon 6 > TFTP_SERVER=192.168.1.3
rommon 7 > TFTP_FILE=c2600-advipservicesk9-mz.123-4.T4.bin
rommon 8 > TFTP_RETRY_COUNT=20
rommon 9 > sync
rommon 10 > tftpdnld

        IP_ADDRESS: 192.168.1.1
    IP_SUBNET_MASK: 255.255.255.0
   DEFAULT_GATEWAY: 192.168.1.254
       TFTP_SERVER: 192.168.1.3
         TFTP_FILE: c2600-advipservicesk9-mz.123-4.T4.bin

Invoke this command for disaster recovery only.
WARNING: all existing data in all partitions on flash will be lost!
Do you wish to continue? y/n:  [n]:  y
.....
Receiving c2600-advipservicesk9-mz.123-4.T4.bin from 192.168.1.3 !!!!!!!!!!!!!!!!
    !!!!!!!!!!!!!!!!!!!!!!!!!!!!!!!!!!!!!!!!!!!!!!!!!!!!!!!!!!!!!!!!!!!!!!!!!!!!!!!!
    !!!!!!!!!!!!!!!!!!!!!!!!!!!!!!!!!!!!!!!!!!!!!!!!!!!!!!!!!!!!!!!!!!!!!!!!!!!!!!!!
    !!!!!!!!!!!!!!!!!!!!!!!!!!!!!!!!!!!!!!!!!!!!!!!!!!!!!!!!!!!!!!!!!!!!!!!!!!!!!!!!
    !!!!!!!!!!!!!
File reception completed.
Copying file c2600-advipservicesk9-mz.123-4.T4.bin to flash.
Erasing flash at 0x61380000
program flash location 0x609b0000
rommon 11 > reset
```

If you want to test an IOS image file prior to deploying but you do not have enough space on Flash to store it, you can use `tftpdnld -r` to load and run it from Dynamic Random Access Memory (DRAM).

This process would then completely restore the selected image to the Cisco device. If there were other files (such as the SDM or ASDM files, or other files you send to clients) on the device, you would need to restore them. Take note the last line in the preceding code, you restart the device with the `reset` command.

Choosing a boot image

If you have more than one IOS image on your device, you would normally choose which one you want to use by setting the boot configuration options in the `startup-config` file, rather than relying on the first valid IOS that is found. You will have to wait until after you have a running IOS as this is set in the configuration that is stored in NVRAM. To change the boot image that you are using, enter Configuration mode, as in the following code:

```
Router1>enable
Password:
Router1#configure terminal
Enter configuration commands, one per line.  End with CNTL/Z.
Router1(config)#boot system flash c2600-advipservicesk9-mz.123-4.T4.bin
Router1(config)#exit
Router1#
*Mar  1 10:49:38.095: %SYS-5-CONFIG_I: Configured from console by console
Router1#copy running-config startup-config
Router1#reload
Proceed with reload? [confirm]
*Mar  1 10:51:27.247: %SYS-5-RELOAD: Reload requested by console. Reload Reason:
    Reload command.
```

The boot image specified is loaded as long as it exists on Flash. If the file is deleted from Flash, the boot process continues with the next boot parameter in the configuration file or the first valid IOS file that is located on Flash.

Recovering a device with a lost password

In this section, I show you another common function that you may need to use the ROMmon interface for. You may already have an old Cisco router or switch on your storage shelf that you cannot use because you do not have the enable password for it. Well, with your trusty Cisco rollover cable, you can use ROMmon to recover the password. Recovering the password may differ slightly based on your device, but most devices use the process described here to tweak the configuration register. If you have a running device of the same type (same model, such as a 2900 Series Router), you can run `show version` to find out what the default configuration register value is set to. In most cases, the register is set to 0x2102. Let me explain what that means.

Several settings can be stored in the configuration register, and they are totaled into a single value. So all the 16-bit values are added together to give you the value that is stored in the register. In the following bullets, I give a brief summary of the main values to worry about.

The lowest four bits control the boot settings:

+ **Boot field equals 0000:** Do not load a system image; enter into ROMmon mode. This allows you to manually load an image to boot.

+ **Boot field equals 0001:** Load the first valid image in Flash.

+ **Boot field between 0010 and 1111:** Load the image specified in the `boot` command in the configuration file stored in NVRAM; if this is not possible, stay in ROMmon.

In addition to the boot values, other values that are of interest include

+ **Bit 6 (0x0040):** Clear the NVRAM contents, this value will be the value to use to clear the existing enable password. Clear the entire contents of NVRAM.

+ **Bit 8 (0x0100):** Disable the `break` command.

+ **Bit 13 (0x2000):** Boot the IOS image on Flash if network boot fails or is not used.

You can use the `show version` command to find out what your configuration register is set to. So if the default register value is 0x2102 (Boot Flash IOS if no network boot, disable Break after system is running, and load items listed in boot configuration), change it to 0x2142 (Boot Flash IOS if no network boot, clear NVRAM, disable Break after system is running, and load items listed in boot configuration). To perform password recovery, follow this process, reload your router, and break into ROMmon, as I describe earlier:

```
System Bootstrap, Version 12.2(8r) [cmong 8r], RELEASE SOFTWARE (fc1)
Copyright (c) 2003 by cisco Systems, Inc.
PC = 0xfff0ac3c, Vector = 0x500, SP = 0x680127d0
PC = 0xfff0ac3c, Vector = 0x500, SP = 0x680127c0
C2600 platform with 131072 Kbytes of main memory

PC = 0xfff0ac3c, Vector = 0x500, SP = 0x80004884

monitor: command "boot" aborted due to user interrupt
rommon 1 > confreg 0x2142
rommon 2 > reset
```

After the reset, you are asked to go through the setup process again. Answer "no" to these requests and then follow this process.

```
Router>enable
Router#copy startup-config running-config
Router1#show running-config
Router1#configure terminal
Enter configuration commands, one per line.  End with CNTL/Z.
Router1(config)#enable secret <password>
Router1(config)#config-register 0x2102
Router1(config)#exit
```

```
Router1#
*Mar  1 10:49:38.095: %SYS-5-CONFIG_I: Configured from console by console
Router1#copy running-config startup-config
Building configuration...
[OK]
Router1#reload
Proceed with reload? [confirm]
*Mar  1 10:51:27.247: %SYS-5-RELOAD: Reload requested by console. Reload Reason:
    Reload command.
```

Because you have changed the configuration register from the configuration screen, you do not need to enter ROMmon to change back. It is not uncommon for this step to be forgotten, so each time you boot the device, you continually enter Setup mode. Do not worry; if you still have a valid startup-config file in NVRAM, follow the immediately preceding code to the end. If you do not have the startup-config file, run setup to restore your settings and change the config-register value.

Book II

Internet Protocols

The 5th Wave

By Rich Tennant

©RICHTENNANT

"It's a wonderful idea, Ralph. But do you really think 'AnnoyPersonTP' and 'DumbMemoTP' will work as protocols on our TCP/IP suite?"

Contents at a Glance

Chapter 1: Making the Most of IPv4

Internet Protocol (IP) version 4 (IPv4) is the current standard "IP" protocol used with TCP/IP — Transmission Control Protocol/Internet Protocol — which is the protocol for Internet addressing. In this chapter, you see how IP addresses are structured and broken down into categories and then further broken down for management. None of this information should strike you as too difficult, especially if you have already made your way through Book I.

In this chapter, when I refer to *IP,* I mean IPv4. I discuss IP version 6 (IPv6) (the new standard that is just starting to be rolled out as of this writing), in detail in Chapter 4 of this minibook.

By the end of this chapter, you

✦ **Have a basic idea of an IP address and its structure.**

✦ **Know the purpose of the subnet mask.**

The preceding two items, in particular, play a big role in TCP/IP, as well as most actions that you will perform with your Cisco devices, especially your routers and firewalls.

✦ **Be able to identify the class to which any address belongs and how the classes relate.**

✦ **Know how to reconfigure networks into smaller or larger pieces by manipulating the subnet mask.**

Getting the lowdown on Internet standards

The Internet Architecture Board (IAB) manages the rules and regulations regarding the structure of the Internet. The IAB manages several working groups, the two largest being the Internet Engineering Task Force (IETF) and the Internet Research Task Force (IRTF). The IETF develops and promotes Internet standards, such as TCP/IP, whereas IRTF works on long-term research and development projects. As protocols and processes are developed, they are documented in Request for Comments (RFC) documents.

Note that all RFCs (currently, more than 6,000) are available from www.ietf.org. Technologies in RFCs sometimes make it into Standards (STD) documents, of which there are currently fewer than 70. An index of the standards can be found at

www.rfc-editor.org/std-index.html

The last half of this chapter has you diving into subnetting pretty heavily, but before you start wading in that direction, first check out the nearby sidebar for a brief history of the Internet as a leisurely distraction for your inner geek.

Meeting TCP/IP, Belle of the Networking Ball

TCP/IP, the protocol suite used to connect computers on the Internet, comprises many protocols that function at different levels of the network model. There are network protocols, transport protocols, and application protocols. In fact, the number of protocols is innumerable:

✦ **SMTP:** Simple Mail Transport Protocol

✦ **POP3:** Post Office Protocol version 3

✦ **HTTP:** HyperText Transfer Protocol

✦ **FTP:** File Transfer Protocol

✦ **IMAP:** Internet Message Access Protocol

TCP/IP is actually a suite of protocols that covers all aspects of the communication process.

Comparing TCP/IP with the OSI Network Model

Like the Open System Interconnection (OSI) model, TCP/IP has its own model. The OSI model and the TCP/IP models were both created independently. The TCP/IP network model represents reality in the world, whereas the OSI mode represents an ideal. With that said, the TCP/IP network model matches the standard layered network model as it should.

Examining Figure 1-1 shows the relationship between the OSI model and the TCP/IP model. This chapter focuses on the IP layer of the model, and Chapter 2 of this minibook examines the TCP and User Diagram Protocol (UDP) layer.

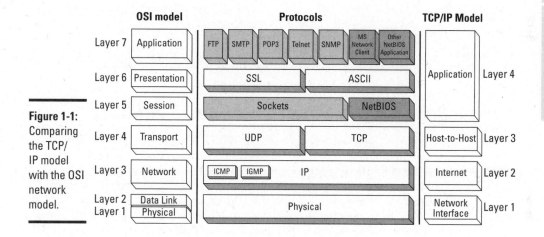

Figure 1-1:
Comparing the TCP/IP model with the OSI network model.

The TCP/IP network model has four basic layers:

+ **Network interface (layer 1):** Deals with all physical components of network connectivity between the network and the IP protocol

+ **Internet (layer 2):** Contains all functionality that manages the movement of data between two network devices over a routed network

+ **Host-to-host (layer 3):** Manages the flow of traffic between two hosts or devices, ensuring that data arrives at the application on the host for which it is targeted

+ **Application (layer 4):** Acts as final endpoints at either end of a communication session between two network hosts

Defining the "host"

Most of the time when you think of a device on your network, you think of a computer. Using *computer* to refer to a device on your network is technically incorrect though. Not all computers have network cards, so not all computers are network devices; conversely, not all network devices are computers because network devices also include printers, routers, switches, hubs, and bridges. So, when possible, without the text sounding too awkward, I use the term *network device* instead of computer.

This chapter is all about IP and the devices on your network that support or operate using IP.

Just as not all computers are network devices, not all network devices are IP-based network devices. Any device on your network that operates using IP as a network layer protocol and can be configured with an IP address is an IP network device; this could include computers, printers, routers, switches, video cameras, and firewalls. The commonly used term for a generic IP-based network device is a *host.* So when discussing communication related to a generic IP-based network device in this book, I use the term *host.*

Comprehending the Structure of an IP Address

At its heart, an IP address is just a 32-bit (or 32-digit binary) number. Although you typically see IP addresses written in dotted decimal notation (192.0.2.205), the IP address can also be written in binary (see Figure 1-2). To understand concepts, such as subnetting, in this chapter, it is easier to understand when working with the addresses in binary, so for much of what you look at in this chapter, I go back to binary several times; things just seem to make more sense that way. You are likely accustomed to seeing IP addresses converted from binary to decimal (see Book I, Chapter 3).

The 32 bits in an IP address are separated into four groups, with each group having eight bits. Eight bits is a *byte,* which can also be referred to as an *octet.* When working with IP addresses, the term *octet* is pretty well the exclusive way to refer to each section of the address. From left to right, that would be octet one, two, three, and four.

Figure 1-2:
A binary and decimal representation of an IP address.

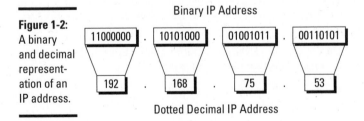

Binary IP Address

| 11000000 | . | 10101000 | . | 01001011 | . | 00110101 |

| 192 | . | 168 | . | 75 | . | 53 |

Dotted Decimal IP Address

As you progress through the next section, you can see exactly how the address structure is used.

Knowing Your Network Classes

IP networking has five main network classes — A through E — and knowing network classes becomes an issue when you deal with routing.

All actual network IDs and addresses are managed and distributed by the *Internet Assigned Number Authority (IANA),* which manages the entire pool of addresses. Addresses used to be permanently assigned to organizations, and any organizations (government, universities, or corporations) could purchase an address block (typically, a class network). During the 1990's, IANA and IAB realized that IP addresses were being consumed faster than expected and in light of the shortage of IP addresses, this practice has slowed to almost a stop. Currently, if you need public IP addresses, your Internet service provider (ISP) usually lease you an appropriately sized block while you get your Internet services from that ISP. The day of companies purchasing IP addresses are in the past.

This section looks at the address classes in descending size order, from Class A to Class E.

Class A

Class A addresses are IP addresses that are assigned to network devices, such as computers, and include all addresses in which the first bit of the first octet is set to 0 (zero). This includes all values from 00000001 to 01111111, or 1 to 127. For Class A networks, the first octet represents a network ID that is defined in the address by a subnet mask, but I cover that in the section "Breaking Up Networks with Subnetting" later in this chapter.

The network ID is not allowed to have all its bits set to 0 or all bits set to 1. You will also find out shortly (in the "Examining special IP addresses" section) why the 127 network ID is excluded from this address class.

Thus, 126 possible Class A networks are available to organizations around the world. With only 126 Class A networks, owning one puts you in an exclusive club. (As I mention earlier, you can no longer acquire a network block of addresses, and when possible, IANA gets them back from the registered owners. Getting addresses back allows IANA to redistribute addresses in a more efficient and temporary manner.)

Class B

Class B addresses are IP addresses that are assigned to network devices, such as computers, and include all addresses in which the first two bits of the first octet are 10. This includes all values from 10000000 to 10111111, or 128 to 191. The definition of the Class B network is represented with a subnet mask (which I discuss in the section "Breaking Up Networks with Subnetting" later in this chapter), but the Class B network ID is made up of the values in the first two octets. Unlike Class A networks, all network IDs in this range are available for use.

Class C

Class C addresses are IP addresses that are assigned to network devices, such as computers, and include all addresses in which the first three bits of the first octet are set to 110. This includes all values from 11000000 to 11011111, or 192 to 223. The default subnet mask for Class C networks defines the first three octets as the network ID for these networks. Like with Class B networks, all the network IDs are available for use on networks. This is the last of the network classes that will be used for network devices on a TCP/IP network.

Class D

Class D network addresses are not assigned to devices on a network. These addresses are used for special-purpose, multicast applications (such as video- and audio-streaming applications). I discuss multicast addresses in Book IV, Chapter 9 when I discuss multicast routing; many processes are used on network devices that communicate with other devices via multicast addresses.

These addresses all need to be registered with IANA to be used globally. Addresses in this class have the first bits of the first octet set to 1110, yielding addresses in the first octet ranging from 11100000 to 11101111, or 224 to 239. These addresses are not defined by a normal subnet mask; instead, each address is used for a specific purpose. And because each address is individually used, it uses a 255.255.255.255 mask, which I discuss later in this chapter in the section "Breaking Up Networks with Subnetting."

Class E

If Class D is special, Class E addresses are even more special. There is no defined use for this address class. Officially, it is listed as reserved for usage and testing by IANA and the Internet Research Task Force (IRTF). In fact, as of RFC3330 in 2002, Class E was updated to "reserved for future use."

Network destination addresses

In Book I, Chapter 2, you look briefly at the data link layer address classifications of unicast, multicast, and broadcast. These three classifications of addresses also apply to the network layer, and specifically to the IP protocol. At the network level, here is how these three address classes work:

✔ **Unicast:** Unique IP address from the Class A, B, or C address ranges. A unicast IP address is always associated with a MAC address for the network interface on which it operates. So if your network device has a network interface for which you have configured an IP address, the IP address uniquely identifies your computer at the network layer. At the same time, at the data link layer, the MAC address associated with the configured network interface uniquely identifies the network device at the data link layer. So there is a one-to-one relationship between unicast addresses at the data link and network layers, and data being sent to a unicast address is processed only by one device on the network.

✔ **Multicast:** Of the three IP address categories, this is the one that is tough to understand. A *multicast* address, which is a Class D address, is associated with a group of network devices. When you send data to the multicast address, it is received by all the devices that are a member of the multicast group. Unlike the unicast address, multiple network devices can be configured to receive data sent to this address. This is useful when sending the same data to multiple devices, such as streaming music or installing a disk image on 50 computers. Instead of sending 50 copies of the data to 50 unicast addresses, multicast allows you to send one copy of the data, and all 50 computers receive it. Unlike broadcast, covered in just a bit, this

data is processed only by the devices that are in the group, and not all devices on the network.

At the data link layer, IANA has registered an Organizationally Unique Identifier (OUI) like how a network card manufacturer would register (read Book I, Chapter 4 to find out more about manufacturer IDs). In this case, instead of using this MAC address block to be assigned to network cards, IANA uses this MAC address range (01:00:5e:00:00:00 to 01:00:5e:7f:ff:ff) to associate IP multicast addresses at the network layer to MAC addresses at the data link layer. This MAC address range is a little smaller than the IP address range, so there is small potential overlap, but this does not present an issue for the multicast traffic.

The registration of the IANA MAC range allows an IP multicast address to map to a MAC address at the data link layer, but it does require that your network switch supports the IANA multicast range; if it does not, the switch treats IP multicast traffic as broadcast traffic (see the next point) at the data link layer.

✔ **Broadcast:** Special group IP addresses technically include all IP network devices in the world but actually map directly to the MAC broadcast address on your current data link. If you look at the broadcast IP address in binary, all the bits are set to 1, which is 255.255.255.255 in the standard dotted decimal notation. The broadcast MAC address that this IP broadcast maps to also has all its binary bits set to 1, so the address is FF:FF:FF:FF:FF:FF.

Any network frames that are sent to the broadcast address are read or processed by every device on that network segment.

Class E comprises absolutely all valid addresses with 240 or higher in the first octet. The first bits of the first octet is 1111, which yields addresses from 11110000 to 11111110 — or technically, 11111111 — which, in decimals, are 240 to 254 — or 255. Because this address class is not being used for address allocation, you cannot know what the *network ID*, which defines the valid addresses in a range, is. So the inclusion of 255 at the end of the range is moot because this address range is not available for you to use. All you need to know is that by definition Class E includes all valid addresses higher than Class D.

Public, private, and automatic IP addresses

Space is running out for people to assign addresses to their devices. Companies or organizations acquire addresses to assign to their network devices, such as smartphones, PCs, servers, routers, and tablets, just to name a few. As these devices proliferate, the number of available addresses can drop dramatically.

As a solution to that issue, in 1996, IANA and IETF came up with *private addressing*, which allows organizations to use a large address space internally on their network while using only a few public addresses, rather than using only public addresses. For this to happen, IANA requires that some public addresses be removed from the global pool. These addresses were either pulled back or voluntarily surrendered by address holders. (This address space change was documented in RFC1918.) The addresses available for usage include 1 Class A network, 16 Class B networks, and 255 Class C networks, which I summarize in Table 1-1. These addresses are now widely used by all organizations on the Internet. These addresses and others can be found in RFC5735, *Special Use IPv4 Addresses*.

Table 1-1	Private IP Address Ranges
Address Class	*Address Range*
Class A	10.0.0.0–10.255.255.255
Class B	172.16.0.0–172.31.255.255
Class C	192.168.0.0–192.168.255.255

Private addresses are not allowed to be routed out to the Internet, so devices using private addresses cannot communicate directly with devices on the Internet. To make private IP addressing functional and resolve this issue, at least one public address is required, which will be used with Network Address Translation (NAT) or Port Address Translation (PAT).

(I cover NAT and PAT in Book VI, Chapter 3.) So a company using private addresses internally still requires at least one address to connect their private network with the Internet.

In addition to the private addresses, Microsoft took a leading role in defining RFC3927 *Dynamic Configuration of IPv4 Link-Local Addresses*. This defines the process that computers should take in situations where there are no other methods of applying dynamic IP address assignments. This process was created to deal with situations where you do not want to — or cannot — manually assign static IP addresses and there is no Dynamic Host Configuration Protocol (DHCP) server on your network to automatically assign addresses.

The solution was to use another IP address range — in this case, a Class B network of 169.254.0.0 — to let IP hosts choose their own address. In this range, there are approximately 65,000 addresses from which the IP host can choose, so the basic process for the host is as follows:

1. Randomly choose an address from the range 169.254.0.1–169.254.255.254.

2. Send an Address Resolution Protocol (ARP) request for the MAC address that has the chosen address to eliminate the chance of duplicate IP address conflicts.

   If no response is received to the ARP request, no other computer is using that IP address so the host can start using the IP address chosen in Step 1.

The preceding steps outline the Automatic Private IP Addressing (APIPA) process. When two or more computers on the same data link support the use of, and are configured to use, APIPA, these hosts can communicate with each other. This process was created to simplify *ad hoc* (or temporary) networks in which TCP/IP is the primary networking protocol because APIPA eliminates the need to manually assign addresses to hosts.

Examining special IP addresses

When networking with TCP/IP, you can work with some special IP addresses. When working with each network segment, here are two special addresses that you deal with:

✦ The IP address of the network ID

✦ The IP address of the network broadcast address

Although both the network ID and network broadcast address look like IP addresses, because of their special purposes, they are not valid addresses that can be assigned to IP hosts to devices on your network. To identify these two special addresses, start by taking an IP address and writing it in binary rather than dotted decimal notation. So for the address 192.0.2.242, binary looks like this:

```
11000000.00000000.00000001.11110010
```

If you refer to the "Class C" section earlier in this chapter, addresses starting with 192 in the first octet are Class C and the first three octets are used for the network ID. If you leave the bits in the network ID portion of the address alone but set the remaining bits (the host portion of the address) to all binary 0s, you are looking at the network ID of the network. Here is what this looks like in binary.

```
11000000.00000000.00000001.00000000
```

In dotted decimal notation, that address looks like 192.0.2.0, which is the network ID for the network that contains 192.0.2.242.

When the host portion of the address is set to all binary 1s, it looks like this:

```
11000000.00000000.00000001.11111111
```

In dotted decimal notation, this address looks like 192.0.2.255; that is the network broadcast address, or the broadcast address for the 192.0.2.0 network. The broadcast address here is slightly different from the broadcast address I define earlier in the sidebar "Network destination addresses;" rather than going to all IP hosts on the current network segment, it is processed only by those whose IP network ID is 192.0.2.0, which is a small difference because I will typically have only one network ID in use on a network segment.

In addition to these two special addresses per network segment, three other addresses are of interest:

✦ **127.0.0.1:** In electronics, a *loopback* is used to take data that you send from a device and pass it back to the receiving side of the device. A loopback tests that both the sending and receiving sides of the device are functioning. The *loopback address* in TCP/IP serves the same function; it verifies that IP on the local host can communicate with IP on the local host. This ensures that your TCP/IP protocol is properly installed and working on your network device. In most operating systems, this address is configured on a virtual network interface — *the loopback adapter* (think loopback network card). In actuality, the loopback address space is the entire Class A network of 127.0.0.0, so you can technically use any of the addresses in this range for loopback testing.

✦ **255.255.255.255:** This is the general broadcast or all-networks broad-cast address, which I discuss earlier in the sidebar "Network destina-tion addresses". Unlike the network broadcast address in which the host portion of an IP address is set to binary 1s and the network por-tion of the address remains the same, this address sets the network portion to binary 1s as well. Having both the host and network ID por-tions of the address set to binary 1s means that the destination of the 255.255.255.255 address is all hosts on all networks. By definition, all hosts on all networks means all networks in the world, but a router will not forward a broadcast from one network to another network; so in actuality this really means all hosts using any network ID on this network segment. Although it is normal to have only one network ID in operation on each network segment of your network, the use of the general broadcast address (instead of the network broadcast address), ensures that devices using other network IDs on the network segment will receive the data being set to the broadcast address.

✦ **0.0.0.0:** This is the opposite of a general broadcast, which goes out to all devices or "them;" this address represents "me" or "this." This concept is very abstract, in that this address is not an address you can test con-nectivity to. The time when you will typically see this address is when set-ting up a default route, which matches all the me's that exist in the world, using the address of 0.0.0.0 and the mask of 0.0.0.0. Just remember that 0.0.0.0 is a special address and move on with your life, and this book.

Breaking Up Networks with Subnetting

Subnet is short for subnetwork, or a portion of the complete network. In theory, all IP addresses belong to one large network that has been initially broken up into the class-based segments (flip back to the section "Knowing Your Network Classes") with the size of the networks in each class identi-fied by a default subnet mask. The *subnet mask* defines what portion of the IP address is used as a network ID and which portion is used as a host ID. By adjusting the default subnet mask, you can take the class-based network and break it into smaller network pieces (or subnetworks) for use across your network devices.

The main reason you want to perform this breakup of your network addresses occurs when you have a router on your network. Your router requires a *network ID* (or a distinct range of addresses) to be associated with each network interface on the router. If you have only one block of IP addresses in the form of a network ID and subnet mask, you need to split the block into at least two pieces for use with your router. *Subnetting* then is the action of splitting your network's IP address block into pieces.

One concept that may help you here is the concept of ANDing, which I cover in Chapter 3 of this minibook. *ANDing* is a mathematical or logical process used to work with binary numbers to determine the scope of a network, indentifying what computers are on a network verses those that are on another network. If you end up being a little confused here, you can skip ahead and come back here.

Subnetting 101

If you have worked with IP for very long, you know that the three big things that you configure for a TCP/IP host are

+ **IP address:** The specific unique IP address used to identify the host on the network

+ **Subnet mask:** Used to define how many hosts can exist on a network

+ **Default gateway:** The IP address assigned to your router, which is the device you use to send data to hosts on other networks

Here is the output of `ipconfig.exe` on a Microsoft Windows computer showing this information:

```
C:\>ipconfig

Windows IP Configuration

Ethernet adapter Local Area Connection:

        Connection-specific DNS Suffix  . : edtetz.net
        IP Address. . . . . . . . . . . : 10.0.1.12
        Subnet Mask . . . . . . . . . . : 255.255.255.0
        Default Gateway . . . . . . . . : 10.0.1.254
```

If you have been working with IP on computers for a while, you might want to say that a Domain Name Server (DNS) is pretty critical, but that relates to resolving names like `www.edtetz.net` to an IP address, not allowing two IP addresses on different networks to communicate.

One of the three important pieces of information is the subnet mask. Each classed network has a default subnet mask. Table 1-2 summarizes some of this information based upon these two rules:

+ All bits in the network portion of the address are not allowed to be set to 0s or 1s.

+ All bits in the host portion of the address are not allowed to be set to 0s or 1s.

Table 1-2		Default Subnet Masks and Hosts		
Address Class	*First Octet Range*	*Default Mask*	*Number of Networks*	*Number of Hosts*
Class A	1–126	255.0.0.0	126	16,777,214
Class B	129–191	255.255.0.0	16,065	65,534
Class C	192–223	255.255.255.0	2,097,152	254

Mulling the number of hosts

Here is where the fourth column of Table 1-2 came from. When looking at the subnet mask, there are two binary numbers at work: 1s and 0s. Here is the Class A mask written in binary:

```
11111111.00000000.00000000.00000000
```

In this mask, the 1s represent the part of the mask that identifies the network ID, and the 0s represent the part of the address used as a host ID. So, given an address like 10.75.24.14, the network ID is 10, and the host ID is 75.24.14, uniquely identifying the host on the specific network. Because only the first octet is used as part of the network ID, the only possible network IDs are 1 to 126.

When dealing with Class B networks, where the default subnet mask is 255.255.0.0 and with all the bits in the first two octets being 1s, the network ID is made up of the first two octets with the host ID being in the last two octets. Going one step further, the Class C networks have a default subnet mask of 255.255.255.0 in which the network ID is made up of the first three octets, and the host ID is made up of the last octet.

Earlier in this chapter, I have listed private addresses that I can use internally on my network, such as a single Class A (10.0.0.0), 16 Class B networks (starting at 172.16.0.0), or 256 Class C networks (all 192.168.0.0 networks); Table 1-2 shows the number of hosts that can exist on any network segment. Although 254 hosts represent a reasonable number of devices on a network segment, such as on the Class C network segments, because of network traffic and congestion caused by devices, it is unreasonable to think that you will ever have a network segment that contains 65,534 hosts or 16,777,214 hosts on the Class B or Class A segments. Because you will not have that many hosts on any segment, you can break those large network address block into more — smaller — network address blocks that you will use to assign addresses to a number of smaller network segments.

When you get into the minibook on routing (Book IV), you see that some routing protocols require that the same subnet mask be used on every segment on your network. This next section focuses on that; whereas in the upcoming section "Explaining Classless InterDomain Routing (CIDR)," you read about varying the size of your subnets.

Modifying the subnet mask

To break your network into smaller segments, simply modify the subnet mask. It is really as easy as that. You can *subnet* any of the network classes, even the smaller Class C networks.

So how is this done? Simply, when looking at the subnet mask in binary, take host bits (the 0s) and turn them into subnet bits (the 1s).This action reduces the number of hosts you can put on a network segment, but allows you to have more than one network segment.

By converting bits in the subnet mask, you have created a new section — the *subnet section* — which is between the network section of the mask and the host section of the mask. The three types of bits in the new subnet mask are network bits, subnet bits, and host bits. This also expands the subnet mask rules that were introduced in the "Subnetting 101" section. The expanded rules are

✦ All bits in the network portion of the address are not allowed to be set to zero or ones.

✦ All bits in the host portion of the address are not allowed to be set to zero or ones.

✦ All bits in the subnet portion of the address are not allowed to be set to all zero or ones. See the upcoming section, "Class C subnetting" for more about the current status of this last rule.

You can see the similarity to the previous rules for addresses, with the addition of the rule around the subnet portion of the address. If I take only one bit from the host and convert it to a subnet bit, it has only two possible combinations — 1 or 0, which is all 1s or all 0s — which is not allowed based on the preceding third rule — so I need to take at least two bits when starting to subnet. I begin by showing you how this would look with the Class A network of 10.0.0.0.

When you start, the default subnet mask for a Class A network looks like this:

```
11111111.00000000.00000000.00000000
```

Going forward, take a minimum of two bits from the host range and use them as the subnet. These two bits give you the possible networks, as defined in Table 1-3.

Table 1-3	Network Ranges for a Two-Bit Subnet Mask		
Subnet ID	*Subnet Mask*	*New Network ID*	*Allowed*
00	255.192.0.0	10.0.0.0	No
01	255.192.0.0	10.64.0.0	Yes
10	255.192.0.0	10.128.0.0	Yes
11	255.192.0.0	10.192.0.0	No

**Book II
Chapter 1**

**Making the Most
of IPv4**

Two subnets — ID 00 and 11 — are not allowed because the subnet ID is all 1s or all 0s. By subnetting this network, you have two network blocks of addresses that you can assign to your network segments. If two network address blocks were not enough to assign unique blocks to each of your network segments — because you have five network segments — you could take another bit from the host range and use that for the subnet range, which I show in Table 1-4.

Table 1-4	Network Ranges for a Three-Bit Subnet Mask		
Subnet ID	*Subnet Mask*	*New Network ID*	*Allowed*
000	255.224.0.0	10.0.0.0	No
001	255.224.0.0	10.32.0.0	Yes
010	255.224.0.0	10.64.0.0	Yes
011	255.224.0.0	10.96.0.0	Yes
100	255.224.0.0	10.128.0.0	Yes
101	255.224.0.0	10.160.0.0	Yes
110	255.224.0.0	10.192.0.0	Yes
111	255.224.0.0	10.224.0.0	No

You might ask how far you can go with this. Keep reading.

Class A subnetting

On a Class A network, you can indeed go quite far because you can continue down to the two bits of the host address space. I have shown the 32-bit address space here, using N for the network ID, S for the subnet ID, and H for the host ID. The two choices here show the lowest number of bits to the largest number of subnet bits:

NNNNNNNN.SSHHHHHH.HHHHHHHH.HHHHHHHH

and

NNNNNNNN.SSSSSSSS.SSSSSSSS.SSSSSSHH

The first example shows 2 subnet bits and 22 host bits, so this would work out to 2^2-2 (or 2) subnets and $2^{22}-2$ hosts per subnet (or 4,194,302), which represents the fewest number of subnets. You could then increase the number of subnets and reduce the number of hosts all the way down to the second example, which has 22 bits for the subnets and only 2 bits for the hosts, giving you 4,194,302 networks of two hosts. This is almost absurd because one of those two hosts would be a router unless you were using these subnets to address the link between two routers.

Class B subnetting

You are not limited to subnetting Class A networks; if you were to look at a Class B network, you would get a range running from these two extremes on the 172.16.0.0 network:

NNNNNNNN.NNNNNNNN.SSHHHHHH.HHHHHHHH

and

NNNNNNNN.NNNNNNNN.SSSSSSSS.SSSSSSHH

In this case, you would still start with two possible subnets, using 2^2-2 (or 2) subnets, but your host bits would be $2^{14}-2$ hosts (or 16,382). Then you would go all the way to 14 bits for the subnet and 2 bits for the host, giving you 16,382 networks of two hosts each. Because you started with a much smaller number of bits, your total number of networks will be far less.

Class C subnetting

Finally, looking at a Class C network, your numbers would look like the following:

NNNNNNNN.NNNNNNNN.NNNNNNNN.SSHHHHHH

and

NNNNNNNN.NNNNNNNN.NNNNNNNN.SSSSSSHH

This scenario would provide you with anything from 2^2–2 (or 2) networks of 2^6 or 62 hosts, down to a low number of 62 networks of 2 hosts.

To quickly summarize, which I do with a Class C network to minimize complexity, you can break down a classed network into smaller pieces, which allows you to use these address blocks to assign addresses to each of your physical network segments. This process of breaking down the network into smaller pieces takes host bits — working from left to right — and using them as subnet bits. Table 1-5 shows you all the possible addresses when subnetting the Class C network of 192.168.1.0.

Similar tables are freely available on the Internet for any network class you choose to subnet, or subnet calculators can give you the figures on the fly. A downloadable calculator is available from www.boson.com/free utilities.html, and an online calculator is available at www.subnet-calculator.com.

As I mention earlier in the chapter, although you used to not be allowed to use the all 0s subnet or the all 1s subnet, this is no longer the case. Older routing protocols (such as RIP version 1) had an issue distinguishing a subnet ID of 192.168.1.0/24 from 192.168.1.0/28. Since the advent of Cisco IOS 12.0, *subnet zero* (and the all ones subnet) has been allowed for usable subnets; and prior to that, you could add the directive in Global Configuration mode of ip subnet-zero to enable you to use all of the 1s and all 0s subnet.

Table 1-5	IP Subnet Table for Class C Networks		
Bits Used for Subnet	*Subnet Mask*	*Number of Subnetworks*	*Computers per Subnet*
1	255.255.255.128	2	126
2	255.255.255.192	4	62
3	255.255.255..224	8	30
4	255.255.255.240	16	14
5	255.255.255.248	32	6
6	255.255.255.252	64	2

By selecting one of these subnets levels, I show you the exact addresses available on each of the network segments. This data is shown in Table 1-6 for the 192.168.1.0 network, using 3 bits in the subnet mask or a mask of 255.255.255.224. Based on the previous table, this gives you eight networks of 30 devices if you allow for the all 0s and all 1s subnets. Although I calculated this by hand, you can easily find tables similar to this on the Internet.

Table 1-6	Available Subnets for 192.168.1.0 Using Mask 255.255.255.224		
Network ID	*First Host Address*	*Last Host Address*	*Broadcast Address*
192.168.1.0	192.168.1.1	192.168.1.30	192.168.1.31
192.168.1.32	192.168.1.33	192.168.1.62	192.168.1.63
192.168.1.64	192.168.1.65	192.168.1.94	192.168.1.95
192.168.1.96	192.168.1.97	192.168.1.126	192.168.1.127
192.168.1.128	192.168.1.129	192.168.1.158	192.168.1.159
192.168.1.160	192.168.1.161	192.168.1.190	192.168.1.191
192.168.1.192	192.168.1.193	192.168.1.222	192.168.1.223
192.168.1.224	192.168.1.225	192.168.1.254	192.168.1.255

You can see from this table that for each subnetwork, there is a network ID address and a broadcast address. You read in the earlier section "Examining special IP addresses" that these two addresses are not allowed to be used for host addresses because they each have a special purpose; the network ID identifies the network, and the broadcast address sends IP packets to all hosts on the network.

Because current networking says that all your subnets are available, rather than excluding the all-0s and all-1s subnets, that leads into the next topic.

Explaining Classless InterDomain Routing (CIDR)

The inclusion of subnet zero changes the management of your subnet divisions by including two additional subnets, regardless of how many bits you choose to use. This also allows splitting of a network ID into as little as two pieces.

The next big change that happened with subnet management is the removal of network classes. In 1995, a system was proposed to eliminate class-based allocation of IP addresses; this process was updated as a best practice in 2006. With the elimination of classes, which is a paradigm shift for most people, you really start working with addresses as simply blocks of addresses. This means that IP address space, which is used to assign addresses to hosts (Class A, B, and C), is treated as one block of addresses, from 1.0.0.0 to 223.255.255.255, which can be broken along any boundaries defined by a valid subnet mask. Assignment of addresses to organizations is still managed by IANA, with existing assignments remaining in place; but they now have more flexibility in how new addresses are assigned because assignments do not need to follow previous class-based boundaries.

In the minibook on routing (Book IV), you can see that you are limited in your choice of routing protocols if you want to use classless routing. In this section, I focus on a few key elements of CIDR, including

+ CIDR notation

+ Variable Length Subnet Masks (VLSM)

+ Route summarization

+ Supernetting

The key to CIDR is that rather than using network classes, defining how big each network segment should be, you ignore the class boundaries and treat the entire address space from 1.0.0.0–223.255.255.255 as one continuous address space that can have blocks of addresses separated by specifying a correct starting address and a subnet mask.

This still allows you to follow boundaries that existed prior to going class-less, but then gives you flexibility to expand ranges beyond ordinary class boundaries, or work with sections of the network smaller than the ordinary class boundaries. When working with segments smaller than class bound-aries, you do not need to worry about eliminating the first and last ranges when subnetting because you did not start with a class-based network. Thus, there is not really a first and last block of addresses in that numeric range but rather just a block of numbers, defined by a starting address and a subnet mask.

CIDR notation

When you are writing a long list of subnets or network addresses, you can easily get a cramp in your hand writing all the subnet masks, for example, if you have to write this list of network IDs:

```
network ID: 192.168.0.0,   Subnet Mask: 255.255.255.0
network ID: 192.168.3.0,   Subnet Mask: 255.255.255.0
network ID: 192.168.6.0,   Subnet Mask: 255.255.255.0
network ID: 192.168.45.0,  Subnet Mask: 255.255.255.0
network ID: 192.168.93.0,  Subnet Mask: 255.255.255.0
network ID: 192.168.115.0, Subnet Mask: 255.255.255.0
```

CIDR notation makes this a little easier for you by allowing you to specify a subnet mask as a number of bits that exist in the subnet mask. The CIDR list of network IDs would look like this:

```
network ID: 192.168.0.0/24
network ID: 192.168.3.0/24
network ID: 192.168.6.0/24
network ID: 192.168.45.0/24
network ID: 192.168.93.0/24
```

Table 1-7 lists all possible masks you will encounter during your use of IP and the CIDR notation for them.

Table 1-7		CIDR to Subnet Mask Conversions	
Subnet Mask	*CIDR Notation*	*Subnet Mask*	*CIDR Notation*
0.0.0.0	/0	255.255.128.0	/17
128.0.0.0	/1	255.255.192.0	/18
192.0.0.0	/2	255.255.224.0	/19
224.0.0.0	/3	255.255.240.0	/20
240.0.0.0	/4	255.255.248.0	/21
248.0.0.0	/5	255.255.252.0	/22
252.0.0.0	/6	255.255.254.0	/23
254.0.0.0	/7	255.255.255.0	/24
255.0.0.0	/8	255.255.255.128	/25
255.128.0.0	/9	255.255.255.192	/26
255.192.0.0	/10	255.255.255.224	/27
255.224.0.0	/11	255.255.255.240	/28
255.240.0.0	/12	255.255.255.248	/29
255.248.0.0	/13	255.255.255.252	/30
255.252.0.0	/14	255.255.255.254	/31
255.254.0.0	/15	255.255.255.255	/32
255.255.0.0	/16		

This means that if I want to relay information to you about a Class A network, I can refer to my network as 10.0.0.0/8 rather than 10.0.0.0 255.0.0.0, a Class B network as 172.16.0.0/16, or a Class C network as 192.168.1.0/24. This reference of the bits used in the subnet mask, rather than writing the entire mask, makes life much easier.

Variable Length Subnet Masks (VLSM)

When first working with subnetting, and in order to support certain routing protocols, all network segments on the network must use the same subnet mask. Some early routing protocols made decisions on what they expected remote subnet masks to be based on what their subnet mask was, thereby requiring that all subnets of that network use the same mask. With the inclusion of subnet masks in all routing tables, you allow the routing protocol to support Variable Length Subnet Masks (VLSM) with which, simply put, you do not need to use the same subnet mask on all your network segments and can vary the mask from segment to segment. This concept is covered in RFC1878 *Variable Length Subnet Table for IPv4,* which effectively says devices should be smart enough to define each subnet individually.

So how does this work? Say that I take an address block, such as 192.168.1.0/24. From this block, I need to provision a network, as shown in Figure 1-3, and determine that I need eight segments used as interconnects between networks on serial links and also I need to support a main office of 60 computers, two regional offices of 25 computers, and 6 other offices with computers each.

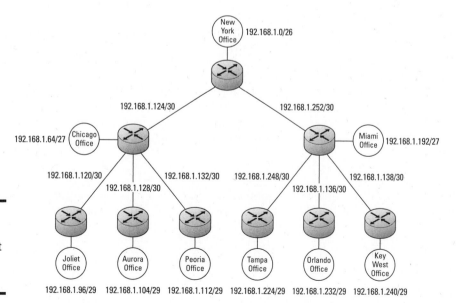

Figure 1-3: VLSM deployment of network addresses.

Book II
Chapter 1

Making the Most of IPv4

If you review the address blocks that are assigned in this figure, you see that a few gaps are still available. One block of addresses, from 192.168.1.144 to 191.168.1.191, is available. The size of the blocks that can be carved from this range are dependent upon the pieces that have been removed already. The largest single block that can be used out of this range is 192.168.1.160–192.168.1.191 (or 192.168.1.160/27), followed by 192.168.1.144–192.168.1.159 (or 192.168.144/28), and either of these can be deployed as smaller segments.

By switching from fixed-length subnet masks to VSMLs, you can use far more addresses that you can with fixed-length subnet masks. To use a subnet mask on a traditional network, you would have had to subnet 17 blocks of 62 addresses (the largest single segment), which would have used the equivalent of five Class C address blocks, resulting in 192.168.1.0/24, 192.168.2.0/24, 192.168.3.0/24, 192.168.4.0/24 and 192.168.5.0/24, with three of four blocks in the last network block still available. This represents a large waste of addresses in the overall IP address space. So, as you can see, VLSM yields a large savings in the utilization of IP address space.

Supernetting

The concept of *supernetting* lends itself nicely to CIDR because it also allows you to ignore class boundaries. When you started your office network, you may have chosen to use the private Class C address space to assign host addresses for your network devices. At the beginning of this running example, your central office had fewer than 60 devices, so you allocated a network of 192.168.0.0/26 to that segment. Over time, the number of devices on the network increased. If you did not yet allocate the address space of 192.168.0.64/26 to any other network segment, you can join 192.168.0.0/26 and 192.168.0.64/26 into a single larger network segment by reassigning the subnet masks to all your hosts, giving you a network of 129.168.0.0/25. This is, however, still in the realm of subnetting because you are dealing with networks smaller than the default class-based network blocks.

Playing out this scenario further, the number of devices increases over time, and you need to repeat the process. If the address blocks of 192.168.0.128/26 and 192.168.0.192/26 or 192.168.0.128/25 are still available, you can merge the address spaces again, but reassign the subnet masks of your network devices to 192.168.0.0/24, which is the default class-based mask for a Class C network.

Things are now stable on your network until the number of devices on the central office network approached the 254 limit of the network segment. When that occurs, you have a choice.

Say that you decided to use the Class C private address space for your network segments, but now your devices have increased to a level that goes beyond the size of a Class C segment. You could break down and use a Class B address block, which is easy enough if you are using private addresses; however, if this network used public addresses, this would not happen because you would never convince IANA or your Internet service provider (ISP) to let you have a Class B address block — even if you were going to try to get a second Class C address block address, you would not have a chance.

So back to the private address space. If you have not allocated the private Class C address block of 192.168.1.0 to any other devices on your network, you can continue the process of joining address blocks by changing the mask from 24 bits to 23 bits. Thus, the network block assignment of 192.168.0.0/23 would include all addresses from 192.168.0.1–192.168.1.254, essentially joining those two Class C blocks into a single address block. This is *supernetting*.

Notice that when you think in classless terms, supernetting is not a big stretch in thought; after all, you just modify the mask to include a larger address block. For people stuck in the class-based world, this is a huge logical jump.

You are limited by the binary network IDs as to which network segments can be joined. For example, 192.168.1.0/24 can be merged with 192.168.0.0/24, but not 192.168.2.0/24. If you convert everything to binary, network address, and masks, you easily see which two network blocks yield the same network ID when supernetting. Look at the three example network IDs along with the 23-bit subnet mask (255.255.254.0), and you see which network IDs have the first 23 bits that match. Because 192.168.0.0 and 192.168.1.0 match for the first 23 bits, they can be combined into the 192.168.0.0/23 network:

```
11000000.10101000.0000000.00000000 (192.168.0.0)
11000000.10101000.0000001.00000000 (192.168.1.0)
11000000.10101000.0000010.00000000 (192.168.2.0)
```

11111111.11111111.1111110.00000000 (255.255.254.0) route summarization

Continuing from supernetting, route summarization should be very easy to follow. *Route summarization* can take place on routers to reduce the size of their routing tables. A *routing table* is a list of routing entries, each of which includes a network ID of a network segment and the address of the next closest router to that network segment. You see how the routing tables work in Book IV, but now is a good time to introduce you to the technical side of route summarization.

A basic router table entry has three basic elements:

+ A network ID
+ A subnet mask
+ The address of the next router to get you to that network

Referring to Figure 1-3, you can assign the lowest address in router-to-router connection at the central office connections to the central office router. This means that the regional office routers (in Chicago and Miami) will be addressed as 192.168.1.134 and 192.168.1.138. And that means that the routing table on the New York office router would look something like this:

```
network ID          Mask                 Gateway
192.168.1.0         255.255.255.192      192.168.1.1
192.168.1.64        255.255.255.224      192.168.1.134
192.168.1.96        255.255.255.248      192.168.1.134
192.168.1.104       255.255.255.248      192.168.1.134
192.168.1.112       255.255.255.248      192.168.1.134
192.168.1.120       255.255.255.252      192.168.1.134
192.168.1.124       255.255.255.252      192.168.1.134
192.168.1.128       255.255.255.252      192.168.1.134
192.168.1.132       255.255.255.252      192.168.1.133
192.168.1.136       255.255.255.252      192.168.1.137
192.168.1.140       255.255.255.252      192.168.1.138
192.168.1.192       255.255.255.224      192.168.1.138
192.168.1.224       255.255.255.248      192.168.1.138
192.168.1.232       255.255.255.248      192.168.1.138
192.168.1.240       255.255.255.248      192.168.1.138
192.168.1.248       255.255.255.252      192.168.1.138
192.168.1.252       255.255.255.252      192.168.1.138
```

Each character takes up memory on your router. So, as your network size increases, the amount of storage required for your routing table increases. Route summarization reduces the number of entries in the table, and follows the same basic process of supernetting.

If you were to take all the addresses in the previous listing and convert all the network IDs over to binary (as I did in the example at the end of the "Supernetting" section), and then compared all the addresses going to a single destination, you would find that bit patterns in the network IDs would allow you to combine entries by reducing the length of the subnet mask. To take a small section of the table as an example, I work with the entries that use the gateway of 192.168.1.134. Here are all the entries in binary:

```
11000000.10101000.0000001.00011000  (192.168.1.64)
11000000.10101000.0000001.01100000  (192.168.1.96)
11000000.10101000.0000001.01101000  (192.168.1.104)
11000000.10101000.0000001.01110000  (192.168.1.112)
11000000.10101000.0000001.01111000  (192.168.1.120)
11000000.10101000.0000001.01111100  (192.168.1.124)
11000000.10101000.0000001.10000000  (192.168.1.128)
```

Reviewing this list, you may have noticed that the first six addresses match the first 25-bits in their addresses. Referring back to Table 1-7, you find out that the 25-bit subnet mask is 255.255.255.192, so the first six entries can be combined into a single entry defined by the network ID of 192.168.1.64 and a mask of 255.255.255.192. If you continued this process of summarization for the entire previous routing table, you could summarize the entire table to the following:

```
network ID         Mask                  Gateway
192.168.1.0        255.255.255.192       192.168.1.1
192.168.1.64       255.255.255.192       192.168.1.134
192.168.1.128      255.255.255.252       192.168.1.134
192.168.1.132      255.255.255.252       192.168.1.133
192.168.1.136      255.255.255.252       192.168.1.137
192.168.1.140      55.255.255.252        192.168.1.138
192.168.1.192      255.255.255.192       192.168.1.138
```

By summarizing the routes, you can reduce the routing table size from 17 entries to 7 entries. If in this example, you had chosen to lay out the addresses slightly differently or used addresses from two Class C blocks, rather than limiting yourself to one, additional summarization would have been possible.

Chapter 2: Choosing between Protocols: TCP and UDP

In This Chapter

✓ Comparing TCP versus UDP for network communication

✓ Examining the header structures

✓ Figuring out when to use TCP and UDP

✓ Getting familiar with three-way handshaking

✓ Understanding how TCP sliding windows operate

As I mention in earlier chapters when discussing the Open System Interconnection (OSI) model and the Internet Protocol (IP) network model, Transmission Control Protocol (TCP) and User Datagram Protocol (UDP) are network protocols that operate at the transport or host-to-host layer, depending on the model you are using. They are responsible for the delivery control mechanisms in use with the TCP/IP suite of protocols.

In this chapter, I show you how TCP and UDP allow you to send data over a large IP-based network and the significance of choosing one transport layer protocol over another. In showing you how these two protocols operate, you see where they fit into the IP packet (which I also discuss in Chapter 1 of this minibook) and you find out about the structure of both TCP and UDP by examining the information found in their headers. When an IP host makes a connection to another IP host, they establish the connection through an access path, or *port,* so I discuss ports and how they relate to a socket in this chapter. I wrap up this chapter by looking at the mechanisms that TCP uses to guarantee delivery of data and why you would want to use UDP instead of TCP in certain cases.

Understanding the UDP and TCP Structure

TCP and UDP are host-to-host layer protocols in the IP network model. TCP and UDP manage the data that is sent to or from the application layer protocols and is delivered using an Internet layer protocol to another host on the network. Although they both have a role in managing the data flow between the application layer protocols on both the sending and receiving hosts, here are some differences between how TCP and UDP operate:

✦ **TCP** manages the process of transferring data from the application layer protocol on one host to the application layer protocols on another host. Not only does TCP facilitate the delivery of data to the application layer protocol, but it confirms delivery with the sending host, verifies that data was not changed during transmission, and ensures that data is received in order. This full service data management is referred to as guaranteed or reliable delivery.

✦ **UDP** also manages the process of transferring data from the application layer protocol on one host to the application layer protocols on another host, but this is where it deviates from TCP. UDP accepts data from the Internet layer protocol, verifies that it has not been modified in transmission, by way of a checksum (see Book I, Chapter 4), and delivers it to the application layer protocol. Although UDP verifies that the data that arrived matches what was sent, it does not notify the sending host that it arrived, nor does it verify that it arrived in order. The lack of the last two functions (notifications and order) makes UDP functions a best-effort transport protocol, or non-guaranteed or unreliable delivery.

Examining packet structure

TCP and UDP headers and data reside in the data section of the IP packet. In Book I, Chapter 4, I discuss the data link layer structure, or *frame.* When using IP at the network layer, the contents of the frame data field are called a *packet.* The packet is the network layer IP structure, which also has a data section, but in this case, the data section of the IP packet contains a structure dubbed a *segment,* which is either a TCP or UDP segment and is defined by a set of headers.

The official name for TCP and UDP data is a *segment.*

In this section, I show you what makes up the IP packet— or, more specifically, what makes up the header of an IP packet. Figure 2-1 shows an IP packet; the sections of the header are as follows.

Figure 2-1:
The
structure
of an IP
packet.

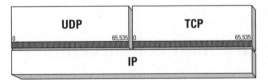

✦ **Version:** This number identifies the version of IP being used for this packet. Because this packet will be using IPv4, you will find a value of 4 in this field. IPv4 is the current standard, but the world is on their way to converting to IPv6. To find out about IPv6 and its header structure read through Chapter 4 of this minibook.

✦ **Internet Header Length (IHL):** This value denotes the overall size of the IP header for this packet, measured in bytes. Because the options (covered later in this bulleted list) listed in the header may vary, this value tells the packet receiver where to expect the data to start.

✦ **Differentiated Services Code Point (DSCP):** RFC2474 defines this field as Differentiated Services, or DiffServ, but it used to be known as the Type of Service (ToS) field. This field is used to identify the type of data found in the IP packet and may be used to classify the data for network Quality of Service (QoS). More and more systems these days want to have their traffic given priority, and this field allows for the classification of QoS data. Your network switches and routers then uses the QoS data to allocate data to higher or lower priority internal queues, processing data at a higher rate from the higher priority queues.

✦ **Explicit Congestion Notification (ECN):** If both ends of an IP connection support this option, they allow for network congestion to occur but adjust the flow of traffic without dropping any data packets. This technology is defined in RFC3168.

✦ **Total Length:** Total Length identifies the total size of the IP packet or datagram, including both the header and data found in the data structure. The smallest this can be is 20 bytes of IP header data, but it can grow up to 65,535 bytes. Every IP host is required to handle datagrams or packets of 576 bytes, but most will support larger blocks of data.

If the *datagram* — the data found in the data portion of the IP packet — is larger than the size of the network frame, the IP data in the network frame will be fragmented. Fragmenting data occurs at the IP layer, and the data is divided into multiple network frames and sent to the destination where it is reassembled. Fragmentation happens as the IP crosses from one interface on a router to another interface on the router, and will happen only if the maximum transmission unit (MTU) on the network segment the network frame is being transferred to is smaller than the MTU on the original network segment.

Even if the network frame size increases along the way, reassembly happens only at the final destination, which makes sense because there may end up being smaller segments along the way, causing it to be fragmented again.

✦ **Identification:** The Identification field is used to identify fragments that belong to an IP datagram.

✦ **Flags:** This three-bit field is used to manage or identify IP datagrams that were fragmented. The bits (in order) are

- *Reserved:* This flag is reserved for future use, so it will be 0 (zero).

- *Don't Fragment (DF):* If the DF flag is set and the packet needs to cross a network segment that has a smaller MTU, which would require the datagram from the packet to be fragmented, the IP packet will be discarded rather than fragmented. When the frame is discarded, the router throws out the packet and sends a delivery failure message to the sending host through Internet Control Message Protocol (ICMP).

- *More Fragments (MF):* If the datagram was fragmented, the MF flag would identify that there are still more portions of the original datagram to follow. If the MF flag is 0 and the fragment offset (see next bullet) is 0, the datagram was never fragmented, whereas the packet containing the last portion of a fragmented datagram will have MF set to 0 with a non-0 offset.

✦ **Fragment Offset:** The offset is used with fragmented datagrams and identifies where this portion of the datagram fits into the whole. This section of the header stores an *integer* (a number without decimal places) representing the number of 8-byte blocks. The portion of the datagram in the current packet is from the beginning of the data in the original, unfragmented datagram.

✦ **Time to Live (TTL):** TTL is an 8-bit field that can hold a value up to 255. This is the number of hops, or routers, that the packet can cross or traverse, before being discarded from the network. Rather than a straight hop count being used to decrement the counter, the router reduces the count by the number of seconds that it takes to handle and forward the packet to its destination, always rounding up to the next second. In most cases, this decrements the count by 1 per router. If the TTL is set to 0, the router handling the packet sends an `ICMP - Time Exceeded` message to the sender, informing it as to the packet's ill-fated destiny.

✦ **Protocol**: The host-to-host layer protocol that will receive the contents of the data portion of the packet. RFC1700 identifies the possible protocol values that can be used in an IP packet. The most common protocols are 1 (ICMP), 6 (TCP), and 17 (UDP).

✦ **Header Checksum:** This checksum (which I introduce in Book I, Chapter 4) consists only of header data. If the header data fails the checksum, the entire packet is discarded because it would be expected to contain errors as well. In addition, the data field of the IP packet (either UDP or TCP) would calculate checksums on the data contained in the IP frame. The IP packet is concerned only with errors in the header because the upper-level protocols would take care of errors in the data. In this case, all the bits in the header are broken into 16-bit words, and all the words are summed. This value is then stored in this field.

✦ **Source IP Address:** This holds the IPv4 address of the host that sent this IP packet.

✦ **Destination IP Address:** This holds the IPv4 address of the host to which the IP packet is being sent.

✦ **Options:** This field allows the inclusion of options in the IP packet, such as header copy settings, requiring the entire IP header to be copied to all packet fragments if the IP packet needs to be split or source route settings.

✦ **Data:** This is the payload of the frame — it is not included in the checksum calculation; the transport layer protocol or higher layer protocols take care of that function. The length of the data in the IP packet can be from 0 bytes up to the maximum amount of data that network frame can hold. For an Ethernet network frame, this is 1500 bytes minus the size of the IP header, which leaves 1308 bytes for data.

Not being put off by Offsets

As part of the management process of data transmission, both IP and TCP use control numbers, and one of these numbers is an offset. An *offset* is a way of telling IP or TCP on the receiving host how to manage the data it is receiving. In most cases, the offset is an identifier of where a block of data fits in relation to a control block. For example, this block of data is set away (or set off) from the control block of data by 100 bytes.

When working with IP, one of the places you see offsets is when an IP moves from a network with a larger maximum transmission unit (MTU) to a network with a smaller MTU. When this happens, the IP packet needs to be split into units small enough to be sent over the network with the smaller MTU, but it also needs to keep track of the IP packets so that they can be reassembled at the destination host. To split the packet into units, IP sets the fragmentation flag and records how far the current IP packet is from the start of the first fragment measured in 8 byte units. So an IP packet of

1000 bytes, moving to a network that allows only the Ethernet frames to be 400 bytes in size, ends up with three pieces for this IP packet. The first two IP packets have more fragments flag set and has fragment offsets of 0 and 50 (400 divided by 8), respectively, while the third packet does not have more fragments flag set because it is the last packet of the set and has a fragment offset of 100 (800/8).

When working with TCP, you see an offset when you work with the urgent (URG) flag. If a group of three TCP segments are marked as urgent, all three segments have the URG flag set, but in this case, the offset is the number of remaining TCP segments that are still considered urgent. That means the offset values for these three segments, in order, would be two, one, and zero.

So an offset value varies based on how the developer of an application or protocol has decided to use it, but it will also be a value to denote how far one item is from another; for instance, the offset from three to nine is six.

TCP and UDP header structures

Just as the data portion of the network frame contains a structure that is an IP packet, the data portion of the IP packet contains a structure that is a segment. The segment could be a TCP or UDP segment depending on which host-to-host service was used. Like the frames and packets, the segment has a header structure and data. The header is used by the TCP or UDP, whereas the data is forwarded to the application layer protocol associated with a port number (which I discuss in the section "Sockets and ports" later in this chapter). The following sections show you the structure and contents of TCP and UDP headers, respectively.

TCP headers

A copy of the RFC793 compatible TCP header is shown in Figure 2-2, and includes the following fields.

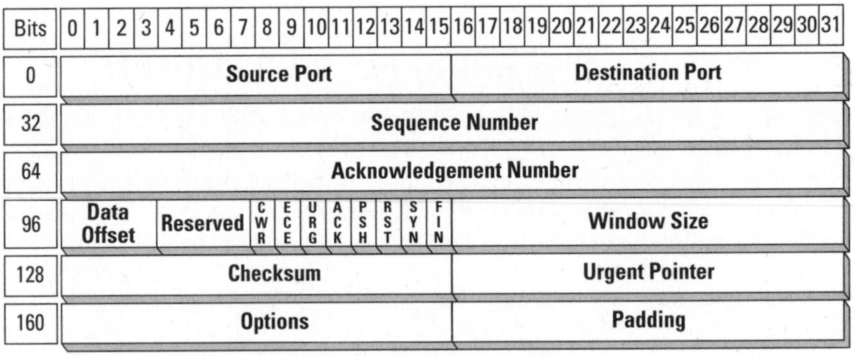

Figure 2-2: The structure of the TCP header.

Bits	0	1	2	3	4	5	6	7	8	9	10	11	12	13	14	15	16	17	18	19	20	21	22	23	24	25	26	27	28	29	30	31
0	Source Port																Destination Port															
32	Sequence Number																															
64	Acknowledgement Number																															
96	Data Offset				Reserved				C W R	E C E	U R G	A C K	P S H	R S T	S Y N	F I N	Window Size															
128	Checksum																Urgent Pointer															
160	Options																Padding															

REMEMBER

✦ **Source Port:** This is the TCP port used on the sending computer.

The connection between two hosts is made between two TCP ports: one for the source host, and one for the destination host.

✦ **Destination Port:** This is the TCP port being connected to the target host.

✦ **Sequence Number:** All TCP data is sent sequentially. The sequence number is used to ensure that all data is received and is in order.

✦ **Acknowledgement Number:** When data is received, an acknowledgement is sent back to the sender, letting the sender know that the last complete piece of data was received.

✦ **Data Offset:** For large pieces of data that needed to be fragmented, this shows where in the overall piece of data this particular piece fits.

✦ **Reserved:** This space has not been designated to hold any data, but is reserved for future use.

✦ **Flags:** Eight flags can be set on a TCP segment, which deal with session control with the remote host:

  • *CWR (Congestion Window Reduced):* Acknowledges a congestion notification received from a TCP segment with the ECE flag enabled.

  • *ECE (ECN Echo):* Explicit Congestion Notification (ECN), alerting the sending host that there is congestion on the network between the sending and receiving host.

  • *URG (Urgent):* Indicates that information in the Urgent Pointer field should be used.

  • *ACK (Acknowledge):* Acknowledges the receipt of a TCP segment with the SYN flag set. This is part of the three-handshake process covered in the "Three-way handshaking" section of this chapter.

  • *PSH (Push):* Requests that any data the receiving host has received be pushed to the receiving application.

  • *RST (Reset):* Notifies that host receiving this TCP segment that the connection has been reset (or unexpectedly terminated) and needs to be reestablished with another three-way handshake.

  • *SYN (Synchronize Sequence Numbers):* TCP guarantees data is received in order by number segments. This flag is used to synchronize the initial sequence number for both the sending and receiving host.

  • *FIN (Finished):* Indicates that the TCP communication session is complete and is going to be cleanly terminated, unlike the reset, which is an unexpected termination.

✦ **Window Size:** Window Size tells the sending device how much data the receiver is willing to receive in a single transmission burst. Read more later in this chapter.

✦ **Checksum:** Checksums are generated on the TCP data and stored in this field, guaranteeing that data has not been corrupted.

✦ **Urgent Pointer:** This field holds an integer indicating the offset, from the current sequence number to the end of the urgent data. In other words, this is the number of remaining segments that have urgent data.

✦ **Options:** Any additional options are specified by this field. They may be of varying length, which is specified by the value in the second byte of this field. The options specified here would control the flow of segment data, such as specifying the maximum size of the TCP segments.

✦ **Padding:** The specifications for TCP state that the total header size needs to end at a 32-bit boundary, so the padding field is used to round off the header to a proper size after the variable length options have been specified. Because this is a padding field, it is filled with zeros.

UDP header

In Figure 2-3, you can see that the header is compliant with RFC768 and contains only four fields, taking up a total of 64 bits:

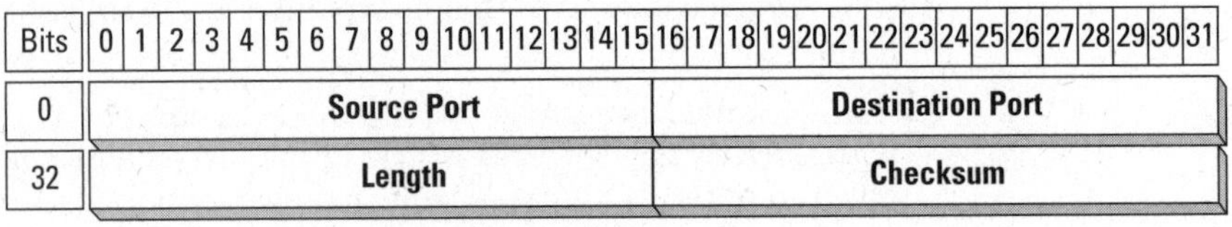

Figure 2-3: The structure of the UDP header.

Bits	0	1	2	3	4	5	6	7	8	9	10	11	12	13	14	15	16	17	18	19	20	21	22	23	24	25	26	27	28	29	30	31
0	Source Port																Destination Port															
32	Length																Checksum															

✦ **Source Port:** This is the TCP port used on the sending computer.

✦ **Destination Port:** This is the TCP port being connected on the target host.

✦ **Length:** The length of the overall frame is stored here. This is used to verify that the full frame has arrived intact.

✦ **Checksum:** A checksum is generated on the UDP data and stored in this field, ensuring that data has not been corrupted during transit. UDP does verify that the data that arrives has arrived intact, whereas TCP ensure that the data arrived, arrived intact, and arrived in order.

Sockets and ports

TCP and UDP operate at the host-to-host layer in the IP communication model and provide host-to-host communication services for the application layer protocol. This means an application layer protocol is on one IP host connecting to an application layer protocol on another IP host. In most situations, these host-to-host connections have a sever process running on one host and a client process running on the other host. Examples of this host-to-host connection include a web browser (such as Mozilla Firefox) connecting to a web server; an e-mail client (such as Outlook Express) connecting to a Simple Mail Transfer Protocol (SMTP) mail server; or a Secure Copy Protocol (SCP) client (such as WinSCP) connecting to an SCP server. To manage the connection between these application layer protocols, TCP and UDP use ports and sockets, which I look at in this section.

A *port* is a TCP or UDP connection point. Think of them as receptacles on an old-fashioned telephone switchboard. There are 65,536 (or 2^16) ports available for a host to manage connections, numbered from 0 to 65,535 for each TCP and UDP. When you establish an application server running on an IP host, you configure that server to be used (or bound to) a specific TCP or UDP port. By associating the application layer server to use a specific port, you have created a destination that a remote IP host can connect to.

When the remote IP host connects to an application layer server, the connection the host makes is to a port operating on a specific IP host (identified by an IP address). This pairing of an IP address and a port as a connection endpoint is a *socket*. In that old-fashioned switchboard analogy, the socket has two connectors connected to each client's phone: one is a receptacle, and the other is a plug. Think of these connectors as the ports, but because the port is associated with a phone, together they make a socket, such as the TCP or UDP port, when paired with an IP address is a socket. To make a phone connection for a client, the "operator" takes the plug for one client and connects it to the socket for the other client. With IP, the client application has a port that it operates on, so on the client host, there is an IP address and port for the client side of the connection; this is a socket. On the server side of the connection is an IP address for the server and a port to make a socket on the server host. To establish a connection between the client application layer and the server application layer is a virtual connection between these two sockets.

As an example of this connection process, I walk you through the process of connecting to a website, such as `www.wiley.com`. You would open your web browser (like Mozilla Firefox) and type **www.wiley.com** into the address bar. I do not go into the details here, but your web browser uses a Domain Name System (DNS) server to look up the name `www.wiley.com` and find out what its IP address is. For this example, the address is 192.0.2.100.

Firefox makes a connection to the 192.0.2.100 address and to the port where the application layer web server is operating. Firefox knows what port to expect because it is a *well-known port* (which I discuss later in this section). The well-known port for a web server is *TCP port 80.* The destination socket that Firefox attempts to connect is written as *socket:port,* or in this example, 192.0.2.100:80. This is the server side of the connect, but the server needs to know where to send the web page you want to view in Mozilla Firefox, so you have a socket for the client side of the connection also.

The client side connection is made up of your IP address, such as 192.168.1.25, and a randomly chosen dynamic port number (keep reading this section to find out more about a dynamic port). The socket associated with Firefox looks like 192.168.1.25:49175. Because web servers operate on

TCP port 80, both of these sockets are TCP sockets, whereas if you were connecting to a server operating on a UDP port, both the server and client sockets would be UDP sockets.

When you refer to sockets, you always base the names on your current point of view. Here are the two types of sockets, based on your point of view. They are

✦ **Local sockets:** Sockets or connection endpoints on your current host.

✦ **Foreign, or remote, sockets:** Foreign, or remote, sockets are on another host.

If you use a command, such as `netstat -n` on Microsoft Windows or Linux, you see a listing of the local addresses (and ports) and the foreign addresses (and ports) to which they are connected.

The three categories of TCP and UDP ports are

✦ **Well-known ports:** When IP was being implemented, there was a slow start of assigning services that needed to use specific ports. The ports were initially assigned from the lowest port number and worked their way up. Ports 0–1023 are considered well-known ports because they were used by many of the core services on the Unix servers, and most required privilege permissions on the server to implement. Telnet (23) and Simple Mail Transport Protocol (SMTP) (25) are two examples of these services.

✦ **Registered ports:** The Internet Assigned Numbers Authority (IANA) keeps the list of all services that run on both the well-known ports and on all registered ports. The registration process puts a permanent association in place with the port number and the service. These services are all long-running services and would be assigned to ports between 1,024 and 49,151. The Microsoft Remote Desktop Protocol (RDP) (3389) and Network File System (NFS) (2049) are two examples of registered ports.

✦ **Dynamic and/or private ports:** All other ports, from 49,152 to 65,535, are referred to as dynamic, or private ports. These ports are not permanently associated to any service. If I write my own service, I can configure it to use any dynamic port that I want, but someone else may write his own service and use the same port. This will not cause any issue until you install both services on the same IP host because they are both going to want to use the same port, and that is just not possible. It would be like two people having their phones hooked up to the same plug and receptacle at the operator's office; it is not possible. This problem should not happen, though, if you have a registered port to work with because the other developer cannot use the same service.

Checking out which services use which ports

So what services use what ports in the world of TCP and UDP? Here is a short list (from the `hosts` file on my computer) of some of the major services in the well-known ports registered range. You may notice that some of the ports are used by the services on both UDP and TCP, but this is not true in all cases. As you scan through the list, you may notice that most of these service names are application layer protocols and either have come up in this book, or will come up in this book. Some protocols, such as FTP, use two ports, and Kerberos operates on either TCP or UDP (which typically means that one port functions as a backup port).

```
ftp-data       20/tcp                              #FTP, data
ftp            21/tcp                              #FTP. control
telnet         23/tcp
domain         53/tcp                              #Domain Name Server
domain         53/udp                              #Domain Name Server
bootps         67/udp     dhcps                    #Bootstrap Protocol Server
bootpc         68/udp     dhcpc                    #Bootstrap Protocol Client
tftp           69/udp                              #Trivial File Transfer
http           80/tcp     www www-http             #World Wide Web
kerberos       88/tcp     krb5 kerberos-sec        #Kerberos
kerberos       88/udp     krb5 kerberos-sec        #Kerberos
ntp            123/udp                             #Network Time Protocol
netbios-ns     137/tcp    nbname                   #NETBIOS Name Service
netbios-ns     137/udp    nbname                   #NETBIOS Name Service
netbios-dgm    138/udp    nbdatagram               #NETBIOS Datagram Service
netbios-ssn    139/tcp    nbsession                #NETBIOS Session Service
```

Knowing When to Use TCP

When you have a large amount of data to send over a network connection, use TCP because the data is guaranteed to arrive in order and intact. Yes, you could send that data over UDP, but you need to build into your application a process for checking and verifying that all the data has arrived or to deal with the fact that some data may not show up. With TCP, all this checking for order and data accuracy is built into the TCP transport layer protocol. By having these checks built into the transport protocol, less work is required by the developer of the application protocols because the receiver is already guaranteed to receive consistent data from the network.

The greatest strength of TCP is when you are sending large blocks of data over an unreliable network that may be experiencing a high number of dropped packets. With TCP, you are guaranteed that all the data will arrive and will be in order. TCP guarantees this level of data accuracy by sending a series of acknowledgements for each piece of data that the client device receives.

TCP is good to use for large data blocks, broken into several data packets, arriving at their destination for reassembly to the large data block with a guarantee that it will be done in such a manner. The following sections describe some services that work with TCP.

Services that use TCP

TCP is used by such protocols as

+ File Transfer Protocol (20, 21)
+ Telnet (23)
+ Simple Mail Transfer Protocol (25)
+ Post Office Protocol 3 (110)
+ Network News Transfer Protocol retrieval of newsgroup messages (119)
+ HyperText Transfer Protocol over SSL/TLS (443)
+ Microsoft-DS Server Message Block file sharing (445)
+ SolarWinds Kiwi Log Server (1470)
+ Citrix XenApp Independent Computing Architecture thin client protocol (1494)

In addition to the preceding are several services that operate on, or at least have been registered for, both TCP and UDP connections. These include

+ Secure Shell (22)
+ Domain Name System (53)
+ HyperText Transfer Protocol (80)
+ Lightweight Directory Access Protocol (389)
+ Timbuktu service ports (1417–1420)
+ Microsoft Windows Internet Name Service (1512)
+ Cisco Skinny Call Control Protocol (2000)

Three-way handshaking

To send data over TCP, follow the required session establishment process, known as *handshaking,* or more specifically, a *three-way handshake* because it involves completing three IP packets. The three-way handshake is illustrated in Figure 2-4 and involves these three frames.

♦ **SYN:** This is the synchronization phase. This TCP segment sets the sequence number to be used for the upcoming data transfer.

♦ **SYN-ACK:** The reply from the remote host does two things:

 • *Verifies the sequence number that will be used.*

 • *Acknowledges the original request.*

♦ **ACK:** This data is sent from the originating host, and acknowledges the sequence number and the acknowledgement from the targeted host.

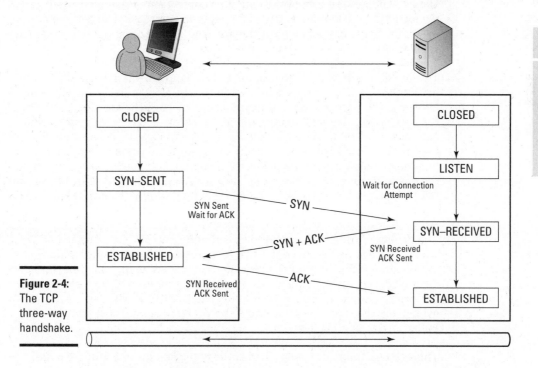

Figure 2-4:
The TCP
three-way
handshake.

After being established through the handshaking process, the TCP sequence numbers will be used in sequential order until the session is terminated. The sequence numbers allow all the data to arrive in order (or in the correct sequence).

There is a process to start a session, and there is also a process to terminate the TCP session. To terminate the session, a Finish frame is sent from one host to the other:

✦ **FIN:** The Finish frame is a request that the session be terminated.

✦ **FIN-ACK:** The response to a finish request is an agreement for finishing and an acknowledgement. Unlike session setup, there is no follow-up acknowledgement; this end of the session is closed when the data is sent. The remote host closes its end of the connection when it receives FIN-ACK.

Sliding windows

Sliding windows are part of the data flow control and are implemented through TCP. If you refer to the TCP header in Figure 2-2, you can see that one of the fields in the header is the Window Size, in addition to a Sequence Number and an Acknowledgement Number.

To send data across the network, there is a happy medium between sending 100MB in one go versus sending 1 byte. The answer lies somewhere in-between. The *sliding window* is how you can manage the amount of data on the network for delivery at any given time. Think of a delivery courier who can carry a set number of packages in his truck. When he leaves to deliver them, you do not know what is going on (prior to couriers using wireless handheld computers that constantly update your package status). When he returns to the sorting station, you know what was delivered, and you can put more packages on his truck for delivery. Sliding windows set the size of his truck.

The benefit of using sliding windows is that it controls overall speed at which data can be delivered. Its size is represented as a number of data packets that can be out for delivery on the network at any one time. In Figure 2-5, I set up a sliding window size of six frames, which would equate to the size of the data on my computer. The size of the window is the smallest between the announced window size of the receiving host and the send buffer on the sending host.

This process then starts with the sending host sending a complete buffer of data — or in this case, six frames. Those frames take a period of time to cross the network to the destination. When they arrive at the destination, the recipient host accepts all the frames and sends back an acknowledgement for the last frame that it receives. If something went wrong with some of the packets, or they suffered an abnormal delay, the acknowledgement may not be for the entire size of the window. Although each frame could have a separate acknowledgement, more typically, the frames will arrive in close enough succession that only one acknowledgement will be sent.

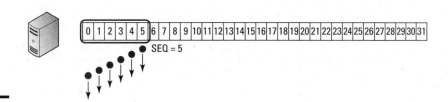

Figure 2-5:
Sending a window full of data with sliding windows.

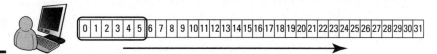

Book II
Chapter 2

Choosing between
Protocols: TCP
and UDP

In this case, Figure 2-6 shows the acknowledgement being returned to the sender. Also, note that the window has moved along to the next block of data that it expects to receive from the sender. If the acknowledgement had been for only part of the window — say, that only three frames were received — the acknowledgement would have been for frame 4 as the next frame. The sender would have moved its window to send — or resend — frame 4 with five other frames.

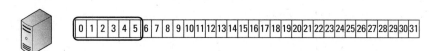

Figure 2-6:
Acknow-ledging a full window with a single acknow-ledgement.

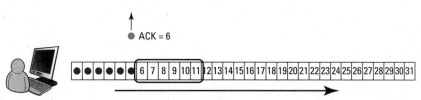

Figure 2-7 shows the follow-up set of data being sent to the receiving host. This process continues until all the data has been received by the receiving host.

Based on the reliability of the underlying network, the speed of the network, and the Round Trip Time (RTT) for data, you may want to adjust the window size to achieve an optimal data transmission rate. Here are a few examples of how the window size adjusts data transmission time:

✦ With the network being reliable, set the RTT to 10 milliseconds (ms) to send 32 blocks of data with a window size of 1, waiting 10 ms after sending each frame. The wait would be for the acknowledgment. To send all the data, you would be looking at a total time of 320ms and a total transmission on the sender of 32 frames.

✦ With the same reliable network and RTT, set the window size to 10. If all data gets through in each transmission cycle, the sending host would have sent 32 frames in no less than 40ms. That time being made up of transmitting three blocks of 10 frames and one block of 2 frames, with the 10ms RTT for the acknowledgement to be received.

✦ Finally, with an unreliable network, allowing only two of every ten packets to make it through and the same RTT, making a valid estimate is very hard. But, with a sliding window of 10 frames, and assuming that 1 of those 10 frames that makes it through is the first frame, the best time you would likely be able to transmit the data during is 320ms, although likely much longer. During that 320ms, you likely have transmitted approximately 275 frames of data. In this scenario, a smaller window size would have gotten the data through just as quickly but with the transmission of far fewer frames.

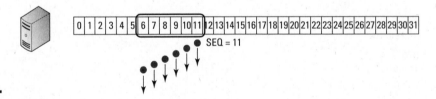

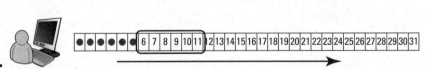

Figure 2-7:
Sending
a second
window
worth of
information.

Knowing When to Use UDP

So why would you ever want to use a best-effort delivery transport protocol when you have the guaranteed option available to you? With the guarantee of delivery that TCP provides, there is extra overhead, just like how guaranteed delivery with Express Post requires completing an extra form and costs you more money. This overhead can be overwhelming when the data that you are delivering is either small or requires no delays. So, UDP is useful when you care less about the data arriving in particular sequence because it all fits in one data packet. Or, perhaps you can deal with missing data, as in the case of streaming video, where you can deal with a lost frame or two and see a video properly over huge delays that cause stuttered playback.

And what uses UDP? UDP is used by such protocols as

✦ Dynamic Host Configuration Protocol (67, 68)

✦ Trivial File Transfer Protocol (69)

✦ Network Time Protocol (123)

✦ Simple Network Management Protocol (161)

✦ Internet Security Association and Key Management Protocol (500)

✦ *Doom,* popular 3D online first-person shooter (666)

✦ Layer 2 Tunneling Protocol (1701)

✦ Microsoft Simple Service Discover Protocol (1900)

✦ Cisco Hot Standby Router Protocol (1985)

✦ Cisco Media Gateway Control Protocol (2427)

Some services can run with TCP and UDP, as listed in the "Knowing When to Use TCP" section, earlier in this chapter.

So is UDP really all that unreliable? Perhaps in the past it was, when you were sending data over all kinds of links in which data bits would regularly run the risk of being lost or delayed. In most modern networks, though, this tends not to be the case. With highly reliable underlying networks, the role of UDP is now really to reduce overhead; in some cases where unreliable connections persist, it still offers utility.

UDP offers a great advantage in situations where you are sending only a small amount of data. As mentioned, between the handshaking process of TCP and its larger headers, there is more overhead and less data sent per packet. If you have a small amount of data — less than about 1,400 bytes — using UDP is for you. The data will either get there or not. And because the data is small enough to fit in a packet, it will arrive in order.

Some systems using UDP include *Trivial File Transfer Protocol (TFTP),* a UDP version of FTP, which allows you to use UDP for large pieces of data. If data does not arrive intact or in order, it is not the job of the protocol to deal with it, but rather the application that needs to deal with the issue. In the case of TFTP as an application/protocol, TFTP can build checking into its protocol, placing data order information into what UDP sees as data but TFTP sees as its protocol information. Because the order of the big file is important, the data in the file needs to be kept in sequence; in TFTP, though, this job is done outside the transport layer.

Error checking is another function that needs to be done by an application protocol when using UDP as a transport layer protocol. If needed, UDP is required to retransmit entire data blocks to get complete data. Again, this is good for fairly reliable networks in which retransmission will be low.

Chapter 3: Working with ARP, the IP Communication Model, and Data Link Layer Troubleshooting

In This Chapter

✔ **Seeing the ARP process in action**

✔ **Understanding how ANDing works and where it is used**

✔ **Troubleshooting with ARP**

✔ **Reviewing other ICMP-based troubleshooting tools**

*I*n earlier chapters, I show you the lower levels of the Open System Interconnection (OSI) model. I discuss how every network card on the network, whether integrated on computer motherboards, installed in printers, or found in your network routers, has a unique address that is used for network communications. This unique address — its Media Access Control (MAC) address — is used to identify each device on a network segment, between two routers, and may be filtered by switches or bridges. In general terms, all devices on that network segment will see all traffic on that segment. However, when a network device receives an Ethernet frame, it checks the destination address in the frames' header; if the destination address referenced in the network frame is not a broadcast address, or their own address, the network device ignores the frame.

Well, this works at the MAC level of the data link layer of the OSI model. The issue here is that you do not know the MAC addresses of any computers on the network, so you need a way of converting the addresses that you do know into MAC addresses to communicate with devices on the network. This chapter delves deeper into this process to examine exactly how you locate these MAC addresses and establish communication sessions with other network devices.

Toward the end of the chapter, I show you tools that you can use to help troubleshoot issues on the network while working at the data link layer of the network.

After you finish this chapter, you will have seen the role that Address Resolution Protocol (ARP) plays in the basic IP communication process in addition to the AND process, which is critical in deciding where to send data. In addition to this critical process, you also review using troubleshooting tools, such as `ping`, `traceroute`, and `pathping`. With this knowledge, you can help to diagnose where some of your problems reside.

Watching Address Resolution Protocol in Action

To communicate with a network device, you need to know its MAC address. If you know only a network layer address, such as the IP address, you need to have a process to locate the MAC address; or in other words, resolve the IP address to a MAC address. ARP is the main process used to resolve IP addresses to MAC addresses. As ARP's name suggests, this set of rules defines how a MAC address is determined, given that you know the IP address of the destination device. This device may be local or remote to the network segment that your computer or device is on. (In (Chapter 1 of this minibook, I introduce network classes and subnetting, which are used in the ARP process.)

To understand the ARP process, examine Figure 3-1, which is the logic tree followed for ARP-related network communications. Any communication session always has two IP addresses of importance:

✦ Your IP address

✦ The IP address of the device you are trying to communicate with

As you see in the next section "The logical AND," these two addresses and your subnet mask determine whether the device you are trying to talk to is on the same network.

The logical AND

In Book I, Chapter 3, I introduce you to a *logic gate*. One of those gates was an AND gate, and it is this AND operation that determines whether the other device is local or remote. Just as when you perform an ADD operation, dubbed ADDing, when you perform an AND operation, you are ANDing. To determine whether two IP addresses are on the same network segment (your IP address and a second IP address), follow this general process:

1. Perform an AND calculation with your IP address and your subnet mask.

2. Perform an AND calculation with the second IP address and your subnet mask.

3. Compare the two results.

Each AND calculation results in numbers that can be compared visually to see whether they are equal. If the two results are the same, the two devices are on the same network segment. Conversely, if the results differ, the two devices are on different network segments. When the devices are on different network segments, use a router to allow communication between the two devices.

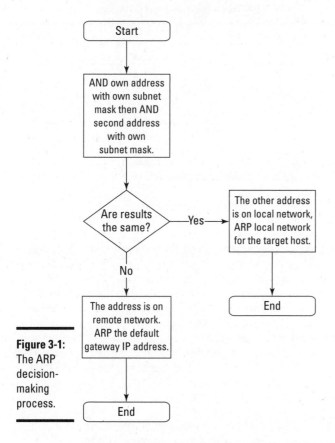

Figure 3-1:
The ARP decision-making process.

The rest of this section explains the exact process of the AND logical operation and shows you this operation in action, including the result of performing the AND operation with your IP address and your subnet mask.

Start by taking a closer look at the AND operation. *AND* is an operator in a logic, or Boolean, calculation. (You can find out more about logical operators in Book I, Chapter 3.) Most logic operators work only when dealing with binary values because you can have only two states — either 0 or 1. Table 3-1 shows the AND results based on two values. The table shows the four possible calculations when using two 1-bit numbers.

Table 3-1	ANDing Inputs and Results	
Bit Value 1	*Bit Value 2*	*Result*
0	0	0
0	1	0
1	0	0
1	1	1

Notice that if you have two 1s, or all 1s in the calculation, the result is a 1. And if you have any 0s in your calculation, the result is 0.

Take this a step further and compare two IP addresses that exist on the same network, as shown in Tables 3-2 and 3-3. Table 3-2 works with 192.168.1.54/24, and Table 3-3 works with 192.168.1.129. If you view the addresses from the perspective that 192.168.1.54/24 is the address of your computer, you know what your IP address and subnet mask is. The address of 192.168.1.129 represents another host (I call it the *target host*) on an unknown network segment (because you do not know whether it is your local network segment or some other network segment). However, these tables prove that 192.168.1.129 and 192.168.1.54/24 are on the same network segment. You know the address you want to connect to, 192.168.1.129, but because it is a remote computer (as opposed to your computer), you do not know what subnet mask that computer is using. Because you cannot know the other subnet mask, the ARP process conducts both AND operations using your subnet mask.

Table 3-2 performs the AND operation with your IP address and your subnet mask. This first step is to convert your address and your subnet mask to binary, and then conduct the AND operation on each bit of the binary address and subnet mask, in columns through the number. Whether you move left to right (or right to left) through the number does not matter; unlike mathematical operations, there are no numbers to carry from one column to the next. For the first four bits in the first octet, the operation is 1 AND 1 is 1, 1 AND 1 is 1, 0 AND 1 is 0, 0 AND 1 is 0. Follow this operation through to the end of the last octet.

In Chapter 1 of this minibook, I mention that /24 defines the subnet mask to be 24 bits, or 255.255.255.0.

Table 3-2	ANDing of 192.168.1.54/24			
Item	*First Octet*	*Second Octet*	*Third Octet*	*Fourth Octet*
Decimal	192	168	1	54
Binary	11000000	10101000	00000001	00110110
Subnet mask	11111111	11111111	11111111	00000000
AND result	11000000	10101000	00000001	00000000

Table 3-3 performs the same AND operation, but you are now working with the IP address of the target host and your subnet mask. You follow the same operations, first convert the address and your subnet mask to binary; then bit by bit, move through the number and perform an AND operation on each set of bits. The results are in the last row of the table.

Table 3-3	ANDing of 192.168.1.129			
Item	*First Octet*	*Second Octet*	*Third Octet*	*Fourth Octet*
Decimal	192	168	1	129
Binary	11000000	10101000	00000001	10000001
Subnet mask	11111111	11111111	11111111	00000000
AND result	11000000	10101000	00000001	00000000

If you compare these AND results from the last row in Tables 3-2 and 3-3, note that the results are the same (11000000.10101000.00000001.00000000). And because these results are the same, the two addresses are on the same network or network segment.

Take this a step further and compare the two IP addresses that exist on different networks, as shown in Tables 3-4 and 3-5. Table 3-4 works with 192.168.1.54/24, which is your address. This table will perform the same calculation as Table 3-2, but I wanted to keep them next to each other in the book to make it easier for you to follow along. Remember, this table uses your address and your subnet mask.

Table 3-4		ANDing of 192.168.1.54/24		
Item	*First Octet*	*Second Octet*	*Third Octet*	*Fourth Octet*
Decimal	192	168	1	54
Binary	11000000	10101000	00000001	00110110
Subnet mask	11111111	11111111	11111111	00000000
AND result	11000000	10101000	00000001	00000000

Table 3-5 works with 10.45.11.54, which represents the IP address of the target host on a network, and at this point, you do not know whether that network is your network or another network segment. You know the address you are attempting to communicate with and you know your subnet mask, so these are the numbers you use in the AND operation.

Table 3-5		ANDing of 10.45.11.54		
Item	*First Octet*	*Second Octet*	*Third Octet*	*Fourth Octet*
Decimal	10	45	11	54
Binary	00001010	00101101	00001011	00110110
Subnet mask	11111111	11111111	11111111	00000000
AND result	00001010	00101101	00001011	00000000

When you compare the results found in the last row of Tables 3-4 and 3-5, you have 11000000.10101000.00000001.00000000 from Table 3-4 and 00001010.00101101.00001011.00000000 from Table 3-5. These two numbers are not the same. Because the results do not match, these two addresses are on different networks.

Using ARP

After you identify whether the target host is local to your network or a remote network, I show the next step the ARP process takes. Refer to Figure 3-1 to see that if the target computer is your local network, your computer will use the ARP protocol and request the MAC address for the target host's IP address. After your computer has the MAC address, it can send data to the target host.

So what exactly is ARP? Start by taking that right down to the OSI model. Figure 3-2 shows the field breakdown of the entire *Ethernet frame,* which is the entire piece of data transferred at the network level. (See Book I, Chapter 4.) The ARP-specific information is found within that Ethernet frame in the Type and Data fields. Figure 3-2 shows sample information in the ARP header and Data fields. Here is a list of the header fields and what type of information you can expect to see:

✦ **Type:** Stores the Type number of the protocol data that is found in the Data field of the Ethernet frame. I have shown this in the ARP data, but this field is actually part of the Ethernet frame structure. For most IP data, the type is 0x0800, but ARP has its own type, 0x0806. This means that even at the network interface layer of the IP network model, the data found in this packet is identified as ARP data.

✦ **Hardware Type:** Within the ARP header, this identifies the physical hardware classification of the network, such as Ethernet or Token Ring. Because most networks are Ethernet networks, you can expect to see a 0x0001 value in this field.

✦ **Protocol Type:** Identifies the Internet layer protocol, typically IP, that is in use. Expect to see a value of 0x0800, which stands for IP, in this field.

✦ **Hardware Size:** The size (in bytes) of the hardware or MAC address. In Book I, Chapter 4, a MAC address is 48 bits in length, which is equal to 6 bytes.

✦ **Protocol Size:** The size (in bytes) of the protocol or IP address. In Book I, Chapter 4, an IP address is a 32-bit number, which is equal to 4 bytes.

✦ **Opcode:** The *opcode,* or operation code, specifies what type of ARP packet is being sent. You can expect to see Request (0x0001) and Reply (0x0002).

✦ **Gratuitous:** Some hosts may send ARP reply to announce their IP and MAC addresses. If they send this type of ARP packet, this field is set to True. This type of ARP announcement is a Gratuitous ARP because it is typically not needed.

✦ **Sender Hardware Address:** The hardware address of the sending host, for an Ethernet network is the MAC address of network card. Every ARP packet contains the hardware address of the sending host.

✦ **Sender Protocol Address:** The protocol address of the sending host. For IP networks, this is the IP address. Every ARP packet contains the IP address of the sending host.

✦ **Target Hardware Address:** The hardware address of the target host. As with the Sender Hardware Address field, this field contains the MAC address of the target host. In an ART request, this field is the hardware broadcast address (FF:FF:FF:FF:FF:FF for Ethernet) because the purpose of the ART request is to locate the MAC address of another host on the network. In an ARP reply, this field contains the MAC address of the host that sent the original ART request.

✦ **Target Protocol Address:** The protocol (or IP) address of the target host. In an ART request, this field contains the IP address of the host for whom you attempt to locate a MAC address. In an ARP reply, this field contains the IP address of the host that sent the original ART request.

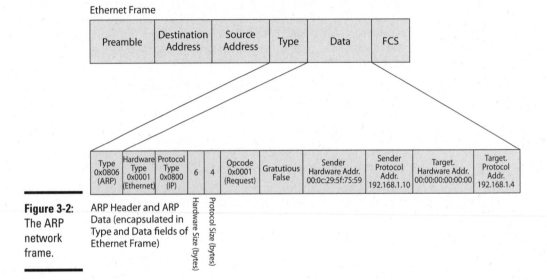

Figure 3-2:
The ARP network frame.

ARP Header and ARP Data (encapsulated in Type and Data fields of Ethernet Frame)

ARP requests for local hosts

For *local hosts* (hosts on your network segment), an ARP request starts with some type of network communication request between the two computers. This could be `ping`, the establishment of a Transmission Control Protocol (TCP) session, or a User Diagram Protocol (UDP) session. Regardless of the reason, the net result is the following process:

1. The first host contacts another host.

   The first host performs an AND operation on its address and subnet mask, as well as the second host's address and its subnet mask, as I describe in the earlier section "The logical AND." This determines that the IP addresses belong on the same network, so the second host should be on the same network segment.

2. This request goes down through the OSI layers until it hits the network layer (or the Internet layer in the IP network model). At that layer, the target IP address must to be matched to a MAC or hardware address.

3. The decision tree in Figure 3-1 is followed.

The very first thing that is checked is the local ARP cache.

The following section takes a closer look at what happens during that process.

By default, items will not remain the ARP cache of a computer for longer than ten minutes but are in the ARP cache of a Cisco network device for four hours. On a computer, the ARP cache contains only recent hosts that have had communication sessions. You examine how to review and manipulate the ARP cache on a computer later in this chapter in the section "Troubleshooting with ARP."

4. If the IP address you are trying to communicate with is not in the ARP cache, the address needs to be resolved.

Figure 3-3 shows the first step in this process. Notice that the target hardware address is the broadcast address for Ethernet.

5. The data request is placed on hold until the address is resolved and an ARP request is generated and sent onto the network.

All ARP requests have the same basic format: two hardware (or MAC) addresses and two protocol (or IP) addresses (source and target).

The data request includes the sending host's MAC and IP information as well as the IP address of the targeted host. The opcode for this type of packet is 0x0001, denoting that this is a request.

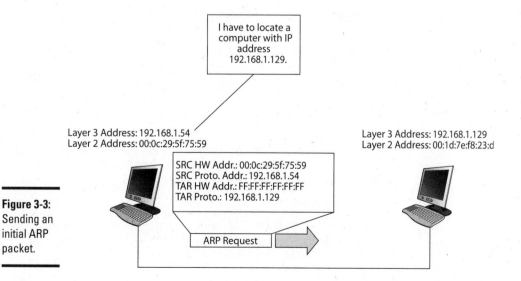

I have to locate a computer with IP address 192.168.1.129.

Layer 3 Address: 192.168.1.54
Layer 2 Address: 00:0c:29:5f:75:59

Layer 3 Address: 192.168.1.129
Layer 2 Address: 00:1d:7e:f8:23:d

SRC HW Addr.: 00:0c:29:5f:75:59
SRC Proto. Addr.: 192.168.1.54
TAR HW Addr.: FF:FF:FF:FF:FF:FF
TAR Proto.: 192.168.1.129

ARP Request

Figure 3-3: Sending an initial ARP packet.

6. The packet is sent to the local hardware broadcast address, so every computer on the local network segment sees that frame and processes it.

   Upon processing the frame and reading the packet information, most computers discard the data because their IP address does not match the one being searched.

7. If by chance, a host does have that address, it records the source MAC and IP address in its own ARP cache, knowing that if someone wants to talk to it, it will likely need to send data shortly, so it then builds its own ARP packet in response.

   The response ARP packet has an opcode of 0x0002, denoting that it is a reply. The ARP reply's structure, looks the same as the ARP request, except that all four address fields are filled out and completed. Logically, it uses its address as the sender address and the sender of ARP request as the target. Figure 3-4 gives you an idea of what this looks like.

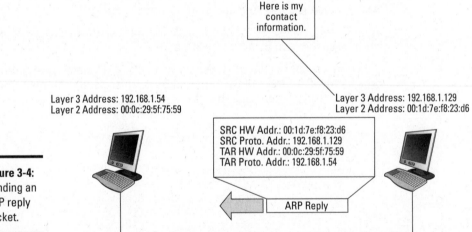

Here is my contact information.

Layer 3 Address: 192.168.1.54
Layer 2 Address: 00:0c:29:5f:75:59

Layer 3 Address: 192.168.1.129
Layer 2 Address: 00:1d:7e:f8:23:d6

SRC HW Addr.: 00:1d:7e:f8:23:d6
SRC Proto. Addr.: 192.168.1.129
TAR HW Addr.: 00:0c:29:5f:75:59
TAR Proto. Addr.: 192.168.1.54

ARP Reply

Figure 3-4:
Sending an
ARP reply
packet.

8. With the response sent, the original host sees a frame on the local network segment that is addressed directly to its MAC address; it opens that frame and processes the ARP packet.

   The original host then knows the target MAC it needs to send its data to.

9. The original host adds the ARP information to its ARP cache and then releases the data it had placed on hold, sending it to the target MAC address over the local network segment.

ARP requests for remote hosts

The process from the preceding section is a little different if the targeted host is not on the local subnet. Figure 3-5 shows you a rough overview of that process, which starts with an ARP to the default gateway that triggers a series of ARPs from that gateway or router through all the routers that connect these two hosts. For simplicity, the figure shows only one router, but there could be any number of routers between these two hosts. The following steps explain this process:

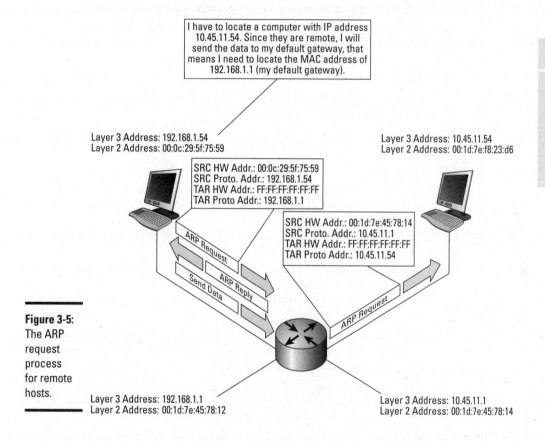

Figure 3-5:
The ARP request process for remote hosts.

1. The first host has data to send to the second host, the data is placed on hold, and two AND operations are performed.

One operation uses the IP address and subnet mask of the first host, and the second uses the IP address of the second host and the subnet mask of the first host.

The result is that two hosts are on separate network segments.

2. A communication session needs to be established through the network routers.

   The closest router that is known is the default gateway (192.168.1.1). To be able to send data through the router, the first host needs to know the MAC address of the router. The host checks the ARP cache, and if the MAC address for 192.168.1.1 is not there, it sends an ARP request for the 192.168.1.1 IP address.

3. After the first host gets the ARP reply from the router, the first host releases the data that needs sent to the second host.

   Because the data is going to a host on a remote network segment, the data is sent through the router.

4. The data arrives at the router, and the router determines whether the second host is local to any of its attached network interfaces or network segments.

5. If the second host is on a connected network segment, the router can send an ARP request looking for the MAC address of the host with the 10.45.11.54 IP address; however, if the second host is not on a connected network segment, the router needs to send the ARP request to another router that the router thinks is closer to the second host.

   In this case, the second host is directly attached to the required network segment, and the router would know that by going through the AND operation for all its network interfaces and the IP address of the second host.

6. After the router identifies the network connection or network interface where the router expects to find the second host, the router sends the ARP request to that network segment.

7. The second host, as shown in Figure 3-6, now knows that another host is attempting to communicate with it. The second host records the IP address and MAC information for the router in its ARP cache.

   However, the second host does not know the first host's MAC address; it never needs to know this info.

8. The second host sends the ARP reply back to the router on its network.

9. After the router receives the ARP reply from the second host, it knows how to get the pending data to the second host, and that data is then sent over the shared network segment to the second host.

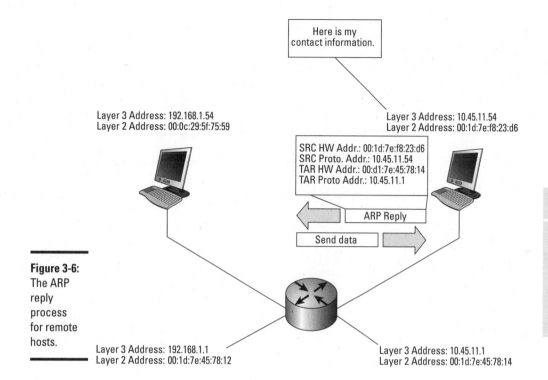

Figure 3-6:
The ARP
reply
process
for remote
hosts.

Troubleshooting with ARP

This ARP process happens very fast and is built into the lowest levels of the networking protocol. In the end, the process appears to be almost transparent, but knowing how it works can greatly help with network troubleshooting. When I look at the address database on any device or host on the network, I only ever see systems on the local network segment listed in the ARP cache.

Many troubleshooting tools are available on most workstations, and although they vary somewhat between operating systems, `arp` is one of the standard commands. In this section, you see how to use the `arp` command on a Windows-based computer, but the main options for this command work the same regardless of the operating system.

Checking out arp command options

Running `arp` without any options displays help for the `arp` command, which is as follows:

```
C:\>arp
```

Displays and modifies the IP-to-Physical address translation tables used by
address resolution protocol (ARP).

```
ARP -s inet_addr eth_addr [if_addr]
ARP -d inet_addr [if_addr]
ARP -a [inet_addr] [-N if_addr]
```

```
  -a          Displays current ARP entries by interrogating the current
              protocol data.  If inet_addr is specified, the IP and Physical
              addresses for only the specified computer are displayed.  If
              more than one network interface uses ARP, entries for each ARP
              table are displayed.
  -g          Same as -a.
  inet_addr   Specifies an internet address.
  -N if_addr  Displays the ARP entries for the network interface specified
              by if_addr.
  -d          Deletes the host specified by inet_addr. inet_addr may be
              wildcarded with * to delete all hosts.
  -s          Adds the host and associates the Internet address inet_addr
              with the Physical address eth_addr.  The Physical address is
              given as 6 hexadecimal bytes separated by hyphens. The entry
              is permanent.
  eth_addr    Specifies a physical address.
  if_addr     If present, this specifies the Internet address of the
              interface whose address translation table should be modified.
              If not present, the first applicable interface will be used.
Example:
  > arp -s 157.55.85.212   00-aa-00-62-c6-09  .... Adds a static entry.
  > arp -a                                    .... Displays the arp table.
```

Looking through your ARP cache with arp -a

Take a look at the most-used `arp` command, which is `arp -a`. Issuing this
command displays the contents of your ARP cache, which is sometimes critical when troubleshooting local communications. The output from this command looks like the following:

```
C:\>arp -a

Interface: 192.168.1.137 --- 0x60005
  Internet Address      Physical Address      Type
  192.168.1.254         00-1d-7e-f8-23-d6     dynamic

Interface: 10.42.200.22 --- 0x200007
  Internet Address      Physical Address      Type
  10.42.0.3             00-11-22-33-44-55     dynamic
  10.42.0.4             00-11-22-33-44-55     dynamic
```

This shows you the IP addresses that are found in the ARP cache for each
network interface in your computer. In this case, there are two network
interfaces, with a combined total of three addresses that are cached. Now, if
you want to get another entry into the cache, you simply need to attempt to
communicate with another device on the network. A simple `ping` command

would suffice for this, but any network request would work. After attempting this with two other addresses (192.168.1.5 and 192.168.1.30), those systems appear in the ARP cache:

```
C:\>arp -a

Interface: 192.168.1.137 --- 0x60005
  Internet Address       Physical Address      Type
  192.168.1.5            00-22-15-ba-93-1c      dynamic
  192.168.1.30           20-cf-30-3a-f7-c9      dynamic
  192.168.1.254          00-1d-7e-f8-23-d6      dynamic
```

These systems are listed as *dynamic,* which means that they were added and removed automatically. After waiting for two minutes, the systems time out of the ARP cache, and the cache will not include the MAC addresses of those other two systems. If there has been communication with that host over that two-minute period, it will remain in the cache for up to ten minutes.

Adding a static ARP entry

You may rarely want to add a static ARP entry. The *static ARP entry* is a permanent (until you delete it) entry into your ARP cache. One reason you may want to add static ARP entries is if you have two hosts that communicate with each other constantly throughout the day; by adding static ARP entries for both systems in each other's ARP cache, you reduce some network overhead, in the form of ARP requests and ARP replies. The additional management work you need to do in adding and maintaining static ARP cache entries usually exceeds the network bandwidth that you save because ARP traffic consumes very little bandwidth. To add a static ARP cache entry, simply use a command like this:

```
C:\>arp -s 192.168.1.30 20-cf-30-3a-f7-c9
```

This command creates a static entry in your ARP cache, so to start a communication session with the host that has a 192.168.1.30 IP address, you do not need to start the process with an ARP request; you already know the target host's MAC address. If a similar ARP entry has not been added to the target host, the target host needs to send an ARP request to your computer to find out your MAC address.

After adding the static ARP entry, the ARP cache on your computer looks like this (notice the static entry that has been created):

```
C:\>arp -a

Interface: 192.168.1.137 --- 0x60005
  Internet Address       Physical Address      Type
  192.168.1.30           20-cf-30-3a-f7-c9      static
  192.168.1.254          00-1d-7e-f8-23-d6      dynamic
```

Communication with the host at 192.168.1.30 would work fine until the MAC address of the target computer changes, which could be because of a network card being changed or some other operation that changes the MAC address. When this happens, you need to delete the invalid ARP entry with an `arp -d` command, such as `arp -d 192.168.1.30`.

If you are using a Cicso router, it will also have an option to examine your ARP information. Connect to your Cisco router and enter Privileged EXEC mode. From here, you can run the command `show arp` to display your current ARP cache:

```
Router#show arp
Protocol  Address          Age (min)  Hardware Addr   Type   Interface
Internet  192.168.1.1          -      0005.32af.8d72  ARPA   Ethernet0
```

The preceding code shows that only the router's own information is in the ARP cache, and thus that there have not been any other local devices talking to this router. Note the dash in the Age column, which indicates the age of the entry. The hyphen denotes that this entry will not age-out of the cache. If your router has been routing traffic for several computers, the ARP cache looks like this:

```
Router#show arp
Protocol  Address          Age (min)  Hardware Addr   Type   Interface
Internet  192.168.1.8          0      000c.2960.4479  ARPA   Ethernet0
Internet  192.168.1.1          -      0005.32af.8d72  ARPA   Ethernet0
Internet  192.168.1.3          2      0021.2f31.0c64  ARPA   Ethernet0
Internet  192.168.1.5         13      0022.15ba.931c  ARPA   Ethernet0
Internet  192.168.1.254        1      001d.7ef8.23d6  ARPA   Ethernet0
```

Unlike Windows workstations, which keep ARP entries for a maximum of ten minutes, the ARP entry on a Cisco router remains in the cache for four hours (240 minutes), which is not uncommon because routers tend to spend most of their time dealing with the same hosts. Each time there is a communication session with that device, the counter is reset to 0. A router is often configured as a default gateway for network devices, which is why they see the same hosts communicating with that for most of a day, and as long as those hosts keep sending data through the router, they will remain in the ARP cache. For a router connected to large network segments, this would result in a rather large ARP listing or ARP table. A large ARP table consumes more of the router's memory, so the caching time (or age) that Cisco has chosen was the result of a tradeoff of memory consumed by the ARP cache versus ARP's need for fresh MAC information.

Similar to the earlier discussion on using ARP for the workstation, there may be times when you want to specify a static ARP entry for a router. This can be done by entering Global Configuration mode. From that mode, the `arp` command looks like this:

```
Router(config)#arp 192.168.1.30 20cf.303a.f7c9 arpa
```

After typing that command, your ARP cache includes that IP-MAC address pair, which would not age-out of the cache. This can be seen by the dash in the Age column. Static ARP entries are not usually identified to an interface like the dynamic entries are.

```
Router#show arp
Protocol  Address         Age (min)  Hardware Addr   Type   Interface
Internet  192.168.1.1        -       0005.32af.8d72  ARPA   Ethernet0
Internet  192.168.1.30       -       20cf.303a.f7c9  ARPA
```

If you no longer need the entry, or if you need to change to something else, remove the original entry with the no arp command:

```
Router(config)#no arp 192.168.1.30
```

After removing the entry, you can re-run the show arp command to see that it has been removed from the table:

```
Router#show arp
Protocol  Address         Age (min)  Hardware Addr   Type   Interface
Internet  192.168.1.1        -       0005.32af.8d72  ARPA   Ethernet0
```

Seeing how ARP is useful

Now that you have seen the arp command in action, what does that tell you? Here are a few areas where you might find this command helpful:

✦ **Cannot ping host on network:** Using arp tells you whether the host is on the network but just not responding to the ping request. Some devices, such as firewalls, do not respond to any Internet Control Message Protocol (ICMP) echo packets. They are configured this way for enhanced security, but it does make it difficult when troubleshooting. So if you attempt a ping and then see the address in your ARP cache, you know that the device or host is alive on the network — from the IP layer, anyway.

✦ **Cannot ping host on remote network:** Using arp tells you whether you are connecting to your default gateway properly. If you attempt to ping that remote system, your host should immediately identify the other host as a remote system and send an ARP request for the IP address of your default gateway or a local router. By checking your ARP cache, you can find your router in the list of known address pairs. If the router does not appear in the ARP table, the problem may be with the router not being available, or perhaps an error with your subnet mask. And if your subnet mask is wrong, you might think that there are more systems on your local network segment than there really are.

✦ **Sporadic communication:** Using `arp` tells you the hardware address that you are seeing. You can check the configuration of the target host to find out its hardware address and then verify what you are seeing in your ARP cache. If not, you might have a duplicate IP address on your network. The good thing is that you now know the MAC address of the duplicated computer, you can search for that MAC address on your network. Be aware, when you have a duplicate IP address situation, the IP-MAC address pair in your ARP cache may toggle back and forth between the correct and wrong MAC addresses while the two hosts with that IP address fight for control.

Using Other Troubleshooting Tools

When troubleshooting networking connectivity, you can use other tools, either at the OS level or at the Cisco router or switch level. In this section, you see how to make use of some of these tools, including

✦ `ping`

✦ `traceroute`

✦ `pathping`

These tools can help you identify exactly where the source of the issue is.

ping

Ping's name comes from usage in sonar in which a sound pulse (literally, a *ping*) is sent and then the response echo is listened for in reflected sound waves. The distance to the target is gauged by the amount of time that passes between the ping and the reflected echo. Just like with a sonar ping, IP `ping` is used to test whether another device exists on a connected network.

And like the other commands in this section, `ping` uses ICMP to test this connection. *ICMP* passes control messages between routers on the network. They include items, such as Source Quench (if someone is sending data faster than the router can process) and Echo Request and Echo Reply (which are used by `ping`).

From the Windows OS, the `ping` command generates this help information from the command line:

```
C:\>ping

Usage: ping [-t] [-a] [-n count] [-l size] [-f] [-i TTL] [-v TOS]
            [-r count] [-s count] [[-j host-list] | [-k host-list]]
            [-w timeout] target_name
```

```
Options:
    -t              Ping the specified host until stopped.
                    To see statistics and continue - type Control-Break;
                    To stop - type Control-C.
    -a              Resolve addresses to hostnames.
    -n count        Number of echo requests to send.
    -l size         Send buffer size.
    -f              Set Don't Fragment flag in packet.
    -i TTL          Time To Live.
    -v TOS          Type Of Service.
    -r count        Record route for count hops.
    -s count        Timestamp for count hops.
    -j host-list    Loose source route along host-list.
    -k host-list    Strict source route along host-list.
    -w timeout      Timeout in milliseconds to wait for each reply.
```

To test for connectivity, use `ping` with the IP address of the device that you want to test for connectivity. Here is an example, connecting to `www.cisco.com`:

```
C:\>ping www.cisco.com

Pinging origin-www.cisco.com [72.163.4.161] with 32 bytes of data:

Reply from 72.163.4.161: bytes=32 time=74ms TTL=105
Reply from 72.163.4.161: bytes=32 time=97ms TTL=105
Reply from 72.163.4.161: bytes=32 time=71ms TTL=105
Reply from 72.163.4.161: bytes=32 time=89ms TTL=105

Ping statistics for 72.163.4.161:
    Packets: Sent = 4, Received = 4, Lost = 0 (0% loss),
Approximate round trip times in milli-seconds:
    Minimum = 71ms, Maximum = 97ms, Average = 82ms
```

Note a few things from this response. For starters, each response is sent from a remote system and has nothing to do with the system you sent it from. In this example, I started with a `ping` to a computer name; so, for this to work right from the start, I had to rely on a Domain Name Server (DNS) to resolve that name to a proper IP address, which worked in my case. The Echo Request then went to the listed IP address. Four requests were sent, and the time for each Echo Response was listed.

Also, note the Time to Live (TTL). Every IP packet that is sent on the network has a TTL. The TTL on a packet is reduced by one as it is handled by each router on the network. When this value is set to 0, the router that is handling it at the time discards the packet and sends an ICMP message back to the originating IP address, stating that the packet `Expired in transit`. The TTL starts from one of the well-known binary numbers, such as 32, 64, 128, or 256. Because most devices on the Internet are usually less than 15 router hops from each other, I suggest that the server at Cisco starts its TTL 128, which would put it about 23 routers away from me. (I take another look at that when I discuss `traceroute`.)

Here are some error messages that you likely encounter using `ping`:

✦ `TTL Expired in Transit`: This rather uncommon error message means that the data packet had its TTL set to 0 during transmission. Typically, this happens only if have a routing loop of some sort on the network, and you are trying to get to an address forwarded in the loop. For example, if RouterA and RouterB have each other set as the gateway of last resort or default gateway, and you `ping` an address that does not exist, each router will say, "I do not know that address; here, you take it" — and this will happen until the TTL hits 0. You will see a response like `Reply from 24.215.102.133: TTL expired in transit`. This is the reason why this TTL process was implemented in the IP protocol: to prevent loops allowing packets to forever loop around the Internet.

✦ `Destination Host Unreachable`: When you see this message, it means that for some reason, the host is not deemed reachable by one of the routers or devices on path. This is different from the upcoming error message `Request Timed Out` in that you are being told specifically that the device cannot be contacted. Typically, this message comes from a router that is directly attached to the network segment that should have the host. It is telling you that you have reached the remote network segment, but there is no host there.

✦ `Destination Net Unreachable`: Like the `Destination Host Unreachable` error message, this message tells you that the network on which the host you are attempting to connect is not reachable. Typically, this message will come from a router along the path to the destination network. This would be a router that should be able to directly pass data to that segment — but it cannot. This sometimes occurs when you are guessing at remote segments based on a known pattern or network numbering scheme, but the segment you are attempting to contact does not actually exist, or you were given the wrong IP information.

An example of a number scheme might be the case of having five regional offices, New York, Chicago, Los Angeles, Houston, and Miami. I know the network IDs for New York, Chicago, and Los Angeles are 10.10.0.0/16, 10.20.0.0/16, and 10.30.0.0/16. That may lead me to believe that Houston and Miami would be 10.40.0.0/16 and 10.50.0.0/16, respectively. I also know that office routers start at 1, so if the New York router is 10.10.0.1, the Houston router should be 10.40.0.1 or 10.50.0.1. If the Houston network ID is actually 10.70.0.0/16, and there are not actual 10.40.0.0/16 or 10.50.0.0/16 networks, my attempt to ping the Houston network using 10.40.0.1 would yield me a `Destination Net Unreachable` error message.

✦ `Request Timed Out`: When you receive this error message, it means that the packet was sent, but no response was ever received. This is the most common error message. Unfortunately, it does not tell you exactly what the issue is; rather, you did not get a response. The problem could be with your configuration, missing a default gateway or a router, or an incorrect subnet mask, so you are looking for other hosts on a remote segment, or expecting them to be on the local network segment when they are not supposed to be. Your Echo Request may be making it to the target host, but the target host is not configured correctly, so the target host cannot send a message back to you. The problem could also be with the address that you are trying to contact, in that it is not correct or changed without your knowing the new address.

The problem could also be a firewall issue, which may be blocking ICMP data yet allowing other data through. Finally, it could just be that the target host is too busy to respond. Even though an ICMP response is quick and easy, if a host is too busy, it will drop these packets because, after all, they are simply diagnostic messages and not really important.

✦ `Unknown Host`: This is not an ICMP error, but rather `ping` reporting a DNS error.

With your Windows-based `ping`, here are some additional options to examine. The most common ones are

✦ `ping -t www.cisco.com`: Ping until stopped with a break (Ctrl+C). This is useful when you are making configuration changes and want to see when they take effect, or if you are waiting for a system to reboot.

✦ `ping -n 15 www.cisco.com`: Ping for a specific number attempts, rather than the default four attempts.

✦ `ping -l 3000 www.cisco.com`: Specifies to send a larger payload. With Windows computers, 32 bytes are sent by default, and that is a portion of the alphabet repeated as many times as necessary. If you want to see the largest block of data you can send between two hosts without having IP fragment the packet, you can adjust the size and add the `-f` option. If the packet is fragmented, you will get a response like `Packet needs to be fragmented but DF set`.

✦ `ping -r 9 www.google.ca`: Specifies that you should list the routers along the path, up to a maximum of nine routers. This is an alternative to using `traceroute` (discussed in the next section), and it is interesting when compared with `traceroute` because it typically shows the IP addresses of the routers facing the target rather than you. The output of this command looks like the following:

Book II
Chapter 3

Working with ARP

```
Reply from 74.125.226.81: bytes=32 time=51ms TTL=55
    Route: 71.7.162.168 ->
           24.215.102.134 ->
           24.215.102.6 ->
           24.215.102.10 ->
           24.215.101.9 ->
           216.239.49.219 ->
           64.233.175.99 ->
           10.252.162.94 ->
           74.125.226.81
```

✦ `ping -i 10 www.cisco.com`: Sets the TTL flag on your outgoing ICMP Echo Request. This means that after the TTL hits 0, you get the error message about the packet expiring in transit. For your internal network, you may know how many routers you should pass through between two points, and using this option can let you closely identify the exact location of looping errors because you see what router expired the packet. With this option, you get either the expired message or a response from the target.

When you get the reply, it lists the TTL set by the remote host, and not the one you specified on your outgoing request.

✦ `ping -w 4000 www.wiley.com`: Sets the amount of time to wait for a reply before reporting that the `Request timed out`. The default time to wait is four seconds, which is sufficient for most well-connected networks. Some slow links, such as cellular or satellite connections, may require longer wait times.

If you are using your Cisco router, enter Privileged EXEC mode to gain access to the `ping` command. Here is an example of the output:

```
Router#ping www.cisco.com
Translating "www.cisco.com"...domain server (192.168.1.254) [OK]

Type escape sequence to abort.
Sending 5, 100-byte ICMP Echos to 72.163.4.161, timeout is 2 seconds:
!!!!!
Success rate is 100 percent (5/5), round-trip min/avg/max = 72/79/92 ms
```

Notice the series of exclamation marks in the output; these identify successful responses from the remote host. The following shows the periods of unsuccessful echo attempts:

```
Router#ping www.wiley.com
Translating "www.wiley.com"...domain server (192.168.1.254) [OK]

Type escape sequence to abort.
Sending 5, 100-byte ICMP Echos to 208.215.179.146, timeout is 2 seconds:
.....
Success rate is 0 percent (0/5)
```

traceroute/tracert

Although using `ping` can tell you whether a host is up, all the firewalls that block ICMP requests can make it tough to tell whether you have a correct address that you are attempting to communicate with.

Enter `traceroute`, which displays the routers that exist between you and the remote host that you are attempting to communicate with. Because this information is not found in the ICMP data, it ingeniously makes use of the expired TTL functionality of IP. `traceroute` sends three ICMP requests to the destination, but sets the TTL of the ICMP request to 1, which is set to 0 by the first router. The ICMP message that it receives telling it that the packet expired includes the routers address. It then sends three more requests with a TTL of one higher number until it successfully reaches the destination or hits 30 routers.

**Book II
Chapter 3**

Working with ARP

Although you use `traceroute` on a Cisco router and on a Linux computer, on a Windows computer, the `traceroute` command is shortened to the 8.3-naming convention as `tracert.exe` and has the following options:

```
C:\>tracert.exe

Usage: tracert [-d] [-h maximum_hops] [-j host-list] [-w timeout] target_name

Options:
    -d                 Do not resolve addresses to hostnames.
    -h maximum_hops    Maximum number of hops to search for target.
    -j host-list       Loose source route along host-list.
    -w timeout         Wait timeout milliseconds for each reply.
```

The basic `traceroute` command is something like this request to www. google.ca:

```
C:\>tracert.exe www.google.ca

Tracing route to www.l.google.com [74.125.226.81]
over a maximum of 30 hops:

  1    1 ms    1 ms    1 ms  fw1.edtetz.net [192.168.1.254]
  2   55 ms   23 ms   21 ms  blk-7-160-1.eastlink.ca [71.7.160.1]
  3   12 ms   25 ms    9 ms  skvl-asr2.eastlink.ca [24.222.226.165]
  4   27 ms   10 ms   11 ms  ns-hlfx-dr002.eastlink.ca [24.215.102.133]
  5   12 ms   33 ms   37 ms  ns-hlfx-br002.eastlink.ca [24.215.102.5]
  6   39 ms   16 ms   15 ms  ns-hlfx-br001.eastlink.ca [24.215.102.9]
  7   44 ms   38 ms   37 ms  google.eastlink.ca [24.215.101.10]
  8   37 ms   37 ms   34 ms  216.239.47.114
  9   37 ms   49 ms   38 ms  64.233.175.98
 10   50 ms   54 ms   39 ms  74.125.226.81

Trace complete.
```

In the following output, note that you see the time for each three responses at each router, with the * (on line 7) denoting a request that timed out. This lets you see if one router is overly busy, as it would have substantially higher response times. By default, the command also performs a reverse DNS lookup for each router IP address along the path. The DNS lookups provide you names for routers that have their names registered in DNS. The reverse DNS lookup function can be disabled with the –d option as shown here:

```
C:\>tracert.exe -d www.google.ca


Tracing route to www.l.google.com [74.125.226.81]
over a maximum of 30 hops:

    1     1 ms     1 ms     1 ms  192.168.1.254
    2    29 ms    45 ms    15 ms  71.7.160.1
    3     9 ms    26 ms    11 ms  24.222.226.165
    4     9 ms    13 ms     9 ms  24.215.102.133
    5     9 ms    13 ms     9 ms  24.215.102.5
    6    15 ms    11 ms    31 ms  24.215.102.9
    7    33 ms       *      35 ms  24.215.101.10
    8    71 ms    34 ms    33 ms  216.239.47.114
    9    32 ms    36 ms    32 ms  64.233.175.98
   10    34 ms    33 ms    36 ms  74.125.226.81

Trace complete.
```

Like with the `ping` command, you can also specify the maximum number of routers to pass through, as well as the amount of time to wait before failing the request packets.

If using a Cisco router, the `traceroute` command has a slightly different appearance to its output, but even though the format of the output is some-what different, `traceroute` provides all the same information:

```
Router#traceroute www.google.ca
Translating "www.google.ca"...domain server (192.168.1.254) [OK]

Type escape sequence to abort.
Tracing the route to www.l.google.com (74.125.226.84)

  1 fw1.edtetz.net (192.168.1.254) 4 msec 4 msec 0 msec
  2 blk-7-160-1.eastlink.ca (71.7.160.1) 32 msec 28 msec 28 msec
  3 skvl-asr2.eastlink.ca (24.222.226.165) 16 msec 12 msec 48 msec
  4 ns-hlfx-dr002.eastlink.ca (24.215.102.133) 24 msec 28 msec 8 msec
  5 ns-hlfx-br002.eastlink.ca (24.215.102.5) 8 msec 8 msec 8 msec
  6 ns-hlfx-br001.eastlink.ca (24.215.102.9) 44 msec 24 msec 12 msec
  7 google.eastlink.ca (24.215.101.10) 36 msec 36 msec 32 msec
  8 216.239.47.114 36 msec 32 msec 36 msec
  9 64.233.175.98 40 msec 32 msec 36 msec
 10 www.l.google.com (74.125.226.84) 36 msec 48 msec 32 msec
```

If you encounter a firewall that blocks your ICMP requests, you will find that at some point, all further requests time out. If you do not want to wait for it to complete the default 30 hops, you can cancel the trace by pressing Ctrl+C on a Windows computer or Ctrl+Shift+6 twice for your Cisco router.

PathPing

PathPing is a Windows utility that mixes the standard `ping` and `traceroute` commands. PathPing is useful for locating sporadic errors that occur along a path between two devices. In essence, it sends multiple `ping`s to each router along a path and then displays statistics on packet loss. You should note from the PathPing help info that many of the options are similar to the basic `ping` command:

```
C:\>pathping

Usage: pathping [-g host-list] [-h maximum_hops] [-i address] [-n]
                [-p period] [-q num_queries] [-w timeout] [-P] [-R] [-T]
                [-4] [-6] target_name

Options:
    -g host-list     Loose source route along host-list.
    -h maximum_hops  Maximum number of hops to search for target.
    -i address       Use the specified source address.
    -n               Do not resolve addresses to hostnames.
    -p period        Wait period milliseconds between pings.
    -q num_queries   Number of queries per hop.
    -w timeout       Wait timeout milliseconds for each reply.
    -P               Test for RSVP PATH connectivity.
    -R               Test if each hop is RSVP aware.
    -T               Test connectivity to each hop with Layer-2 priority tags.
    -4               Force using IPv4.
    -6               Force using IPv6.
```

The following options should be of interest:

✦ `-p`: Reduces the load on devices by waiting briefly between `ping` requests. This is different from the `-w` option, which identifies how long to wait before failing a request. This is the delay between successive ICMP requests.

✦ `-q`: Specifies the number of pings per hop in the path. The default is 100.

The default output of `pathping` looks similar to the following request to `www.google.ca`:

```
C:\>pathping -n www.google.ca

Tracing route to www.l.google.com [74.125.226.81]
over a maximum of 30 hops:
  0  192.168.1.137
  1  192.168.1.254
```

**Book II
Chapter 3**

Working with ARP

```
 2  71.7.160.1
 3  24.222.226.165
 4  24.215.102.133
 5  24.215.102.5
 6  24.215.102.9
 7  24.215.101.10
 8  216.239.47.114
 9  64.233.175.98
10  74.125.226.81

Computing statistics for 250 seconds...
                   Source to Here   This Node/Link
Hop  RTT    Lost/Sent = Pct    Lost/Sent = Pct   Address
 0                                                192.168.1.137
                                    0/ 100 =  0%    |
 1   1ms     0/ 100 =  0%       0/ 100 =  0%   192.168.1.254
                                    0/ 100 =  0%    |
 2   19ms    2/ 100 =  2%       2/ 100 =  2%   71.7.160.1
                                    0/ 100 =  0%    |
 3   15ms    0/ 100 =  0%       0/ 100 =  0%   24.222.226.165
                                    0/ 100 =  0%    |
 4   23ms    1/ 100 =  1%       1/ 100 =  1%   24.215.102.133
                                    0/ 100 =  0%    |
 5   14ms    0/ 100 =  0%       0/ 100 =  0%   24.215.102.5
                                    0/ 100 =  0%    |
 6   16ms    0/ 100 =  0%       0/ 100 =  0%   24.215.102.9
                                    0/ 100 =  0%    |
 7   42ms    0/ 100 =  0%       0/ 100 =  0%   24.215.101.10
                                    0/ 100 =  0%    |
 8   40ms    0/ 100 =  0%       0/ 100 =  0%   216.239.47.114
                                    1/ 100 =  1%    |
 9   39ms    1/ 100 =  1%       0/ 100 =  0%   64.233.175.98
                                    0/ 100 =  0%    |
10   38ms    1/ 100 =  1%       0/ 100 =  0%   74.125.226.81

Trace complete.
```

So to review that output, the `pathping` command starts with a summary of the path, and then provides your average response time and the number of packets that failed with their average for each node in the path. This process of multiple pings to each hop does take some time to generate.

Chapter 4: Preparing for the Advent of IPv6

In This Chapter

✔ Grasping the basic IPv6 address structure

✔ Collapsing, identifying, and assigning addresses

✔ Integrating with IPv4 and IPv6 networks

The first question you may ask about Internet Protocol version 6 (IPv6) is, "What is wrong with IPv4? Why do we need a new type of IP addressing structure?" Well, the answer is really a testament as to the popularity of the Internet. IPv4 has been around since the late 1970s when most computers were mainframes and minicomputers. Minicomputers tended to have a couple of network connections, but most devices — such as terminals and printers — were connected to it via serial connections. The expectation of the time was that if all the computers in the world started using TCP/IP, there would still be millions of addresses left available.

Well, who knew that 40 years later, not only would there be at least one computer in every household, but multiple computing devices that needed their own addresses, too. For example, my house has a media server, three media server front ends, five computers, three smartphones (with Wi-Fi), three iPods (with Wi-Fi), a Nintendo Wii, and a Microsoft Xbox, bringing my five-person household to 17 active IP addresses.

You look at private addresses in Chapter 1 of this minibook and Network Address Translation/Port Address Translation (NAT/PAT) in Book VI, Chapter 3 as alternatives to save addresses, but they do not work in every situation. Moving forward, you need a much bigger address space to work with, and that is the biggest gift IPv6 offers.

The transition to IPv6 was a slow one because it was conceived with a working IP name: Next Generation (IPng) in RFC 1550 in 1993. IPv6 underwent a few tweaks and was given the designation of IP version 6 (IPv6) in RFC 1883 in 1995. (IPv6 was used as the designation because IPv5 had already been assigned to another protocol that was being tested.) Over the years, IPv6 has been fine-tuned and supporting protocols have been designed and tested, with the largest hurdle being how to actually implement and migrate the world over to IPv6. Well, that has mostly been worked out; more products support IPv6, such as Microsoft Windows 7. In another 16 years or so, IPv6 will be standard.

I recommend having some concept as to what IPv6 is and how it works. It may still be quite a while before you are forced to move to IPv6 because of application requirements or your Internet service provider (ISP). Until that time, try not to sweat it too much. The change will happen eventually, and there is nothing to worry about. This chapter gives you the basic orientation that you need to prepare yourself for that time.

Reviewing Address Structure

When working with IPv4, you have a 32-bit address format broken into byte size units, or *octets*. IPv4 allows for a total of 4.3 billion addresses (2^{32}). After you get rid of special address spaces such as loopback, multicast, and reserved blocks, you have only about 3.7 billion addresses to work with. Of that, approximately 2.4 billion are already assigned to exiting users, so you do not end up with very many left for all the new people and their myriad of devices. Well, IPv6 increases that address space up to 128 bits, or 2^{128} addresses, or 3.4×10^{38} addresses. Now that *is* a lot. Check out Table 4-1, where it might make a little more sense.

Table 4-1	IPv4 and IPv6 Comparison	
	IPv4	*IPv6*
Bits	32	128
Octets	4	16
Binary address	10011101.10010001.111 11011.01101110	10011101.10000010.00010010.10010010. 00011101.00111011.10001101.11110001. 00111011.11000111.11000011.10001110. 11001111.00001111.00111110. 00001110
Alternate address display	157.145.251.110	9D82:1292:1D3B:8DF1:3BC7:C38E:CF0 F:3E0E
Total number of addresses	4.3×10^9	3.4×10^{38}

You may have noticed the rather odd-looking alternate IPv6 address in the table. That is done to keep you from getting a cramp in your hand when writing decimal numbers. This is *hex-colon notation,* which takes 16 bits and converts them to four hexadecimal numbers, rather than six decimal numbers in dotted-decimal notation. You can find a primer on other number systems in Book I, Chapter 3.

Collapsing Addresses

When working with IPv6 address, it can take a lot to write your addresses — after all, they are 128 bits long. To make life simpler, here are some rules you can use to condense this notation:

**Book II
Chapter 4**

Preparing for the
Advent of IPv6

✦ Leading zeros in the address are optional. So, for an address block, 0A45 would be equal to A45, and 0000 would be equal to 0.

✦ Multiple fields of zeros can be expressed as : :, but this can be done only once per address.

✦ An unknown or unspecified address, even in IPv4, is typed as all zeros; as such, it can be represented in IPv6 as : :.

Most addresses that you write can likely be compressed in some fashion. Table 4-2 shows some examples of this type of compression.

Table 4-2	IPv6 Address Reduction
IPv6 Address	*Simplified Notation*
FF01:0000:0000:0000:0000:0000:0000:0001	FF01::1
2031:0000:130F:0000:0000:09C0:876A:130B	2031:0:130F::9C0:876A:130B
0000:0000:0000:0000:0000:0000:0000:0001	::1
FE80:0000:0000:5EFE:0192.0168.0001.0123	FE80::5EFE:192.168.1.123
FE80: 0000:0000:0000:1585:4868:495F:D521	FE80::1585:4868:495F:D521

Identifying Special Addresses

With IPv4, you have seen that there may be special address groups that existed within the total IP address space. In addition to Class A, B, and C addressees, you also have the loopback address block (anything starting with 127) as well as multicast address space and Automatic Private IP

Addressing (APIPA) addresses. Well, IPv6 handles addresses a little differently. Within IPv6 are three main types of addresses, which are

✦ **Unicast:** A single unique address for a network interface. There are several types of unicast addresses, which I discuss in just a bit.

✦ **Multicast:** A one-to-many relationship in which the IP address is actually a group address and many devices can belong to the group. (See Chapter 1 in this minibook for more details). Unlike IPv4, there is no such thing as a broadcast address that is processed by every device on a network; instead, IPv6 relies on multicast and anycast addresses to be able to send data to more than a single unicast device on your network. Also, unlike IPv4, this new multicast address range is substantially larger than its predecessor, so it should be a long time before anyone runs into address limitations.

✦ **Anycast:** A one-to-nearest relationship using unicast addresses. The difference between this and normal unicast traffic is that multiple devices use the same address, similar to a multicast group address. Communication might start with a unicast packet being sent to a multicast address in which the device that is closest to the sender would answer the request. Anycast addresses are a perfect solution for load-balancing problems (such as a web server farm) because multiple devices can use and share the same address, and only one device will respond to network requests from each client device. Because anycast addresses are allocated from the unicast pool, the address format for them is the same as that of the unicast addresses.

When configuring network interfaces for IPv6, a single network interface could have a number of addresses associated with it. This may be a mixture of these address types. Within the unicast type there are three main address groups:

✦ **Global addresses:** These globally routable addresses are the addresses that are assigned by your ISP and include addresses in the 2000::/3 range. This range would include from 2000:: through to 39FF:FFFF:FFFF:F FFF:FFFF:FFFF:FFFF:FFFF. Global addresses represent about one-eighth of all IPv6 addresses, and the numbers are handed out by the IANA, as they are with IPv4.

✦ **Reserved addresses:** The Internet Engineering Task Force (IETF) reserved several addresses of the global address space to be implemented if it decides to introduce new features. This reserved space amounts to approximately 1 of every 256 IPv6 addresses.

✦ **Private addresses:** All private addresses start with FE in the first two positions of this address, followed by another digit from 8 to F. This could also be written as FE80::/9. Like with IPv4, these addresses cannot be routed over the Internet. These private addresses fall into these major categories:

- *Site-local addresses* are a section of the main private address space and include addresses in the FEC0::/10 block, which are all addresses that start with FE and have C, D, E, or F for their third character. These addresses are used to assigned IPv6 addresses to a site or organization (using an IPv6 DHCP server), and do not route outside that area or to the Internet. Internal routers forward data to these addresses on internal interfaces, but routers do not forward data to these out to the Internet. Because of a lack of definition around how site-local addresses were to be used, they were *deprecated* (marked and obsolete) in 2004, and replaced with a *unique-local address* in 2005.

  I continue to mention site-local addresses to you because, although deprecated, you will likely encounter the term from time to time and in older documentation.

- *Unique-local addresses* are designed for an organization to assign internal addresses across its organization. These addresses are defined by the FC00::/7 address block, with the second half of the block, FD00::/8, allocated for use on networks and a description for FC00::/8 address block still in the works. As with the description of site-local addresses, these addresses are for internal-use only and are never routed out to the Internet.

- *Local-link addresses* are similar to APIPA addresses, which I cover in Chapter 1 of this minibook, because they are self-generated and allow for IPv6 communications with other devices on that data link or network segment. These addresses all start with FE, and the third digit is 8, 9, A, or B, or FE80::/10. All IPv6 within a given data link that have local-link addresses can talk to each other. No routers, internal or external, forward traffic to or from these addresses.

Assigning Addresses

When assigning addresses to your IPv6 network cards, you need to know that just like IPv4 addresses (see Chapter 1 of this minibook), there is a network portion of the address and a host portion of the address. Both portions are 64-bits long, so the first 64-bits of an IPv6 address is the *network address* (sometimes referred to as a network ID or network prefix), and the last 64-bits of an IPv6 address is a *unique host ID* for the specific network ID. The four methods of assigning IPv6 addresses are

✦ **Manual Interface ID Assignment:** An address is manually assigned to an interface. This is fairly easy to do with most Cisco devices from the interface configuration with a command like

```
Router1(config-if)# ipv6 address 2001:DB8:1111:2222::54/64
```

As with any manual system, it is easy to assign one address to one interface; but you may not want to manually assign addresses to every device on your network manually.

✦ **EUI-64 Interface ID Assignment:** This is similar to a full manual address, but instead of specifying full address, you configure only the network portion of the address, and the remainder of the address is derived from the interface's Media Access Control (MAC) address. When configuring this from the interface prompt, the command looks like this:

```
Router1(config-if)# ipv6 address 2001:DB8:1111:2222::/64 eui-64
```

The MAC address on your network interface is a 48-bit number and may sometimes be referenced as MAC-48 to denote the length. Because the MAC address is a unique identifier, it can also be referred to as an Extended Unique Identifier (EUI) of 48-bits or EUI-48. *MAC* refers to a network interface identifier, whereas EUI-48 could be assigned to other devices. When designing IPv6, the designers wanted to have unique identifiers that were larger than the current EUI-48, so they lengthened the identifier to 64-bit and created the EUI-64 identifier. So an EUI-64 is simply a globally unique identifier.

This configuration makes address assignment much easier because all devices on the same data link share the same network ID, and all you need to have automatically assigned is the host ID, which is guaranteed unique because it is based on the already globally unique MAC address.

✦ **Stateless Auto-Configuration:** This is by far the easiest way to configure an IP address on an interface, allowing full automatic configuration. This configuration mode was created to allow all devices on the same data link to automatically configure themselves, reducing administrative overhead for the network administrators. In addition to full autoconfiguration, Stateless Auto-Configuration sends a request for a router advertisement (RA), which is used by the client as a 64-bit network ID prefix to the client's IP address. This means that if you have configured your routers with their 64-bit network IDs, your network devices use those network IDs; otherwise, all your network IDs for your internal network are assigned automatically. The 64-bit network ID could be a global or private address, but the remaining 64 bits of the address are chosen automatically by the client.

✦ **DHCPv6 (Stateful):** Dynamic Host Configuration Protocol (DHCP) servers that have the appropriate extensions installed for IPv6 can process DHCP address requests. This process for handing out addresses is similar to IPv4; the server is configured with an address pool to hand out, and it randomly fills the address requests from this pool. This process allows for complete control over the assigned client IP address, as well as being able to view the list of assigned addresses. In DHCPv6, the client first checks for a router advertisement; and if there is, the client is allowed to use DHCP. If there is no router or the router allows for DCHP, the client sends a multicast request to all DHCP agents on the network; if there are no router advertisements or DHCP responses, the client uses the local-link address.

Integration with IPv4

Because the entire world is currently running IPv4, one of the big questions that have been haunting the staff at IANA and IEFT is how to move people from IPv4 over to IPv6. It is not like they can just announce that on January 1 the Internet will use only IPv6. That just would not work. So instead, they had to come up with a way to slowly migrate people to the new addressing scheme while allowing them to keep everything that they currently have in place. To that goal, there are three basic methods of compatibility:

✦ **Dual-stack:** In dual-stack configuration, the device is configured for both IPv4 and IPv6 network stacks like the routers in Figure 4-1. The dual-stack configuration can be implemented on a single interface or with multiple interfaces. In this configuration, the device decides how to send the traffic based on the destination address of the other device.

As of IOS 12.2(2), Cisco is IPv6-ready. To support dual-stack routing on a single interface, you need to configure IPv6 on your routing device. The following commands allow for forwarding of IPv6 data packets:

```
Router1> enable
Router1# configure terminal
Router1(config)# ipv6 unicast-routing
Router1(config)# interface ethernet0
Router1(config-if)# ip address 192.168.75.1 255.255.255.0
Router1(config-if)# ipv6 address 2123:AFFF::192:168:75:1/120
Router1(config-if)# exit
Router1(config)# exit
Router1# copy running-config startup-config
```

✦ **Tunneling:** Tunneling refers to passing IPv6 data over an IPv4 network by placing the IPv6 packet into the data section of an IPv4 packet, as shown in Figure 4-2. The four main types of tunneling are

• *Manual IPv6-to-IPv4 tunneling* encapsulates an IPv6 packet in an IPv4 packet. So as to not fragment the packet from adding the IPv4 header to it, the data packet needs to be reduced by 20 bytes if the IPv4 has an optional protocol field, or 20 octets if it does not, as well as require routers support both IP stacks.

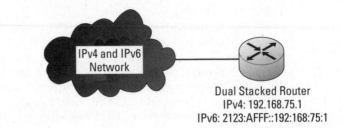

Figure 4-1:
Two options
for a dual-
stacked
router.

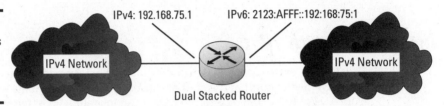

- *Dynamic 6-to-4 tunneling* routes data between islands of IPv6 routers across your network.

- *Intra-Site Automatic Tunnel Addressing Protocol (ISATAP) tunneling* uses the existing IPv4 network as the link layer of the IPv6 network and routes the data between the IP networks via routers supporting both IP stacks.

- *Teredo tunneling* performs the tunneling work at the dual-stacked host on either end of the connection rather than at a gateway router.

Figure 4-2:
IPv6 data
being
tunneled
over an IPv4
network.

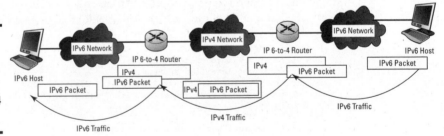

✦ **Proxying and translation (NAT-PT)**: Network Address Translation-Protocol Translation (NAT-PT) places a translation mechanism on the network, which translates traffic going back and forth between IPv4 and IPv6.

With these methods available to companies, ISPs, and users, the path to migrate your network to IPv6 does not need to be long or difficult.

Book III

Switching

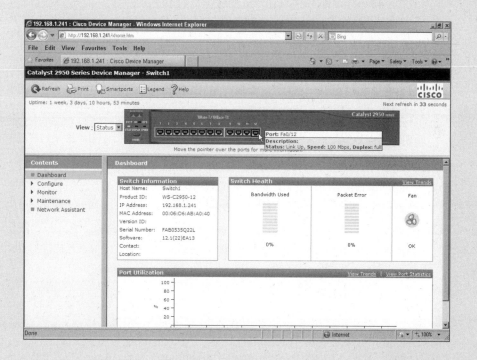

Contents at a Glance

Chapter 1: Reviewing the Enterprise LAN

In This Chapter

✔ Checking out features that make up the enterprise LAN

✔ Looking at Cisco hardware options for your LAN

✔ Reviewing standard features of switches

✔ Evaluating Cisco service options

Most organizations have a LAN, but what makes a LAN an enterprise LAN is the level of reliance that the organization has on that network. When an organization has a high reliance on the LAN, high-quality equipment with redundant features is used on the network to reduce the chance of interruption to the services provided to the organization's users. Cisco has an Enterprise category in their product catalog that provides numerous products supporting enterprise LAN.

In this chapter, I introduce you to the features that make up an enterprise LAN, which include such features as Spanning Tree Protocol (STP), VLAN Trunking Protocol (VTP), and EtherChannel. In addition, I show you some basics about how this technology works and the standards that relate to these technologies.

If your network is small, you may be interested in only a few of these features, but if you have more than one switch and thus more than 50 network devices, you will likely make use of the data in this minibook.

Although I introduce you to features of the enterprise LAN in this chapter, you will gather further knowledge on the subject by reading the rest of the chapters in this minibook.

Identifying Features of an Enterprise LAN

Certain features clearly identify an enterprise LAN. In my job, I see networks large enough to be considered enterprise LANs, except that, for reasons of their own, the administrators decided not to implement any of the real features of an enterprise LAN — perhaps because setting up an enterprise LAN can be complicated and, frankly, one heck of a lot of work.

Most of the features of an enterprise LAN take a bit of planning and configuration, but once you have them set up, you should find that implementing them is not very complicated at all.

So what features or characteristics will enable you to really call your network an enterprise LAN? Some of those features include the following:

✦ **Number of nodes:** One significant factor that can identify an enterprise LAN is the number of devices on your network. On the other hand, I have seen enterprise-LAN-sized networks, in terms of the number of nodes that were not managed as an enterprise LAN, so using the number of nodes as the sole criterion for an enterprise LAN is ill-advised. What is the magic number of nodes; is it 100, 200, 500, 1,000, 5,000? The answer to that question is still open for discussion, but even on networks as small as 200, you can implement the enterprise-class features listed in this bulleted list. If you have hit 5,000 nodes, I *really* hope that you have implemented the features in this bulleted list already.

✦ **Managed devices:** I am more inclined to call your network an enterprise LAN if you deploy managed switches on your network. However, it is not enough to have managed devices — you really need to be managing them. Cisco has a line of unmanaged switches that you can deploy on small networks, but when you use unmanaged devices, you will not be deploying any of the enterprise LAN features. So, the first step on your path to an enterprise LAN is to deploy managed devices.

✦ **Virtual LAN (VLAN):** A VLAN allows you to create many smaller logical networks over the area of your physical LAN. This allows you to create groupings of devices and isolate them from each other, thereby enabling you to control traffic from one VLAN to another VLAN through routers. You will even be able to filter traffic and control data flow among these network segments. In the past, this separation of network devices could have been managed only in a less flexible static solution using physical switches.

✦ **Spanning Tree:** Loops are common on your network when you have deployed a large number of switches, but when a loop is created, it can stop all traffic until the loop is removed. Sometimes the network administrator causes these by making mistakes in the wiring closet; other times, loops can occur when a user has access to multiple network ports, but has a lack of knowledge about them. The enterprise solution to protect you from loops in your network is Spanning Tree Protocol (STP), which is only implemented on manage network devices. STP evaluates all the devices connected to a network, and if it identifies a network loop, it shuts down (or actually just blocks) a network port on your managed device. This prevents loops from being an issue on your enterprise LAN.

✦ **Port-based security settings:** Most enterprise LAN switches allow you to implement some level of security around your switch port access. This may involve limiting the number of devices attached or forcing the user to log on before being allowed to use the data network.

✦ **EtherChannel:** Single links connecting your switches together may cause bottlenecks, so technologies such as EtherChannel and LinkAggregation allow you to combine multiple links or ports so that they act as a single, larger link.

When implemented, these features help move your small LAN into an enterprise LAN. As I said, many people are afraid to implement these features, often simply because of a fear of the unknown. Implementing some or all of these will make your network more redundant and self-correcting, allowing you to have a more reliable and trouble-free network.

Working with Cisco Switching Technologies

Cisco offers a wide variety of products to meet your switching needs on your network:

✦ **Small-to-medium business products:** These tend to be scaled down enterprise products that offer a smaller set of features at a lower price point for cost conscious small business owners. The products in this category often come with simplified management tools because many small business clients do not have Cisco management expertise in-house. Usually, you will find the high end of this product set is actually the low end of the Classical enterprise products.

✦ **Classical enterprise products:** Cisco already has a major presence in the enterprise market, which has supported Cisco for most of its life as a corporation. In this product range, you find very powerful and reliable devices capable of supporting the largest of enterprises without fail. If you walk into any large organization that depends on its network to support its business operations, you will likely find that the network infrastructure is dominated by Cisco enterprise equipment.

✦ **Carrier-grade products:** As a reader of this book, I venture to guess that you are not in the carrier-grade market. This market includes telephone carriers who cannot afford any downtime on their networks. The amount of traffic that needs passed by these high-traffic network users comes at a price that even many enterprises are not willing to pay.

The following two sections describe small-to-medium business products and classical enterprise products, respectively; carrier-grade products are beyond the scope of this book.

**Book III
Chapter 1**

Reviewing the
Enterprise LAN

Small-to-medium business products

In the small-to-medium business part of the product line, Cisco offers the following:

+ **100 Series:** This series ranges from 5-port 10/100 switches up to 24-port 10/100/1000 switches in either a desktop or rack mount configuration. These switches are unmanaged, which means they lack all of the advanced functionality that enterprise LANs require.

+ **200 Series:** These switches come in configurations that support from 18 to 50 ports up to gigabit speeds. These switches start the product lines moving toward management by supporting QoS priority queues and 802.1x network authentication. This series supports some of the enterprise features, but not them all.

+ **300 Series:** Provides even more management capabilities. These switches support 24- or 48-port configurations and allow for complex Access Control Lists (ACLs) for security, inter-VLAN routing, and basic VLAN implementations. Although these switches are not ready to support a large enterprise, they have a subset of the features that the enterprise products will have.

+ **Cisco Catalyst 2960 series:** At the top of the small business market is a series of mid-range enterprise LAN switches, which support full management and come in configurations from 8 ports to 48 ports. In addition to functionality of the 300 series, these switches offer Power over Ethernet (PoE) on up to 48 ports, stacking options, and 10GB uplink ports. Stacking allows for high-speed connections between switches through a single management interface. These switches also support Layer 3 switching.

Classical enterprise products

When moving up into the purely enterprise class devices, here are a few key product classes:

+ **Catalyst Compact Switches:** Cisco has a new line of Catalyst Compact Switches sporting up to 12 ports of gigabit connectivity and PoE ports. These switches are physically smaller than other enterprise Catalyst switches and have reduced power requirements that will save you money and a fanless construction, which means that they can reside in user areas with few complaints about noise.

+ **Catalyst 2960 Switches:** This series of fixed configuration switches offers 24 to 48 ports of Fast Ethernet or Gigabit Ethernet connectivity. They support Power over Ethernet (PoE) and come with fixed power supplies. Because of their features and price, they are the workhorses of many enterprise networks. The largest of these switches, the 4510R, is a 10-slot chassis that holds two controllers and up to eight line cards.

Each line card can contain up to 48 ports, which gives you a huge 384-port switch.

✦ **Catalyst 3560-X Series Switches and Catalyst 3560-E Series Switches:** These series of switches offer 24 to 48 ports of Gigabit Ethernet and PoE connectivity. This switch offers enhancements over the Catalyst 2960 Series by supporting a larger set of IOS features and dual redundant power supplies. Dual power supplies increase its availability because it can continue to operate in the case of a single power supply failure.

✦ **Catalyst 4500E Series Switches:** The largest of this series of enterprise switches is the 4510R. This 10-slot chassis holds two controllers and up to eight line cards. Each line card can contain up to 48 ports, which gives you a huge 384-port switch. Unlike standalone switches, these modular switches offer benefits in large-scale wiring closets where you only need to install and supply power to a single chassis in order to support a huge number of switch ports.

✦ **Catalyst 6500 Series Switches:** Designed for the core of your network, Cisco's core and distribution switches take it up another step in the form of the Catalyst 6500 Series Switches with its 13-slot 6513-E switches occupying 21 rack units in a communications cabinet. These powerhouse switches operate across network layers from 2 to 4, performing more functions than your standard level two switches.

Cisco provides switching products scaling from the smallest of organizations to the largest of enterprises. It is likely that your organization will fall somewhere within that range.

Examine the whole Cisco catalog online at www.cisco.com to review the products and evaluate what will work best for you.

Reviewing Switching Standards

When shopping for your switch, you will find that a lot of feeds and speeds are mentioned. In this section, I introduce you to many of the terms you will see in switch specifications. Rather than stalling, I will dive right in.

✦ **Ports:** Ethernet (10 Mbps, not likely any more), Fast Ethernet (100 Mbps), Gigabit Ethernet (1 Gbps), and 10 Gigabit Ethernet (10 Gbps) speeds, using connectors such as RJ45 copper, Fiber (such as LC connectors), and more likely, Small Form-Factor Pluggable (SFP) and Small Form-Factor Pluggable Plus (SFP+), with the latter allowing you to mix and match connector types through pluggable connectors.

✦ **Stacking:** There is always some way of connecting switches together to make a large network segment. You can always connect them via front side data ports, but many switches support high-speed stacking solutions using special ports and cables. Cisco's current stacking solution is FlexStack, which offers a 40 Gbps connection between switches and allows all switches in a stack to be managed as if they are one switch. If you are concerned about network throughput and switching speed, when purchasing your switches, ensure that they support a common stacking solution and purchase the gear that you require to implement the solution, which may involve interface cards and technology-specific cables.

✦ **PoE and PoE+:** Power over Ethernet (PoE) allows you to provide power to remote devices over the same connection that you are providing data services. This allows for simplified deployments for IP-based phones for your telephony infrastructure or when deploying wireless access points. Both phones and access points can have all of their power needs met by a PoE switch. Standard PoE will supply up to 15.4 watts per port, whereas PoE+ is capable of supplying 30 watts per port. A PoE switch will cost you more than a non-PoE switch, but if you are considering an IP telephony deployment in the near future, you should consider the extra cost as an investment in the future.

✦ **Power supplies:** There are a few options for powering your switches. Cisco has standard switches that have universal power supplies that accept standard utility power, between 110 or 240 volts, but you should check the rating on the power supply before connecting it to your power source. Cisco also has switches that take only 12-volt power. In some cases, companies have changed their communications racks over to 12-volt power in places such as ships. Figure 1-1 shows a power connector. Power supplies in some switches are fixed rather than modular (and hot swappable). If a fixed power supply in a switch becomes defective, you will have to replace the switch with a new one, whereas models of switches that have modular power supplies allow you to replace a defective power supply in seconds rather than replacing the entire switch. Modular power supplies typically are found only on the larger, more expensive switches and chassis-based systems.

Another consideration is whether the switch has — or supports — single or dual power supplies. Dual power supplies give you some level of redundancy in the event of a failed power supply. Some switches also support a Redundant Power Supply (RPS) system, which uses a 12-volt power supply system through special RPS power connectors.

✦ **USB storage:** Some of the new switches on the market sport a USB connector for storage. This gives you another option for backing up configurations or installing IOS and software upgrades.

Figure 1-1:
A secondary DC power supply input on a Cisco Catalyst 2950 switch.

✦ **Uplink:** Similar to the stacking options I just mentioned, switches will often have special-purpose ports on the front to allow for interconnecting your switches. These are sometimes higher speed ports than the other ports on the switch or allow for flexible connections through SFP slots.

✦ **Port bonding:** Book III, Chapter 7, covers EtherChannel, which allows you to treat multiple ports as a single data transfer unit. Port bonding makes use of two main technologies, Port Aggregation Protocol (PAgP) and Link Aggregation Control Protocol (LACP).

✦ **Media-Dependent Interface Crossover (MDIX):** The standard cable that you use to connect your computer to a switch is called a straight-through cable because the eight wires in the connector on one end of the cable match up with the eight wires on the connector at the other end of the cable. A crossover cable swaps the position of two of the wires on the connector at one end of the cable (connecting the send wire on the end of the cable to the receive wire on the other end of the cable). Older switches use straight-through cables to connect end-user computing devices, while requiring a crossover cable for switch-to-switch links. All of your newer switches support *medium dependent* *interface crossover* (MDIX) or Auto-MDIX, which detects whether a straight-through or crossover connection is required for the device as it is connected. This means that you no longer need to worry about special cables for your inter-switch connections.

✦ **802.1x authentication:** 802.1x is a standardized authentication protocol. It enables you to implement port-based security requiring users to log on or authenticate before being allowed to send data on the network switchport.

✦ **Port-Base ACLs:** Access Control Lists (ACLs) allow you to control where devices connected to a switchport are able to send their data or what other devices they are able to communicate with on the network.

✦ **SSH:** Telnet is standard remote access protocol for switch management, but it is not a secure communication method. Secure Shell (SSH) is a secure communication protocol that should be used for all switches.

✦ **SNMPv3:** There have been several versions of SNMP, with version 3 being the latest. Version 3 supports additional security and authorization features.

✦ **TACACS+ and RADIUS:** If you are implementing 802.1x authentication, you need a source of accounts to authenticate against. This authentication source will be a Terminal Access Controller Access-Control System (TACACS+) or Remote Authentication Dial In User Service (RADIUS) server.

✦ **QoS:** Quality of Service (QoS) controls the speed of data transmission by a series of rating data and queuing of rated data. This allows important traffic to move through the network faster than unimportant traffic.

✦ **Forwarding bandwidth:** A rating of the speed at which data can be forwarded to the destination port.

✦ **Flash and DRAM memory:** Both of these represent the amount of storage in your switch, either to store your IOS software image or as processing memory.

✦ **Maximum VLANs:** The highest number of VLANs that are supported by the device. This may be as low as eight or into the thousands, with 256 being fairly common.

✦ **VLAN IDs:** Separate from the number of VLANs supported is the range of IDs that can be used. Typically, even if a switch supports only eight VLANs, it will support VLAN IDs from one to 4096. Therefore, the eight VLANs a switch would use may have VLAN IDs of 5, 250, 1495, and 3750.

✦ **MTU:** The Maximum Transmission Unit (MTU) is the largest frame that the switch will support passing on the network. All switches support the standard Ethernet II frame size of 1500 bytes.

✦ **Jumbo frames:** Some switches will support jumbo frames, which are oversized data frames — up to 9000 bytes, depending on hardware. These are used for specialized purposes such as iSCSI storage area networks (SANs).

✦ **Forwarding rate:** Similar to the forwarding bandwidth, the forwarding rate is measured in million packets per second (mpps).

✦ **Unicast MAC addresses:** A switch address database has a limited size. For small switches, you may want to ensure that the switch will be capable of holding all of the addresses that are attached to the switch's network segment. This is not typically a problem unless you have overly large network segments running into the thousands.

✦ **List of standards:** Usually the information on the switch's data sheet or specification sheet will have a laundry list of standards that the switch supports. Scan this information for any technologies that you really care about.

✦ **List of compliant RFCs:** All standards around the TCP/IP are documented in a series of documents called Request for Comments (RFC). Similar to the previous item, your switch will support several standard protocols and features that are found in the RFCs. Review this list for important requirements that you may have.

The list you have just reviewed represents the major points or features on which you will want to evaluate your switches for purchase. This selection or evaluation process is a task that I regularly perform when selecting products that will match a customer's environment. That process will start by evaluating their goals and requirements and then identifying which products have the features that they require. When ranking the possible products, the switch characteristics from the previous list play a role in what product makes it through the final selection process.

Purchasing Support

When purchasing a Cisco product, you do not need to purchase Cisco service options. If you run into issues when you get the switch unboxed and are attempting to connect it to your network, you may wish you had purchased support. I cover the major levels of support from Cisco in this section.

Cisco SMARTnet Service

This is the premier level of service for enterprise customers of Cisco. It provides IT staff immediate access to Cisco support engineers and a range of online resources. If you have a problem on your network that you are not able to resolve, this fast and efficient access to Cisco resources will be a great benefit. Some of the features included in Cisco SMARTnet Service include

✦ Around-the-clock, global access to Cisco's Technical Assistance Center (TAC)

✦ Unrestricted access to the extensive Cisco.com knowledge base and tools

✦ Next-business-day, 8x5x4, 24x7x4, or 24x7x2 advance hardware replacement and onsite parts replacement and installation available, depending on options purchased. 8x5x4 means that you call support 8 hours a day, 5 days a week, and you have a replacement product within 4 hours, the other times listed work the same way. As these levels reduce your downtime, your cost for the coverage goes up.

✦ Ongoing operating system software updates within the licensed feature set

Cisco Smart Foundation Service

This is a reduced service level from the Cisco SMARTnet Service. This support offering is aimed at small-to-medium size businesses that do not have the requirement to have all network services running around the clock and can manage with the reduced window of access to Cisco support services. The features included in Cisco Smart Foundation Service include

✦ Next-business-day advance hardware replacement as available

✦ Access to Small Medium Business (SMB) Technical Assistance Center (TAC) during business hours (access levels vary by region)

✦ Access to Cisco's SMB knowledge base

✦ Online technical resources through Smart Foundation Portal

✦ Operating system software bug fixes and patches

Cisco Smart Care Service

This support option is only available in North America and Europe and is aimed toward small and medium size businesses. The service offering provides a higher level of service through proactive health checks conducted on your network. This allows for a higher level of network availability and reduced downtime through proactive network management. The features included in Cisco Smart Care Service include

✦ Network-level coverage for the needs of small and medium-sized businesses

✦ Proactive health checks and periodic assessments of Cisco network foundation, voice, and security technologies

✦ Technical support for eligible Cisco hardware and software through Smart Care Portal

✦ Cisco operating system and application software updates and upgrades

✦ Next-business-day advance hardware replacement as available, 24x7x4 option available

Cisco SP Base Service

Through the available support options, Cisco SP Base Service will assist you with problem resolution from simple problem to complex problems. With this service, you will be able to increase network availability and reduce network downtime. This is important to keep your mission critical applications running. The features included in Cisco SP Base Service are

✦ Around-the-clock, global access to the Cisco TAC

✦ Registered access to Cisco.com

✦ Next-business-day, 8x5x4, 24x7x4, and 24x7x2 advance hardware replacement. Return to factory option available.

✦ Ongoing operating system software updates

When purchasing your support options, pay attention to the software updates. The base service gives you software updates for the operating system, but not necessarily for other software that may be included on your router. So if your switch comes with other software components, such as integrated switch management software, they may not be included in the software updates. Moreover, when working with a product like the Cisco Adaptive Security Appliance (ASA), in addition to the IOS installed on the ASA, you have VPN client software and the Adaptive Security Device Manager (ASDM), which you will likely want to upgrade; however, the Cisco SP Base Service and Smart Foundation Service cover updates only to the IOS.

**Book III
Chapter 1**

**Reviewing the
Enterprise LAN**

Chapter 2: Switching Basics

In This Chapter

✔ **Viewing the switch's location in the OSI model**

✔ **Seeing how a switch forwards traffic**

✔ **Booting your switch into operation**

✔ **Connecting client devices to your switch**

*P*revious chapters in this book explain where switches fit into the overall structure of the enterprise environment. In this chapter and the remainder of this minibook, you are introduced to advanced configuration of the switch.

In particular, this chapter covers how the switch functions in the OSI network model, as well as the methods the switch uses to forward traffic. You also look at the following:

✦ The benefits of the full duplex operation

✦ How a switch can speed up traffic over the operation of a hub

✦ The power-up process of the switch and what all of the status lights on the front of the unit mean

✦ The process of connecting client devices to the switch

The next chapter in Book III walks you through the configuration process, and the rest of the chapters in this minibook take you through the configuration process, both the basic configuration and some of the advanced configuration topics, such as VLANs, Spanning Tree Protocol, and EtherChannel.

Switching and the OSI Model

As you may now be aware, switching fits into the OSI model at Layer 2. If this surprises you, read Book I, Chapters 1 and 4. With switching and bridging happening at Layer 2, they deal with the MAC address information found in the Ethernet frames. If you go down to Layer 1, a device such as a repeater or hub simply takes the electrical impulse on the wire and amplifies the signal. A switch, on the other hand, reads the Ethernet frame into memory, reconstructs it, and retransmits it out of the destination port (or all ports, in the case of a broadcast frame).

Switches support the following three basic types of forwarding mechanisms:

✦ **Store-and-forward switching:** A process by which the switch reads the entire Ethernet frame into memory before examining it, at which time the switch will identify the destination address and make a forwarding decision. This type of switching provides two benefits: The switch is assured of a complete frame and no collision will occur on the network before sending the data. The drawback is a slight delay on forwarding of the data.

✦ **Cut-through switching:** With this process, a forwarding decision is made as soon as enough of the frame is read, which can be as little as 17 bytes of data past the preamble. From that much data, the switch can identify the difference among Ethernet II, IEEE 802.3, IEEE 802.2, and Ethernet_SNAP frame types. After this difference is identified, the process of forwarding the frame to its destination can begin. Depending on the type of frame and the use of Access Control Lists (ACLs), a total of 54 bytes of data can be read. This condition can significantly reduce the delay in forwarding data to its destination, because without the store-and-forward delay, you can approach true wire speed. The problem occurs when you experience a collision on your network for a data frame that is partially forwarded, making the work done forwarding the frame useless. This issue is mitigated on networks that are entirely switched because collisions will occur only when you have two or more devices connected with a hub (covered in Book I, Chapter I) that is then connected to a port on a switch. By eliminating hubs on your network, you eliminate collisions.

✦ **Fragment-free switching:** This process is similar to cut-through, with the exception that the forwarding decision is not made until the first 64 bytes of the data frame are read and are collision free. After 64 bytes are read, the switch has enough data to forward a legal frame because Ethernet requires frames to be at least 64 bytes. On a fully switched network, this process does not provide a benefit over cut-through switching. However, if the chance for collisions is high, this process is preferable to cut-through switching because it prevents forwarding frames that are less than the minimum Ethernet size. (These illegally sized frames are called *runts*.)

Both switching methods that forward data before the entire frame is read into the switch have a critical flaw when dealing with the integrity of the Ethernet frame. The last piece of data is the FCS, or Frame CheckSum, which is used to verify that the Ethernet frame that has arrived at the switch has not been altered or changed through a network error. Because the switch has not read the entire frame, the switch is not able to calculate a checksum or compare it to the FCS found at the end of the frame. Frames with a failed checksum should not be forwarded; but in this case, most of the switch has already been forwarded by the time the switch knows the checksum is wrong.

Because of the speed of the current switches, you will likely find that most switches on the market, like Cisco's switches, use the store-and-forward method of passing data because the new speeds of moving data internally in the switch outweigh the cost of forwarding bad data.

Communicating with Duplex/Simplex

The terms *duplex* and *full duplex* are synonyms, as are *simplex* and *half duplex*. A simplex device is not capable of sending and receiving data at the same time. Think of the old CB radios or most of the FRS radios on the market. These devices can transmit your voice, or they can listen to the other people on the channel, but they are not able to do both at the same time, ever. The same is true for half duplex or simplex devices. These devices are only capable of sending or receiving data at any given time, so they are constantly changing from sending to receiving. This prevents them from sending data as fast as they possibly can, because after sending data, they need to wait for responses from the target systems.

The other option, *full duplex,* or *duplex,* enables network devices to send and receive data at the same time and to send it continuously, because they can receive responses to the sent packets as they are returned. When dealing with inter-switch links, or connections between switches, full duplex is the way the links need to be configured.

Using half duplex links between switches will have a grave impact on your data throughput. For example, if your network is composed of two switches with your clients' computers on one switch, your servers on the other, and the ports linking the two switches are set to half duplex, you have a recipe for disaster. Similar to a repaving project where traffic in both directions shares one lane on the road, as traffic queues up to pass over the one-way-at-a-time link between the switches, the clients' devices on one switch will constantly be delayed trying to "talk" to the servers on the opposite switch. I have seen networks where this has been the case, and simply changing the switches to full duplex on that inter-switch link dramatically changes the performance of the network.

Colliding and Broadcasting

Book I, Chapter 4 examines the concept of collisions on a network. However, permit me to reiterate. A *collision* occurs on your network when something happens to the data sent from the physical network medium that prevents it from reaching its destination. Mainly, it encounters another signal from another host on the network that yields a resulting useless signal on the network when the signals combine. The collision occurs when the sending device does not receive a clear response back within the allotted time. This causes an issue for both network devices because they both need to wait for an ever-increasing period until they are able to transmit the data clearly. If the network is busy enough, the network devices can spend an inordinate amount of time retransmitting data.

A collision can only occur at the physical layer in the OSI model (see Book I, Chapter 4). When multiple devices share a common media at the physical layer, which happens when you have multiple devices connected with a hub, there is a possibility that you will have a collision. The network area where a collision may occur is called a *collision domain*.

So, what benefit do you get from the switch? The switch acts like a multi-port bridge that, yes, *bridges* two collision domains. What happens with the introduction of the bridge? The bridge breaks the network into two or more pieces, with each piece being a separate collision domain. Fewer network devices in a collision domain reduce the chance of a collision, just like fewer cars on a street reduce the chance of an accident. Figure 2-1 shows a network before and after a bridge is added. The addition of the bridge reduces the collisions on the network by reducing the number of devices sharing either portion of the shared media. No special configuration is required to implement a switch or bridge onto your network, and since it is so easy to implement this product, I will introduce you to the flow of traffic in this scenario.

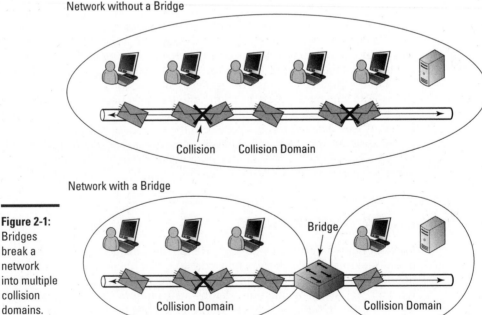

Network without a Bridge

Collision   Collision Domain

Network with a Bridge

Figure 2-1:
Bridges
break a
network
into multiple
collision
domains.

Bridge

Collision Domain   Collision Domain

Broadcast domains

In addition to hearing network support professionals talking about collision domains, you will hear them talk about broadcast domains, too. A broadcast is a message sent to a data link address of FF:FF:FF:FF:FF:FF. All devices on a network that see the same broadcast are part of the same broadcast domain. Because the broadcast is sent to a data link layer component, all the devices that have a common or shared data link layer will see it. Ports on a bridge or a switch are on the same data link, so they are all in the same broadcast domain. Adding a switch to a network does not reduce the number of devices that see a broadcast. To do that, you need to move up a layer in the OSI model and add a router to your network. Each port on a router will connect to a different broadcast domain, and broadcasts sent over the data link layer on one port of the router will not be seen by devices connected to the other ports.

1. A network host sends an Ethernet frame destined for another host.

2. Regardless of where the destination host is, the bridge looks at the source address of the frame, and if the bridge does not recognize the MAC address of the source host, the bridge records the MAC address in the bridge's Address Database, which includes the port on which the address is found.

3. The bridge looks at the destination MAC address in the Ethernet frame and does one of the following.

   - If the bridge does not know where the destination host is, it will flood the frame out to all ports on the bridge.

   - If the bridge does know where the destination host is, it will send the frame out on the port on which the destination host is located, unless it is the port on which the frame originally came from, as the destination host will already have received the frame.

4. The data should arrive at the host to which it was targeted, and the destination host will send data back to the original source host. At this point, if the bridge did not know where this host was, Step 2 will place the original destination host's MAC address in the Address Database.

The great thing about switches and bridges is that they require almost no configuration to function. If you have a heavily congested network, adding a switch to the middle of the network reduces the collision rate on the network (refer to Figure 2-1) and you achieve an increase in network performance and throughput. This process has no impact on your network layer protocols because it takes place at Layer 2, and your network-level devices (Layer 3) will not see any difference in the traffic that they see. If you replace your network hubs with switches, each network device will be in a collision domain by itself, and your rate of collisions should reduce to zero.

Book III
Chapter 2

Switching Basics

Powering Up Your Switch

The first step on getting a switch integrated into a network is to get it powered up. There are several options for getting power to your switch, but the most common is the universal power cords used on enterprise products — the same power cord you find on your IT equipment and computers.

Some switches have power switches, whereas many switches are fixed to power up as soon as the power plug is attached to the system.

Viewing status lights

When you power up your switch, several things happen, and the status lights on the front of the unit tell you what is going on. (They are similar to the lights that show up briefly on your dashboard when you start your car to let you know what is working.) Every LED lights temporarily and then goes out. The system (SYST) LED turns to amber, as do all the switch ports that have devices connected. Then the Power On Self Test (POST) process takes place, which may require some time if you are dealing with a large switch. You may see LEDs flash during the POST process, but this is normal.

When the switch successfully completes the POST process, the SYST and status (STAT) LEDs become green. Switch ports that have devices remain amber for a period because Spanning Tree Protocol (STP), which is enabled by default, is in *Learning* mode (a feature of STP covered in Book III, Chapter 6) on those ports before they transition to green and allow forwarding of traffic. After these lights transition to green, your switch will be fully up and running.

Typically, a group of LEDs with a Mode selector button is on the left side of the Cisco switch, as shown in Figure 2-2. Press the button, and you see that the mode LEDs cycle through STAT, UTIL, DUPLX, and SPEED. With the change in the mode LED, you may see a change in the switch port LEDs.

✦ **SYST:** If SYST is off, the switch is off; if green, the switch is operating normally; if amber, the switch is not functioning properly, which is the case during the boot process.

✦ **RPS:** If RPS is off, a Redundant Power Supply (RPS) has not been installed or is turned off. If solid green, an RPS is connected and ready to provide power in the event of a failure of the main power supply. If flashing green, the RPS is connected but currently unavailable because of powering another device. If solid amber, the RPS has a fault or is in standby mode. If flashing amber, the RPS is functioning, and the main power supply in the switch has failed.

Figure 2-2:
The Mode button will tell you more about your switch status.

✦ **STAT:** When STAT is selected, you see the status of the actual switch ports. If the switch port is off, there is no link. If the switch port is solid green, a link is present. If the switch port is flashing green, there is activity on the port. If the switch port is alternating green and amber, there is a link problem, such as excessive errors. If the switch port is solid amber, the port has been disabled. A port may be disabled automatically by a policy, manually by the administrator, or because of Spanning Tree Protocol (STP).

After you bring a port up, it could be amber for up to 30 seconds because of Spanning Tree Protocol (STP).

✦ **UTIL:** When UTIL is selected, you see the status of the actual switch ports. This one is a little complicated. When using this mode, all of the switch ports on the front of your switch are used like a big bar graph using a logarithmic scale. The green lights represent current backplane utilization. If the lights are amber, you are looking at the maximum backplane utilization since the switch was powered on. So, typically, a few amber LEDs might follow the green LEDs. If the LEDs are green and amber, the current utilization is greater than the maximum, and the maximum is being updated as you watch the LEDs.

✦ **DUPLX:** When DUPLX is selected, you see the status of the actual switch ports. If the switch port is off, the port is running in Half Duplex mode; if the switch port is green, the port is running in Full Duplex mode. You want as many ports as possible running in Full Duplex mode, especially if they are inter-switch links or trunk ports between switches.

✦ **SPEED:** When SPEED is selected, you see the status of the actual switch ports. If the switch port is off, the port is running at 10 Mbps; if the switch port is green, the port is running at 100 Mbps; if the switch port is flashing green, the port is running at 1000 Mbps.

If you press the Mode button on a switch for three seconds and all the mode LEDs start to blink in unison, the switch has already completed Express Setup mode.

If you have attached a rollover cable (Book I, Chapter 5 covers rollover cables and managing your switch) to the console port, as discussed in the next chapter, you will see that the boot process is as follows:

```
C2950 Boot Loader (C2950-HBOOT-M) Version 12.1(11r)EA1, RELEASE SOFTWARE (fc1)
Compiled Mon 22-Jul-02 18:57 by antonino
WS-C2950-12 starting...
Base ethernet MAC Address: 00:06:d6:ab:a0:40
Xmodem file system is available.
Initializing Flash...
flashfs[0]: 328 files, 5 directories
flashfs[0]: 0 orphaned files, 0 orphaned directories
flashfs[0]: Total bytes: 7741440
flashfs[0]: Bytes used: 6682624
flashfs[0]: Bytes available: 1058816
flashfs[0]: flashfs fsck took 8 seconds.
...done initializing flash.
Boot Sector Filesystem (bs:) installed, fsid: 3
Parameter Block Filesystem (pb:) installed, fsid: 4
Loading "flash:c2950-i6q4l2-mz.121-22.EA13.bin"...##############################
    ###########################################################################
    ###########################################################################
    ####################

File "flash:c2950-i6q4l2-mz.121-22.EA13.bin" uncompressed and installed, entry
    point: 0x80010000
executing...

                Restricted Rights Legend

Use, duplication, or disclosure by the Government is
subject to restrictions as set forth in subparagraph
(c) of the Commercial Computer Software - Restricted
Rights clause at FAR sec. 52.227-19 and subparagraph
(c) (1) (ii) of the Rights in Technical Data and Computer
Software clause at DFARS sec. 252.227-7013.

            cisco Systems, Inc.
            170 West Tasman Drive
            San Jose, California 95134-1706
```

```
Cisco Internetwork Operating System Software
IOS (tm) C2950 Software (C2950-I6Q4L2-M), Version 12.1(22)EA13, RELEASE SOFTWARE
    (fc2)
Technical Support: http://www.cisco.com/techsupport
Copyright (c) 1986-2009 by cisco Systems, Inc.
Compiled Fri 27-Feb-09 22:20 by amvarma
Image text-base: 0x80010000, data-base: 0x80570000


Initializing flashfs...
flashfs[1]: 328 files, 5 directories
flashfs[1]: 0 orphaned files, 0 orphaned directories
flashfs[1]: Total bytes: 7741440
flashfs[1]: Bytes used: 6682624
flashfs[1]: Bytes available: 1058816
flashfs[1]: flashfs fsck took 8 seconds.
flashfs[1]: Initialization complete.
Done initializing flashfs.
POST: System Board Test : Passed
POST: Ethernet Controller Test : Passed
ASIC Initialization Passed

POST: FRONT-END LOOPBACK TEST : Passedcisco WS-C2950-12 (RC32300) processor
    (revision B0) with 20957K bytes of memory.
Processor board ID FAB0535Q22L
Last reset from system-reset
Running Standard Image
12 FastEthernet/IEEE 802.3 interface(s)

32K bytes of flash-simulated non-volatile configuration memory.
Base ethernet MAC Address: 00:06:D6:AB:A0:40
Motherboard assembly number: 73-5782-08
Motherboard serial number: FAB0535BC1K
Model revision number: B0
Model number: WS-C2950-12
System serial number: FAB0535Q22L


Press RETURN to get started!


00:00:15: %SPANTREE-5-EXTENDED_SYSID: Extended SysId enabled for type vlan
00:00:17: %SYS-5-CONFIG_I: Configured from memory by console
00:00:17: %SYS-5-RESTART: System restarted --
Cisco Internetwork Operating System Software
IOS (tm) C2950 Software (C2950-I6Q4L2-M), Version 12.1(22)EA13, RELEASE SOFTWARE
    (fc2)
Technical Support: http://www.cisco.com/techsupport
Copyright (c) 1986-2009 by cisco Systems, Inc.
Compiled Fri 27-Feb-09 22:20 by amvarma
00:00:17: %SNMP-5-COLDSTART: SNMP agent on host Switch1 is undergoing a cold
    start
00:00:21: %LINK-3-UPDOWN: Interface FastEthernet0/3, changed state to up
00:00:21: %LINK-3-UPDOWN: Interface FastEthernet0/8, changed state to up
00:00:21: %LINK-3-UPDOWN: Interface FastEthernet0/10, changed state to
    up00:00:21: %LINK-3-UPDOWN: Interface FastEthernet0/11, changed state to up
00:00:21: %LINK-3-UPDOWN: Interface FastEthernet0/12, changed state to up
00:00:21: %LINK-3-UPDOWN: Interface FastEthernet0/1, changed state to up
00:00:21: %LINK-3-UPDOWN: Interface FastEthernet0/2, changed state to up
00:00:21: %LINK-3-UPDOWN: Interface FastEthernet0/9, changed state to up
00:00:23: %LINEPROTO-5-UPDOWN: Line protocol on Interface FastEthernet0/3,
    changed state to up
```

```
00:00:23: %LINEPROTO-5-UPDOWN: Line protocol on Interface FastEthernet0/8,
    changed state to up
00:00:23: %LINEPROTO-5-UPDOWN: Line protocol on Interface FastEthernet0/10,
    changed state to up
00:00:23: %LINEPROTO-5-UPDOWN: Line protocol on Interface FastEthernet0/11,
    changed state to up
00:00:23: %LINEPROTO-5-UPDOWN: Line protocol on Interface FastEthernet0/12,
    changed state to up
00:00:23: %LINEPROTO-5-UPDOWN: Line protocol on Interface FastEthernet0/1,
    changed state to up
00:00:23: %LINEPROTO-5-UPDOWN: Line protocol on Interface FastEthernet0/2,
    changed state to up
00:00:23: %LINEPROTO-5-UPDOWN: Line protocol on Interface FastEthernet0/9,
    changed state to up
00:00:53: %LINEPROTO-5-UPDOWN: Line protocol on Interface Vlan1, changed state to
    up
```

Refer to the preceding boot process code, and notice these sections:

+ Hardware initialization

+ Boot loader and the selection of an IOS image

+ System POST

After you see the Press ENTER message, the system has finished loading the IOS and completed the post. At this point, the switch loads its configuration into memory and enables all switch ports. Because the switch ports have just come up, they must be treated as any newly connected switch port and adhere to Spanning Tree Protocol (STP) or any other feature that applies to a switch port. You will see that the link state on all connected ports is changed to up, and after the required wait time, the line protocol is brought to an up state as well.

Connecting the client cables

You will find two main types of cables in any bundle of cables lying around your office. The majority of the cables will be *straight-through cables*, but some may be *crossover cables*. In straight-through cables, the eight pins or wires that make up the cable match directly from one side of the cable to the other. With crossover cables, the send and receive wires are exchanged with each other or are crossed. In most cases, you will want to use the standard cable because these cables are designed for connecting devices or hosts to a switch. Crossover cables are designed for switch-to-switch connections.

Many of the switches in Cisco's product line support Auto-MDIX, which allows you to use a straight-through cable to connect two switches. If your switch does not support Auto-MDIX (or has it disabled), using a straight-through cable will not work to connect the switches, and the LED on that port will not illuminate. If you forget this, remember to check the cable when interconnecting the switch.

These cables will have either fiber connectors or some type of RJ45 connectors. Typically, you will use RJ45 connectors in ports, as shown in Figure 2-3. In this figure, notice that each switch port is numbered and illuminates when a running device is connected to the switch. Also, ensure that your cables still have their retaining clips on them and that the connectors are fully seated in the switch port socket. On several occasions, I have been troubleshooting connectivity issues, only to find a cable was not pushed all the way into the switch port socket.

Figure 2-3:
The most common port on a switch is the RJ45 port.

**Book III
Chapter 2**

Switching Basics

Just as straight-through cables will not connect switches with auto-MDIX disabled, crossover cables will not connect devices to switches with auto-MDIX disabled.

After you have connected your client device to the switch, do not expect to be able to communicate with your new network neighbors right away.

By default, Spanning Tree Protocol (STP) is enabled on all of your ports, which means that new devices are not allowed to communicate until the switch is sure that the connected device is not another switch. STP does this by implementing a listening phase during which the switch is not allowed to send traffic to main data network. If the switch passes the test, then the port transitions into a forwarding state. You will see the light for that port change from amber (blocking) to green (forwarding).

If you are powering up a switch from your shelf, do not connect it to the main network until you read the rest of this minibook about switching, especially Chapter 5 on VLANs and the VLAN Trunking Protocol (VTP). If the switch you are powering up has a VLAN database with a higher reversion number than your production switches, it will overwrite your production configuration, possibly deleting all of your production VLANs.

Chapter 3: Configuring Switches

In This Chapter

✔ **Configuring a basic switch with the most common options**

✔ **Configuring passwords for different interfaces**

✔ **Running the Setup Wizard**

✔ **Setting up a new user**

Switch configuration is important to maximizing the performance of your network. Although, in many cases, you can just take your new switch out of the box and plug it into a port on an existing switch and be fine, if you have not changed any of the settings on your other switches, you will not be getting the best performance from these switches or your network.

In this chapter, you find out how to apply a basic configuration on your switch and gain a firm grasp on what you need to do to complete your switch configuration, from examining ports to creating users to managing switches. I show you what you need to do from the command line as well as some of the graphical tools that are available to you with Cisco products. Later chapters in this minibook cover some of the more advanced switching topics.

Switching with the Internetwork Operating System (IOS)

The first step is to connect to your switch so you can make configuration changes. You will want to focus on different features, depending on whether you are working on a switch, router, or security device; however, the general IOS is the same regardless of what device you are managing (you may want to refer to Book I, Chapter 5, where I introduce IOS). Book I, Chapter 5 does not cover very many commands, but you follow the same process for entering the User EXEC mode, the Privileged EXEC mode, the Global Configuration mode, and for saving your configuration changes. This chapter will also show you Interface Configuration mode.

To get help from the IOS, type a question mark at any point on the command line to see what commands are available or to find out how to complete a command that you are working on. Tab auto-completion of commands is also a default feature of the IOS, to use tab auto-completion just type enough of a command's name to distinguish it from other commands, press the Tab key, and the command's full name should appear automatically. Generally, by using these two features, you can quickly figure out most commands.

If you are entirely new to switch configuration, you can download a complete command reference guide for each IOS routing component; just go to Cisco's website at www.cisco.com/cisco/web/psa/reference.html. On the page that appears, select your IOS version from the Products selection list. You may also find the LAN Switching guide for the current IOS version at the following link:

www.cisco.com/en/US/docs/ios/lanswitch/command/reference/lsw_book.html

Connecting to Your Switch

A few basic methods of making configuration changes to a switch are available, as shown here:

✦ **Console connection:** This method involves having direct physical access to the switch and making changes through your computer's serial port and a rollover cable. This is command-line access to a switch and, typically, is the way you will configure an IP address on a new switch — because this method is a bit easier than trying to locate the new address that appears in DHCP or some other source.

✦ **Telnet or SSH:** These options give you remote command-line access to the switch to make configuration changes. There are a few requirements when using these features. The switch needs to be configured with an IP address, and the protocol that you want to use needs to be enabled.

✦ **CiscoWorks:** CiscoWorks LAN Management Solution (LMS) 4.0 is an enterprise workflow, monitoring, troubleshooting, reporting, and configuration management tool. With CiscoWorks, you have a true management tool for your entire network; but it comes with a price tag of approximately $10,000 with licenses to manage 300 network devices.

✦ **Cisco Web Console:** Represents the most popular, easy-to-use graphical user interface (GUI) that lets you configure your switches' interfaces using a web browser, mouse, and keyboard, just like you navigate any website (see Figure 3-1).

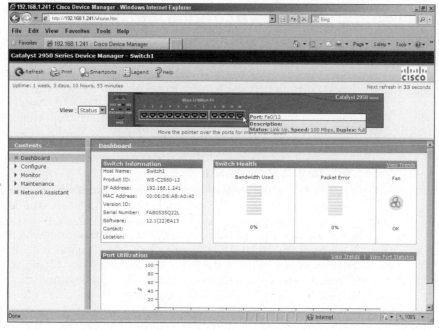

Figure 3-1:
Cisco's Web Console is an easy-to-use GUI-based tool integrated into IOS.

Because you can always make a console connection to your switch, take a few minutes to locate a rollover cable for your switch as well as the console port on the switch. If you do not have a serial port on your computer, make plans to get a USB serial port adapter for your computer and test it with your Cisco devices. It is best to do this before you need to make an emergency connection to your switch.

If you have already enabled SSH access to your switch, ensure that you also disabled Telnet access. SSH is as easy to use as Telnet and the only secure remote access option to the command-line interface (CLI). If by chance you do not see a console port on your switch, check your documentation to see if you purchased a managed switch. An unmanaged switch does not support the advanced features covered in this minibook and does not allow configuration changes to be made to the switch; as such, it will not have a console port.

In addition to the reliable command line, which is found on all Cisco devices, and the easier to use but sometimes less functional web-based interface that is found on some devices, Cisco has a variety of graphical management tools that you can use to manage configurations and to monitor network devices. At Cisco, you can find these tools, including (enterprise tool) CiscoWorks LAN Management Solution (LMS) and (small business tool) Cisco Configuration Professional, by going to ww.cisco.com/en/US/products/sw/netmgtsw/ index.html. Be sure to check them out — as either of them may make your life easier.

Revealing Basic Switch Configuration

You really do not need to do anything to your switch to get it working — just take it out of the box and connect it to your network. Unlike the router (covered in Book IV), all the ports on your switch are enabled by default, unless you disable them (see the "Configure" section, later in this chapter, for more on disabling switch ports). To get the most out of your switch, you need to do a bit of work, though none of it is too scary. The following sections discuss each of the major configuration items.

Setting a hostname

The `hostname` does not change how the switch functions, but when making remote connections to the switch, be sure that you are working on the correct device on the network. You do not want to think you are disabling an unused port on a remote switch, only to find out that you disabled the switch port to which the company president is connected, for example. Some people would call that a Career Limiting Move (CLM), and you do want to avoid those. To set the `hostname`, follow this example. Notice that `exit` is used to leave Global Configuration mode.

This book uses code examples like the following one. In this example, you will see that some of the text is bold. The full example shows what is taking place in a console screen using the Cisco CLI, while the bold text shows what I typed.

```
Switch>enable
Password:
Switch#configure terminal
Enter configuration commands, one per line.  End with CNTL/Z.
Switch(config)#hostname Switch1
Switch1(config)#exit
```

Examining ports and speeds

You will find several ports on your switch, including these:

+ **Stacking port:** Used to connect switches together for common management and high-speed data transfer.

+ **Ethernet/FastEthernet/GigabitEthernet:** Standard network interfaces used to connect different devices to your network. You see these along the front side of the switch, each numbered based on type, normally ranging from 8 to 50 ports.

+ **Console:** Serial configuration port for command-line access to switch management and configuration.

+ **Power connector:** This may accept a standard universal power cable — common on all computer equipment — supporting 110 to 220 volts or a 12V DC connector, as shown in Figure 3-2.

Figure 3-2:
A typical
12V power
connector
for a switch.

Configuring interfaces

In previous chapters, I talk about switches and the series of ports you attach network devices to. When you enter the configuration of the Cisco IOS, these physical ports are *logical interfaces,* so you specify an interface by describing the physical location of a port. I will fully explain this while I walk you through the process.

In this section, I examine the basics of configuring Ethernet, Fast Ethernet, and Gigabit Ethernet connections because they are typically the interfaces you see on your switch. There is not a substantial difference between copper or fiber connectors.

To configure the switch so that you can connect an appropriate device to a port and have it work, follow these steps:

1. **Connect to your switch and get into Configuration mode using a set of commands like the following:**

```
Switch1>enable
Password:
Switch1#configure terminal
Enter configuration commands, one per line. End with CNTL/Z.
```

2. **Choose the interface by number.**

You are able to choose from Ethernet, FastEthernet, or Gigabit Ethernet type interfaces.

3. **Specify the interface number.**

   All ports in current IOS versions are numbered, starting at the motherboard in one of these formats: `network-module-slot/port`, `0/interface-card-slot/port`, or `network-module-slot/interface-card-slot/port`. To specify an interface, you specify the location of the port that represents the interface. Effectively, all modules are connected to the motherboard slot on the switch, which is always slot `0` and the first zero in the interface name.

   If you have a switch installed in a router HWIC or working with a chassis-based system, specify the slot that the card is installed into and then the interface in the format of `0/0/1` — `0` for the motherboard, `0` for the first HWIC slot, `1` for the first port on the network module.

   In my case, the switch does not have an expansion module, so I specify `0` for the motherboard and `1` for the first port on the switch.

   ```
   Switch1(config)#interface fastEthernet 0/1
   ```

   When working with switches, the first interface is numbered one, whereas when you work with most other Cisco devices, you find the first interface is zero.

4. **Set the specifics of the network connection or use the Auto settings for medium dependent interface crossover (MDIX), Duplex, and Speed settings.**

   MDIX modes include Auto or Off, Duplex modes include Full Duplex or Half Duplex, while speeds will typically be from 10 Mbps up to the speed of the interface. (I cover MDIX in Book III, Chapter 1.)

   ```
   Switch1(config-if)#mdix auto
   Switch1(config-if)#duplex auto
   Switch1(config-if)#speed auto
   ```

5. **Add a description to the interface.**

   ```
   Switch1(config-if)#description Firewall Connection
   ```

   It is a good idea, at least for important interfaces, to add a description. But because most ports will have computers belonging to ordinary network users, you may not want to add descriptions like "Bob's office" for these ports. Important ports might include access points, routers, uplinks, or firewalls. Giving yourself a description may prevent you from changing the configuration on the wrong interface. These descriptions do not assist with the configuration; they just help prevent human error.

   If you disable MDIX, be sure that you use the correct cable. If you have a computing device such as a computer, printer, or router, use a straight-through cable; if you want to connect two switches, you need a crossover cable. I discuss these cables in Book III, Chapter 1.

If you are concerned about security in respect to how many computers a user connects, disable the MDIX setting so that the user will not be able to connect a personal switch or access point to their office network jack. Of course, the user could use a crossover cable if they are in the know, in which case public flogging of that user should be performed.

Configuring the management interface

Before you can manage your switch, you need to configure a management interface. Unlike the routers in Book IV that allow for management on any configured interface, you are not able to associate IP addresses to the physical ports or interface; rather, you associate the IP address to a virtual interface that is implicitly created with a Virtual LAN (VLAN). Book III, Chapter 5, discusses VLANs, so in this section, I just cover the basics to get to the management interface of your switch. You need a switchport configured for the same VLAN as your management VLAN will be configured. If you want to manage your switch over the default VLAN, just follow these steps (notice end is used in this case to exit Global Configuration mode:

1. **Create a new VLAN with the following command:**

```
Switch1>enable
Switch1#configure terminal
Enter configuration commands, one per line.  End with CNTL/Z.
Switch1#interface VLAN 1
Switch1(config-if)#ip address 192.168.1.241 255.255.255.0
Switch1(config-if)#end
```

You do have the option of configuring your switch to use DHCP using the command ip address dhcp. This option can work well if you want to set reservations for the switch's MAC address, but in most of the organizations that I deal with, all managed network devices are assigned static addresses for consistency and ensured connectivity. It would be a danger to network-management if I lost the ability to manage my network because a DHCP server went offline for too long.

If you were to exit the configuration now and check your running configuration, you would notice one configuration item a little strange:

```
Switch1>enable
Switch1#show running-config interface VLAN 1
Building configuration...

Current configuration : 82 bytes
!
interface Vlan1
 ip address 192.168.1.241 255.255.255.0
 no ip route-cache
end
```

This output clues you in that one important item is missing or, rather, that something is present that should not be. Unlike the reset of the switch ports, the VLAN interfaces are not enabled by default. You can have only one management interface or VLAN enabled at a time, so if you configure a second VLAN interface for management, the first one will be shut down or disabled. It will not be deleted, but it will be disabled. You will have to disable it and enable the other one.

2. **Enter the following commands to start using the first VLAN interface again and shut down the second one:**

```
Switch1>enable
Switch1#configure terminal
Enter configuration commands, one per line.  End with CNTL/Z.
Switch1(config)#interface vlan 1
Switch1(config-if)#no shutdown
Switch1(config-if)#end
```

If you are working on the console or have `terminal monitor` running, you will receive a status message telling you that the interface has been enabled and can be used again. The message will be similar to the following:

```
00:00:52: %LINEPROTO-5-UPDOWN: Line protocol on Interface Vlan1, changed
     state to up
```

Now you have all the information required (and then some) to configure a switch interface. If you trust the default settings for the MDIX, Speed, and Duplex settings, you likely just need to assign an IP address and bring the management interface up. A description is nice to have and other configuration options are required based on configuration of other parts of your network, such as VLAN configuration.

Once you have the interface up and running, if you are using defaults for your MDIX, Speed, and Duplex settings, examine the interface to ensure that it has detected settings that you are happy with. Do this with the `show interfaces` command, as shown here. This switch does not support MDIX, but you should be able to locate the other settings.

```
Switch1>enable
Switch1#show interfaces  fastEthernet 0/1
FastEthernet0/1 is up, line protocol is up (connected)
  Hardware is Fast Ethernet, address is 0006.d6ab.a041 (bia 0006.d6ab.a041)
  MTU 1500 bytes, BW 100000 Kbit, DLY 100 usec,
     reliability 255/255, txload 1/255, rxload 1/255
  Encapsulation ARPA, loopback not set
  Keepalive set (10 sec)
  Full-duplex, 100Mb/s, media type is 100BaseTX
  input flow-control is unsupported output flow-control is unsupported
  ARP type: ARPA, ARP Timeout 04:00:00
  Last input 00:00:24, output 00:00:01, output hang never
  Last clearing of "show interface" counters never
  Input queue: 0/75/0/0 (size/max/drops/flushes); Total output drops: 0
  Queueing strategy: fifo
  Output queue: 0/40 (size/max)
  5 minute input rate 0 bits/sec, 0 packets/sec
  5 minute output rate 0 bits/sec, 0 packets/sec
     2577 packets input, 213622 bytes, 2 no buffer
     Received 2574 broadcasts (420 multicast)
     0 runts, 0 giants, 0 throttles
```

```
0 input errors, 0 CRC, 0 frame, 0 overrun, 2 ignored
0 watchdog, 420 multicast, 0 pause input
0 input packets with dribble condition detected
2090 packets output, 157557 bytes, 0 underruns
0 output errors, 0 collisions, 2 interface resets
0 babbles, 0 late collision, 0 deferred
0 lost carrier, 0 no carrier, 0 PAUSE output
0 output buffer failures, 0 output buffers swapped out
```

Pay attention to the values at the end of the previous command, because most of them will help you identify configuration issues.

Within all this information, notice that the interface and line protocols should both be Up. In my case, the interface detected Full Duplex as well as a speed of 100 Mbps. When working with a switch, I will see only an IP address on the VLAN interface, which for Layer 2 switches will be the management interface, but will be considered a routing interface for Layer 3 switches. I can verify the IP address of the interface, and I can see if there are any packet errors on the interface. Incorrect Duplex settings between ends of a connection can cause packet errors.

If you are working with a Layer 3 router, you have two types of configuration changes to work with: a full set of switch configuration commands in addition to a full set of routing commands. (Routing commands are covered in Book IV.)

Setting the default gateway

The IP address on the management interface is already set, but that is not everything that you need to do. In most cases, as with the configuration of network devices, you need to configure at least a default gateway. In this case, the default gateway is not set in the interface, but for the entire switch.

**Book III
Chapter 3**

**Configuring
Switches**

Viewing terminal messages

When you are working on the console of a switch, you will often see status messages from various things that happen on the switch, such as when a device is connected to a port and the link is enabled. If you are using a remote terminal session through Telnet or SSH, then you do not see these status messages. If you want to see these messages, enter Privileged EXEC mode and type **terminal monitor**. This copies all terminal messages to your remote terminal session.

To set the gateway of last resort, you enter Global Configuration mode and use the `ip default-gateway` command to set a route to a universal system. Remember, this needs to target a router that is directly connected to a network or segment to which your router is connected. The complete command looks like this:

```
Switch1>enable
Switch1#configure terminal
Enter configuration commands, one per line.  End with CNTL/Z.
Switch1(config)#ip default-gateway 192.168.1.254
Switch1(config)#end
```

Setting passwords

Although it is not actually necessary to have a password on your switch, it is a very good idea to create one, especially if you configured the switch with an IP address on the management interface. If you do not configure a password but have enabled Telnet, anyone can connect to your switch from any interface and reconfigure your switch to their heart's desire, giving themselves access to your entire internal network.

The last several versions of the Cisco IOS for routers force you to set up passwords on your first boot, if you have not already enabled passwords.

Several types of passwords can be configured on your Cisco switch, such as Telnet and SSH connections, the console port, and the enable password. These password locations are good places to have password protection, but at the least, you should have an enable password because this acts as a master password on the switch and is required by any person who wants to enter Privileged EXEC mode.

I have stopped being surprised when I visit a new client's network and find that their network devices have no passwords or default factory passwords. It does, however, make my initial connections easier to accomplish. Always set or change system default passwords to prevent unauthorized changes to your network devices.

Setting the enable password

The enable password is used every time you move from User EXEC mode to Privileged EXEC mode. This condition gives you security on your switch because Privileged EXEC mode is where all the dangerous commands are, including Global Configuration mode. To set an enable password you would use the following command:

```
Switch1>enable
Switch1#configure terminal
Switch1(config)#enable password mypass
```

This command creates an enable password that is stored in the configuration file. To view this password, show your running configuration using the following command:

```
Switch1>enable
Password:
Switch1#show running-config | include enable password
enable password mypass
```

The problem with the enable password is that it is stored in plain text in the configuration file. Anyone with access to your configuration file can read your password without any trouble. Cisco's solution to this problem was to create a new type of password called the *secret password*. When you configure both an enable and a secret password, the secret password is the password that will be used to change from User EXEC mode to Privileged EXEC mode, instead of the weaker enable password. The following code sets both passwords for your switch:

```
Switch1>enable
Switch1#configure terminal
Switch1(config)#enable password mypass
Switch1(config)#enable secret mysecret
```

To see this in your configuration, use the following command:

```
Switch1>enable
Password:
Switch1#show running-config | include enable
enable secret 5 $1$BSX4$FZp.ZFvYSAGUEDn8dvr140
enable password mypass
```

 Most encrypted passwords in your configuration file use a weak reversible encryption and will be identified by a 7 in the password line, whereas the secret password is encrypted with a one-way MD5 hash with a 5 denoted in the password line. You may also see a 0 that identifies it as an unencrypted password.

Setting the Telnet password

If you need to remotely manage your switch, you will be able to choose between Telnet and SSH. Earlier in the chapter, I discussed the dangers of Telnet — that is, that it sends data over the network in plain text, which makes Telnet less secure when compared to SSH. Some people will make a justification for Telnet, and if they are running it only within a secured management network, then some of the risks are indeed mitigated.

In spite of risks, you should know how Telnet works and how to administer it, so I will show you how to do the setup. Telnet accesses the switch through the Virtual Terminal ports or vty ports. To see whether you are set up with vty ports on your switch, use the following command:

```
Switch1>enable
Password:
Switch1#show running-config | include line vty
line vty 0 4
```

The fourth line in the preceding code indicates that I have five vty ports on my switch, numbered from 0 to 4. This means that I can host up to five concurrent Telnet connections simultaneously on my switch. The chance of having five network administrators making connections to this switch at the same time is somewhat low. If you want to know how many connections your switch will support, use the following command to find out.

```
Switch1>enable
Password:
Switch1#configure terminal
Enter configuration commands, one per line.  End with CNTL/Z.
Switch1(config)#line vty 0 ?
  <1-181>  Last Line number
  <cr>
```

The preceding output tells you that the switch will support up to 182 total vty ports, but I can configure it to as low as 1 port by inserting a carriage return (pressing Enter).

To set the password for Telnet or vty port, use the following commands.

```
Switch1>enable
Password:
Switch1#configure terminal
Enter configuration commands, one per line.  End with CNTL/Z.
Switch1(config)#line vty 0 4
Switch1(config-line)#password vtypass
Switch1(config-line)#exit
Switch1(config)#exit
```

Note the appearance of the Line Configuration mode prompt (config-line). This is the first time you have seen this in this book. Line Configuration mode configures different command line interfaces, such as the console and virtual terminal ports (vty).

To have access to the switch for Telnet, you need to specify both an enable password and the Telnet password in your configuration.

Setting the SSH password

To set up access to the switch for SSH, a few additional steps are needed. SSH access is not possible with only a password; you need to have a user account created on your switch. You will see how to create users in the section "Working with Users", later in this chapter. For now, I will assume that you have a user named *remote* with a password named *remote*. (**Note:** Do *not* use this type of password policy on your production network!)

To set up SSH access, you need to change the default vty terminal or create a new one. In this case, I will create a new vty for SSH access using the following commands:

```
Switch1>enable
Password:
Switch1#configure terminal
Enter configuration commands, one per line.  End with CNTL/Z.
Switch1(config)#ip domain-name edtetz.net
Switch1(config)#crypto key generate rsa
The name for the keys will be: Switch1.edtetz.net
Choose the size of the key modulus in the range of 360 to 2048 for your
  General Purpose Keys. Choosing a key modulus greater than 512 may take
  a few minutes.

How many bits in the modulus [512]: 1024
% Generating 1024 bit RSA keys ...[OK]

Switch1(config)#
*Mar 17 00:59:53.971: %SSH-5-ENABLED: SSH 1.99 has been enabled
Switch1(config)#line vty 5
Switch1(config-line)#login local
Switch1(config-line)#transport input ssh
Switch1(config-line)#exit
Switch1(config)#exit
```

The preceding commands have completed four key tasks:

✦ Created a set of Secure Sockets Layer (SSL) encryption keys and enabled SSH access with the `crypto` command.

✦ Created a vty terminal pool of one terminal to be used specifically with SSH.

✦ Enabled the incoming transport to SSH rather than Telnet or the other supported protocols using the `transport` command.

✦ Set the login option to use the local users database. This authenticates SSH users by checking their credentials against the users found in the local users database.

The `crypto key` command needs to be issued only one time on the switch. Once the key is generated, it can be used by all services that require cryptography or encryption services.

At this point, you can use an SSH client program (like PuTTY) to connect to the command-line interface on this switch on TCP port 22. Because Telnet is still enabled on vty ports 0 through 4, I can use the following command to disable Telnet access, or actually all remote access through that set of vty ports. By disabling the four default vty ports, I have reduced remote management of this switch to one SSH user at a time and eliminated unencrypted Telnet management traffic on my network. Therefore, I can still manage my switch remotely, but I will be required to use SSH.

**Book III
Chapter 3**

**Configuring
Switches**

```
Switch1>enable
Password:
Switch1#configure terminal
Enter configuration commands, one per line.  End with CNTL/Z.
Switch1(config)#line vty 0 4
Switch1(config-line)#transport input none
Switch1(config-line)#exit
Switch1(config)#exit
```

Setting the console port password

Anyone with access to the console port on your switch can connect to it and have at least User EXEC mode access. If they happen to know the enable or secret password, they can enter Privileged EXEC mode. To prevent this, you can add an additional password to the configuration that will require password access to the console port. Of course, the bigger security question in a situation like this is why does this strange person have physical access to your switch, but that is covered in Book VI, Chapter 4.

To place a password on the console port, you use a system that is very similar to that of the vty ports. To do so, use the following commands:

```
SSH client program like putty Switch1>enable
Switch1#configure terminal
Enter configuration commands, one per line.  End with CNTL/Z.
Switch1(config)#line con 0
Switch1(config-line)#password conpass
Switch1(config-line)#login
Switch1(config-line)#exit
Switch1(config)#exit
```

These commands add an extra layer of security on connection to this port.

Knowing where passwords sleep

Now that you have looked at all the available passwords, take a look at the running configuration to see how they are stored.

```
Switch1>enable
Switch1#show running-config
Building configuration...

Current configuration : 921 bytes
!
version 12.3
!
(Output truncated for brevity)
!
enable secret 5 $1$exG2$cxsOWeiMWa7a8SMo5dw51/
enable password enablepass
!
(Output truncated for brevity)
!
line con 0
 password conpass
 login
```

```
line vty 0 4
 password termpass
 login
!
end
Switch1#
```

Notice that the only password that is not stored in plain text is the enable secret password. All of the other passwords are clearly readable to anyone who has access to the configuration file or command and are thus not very secure. Your configuration file has an option to encrypt all passwords, and in Book VI, Chapter 4, you read more about using encrypted passwords as a security best practice.

Banners

A *banner* is a message presented to a user who is using the switch. The type of banner you configured for use determines when this message is shown. You can configure three main types of banners on your Cisco switch, as shown here:

✦ **Message of the Day (MOTD):** This type of logon message has been around for a long time on Unix and mainframe systems. The idea of the message is to display a temporary notice to users, such as issues with system availability. However, because the message displays when a user connects to the device prior to login, most network administrators are now using it to display legal notices regarding access to the switch, such as `unauthorized access to this device is prohibited and violators will be prosecuted to the full extent of the law` and other such cheery endearments.

✦ **Login:** This banner is displayed before login to the system, but after the MOTD banner is displayed. Typically, this banner is used to display a permanent message to the users.

✦ **Exec:** This banner displays after the login is complete when the connecting user enters User EXEC mode. Whereas all users who attempt to connect to the switch see the other banners, only users who successfully log on to the switch see this banner, which can be used to post reminders to your network administrators.

To configure each of these banners and set them up on your switch, follow these commands:

```
Switch1>enable
Switch1#configure terminal
Enter configuration commands, one per line.  End with CNTL/Z.
Switch1(config)#banner motd #
Enter TEXT message. End with the character '#'.
This device is for authorized personnel only.
If you have not been provided with permission to
access this device - disconnect at once.
```

```
#
Switch1(config)#banner login #
Enter TEXT message. End with the character '#'.
*** Login Required. Unauthorized use is prohibited ***
#
Switch1(config)#banner exec #
Enter TEXT message.  End with the character '#'.
*** Ensure that you update the system configuration ***
*** documentation after making system changes.      ***
#
Switch1(config)#exit
```

Notice that each of the banner lines ends with a # symbol; this is a delimiter to identify the end of the message. You can specify any character you want, but the character you choose is the one you will use to end the banner message. Here is what these messages look like when you connect to the switch:

```
Switch1 Con0 is now available
Press RETURN to get started!

This device is for authorized personnel only.
If you have not been provided with permission to
access this device - disconnect at once.

*** Login Required.  Unauthorized use is prohibited ***

User Access Verification

Password:
*** Ensure that you update the system configuration ***
*** documentation after making system changes.      ***

Switch1>
```

Working with Users

I mention in the earlier "Setting the SSH password" section that with SSH, user accounts are required in order to log on. These accounts can be stored in a local database on the switch or on a central access server named *Terminal Access Controller Access-Control System (TACACS)*, which is an industry-standard authentication server. Most small organizations and even some larger ones rely on the local database for user authentication, so I describe this user creation option in this minibook.

To use the local database for authentication, you need to do two things in this order:

1. **Create at least one user account.**

2. **Configure your switch to use the local database rather than a password, which is done on an interface basis.**

Creating a user in the account database

To create a user in the account database, use a command like the following to specify the username and password:

```
Switch1>enable
Password:
Switch1#configure terminal
Enter configuration commands, one per line.  End with CNTL/Z.
Switch1(config)#username remoteuser password remotepass
Switch1(config)#username edt password edpass
Switch1(config)#exit
```

Removing a user

To remove a user, you can use the standard no command and then specify the username in the same way that the following command removes the user named remoteuser from the local database.

```
Switch1>enable
Password:
Switch1#configure terminal
Enter configuration commands, one per line.  End with CNTL/Z.
Switch1(config)#no username remoteuser
Switch1(config)#exit
```

Enable user-level protection

Finally, you need to enable the login local setting on the interfaces you want to protect with this user-level protection, using a command similar to the following:

```
Switch1>enable
Password:
Switch1#configure terminal
Enter configuration commands, one per line.  End with CNTL/Z.
Switch1(config)#line aux 0
Switch1(config-line)#login local
Switch1(config-line)#exit
Switch1(config)#exit
```

**Book III
Chapter 3**

**Configuring
Switches**

Running Setup Wizard

If you unpack your switch and plug it in, you will be running the generic factory configuration. This configuration is enough to allow you to use the switch on the default VLAN — vlan 1 — and will have all auto options enabled for each port. There will not be a management interface for Telnet or SSH; but once a management IP is configured, you can connect with Telnet and the web browser to make configuration changes. The complete configuration is shown here:

```
Switch1>enable
Switch1#show running-config
Building configuration...

Current configuration : 723 bytes
!
version 12.1
no service pad
service timestamps debug uptime
service timestamps log uptime
no service password-encryption
!
hostname Switch
!
!
ip subnet-zero
!
!
spanning-tree mode pvst
no spanning-tree optimize bpdu transmission
spanning-tree extend system-id
!
!
interface FastEthernet0/1
!
interface FastEthernet0/2
!
(Omitted for brevity)
!
interface FastEthernet0/11
!
interface FastEthernet0/12
!
interface Vlan1
 no ip address
 no ip route-cache
 shutdown
!
ip http server
!
line con 0
line vty 5 15
!
!
end
```

When you first unpack a new switch or if you have erased the configuration, when the switch boots for the first time, it will automatically enter setup. If your switch does not, you have the option of running setup from Privileged EXEC mode. Here is the basic setup process; within just a few minutes, you can have the management interface on your switch up and running:

```
Switch>enable
Switch#setup
         --- System Configuration Dialog ---

Continue with configuration dialog? [yes/no]: yes

At any point you may enter a question mark '?' for help.
Use ctrl-c to abort configuration dialog at any prompt.
```

Default settings are in square brackets '[]'.

Basic management setup configures only enough connectivity
for management of the system, extended setup will ask you
to configure each interface on the system

Would you like to enter basic management setup? [yes/no]: **yes**
Configuring global parameters:

  Enter host name [Switch]: **Switch1**

  The enable secret is a password used to protect access to
  privileged EXEC and configuration modes. This password, after
  entered, becomes encrypted in the configuration.
  Enter enable secret: **secretpass**

  The enable password is used when you do not specify an
  enable secret password, with some older software versions, and
  some boot images.
  Enter enable password: **enablepass**
% Please choose a password that is different from the enable secret
  Enter enable password: enable

  The virtual terminal password is used to protect
  access to the switch over a network interface.
  Enter virtual terminal password: **termpass**
  Configure SNMP Network Management? [no]:

Current interface summary

Interface	IP-Address	OK?	Method	Status	Protocol
Vlan1	unassigned	YES	unset	administratively down	down
FastEthernet0/1	unassigned	YES	unset	up	up
FastEthernet0/2	unassigned	YES	unset	up	up
FastEthernet0/3	unassigned	YES	unset	up	up
FastEthernet0/4	unassigned	YES	unset	down	down
FastEthernet0/5	unassigned	YES	unset	down	down
FastEthernet0/6	unassigned	YES	unset	down	down
FastEthernet0/7	unassigned	YES	unset	down	down
FastEthernet0/8	unassigned	YES	unset	up	up
FastEthernet0/9	unassigned	YES	unset	up	up
FastEthernet0/10	unassigned	YES	unset	up	up
FastEthernet0/11	unassigned	YES	unset	up	up
FastEthernet0/12	unassigned	YES	unset	up	up

Enter interface name used to connect to the
management network from the above interface summary: **vlan1**

Configuring interface Vlan1:
  Configure IP on this interface? [no]: **yes**
    IP address for this interface: **192.168.1.241**
    Subnet mask for this interface [255.255.255.0] :
    Class C network is 192.168.1.0, 24 subnet bits; mask is /24
Would you like to enable as a cluster command switch? [yes/no]: **no**

The following configuration command script was created:

hostname Switch1
enable secret 5 1HXb6$RZPOXPyDvYuOWOhvYUP1d.
enable password enablepass
line vty 0 15

```
password termpass
no snmp-server
!
!
interface Vlan1
no shutdown
ip address 192.168.1.241 255.255.255.0
!
interface FastEthernet0/1
!
interface FastEthernet0/2
!
(Omitted for brevity)
!
interface FastEthernet0/11
!
interface FastEthernet0/12
!
end


[0] Go to the IOS command prompt without saving this config.
[1] Return back to the setup without saving this config.
[2] Save this configuration to nvram and exit.

Enter your selection: [2]
Building configuration...
[OK]
Use the enabled mode 'configure' command to modify this configuration.

Switch1#
00:09:12: %LINK-3-UPDOWN: Interface Vlan1, changed state to up
00:09:13: %LINEPROTO-5-UPDOWN: Line protocol on Interface Vlan1, changed state to
    up
(Omitted for brevity)
Switch1#
```

Notice how little information you need to enter to get basic management access to your switch over the network. This includes Telnet access to switch.

After the setup wizard is complete, enter Configuration mode to update your configuration to disable Telnet in favor of SSH (as a secure option) and configure your other network interfaces.

Working with Web Console

If you refer to the default factory configuration, you will see a line that reads ip http server. This line enables a web server on your switch that lets you use your web browser — such as Firefox, Internet Explorer, or Google Chrome — with Java support to configure and manage your switch. So, if you are uncertain about using the command line, Web Console gives you the ability to make all of your configuration changes through a friendly Web GUI. There is even a spot where you can pass through command-line items for changes that do not exist in the GUI.

To start this process, open your web browser and connect to `http://` `<management address of switch>`. You will need to know the enable or secret password to connect this interface (see the earlier "Setting passwords" section). When you are presented with the authentication dialog box, you can ignore the username field and fill in the password field, unless you have created user accounts on your switch, in which case provide credentials for a valid user.

Dashboard

The dashboard is the main page that opens when you log on to Web Console (refer to Figure 3-1 to see the dashboard). In addition to showing you a graphical image of the switch with its active ports, the console gives you a brief look at the health of your switch:

✦ The Switch Information section gives you all the information you need to get warranty information about your product.

✦ The Switch Health section lets you identify any major problems related to bandwidth, packet errors, or the system fans.

✦ The Port Utilization section identifies which port(s) are being over-utilized if you have a bandwidth issue.

In Book III, Chapter 2, you read about the Mode button on the front of your switch. Next to the image of the switch at the top of Web Console is a View menu that lets you change the display of the port colors to identify the ports as the Mode button would. Here are the three items that can be displayed in the View drop-down list:

✦ **Status:** Sets active ports to green.

✦ **Speed:** Sets the port color based on the connected port speed.

✦ **Duplex:** Sets the port color based on the Duplex settings of the port.

If you mouse over any of the ports, this web page has a pop-up window that shows the same settings as the View menu in one convenient display (refer to Figure 3-1).

Configure

The Configure navigation menu has four options, Smartports, Port Settings, Express Setup, and Restart/Reboot. This menu gives you access to the main settings that you will likely want to configure on your switch. I discuss these settings briefly in the following sections.

Smartports

Because port configuration requires a bit of knowledge, Cisco simplified the process by creating *Smartports*, which are preconfigured settings you can easily apply to your switchports. Figure 3-3 shows you what the Smartports configuration looks like through the web GUI. You select the type of port you want to apply and then select the ports to which you want to apply this configuration.

Smartports are really just a series of macros (which you can modify) that Cisco has preconfigured on your switch. (I examine Smartport macros in detail in Book III, Chapter 8.) The mysterious engineers at Cisco determined that for most networks, these base configurations for ports make a lot of sense. It is a bit of an all-or-nothing in that you can use Smartports to do your configuration, or you can do all of the configuration by hand; however, if you do some by hand, your configuration may be overwritten or incompatible with other Smartport configurations. Table 3-1 summarizes the Smartport roles that you will find on your switch.

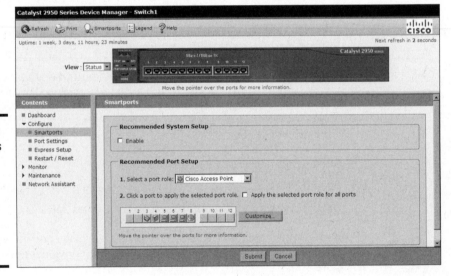

Figure 3-3: Smartports make complex port configuration much easier.

Table 3-1	Smartport Roles
Smartport Role	*Description*
Desktop	Suitable for access devices, such as desktop computers and printers. Implementation increases security on your network ports. This role is not suitable for routers and switches.
Cisco Switch	Configures the port in Trunk mode with the other connected device that is expected to be a switch. I talk about Trunk mode in Book III, Chapter 5.
Cisco Router	Configures settings that are compatible with a network router.
Cisco Phone + Desktop	Compatible with Cisco IP phones. Because phones have built-in switches to support a desktop connection and the IP phones typically operate on different VLANs and have QoS configured, these ports have special configuration requirements.
Cisco Access Point	If you are using Cisco IOS 12.2 or later, this role can be used for access points that you may have on your network.
None	Removes all custom settings from the port.

The following code shows you the settings that are applied for each one of these types of ports in the order they are applied. Note that the configuration on the port even shows you which macro runs to apply the setting. Although you have not yet looked at all these settings, spend a few minutes reviewing the changes that are made to the ports in each of these configurations. Note that trunk ports are used for the router, access points, and switches. This topic comes into play in Book III, Chapter 5, which introduces VLANs and their relationship to trunk ports. Also note the prevalence of spanning tree in this configuration, which you see in Book III, Chapter 6.

```
interface FastEthernet0/4
 switchport mode access
 switchport port-security
 switchport port-security aging time 2
 switchport port-security violation restrict
 switchport port-security aging type inactivity
mls qos cos override
 macro description cisco-desktop
 spanning-tree portfast
 spanning-tree bpduguard enable
!
interface FastEthernet0/5
 switchport mode trunk
 switchport nonegotiate
 mls qos trust cos
 macro description cisco-switch
```

**Book III
Chapter 3**

**Configuring
Switches**

```
  spanning-tree link-type point-to-point
!
interface FastEthernet0/6
 switchport mode trunk
 switchport nonegotiate
 mls qos trust cos
 macro description cisco-router
 spanning-tree portfast trunk
 spanning-tree bpduguard enable
!
interface FastEthernet0/7
 switchport mode access
 switchport voice vlan 1
 switchport port-security
 switchport port-security maximum 2
 switchport port-security aging time 2
 switchport port-security violation restrict
 switchport port-security aging type inactivity
 mls qos trust device cisco-phone
 macro description cisco-phone
 spanning-tree portfast
 spanning-tree bpduguard enable
!
interface FastEthernet0/8
 switchport mode trunk
 switchport nonegotiate
 mls qos trust cos
 macro description cisco-wireless
 spanning-tree bpduguard enable
!
```

The Smartports page also has a Recommended System Setup check box. By selecting this check box, the macro will modify the default configuration on your switch to ensure that the following settings are in place. (***Note:*** Someone at Cisco decided that these changes are important to an operating network. Although this decision may be debatable, these settings will not hurt your networks.)

```
errdisable recovery cause link-flap
errdisable recovery interval 60

udld aggressive

spanning-tree mode rapid-pvst
spanning-tree loopguard default

macro global description cisco-global
```

Port Settings

The Port Settings page allows you to configure your port settings as shown in Figure 3-4. These settings include the Speed and Duplex settings. Port settings also give you an easy way to set a description on your ports. Descriptions help you avoid configuring incorrect ports and make you pay close attention when making changes. Finally, you have the option to enable or disable a port here, which is the same as issuing the shutdown or no shutdown command.

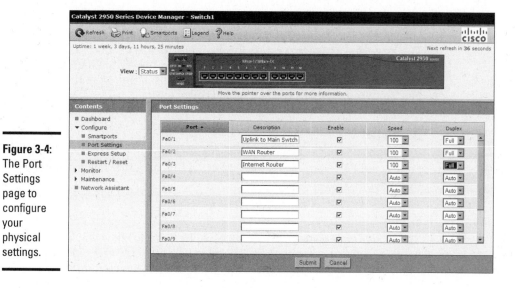

Figure 3-4:
The Port Settings page to configure your physical settings.

Express Setup

The Express Setup settings are shown in Figure 3-5. They give you an easy way to configure the management interfaces for your switch. These interfaces include the management interface, VLAN, IP configuration, and password. Other settings include the switch name and methods of making remote connections, such as Telnet, SSH, or http.

**Book III
Chapter 3**

**Configuring
Switches**

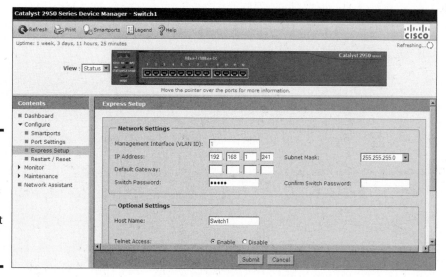

Figure 3-5:
Express Setup provides you with management configur-ation.

Restart and Reset

Finally, you finish the "Configure" section with the Restart and Reset page. This page allows you to restart the switch, which is needed from time to time, but more importantly, here you can reset the switch back to the factory configuration. Even though performing this action from the command line is not too difficult, Web Console is even easier.

Monitor

The monitor section gives you access to three main items: Trends, Port Status, and Port Statistics. Again, much of this data is available to you through the console.

Trends

The Trends page gives you three nice graphs that can show you some of the issues you may be experiencing. The main items that Cisco decided to graph are Bandwidth Utilization, Packet Errors, and Port Utilization for a specific port.

Port Status

Whereas Port Settings allows you to set the configuration of a port, Port Status allows you to see how those settings are currently operating. When working with port settings that are in Auto mode, Port Status allows you to see how those ports negotiated their settings. As seen in Figure 3-6, the status includes the Description, current connection Status, VLAN, Speed, and Duplex.

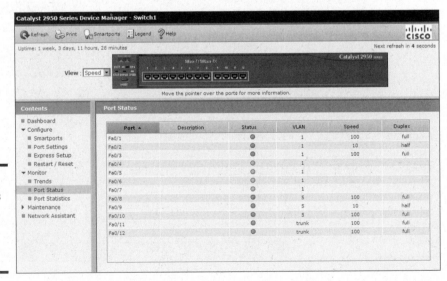

Figure 3-6: Port Status displays current operating settings.

Port Statistics

Port Statistics can be valuable when attempting to troubleshoot switch issues. High numbers of errors over a period of time are indicators of a problem. From this page, you can clear the counters on a port and watch them go back up, expecting the error values on transmitted or received packets to be quite lower than the total transmitted or received.

Maintenance

There is only one item in the Maintenance menu, and it is for Telnet. This option gives you a single link that launches a Telnet session using your locally installed version of Telnet, if it is linked to your web browser, to open links with the `telnet://` directive.

Network Assistant

Finally, the last link in Cisco's Web Console is a promotion for Cisco's Network Assistant, which is a graphical application that you can use to manage your network devices, such as routers, switches, and access points. The goal of this application is to make your network management tasks even easier by centralizing all of your management in one application. It even has an easy-to-click link that takes you to Cisco's website to download a copy of the tool. You will need to create a Cisco ID to download this tool.

Chapter 4: Easing Device Discovery with CDP

In This Chapter

✔ Learning what CDP is and how it operates

✔ Configuring CDP settings for your network devices

✔ Building a network diagram from CDP information

Cisco Discovery Protocol (CDP) is data link layer protocol that allows you to find information about the connections between devices. This chapter provides the basic information on how the protocol works and how to enable it on your devices. You also find out how to get information from your devices, including how they are connected to each other, how to view the debugging information, what you need to do if you encounter devices on which CDP is not running, and how to retrieve information from the system.

CDP is useful and easy to use, so you should start exploring a bit of your network using this default tool from Cisco. Because CDP runs on all modern Cisco equipment, you may as well work with this tool or at least know what it is doing over your network, even if you do not use the information it generates.

Discovering How CDP Operates

Cisco Discovery Protocol (CDP) is a nifty tool from Cisco that gives you a boost if your network is primarily made of Cisco devices because Cisco devices use this communication protocol to identify other Cisco devices. Most Cisco Enterprise devices support CDP. CDP essentially allows you to identify Cisco devices on your network and see how they are connected.

CDP becomes very useful if you have inherited or been brought in to work with an unfamiliar network. Within a few minutes, you have a picture of the network with a level of clarity that the previous administrator who did not use CDP would have had because many network administrators make connections to devices at the spur of a moment and then forget that those connected devices exist.

CDP has been enabled by default on Cisco routers and switches since IOS 10.0 (circa 1996), so unless you have turned it off, it should be running on your network devices. At periodic intervals, the CDP device sends out a packet on all of its interfaces. By default, the CDP packets are sent to a multicast address every 60 seconds. The receiving device's *holdtime* (the amount of time which it retains the data) is 180 seconds by default. The size of these packets is less than 500 bytes, which means that although they are on your network often, they do not amass a large amount of data — no more bandwidth is consumed with CDP than with Spanning Tree Protocol (STP) management packets (see Chapter 6 in this minibook for more information on STP).

Table 4-1 shows the type of information found in the Type Length Value (TLV) definitions, which is the main data found in the CDP frame. TLV is a standard data storage structure designed to encode data inside of protocol frames.

Table 4-1	CDP TLV Definitions
TLV	*Definition*
Device-ID	The name of the device that is stored as a string.
Address	A list of network addresses of both transmitting and receiving devices.
Port-ID	Displays the port identifier used to send the CDP frame.
Capabilities	Represents the type of devices, such as a switch or router.
Version	Displays the software release or version operating on the device.
Platform	Identifies the hardware platform for the transmitting device, such as Cisco ASA 2200 or Catalyst 2950.
IP Network Prefix	Contains a list of network prefixes that the transmitting device can send IP packets. Data can be sent to this physical interface as an interface type and port number, such as Eth 0/2.
VTP Management Domain	VLAN Trunking Protocol (VTP) makes use of CDP to distribute information, so this contains the name of the VTP management domain, of which a switch can be a member of only one domain. This allows the device to verify the VTP configuration of neighboring devices.
Native VLAN	Identifies the VLAN on the identified interface that will be used when untagged data is received on that port as specified in the IEEE 802.1Q specification.
Full/Half Duplex	Shows the status of the Duplex configuration for the interface used to send the CDP data. This information can be used for troubleshooting.

The data being passed around the network allows you to build a topological map of the connected devices, and if you move from node to node of that map (by connecting to the CLI on each switch or router you discover), you can build an entire map of the network. Therefore, if you are in the middle of troubleshooting and need to know how a few of the devices on your network are connected (or if you are documenting your entire network design), CDP is for you.

Working with CDP

Basic CDP commands are easy to work with. From Global Configuration mode, there are only a few CDP options to set, which you see shortly in the section "Enabling CDP". With very little configuration, you can have the entire system in operation. In fact, the biggest CDP configuration requirement is disabling CDP where you do not want it.

Seeing whether CDP is operating on a device

You can use the show command to see whether CDP is currently operating on your device. The following output shows the currently configured CDP settings on Switch1, which are actually the default settings. The default settings send CDP packets every 60 seconds, using CDPv2 as the protocol version, and the receiving device retains that information for 180 seconds.

Book III
Chapter 4

```
Switch1>enable
Switch1#configure terminal
Enter configuration commands, one per line.  End with CNTL/Z.
Switch1#show cdp
Global CDP information:
        Sending CDP packets every 60 seconds
        Sending a holdtime value of 180 seconds
        Sending CDPv2 advertisements is enabled
```

If you want to change from the default values, you can set CDP packets to send every 5 to 254 seconds (Book I, Chapter 3 deals with the pesky binary number limits that show up). The CDP hold timer can be configured from 10 seconds to 255 seconds, with the holdtime always larger than the CDP packet timer; otherwise, other devices could remove the information about their neighbor right before getting the second CDP packet, which does not make much sense.

The standard recommendation is that the holdtime be at least three times the value of the CDP time. That way, information about neighboring devices will remain in your CDP data even if you fail to receive two out of the three CDP data frames that are sent.

Enabling CDP

Even though CDP is enabled by default on your Cisco devices, you might inherit a network where the previous administrator had disabled CDP because he disliked three letter protocols (or for some other equally valid reason).

If you find that CDP is not running on your device, you can enable CDP using the cdp run command as follows:

```
Switch1>enable
Switch1#configure terminal
Enter configuration commands, one per line.  End with CNTL/Z.
Switch1(config)#cdp ?
  advertise-v2  CDP sends version-2 advertisements
  holdtime      Specify the holdtime (in sec) to be sent in packets
  run           Enable CDP
  timer         Specify the rate at which CDP packets are sent      (in sec)
Switch1(config)#cdp run
Switch1(config)#end
```

Disabling CDP

After CDP is running on your device, by default, CDP is enabled on all interfaces of the device. At times, you may want to disable CDP — for example, on the external interface of the Internet router connected to your ISP because the ISP does not need the details about the internal network configuration. Using this method only disables CDP on a specific interface where you choose not to transmit CDP data, but leaves it enabled on the device, so you are still able to receive CDP data. To disable CDP on an interface, use Interface Configuration mode, as shown here:

```
Switch1>enable
Switch1#configure terminal
Enter configuration commands, one per line.  End with CNTL/Z.
Switch1(config)#interface fastEthernet 0/1
Switch1(config-if)#no cdp enable
Switch1(config)#end
```

Viewing information about devices

Once you have CDP running and collecting data about your neighboring devices, you may want to view information about those devices, which you obtain by using the show cdp neighbors command. The following is a list of options that go with that command. You can be specific about which neighbors you want to see, or you can show them all, and you can view summary data or detailed data.

```
Switch1>enable
Switch1#show cdp neighbors ?
  Async             Async interface
  BVI               Bridge-Group Virtual Interface
  Dialer            Dialer interface
  FastEthernet      FastEthernet IEEE 802.3
  Lex               Lex interface
  Multilink         Multilink-group interface
  Port-channel      Ethernet Channel of interfaces
  Tunnel            Tunnel interface
  Virtual-Template  Virtual Template interface
  Virtual-TokenRing Virtual TokenRing
  Vlan              Catalyst Vlans
  detail            Show detailed information
  |                 Output modifiers
  <cr>
```

You can get detailed data with the cdp command. Here is detailed information that I can see about my neighboring devices. Look through the output for the information listed in Table 4-1.

Notice the device type of RootBridge.edtetz.net; pick out which switch port can see Router2; and decode what IOS version is running on Switch2.

```
Switch1>enable
Switch1#show cdp neighbors detail
-------------------------
Device ID: Switch2
Entry address(es):
  IP address: 192.168.1.243
Platform: cisco WS-C2950-12,   Capabilities: Trans-Bridge Switch
Interface: FastEthernet0/12,   Port ID (outgoing port): FastEthernet0/1
Holdtime : 137 sec

Version :
Cisco Internetwork Operating System Software
IOS (tm) C2950 Software (C2950-C3H2S-M), Version 12.0(5.3)WC(1), MAINTENANCE
    INTERIM SOFTWARE
Copyright (c) 1986-2001 by cisco Systems, Inc.
Compiled Mon 30-Apr-01 07:56 by devgoyal

advertisement version: 2
Protocol Hello:  OUI=0x00000C, Protocol ID=0x0112; payload len=27, value=00000000
    FFFFFFFF010121FF0000000000000006D6AC46C0FF0001
VTP Management Domain: ''
Management address(es):

-------------------------
Device ID: Router2
Entry address(es):
  IP address: 192.168.1.240
Platform: Cisco 2621XM,  Capabilities: Switch IGMP
Interface: FastEthernet0/3,  Port ID (outgoing port): FastEthernet0/0
Holdtime : 142 sec

Version :

Cisco IOS Software, C2600 Software (C2600-ADVIPSERVICESK9-M), Version 12.3(4)T4,
    RELEASE SOFTWARE (fc2)
Technical Support: http://www.cisco.com/techsupport
```

```
Copyright (c) 1986-2004 by Cisco Systems, Inc.
Compiled Thu 11-Mar-04 19:57 by eaarmas

advertisement version: 2
VTP Management Domain: ''
Duplex: full
Management address(es):

------------------------
Device ID: RootBridge.edtetz.net
Entry address(es):
  IP address: 192.168.1.103
Platform: AIR-AP350,  Capabilities:
Interface: FastEthernet0/1,  Port ID (outgoing port): fec0
Holdtime : 131 sec

Version :
Cisco 350 Series AP 12.03T

advertisement version: 2
Duplex: full
Power drawn: 6.000 Watts
Management address(es):
```

After reviewing the code, you should now know

- ✦ RootBridge.edtetz.net is an AIR-AP350 — an Aironet 350 series access point

- ✦ Router2 is seen by port `FastEthernet0/3` — Router2 is using `FastEthernet0/0`

- ✦ Switch2 is running IOS version 12.0

The `show` command offers a long list of items you can see information about. One of those items is `cdp interface`. The `show cdp interface` command provides you with detailed information about the interfaces CDP is running on. I shortened the output to show only the first four switch interfaces. Notice that all the interfaces are still running at the default CDP configuration.

```
Switch1>enable
Switch1#show cdp interface
FastEthernet0/1 is up, line protocol is up
  Encapsulation ARPA
  Sending CDP packets every 60 seconds
  Holdtime is 180 seconds
FastEthernet0/2 is up, line protocol is up
  Encapsulation ARPA
  Sending CDP packets every 60 seconds
  Holdtime is 180 seconds
FastEthernet0/3 is up, line protocol is up
  Encapsulation ARPA
  Sending CDP packets every 60 seconds
  Holdtime is 180 seconds
FastEthernet0/4 is down, line protocol is down
  Encapsulation ARPA
  Sending CDP packets every 60 seconds
  Holdtime is 180 seconds
```

CDP versions

Cisco has enabled CDP since IOS 10.0. This version of CDP is 1. With the release of Cisco IOS 12.0, Cisco added some additional information to the protocol and updated the version to 2. By default, any devices running IOS 12.0 or newer will automatically have CDP version 2 enabled by default. There is no problem having a mix of CDP versions on your network.

Checking traffic data

If you are curious about the amount of CDP data that has gone through your devices, you can use the `traffic` option, which provides a summary about that data. Here is a copy of the output for my switch. Notice that it shows separate data for CDPv1 and CDPv2 protocols.

```
Switch1>enable
Switch1#show cdp traffic
CDP counters :
        Total packets output: 25123, Input: 8011
        Hdr syntax: 0, Chksum error: 0, Encaps failed: 0
        No memory: 0, Invalid packet: 0, Fragmented: 0
        CDP version 1 advertisements output: 0, Input: 0
        CDP version 2 advertisements output: 25123, Input: 8011
```

Ogling CDP's debug options

No protocol information would be complete in a Cisco book without a run-through of the debug options for that protocol. As with all other protocols, CDP has specific debug commands that can help you to identify errors or problems with the protocol. You can display debugging information for the following items (as shown by the context help for the command):

```
Switch1>enable
Switch1#debug cdp ?
  adjacency   CDP neighbor info
  events      CDP events
  ip          CDP ip info
  packets     CDP packet-related information
```

To see `debug cdp` in action, the following shows the output for `debug cdp events`:

```
Switch1>enable
Switch1#debug cdp events
CDP events debugging is on
Switch1#
CDP-EV:  CDP sending protocol-hello notification
  CDP-EV: protocol-hello notification, contents:
  CDP-EV: notification_count = 1
  CDP-EV: OUI =0x00000C, Protocol ID=0x0112
  CDP-EV: payload len=27, value=00000000FFFFFFFF010121FF0000000000000000006D6AC46C
    0FF0001
```

```
CDP-EV: receiving IDB name = 'FastEthernet0/12'
CDP-EV: remote device name = 'Switch2', CDP device number = 4
CDP-EV: remote interface name = 'FastEthernet0/1'
CDP-EV: src_mac = 0006.D6AC.46C1, capabilities = A
CDP-EV: duplex = 1, native-vlan = 0
CDP-EV: received_vtp_mgmt_domain = 1, vtp_mgmt_domain_length = 0
CDP-EV: vtp-management-domain-name = ''

CDP-EV:  CDP sending protocol-hello notification
  CDP-EV: protocol-hello notification, contents:
  CDP-EV: notification_count = 1
  CDP-EV: OUI =0x00000C, Protocol ID=0x0112
  CDP-EV: payload len=27, value=00000000FFFFFFFF010121FF0000000000000006D6AC46C
    0FF0001
  CDP-EV: receiving IDB name = 'FastEthernet0/12'
  CDP-EV: remote device name = 'Switch2', CDP device number = 4
  CDP-EV: remote interface name = 'FastEthernet0/1'
  CDP-EV: src_mac = 0006.D6AC.46C1, capabilities = A
  CDP-EV: duplex = 1, native-vlan = 0
  CDP-EV: received_vtp_mgmt_domain = 1, vtp_mgmt_domain_length = 0
  CDP-EV: vtp-management-domain-name = ''
Switch1#no debug all
All possible debugging has been turned off
```

Scanning through the preceding output, you can identify the following:

✦ Switch1 can see Switch2.

✦ The interfaces on Switch1 are connected to the interfaces on Switch2.

✦ The MAC address of Switch1.

✦ The VLAN that the switches are likely using to communicate.

✦ The VTP domain to which switches belong.

Overlooking CDP miscellany

Finally, there are a few more commands to manage CDP on your devices, such as the `clear` command, which you execute in Privileged EXEC mode. The clear command will reset your counters or remove all collected CDP data so it can be recollected from scratch. These commands are as follows:

```
Switch1>enable
Switch1#clear cdp ?
  counters  Clear CDP counters
  table     Clear cdp table
```

There is also the `counters` option for the `clear` command, which resets all the CDP counters to zero. You saw these counters when you ran the `show cdp traffic` command (see the earlier "Checking traffic data" section). The `table` option removes all entries from your neighbor's table. Because this data is sent every 60 seconds, it is rebuilt very quickly.

Building Your Network Layout

I have spent a lot of time at client sites documenting their network configuration. This task sometimes involves hours in wiring closets tracing cables and documenting ports. In some cases, the wiring closet is a real rat's nest of cables, and it can take hours of navigating to find out what switches are connected to which switches, to which routers, and on and on, *ad infinitum*.

Even a small network of a dozen switches with four WAN connections from different routers can take a long time to decipher. But with CDP, in a few minutes, you can have a network diagram — without the need of tracing cables through a network closet with a rat's nest of cables.

This exercise is also good for determining whether any Cisco switches you may not be aware of are kicking around your network. This is possible because you are going to build a table of all connections between devices. This means you will learn about all connected Cisco devices on your network, not just the ones you know are there.

The other nice piece of this puzzle is that, although I suggested that these devices are all in one wiring closet, you could obtain the same information if they were in wiring closets on the fourth and seventeenth floors, or in an office four blocks away connected with a LAN extension.

Examine Figure 4-1 as I walk you through the process.

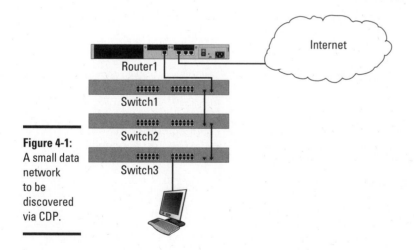

Figure 4-1:
A small data
network
to be
discovered
via CDP.

1. **Choose a starting point, in this case, Switch2.**

   It does not matter where that starting point is, just that you have one.

2. **Connect to the starting point device and run the command to see the CDP neighbors:**

```
Switch2>enable
Switch2#show cdp neighbors
Capability Codes: R - Router, T - Trans Bridge, B - Source Route Bridge
                  S - Switch, H - Host, I - IGMP, r - Repeater, P - Phone

Device ID       Local Intrfce    Holdtme    Capability  Platform  Port
   ID
Switch1         Gig 0/1          155            S I     WS-C2960-1Gig
   0/1
Switch3         Gig 0/2          120            S I     WS-C2960-1Gig
   0/2
```

   From this output, you know

   - There are two other switches named Switch1 and Switch3.

   - These 3 switches are connected through the two Gigabit ports on the front of the switches, rather than through any of the 24 FastEthernet ports.

   - This company probably does not have other Cisco equipment on this portion of the network because you do not see that they have any access points or IP phones.

3. **On Switch3, view the `show cdp neighbors` command to see what it has connected:**

```
Switch3>enable
Switch3#show cdp neighbors
Capability Codes: R - Router, T - Trans Bridge, B - Source Route Bridge
                  S - Switch, H - Host, I - IGMP, r - Repeater, P - Phone

Device ID       Local Intrfce    Holdtme    Capability  Platform  Port
   ID
Switch2         Gig 0/2          145            S I     WS-C2960-1Gig
   0/2
```

   You see that Switch3 is alone. The client computer that is connected to the switch does not send CDP data, so you do not need to worry about it.

4. **Run `show cdp neighbors` on Switch1.**

```
Switch1>enable
Switch1#show cdp neighbors
Capability Codes: R - Router, T - Trans Bridge, B - Source Route Bridge
                  S - Switch, H - Host, I - IGMP, r - Repeater, P - Phone

Device ID       Local Intrfce    Holdtme    Capability  Platform  Port
   ID
Switch2         Gig 0/1          155            S I     WS-C2960-1Gig
   0/1
Router1         Gig 0/2          154            R I     2611      Fas
   0/1
```

Switch1 offers no real surprises. It confirms the connection to Switch2 that you documented on the connection at Switch 2 and shows the connection you have with Router 1.

5. **Connect to Router 1 and run the `show cdp neighbors` command.**

If you (or your service provider) are on the ball, you will not see the service provider equipment listed in the `show cdp neighbors` command.

To complete the exercise, it would be wise to run the `show cdp neighbors` command on your router. You do not expect to see information about your ISP's devices, but there is a possibility that your router has interfaces that are not listed in your documentation, such as a Demilitarized Zone (DMZ) supporting publicly accessible Internet resources.

Book III
Chapter 4

Easing Device Discovery with CDP

Chapter 5: Virtualizing Networks with VLANs and VTP

In This Chapter

✔ **Understanding VLANs**

✔ **Configuring VLANs**

✔ **Easing management of VLANs with VTP**

*O*nce upon a time not so very long ago (*cue:* sparkly sounds of a fantasy, animated movie opening sequence), in order to separate users into individual network segments for security or other reasons, you had to provide them with their own network switch. If these users were in separate areas of your office, going to separate wiring closets, you also had to give them a separate cable for uplink or backhauling between wiring closets. This process created a ton of extra work and quickly became annoying.

Enter virtual LANs (VLANs): a solution to fix these ills. In this chapter, I show you how to set up VLANs, as well as how to automate the process of propagating VLAN information among your switches, which can quickly turn into work. I then show you how to implement trunk links among the switches, which is the easiest way to interconnect switches supporting the configured VLANs. Finally, I discuss VLAN configuration and implementing VLAN Trunking Protocol (VTP) to make VLAN management easier. Although you can manage VLAN deployment without VTP, using it does diminish the legwork on large networks, and by the end of this chapter, you will be able to lay out a simple network deployment with VLANs and VTP.

Implementing Virtual Local Area Networks (VLANs)

With the cost per port for switches following the same economies of scale as most other items in the world, it makes sense to purchase switches with the highest port count — so to save money, get one 48-port switch rather than two 24-port switches. But what about those four users who need to be isolated from everyone else? If you have a standardized switch model used in your organization, you may be forced to get those users another 12-port or 24-port switch in the same series and, of course, wasting the additional ports. I would if I were not using a managed switch that supports VLAN technology.

By using VLANs, you can take four ports on one switch and associate them with a VLAN, which means you treat those four ports as their own separate switch. Doing so allows you to isolate them and save money on a new hardware purchase. Even better, by being careful with VLAN and port assignments, those four ports do not need to be on the same switch or in the same wiring closet, because you can interconnect all the ports belonging to a single VLAN over inter-switch links that have been configured for Trunk mode. A port configured for Trunk mode is also called a *trunk port* and, by default, it will pass traffic for all VLANs. You will hear about trunk ports throughout this chapter.

In short, VLANs allow you to break up devices on your network regardless of their location. Figure 5-1 illustrates separating users' computers and servers into functional groups. The servers are isolated in VLAN1; VLAN5 is a department with its own departmental server; and VLAN2, VLAN3, and VLAN4 separate users into functional groups, say sales, finance, and manufacturing. Each device can operate on their own VLAN regardless of the location they are connecting on the network. In most cases, these devices are spread over the switches in some manner, but they could also reside all in one location (like the servers do).

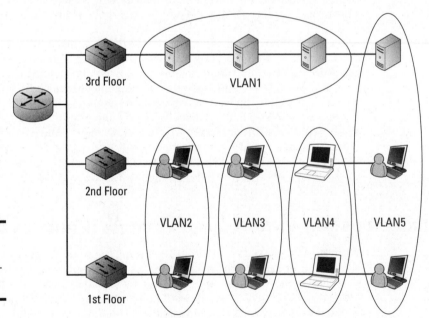

Figure 5-1:
A typical
VLAN infra-
structure.

You now know that you can break up your network into smaller virtual chunks. If you want to know how this all works in the end, keep reading.

Understanding how VLANs work

The magic of VLANs is found in the Ethernet headers. When a switch receives an Ethernet frame, the frame will either already have a VLAN tag or the switch will insert a VLAN tag into the Ethernet header. If the frame was received from another switch, that switch will have already inserted the VLAN tag; while frames come from network devices, such as computers, the frame will not have a VLAN tag. If you are using the switch defaults for VLANs, the VLAN tag that will be placed on the frame is VLAN1. Book I, Chapter 4, covers the basic structure of the frame, but not where the VLAN information is placed. When placing a VLAN tag (also known as an IEEE 802.1Q tag) on the Ethernet frame, the four bytes of data, which make up the VLAN tag, are inserted before the Type field, as shown in Figure 5-2. This 4-byte header includes several pieces of information:

✦ A 2-byte Tag Protocol Identifier (TPID), which will be set to a value of 0x8100 to denote that this frame carries 802.1Q or 802.1p tag information.

✦ A 2-byte Tag Control Information (TCI), which is made of the following:

  • A 3-bit user Priority Code Point (PCP) that sets a priority value between 0 and 7, which can be used for Quality of Service (QoS) priority traffic delivery.

  • A 1-bit Canonical Format Indicator (CFI) that is a compatibility bit between Ethernet and other network structures, such as Token Ring. For Ethernet networks, this value will also be set to zero.

  • A 12-bit VLAN Identifier (VID) that identifies the VLAN the frame belongs to.

**Book III
Chapter 5**

Virtualizing
Networks with
VLANs and VTP

Figure 5-2:
VLAN tagging is supported by implementing an additional Ethernet frame header.

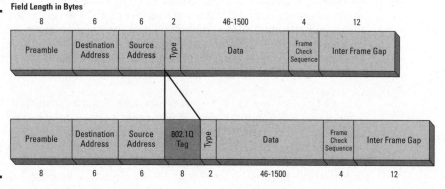

Haggling with gargantuan packet sizes

An unfortunate error can happen when tagging VLANs on a frame. The maximum size of an IEEE 802.3 Ethernet frame is 1518 bytes, which I discuss in Book I, Chapter 4. If the payload or data portion contains its full 1500 bytes of data and the additional 4-byte header into the frame, the frame would be 1,522 bytes in size. To deal with this situation, IEEE released a new standard for Ethernet in 1998 (IEEE 802.3ac) that increased the maximum size of an Ethernet frame to 1,522 bytes. If you have older switches that do not support the larger IEEE 802.3ac frame size, your switches might drop these unsupported frames with notification or might report them as *baby giants*, or overly sized frames.

Prior to the IEEE 802.1Q standard defining VLAN tagging, some vendors took matters into their own hands with proprietary solutions. Cisco's answer to the problem was *Inter-Switch Link (ISL),* which now runs on switchports configured for Trunk mode. In addition to switches, Cisco has supported ISL with router connections since Cisco IOS Release 11.1. ISL implements support for VLAN information in a completely different manner than IEEE 802.1Q; instead of inserting a header into the Ethernet frame it encapsulates the entire existing Ethernet frame into an ISL frame with a new header used to transport the Ethernet frame between switches. The ISL frame adds an extra 30 bytes to the size of the Ethernet frame with a 26-byte ISL header containing the VLAN ID and a 4-byte checksum at the end of the frame. This overhead exists only if the frame goes out over an ISL link.

When the ISL frame leaves the switch, the switch examines the port type of the exiting port. If the port is not part of an ISL link, the ISL encapsulation is stripped from the frame, and the standard 802.1Q tag is inserted into the Ethernet frame.

VLAN frames

Now you know how to move VLAN traffic from one switch to another by using IEEE 802.1Q tags or ISL frames across ISL links, but how does VLAN information get onto the frames in the first place? There are both manual and automatic methods for doing this, but the most common method is the manual method of configuring a port-based VLAN. With a port-based VLAN, your switch examines data that comes in on a port, and if the data is not already tagged with a VLAN, the switch then places a VLAN tag on the data.

When implementing VLANs on your network, you use trunk ports for your inter-switch links, but for your client access ports, you use Access mode instead of Trunk mode. When you unbox your new switch, all ports are in Access mode by default; that means that they expect to have computing devices connected to them, and they will automatically insert IEEE 802.1Q tags into any Ethernet frames that do not already have tags. Typically, ports in Access mode expect to see untagged traffic because computers and other devices do not know how to pre-tag Ethernet frames. If you have implemented IP telephony, IP phones are capable of tagging their own traffic through an integrated two-port switch, as shown in Figure 5-3.

Figure 5-3:
The two-
port switch
integrated
into Cisco IP
phones.

A switch does not expect to see traffic with VLAN tags on ports in Access
mode because most devices on those ports do not tag their own traffic; traffic on Trunk mode ports automatically allow traffic tagged for any VLANs
to be sent to connected switches. Because Trunk mode ports send traffic
tagged for any VLAN, they expect to see traffic arriving from connected
switches tagged for any VLAN.

Passing traffic from VLAN to VLAN

If you read about VLAN information in Book III, you likely expect all of this
VLAN information to be Layer 2 or at the data link layer; it is. VLANs allow
you to isolate users from each other by placing them in different VLANs,
but now how do you pass traffic from one VLAN to another VLAN? Doing so
involves the use of a Layer 3 device to route the traffic from one VLAN to
another; yes, that would be router. Therefore, if your router does not support VLANs or VLAN tagging, this process will require an interface configured on each VLAN, which can be an expensive proposition. For example, in
my case, I would have to purchase a router to support an interface for each
VLAN running on my network. The better solution is to purchase a router
that supports VLANs, which means you can connect a single interface on
your router to a Trunk mode port on your switch, which allows the router to
internally route between virtual VLAN interfaces. The other option you have
available to you is to purchase a Layer 3 switch, which is a switch with routing functions built into it. That is, they are capable of providing all the inter-
VLAN routing functionality, without leaving the switching device.

A managed Layer 2 switch will see tagged or untagged data, and the switch
may be configured to allow traffic on specified VLANs to be forwarded or
blocked. If there is untagged traffic, this switch can place a VLAN tag into the
existing header or encapsulate the frame if sending it over an ISL link. Finally,
trunk ports will pass traffic for all VLANs by default, unless told otherwise.

**Book III
Chapter 5**

**Virtualizing
Networks with
VLANs and VTP**

Several default VLANs are created on your switch that cannot be removed. These include VLANs 1 and 1002–1005. The latter VLANs are used for Token Ring and FDDI networks; VLAN 1 is the default VLAN and is used for Ethernet.

Although supporting 4096 Per VLAN Spanning Tree (PVST) would be nice, one for each VLAN, there is an IOS limit of 64 instances of spanning tree instances. So if you are using PVST, as you do in the next chapter, only the first 64 VLANs will have spanning tree enabled, and it will be disabled for the remaining VLANs.

Setting up VLANs

To create a VLAN on your switch, you can type only one command in Global Configuration mode: `set vlan VID`, which puts the switch into VLAN Configuration mode. However, typically you type a second command, the `name` command, for clarity while in VLAN Configuration mode. That is all you need to do to create a new VLAN. The bigger part of the job includes ensuring that it is available on all the other switches and assigning ports on the switches to VLAN. The following code creates a test VLAN with an ID of 20:

```
Switch1>enable
Switch1#configure terminal
Switch1(config)#set vlan 20
Switch1(config-vlan)#name Test_VLAN
Switch1(config-vlan)#end
```

Now that you have created this VLAN, you can use it as a management interface for this switch. To use it as a management interface, you assign an IP address to the network interface, as opposed to the VLAN interface. You do so with the `interface` command, which you will use to configure a router interface with an IP address. (You can refer to Book III, Chapter 3, which includes how to set the default gateway.)

```
Switch1>enable
Switch1#configure terminal
Switch1(config)#interface vlan 20
Switch1(config-if)#description Test VLAN
Switch1(config-if)#ip address 192.168.20.1 255.255.255.0
Switch1(config-if)#end
```

Using a computer connected to a port on the switch and configured for the same VLAN, you can attempt to ping this address (192.168.20.1). You should find that you could not access the address because the VLAN interface is not enabled. Showing the running configuration sheds light on the issue. Here is the issue and the corrective action:

```
Switch1>enable
Switch1#show running-config interface vlan 6
Building configuration...

Current configuration : 113 bytes
!
interface Vlan20
 description Test VLAN
 ip address 192.168.20.1 255.255.255.0
 no ip route-cache
 shutdown
end
Switch1#configure terminal
Switch1(config)#int vlan 20
Switch1(config-if)#no shutdown
Switch1(config-if)#
1w4d: %LINK-3-UPDOWN: Interface Vlan20, changed state to up
1w4d: %LINK-5-CHANGED: Interface Vlan1, changed state to administratively down
1w4d: %LINEPROTO-5-UPDOWN: Line protocol on Interface Vlan20, changed state to up
1w4d: %LINEPROTO-5-UPDOWN: Line protocol on Interface Vlan1, changed state to down
```

This code brings up VLAN 20 as the management VLAN, but look what happened to VLAN 1, which was the previous management VLAN — it is now disabled. Unlike routing interfaces, which allow multiple interfaces to be up and running, in this case, you are looking at just the management VLAN, and there can only be one. So as you enable another VLAN as the management VLAN, the existing management interface and VLAN are disabled. If you really want to, or need to, use VLAN 1 for your management VLAN, you must issue the no shutdown command for interface vlan 1. I cover the shutdown and no shutdown commands in Chapter 3 of this minibook.

The last step in this exercise is to assign other ports to the VLAN. Here are two common ways:

✦ **Dynamic Assignment with RADIUS Server:** A complicated process of storing MAC addresses in a RADIUS server and passing VLAN assignments back to a switch with a computer attached.

✦ **Port-based assignments:** The most common method for VLAN assignments are port-based assignments. If you connect a device to a specific port on a switch, it will be associated with a specific VLAN. If you plug it into the incorrect port, it will be associated with an incorrect VLAN.

Configuring a range of interfaces

Configuring a range of interfaces or ports on your switch prevents you from having to configure each of these interfaces individually.

Putting your switch into Interface Range Configuration mode allows you to configure multiple ports at the same time, reducing your work when making major configuration changes on your switch. You denote a range for interfaces by specifying the starting interface and the last interface in the range. The following code example uses this technique to configure interfaces 8 through 12. Once the proper Configuration mode is specified, you use the `switchport access` command to place these ports in `vlan 5`. Trunk ports are ports used for inter-switch connections, while access ports are used to connect devices to your switch. The `switchport` command is used to change between Trunk mode and Access mode. The following example lists the other directives available to the `switchport` command:

```
Switch1>enable
Switch1#configure terminal
Switch1(config)#interface range fastEthernet 0/8 , fastEthernet 0/12
Switch1(config-if-range)#switchport ?
  access        Set access mode characteristics of the interface
  host          Set port host
  mode          Set trunking mode of the interface
  nonegotiate   Device will not engage in negotiation protocol on this
                interface
  port-security Security related command
  priority      Set appliance 802.1p priority
  protected     Configure an interface to be a protected port
  trunk         Set trunking characteristics of the interface
  voice         Voice appliance attributes
Switch1(config-if-range)#switchport access vlan 5
Switch1(config-if-range)#end
```

With ports 8 through 12 now associated with VLAN 5, you can verify this configuration using the trusty `show` command. In this case, the most appropriate command is `show vlan brief`, whose output appears in the next command example. Be sure to notice the difference in the VLAN names that appear in this listing. VLAN 2 is assigned a descriptive name; VLAN 15 is assigned a name that is not very descriptive; VLAN 10 is not assigned a name at all, making it even less descriptive. If you want to ensure the proper devices and ports are assigned to the proper VLANs, use descriptive names on your VLANs.

```
Switch1>enable
Switch1#show vlan brief

VLAN Name                             Status    Ports
---- -------------------------------- --------- -------------------------------
1    default                          active    Fa0/1, Fa0/2, Fa0/3, Fa0/4
                                                Fa0/5, Fa0/6, Fa0/7
2    Executives                       active
5    VLAN0005                         active    Fa0/8, Fa0/9, Fa0/10, Fa0/11
                                                Fa0/12
10   VLAN0010                         active
15   VLAN_15                          active
20   Test_VLAN                        active
1002 fddi-default                     act/unsup
1003 trcrf-default                    act/unsup
1004 fddinet-default                  act/unsup
1005 trbrf-default                    act/unsup
```

VLAN database

All of the VLAN information is stored in the VLAN database. This database is on your flash memory and is shown in this directory listing:

```
Switch1>enable
Switch1#dir flash:/vlan.dat
Directory of flash:/vlan.dat

    3  -rwx        780  Mar 13 1993 22:52:09 +00:00  vlan.dat

7741440 bytes total (1058816 bytes free)
```

If you want to enter the VLAN database and make changes to that data directly, you can enter the Configuration mode by typing **vlan database,** but this is a depreciated method of making changes to the data, so you want to limit your changes to one of the standard modes.

```
Switch1>enable
Switch1#vlan database
% Warning: It is recommended to configure VLAN from config mode,
  as VLAN database mode is being deprecated. Please consult user
  documentation for configuring VTP/VLAN in config mode.
```

If you delete the VLAN database, you will remove all VLAN information on your switch. This is not recommended. If you remove all your VLANs, systems that were configured for specific VLANs will no longer be able to communicate properly.

Getting Started with VLAN Trunking Protocol (VTP)

While working with VLANs, you have probably found that it is not difficult to add a VLAN to a switch. It is also not very difficult to configure trunk links between switches, which by default, carry all VLAN traffic; however, the problem you may run into is adding the VLANs to all of your switches. I have worked with switches from other manufacturers that do not include a facility like VTP. Ensuring that all VLANs are configured on all switches is important because if you are not careful with the configuration, you can find that systems on the same VLAN are not able to communicate with each other. Figure 5-4 illustrates how this problem can happen. Notice that Switch 1 and Switch 3 are configured for VLAN2 and both have users; but these devices cannot communicate with each other because Switch 2 is not configured to support VLAN2. Because Switch2 is not configured for VLAN2, it will not pass traffic for VLAN2. The users on Switch 1 and Switch 2 on VLAN3 are able to communicate with each other without an issue because there is a direct link on the correct VLAN between the systems.

**Book III
Chapter 5**

**Virtualizing
Networks with
VLANs and VTP**

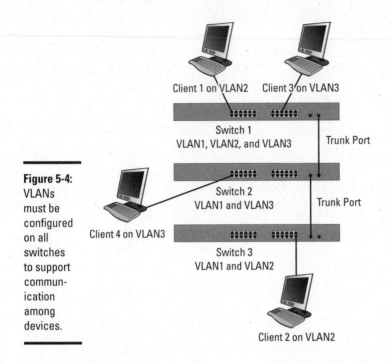

Client 1 on VLAN2   Client 3 on VLAN3

Switch 1
VLAN1, VLAN2, and VLAN3   Trunk Port

Figure 5-4:
VLANs
must be
configured
on all
switches
to support
commun-
ication
among
devices.

Switch 2
VLAN1 and VLAN3   Trunk Port

Client 4 on VLAN3

Switch 3
VLAN1 and VLAN2

Client 2 on VLAN2

VTP alleviates this issue by automatically replicating information about your
VLANs from one switch to another so that all switches on your network are
aware of all VLANs on your network.

Learning how VTP works

As I mentioned when discussing Figure 5-4, a lack of consistency in how you
apply the VLAN configuration across your network can lead to communication
errors or security issues on your network. One security issue that can arise
is having two groups in different parts of the network using the same VLAN
ID. Initially, this is not an issue, but if a link is established between the VLANs,
users you want to keep separate will be combined. To resolve this issue, Cisco
created a protocol to be used on their switching devices. Because switching
operates at Layer 2, this new solution operates at Layer 2 as well.

By making use of trunk links between switches, Cisco added some new
network frames to be sent over those links. These additional frames were
designed to pass VLAN information over the trunk links — thereby being
a VLAN Trunking Protocol. So the information that is sent over these links
allows modification of VLAN information between switches on either side of
the trunk link, including adding, removing, and renaming VLANs, assuming
they all belong to a common VTP domain.

A *VTP domain* is a grouping mechanism used to amalgamate a group of switches into a single management unit. Depending on the roles assigned to each switch, you can create and manage the VLAN configuration on any switch, and those changes will be relayed to all other switches on your network. This also eliminates the chance of having duplicate names or VLAN IDs intended for different types of users or roles.

Without using VTP, I have had to document VLAN configurations for clients or deploy a new VLAN out to their corporate network consisting of numerous switches. Both of these jobs can be daunting. Similarly, when adding a new switch to a network, ensuring that it has your entire current network VLANs added to its configuration is very important. VTP makes this last task as easy as plug-and-play.

Implementing VTP

The first step in implementing VTP is to configure or create a VTP domain. All switches within the same VTP domain will share VLAN information. If you have groups of switches that you do not want to share information, just be sure to use two different VTP domains. Remember though, if you have a switch that has never been configured and you connect it via a trunk port, it will automatically take the VTP domain of the switch on the other end of the trunk port. In this case, you need to configure the VTP domain prior to configuring the trunk port.

**Book III
Chapter 5**

**Virtualizing
Networks with
VLANs and VTP**

The information shared through VTP includes the following:

✦ Management Domain
✦ Known VLANs and VLAN configuration
✦ VTP configuration revision number

Being leery of the VTP configuration revision number

The *VTP revision number* is important because it determines which updates are to be used. When you set a VTP Domain Name, the revision number is set to zero, after which each change to the VLAN database increases the revision number by one. When a switch receives VTP information from a neighboring switch, the first switch processes data only for the same domain when the revision number is higher than its own.

Always check your VTP revision numbers before adding a switch to your network or when adding a switch back to your network. If you remove a switch and place it in your lab, you may create additional VLANs or delete all configured VLANs — either of which will increase the revision number. When you add that switch back into your production network, the switch will have the highest revision number of any device on the network. This forces the deletion of all existing VLANs to all other switches because they will have a lower revision number. Having all of your VLAN information deleted could be ruinous for your data network. Always use `show vtp status` to check revision numbers. You can reset your revision number on the switch you are adding to the network by changing the VTP domain to something else and then changing it back.

Pruning in the VTP tree

VTP solves one problem for you — and immediately creates a new one. Without VTP, you would need to manually create VLANs on all your switches or at least on switches that support devices or pass traffic for that VLAN. This allows traffic, especially broadcast traffic, for that VLAN to pass only through switches that are required in the communication process. The issue you encounter when using VTP is that the VLAN is propagated over trunk links to all of your network switches. The result is that broadcast traffic, as shown in Figure 5-5, will be sent to all switches on your network. This would not be a concern if you had network devices in that VLAN existing on all switches, but you do not; therefore, you have created extra network traffic for no reason. In this case, there is a VLAN2 user on only two switches, interconnected by a third; you need to have the VLAN visible only on switches 1, 3, and 6.

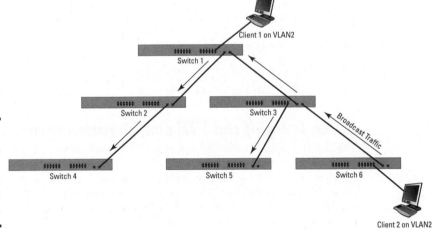

Figure 5-5:
VTP allows
all VLAN
traffic to be
dispersed to
all switches.

Enter *VTP pruning*, a solution that eliminates the need to manually maintain the VLAN information on switches. The pruning feature prevents VLAN data from traversing needless links by monitoring traffic. You enable VLAN pruning on your switch in Global Configuration mode. After you enable VTP pruning, VLAN traffic will be evaluated for a very short time. After VTP determines what switches require what VLAN traffic to send to the switches, it will filter the traffic. After the filtering process starts, much of the background traffic (such as broadcasts) on your network will be reduced, as shown in Figure 5-6. This filtering is not a permanent state because when ports on the other switches are put in the VLAN, the required VLANs for those switches will be unpruned.

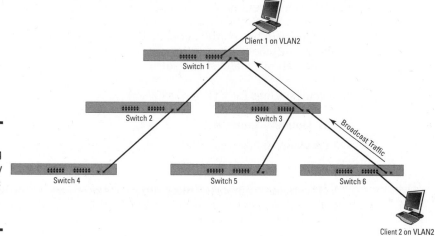

Figure 5-6:
VTP Pruning automatically filters traffic to where it is needed.

Only VLANs 2 to 1001 are pruned by default. VLAN1 is used for system tasks, such as carrying management data, so it will never be pruned. VTP pruning is not compatible with switches that are running in Transparent mode (because it is not able to manage them).

Configuring VTP

You must do a few things to configure VTP. You need to configure a port on your switch as a trunk (refer to Book III, Chapter 3, for the steps to complete this process); then you need to enable VTP. You use three operating modes with VTP that you designate in Global Configuration mode:

✦ **VTP Client mode:** When running in Client mode, your switch will only receive configurations from other devices and will not allow changes to VLANs to be made on that specific switch.

✦ **VTP Server mode:** This mode allows you to make changes and propagate those changes out to all other switches in the domain. This is the default mode on your switches when you unpack them. How many servers can you have on your network? Well, as many as you want. Your VTP server will send VTP advertisements through 802.1Q trunk links to other switches, keeping them aware of any changes that occur on the switch. VTP Server mode switches will also accept VTP advertisements from other switches and apply revisions that are more recent.

✦ **VTP Transparent mode:** When a switch is running in this mode, you can create and modify VLANs on that switch, but those changes are not sent to other switches on the network. You can pass VTP through the switch, but the switch will not participate with VTP; rather it will have its VLAN configuration set and stored locally.

The default settings for VTP are as follows:

✦ **VTP Domain Name:** Null

✦ **VTP Mode:** Server

✦ **VTP Version 2 State:** Disabled.

VTP version 2 supports Token Ring: This represents the only difference between version 1 and version 2. If you are not using Token Ring, then you should use version 1.

✦ **VTP Password:** None

✦ **VTP Pruning:** Disabled

The other commands you will want to use in Global Configuration mode are listed here. In order to configure VTP, you only need to specify a domain name and a password. The rest of the options do not need to be changed. These two commands will modify the default options.

```
Switch1(config)#vtp domain MyVtpDomain
Switch1(config)#vtp password MyVtpPassword
```

Now, walk through a brief configuration. Note that a switch currently does not have any special VLANs configured, as shown here:

```
Switch2>enable
Switch2#show vlan brief

VLAN Name                             Status    Ports
---- -------------------------------- --------- -------------------------------
1    default                          active    Fa0/2, Fa0/3, Fa0/4, Fa0/5
                                                Fa0/6, Fa0/7, Fa0/8, Fa0/9
                                                Fa0/10, Fa0/11, Fa0/12
1002 fddi-default                     act/unsup
1003 token-ring-default               act/unsup
1004 fddinet-default                  act/unsup
1005 trnet-default                    act/unsup
```

Because you want the entire VLAN configuration copied to this switch, you will want to use VTP. However, you have determined that you will not need to be able to make changes to the overall network VLAN configuration from this switch, which is ideal for VTP Client mode. You also configure it for the network VTP domain that you are working with here, which includes a password. Notice the status messages you get as you make the configuration changes:

```
Switch2>enable
Switch2#configure terminal
Enter configuration commands, one per line.  End with CNTL/Z.
Switch2(config)#vtp mode client
Setting device to VTP CLIENT mode.
Switch2(config)#vtp domain edtetz.net
Changing VTP domain name from NULL to edtetz.net
Switch2(config)#vtp password MyVtpPass
Setting device VLAN database password to MyVtpPass
Switch2(config)#end
```

Even though you made these changes, if you check the VLAN configuration on the switch, you will not see any changes. That is because VTP information passes only through trunk ports, which have not been configured on this switch. You have already made the necessary changes on your other network switches, like Switch 1, so you just need to make the change here. Now, make sure that all ports that interconnect switches are configured as trunks and are actually trunking:

```
Switch2>enable
Switch2#configure terminal
Enter configuration commands, one per line.  End with CNTL/Z.
Switch2(config)#interface fastEthernet 0/1
Switch2(config-if)#switchport mode trunk
Switch2(config-if)#end
```

Wait just a few seconds, and the VTP traffic will start flowing through to this switch. Once that happens, you are able to check the status of the VLANs and see the change based on the VLAN data that comes through from Switch 1. Here is how `show vlan brief` looks now.

**Book III
Chapter 5**

**Virtualizing
Networks with
VLANs and VTP**

```
Switch2>enable
Switch2#show vlan brief

VLAN Name                             Status    Ports
---- -------------------------------- --------- -------------------------------
1    default                          active    Fa0/2, Fa0/3, Fa0/4, Fa0/5
                                                Fa0/6, Fa0/7, Fa0/8, Fa0/9
                                                Fa0/10, Fa0/11, Fa0/12

2    Executives                       active
5    VLAN0005                         active
10   VLAN0010                         active
15   VLAN_15                          active
20   Test_VLAN                        active
1002 fddi-default                     act/unsup
1003 token-ring-default               act/unsup
1004 fddinet-default                  act/unsup
1005 trnet-default                    act/unsup
```

Viewing your VTP settings

VTP changes the VLAN database of your switch; therefore, you will not see VTP information in your running configuration. This is sometimes confusing because whenever you make changes in Global Configuration mode, the changes show up in your running configuration — except your VTP settings. To see the VTP settings, use the show command. Passwords are listed with the password command.

```
Switch1>enable
Switch1#show vtp ?
  counters  VTP statistics
  password  VTP password
  status    VTP domain status
```

The most useful option probably is status, which shows you the VTP configuration — minus the password — for your switch. Note that you see the revision number here, as well as the mode and domain name:

```
Switch1>enable
Switch1#show vtp status
VTP Version                     : 2
Configuration Revision          : 1
Maximum VLANs supported locally : 128
Number of existing VLANs        : 11
VTP Operating Mode              : Server
VTP Domain Name                 : edtetz.net
VTP Pruning Mode                : Disabled
VTP V2 Mode                     : Disabled
VTP Traps Generation            : Disabled
MD5 digest                      : 0xBC 0x8C 0xD6 0xE4 0x2F 0xA4 0x5D 0x28
Configuration last modified by 192.168.1.243 at 3-20-11 22:27:26
Local updater ID is 192.168.1.243 on interface Vl1 (lowest numbered VLAN
     interface found)
```

counters is a little less useful — unless you are not seeing any of the VLAN updates from neighboring switches. In that case, counters is very useful because it shows you the advertisements that you sent and received. If you are not receiving these, check the Trunk settings. The last thing you see in counters is the pruning information, which again will be useful if you have VTP pruning enabled because it shows where the pruning occurs on the network.

```
Switch1>enable
Switch1#configure terminal
Switch1#show vtp counters
VTP statistics:
Summary advertisements received    : 6
Subset advertisements received     : 1
Request advertisements received    : 0
Summary advertisements transmitted : 7
Subset advertisements transmitted  : 2
Request advertisements transmitted : 0
Number of config revision errors   : 5
Number of config digest errors     : 0
Number of V1 summary errors        : 0


VTP pruning statistics:

Trunk            Join Transmitted Join Received    Summary advts received from
                                                   non-pruning-capable device
---------------- ---------------- ---------------- ---------------------------
Fa0/1                   0                0                 0
```

**Virtualizing
Networks with
VLANs and VTP**

Chapter 6: Adding Fault Tolerance with STP

In This Chapter

✏ **Examining the basic role of STP on your network**

✏ **Setting up STP on your network**

✏ **Troubleshooting and debugging STP on your network**

A network segment is allowed to be only so long from end to end, because there is a required limit to how long it takes for the collision notification. If you create a network loop, which can happen accidentally, a problem will occur on the network as soon as a piece of data is sent on the network. The data is sent in a never-ending loop until the switch is crushed under the volume of data that it is attempting to forward to its destination, even though it is the same packet, again, and again, and again. If this data is broadcast data, it will span the entire network segment, regardless of how many switches make up the network.

Digital Equipment Corporation (DEC) created a protocol to deal with this problem and called it *Spanning Tree Protocol* or STP, and IEEE published it as a standard called 802.1D. This protocol has been improved multiple times over the years, mostly to deal with shortening the time it takes for the protocol to respond to changes on the network.

If you have or are planning to implement STP on your network, you will find the information in this chapter helpful because it explains the benefits of STP and possible issues involved in its normal course of operation.

Working with Spanning Tree Protocol (STP)

STP was developed before switches were created in order to deal with an issue that occurred with networks that were implementing network bridges. STP serves two purposes: First, it prevents problems caused by loops on a network. Second, when redundant loops are planned on a network, STP deals with remediation of network changes or failures.

The difference between a bridge and a switch is that a switch functions like a multiport bridge; whereas a bridge might have two to four ports, a switch looks like a hub and, on an enterprise network, will usually have 12 to 48 ports. As you go through this chapter, note that STP technology uses the term *bridges,* when you are actually placing switches (multiport bridges). At the time STP was created, switches did not exist. Clear as mud?

Building the initial topology

STP is a Layer 2 protocol that passes data back and forth to find out how the switches are organized on the network and then takes all the information it gathers and uses it to create a logical tree. Part of the information STP receives defines exactly how all the network switches are interconnected. STP builds this information by sending out network packets called Bridge Protocol Data Units (BPDUs or sometimes BDUs). These BPDUs — or rather the data in them — control the way STP determines the network topology.

Figure 6-1 shows a basic network with simplified 4-digit MAC addresses for the switches. All the switches on the network will send BPDU frames to the entire network, even if a network that does not have any loops. These packets, by default, are sent out on the network every two seconds, are very small, and do not negatively affect the network traffic. If you are performing a packet capture on a network, however, be aware that these packets fill your capture screen quickly and can be distracting when reviewing your captured data. The initial process of sending BPDU frames will determine which switch will be the *Root Bridge* and act as the controller or manager for STP on the network. By default, the Root Bridge is the switch with the numerically lowest MAC address.

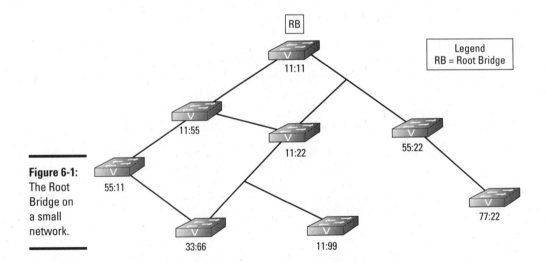

Figure 6-1:
The Root
Bridge on
a small
network.

Identifying Root Ports

The BPDU, which every switch sends, contains information about the switch and its *Bridge ID* that uniquely identifies the switch on the network. The Bridge ID is made of two components: a configurable Bridge Priority value (which is 32,769 by default) and the switch MAC address. If none of the switches on your network has had its Bridge Priority values adjusted, then the switch with the lowest MAC address will be the Root Bridge; but if the Bridge Priority values on your network have been modified, the Root Bridge will be the switch with the lowest Bridge Priority value. The Root Bridge shown in Figure 6-1 is switch 11:11.

After the Root Bridge is identified, all other switches determine the quickest path from themselves to the Root Bridge. Some switches have more than one path to the Root Bridge due to a network loop. In Figure 6-1, switch 11:22 has two paths, one that is two hops away from the Root Bridge and one that is one hop away. If the speed of the networking technology is the same for all network segments, the path with the fewest number of hops is designated as the Root Port.

The switch will identify which of its interfaces is the Root Port. Each network technology has a rated speed, so based on the technology of each network segment between the switch and the Root Bridge, the switch is able to calculate the cost of each available path. Table 6-1 lists the STP cost associated with each network technology speed. Notice in the table that the data rate is inversely proportional to the STP cost.

Table 6-1	Network Speeds and STP Costs
Data Rate	**STP Cost**
4 Mbps	5,000,000
10 Mbps	2,000,000
16 Mbps	1,250,000
100 Mbps	200,000
1 Gbps	20,000
2 Gbps	10,000
10 Gbps	2,000

In Figure 6-2, all the Root Ports are identified. In the event that a switch has two paths to the Root Bridge and each path has the same cost, then the switch will look at the BPDU frames from its closet neighbor on each of the paths. The switch will designate its Root Port based on the neighbor with the lowest Bridge ID.

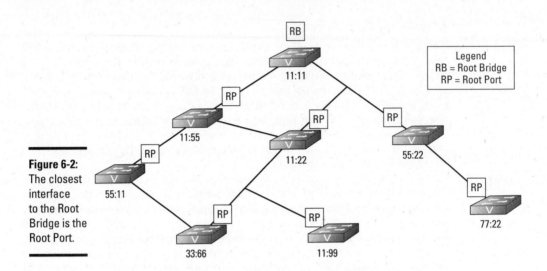

Figure 6-2:
The closest
interface
to the Root
Bridge is the
Root Port.

Identifying Designated Ports

Each switch knows the least cost path to take to get to the Root Bridge, which may require passing data to another switch's interface. For the sake of this example, I call the main switch that I am using in my example the reference switch and its neighbor the neighbor switch. The port on the next closest switch (neighbor switch) to the Root Bridge that is facing the reference switch is called the *Designated Port*. The reference switch will use the Designated Port as its path to get to the Root Bridge. Figure 6-3 identifies all the Designated Ports that the downstream switches will use to send data to the Root Bridge.

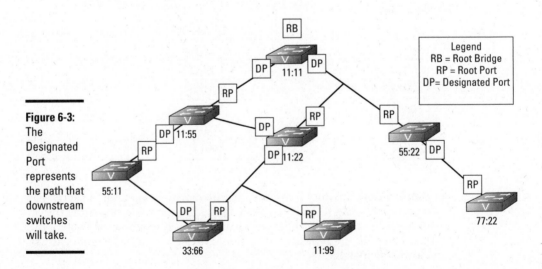

Figure 6-3:
The
Designated
Port
represents
the path that
downstream
switches
will take.

Blocking loops

You still have one outstanding problem to resolve. There are still loops on this network that threaten to bring the current network down; however, by working through how all the Root Ports and Designated Ports are assigned, you have actually completed the work to resolve the loop issue on the network. In Figure 6-3, only two ports are used to connect to neighboring switches that are neither Root Ports nor Designated Ports. Because these ports do not have either role assigned to them, they are part of a loop on the network. If you review Figure 6-3, you should be able to identify the loops on the network. To resolve the loop issue, STP puts these ports without a role into Blocking state, which means these are *Blocking Ports*. Blocking Ports are ports that do not allow traffic to be sent or received through the port; it is blocking the traffic. Essentially, you could say that the Blocking Ports have been disabled, but they are not disabled. Since the ports are not disabled, the switch on the other end of the link still sees the link as active, but frames that are sent over that link (excluding BPDU frames) are dropped (blocked). Figure 6-4 shows you the completed STP diagram, including the Blocking Ports.

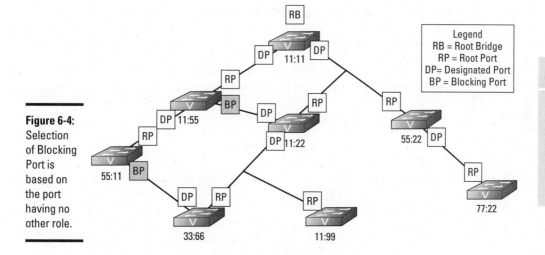

Figure 6-4:
Selection of Blocking Port is based on the port having no other role.

Dealing with network changes

What happens when you connect a new hub or switch to this sample network? I will use a hub for this example because it lacks any network intelligence. In Figure 6-5, I connected a hub to a port on both switch 11:99 and switch 77:22.

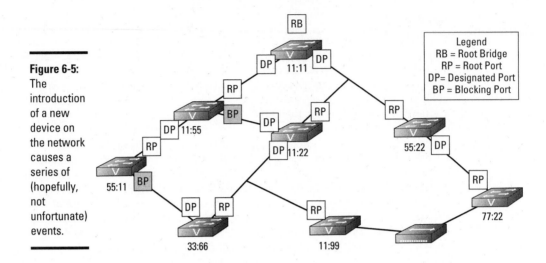

Figure 6-5:
The introduction of a new device on the network causes a series of (hopefully, not unfortunate) events.

The net effect is actually the same as directly connecting these two switches with a standard network cable; I have created a loop on the network through switches 11:99, 11:22, 55:22, and 77:22. The hub operates at Layer 1 and does not know anything about Layer 2 or STP, so the hub treats the links of both of the ports, which were just connected as active and will happily pass data back and forth through this connection. The switches, on the other hand, do *not* treat this connection as active. Anytime an interface or port has its state changed to Up because either you connect a device or issue a `no shutdown` command on the interface, a switch follows a strict process, placing the port into one of the four STP port states shown in Table 6-2.

Table 6-2	STP Port States
State	*Description*
Blocking	If there is a loop after STP topology is learned and known, a port is placed in Blocking state to prevent the loop from being detrimental to the network.
Listening	When a port's state changes to Up, it is placed in a Listening state, which allows it to process and forward BPDU data, but it will drop all other data that it sees.
Learning	After listening, if the switch decides that the connection did not cause a loop, it learns what addresses are on the network segment and adds them to its address database to prevent some of the flooding that would otherwise take place on the switch.
Forwarding	If no loops are caused by the interface, any data going to or from that interface is forwarded as normal on a switch.

Here is what happens when a port's state changes to Up:

1. Each switch to which the hub has been connected (switches 11:99 and 77:22) notices that the link state of one of their ports has changed to Up. Each switch puts the newly linked port in Listening state, which means that it sees and forwards BPDU frames, but does not pass other traffic. At this time, each switch does not know if this new link will create a loop on the network.

2. After a delay of 30 seconds, if the newly linked port does not see any BPDUs, or if the result of those BPDUs does not indicate a loop, the port goes into Learning state for 15 seconds and then transitions to Forwarding state. In this case, each switch 11:99 will have sent BPDUs on the port to which the hub is connected and switch 77:22 will have seen the BPDU frames, and vice-versa. Because of seeing each other's BPDUs, these switches will know that they are connected to each other and are creating a loop. With this knowledge, they will start the process of calculating the path cost to the root bridge, which in this is a case of equal cost paths to Root Bridge; the path from each switch, through the hub will pass through two other switches. Because there are equal path costs, the tie is solved by designating the lowest priority switch as a Designated Port and blocking on the other port, as shown in Figure 6-6. With the assignment of a new Root Port, Designated Port, or identification a new Root Bridge, a change has been made to the STP structure on the network. Any change to the STP structure on the network is called a *topology change,* and the layout of the STP structure is called the STP *topology.*

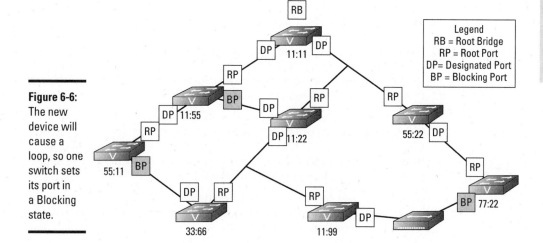

Figure 6-6: The new device will cause a loop, so one switch sets its port in a Blocking state.

Effect of a network loop

So what happens when there is a loop on your network and you do not have spanning tree running? Well, if you have no network traffic on your network, then nothing. If you have a hub-based network, as soon as the first piece of data is sent on the network, a single Ethernet frame will cycle through the loop repeatedly. A single network frame will cycle around the network and actually consume 100% of the possible network bandwidth.

If you have a switch-based network, then it may actually take a broadcast packet to cause a problem with a network loop. When a switch gets a broadcast from a network device, it forwards it out through all ports. The neighboring switch will get that broadcast and forward the broadcast through all other ports, and due to the loop, this broadcast will make its way to the original switch that received the broadcast from the network device. When the broadcast arrives, it will not know that it has seen it before, so it will forward it to all other ports. This process will be repeated thousands of times per second, causing a huge volume of traffic from a single broadcasted Ethernet frame. When this happens on your network, everyone will lose the ability to communicate on the network, and the activity lights on your switches will be solid (on) rather than blinking (on and off). If you break the loop, your network will return to normal in a few minutes.

In Figure 6-7, I created an interface problem in switch 11:55. I either typed the shutdown command in the interface or unplugged the cable; either way, the state of the port has changed to Down. Suddenly, the other devices connected to switch 55:11 do not have a path to the rest of the network as they were using that inter-switch connection and the other inter-switch connection is in a Blocking state. The following process occurs:

1. Switch 55:11 detects a change on an interface or notices that the BPDU data stops showing up, so the switch will flood the change in its BPDU frames and send them out through all switch ports, including the Blocking Port that it knew had a connection to the rest of the network at one time.

2. In the review of the topology, switch 55:11 actually announces via its BPDU frame that a topology change has occurred by sending a Topology Change Notification (TCN) BPDU. This data goes directly to the Root Bridge, which sends BPDU updates to the rest of the network. Because of this topology change, a few things happen:

   a. Switch 55:11 takes the port on Segment A (see Figure 6-7) and places it in Forwarding state, after identifying this action as the way to correct the isolation it is undergoing.

   b. The Root Bridge receives notification of the change.

   c. Other switches on the network receive notification of the change.

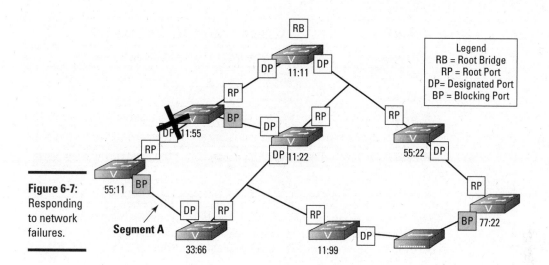

Figure 6-7:
Responding
to network
failures.

This activation process happens quickly after a failure is noticed, but detecting the failure can take several seconds. The delay in detecting a failure is because the switch should not have received several of the expected BPDU frames over the link before transitioning the relevant ports from Blocking to Forwarding. Even with this small delay, which may create a problem for some of your network-based applications, the corrective action taken by STP is much faster than your locating the interface at issue and establishing the links manually.

Setting Up STP

All switches from Cisco ship with STP enabled by default, but if STP is misconfigured for any reason, you can easily enable it. To enable spanning tree, connect to your switch and type spanning-tree mode <*selected mode*> while in Global Configuration mode. Table 6-3 lists some of the differences among the different versions of spanning tree. The current version of the IOS supports the following modes and defaults to PVST mode.

```
Switch2> enable
Switch2# configure terminal
Switch2(config)#spanning-tree mode ?
  mst        Multiple spanning tree mode
  pvst       Per-Vlan spanning tree mode
  rapid-pvst Per-Vlan rapid spanning tree mode
```

**Book III
Chapter 6**

**Adding Fault
Tolerance
with STP**

Table 6-3	**Comparison of STP Versions**	
STP Version	*IEEE Identifier*	*Failover Interval*
STP	802.1D	30–50 seconds
RSTP (Rapid)	802.1w	6 seconds (3 Hello intervals)
MSTP or MST (Multiple)	802.1s or 802.1Q-2005	6 seconds (3 Hello intervals)
PVST (Per VLAN)	Cisco Proprietary	6 seconds (3 Hello intervals)
R-PVST (Rapid)	Cisco Proprietary	6 seconds (3 Hello intervals)

After you enable a version of STP on your switch, you need to configure some of the options for the STP, with the biggest option being one of the fast technologies. One the most popular of these options is PortFast, which I cover in the upcoming "STP and PortFast" section.

```
Switch2> enable
Switch2# configure terminal
Switch2(config)#spanning-tree ?
  backbonefast   Enable BackboneFast Feature
  etherchannel   Spanning tree etherchannel specific configuration
  extend         Spanning Tree 802.1t extensions
  loopguard      Spanning tree loopguard options
  mode           Spanning tree operating mode
  mst            Multiple spanning tree configuration
  pathcost       Spanning tree pathcost options
  portfast       Spanning tree portfast options
  uplinkfast     Enable UplinkFast Feature
  vlan           VLAN Switch Spanning Tree
```

STP and issues with VLANs

Before talking about PortFast, I want to discuss the issue that you encounter when implementing VLANs on a network that is supporting STP. When STP was developed, the concept of a VLAN had not even entered anyone's thoughts. When VLANs started to become popular, the issue with mixing these two technologies on the same network became apparent; STP only expects to support one network.

Examine Figure 6-8 for a moment. If you had to live with the original version of STP, the port that will be blocked is identified on switch 11:55. In this implementation, VLAN1 is configured to run on all network segments, but VLAN2 is implemented on only two of the three network segments. However, now spanning tree has blocked access to the two portions of VLAN2. The upshot is that computers on these segments, if they are part of VLAN2, will not be able to communicate. To resolve this problem, Per VLAN Spanning Tree (PVST) implements an instance of STP for each VLAN. With PVST, the STP topology for VLAN1 will remain the same; but because VLAN2 is implanted on two segments, it will not form a loop because there is a break in the network between switches 11:11 and 11:22. In the case of the STP topology for VLAN2, there would be no Blocking Ports.

Figure 6-8:
VLAN
and STP
interaction.

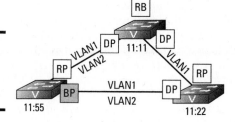 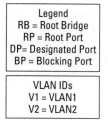

> **Legend**
> RB = Root Bridge
> RP = Root Port
> DP= Designated Port
> BP = Blocking Port

> **VLAN IDs**
> V1 = VLAN1
> V2 = VLAN2

When providing VLAN support for STP you encounter two protocols on your Cisco switches:

+ **MSTP:** An open standards version of STP that allows you to initiate multiple copies of STP on your switch and manually configure separate zones or implementations. MSTP uses the same basic frame structure as RSTP but after the RSTP data in the frame concludes, MSTP adds an additional section to support VLANs on your network. This structure makes it backwards compatible with RSTP, which may be running on your network.

+ **PVST:** *Per VLAN Spanning Tree* is more popular than MSTP, especially if a very structured VLAN solution is implemented on your network. Per VLAN creates an instance of STP for each VLAN running on your network, up to a limit of 64 VLANs. If you need to implement more than 64 VLANs on your network, only 64 VLANs can have an instance of STP operating.

STP and PortFast

Another problem that you may encounter with spanning tree relates to the time it takes to transition ports over to the Forwarding state. This factor of time is not an issue for many people, but it can cause problems for some. If I power up my computer in the morning, power goes to the network card immediately (earlier, if I have Wake-on-LAN for my NIC), and the port on the switch enters the Listening state. By the time the OS wants to start up the network card drivers and get an address from DHCP, the port on the switch is in Forwarding state, which works well most of the time. If, however, I unplugged the NIC on my laptop to move it to another desk, Windows will tell me that it has a problem communicating on the network. Why? The NIC connected to the port changed the link state of the port to Up, Windows immediately tried to get a DHCP address, but the port is not yet in a Forwarding state. This is a common problem when using STP on your network. In a few more seconds, Windows will attempt to get an IP address again, and it will succeed.

The other time you may see this issue is with Pre-Boot Execution (PXE) devices, such as Windows Deployment Services. Figure 6-9 shows a typical PXE implementation. Here is what happens with PXE: You apply power to your computer, which activates the NIC, but less than five seconds later, the computer's POST finishes and the NIC attempts to get an IP address from DHCP so that it can load a boot image directly from the PXE server, which fails. The computer attempts to get an IP address from a DHCP server several times within approximately 10 seconds, after which it gives up and moves onto another boot device, such as the hard drive. The unfortunate part of this process is that because it fails to get an IP address or connect with the PXE server, you are not able to install your new operating system image on that computer. The problem with this scenario is that because STP makes the computer wait 45 seconds prior to forwarding traffic on the port, the PXE network boot has timed out.

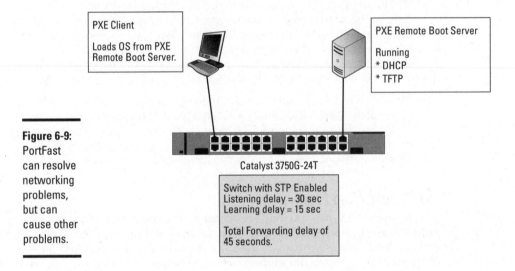

PXE Client

Loads OS from PXE Remote Boot Server.

PXE Remote Boot Server

Running
* DHCP
* TFTP

Catalyst 3750G-24T

Switch with STP Enabled
Listening delay = 30 sec
Learning delay = 15 sec

Total Forwarding delay of 45 seconds.

Figure 6-9: PortFast can resolve networking problems, but can cause other problems.

PortFast is the solution to this problem of delays when client computers are connecting to switches. PortFast is not enabled by default. With PortFast enabled on a port, you effectively take the port and tell spanning tree not to implement STP on that port. This solution is not a bad one if only one computer is plugged into the port — so that people will not be creating accidental loops on the network, which can be frighteningly easy to do. I once had a whole network sporadically brought down for the better part of a week, thanks to a Windows Tablet PC that was set to bridge the wireless connection and the wired connection. Both of these networks were implemented on the same VLAN. When the user left the wireless card enabled and plugged into the wired network, a loop was created, bringing down the network. In this case, STP was enabled, but PortFast was also enabled on the end-user ports so the STP port evaluation process was not conducted.

Setting PortFast on all ports

While there may be some ports you want to exclude from the PortFast configuration (you will see how to handle them in the next sub-section), if you want most ports to use PortFast you make that default setting. To set PortFast on all ports from Global Configuration mode, use the command spanning-tree portfast default:

```
Switch2> enable
Switch2# configure terminal
Switch2(config)#spanning-tree portfast ?
  bpdufilter  Enable portfast bdpu filter on this switch
  bpduguard   Enable portfast bpdu guard on this switch
  default     Enable portfast by default on all access ports
```

Setting PortFast on specific ports

You can also implement PortFast on specific ports, as illustrated here, where the following command enables PortFast for FastEthernet ports 1 through 10. Notice the big warning about the dangers of PortFast.

```
Switch2#configure terminal
Enter configuration commands, one per line.  End with CNTL/Z.
Switch2(config)#interface range
Switch2(config)#interface range fastEthernet 0/1 -10
Switch2(config-if-range)#spanning-tree portfast
%Warning: portfast should only be enabled on ports connected to a single
 host. Connecting hubs, concentrators, switches, bridges, etc... to this
 interface when portfast is enabled, can cause temporary bridging loops.
 Use with CAUTION

%Portfast will be configured in 10 interfaces due to the range command
 but will only have effect when the interfaces are in a non-trunking mode.
Switch2(config-if-range)#end
```

The BPDU Guard option removes the danger expressed in the warning. In this case, I incorrectly selected my ports, and ports 1 and 2 should have spanning tree enabled normally on them. BPDU Guard throws up warnings right away to prevent the loop that has been created from causing a problem on my network. When a PortFast port with BPDU Guard on it sees a BPDU frame, the action causes the switch to say, "Hey, this port is configured incorrectly!" and immediately the switch puts that port in an error state.

```
Switch2#configure terminal
Enter configuration commands, one per line.  End with CNTL/Z.
Switch2(config)#interface range fastEthernet 0/1 -10
Switch2(config-if-range)#spanning-tree bpduguard enable
Switch2(config-if-range)#
3d14h: %SPANTREE-2-BLOCK_BPDUGUARD: Received BPDU on port FastEthernet0/2 with
    BPDU Guard enabled. Disabling port.
3d14h: %PM-4-ERR_DISABLE: bpduguard error detected on Fa0/2, putting Fa0/2 in
    err-disable state
3d14h: %SPANTREE-2-BLOCK_BPDUGUARD: Received BPDU on port FastEthernet0/1 with
    BPDU Guard enabled. Disabling port.
3d14h: %PM-4-ERR_DISABLE: bpduguard error detected on Fa0/1, putting Fa0/1 in
    err-disable state
3d14h: %LINEPROTO-5-UPDOWN: Line protocol on Interface FastEthernet0/2, changed
    state to down
3d14h: %LINEPROTO-5-UPDOWN: Line protocol on Interface FastEthernet0/1, changed
    state to down
3d14h: %LINK-3-UPDOWN: Interface FastEthernet0/2, changed state to down
3d14h: %LINK-3-UPDOWN: Interface FastEthernet0/1, changed state to down
Switch2(config-if-range)#end
```

To correct the error state on the port, connect to that port in Interface Configuration mode and then shut down and re-enable those ports as shown here:

```
Switch2#configure terminal
Enter configuration commands, one per line.  End with CNTL/Z.
Switch2(config)#interface range
Switch2(config)#interface range fastEthernet 0/1 -10
Switch2(config-if-range)#shutdown
Switch2(config-if-range)#no shutdown
```

Troubleshooting STP

The first part of troubleshooting STP is to gather additional information about the running protocol. Our good buddy show will get you started. If you have read other chapters on protocols, you will know that the show command has a great deal of information to display, and STP is no different.

Here is a list of the show options available to STP on Cisco switches:

```
Switch2> enable
Switch2#show spanning-tree ?
  active             Report on active interfaces only
  backbonefast       Show spanning tree backbonefast status
  blockedports       Show blocked ports
  bridge             Status and configuration of this bridge
  detail             Detailed information
  inconsistentports  Show inconsistent ports
  interface          Spanning Tree interface status and configuration
  mst                Multiple spanning trees
  pathcost           Show Spanning pathcost options
  root               Status and configuration of the root bridge
  summary            Summary of port states
  uplinkfast         Show spanning tree uplinkfast status
  vlan               VLAN Switch Spanning Trees
  |                  Output modifiers
  <cr>
```

Because PVST is the default STP version, it also includes statistical information about the VLANs for which STP is running.

```
Switch2> enable
Switch2#show spanning-tree summary
Switch is in pvst mode
Root bridge for: none
EtherChannel misconfig guard is enabled
Extended system ID          is enabled
Portfast Default            is disabled
PortFast BPDU Guard Default is disabled
Portfast BPDU Filter Default is disabled
Loopguard Default           is disabled
UplinkFast                  is disabled
BackboneFast                is disabled
Pathcost method used        is short

Name                 Blocking Listening Learning Forwarding STP Active
-------------------- -------- --------- -------- ---------- ----------
VLAN0001                  1       0        0          2          3
VLAN0002                  1       0        0          1          2
VLAN0005                  1       0        0          1          2
VLAN0010                  1       0        0          1          2
VLAN0015                  1       0        0          1          2
VLAN0020                  1       0        0          1          2
-------------------- -------- --------- -------- ---------- ----------
6 vlans                   6       0        0          7         13

Switch2> enable
Switch2#show spanning-tree root

                                Root Hello Max Fwd
Vlan              Root ID       Cost Time Age Dly  Root Port
---------------- -------------------- ------ ----- --- ---  ----------------
VLAN0001         32769 0006.d6ab.a040   19     2   20  15   Fa0/2
VLAN0002         32770 0006.d6ab.a040   19     2   20  15   Fa0/2
VLAN0005         32773 0006.d6ab.a040   19     2   20  15   Fa0/2
VLAN0010         32778 0006.d6ab.a040   19     2   20  15   Fa0/2
VLAN0015         32783 0006.d6ab.a040   19     2   20  15   Fa0/2
VLAN0020         32788 0006.d6ab.a040   19     2   20  15   Fa0/2
```

This output shows much more information. To abridge the output, I show only the STP information for VLAN1. Here are some of the major pieces of information in this output:

✦ **Bridge address:** The MAC address of the current switch

✦ **Address of the Root Bridge:** The MAC address of the current Root Bridge

✦ **Delays and forwarding times:** The current configured values of the forwarding and delay timers

✦ **Port status for that VLAN:** Status of the ports configured in the displayed VLAN

In the following output of show spanning-tree from Switch1, note that all listed ports are in a Forwarding (FWD) state. Currently, port 11 and port 12 are connected to Switch2, creating a loop.

```
Switch1>enable
Switch1#show spanning-tree
VLAN0001
  Spanning tree enabled protocol ieee
  Root ID    Priority    32769
             Address     0006.d6ab.a040
             This bridge is the root
             Hello Time   2 sec  Max Age 20 sec  Forward Delay 15 sec

  Bridge ID  Priority    32769  (priority 32768 sys-id-ext 1)
             Address     0006.d6ab.a040
             Hello Time   2 sec  Max Age 20 sec  Forward Delay 15 sec
             Aging Time 300

Interface        Role Sts Cost      Prio.Nbr Type
---------------- ---- --- --------- -------- --------------------------------
Fa0/1            Desg FWD 19        128.1    P2p
Fa0/2            Desg FWD 100       128.2    Shr
Fa0/3            Desg FWD 19        128.3    P2p
Fa0/11           Desg FWD 19        128.11   P2p
Fa0/12           Desg FWD 19        128.12   P2p
```

In the following output, you see what the ports look like on Switch2.

```
Switch2>enable
Switch2#show spanning-tree

VLAN0001
  Spanning tree enabled protocol ieee
  Root ID    Priority    32769
             Address     0006.d6ab.a040
             Cost        19
             Port        11 (FastEthernet0/11)
             Hello Time   2 sec  Max Age 20 sec  Forward Delay 15 sec

  Bridge ID  Priority    32769  (priority 32768 sys-id-ext 1)
             Address     0006.d6ac.46c0
             Hello Time   2 sec  Max Age 20 sec  Forward Delay 15 sec
             Aging Time 15

Interface        Role Sts Cost      Prio.Nbr Type
---------------- ---- --- --------- -------- --------------------------------
Fa0/2            Desg FWD 19        128.2    P2p
Fa0/11           Root FWD 19        128.11   P2p
Fa0/12           Altn BLK 19        128.12   P2p
```

If you examine the state of the ports, you see almost the same output as
Switch1, with a few exceptions. Notice that Switch2 knows that it is not the Root
Bridge because the Root ID and Bridge ID on this switch do not match. Port
Fa0/12 is in a Blocking (BLK) state, and a Priority value is defaulting to 32769. If
you want to force a switch to be the Root Bridge or not be the Root Bridge, you
can change this value. A higher value will guarantee that you are not the Root
Bridge, while a lower value will ensure that you are the Root Bridge.

The lowest value achieved by adding the priority MAC address will get to
the Root Bridge. Therefore, if you change this value, you influence the Root
Bridge assignment.

If you have a few core switches that never have a problem with rebooting, adjust the priority so that one of these core switches is your Root Bridge.

Avoid having an edge switch on the far side of a LAN extension as the Root Bridge. An edge switch regularly loses its connection or gets rebooted. When these occur, the entire topology is rebuilt.

Debugging STP

You can collect specific debug information for a number of items related to STP. Consider what you might want to see in your debug data. If you enable debugging for STP or debugging for BPDU items, you will see a BPDU frame for each VLAN every two seconds. This can quickly fill your screen so that you will not be able to see to turn debugging off. Just type the no version of the command that started the debugging. Even if you cannot see it typed, it will work. As a shortcut, you can disable all debugging on your switch with the no debug all command or the shorter u all.

The debug command can be a busy tool if you are not careful. It will fill your screen with output, and you will not be able to see to turn it off. Use u all to disable all available debugging, and be patient.

```
Switch2#debug spanning-tree ?
  all              All Spanning Tree debugging messages
  backbonefast     BackboneFast events
  bpdu             Spanning tree BPDU
  bpdu-opt         Optimized BPDU handling
  config           Spanning tree config changes
  csuf/csrt        STP CSUF/CSRT
  etherchannel     EtherChannel support
  events           Spanning tree topology events
  exceptions       Spanning tree exceptions
  general          Spanning tree general
  mstp             MSTP debug commands
  pvst+            PVST+ events
  root             Spanning tree root events
  snmp             Spanning Tree SNMP handling
  switch           Switch Shim debug commands
  synchronization  STP state sync events
  uplinkfast       UplinkFast events
```

debug all and debug BPDU both quickly backlog the display buffer, so even after you disable the debugging, you may be waiting some time for the output to clear. Most of the data in the output is generated from the BPDU information.

Book III
Chapter 6

Adding Fault Tolerance with STP

```
Switch2#debug spanning-tree all
01:22:46: STP: VLAN0001 rx BPDU: config protocol = ieee, packet from
    FastEthernet0/1  , linktype IEEE_SPANNING , enctype 2, encsize 17
01:22:46: STP: enc 01 80 C2 00 00 00 00 06 D6 AB A0 4C 00 26 42 42 03
01:22:46: STP: Data
    000000000080010006D6ABA040000000000080010006D6ABA040800C0000140002000F00
01:22:46: STP: VLAN0001 Fa0/1:0000 00 00 00 80010006D6ABA040 00000000
    80010006D6ABA040 800C 0000 1400 0200 0F00
01:22:46: STP(1) port Fa0/1 supersedes 0
01:22:46: STP SW: TX: : 0180.c200.0000<-0006.d6ac.46c2 type/len 0026
01:22:46:    encap SAP linktype ieee-st vlan 1 len 60 on v1 Fa0/2
01:22:46:    42 42 03 SPAN
01:22:46:    CFG P:0000 V:00 T:00 F:00 R:8001 0006.d6ab.a040 00000013
01:22:46:    B:8001 0006.d6ac.46c0 80.02 A:0100 M:1400 H:0200 F:0F00
01:22:46: STP: VLAN0001 Fa0/2 tx BPDU: config protocol=ieee
    Data : 0000 00 00 00 80010006D6ABA040 00000013 80010006D6AC46C0 8002 0100
    1400 0200 0F00
01:22:46: STP SW: PROC RX: 0100.0ccc.cccd<-0006.d6ab.a04c type/len 0032
01:22:46:    encap SNAP linktype sstp vlan 2 len 64 on v2 Fa0/1
01:22:46:    AA AA 03 00000C 010B SSTP
01:22:46:    CFG P:0000 V:00 T:00 F:00 R:8002 0006.d6ab.a040 00000000
01:22:46:    B:8002 0006.d6ab.a040 80.0C A:0000 M:1400 H:0200 F:0F00
01:22:46:    T:0000 L:0002 D:0002
```

A much lower throughput item to track, but equally important, is the presence of topology changes. On a stable network, you see these only when switches are being rebooted. In this case, I disabled and re-enabled the ports used in a spanning tree link. Notice how I can see the whole Listening, Learning, and Forwarding transition.

```
Switch2#debug spanning-tree events
Spanning Tree event debugging is on
Switch2#
3d13h: STP: VLAN0001 new root port Fa0/1, cost 19
3d13h: STP: VLAN0001 Fa0/1 -> listening
3d13h: STP: VLAN0002 new root port Fa0/1, cost 19
3d13h: STP: VLAN0002 Fa0/1 -> listening
3d13h: STP: VLAN0005 new root port Fa0/1, cost 19
3d13h: STP: VLAN0005 Fa0/1 -> listening
3d13h: %LINEPROTO-5-UPDOWN: Line protocol on Interface FastEthernet0/2, changed
    state to down
3d13h: STP: VLAN0001 sent Topology Change Notice on Fa0/13d13h: STP: VLAN0002
    sent Topology Change Notice on Fa0/1
3d13h: STP: VLAN0005 sent Topology Change Notice on Fa0/1
3d13h: %LINK-3-UPDOWN: Interface FastEthernet0/2, changed state to down
3d13h: STP: VLAN0001 Fa0/1 -> learning
3d13h: STP: VLAN0002 Fa0/1 -> learning
3d13h: STP: VLAN0005 Fa0/1 -> learning
3d13h: %LINK-3-UPDOWN: Interface FastEthernet0/2, changed state to up
3d13h: set portid: VLAN0001 Fa0/2: new port id 8002
3d13h: STP: VLAN0001 Fa0/2 -> listening
3d13h: set portid: VLAN0002 Fa0/2: new port id 8002
3d13h: STP: VLAN0002 Fa0/2 -> listening
3d13h: set portid: VLAN0005 Fa0/2: new port id 8002
3d13h: STP: VLAN0005 Fa0/2 -> listening
3d13h: STP: VLAN0001 new root port Fa0/2, cost 19
3d13h: STP: VLAN0001 sent Topology Change Notice on Fa0/2
3d13h: STP: VLAN0001 Fa0/1 -> blocking
3d13h: STP: VLAN0005 new root port Fa0/2, cost 19
3d13h: STP: VLAN0005 sent Topology Change Notice on Fa0/2
```

```
3d13h: STP: VLAN0005 Fa0/1 -> blocking
3d13h: STP: VLAN0002 new root port Fa0/2, cost 19
3d13h: STP: VLAN0002 sent Topology Change Notice on Fa0/2
3d13h: STP: VLAN0002 Fa0/1 -> blocking
3d13h: %LINEPROTO-5-UPDOWN: Line protocol on Interface FastEthernet0/2,
       changed state to up
3d13h: STP: VLAN0001 Fa0/2 -> learning
3d13h: STP: VLAN0002 Fa0/2 -> learning
3d13h: STP: VLAN0005 Fa0/2 -> learning
3d13h: STP: VLAN0001 sent Topology Change Notice on Fa0/2
3d13h: STP: VLAN0001 Fa0/2 -> forwarding
3d13h: STP: VLAN0002 Fa0/2 -> forwarding
3d13h: STP: VLAN0005 Fa0/2 -> forwarding
```

Finally, review the following code, which illustrates the terribly chatty BPDU debugging. Note the type of information included in the BPDU frames that steadily crosses your network. In this example, you see where debugging is disabled.

```
Switch2#debug spanning-tree bpdu
Switch2#
3d13h: STP: VLAN0001 rx BPDU: config protocol = ieee, packet from FastEthernet0/2
     , linktype IEEE_SPANNING , enctype 2, encsize 17
3d13h: STP: enc 01 80 C2 00 00 00 00 06 D6 AB A0 4B 00 26 42 42 03
3d13h: STP: Data
       000000000080010006D6ABA0400000000080010006D6ABA040800B0000140002000F00
3d13h: STP: VLAN0001 Fa0/2:0000 00 00 00 80010006D6ABA040 00000000
       80010006D6ABA040 800B 0000 1400 0200 0F00
3d13h: STP(1) port Fa0/2 supersedes 0
3d13h: STP: VLAN0001 Fa0/3 tx BPDU: config protocol=ieee
     Data : 0000 00 00 00 80010006D6ABA040 00000013 80010006D6AC46C0 8003 0100
     1400 0200 0F00
3d13h: STP: VLAN0001 rx BPDU: config protocol = ieee, packet from FastEthernet0/1
     , linktype IEEE_SPANNING , enctype 2, encsize 17
3d13h: STP: enc 01 80 C2 00 00 00 00 06 D6 AB A0 4C 00 26 42 42 03
3d13h: STP: Data
       000000000080010006D6ABA0400000000080010006D6ABA040800C0000140002000F00
3d13h: STP: VLAN0001 Fa0/1:0000 00 00 00 80010006D6ABA040 00000000
       80010006D6ABA040 800C 0000 1400 0200 0F00
3d13h: STP(1) port Fa0/1 supersedes 0
3d13h: STP: VLAN0005 rx BPDU: config protocol = ieee, packet from FastEthernet0/2
     , linktype SSTP , enctype 3, encsize 22
3d13h: STP: enc 01 00 0C CC CC CD 00 06 D6 AB A0 4B 00 32 AA AA 03 00 00 0C 01 0B
3d13h: STP: Data
       000000000080050006D6ABA0400000000080050006D6ABA040800B0000140002000F00
3d13h: STP: VLAN0005 Fa0/2:0000 00 00 00 80050006D6ABA040 00000000
       80050006D6ABA040 800B 0000 1400 0200 0F00
3d13h: STP(5) port Fa0/2 supersedes 0
3d13h: STP: VLAN0005 rx BPDU: config pu allrotocol = ieee, packet from
       FastEthernet0/1  , linktype SSTP , enctype 3, encsize 22
3d13h: STP: enc 01 00 0C CC CC CD 00 06 D6 AB A0 4C 00 32 AA AA 03 00 00 0C 01 0B
3d13h: STP: Data
       000000000080050006D6ABA0400000000080050006D6ABA040800C0000140002000F00
3d13h: STP: VLAN0005 Fa0/1:0000 00 00 00 80050006D6ABA040 00000000
       80050006D6ABA040 800C 0000 1400 0200 0F00
3d13h: STP(5) port Fa0/1 supersedes 0
3d13h: STP: VLAN0002 rx BPDU: config protocol = ieee, packet from FastEthernet0/2
     , linktype SSTP
All possible debugging has been turned off
Switch2# , enctype 3, encsize 22
```

**Book III
Chapter 6**

**Adding Fault
Tolerance
with STP**

```
3d13h: STP: enc 01 00 0C CC CC CD 00 06 D6 AB A0 4B 00 32 AA AA 03 00 00 0C 01 0B
3d13h: STP: Data
       000000000080020006D6ABA040000000000080020006D6ABA040800B0000140002000F00
3d13h: STP: VLAN0002 Fa0/2:0000 00 00 00 80020006D6ABA040 00000000
       80020006D6ABA040 800B 0000 1400 0200 0F00
3d13h: STP(2) port Fa0/2 supersedes 0
3d13h: STP: VLAN0002 rx BPDU: config protocol = ieee, packet from FastEthernet0/1
       , linktype SSTP , enctype 3, encsize 22
3d13h: STP: enc 01 00 0C CC CC CD 00 06 D6 AB A0 4C 00 32 AA AA 03 00 00 0C 01 0B
3d13h: STP: Data
       000000000080020006D6ABA040000000000080020006D6ABA040800C0000140002000F00
3d13h: STP: VLAN0002 Fa0/1:0000 00 00 00 80020006D6ABA040 00000000
       80020006D6ABA040 800C 0000 1400 0200 0F00
3d13h: STP(2) port Fa0/1 supersedes 0
```

Chapter 7: Adding Fault Tolerance with EtherChannel

In This Chapter

✔ Examining the basic role of EtherChannel

✔ Setting up EtherChannel on a Cisco switch

✔ Viewing and troubleshooting your EtherChannel configuration

*E*therChannel allows you to take ports on a switch and combine them to give you a larger data pipe. In this way, you can double, triple, even quadruple, the amount of data you send between two devices. EtherChannel offers great advantages in high-bandwidth situations where you need more throughput.

EtherChannel does not suffer from the delays that Spanning Tree Protocol (STP) does when a failover happens because as long as at least one inter-switch link is still up, there is no interruption (as short as 2 seconds), only reduced bandwidth. (Refer to Book III, Chapter 6, for more on STP.) In situations where absolutely no network interruption can occur, you may prefer EtherChannel to STP. They are not mutually exclusive. You can create two EtherChannel port groups on the same pair of switches, and STP will kick in and do what it is designed to do — prevent this type of loop and block one link while forwarding traffic on the other link.

EtherChannel has been a part of the Cisco IOS for many years, so you should find that all the managed switches you encounter support it. Do not be afraid to enable it on a pair of ports and try it.

After reading this chapter, you will be able to set up EtherChannel on the switches on your network to give you fault tolerance and expanded through-put. I begin by explaining the benefits to using EtherChannel, as well as the cost to implement it (actually, the cost is to your ports, which I discuss in the next section). Then I provide the required steps to set it up, followed by information on how to view your configuration and perform some basic troubleshooting.

Examining How EtherChannel Works

There was a time when the available bandwidth on a switch was limited to a single port. In many cases, a switch came with a couple of faster ports that could be used to connect to another switch. However, this changed in the early 1990s when switch manufacturers decided the way to get more speed out of the switch was to combine physical ports together to form a logical link in a process called *channel bonding* or *Ethernet bonding*.

Today people are still looking for the fastest way to implement inter-switch links. After the release of Fast Ethernet (100 Mbps), you could expect to have a few of these more expensive ports on your switch, allowing you to use them for inter-switch links. The same thing happened after the prices dropped on Fast Ethernet ports, and I started getting 24-port and 48-port Fast Ethernet switches. Gigabit Ethernet came around as a more expensive offering, and rather than getting a switch with 24 or 48 expensive gigabit ports, I could get a switch with two or four Gigabit Ethernet ports to use for inter-switch links. The same process is going on with Gigabit Ethernet switches, which now have ten Gigabit Ethernet ports for supporting inter-switch links. As long as there is a faster but more expensive connection type, you will see it used as a method of interconnecting switches. And when that technology becomes inexpensive, and manufacturers are using it for all their switch ports, there will be new, faster, and more expensive technologies released and used where they can do the most good.

If you have 24 devices running at 100 Mbps on a 24-port switch, they can combine and send up to 2,400 Mbps (2.4 Gbps) — if by chance they all need to send their maximum bandwidth to a remote system at the same time. Additionally, interconnecting with other switches at a lowly 100 Mbps causes a severe bandwidth deficit (2.4 Gbps versus 100 Mbps) when trying to send data. If you add a single Gigabit Ethernet port to the switch, you still have a bandwidth deficit (2.4 Gbps versus 1 Gbps) that is less severe. This is a deficit only if all 24 devices are sending data at their maximum speed, which will not occur normally.

Enter EtherChannel, which allows you to take multiple ports on a pair of switches and interconnect them as a single link. This situation is different from STP, which allows you to connect multiple ports but then blocks traffic on all but one port. With EtherChannel, all ports function as a single combined link. Therefore, if you interconnect two Gigabit Ethernet ports, you get 2 Gbps of throughput, which is slightly lower than the combined potential speed of 2.4 Gbps.

Switches avoid collisions by having only a single host on each collision domain, allowing data transfer at nearly wire speed.

To show a connection deficit situation, I set up a Cisco 2960 switch (WS-C2960-48TT-L) with 48 Fast Ethernet (100 Mbps) ports, and two 1 Gigabit Ethernet copper ports, as well as a Cisco Catalyst 3750G switch (Catalyst 3750G-24T) with twenty-four 1 Gigabit Ethernet ports. During this example, I will adjust the load put on the switch by the client computers.

✦ In Figure 7-1, you see a network with a single client computer streaming data from a video server on a Gigabit Ethernet switch. Having one client on two expensive switches is not typical. When only one client streams the data, the client's computer receives the data at a rate of 60 Mbps. Because a single client computer is on an unencumbered network, you can deduce that 60 Mbps is the maximum speed at which the application can receive data.

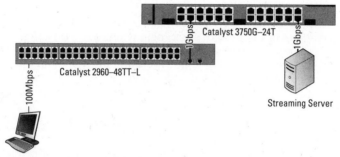

Figure 7-1:
A client streaming data from a video server.

Catalyst 3750G-24T

1Gbps

1Gbps

Catalyst 2960-48TT-L

100Mbps

Streaming Server

Client Streaming at 60Mbps

✦ Figure 7-2 shows a typical network, with 24 clients all streaming video from the server. In this situation, each client receives streamed data at approximately 33 Mbps (1000 Mbps uplink multiplied by 80 percent [network overhead] divided by 24 clients). This is the fastest speed at which clients could possibly get the data. With video streaming at a slower than maximum rate, clients may experience interruptions in their video playback.

✦ In Figure 7-3, a two-port EtherChannel group is enabled between the two switches, which doubles the bandwidth available on the uplink, bringing the link speed up to 2 Gbps. With the inter-switch link at 2 Gbps, the transfer rate for each client goes up to the maximum speed of 60 Mbps per client. To support all 48 clients at that rate, you need two more gigabit ports to add an EtherChannel group — not possible on this switch, but possible with a Cisco Catalyst 3750G switch, which has 48 gigabit ports.

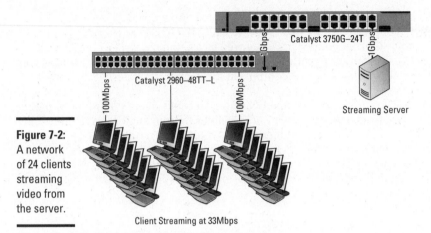

Figure 7-2:
A network
of 24 clients
streaming
video from
the server.

Client Streaming at 33Mbps

You are not limited to combining two ports. You can use EtherChannel to get up to eight active ports in a single channel group and up to six port groups on a switch. Later sections of this chapter walk you through the process of setting up these EtherChannel links.

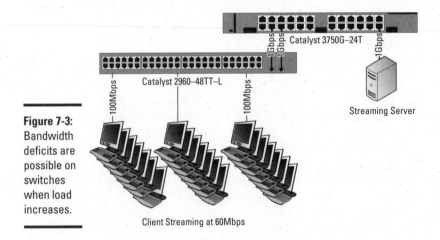

Figure 7-3:
Bandwidth
deficits are
possible on
switches
when load
increases.

Client Streaming at 60Mbps

In the introduction to this chapter, I say that EtherChannel comes with a cost. The cost is the loss of extra ports. If you have two 48-port gigabit switches, and you decide you need an 8 Gbps interconnect, you lose eight ports per switch, whereas you may have budgeted for only one port per switch based on your port counts for servers, and so on. Now your available device ports go from 94 host connections to 80 host connections.

Checking Out EtherChannel Basic Guidelines

Rules, rules, rules, everything in the networking world has rules! EtherChannel is no different; it has a set of restrictions that dictate what you can and cannot do. Before running off to implement EtherChannel, know what the restrictions are so you do not get halfway through and find out it will not work the way you planned. Here are some basic guidelines on setting up EtherChannel:

✦ You can assign up to eight ports to a channel group. Using Link Aggregation Control Protocol (LACP), you can configure 16 ports in the port group, but only eight ports can be active; the other ports are in Standby mode. This is useful when you lose links in the active group, as the standby links will activate immediately. If you happen to configure your ports this way, then you have a very fast, very reliable inter-switch link, with a very high port cost.

✦ You need to configure both switches for the same connection mode: Link Aggregation Control Protocol (LACP), Port Aggregation Protocol (PAgP), or EtherChannel.

✦ PAgP is a Cisco propriety protocol, whereas LACP is an open standard. If you are creating EtherChannel with switches from other vendors, you need to use LACP.

✦ PAgP has two configuration modes, *Auto* and *Desirable*. Auto waits for the other host to start the session, and Desirable attempts to start the session. The Auto setting will minimize the number of PAgP packets sent on the connection. An Auto-configured link can form a session with a Desirable-configured link; a Desirable can form a session with another Desirable-configured link or an Auto-configured link. However, both ends of an inter-switch link cannot be set to Auto, or you would have two hosts on Auto looking rather dumb waiting for each other to start the session.

✦ LACP also has two configuration modes, *Active* and *Passive*. Similar to PAgP's Auto and Desirable, an Active link attempts to start a LACP session by sending out negotiation packets; a Passive link will respond to packets that it receives. As with Auto links in PAgP, the LACP Passive links minimizes the number of LACP packets sent on the connection. Both ends of the link cannot be set to Passive mode, so two Active links can form a session, as can an Active link and a Passive link, but two Passive links will never send out negotiation packets and again will just be standing around looking rather dumb.

✦ All ports in a channel group must have the same configuration for Speed and Duplex settings; otherwise, you have anarchy on your hands. Ports that are 100 Mbps Half Duplex trying to send data when the port they are paired with is a 1 Gbps Full Duplex port is like giving a German person coming to America a translator who only speaks Dutch and Russian.

✦ All ports must be assigned to the same VLAN and have matching switch-port modes.

✦ When STP needs to send data out, it uses only one of the configured ports, instead of sending the data over all the ports.

Setting Up EtherChannel

When setting up an EtherChannel connection, remember the following points; they can help you avoid problems during the configuration process:

✦ You can configure up to eight ports, and all of these ports should be the same type (Fast Ethernet, Gigabit Ethernet).

✦ Set all ports to function at the same Speed and Duplex settings.

✦ Ensure that all ports are enabled and that none have been configured using the `shutdown` command. The `shutdown` command is discussed in Chapter 3 of this minibook.

✦ Switchport settings from the first port in EtherChannel are copied to all other ports in the EtherChannel when the ports are added to the channel group. This is a copy action and not a link, so if you change the settings after the fact, you need to change the settings on all ports. The settings that must remain the same across all ports are

- *Allowed VLAN list*

- *STP path cost*

- *STP port priority*

- *STP PortFast settings*

- *EtherChannel groups*

Cisco's GigaStack, FlexStack, and other proprietary high speed inter-switch links should never be configured as part of an EtherChannel because these stacking ports have specific functionality enabled for stacking functions that is not compatible with EtherChannel. Only use standard connection ports on the front of your switch for EtherChannel connections.

Stepping through EtherChannel configuration

The basic process for configuring your EtherChannel interfaces is as follows:

1. **Connect to the command-line interface (CLI) your switch.**

As discussed in Book I, Chapter 5, this connection may be via SSH, Telnet, or the console port.

2. **Access Privileged EXEC mode.**

   ```
   Switch1> enable
   ```

3. **Access Global Configuration mode.**

   ```
   Switch1# configure terminal
   ```

4. **Access Interface Configuration mode.**

   ```
   Switch1(config)# interface range fasttethernet0/11 -12
   ```

5. **Change `switchport` to `trunk` or `access`, but all ports must be in the same VLAN.**

   ```
   Switch1(config-if-range)# switchport mode access
   Switch1(config-if-range)# switchport access vlan 10
   ```

6. **Assign the port to a channel group, which is an integer between 1 and 6. You also configure PAgP or LCAP at this time by specifying a mode, as listed in Table 7-1.**

   ```
   Switch1(config-if-range)# channel-group 5 mode desirable
   ```

7. **Use the** end **command to exit out of Global Configuration mode.**

Table 7-1		EtherChannel Modes
Mode	*Protocol*	*Description*
Auto	PAgP	Sets the interface to respond to PAgP negotiation packets, but the interface will start negotiations on its own.
Desirable	PAgP	Sets the interface to actively attempt to negotiate a PAgP connection.
On	EtherChannel	Forces the connection to bring all links up without using a protocol to negotiate connections. This mode can only connect to another device that is also set to **on**. When using this mode, the switch does not negotiate the link using either PAgP or LACP.
Active	LACP	Sets the interface to actively attempt to negotiate connections with other LACP devices.
Passive	LACP	Sets the interface to respond to LACP data if it receives negotiation requests from other systems.

The following commands are the setup commands you use for configuring one of the switches for EtherChannel. Notice the keyword "desirable," which means that you will be using the Cisco proprietary protocol of PAgP. This also means that the switch at the other end of the connections needs to be a Cisco switch as well.

```
Switch1> enable
Switch1# configure terminal
Switch1(config)# interface range fasttethernet0/11 -12
Switch1(config-if-range)# switchport mode access
Switch1(config-if-range)# switchport access vlan 10
Switch1(config-if-range)# channel-group 5 mode desirable
Switch1(config-if-range)# end
```

Note that on the second switch, you applied the following configuration. Notice that the channel-group used on this switch is different. Different port groups are allowed because it is simply a local (to the switch) configuration to keep each port group uniquely identified. Many IT administrators do keep the channel-group numbers the same because by matching the port group numbers on either end of the connection, you can avoid confusion for others.

```
Switch2> enable
Switch2# configure terminal
Switch2(config)# interface range fasttethernet0/1 -2
Switch2(config-if-range)# switchport mode access
Switch2(config-if-range)# switchport access vlan 10
Switch2(config-if-range)# channel-group 2 mode auto
Switch2(config-if-range)# end
```

In this configuration, this pair of ports allows you to send data only for VLAN 10 over the EtherChannel link. To pass traffic for all VLANs, you must configure the switchport as a trunk because Access ports will only send traffic for one VLAN.

Configuring EtherChannel load balancing

EtherChannel can use two methods for load balancing connections, with the default load balancing based on the source MAC address of the system sending data. But because it is sometimes more important for some data to be received rather than sent, Cisco gives you a choice. The two methods you can use for load balancing are Source MAC (src-mac) and Destination MAC (dst-mac). So, what exactly does all this mean? When load balancing the connection, the switch takes a look at the MAC addresses in the packet header to determine which link is used for the data. In the src-mac mode (the default load balancing mode), the switch looks at the frame source MAC address, then it passes all frames it sees from the same source MAC address through one of the links. dst-mac works the same way, but it classifies the frames based on the destination and will always pass data from that MAC address through the same link. To configure load balancing, use the following commands:

```
Switch1> enable
Switch1# configure terminal
Switch1(config)# port-channel load-balance dst-mac
Switch1(config)# end
```

To view this setting, use the `show` command, as shown here:

```
Switch1> enable
Switch1# show etherchannel load-balance
Destination MAC address
```

Getting at Diagnostic Information for EtherChannel

To diagnose problems, you first must be able to collect information about your switch and its EtherChannel configuration. To perform this task, you, as always, rely on the `show` and `debug` commands. I start with a brief overview of what you get from the `show` command.

```
Switch1> enable
Switch1# configure terminal
Switch2#show EtherChannel ?
  <1-6>          Channel group number
  detail         Detail information
  load-balance   Load-balance/frame-distribution scheme among ports in
                 port-channel
  port           Port information
  port-channel   Port-channel information
  protocol       protocol enabled
  summary        One-line summary per channel-group
  |              Output modifiers
  <cr>
```

Following the typical Cisco command standard, `detail` gives you more information than you probably want, whereas `summary` gives you little more than the basics. You should check with `summary` first, and if the information you need is there, then you are done; otherwise, load up the screen with information from the `detail` option. The other options for the `show EtherChannel` command give you more information about your ports, port-channels, and protocols (PAgP or LACP) if in your troubleshooting you feel that you need to drill down a little deeper. Here is the summary information for the current connection, which reveals the ports that make up the EtherChannel.

```
Switch1> enable
Switch1# configure terminal
Switch2#show etherchannel summary
Flags:  D - down         P - in port-channel
        I - stand-alone s - suspended
        H - Hot-standby (LACP only)
        R - Layer3       S - Layer2
        u - unsuitable for bundling
        U - in use       f - failed to allocate aggregator
        d - default port

Number of channel-groups in use: 1
Number of aggregators:           1

Group  Port-channel  Protocol    Ports
------+-------------+-----------+-------------------------------------------
2      Po2(SD)        PAgP        Fa0/1(D)    Fa0/2(D)
```

In addition to the EtherChannel information, both PAgP and LACP offer further information via the `show` command. The information can be selected by channel group number and includes counters related to the data that has gone through the links, information about the links that is internal to the switch, and information about the devices on the other side of the EtherChannel links.

```
Switch1> enable
Switch1# configure terminal
Switch2#show PAgP ?
  <1-6>     Channel group number
  counters  Traffic information
  internal  Internal information
  neighbor  Neighbor information
Switch1> enable
Switch1# configure terminal
Switch2#show LACP ?
  <1-6>     Channel group number
  counters  Traffic information
  internal  Internal information
  neighbor  Neighbor information
  sys-id    LACP System ID
```

Here is an example of one of those commands, it is retrieving information about PAgP, using the `internal` option. You can see in the output that even though you configured the switch, one of the cables is not attached (flag is d), and as such, only half of the EtherChannel is up. With the second cable attached, you see both ports with the SC flags and the H timer running.

```
Switch2> enable
Switch2# show pagp internal
Flags:  S - Device is sending Slow hello.  C - Device is in Consistent state.
        A - Device is in Auto mode.         d - PAgP is down
Timers: H - Hello timer is running.         Q - Quit timer is running.
        S - Switching timer is running.     I - Interface timer is running.

Channel group 2
                                  Hello    Partner  PAgP      Learning Group
Port      Flags State  Timers  Interval Count   Priority  Method  Ifindex
Fa0/1     SC    U6/S7    H       30s      1        128      Any      15
Fa0/2     d     U1/S1            1s       0        128      Any      0
```

Debugging EtherChannel

The basic `debug` command options are listed here. As always with the `debug` command, you can use specific options if you have an idea about where the issues are or can enable all of the debug options for the component — if doing so does not generate too much information.

```
Switch2> enable
Switch2#debug etherchannel ?
  all        All debugging
  detail     Step below all
  error      Displaying error messages
  event      Major events
  idb        Agport idb related events
  linecard   SCP messages to linecard
  <cr>
Switch2> enable
Switch2#debug pagp ?
  all      PAgP all debugging
  event    PAgP events
  fsm      PAgP Finite State Machine
  misc     PAgP Miscellaneous
  packet   PAgP activity
  <cr>
Switch2> enable
Switch2#debug lacp ?
  all      LACP all debugging
  event    LACP events
  fsm      LACP Finite State Machine
  misc     LACP Miscellaneous
  packet   LACP activity
  <cr>
```

In this case, both the EtherChannel and PAgP debug commands are enabled,
but not LACP because you do not expect to see any LACP information on the
network. Previously in this chapter, only PAgP was enabled, so if you see
LACP data, something is seriously wrong. In the production network, where
someone else may be configuring the remote end of the connection, it may
not hurt to turn on the LACP option as well. Notice in the output that the
interface is brought up.

```
Switch2> enable
Switch2# debug EtherChannel
Switch2# debug PAgP
3d01h: %LINK-3-UPDOWN: Interface FastEthernet0/1, changed state to up
3d01h: FEC: pagp_switch_agc_compatable: comparing GC values of Fa0/1 Po5 flag =
    1 1
3d01h: FEC: pagp_switch_port_attrib_diff: Fa0/1 Po5 same
3d01h: FEC: pagp_switch_agc_compatable: GC values are compatable
3d01h: PAgP - Fa0/1 failed - not my device_id. 0000.0000.0000 0006.d6ac.46c0
3d01h: FEC: add port (Fa0/1) to agport (Po5)
3d01h: FEC: pagp_switch_add_port_to_agport_internal: msg to PM to bundle port
    Fa0/1 with Po5
3d01h: FEC: pagp_switch_want_to_bundle: Bndl msg to PM for port Fa0/1 to Agport
    Po5
3d01h: %LINEPROTO-5-UPDOWN: Line protocol on Interface FastEthernet0/1, changed
    state to up
3d01h: %LINK-3-UPDOWN: Interface Port-channel5, changed state to up
3d01h: %LINEPROTO-5-UPDOWN: Line protocol on Interface Port-channel5, changed
    state to up
```

**Book III
Chapter 7**

**Adding Fault
Tolerance with
EtherChannel**

Chapter 8: Speeding Configuration with Smartport Macros

In This Chapter

✓ **Defining and understanding the role of Smartport macros**

✓ **Creating your own Smartport macros**

✓ **Working with existing Smartport macros**

✓ **Deleting macros and cleaning up your old work**

For people who actually plan things out — which should be everyone out there — when implementing changes or deploying new network interfaces, Smartport macros can save you a lot of time. As you probably know from previous experience (for example, with the Microsoft Word macros), a *macro* allows you to record and store a series of steps that you can then replay or use later. A macro allows you to execute a keyboard shortcut or click a custom button to perform an entire series of steps with consistent results. In Microsoft Word, you might use a macro to insert your signature block at the end of a letter, to reformat a table, or to fill in a series of placeholders in a report with actual values stored in a different location.

Two of the main benefits of Smartport macros are related to speed and consistency. With a macro in hand, you can quickly and efficiently apply a specific configuration to a series of ports on your network switches with a minimal amount of effort, making configuration changes easier and quicker to implement and helping to ensure that configurations between ports are consistent. In this chapter, I walk you through the process of creating, applying, and monitoring your Smartport macros.

In Book III, Chapter 3, where I introduce the concept of Smartport macros, you examine Smartport macros from the perspective of the web-based management GUI. This chapter discusses how you can modify Smartport macros and use them in many more ways.

If every network interface you bring up is a custom job, and you find yourself using a ton of macros, consider making your network design standardized and start using macros to reach a goal of network standardization.

Viewing Existing Smartport Macros

To examine your existing Smartport macros, you use the ever-popular `show` command — specifically, you use `show parser macro`. This shows you how many macros are on the switch and exactly what commands are in those macros. Some of these macros are easy to execute, whereas others may require parameters to operate correctly.

Viewing macros using the brief option

The first version of this command that I show includes the `brief` option, which lists the macros found on the system and illustrates the types of devices for which a macro can apply, in either Global Configuration mode or Interface Configuration mode.

```
Switch1> enable
Switch1# configure terminal
Switch1#show parser macro brief
     default global    : cisco-global
     default interface: cisco-desktop
     default interface: cisco-phone
     default interface: cisco-switch
     default interface: cisco-router
     default interface: cisco-wireless
```

Viewing macros without the brief option

If you do not use the `brief` option, you see the following output related to all the macros found on your system. The output of the command includes a count of the macros, as well as full details about each macro, from its name to all the commands that make up the macro. This code sample is the output of the default macros found on an IOS 12.x Catalyst 2960 switch:

```
Switch1> enable
Switch1# configure terminal
Switch1# show parser macro
Total number of macros = 6
--------------------------------------------------------------
Macro name : cisco-global
Macro type : default global
# Enable dynamic port error recovery for link state
# failures
errdisable recovery cause link-flap
errdisable recovery interval 60

# Enable aggressive mode UDLD on all fiber uplinks
udld aggressive

# Enable Rapid PVST+ and Loopguard
spanning-tree mode rapid-pvst
spanning-tree loopguard default
spanning-tree extend system-id
--------------------------------------------------------------
```

```
Macro name : cisco-desktop
Macro type : default interface
# macro keywords $access_vlan
# Basic interface - Enable data VLAN only
# Recommended value for access vlan should not be 1
switchport access vlan $access_vlan
switchport mode access

# Enable port security limiting port to a single
# MAC address -- that of desktop
switchport port-security
switchport port-security maximum 1

# Ensure port-security age is greater than one minute
# and use inactivity timer
switchport port-security violation restrict
switchport port-security aging time 2
switchport port-security aging type inactivity

# Configure port as an edge network port
spanning-tree portfast
spanning-tree bpduguard enable

# Remark all inbound data packets with COS=0 & DSCP =0
mls qos cos override
-----------------------------------------------------------------
Macro name : cisco-phone
Macro type : default interface
# Cisco IP phone + desktop template

# macro keywords $access_vlan $voice_vlan

# VoIP enabled interface - Enable data VLAN
# and voice VLAN
# Recommended value for access vlan should not be 1
switchport access vlan $access_vlan
switchport mode access

# Update the Voice VLAN value which should be
# different from data VLAN
# Recommended value for voice vlan should not be 1
switchport voice vlan $voice_vlan

# Enable port security limiting port to 2 MAC
# addresses -- One for desktop and one for phone
switchport port-security
switchport port-security maximum 2

# Ensure port-security age is greater than one minute
# and use inactivity timer
switchport port-security violation restrict
switchport port-security aging time 2
switchport port-security aging type inactivity

# Enable qos to extend trust to attached Cisco phone
mls qos trust device cisco-phone

# Configure port as an edge network port
spanning-tree portfast
spanning-tree bpduguard enable
-----------------------------------------------------------------
```

**Book III
Chapter 8**

**Speeding
Configuration with
Smartport Macros**

```
Macro name : cisco-switch
Macro type : default interface
# macro keywords $native_vlan
# Access Uplink to Distribution
# Do not apply to EtherChannel/Port Group

# Define unique Native VLAN on trunk ports
# Recommended value for native vlan should not be 1
switchport trunk native vlan $native_vlan

# Update the allowed VLAN range (ALL) such that it
# includes data, voice and native VLANs
switchport trunk allowed vlan ALL

# Hardcode trunk and disable negotiation to
# speed up convergence
switchport mode trunk
switchport nonegotiate

# Configure qos to trust this interface
mls qos trust cos

# 802.1w defines the link as pt-pt for rapid convergence
spanning-tree link-type point-to-point
---------------------------------------------------------------
Macro name : cisco-router
Macro type : default interface
# macro keywords $native_vlan
# Access Uplink to Distribution

# Define unique Native VLAN on trunk ports
# Recommended value for native vlan should not be 1
switchport trunk native vlan $native_vlan

# Update the allowed VLAN range (ALL) such that it
# includes data, voice and native VLANs
switchport trunk allowed vlan ALL

# Hardcode trunk and disable negotiation to
# speed up convergence
switchport mode trunk
switchport nonegotiate

# Configure qos to trust this interface
mls qos trust cos

# Ensure fast access to the network when enabling the interface.
# Ensure that switch devices cannot become active on the interface.
spanning-tree portfast trunk
spanning-tree bpduguard enable
---------------------------------------------------------------
Macro name : cisco-wireless
Macro type : default interface
# macro keywords $native_vlan
# Access Uplink to Distribution

# Define unique Native VLAN on trunk ports
# Recommended native vlan should NOT be 1
```

```
switchport trunk native vlan $native_vlan

# Update the allowed VLAN range such that it
# includes data, voice and native VLANs
switchport trunk allowed vlan ALL

# Hardcode trunk and disable negotiation to speed up convergence
switchport mode trunk
switchport nonegotiate

# Configure qos to trust this interface
mls qos trust cos

# Ensure that switch devices cannot become active on the interface.
spanning-tree bpduguard enable
---------------------------------------------------------------
```

That was a lot of data! Now imagine having to type in each set of configuration commands every time you wanted to configure a switch interface for another job role! Macros can save your limbs from unwanted carpal tunnel syndrome.

Viewing details for a single macro

To see the details for only one macro, rather than displaying all the macros every time, use the name option, as shown here, to display just the cisco-desktop macro:

```
Switch1> enable
Switch1#show parser macro name cisco-desktop
Macro name : cisco-desktop
Macro type : default interface
# macro keywords $access_vlan
# Basic interface - Enable data VLAN only
# Recommended value for access vlan should not be 1
switchport access vlan $access_vlan
switchport mode access

# Enable port security limiting port to a single
# MAC address -- that of desktop
switchport port-security
switchport port-security maximum 1

# Ensure port-security age is greater than one minute
# and use inactivity timer
switchport port-security violation restrict
switchport port-security aging time 2
switchport port-security aging type inactivity

# Configure port as an edge network port
spanning-tree portfast
spanning-tree bpduguard enable

# Remark all inbound data packets with COS=0 & DSCP =0
mls qos cos override
```

Working with Macros

Macros are a great time saving tool for you to use to help with your switch configurations. To make them even more powerful, I will show you how to create your own macros from scratch. Before I dive into showing you how to create your macro, you need to be aware of a few things, such as the rules that Cisco has regarding macros.

Before boring you with Cisco's rules though, you should note the following things about macros:

✦ When a macro is applied to an interface, all existing configuration on the interface is retained. This is not a total replacement of the configuration, but an augmentation to the existing configuration.

✦ A macro can contain up to 3,000 characters of text. This is not as limiting as a tweet, say, but it does mean that you need to pay attention to what you want to accomplish and get to the point with your macro.

✦ Macros are case-sensitive, so watch your use of case in the macro name. For example, MyMacro is not the same macro as Mymacro or mymacro, all of which could perform completely different operations.

✦ They will not tie your shoes for you.

Rules for creating your own Smartport macro

You have a lot of latitude when using Smartport macros, but here are a few *Do not's!*

✦ You are not allowed to use `exit` or `end`, which would exit you from Interface Configuration mode or Global Configuration mode. The macro needs to run in the context of one interface.

✦ Similar to the previous rule, you are not allowed to change the command mode with a command such as the `interface` command. All commands for a macro need to execute in the current command mode.

✦ To create a macro, you need to enter the Macro Editor mode using the `macro name` command.

✦ When you want to complete your macro, end it with an @ symbol.

✦ You use the # sign to issue a comment line within a macro. Use comment lines to identify the purpose of your macro statements.

Smartport macros and parameters

When working with Smartport macros, you have the option of creating parameters to use within the macros. You identify these parameters in the macro by using the `macro keywords` directive in your macro. When you run this macro you will use the `macro apply` command to provide the macro your parameters. By using parameters, you can make your macros much more flexible and useful.

Creating a sample macro

You are now ready to create a macro; I created Awesome_Macro for this purpose. This macro uses parameters and assigns some of the settings that are applied with the `cisco-desktop` macro in the earlier "Viewing details for a single macro" section.

```
Switch1> enable
Switch1# configure terminal
Switch1(config)# macro name Awesome_Macro
Enter macro commands one per line. End with the character '@'.
# macro keywords $VLAN_ID
# Basic interface - Enable data VLAN only
# Recommended value for VLAN_ID should not be 1
switchport access vlan $VLAN_ID
switchport mode access

# Configure port as an edge network port
spanning-tree bpduguard enable
@
Switch1(config)#exit

Switch1#show parser macro name Awesome_Macro
Macro name : Awesome_Macro
Macro type : customizable
# macro keywords $VLAN_ID
# Basic interface - Enable data VLAN only
# Recommended value for VLAN_ID should not be 1
switchport access vlan $VLAN_ID
switchport mode access

# Configure port as an edge network port
spanning-tree bpduguard enable
```

> **TIP**
>
> After creating the Smartport macro, use the `show` command to verify that the macro was typed correctly.

Applying a Smartport macro to an interface

Applying a macro to an interface is as easy as creating a macro. You can apply a macro to either a single interface or a range of interfaces. When you apply a macro to an interface range, the macro is individually applied to each interface in the range, sequentially. Even if the macro fails to be applied to an interface, the processing will continue on the other interfaces in the range.

First, look at the interface to which you want to apply Awesome_Macro (in my case `interface FastEthernet0/4`) to see whether any configuration is currently applied to the interface. The interface is completely uncon-figured, as seen by the lack of commands between the lines `interface FastEthernet0/4` and `end`.

```
Switch1> enable
Switch1#show running-config interface FastEthernet 0/4
Building configuration...

Current configuration : 33 bytes
!
interface FastEthernet0/4
end
```

To apply a Smartport macro to an interface, you access Interface Configuration mode on the interface to which you want to apply the macro. As shown in the following output, you use the `macro apply` command to apply a specific macro to the selected interface. In the following example, notice how the `VLAN_ID` parameter is applied, as well as how it is identified when using the context-sensitive help (first shown in Book I, Chapter 5).

```
Switch1> enable
Switch1# configure terminal
Switch1(config)#interface FastEthernet 0/4
Switch1(config-if)#macro apply Awesome_Macro ?
  WORD  Keyword to replace with a value e.g. $VLAN_ID
  <cr>

Switch1(config-if)# macro apply Awesome_Macro $VLAN_ID 5
Switch1(config-if)#end
```

Viewing ports that are using your macro

With the macro applied, you now may be curious to find out which ports are using the new macro. To do so, use the following command, which lists exactly what macro(s) have been applied to which ports:

```
Switch1> enable
Switch1# configure terminal
Switch1#show parser macro description
Global Macro(s): cisco-global

Interface     Macro Description(s)
--------------------------------------------------------------
Fa0/4         Awesome_Macro
Fa0/7         cisco-switch
Fa0/12        cisco-router
--------------------------------------------------------------
```

In reverse, you can use the show command to find out which macros are applied to a specific port, as illustrated here:

```
Switch1> enable
Switch1# configure terminal
Switch1#show parser macro description interface FastEthernet 0/4
Global Macro(s): cisco-global

Interface    Macro Description(s)
----------------------------------------------------------------
Fa0/4        Awesome_Macro
----------------------------------------------------------------
```

Now that you know that Awesome_Macro is applied to interface FastEthernet 0/4, you can review the running-config and see exactly what has been applied. Notice that in addition to the actual macro commands, one additional line appears in the interface configuration: the macro description line. This additional line names the macro that has been applied to the port.

```
Switch1> enable
Switch1# configure terminal
Switch1#show running-config interface FastEthernet 0/4
Building configuration...

Current configuration : 326 bytes
!
interface FastEthernet0/4
 switchport access vlan 5
 switchport mode access
 macro description Awesome_Macro
 spanning-tree portfast
 spanning-tree bpduguard enable
end
```

Removing a macro

Removing a macro from an interface is a little more complicated than applying it in the first place. Nevertheless, you can easily remove the macro from the switch. To remove Awesome_Macro from the switch, use the following command:

```
Switch1> enable
Switch1# configure terminal
Switch1# no macro Awesome_Macro
```

The no macro Awesome_Macro command does not remove the macro configuration from the interfaces where it has already been applied, it only deletes the macro. To remove the commands from where they were applied, you can either reset the interface to the default configuration using a command such as default interface or create a reversal macro that has a no command for every macro command. The latter option increases the number of macros that exist on the switch because you will have both a macro and a reversing macro but this allows you to be surgical in removing the macro configuration. Here you reset interface FastEthernet 0/4 to the default configuration.

```
Switch1> enable
Switch1# configure terminal
Enter configuration commands, one per line.  End with CNTL/Z.
Switch1(config)# default interface FastEthernet 0/4
Interface FastEthernet0/4 set to default configuration
Switch1(config)#end
```

To verify that the interface has been reset to the factory default configuration, use the show running-config.

```
Switch1> enable
Switch1# show running-config interface FastEthernet 0/4
Building configuration...

Current configuration : 33 bytes
!
interface FastEthernet0/4
end
```

Book IV

Routing

"It's okay. One of the routers must have gone down and we had a brief broadcast storm."

Contents at a Glance

Chapter 1: Making the Wide Area Network (WAN) Wide

In This Chapter

✔ Identifying the differences between WAN types

✔ Introducing routing protocols

This minibook on routing logically begins with where you are likely to use routers. Although some people use routers on the interior of a well-connected network to separate a larger number of users or to aid in implementing a set of security features, most people use routers to connect remote offices that are linked through their telephone company's network infrastructure.

This chapter looks at the key elements of technologies you can use to make the connections between all your routers. In addition to covering the infrastructure elements, I introduce you to different routing protocols you can implement for your wide area network (WAN).

Identifying Features of a WAN

First, I want to explain what makes up a WAN. Sometimes people want to identify a WAN by the size of the network or by the devices that compose the network, but I disagree with both methods of classification. For example, if your network has 5,000, or even 100,000, devices and you are not using WAN technologies to interconnect them, you do not necessarily have a WAN. If you have a large campus network using routers and dynamic routing protocols and the infrastructure that it runs over is all internal to your organization, you do not necessarily have a WAN.

So, in case you have not already guessed, a *WAN,* by definition, uses infrastructure that you do not own, but that is owned by a telephone company or another external provider. If your network uses a network infrastructure that is owned by your service provider, implementing WAN technologies, you have a WAN. This infrastructure can fall into many areas or technologies; the big criterion is that the infrastructure is not yours.

Sending data long distances

Although I said that long distances are not criteria for defining a WAN, commonly, WANs do span substantial distances. If your WAN spans only a single city, across town is a long way; nevertheless, your carrier may choose different technologies for that distance than they would if your network spanned a state, country, or continent. So, although distance is not a true criterion for determining whether your network is a WAN, most WANs do span a great distance, and the technologies used in the WAN depend a great deal on the distances involved.

Implementing routing protocols

Routing protocols are also not true criteria for a WAN definition. A WAN can either use manual routing or implement a routing protocol such as RIP or EIRGP, which are discussed in the section, "Choosing a routing protocol," later in this chapter. Although larger, more complex networks like a national WAN may be easier to manage when implementing a routing protocol, their use does not dictate that you have a WAN. A large corporation could have a single (but large) building or a campus of several buildings that causes the network to have several routers. To make life easier on the routing front, you could choose to implement one of the many available routing protocols. So, although most WAN environments make use of routing protocols, not all networks that implement routing protocols are necessarily WANs.

Using carrier equipment

By *carrier equipment,* I mean the equipment from your telephone company that allows you to connect your network to the backbone of its network. These network connections can be digital subscriber line (DSL), frame relay, fiber optic, broadband cable, or another technology used by your telephone company or network provider. This component really turns a network into a WAN, allowing your traffic to travel between your locations while traversing another provider's network, mainly your ISP or telephone company.

In some cases, this traffic may cross several providers' networks. If you are connecting two offices and they are in different countries, you may be crossing networks owned by a regional provider, which connects to a national provider and then crosses borders and travels across the other national provider to another regional provider before finally reaching your other branch office location.

It is this use of other people's networks that really defines use of a large LAN versus a WAN (LANs are covered in the next section). So, a WAN is not related to the size of your network, or to your choice of routing protocols, or to any other factors.

Getting a handle on network size

I spend a fair amount of time in this book talking about Local Area Network (LAN) technologies and devices, with a comprehensive look at LAN technologies in Book III, Chapter 1. A LAN is a private network that typically is made up of a well-connected, reliable, and fast network connection. A WAN is a type of LAN. Alternatives on the LAN framework include CANs, MANs, and WANs. All three of these network options are illustrated in Figure 1-1.

CANs

If you take the LAN network model and make it slightly larger, you end up with several buildings in a single area that are interconnected. This kind of network is referred to as a *campus environment* or a *Campus Area Network (CAN)*. In this case, the interconnections between the buildings may be provided by internal resources or by a telephone company or service provider. In most cases, the interconnection of these buildings is a private investment in a network infrastructure because these links will be used indefinitely.

If you use external network providers, you can still refer to this infrastructure as a WAN. However, because the network is typically a private network structure, many organizations refer to it as a LAN. This LAN may be a flat network with switches connecting all of these buildings on a campus or the floors of a building, but because you want to reduce broadcasts spanning your entire network and passing though remote buildings, you probably will implement a series of routers. These routers perform better than switches when managing network traffic and conserving bandwidth for other applications.

MANs

If your buildings are more dispersed, say around a city, your network increases to a *Metropolitan Area Network (MAN)*. In this case, the odds are very high that you will not own the entire network infrastructure, so you will be buying or leasing network connectivity from a service provider. Because your network connections are fairly short range and may all be hosted by one provider, the technology choices may allow you to utilize higher speed or cheaper technologies over traditional WAN technologies. These choices are entirely dependent on what your service provider can offer.

WANs

Finally, you get into *Wide Area Network (WAN)*, using traditional WAN connectivity options such as Frame Relay and switched circuits. These technologies allow you to create a multi-location LAN, or WAN, that could span the globe. In that case, you are dealing with and negotiating connections in many countries and getting all of your service providers or telephone companies to communicate with each other, so you probably need to rely on a routing protocol to deal with the changing link states and network availability.

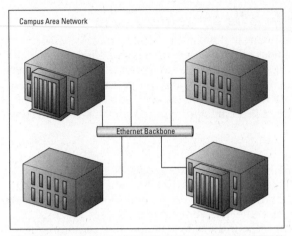

Campus Area Network

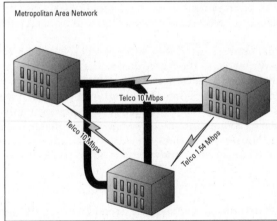

Metropolitan Area Network

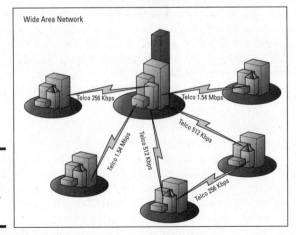

Wide Area Network

Figure 1-1:
Comparing
CAN, MAN,
and WAN.

Choosing Technologies

When you are choosing technologies, you are at the mercy of your service provider, but the provider probably will give you a menu of options to choose from, each with different performance characteristics and prices. Your choices will include an array of physical connection types, which includes technologies such as frame relay or T1 connections. After you have selected a physical medium of connection, you also must choose from myriad routing protocols, including Routing Information Protocol (RIP) and Open Shortest Path First (OSPF).

Revisit your technology choices every few years, because your provider or its competition may be able to give you more performance from less expensive connections.

Getting the physical connection

In almost every connectivity option, you will be using a router to act as the boundary between your network devices and the devices that belong to the telephone company. In many cases in this scenario, you may use two routers, where, as part of your contracted connection, the telephone company provides you with a router that connects directly to your router. In other cases, you may use a router that is supporting T1, ISDN, or another connection type through a WAN Interface Card (WIC), which is an expansion card for your router, allowing your router to connect directly to the telephone company's network. Figure 1-2 shows a router that contains a T1 WIC.

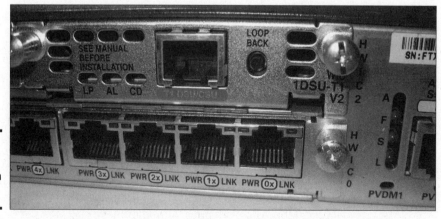

Figure 1-2:
Cisco WIC, installed in a router.

Depending on your router's capabilities and the telephone company's connection options, you may use a Data Service Unit/Channel Service Unit

(DSU/CSU), which is a Layer 1 device that connects the telephone company's network to your router. In Figure 1-2, the DSU/CSU is built into the T1 WIC, whereas in other cases, you will have separate, distinct devices connected to your router. The DSU/CSU can be thought of as a modem in that it connects your digital device (router) to your telephone company's network; however, unlike a modem, the connection is digital on both sides of the DSU/CSU. When the DSU/CSU is a separate device, it typically connects to your router through a serial port.

Here are some of the options to consider for connecting your network to a telephone company's network:

+ **Cable:** Many cable companies have gotten into the service-provider market, with the least expensive of their connections being their standard cable connection. In recent years, these companies have started offering faster and more reliable connection options such as fiber-based services like FiOS.

    Because these companies are fairly new in the market, they tend to have more modern connection options, which may present challenges when setting up a WAN spanning borders of less technologically developed countries.

+ **DSL:** DSL technologies are fast and reliable options when newer options are not available. They have been around long enough to be available in most regions and tend to offer inexpensive connectivity options. This technology changes rapidly. Your local provider supports some DSL types, such as Asymmetric Digital Subscriber Line (ADSL) or Symmetric Digital Subscriber Line (SDSL).

+ **T1/E1/ISDN:** ISDN and T1 connectivity options are typically more readily available than even ADSL because of their level of maturity in the overall network world. T1 connections and Primary Rate Interface (PRI) ISDN connections allow you to put a full, 26-wire pair connection into place and then activate as many pairs of wires as you need, providing you with 64 Kbps per pair. This partially activated connection is called a *fractional connection*.

    The standards on the number of pairs and the speeds vary by region. In the United States, typically you are looking at 24 pairs on a T1 connection with an 8K control channel, yielding 1.544 Mbps of throughput; whereas the European versions (E1) usually provide 32 pairs, providing a connection of 2.048 Mbps. The North American T-Carrier signals go up to five levels, with the top end being 5,760 pairs or channels allowing 400.352 Mbps of throughput. Although these numbers get pretty high, Basic Rate ISDN (BRI ISDN) will run as little as two 64 Kbps data channels with a 16 Kbps control channel.

✦ **Serial connections:** Serial connections are the oldest connection technologies and are available in areas that may be lacking other connection methods. Serial connections are available worldwide. The *frame relay* system is the main method of offering serial connections. When implementing frame relay on a Cisco router, you have two choices for encapsulation methods: Point to Point Protocol (PPP) or High-Level Data Link Control (HDLC), which are discussed in Chapter 5 of this minibook. Your choice depends on what you are using at the other end of the connection, because the same technologies must be used at both ends of the connection.

With the physical part of the connection out of the way, your next choice deals with routing protocols.

Choosing a routing protocol

The one option that is always available when choosing a routing protocol is to not choose one and to use manual routing management. Although manual routing is an option, it is not always a good option. Manual routing is easy to set up if you understand your network, but as your network grows from 2, to 4, to 10, to 100 routers, implementing changes may become so difficult that you stop making them, thus penalizing your users with poor network management. So, even though you have the option of manually maintaining all of your routing tables, you probably want to investigate a dynamic routing protocol as your network grows.

Not all routing protocols are equal, and each has a benefit and a drawback. Although you see the configuration and management of each of these protocols in later chapters of this minibook, as specified in the following list, I introduce you to each of them in later sections of this chapter:

✦ Routing Information Protocol (RIP) version 1 and 2 are covered in Chapter 7.

✦ Enhanced Interior Gateway Routing Protocol (EIGRP) appears in Chapter 7.

✦ Open Shortest Path First (OSPF) is configured in Chapter 8.

✦ Intermediate System to Intermediate System (IS-IS) is described in Chapter 8.

✦ Boarder Gateway Protocol (BGP) appears in Chapter 9.

Routing Information Protocol (RIP)

RIP as a routing protocol is based on methodologies that go back to the beginning of TCP/IP routing with the formation of the ARPANET, which is the precursor of what is now called the Internet. RIP is an open protocol and

**Book IV
Chapter 1**

**Making the Wide
Area Network
(WAN) Wide**

was first published in RFC1058 (and its successor RIPv2 in RFC1723), which was later adopted as Internet Standard 34. RIP is a *distance-vector routing protocol*, which means that each router may not know where the final destination network is, but it does know in which direction it exists and how far away it is.

By *direction,* I mean which routing interface the router will send data through, and by *how far away* or *distance,* I mean how many routers the data will pass through before reaching its destination.

RIP places a limit on the maximum distance to the targeted computer as 16 hops or 16 routers, with each router representing a hop from one network to another. Because the route starts with router 0, you are dealing with routes that touch 15 or fewer other routers. For routers farther away, the routing information is dropped or ignored. You may think that 16 hops is a limitation, but even on a network as large as the Internet, you can usually get to where you want to go within 16 hops. When you `traceroute` (`tracert` on Windows) an address, `traceroute` traces for only 30 hops, and in most cases, it gets you to your destination in fewer than 15 hops. To accomplish this efficiency requires a high level of network planning to ensure that your hop counts are as low as possible.

In terms of sharing routing information with others, RIP version 1 (RIPv1) shared its routing information with other routers by broadcasting its routing table information through all of its configured network interfaces. Each router that received this information stored it in its own routing table with updated hop counts, ignoring or dropping hop counts over 15.

One major issue that RIPv1 had was that it was *classful*, which meant that all network segments on a network had to be the same size. You could not deviate your subnet mask from the default for the class; all network segments needed to use the same mask. Figure 1-3 illustrates this problem in a three-router layout, with five segments, where only the three segments have computers. If you were to use a Class C address space like 192.168.1.0, your mask would have to be 255.255.255.224, which would give you 8 segments of 30 devices; but in case of RIP, you would be able to use only 6 segments, and one of your 30 devices would be the router's interface, leaving you with 29 devices on the network segments. When sending routing information, only the network IDs are sent and not the matching subnet masks.

To deal with some of the limitations of RIP version 1, RIP version 2 (RIPv2) was proposed in RFC1388 and updated in RFC2453, which became Internet Standard 56. RIPv2 allows the protocol to carry subnet information, allowing support of *Classless Inter-Domain Routing (CIDR),* which ignores class-based boundaries when routing and allows each segment to maintain a unique subnet mask. The topic of CIDR and subnetting is covered in Book II, Chapter 1.

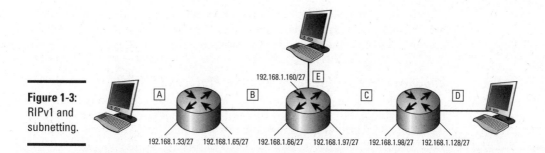

Figure 1-3:
RIPv1 and
subnetting.

192.168.1.160/27 E

A B C D

192.168.1.33/27   192.168.1.65/27   192.168.1.66/27   192.168.1.97/27   192.168.1.98/27   192.168.1.128/27

Without needing to maintain the same subnet mask on all network segments allows conservation of network IP addresses, as shown in Figure 1-4; where an updated network addressing layout exists with appropriate subnet masks on each segment. In this case, you can assign a larger network ID to segment A (192.168.1.0/25) of 126 hosts; a smaller segment D (192.168.1.128/26) of 62 hosts; and a smaller segment E (192.168.1.192/27) of 30 hosts; while assigning smaller addresses spaced to segments B and C of 192.168.1.248/30 and 192.168.1.252/30. You are left with two other small address blocks of 192.168.1.224/28 allowing 14 hosts and 192.168.1.240/29 allowing 6 hosts. In this scenario, you waste few addresses because the router-to-router segments have only the minimum number of addresses assigned to them (2), whereas previously you had two wasted segments of 16 addresses, plus the router-to-router segments that were allocated 14 addresses, when they needed only 2.

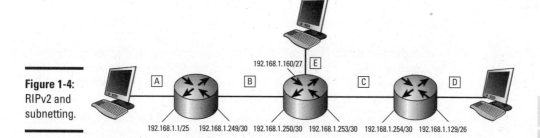

Figure 1-4:
RIPv2 and
subnetting.

192.168.1.160/27 E

A B C D

192.168.1.1/25   192.168.1.249/30   192.168.1.250/30   192.168.1.253/30   192.168.1.254/30   192.168.1.129/26

RIPv2 also switched from using broadcasts to propagate router information over to using multicasts at address 224.0.0.9, thereby reducing network traffic to unneeded systems. To further enhance the protocol, router authentication (to validate the router's participation in RIP) was added so that only routing data from trusted routers is added to the routing tables, thereby preventing corruption of the routing tables from unauthorized routers on your network.

**Book IV
Chapter 1**

Making the Wide
Area Network
(WAN) Wide

With the advent of IPv6, RIP was given another facelift in the form of RIP next generation (RIPng), which increases the size of the address fields, and changed the authentication mechanism to IPSec.

Enhanced Interior Gateway Routing Protocol (EIGRP)

If the world can create a protocol by consensus, you could likely build a better protocol, because you would not need to make concessions with other people. Cisco created the now obsolete Interior Gateway Routing Protocol (IGRP) to overcome issues in RIP. IGRP was still a distance vector routing protocol, but in addition to distance, Cisco allowed the protocol to carry more information about the path, such as bandwidth, delay, load, MTU, and reliability. Cisco also increased the maximum hop count to 255 but allowed it to be configurable.

Rather than broadcasting updates every 30 seconds, IGRP stretched the time out to 90 seconds, reducing load on the network but increasing convergence time.

As with RIPv1, IGRP is a class-based routing protocol, and the data about the routes does not include subnet mask information. Because of the limitations of the protocol, it too has been replaced by a better, newer version in the form of Enhanced Interior Gateway Routing Protocol (EIGRP).

EIGRP reduces the time to convergence by passing data to other routers only when neighboring routers change. If there is a new adjacent router, EIGRP will pass that information out to all of its routing partners or out to all of its network interfaces.

EIGRP stores its routing information in the router in three basic tables:

+ **Neighbor table:** This table stores the addresses of neighbors, those routers that are directly accessible through the routers own local interfaces. If the path to a targeted router has to go through another router, then that targeted router is not a neighbor.

+ **Topology table:** This table stores the routing tables which this router has received from neighboring routers. With this information, this router identifies the best route to each possible destination network, as well as identifying a successor and a feasible successor. The successors will be used when the primary route to the destination fails.

+ **Routing table:** This table is built from the topology table and contains just the routing information to each destination network. It includes successors as the primary route to the destination and feasible successors as backup routes where applicable and depending on the configuration of EIGRP.

Open Shortest Path First (OSPF)

OSPF is a link-state routing protocol, as compared to the distance vector protocols you have been looking at. The main difference here is that a *linked-state protocol* does not send its routing table in the form of updates, but only shared its connectivity configuration. By collecting connectivity information from all of the devices on the network, OSPF can store all this information in a database and use that information to build a topology map. This information will allow OSPF to identify the best or shortest route to every other network segment on the network. The route selection is based on overall hops to the destination, as well as link speed or link cost. The topology not only includes the best route to the destination as calculated by the Dijkstra algorithm (a search algorithm created by Edsger Dijkstra), but also, when possible, it includes a candidate or backup route to the destination.

After creating the topology map, OSPF populates the routing table with the chosen routes to each destination. As traffic passes from router to router, each router evaluates the best path to the destination network. In some cases, this process can lead to routing loops on the network, because each one is evaluating the path based on its own link state database.

The OSPF interior network protocol belongs to a single routing domain (or group of routers) known as an Autonomous System (AS). All routers belonging to the same AS share connection information and build their linked-state database from that information. Specifically with OSPF, as opposed to link-state terminology in general, the primary, or best, route the destination goes through is the Designated Router (DR), although if it fails, the secondary or backup path will be sent to the Backup Designated Router (BDR).

OSPF typically uses multicast to share connection information with its neighbors, and this information is sent to the 224.0.0.5 multicast address.

OSPF is an open protocol and is defined in RFC2328 for version 2 of the protocol. Version 3 of OSPF has been updated to support IPv6 and is defined in RFC5340. Other than for the newly integrated support for IPv6, no major technical differences exist between version 2 and version 3.

Intermediate System to Intermediate System (IS-IS)

IS-IS is another link-state routing protocol, and its technical information is found in RFC1142. It was developed by Digital Equipment Company for DECNet at the same time Internet Engineering Task Force (IETF) was working on OSPF for IP. As such, they do share some similarities in purpose. Since being developed, IS-IS has been extended to support IP and was published as an open standard in RFC1195.

IS-IS is used primarily by service providers on their network to route data, so you will not likely see it or have to work with it. One major difference between IS-IS and other routing protocols is that IS-IS does not rely on IP to distribute routing information traffic. IS-IS, which is independent of the network layer protocols being used, uses any network layer protocol to send its messages; in addition, IS-IS can distribute routing information for any protocol, not just IPv4, which simplified updating the protocol to support IPv6.

IS-IS works with two basic areas, a Level 1 (intra-area) or Level 2 (inter-area). A third area designator is a hybrid Level 1–2 (both areas). Each IS-IS router is only ever part of an area, but Level 1–2 routers can exchange information with routers in both areas. Within an area, the methods that IS-IS uses to manage routing information is similar to that of OSPF.

Border Gateway Protocol (BGP)

BGP is one of the core protocols used by most of the service providers on the Internet. Most core routing decisions on the Internet are made by BGP. The current version (version 4) of the protocol is defined in RFC4271.

BGP can run as either an interior or exterior protocol, and when run as an interior protocol, it may be referred to as IBGP.

As an exterior protocol, BGP's main role is to transmit to other BGP routers any routes being managed by an interior gateway protocol, thereby allowing the routes to be used by all systems in both areas.

To identify the systems for which BGP is supposed to be transferring routing information, BGP makes use of Autonomous Systems (AS) which are groups of routers on your network.

In most cases, you will need to implement this protocol only when attempting to provide redundant routing between you and your service provider.

Chapter 2: Cozying Up to Routing Basics

In This Chapter

✔ Examining where routers fit into the OSI model

✔ Enabling routing on your network

✔ Implementing the DHPC service on your router

In this chapter, I discuss the main purpose of routers and where they fit into your overall physical network infrastructure and, of course, into our old friend, the OSI model. The single main function that routers have in the network world is to move data, so much of this chapter surrounds the fact that data movement is the main goal.

Though routers are excellent in the data movement, they are capable of providing other services for the networks on which they reside. As part of these services, I also show that routers are capable of fulfilling many other network roles, by having you walk through configuring the router to act as a DHCP server for your network.

Of Routers and Routing

When you read Book III, you see how a switch is used to break a collision domain into smaller units, reducing the number of collisions that occur on a network. By reducing the collisions, you increase throughput of busy networks, because network devices do not have to repeatedly retransmit data. This situation, however, does nothing to reduce the amount of broadcast traffic on the network. Broadcast traffic on an Ethernet network is sent to the hardware address FF:FF:FF:FF:FF:FF. Every device in that broadcast domain opens and reads the data packets to the point that the device can decide that the packets do not apply to them.

Windows, rigging the election

The Windows browser service maintains a list of Windows computers on a network segment via a series of broadcast traffic. This process sends "announcement" packets informing the network segment that they are Windows computers and are sending "election" packets, which determines the most reliable computer on the network segment to maintain the master list of all Windows computers.

In the case of an ARP request that is sent to a broadcast address, the network device needs to read the whole packet and examine the MAC address referenced in the data section of the frame. If the MAC address does not match its own address, the packet is ignored. Whereas, in the case of Ethernet frame that contains the Windows browser service election packet, the network device needs to read the network frame and will not know that the frame can be ignored until it gets to the part of the frame that identifies the workgroup or domain name which this election is for. This processing of broadcast frames can cause a great deal of work by every device on the network, and in addition to the number of broadcasts consuming available network bandwidth, negatively affect your data throughput. Enter routers.

Knowing why routers are useful

Although with a small network, you actually do not need routers, if your network is connected to the Internet, you will have at least one router. In addition to a router connecting you to the Internet, you may choose to have internal routers on a network for many reasons, such as the following:

✦ To accommodate a second office that is connected to your network via a telephone company using either a private line or leased lines or over the Internet.

✦ To increase security for systems on your network, which would include any systems where you want to restrict access such as your servers. These segments can have rules on their routers allowing only a certain range of IP addresses to connect to the segments.

✦ To reduce the size of the broadcast domains on your network. If broadcast domains are too large, they can create problems with network performance because of excessive background traffic. Adding routers splits the broadcast into smaller segments. Broadcast domains are covered later in this chapter.

Knowing what routers do

The main purpose of a router is to pass data from one interface on the router to another interface. For many routers, their only job is to pass traffic, and over the years Cisco has perfected the process of moving this data as fast as possible over the router. The router makes decisions about where that data needs to be based on a routing table, which you can think of as an address book.

You can use routers to divide a network into several different broadcast domains. For example, you can break a 1,000-device network into ten 100-device networks that pass data back and forth through one or more routers. Although doing so increases network complexity, because each segment needs its own IP address subnet and default gateway (which is the router), this process reduces the effect of the broadcast traffic from 1,000 devices to 100 devices, which can increase overall throughput.

Switches operate at Layer 2 — the data link layer — in the OSI network model, filtering and passing data based on MAC addresses of the devices. Routers, on the other hand, operate at Layer 3 — the network layer — filtering and passing data based on the network protocol addresses, which these days typically means IP addresses.

Unlike switches, which automatically build address tables, routers rely on a *routing table,* which is a distinct part of the router's firmware that records routing information such as network IDs (covered in Book II, Chapter 1) and the next router or process in the packet. Routing tables must be manually configured or dynamically configured using a routing protocol such as Routing Information Protocol (RIP), described in Chapter 7 of this minibook, or Open Shortest Path First (OSPF), described in Chapter 8 of this minibook. The routing table contains a list of network IDs that look like IP addresses, and for each destination address to which the router needs to send data, the router uses a logical AND operation, which I discuss in Book II, Chapter 3. This AND operation is performed against every entry in the routing table until it finds the entry that most closely represents the destination address. The closest routing entry to the destination IP address is the routing entry that is used.

Examining the routing process

The routing process starts with a source computer that makes the first decision in the routing steps, which is illustrated in Figure 2-1. Not shown in the figure is the implicit route that each router would have for any network segments on which the routers interfaces are directly connected. The routing process goes like this:

1. The source computer at 192.168.1.25 wants to send data to the computer at 192.168.100.75, so it consults its local routing table, which, for simplicity, has only one routing entry for its default gateway (`Router1`).

2. As the data arrives at `Router1`, `Router1` looks at the destination address of the IP packet and then scans through its own routing table to determine that the data should be sent off the network over Router2 as a route to the destination.

3. As the data arrives at `Router2`, `Router2` looks at the destination address of the IP packet and determines that it does not have a specific routing entry to the destination network, but does have a default route or gateway of last resort, so `Router2` passes the data on to `Router3`.

4. As the data arrives at `Router3`, `Router3` has two entries in its routing table: one for the network of 192.168.100.0 through `Router4` and one for the host (denoted by `/32` in the routing table) of 192.168.100.75 through `Router5`. In this case, `Router3` chooses the most specific routing table match to the destination address. `Router3` then sends the data to `Router5`.

5. `Router5` looks at the destination address of the IP packet, reviews its routing table, and finds that it is directly connected to the destination network. In that case, it sends the data directly through the interface configured for the network 192.168.100.0, which gets the data to 192.168.100.75, the final destination.

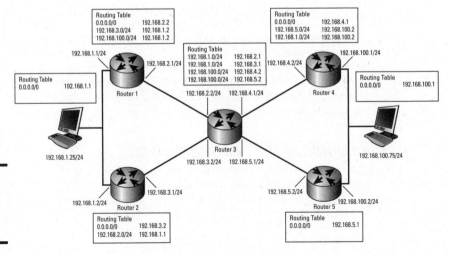

Figure 2-1:
Examining
the routing
process.

Viewing your router's routing table

To view the routing table on your router, you connect to the command-line interface and type the following commands:

```
Router2>enable
Password:
Router2#show ip route
Codes: C - connected, S - static, R - RIP, M - mobile, B - BGP
       D - EIGRP, EX - EIGRP external, O - OSPF, IA - OSPF inter area
       N1 - OSPF NSSA external type 1, N2 - OSPF NSSA external type 2
       E1 - OSPF external type 1, E2 - OSPF external type 2
       i - IS-IS, su - IS-IS summary, L1 - IS-IS level-1, L2 - IS-IS level-2
       ia - IS-IS inter area, * - candidate default, U - per-user static route
       o - ODR, P - periodic downloaded static route

Gateway of last resort is 192.168.5.10 to network 0.0.0.0

C    192.168.5.0/24 is directly connected, FastEthernet0/1
C    192.168.1.0/24 is directly connected, FastEthernet0/0
     192.168.100.0/24 is variably subnetted, 2 subnets, 2 masks
S       192.168.100.0/24 [1/0] via 192.168.5.2
S       192.168.100.75/32 [1/0] via 192.168.5.5
S*   0.0.0.0/0 [1/0] via 192.168.5.10
```

Note that the routing table output includes a list of all known routes and the routing protocol that those routes were learned from. In this case, two networks are directly connected (C) to the routers' interfaces: 192.168.5.0/24 and 192.168.1.0/24. Directly connected interfaces are always added to the routing table. Because the router is directly connected to those networks, the router knows that data can be sent to them. In addition to these directly connected networks are three static ("S") or manually typed routes, one for a network (192.168.100.0/24), one for an IP host (192.168.100.75/32), and one for everything else (0.0.0.0/0). The last route is the default gateway or gateway of last resort, which means that if a better route is not found, this route is chosen.

After you connect your router in a single router network, if you need to route only to directly connected networks, you do not have to worry about setting up static routes or enabling a routing protocol.

In the preceding routing table, you have routes to all systems on the 192.168.1.0/24 and 192.168.5.0/24 networks. For data going to either of these networks, you use the appropriate router interface, FastEthernet0/0 or FastEthernet0/1. If you have data for a system on the 192.168.100.0/24 network, you send that data on to the next router, which is found at 192.168.5.2. Bear in mind that this next router must be on a network to which you are directly connected. There is one routing table entry for the 192.168.100.0/24 network, but there is also the exception for the address of 192.168.100.75/32. The host 192.168.100.75 has a special route and the router

**Book IV
Chapter 2**

Cozying Up to
Routing Basics

passes the data to the router 192.168.5.5, rather than to the normal router for that network (192.168.5.2). You might use a special route such as this one if, for example, you want to use different security settings that make it easier (or harder) to communicate with system 192.168.100.75; or, perhaps the physical links going from that router may be faster (or slower), and based on the role of 192.168.100.75, using links with specific speed settings makes more sense. The point is that you tailor your routing table to pass data for sections of the same network over different paths, and the router always chooses the route based on the route that most closely matches the destination address.

Enabling Routing

It may seem strange, but when you first enable your router and configure IP addresses for its interfaces, the router will not actually route data. First, you must "tell" the router it is allowed to do so by following these steps:

```
Router2>enable
Password:
Router2#configure terminal
Enter configuration commands, one per line.  End with CNTL/Z.
Router2(config)#interface fastEthernet 0/0
Router2(config-if)#ip address 192.168.1.240 255.255.255.0
Router2(config-if)#no shutdown
Router2(config-if)#exit
Router2(config)#interface fastEthernet 0/1
Router2(config-if)#ip address 192.168.5.1 255.255.255.0
Router2(config-if)#no shutdown
Router2(config-if)#exit
Router2(config)#ip routing
Router2(config)#exit
```

The first part of this process sets up your network interfaces. The key to allowing your router to route traffic between its configured interfaces is found in the ip routing command, which turns on the routing processes.

Unlike with switches, where every interface (or port) on a switch is enabled by default, with routers, you have to specifically tell a router to enable an interface, by specifying the no shutdown command when you are in Interface Configuration mode.

Working with DHCP

As I mention in the introduction to this chapter, services that are not router-related are also available on your router — for example, the Dynamic Host Configuration Protocol (DHCP) service. You can use DHCP to hand out IP address configuration to devices on your network. Servers on your network can perform this job, but in some cases, such as in a small office without a server, you can use your router to perform this role. When a DHCP server cannot be placed on a network, your router can also play the role of an IP Helper or DHCP Relay. You can find out more about IP Helper in the later section "Getting DHCP help from the IP Helper."

Here is the basic four-step DHCP address acquisition process (also illustrated in Figure 2-2):

✦ **DHCP Discover:** The client device sends out a request for all DHCP servers available on the network to provide an address if they have one available.

✦ **DHCP Offer:** All DHCP servers on the network that have an available address respond. The client device may receive multiple offers if multiple servers are on the network.

✦ **DHCP Request:** The client chooses one offer and sends a request back to the DHCP server. Because the client is not authorized to use the offered address yet, the DHCP Request is still a broadcast. The client accepts the first offer received unless another offer matches the last IP address that the client had.

✦ **DHCP Ack or DHCP NAck:** Typically, the DHCP server finalizes the process with an acknowledgment, or *Ack,* allowing the client device to start using the address. In rare cases, the server issues a *Negative Acknowledgment,* or *NAck*, because it may have decided that the address is not available in the milliseconds that have passed since it offered the address. Far more likely is that a NAck would come from a second, but malfunctioning, DHCP server, which sees the DHCP Request going to the first DHCP server and refuses it because it was not the address it offered. Its refusal is the malfunctioning part of this scenario because, if the DHCP Request was not offered for the second server, it should have been ignored.

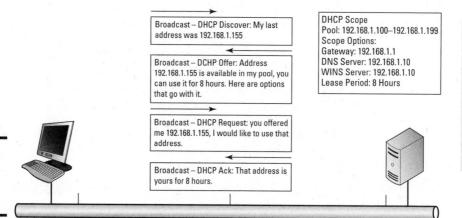

Figure 2-2:
Examining
the DHCP
process.

Broadcast – DHCP Discover: My last address was 192.168.1.155

Broadcast – DCHP Offer: Address 192.168.1.155 is available in my pool, you can use it for 8 hours. Here are options that go with it.

Broadcast – DHCP Request: you offered me 192.168.1.155, I would like to use that address.

Broadcast – DHCP Ack: That address is yours for 8 hours.

DHCP Scope
Pool: 192.168.1.100–192.168.1.199
Scope Options:
Gateway: 192.168.1.1
DNS Server: 192.168.1.10
WINS Server: 192.168.1.10
Lease Period: 8 Hours

**Book IV
Chapter 2**

Cozying Up to
Routing Basics

I have seen cases where multiple DHCP servers on the same network segment are configured for non-overlapping scopes (the DHCP service configuration of the configuration information it will hand out) on that network segment. One server offers an IP address, but when the client requests the address, the other server sees the request and issues a NAck, because it did not offer that address. This situation is not supposed to happen, because a DHCP server should NAck only an address it offers. When this NAck problem starts to happen, typically all computers on your network will slowly lose their IP configuration. You can quickly identify the problem by doing a network packet capture with a tool such as Wireshark (refer to Book I, Chapter 4, for more on Wireshark). Wireshark tells you the IP address and MAC address of the other DHCP server. You can use the information from Wireshark to locate the offending DHCP server and shut it down.

All this traffic is broadcast traffic because until the client device receives the final acknowledgement, it is not allowed to use the offered address; so it does not have a valid IP address on the network.

Once the client has the address, it keeps the address until it reaches eight hours, or whatever the configured lease period is. At the end of the lease period, if the client has not renewed its lease or obtained a lease from another source, it has to relinquish the use of that address and attempt to reach a DHCP server to get another address. At the same time, even if the device is turned off after getting its lease, the DHCP server has "contracted" not to give that address to any other device until the lease period expires.

Before the lease expires, the client will attempt to renew its lease to avoid being in a situation where it does not have a valid working IP address. This process works at these time intervals:

+ **50 Percent — Lease Renewal:** At 50 percent of the lease period, the client will attempt to renew its lease. This renewal is a unicast message directly to the DHCP server, which is allowed because, unlike the original lease process, the client and the server both have valid IP addresses on the network through which they can communicate. The goal is that the client will be able to renew its lease and never be without an IP address. If the lease renewal is successful, it is renewed to the original lease period, providing that it has not been modified on the server.

  So with an eight-hour lease, at four hours, the device will attempt to renew the lease and will end up with a new eight hour lease when successful. If for some reason the device is not able to renew its lease, it will continue to attempt a renewal periodically based on the client configuration.

+ **87.5 Percent — Rebinding:** If the client reaches 87.5 percent of the lease period and still has not managed to renew its lease, it will attempt to locate another DHCP server to acquire a lease. This process is identical to the original lease process. So even though the client has a valid IP address on the network, it will send out a new DHCP discovery broadcast in an attempt to locate a valid DHCP server on the network. All DHCP servers that receive discovery requests will respond with an available address. If there is more than one response, the client will choose one response and send out its request for that address, and then wait to receive an acknowledgement in return. If no servers respond to this discovery request, the client will periodically make additional requests based on the client settings. During this period, the client is still allowed to use the configured IP address that it had received in its original lease.

✦ **100 Percent — Lease Expiry:** If the client has not located another DHCP server by the time it reaches 100 percent of the lease period, the client gives up its leased address and periodically sends out DHCP discovery requests. It continues this process until it receives a response.

Setting up your DHCP server

Setting up your DHCP server is easy, involving only a few lines in your router's configuration file. Just follow these steps:

1. **Determine your network range and any addresses that you do not want to include in your pool of addresses.**

2. **Exclude your reserved addresses.**

3. **Enable the pool.**

4. **Specify the IP network for which to assign addresses.**

5. **Specify options you want to include, such as**

• DNS servers

• WINS servers

• NetBIOS Node Types (b, p, m, or h)

• Lease Duration in days, hours, and minutes

If you want, you can specify the following items also:

✦ A location to store the DHCP database, which could be a network location. In this way, you do not lose your assigned leases if your router experiences a failure.

✦ Statically assign addresses to specific hosts — this is managed through their MAC addresses. In this way, you gain the flexibility to use DHCP as well as the capability to have the same device always obtain the same address, which is ideal for devices such as servers or printers.

The following code walks you through the basic process to get your DHCP server up and running for a basic network of 192.168.1.0:

```
Router2>enable
Password:
Router2#configure terminal
Enter configuration commands, one per line.  End with CNTL/Z.
Router2(config)#ip dhcp excluded-address 192.168.1.1 192.168.1.3
Router2(config)#ip dhcp pool DHCPPool
Router2(config-dhcp)#network 192.168.1.0 255.255.255.0
Router2(config-dhcp)#domain-name cisco.com
Router2(config-dhcp)#dns-server 192.168.1.1 192.168.1.21
Router2(config-dhcp)#dns-server 192.168.1.102 192.168.2.102
Router2(config-dhcp)#netbios-name-server 192.168.1.103 192.168.2.103
Router2(config-dhcp)#netbios-node-type h-node
Router2(config-dhcp)#default-router 192.168.1.1
Router2(config-dhcp)#lease 0 0 10
Router2(config-dhcp)#exit
Router2(config)#exit
```

To specify storing the DHCP database in a remote location, include a line like this one in the previous configuration. This configuration line stores the database 120 seconds after an update to the local database.

```
ip dhcp database ftp://user:password@192.168.1.103/router-dhcp write-delay 120
```

When handing out address information for multiple subnets, at times you will want to specify the same options for all subnets. To do so, you create a pool at a higher level (network-wise) and configure your options there. These options are handed out to the lower level pools as well. The following configuration of three pools illustrates this functionality:

```
Router2>enable
Password:
Router2#configure terminal
Enter configuration commands, one per line.  End with CNTL/Z.
Router2(config)#ip dhcp excluded-address 172.30.1.100 172.30.1.103
Router2(config)#ip dhcp excluded-address 172.30.2.100 172.30.2.103
Router2(config)#ip dhcp pool 0
Router2(config-dhcp)#network 172.30.0.0 /16
Router2(config-dhcp)#domain-name edtetz.net
Router2(config-dhcp)#dns-server 172.30.1.102 172.30.2.102
Router2(config-dhcp)#netbios-name-server 172.30.1.103 172.30.2.103
Router2(config-dhcp)#netbios-node-type h-node
Router2(config-dhcp)#exit
Router2(config)#ip dhcp pool 1
Router2(config-dhcp)#network 172.30.1.0 /24
Router2(config-dhcp)#default-router 172.30.1.100 172.30.1.101
Router2(config-dhcp)#lease 30
Router2(config-dhcp)#exit
Router2(config)#ip dhcp pool 2
Router2(config-dhcp)#network 172.30.2.0 /4
Router2(config-dhcp)#default-router 172.30.2.100 172.30.2.101
Router2(config-dhcp)#lease 30
Router2(config-dhcp)#exit
Router2(config)#exit
```

In addition to the pools and exclusions just listed, a *reservation* is the process by which you statically associate a single computer with an IP address using DHCP. The following code associates Bobs-pc with the address of 172.30.2.25, as long as the MAC address of Bobs-pc remains 04c8.58b0.0b2c. You repeat this process for other computers that need to keep a static address. In these cases, if another pool hands out addresses for the network 172.30.2.0/24 or 172.30.0.0/16, Bob-pc also receives the options assigned to those pools.

```
Router2>enable
Password:
Router2#configure terminal
Enter configuration commands, one per line.  End with CNTL/Z.
Router2(config)#ip dhcp pool Bobs-pc
Router2(config-dhcp)#host 172.30.2.25
Router2(config-dhcp)#hardware-address 04c8.58b0.0b2c ieee802
Router2(config-dhcp)#client-name Bob-pc
Router2(config-dhcp)#exit
Router2(config)#exit
```

Watching the DHCP traffic go by

To see what is happening on your network in regard to DHCP, enable the following debug options. Though you can monitor several options (debug ip dhcp server packet is probably the most useful), you can also choose from others:

✦ ip dhcp server events: Reports address assignments, lease expirations, and other events that take place with the DHCP service

✦ ip dhcp server class: Displays class-based address allocation

✦ ip dhcp server linkage: Displays database linkage

✦ dchp detail: Displays DHCP packet contents

Here is the output for debug ip dhcp server packet:

```
Router2>enable
Password:
Router2#terminal monitor
Router2#debug ip dhcp server packet
DHCPD:DHCPDISCOVER received from client 0b07.1134.a029 through relay 192.168.5.1.
DHCPD:assigned IP address 192.168.5.73 to client 0a06.1335.a126.
DHCPD: DHCPREQUEST received from client 0100.2241.806c.f3.
DHCPD: DHCPDISCOVER received from client 0100.16ec.7a50.d7 on interface
    FastEthernet0/1.
DHCPD: Sending DHCPOFFER to client 0100.16ec.7a50.d7 (192.168.5.20).
DHCPD: broadcasting BOOTREPLY to client 0016.ec7a.50d7.
DHCPD: DHCPREQUEST received from client 0100.16ec.7a50.d7.
DHCPD: Sending DHCPACK to client 0100.16ec.7a50.d7 (192.168.5.20).
DHCPD: DHCPINFORM received from client 0100.1d6a.44f1.c4 (192.168.1.132).
DHCPD: DHCPREQUEST received from client 0100.16ec.7a50.d7.
DHCPD: unicasting BOOTREPLY to client 0016.ec7a.50d7 (192.168.5.20).
Router2#no debug ip dhcp server packet
```

If you enable too many `debug` options, you will affect the performance of your router and may have trouble reading items that are going across the screen. You can use the command `no debug all` to disable all debugging on your router.

If you need to remove a specific address pairing or DHCP lease from your DHCP database, use the `clear` command, like this command removing the lease for 172.30.1.175:

```
Router2# clear ip dhcp binding 172.30.1.175
```

You can also use `clear ip dhcp binding` to remove all automatic bindings (DHCP leases) from your DHCP database:

```
Router2# clear ip dhcp binding *
```

To view the DHCP database (which is common when you are trying to locate a device on the network), use the command that follows. At times, you may have an IP address or device that you need to locate, perhaps you are following up on an issue discovered from a firewall log or other source. The `show` command allows you to identify the MAC address of the device. From there, you can move to network switches to locate the switch port the device is connected to; or refer to client computer documentation, if you happen to record the MAC addresses before giving your network users their computers.

```
Router2#show ip dhcp binding 192.168.5.20
IP address          Client-ID/              Lease expiration        Type
                    Hardware address/
                    User name
192.168.5.20        0100.16ec.7a50.d7       Mar 14 2002 07:40 AM    Automatic
```

To see information about your pools and their usage, use this command:

```
Router2#show ip dhcp pool

Pool DHCP-Pool :
 Utilization mark (high/low)    : 100 / 0
 Subnet size (first/next)       : 0 / 0
 Total addresses                : 254
 Leased addresses               : 4
 Pending event                  : none
 1 subnet is currently in the pool :
 Current index        IP address range                    Leased addresses
 192.168.5.21         192.168.5.1      - 192.168.5.254     4
```

Finally, to determine the amount of work your router is doing to support DHCP, view its statistics for DHCP with the following command:

```
Router2#show ip dhcp server statistics
Memory usage          16566
Address pools         1
Database agents       0
```

```
Automatic bindings    4
Manual bindings       0
Expired bindings      15
Malformed messages    0
Secure arp entries    0

Message               Received
BOOTREQUEST           0
DHCPDISCOVER          67
DHCPREQUEST           230
DHCPDECLINE           0
DHCPRELEASE           0
DHCPINFORM            19

Message               Sent
BOOTREPLY             0
DHCPOFFER             34
DHCPACK               22
DHCPNAK               82
```

Getting DHCP help from the IP Helper

When you have a centralized DHCP server and want the ability to track all DHCP leases, you can implement an *IP Helper address* to forward DHCP broadcasts on to their appropriate destination. In this way, you can implement a single DHCP server as one management point where you can check the leases for any device on your network and manage all the IP subnets on your network. Each subnet that does not have its own DHCP server will be configured with an `ip helper-address` command. The configuration for this command follows; note that you first must change the router interface to which you will be assigning the helper.

```
Router2>enable
Password:
Router2#configure terminal
Enter configuration commands, one per line.  End with CNTL/Z.
Router2(config)#interface fastEthernet 0/1
Router2(config-if)#ip helper-address global 192.168.1.8
Router2(config-if)#exit
Router2(config)#exit
```

When you enable the IP Helper address, all traffic for the UDP ports listed in Table 2-1 are automatically forwarded to the address specified.

Table 2-1	UDP Traffic Forwarded by IP Helper Address
UDP PORT	*Common Name*
69	TFTP
67	BOOTP Client
68	BOOTP Server
37	Time Protocol

(continued)

Table 2-1 *(continued)*

UDP PORT	Common Name
49	TACACS
53	DNS
137	NetBios
138	NetBios Datagram

To restrict the forwarded traffic, you can specify the restrictions by adding any of the following no commands to your configuration at the Global Configuration mode.

```
Router2>enable
Password:
Router2#configure terminal
Enter configuration commands, one per line.  End with CNTL/Z.
Router2(config)#no ip forward-protocol udp 37
Router2(config)#no ip forward-protocol udp 49
Router2(config)#no ip forward-protocol udp 53
Router2(config)#no ip forward-protocol udp 67
Router2(config)#no ip forward-protocol udp 68
Router2(config)#no ip forward-protocol udp 137
Router2(config)#no ip forward-protocol udp 138
Router2(config)#exit
```

Automatic Private IP Addressing (APIPA)

Many network devices that you connect to your network these days have a fallback position when DHCP services are not available on the network but the client devices are configured to use DHCP for their IP address configuration. This fallback is APIPA, a client-side process that has the client device randomly choose one of the 65,534 addresses available in the Class B network address of 169.254.0.0/16. After choosing an address from this range, the computer sends an ARP request to see whether another device on the network is using that address, and if it is not, the client device uses the address. Even though the device uses this made-up address, it continues to send out DHCP Discover broadcasts to locate a DHCP server on the network as soon as the DHCP server becomes available.

While waiting for a valid DHCP-delivered address, the device that is using an APIPA address can communicate with any other device on the network that is using an APIPA address. If two or more devices are connected to a switch and the devices are using APIPA, therefore, all of them can communicate at least with each other, but not with any other devices on the network that are using proper addresses for that network segment.

Chapter 3: Router Configuration

In This Chapter

✔ Configuring a router

✔ Configuring passwords for different interfaces

✔ Running the Setup Wizard

✔ Managing users

*I*n the previous chapter, I discuss in depth what routers do and how they do it. This chapter reviews the steps you take to connect to your router and to make configuration or setup changes. You start this process by making a physical connection to your router (see Book I, Chapter 5 for more on this topic). After you establish the connection, you can make changes to the configuration of your router. This chapter walks you through the basic configurations for both your network and the interfaces. Advanced routing configuration is covered in later chapters of this minibook as you examine each type of routing protocol.

Getting to Know the Internetwork Operating System (IOS) for Routers

I introduce the IOS in Book I, Chapter 5. The command set in the IOS used with routers and switches (see Book III for more on switches) have many of the same commands and share the same basic structure. You should only see a small selection of commands that are specific to a router. You generally follow the same method of navigating the commands on the router and moving between command modes, as you do on any Cisco IOS device. If you are not familiar with User EXEC mode, Privileged EXEC mode, and Global Configuration mode, read the content in Book I, Chapter 5.

Getting help in the IOS is easy: Type a question mark (**?**) at any point on the command line to see the commands that are available or to find out how to complete a command. In conjunction with tab completion, you can usually quickly figure out most commands.

If you are new to router configuration, you can download a complete command reference guide for each IOS routing component from Cisco by going to www.cisco.com/cisco/web/psa/reference.html and selecting the Support section. After you get to the reference page, select your IOS version from the Product selection dialog box.

Making Router Connections

In Book I, Chapter 5, I introduce how to connect to your router and make changes to the configuration. Here are the three basic ways to make configuration changes to a router:

✦ **Console connection:** This method involves having direct access to the router. You make the changes through the computer's serial port and a rollover cable. This is command line access to a router.

Because, initially, you can always make a console connection to the router, be sure to take a few minutes to locate a rollover cable for the router as well as the console port on the router. If you do not have a serial port on your computer, make plans to get a USB serial port adapter for the computer and test it with your Cisco router. Be sure to do this before you need to make an emergency connection to your router.

✦ **Telnet or SSH:** These options give you remote command-line access to the router to make configuration changes.

If you have already enabled SSH access to your router, ensure that you also disabled Telnet access. SSH is as easy to use as Telnet and is the only secure remote access option to the command-line interface.

✦ **Security Device Manager (SDM):** Represents the most popular graphical configuration interface for your routers.

Performing a Basic Configuration

You have only a few issues to worry about in order to get a basic routing configuration on your router. This section looks at each of these issues.

Setting the hostname

The *hostname* is the name the router goes by on your network. The router-name does not change how the router functions, but when you are making remote connections to the router, this name enables you to be sure you are working on the correct device on the network. Few things are worse than applying the incorrect configuration to a central production router.

To apply a descriptive name to your router, you can use code similar to the following snippet, using perhaps an even more descriptive name:

```
Router>enable
Password:
Router#configure terminal
Enter configuration commands, one per line.  End with CNTL/Z.
Router(config)#hostname Router2
Router2(config)#exit
```

Configuring standard router ports

You find several ports on your router; these ports include the ones described in this list:

✦ **Aux port:** This auxiliary port is used to connect a modem to the router, which can then be used to remotely modify the configuration on the router. This port is shown in Figure 3-1.

Figure 3-1:
Most routers have both console and AUX ports.

✦ **Attachment Unit Interface (AUI) port:** Before the WIC became a standard for providing expansion through an add-on port, the AUI allowed transceivers to be used, providing you with the ability to add various types of network connections, such as fiber or copper Ethernet connections.

A *transceiver* is a small electronic device that converts electrical signals from the AUI specification on one side of the transceiver to that of the connection type on the other side of the transceiver. An AUI port is shown in Figure 3-2.

✦ **Serial:** Connects a modem or other serial device to allow a WAN network interface to be used on the router. Two serial ports are shown in Figure 3-2.

✦ **Ethernet/Fast Ethernet/Gigabit Ethernet:** Standard network interfaces used to connect different network segments.

✦ **Console:** Serial configuration port for command-line access to router management and configuration. Refer to Figure 3-1 to see the console port.

Figure 3-2:
Most WAN
interface
or network
interface
connections
are managed
through AUI
and serial
ports.

✦ **WAN Interface Card (WIC) port:** Because a wide variety of WAN connectivity options are available (for example, T1, ISDN, ADSL), you can use this port to add different interfaces to a standard router. See Figure 3-3.

✦ **Hardware WAN Interface Card (HWIC) port:** With the integration of services into routers, the WIC interface became too limiting. The HWIC interface was created to support a wider variety of hardware expansion options, such as switches and service cards. This port is backward compatible with most older WIC hardware.

Figure 3-3:
A T1 WIC
card and
8-port switch
installed
in HWIC
interface
ports.

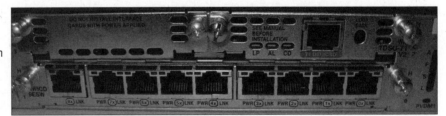

Configuring interfaces

In this section, I examine only the basics of configuring Ethernet, Fast Ethernet, and Gigabit Ethernet connections. Serial connections are covered in Chapter 5 of this minibook.

Connecting to your router

To start your configuration, you need to connect to your router and get into Configuration mode using the following set of commands:

```
Router2>enable
Password:
Router2#configure terminal
Enter configuration commands, one per line.  End with CNTL/Z.
```

The next option is to choose the port by number (it is also known as an *interface* because it is a networking port), which is how to correctly identify the specific interface with which you want to work. You can choose from Ethernet, Fast Ethernet, or Gigabit Ethernet interfaces. Then you specify the port number.

All devices in current IOS versions are numbered starting at the motherboard in one of these formats:

✦ **network-module-slot/port**

✦ **0/interface-card-slot/port**

✦ **network-module-slot/interface-card-slot/port**

All modules are effectively connected to the motherboard slot on the router, which is always slot 0 and is represented by the first 0 in the interface name. After that, the numbers are for an integrated interface, or for another expansion slot in your router. For example, if you have WIC or HWIC installed, you specify the motherboard slot (0), and then the slot into which the card is installed (0), and then you specify the interface number; 0 is the first interface for routers, and 1 is the first interface for switches (which can be installed into a router HWIC). So the first switch port for an HWIC switch is 0/0/1:

```
Router2(config)#interface FastEthernet 0/0
```

Using auto settings

You can set the specifics of the network connection or use the auto settings for duplex and speed settings. Duplex modes include Full Duplex mode or Half Duplex mode, whereas speeds typically are from 10 Mbps up to the speed of the interface.

```
Router2(config-if)#duplex auto
Router2(config-if)#speed auto
```

Adding a description

You might not want to use this feature for switches, but on your router, providing a description helps to prevent changing the configuration on the wrong interface. "Oops, was that the corporate WAN interface I just changed the IP address on? Time to polish up that resumé." A description does not assist with the configuration; it just helps prevent human error.

```
Router2(config-if)#description Internal Interface
```

Configuring a VLAN identifier

Because the interface works similarly to a switchport — and if you do not want to use the access settings on the switch to which you have connected the router — you can configure a VLAN identifier for the interface. You do so with the `vlan-id` or `vlan-range` command:

```
Router2(config-if)#vlan-id dot1q 1
Router2(config-if-vlan-id)#exit
```

Setting a routing interface

Because you plan to route from this interface, you need to give the client devices an IP address to connect to, as follows:

```
Router2(config-if)#ip address 192.168.1.240 255.255.255.0
```

You do have the option of configuring your router to use DHCP using the command `ip address dhcp`, but typically this command is not used for static network devices such as routers. Connecting this router as a Network Address Translation (NAT) device to an ISP represents the only case where a DHCP-configured interface is likely to be used. See Book VI, Chapter 3 for more on NAT.

Enabling your interface

Now, you have done all of this work, and there is a good chance you want to use this interface; however, if you exit the configuration and check the running configuration, you will notice one configuration item that is a little strange.

```
Router2#show running-config interface FastEthernet 0/0
Building configuration...

Current configuration : 199 bytes
!
interface FastEthernet0/0
 description Internal LAN Interface
 ip address 192.168.1.240 255.255.255.0
 shutdown
 speed auto
 full-duplex
 vlan-id dot1q 1
  exit-vlan-config
 !
 no mop enabled
end
```

One important item is missing — or, one item is present that should not be present. Unlike switches, all interfaces on your router should be, by default, shut down using the `shutdown` command. At first, this may seem strange, but think about where routers are used; in many cases, they exist as a gateway between you and the unprotected Internet. Setting the port as disabled gives you some additional security around your router until you are ready to open the flood gates. As with switch interfaces, the command to get rid of the `shutdown` command is `no shutdown`. So you need to complete the configuration of your router interface with the following command:

```
Router2(config-if)#no shutdown
```

If you are working on the console or have `terminal monitor` enabled, you should receive a status message telling you that the interface has been enabled. This message will be similar to the following:

```
%LINK-5-CHANGED: Interface FastEthernet0/0, changed state to up
```

Double-checking your settings

After you have the interface up and running, if you are using an auto setting for the speed and duplex settings, examine the interface to ensure that it has detected settings you are happy with. Do so with the `show interface` command, as shown here:

```
Router2#show interfaces FastEthernet 0/0
FastEthernet0/0 is up, line protocol is up
  Hardware is AmdFE, address is 000f.8f4b.a600 (bia 000f.8f4b.a600)
  Description: Internal LAN Interface
  Internet address is 192.168.1.240/24
  MTU 1500 bytes, BW 100000 Kbit, DLY 100 usec,
     reliability 255/255, txload 1/255, rxload 1/255
  Encapsulation ARPA, loopback not set
  Keepalive set (10 sec)
  Full-duplex, 100Mb/s, 100BaseTX/FX
  ARP type: ARPA, ARP Timeout 04:00:00
  Last input 00:00:07, output 00:00:02, output hang never
  Last clearing of "show interface" counters never
  Input queue: 0/75/0/0 (size/max/drops/flushes); Total output drops: 0
  Queueing strategy: fifo
  Output queue: 0/40 (size/max)
  5 minute input rate 0 bits/sec, 0 packets/sec
  5 minute output rate 0 bits/sec, 0 packets/sec
     417167 packets input, 39317868 bytes
     Received 415431 broadcasts, 0 runts, 0 giants, 0 throttles
     0 input errors, 0 CRC, 0 frame, 0 overrun, 0 ignored
     0 watchdog
     0 input packets with dribble condition detected
     149499 packets output, 17447327 bytes, 0 underruns
     0 output errors, 0 collisions, 3 interface resets
     0 babbles, 0 late collision, 0 deferred
     4 lost carrier, 0 no carrier
     0 output buffer failures, 0 output buffers swapped out
```

In the preceding information, notice that the interface and line protocols should both be up. In this case, the interface detected `Full-duplex` as well as a speed of 100 Mbps. From here, you can verify the IP address of the interface, and you can see if any packet errors are on the interface.

Incorrect duplex settings between ends of a connection can cause packet errors.

Configuring your router's IP settings

You have already set the IP address on the interface, but in most cases, you must do more. For example, with the configuration of network devices, you need to configuration at least a default gateway. In this case, the default gateway is not set in the interface, but for the entire router. The default gateway will appear in the configuration as the *Gateway of last resort*, which means if no specific route is specified, the router uses this gateway. When you look at the routing table with the `show ip route` command, the gateway will appear as the gateway of last resort:

```
Router2#show ip route
Codes: C - connected, S - static, R - RIP, M - mobile, B - BGP
       D - EIGRP, EX - EIGRP external, O - OSPF, IA - OSPF inter area
       N1 - OSPF NSSA external type 1, N2 - OSPF NSSA external type 2
       E1 - OSPF external type 1, E2 - OSPF external type 2
       i - IS-IS, su - IS-IS summary, L1 - IS-IS level-1, L2 - IS-IS level-2
       ia - IS-IS inter area, * - candidate default, U - per-user static route
       o - ODR, P - periodic downloaded static route

Gateway of last resort is 192.168.5.10 to network 0.0.0.0

C    192.168.5.0/24 is directly connected, FastEthernet0/1
C    192.168.1.0/24 is directly connected, FastEthernet0/0
     192.168.100.0/24 is variably subnetted, 2 subnets, 2 masks
S       192.168.100.0/24 [1/0] via 192.168.5.2
S       192.168.100.75/32 [1/0] via 192.168.5.5
S*   0.0.0.0/0 [1/0] via 192.168.5.10
```

To set the gateway of last resort, enter Global Configuration mode and use the `ip route` command to set a route to a universal system. Numerically, it is the opposite of a broadcast address, which is 255.255.255.255. You can specify that you want to route to all systems with the network ID of 0.0.0.0 and mask of 0.0.0.0 or 0.0.0.0/0 in Classless InterDomain Routing (CIDR) notation. So in this case, your network ID is defined as all binary zeros, and your mask says that all bits are host bits, which effectively defines all networks and all hosts. The only other thing that the route command needs is the actual gateway or router to use to get your data one step closer to its destination; this router needs to be on a network segment to which your router is connected. The complete command looks like this:

```
Router2(config)#ip route 0.0.0.0 0.0.0.0 192.168.10.1
```

Enabling routing

You are now in a situation where you should be able to use the `ping` command to test a connection to a remote address through your gateway of last resort. If you configure a device and connect it to your router interface, you can attempt to use the `ping` command to test the connection to a remote host (a host on another router segment). If you attempt to do so, you find that you do not receive a reply. Remember, the remote host needs to have a path back to your network segment, so you must configure the other host to use the other router interface to connect back to your local host, similar to what is shown in Figure 3-4. If this figure is representative of your configuration, with the router configured with two interfaces similar to the preceding description, you still will not able to test the connection from one host to the other.

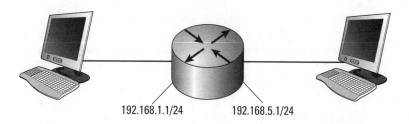

192.168.1.1/24   192.168.5.1/24

Figure 3-4:
A basic two-segment network.

| Local Host
IP Address:
192.168.1.10/24

Default Gateway:
192.168.5.1 |

| Remote Host
IP Address:
192.168.5.10/24

Default Gateway:
192.168.5.1 |

Well, what is missing? Even though you have a router, by default the router will not route traffic. Again, you can think of this as a security feature or as an optional configuration. Some people will install the router as a gateway device, using private addresses inside their network and public addresses outside, and their router will send Network Address Translation (NAT) traffic between the interfaces rather than routing. So until you enable `ip routing` with the following command, your router will not route IP-based traffic.

```
Router2(config)#ip routing
```

Now, you should be able to test the connection (with the `ping` command) from one side of your router to the other side.

Testing your routing by using the `ping` command the remote side of the router is not a good test that everything is working, because even without enabling routing, the router will respond from any of its configured interfaces. The only way to test that routing is actually working through the router is to use a command like `ping` to get a response from a remote host.

Configuring passwords

Although it is not necessary to have a password on your router, doing so is a very good idea. If you do not configure any passwords and enable Telnet, anyone can connect to your router, from any interface, and reconfigure your router to their hearts desire, giving themselves access to your entire internal network.

The last several versions of the Cisco IOS for routers force you to set up passwords on the first boot if you have not already enabled passwords.

Several types of passwords can be configured on a Cisco router, such as for Telnet and SSH connections, the console port, the enable password, and the secret password. All these password locations represent good access locations for passwords, but if you have only one password on only one access location, you should at least have an enable password.

Setting the enable password

You use the enable password every time you move from User EXEC mode to Privileged EXEC mode. This password gives you security on your router, because Privileged EXEC mode is where all the dangerous commands are located, including access to Global Configuration mode. To set an enable password, use the following command:

```
Router2>enable
Router2#configure terminal
Router2(config)#enable password mypassword
```

This command creates an enable password that is stored in your configuration file. To view this password, show the running configuration using the following command:

```
Router2>enable
Password:
Router2#show running-config | include enable password
enable password mypassword
```

You may immediately see the problem here. The password is stored in plain text in your configuration file, thus anyone who has access to your configuration file can easily read the password.

Setting the secret password

Cisco's solution to the enable password's inherent problem was to create a new type of password called the *secret password*. When you configure both an enable and a secret password, the secret password is the password that will be used to switch from User Exec mode to Priv Exec mode. The following code sets both passwords for your router:

```
Router2>enable
Router2#configure terminal
Router2(config)#enable password mypassword
Router2(config)#enable secret mysecretpassword
```

To see your enable passwords in your configuration, use the following command:

```
Router2>enable
Password:
Router2#show running-config | include enable
enable secret 5 $1$BSX4$FZp.ZFvYSAGUEDn8dvr140
enable password mypassword
```

Most encrypted passwords in your configuration file use a weak reversible encryption and are identified by a 7 in the password line, whereas the secret password is encrypted with a one-way MD5 hash with a 5 denoted in the password line. You may also see a 0, which identifies it as an unencrypted password.

Setting the Telnet password

If you need to remotely manage your router, you can choose between Telnet and SSH. I discuss the dangers of Telnet in the section "Connecting remotely via Telnet or SSH," in Book I, Chapter 5 — that is, Telnet sends data over the network in clear text, which makes it less secure than SSH. Some people justify the use of Telnet, and granted, if they are running it on a secured management network, some of the risks are mitigated.

In spite of the risks, it is good to know how Telnet works and how to administer it. Telnet accesses the router through the Virtual Terminal ports or vty ports. To see if you are set up with vty ports on your router, use the following command:

```
Router2>enable
Password:
Router2#show running-config | include line vty
line vty 0 4
```

So, you are set up with five vty ports on your router, numbered from 0 to 4, which means you can host up to five Telnet connections simultaneously on your router. The chance of having five network administrators making connections to this router at the same time is somewhat low. To find out how many connections your router will support, use the following command:

```
Router2>enable
Password:
Router2#configure terminal
Enter configuration commands, one per line. End with CNTL/Z.
Router2(config)#line vty 0 ?
  <1-181>  Last Line number
  <cr>
```

By typing the **?,** the router lets you know that it can support up to 182 total vty ports, but you can configure it to as low as 2 ports by typing **1.**

To set the password for a Telnet or vty port, use the following commands:

```
Router2>enable
Password:
Router2#configure terminal
Enter configuration commands, one per line.  End with CNTL/Z.
Router2(config)#line vty 0 4
Router2(config-line)#password vtypass
Router2(config-line)#exit
Router2(config)#exit
```

Note the appearance of the Line Configuration mode prompt (config-line), which has not yet appeared in this minibook. It is one more mode that you see when managing your router.

To have access to the router for Telnet, you need to have both an enable password and the Telnet password specified in your configuration.

Setting the SSH password

To set up access to the router for SSH, you must perform a few more steps. SSH access is not possible with only a password; you also need a user account created on your router. You discover how to create users in the section "Working with Users," later in this chapter. For now, assume that you have a user named *remote* with a password of *remote*. (Please do not use this type of password policy on your production network!)

To set up SSH access, you must change the default vty terminal or create a new one. In this case, you create a new vty for SSH access using the following commands:

```
Router2>enable
Password:
Router2#configure terminal
Enter configuration commands, one per line.  End with CNTL/Z.
Router2(config)#ip domain-name edtetz.net
Router2(config)#crypto key generate rsa
The name for the keys will be: Router2.edtetz.net
Choose the size of the key modulus in the range of 360 to 2048 for your
  General Purpose Keys. Choosing a key modulus greater than 512 may take
  a few minutes.

How many bits in the modulus [512]: 1024
% Generating 1024 bit RSA keys ...[OK]

Router2(config)#
*Mar 17 00:59:53.971: %SSH-5-ENABLED: SSH 1.99 has been enabled
Router2(config)#line vty 5
Router2(config-line)#login local
Router2(config-line)#transport input ssh
Router2(config-line)#exit
Router2(config)#exit
```

The preceding commands accomplish four key things:

✦ Creates a set of ssl encryption keys and enabled SSH.

✦ Creates a vty terminal pool of one terminal.

✦ Enables the incoming transport to SSH, rather than to Telnet or the other supported protocols.

✦ Sets the login option to use the local user account database.

The `crypto key` command needs to be issued only once on the router.

At this point, you should now be able to use a program like **putty** (discussed in Book I, Chapter 5) to connect to this router on TCP port 22. Because Telnet is still enabled on vty ports 0 through 4, you can use the following command to disable Telnet access or all remote access through that set of vty ports. By disabling the four default vty ports, you reduce the remote management of this switch to one SSH user at a time and eliminate unencrypted Telnet management traffic on the network. So, you can still manage the switch remotely, though you are required to use SSH.

```
Router2>enable
Password:
Router2#configure terminal
Enter configuration commands, one per line.  End with CNTL/Z.
Router2(config)#line vty 0 4
Router2(config-line)#transport input none
Router2(config-line)#exit
Router2(config)#exit
```

Setting the console port password

Anyone with access to the console port on your router can connect to it and have, at least, access to the User Exec mode. If they happen to know the enable or secret password, they can enter Priv Exec mode. To prevent this access, you can add an additional password to the configuration, which require users to enter a password in order to gain access to the console port.

In a case such as this, the bigger security question is why anyone who is not authorized has physical access to your router, which I cover in Book VI, Chapter 4.

To place a password on the console port, you use a system that is very similar to that of the vty ports. Examine the following commands:

```
Router2>enable
Password:
Router2#configure terminal
Enter configuration commands, one per line.  End with CNTL/Z.
Router2(config)#line con 0
Router2(config-line)#password conpass
Router2(config-line)#login
Router2(config-line)#exit
Router2(config)#exit
```

By implementing a console port password you add an extra layer of security on connections to this port.

Setting the Auxiliary Port (AUX) password

The *AUX port* is used to configure a modem to allow dial-in access to the router. You can use this modem connection as a backup configuration interface if you make a configuration error and lose other forms of remote configuration access, such as SSH or Telnet. By having a configured modem attached to the AUX port, you can connect to the router and correct the problem from any location where you have a modem connection.

Unfortunately, by default, anyone is able to dial in to your modem and get access to User Exec mode on your router. To make it more difficult for unauthorized people to access your router, you can configure a password on the AUX port. To do so, use the following configuration commands:

```
Router2>enable
Password:
Router2#configure terminal
Enter configuration commands, one per line.  End with CNTL/Z.
Router2(config)#line aux 0
Router2(config-line)#password conpass
Router2(config-line)#login
Router2(config-line)#exit
Router2(config)#exit
```

Finding out where passwords live

Now that you have looked at all the available types of passwords, display the running configuration to see how they are stored:

```
Router2#show running-config
Building configuration...

Current configuration : 921 bytes
!
version 12.3
!
(output omitted for briefness)
!
enable secret 5 $1$exG2$cxsOWeiMWa7a8SMo5dw51/
enable password enablepass
!
(Output omitted for brevity)
!
line con 0
 password conpass
 login
line aux 0
 password auxpass
 login
line vty 0 4
 password termpass
 login
!
end
```

Notice that the only password that is not stored in clear text is the enable secret password. All other passwords are clearly readable to anyone who has access to the configuration file or command.

Because all of these passwords are stored in the configuration file in clear text, they are not very secure. You have an option to encrypt all passwords in your configuration file, and I cover encrypted passwords in Book VI, Chapter 4 as a security best practice.

Setting banners

A *banner* is a message that is presented to someone using the router. When this message is shown to the user depends on the type of banner you configured. You can configure three main types of banners on a Cisco router.

✦ **Message of the Day (MOTD):** This type of logon message has been around for a long time on Unix and mainframe systems. The idea was to display a temporary notice to users, such as issues with system availability. However, because it displays when you connect to the device prior to login, most network administrators now use it to display legal notices regarding access to the router, such as `unauthorized access to this device is prohibited and violators will be prosecuted to the full extent of the law`.

✦ **Login:** This banner displays before login to the system but after the MOTD banner is displayed. Typically, this banner displays a permanent message to users.

✦ **Exec:** This banner displays after the login is completed when the connecting user enters User EXEC mode. Whereas the other banners are seen by all people who attempt to connect to the router, this banner is seen only by users who successfully log on to the router. This banner can be used to post reminders to network administrators.

To configure each of these banners, examine the following commands, which set all three banners up on your router:

```
Router2(config)#banner motd #
Enter TEXT message. End with the character '#'.
This device is for authorized personnel only.
If you have not been provided with permission to
access this device - disconnect at once.
#
Router2(config)#banner login #
Enter TEXT message. End with the character '#'.
*** Login Required. Unauthorized use is prohibited ***
#
Router2(config)#banner exec #
Enter TEXT message.  End with the character '#'.
*** Ensure that you update the system configuration ***
*** documentation after making system changes.     ***
#
Router2(config)#exit
```

**Book IV
Chapter 3**

**Router
Configuration**

Notice that each of the banner lines ends with a hash symbol (**#**) to delimit the end of the message. You can specify any character you want, but you will be using it to end the banner message. Here is what these messages look like when you connect to the router:

```
Router2 Con0 is now available
Press RETURN to get started!

This device is for authorized personnel only.
If you have not been provided with permission to
access this device - disconnect at once.

*** Login Required.  Unauthorized use is prohibited ***

User Access Verification

Password:
*** Ensure that you update the system configuration ***
*** documentation after making system changes.      ***

Router2>
```

Running Setup Wizard

Although I explain how to configure elements of your router, you have to follow a specific procedure the first time you power up a new router, or when you erase the configuration. When the router boots for the first time, it automatically enters setup. If your router does not, you have the option of running setup from Privileged EXEC mode. Here is the basic setup process; within just a few minutes, you can have your router up and running.

```
Router#setup

        --- System Configuration Dialog ---
Continue with configuration dialog? [yes/no]: yes

At any point you may enter a question mark '?' for help.
Use ctrl-c to abort configuration dialog at any prompt.
Default settings are in square brackets '[]'.

Basic management setup configures only enough connectivity
for management of the system, extended setup will ask you
to configure each interface on the system

Would you like to enter basic management setup? [yes/no]: yes
Configuring global parameters:

  Enter host name [Router]: Router2

  The enable secret is a password used to protect access to
  privileged EXEC and configuration modes. This password, after
  entered, becomes encrypted in the configuration.
  Enter enable secret: secretpass

  The enable password is used when you do not specify an
  enable secret password, with some older software versions, and
```

```
      some boot images.
      Enter enable password: enablepass

      The virtual terminal password is used to protect
      access to the router over a network interface.
      Enter virtual terminal password: termpass
      Configure SNMP Network Management? [no]:

  Current interface summary

  Interface                 IP-Address      OK? Method Status
       Protocol
  FastEthernet0/0           192.168.1.108   YES DHCP   up                          up
  FastEthernet0/1           unassigned      YES unset  administratively down  down

  Enter interface name used to connect to the
  management network from the above interface summary: FastEthernet0/0

  Configuring interface FastEthernet0/0:
    Use the 100 Base-TX (RJ-45) connector? [yes]:
    Operate in full-duplex mode? [no]:yes
    Configure IP on this interface? [yes]:
      IP address for this interface [192.168.1.108]: 192.168.1.240
      Subnet mask for this interface [255.255.255.0] :
      Class C network is 192.168.1.0, 24 subnet bits; mask is /24

  The following configuration command script was created:

  hostname Router2
  enable secret 5 $1$exG2$cxsOWeiMWa7a8SMo5dw51/
  enable password enablepass
  line vty 0 4
  password termpass
  no snmp-server
  !
  no ip routing

  !
  interface FastEthernet0/0
  no shutdown
  media-type 100Base-TX
  full-duplex
  ip address 192.168.1.240 255.255.255.0
  no mop enabled
  !
  interface FastEthernet0/1
  shutdown
  no ip address
  !
  end

  [0] Go to the IOS command prompt without saving this config.
  [1] Return back to the setup without saving this config.
  [2] Save this configuration to nvram and exit.

  Enter your selection [2]:

  Building configuration...
  [OK]
  Use the enabled mode 'configure' command to modify this configuration.
```

Notice how little information you need to enter to get basic management access to your router over the network, including Telnet access to the router. After the Setup Wizard is complete, enter Configuration mode to update your configuration to disable Telnet in favor of SSH, configure your other network interfaces, and enable routing.

Working with Users

As mentioned in the earlier section "Setting the SSH password," with SSH, user accounts are required in order to log in. These accounts can be stored in a local database on the router or on a central access server named *Terminal Access Controller Access-Control System (TACACS)*, which is an industry-standard authentication server.

Most small organizations and even some larger ones rely on the local database for user authentication, so this is the user creation option that I will describe in this book.

To use the local database for authentication, you need to follow these two steps:

1. **Create at least one user account.**
2. **Configure your router to use the local database rather than a password, which is done on an interface basis.**

Creating a user in the account database

To create a user in the account database, use a command like the following to specify the username and password:

```
Router2>enable
Password:
Router2#configure terminal
Enter configuration commands, one per line.  End with CNTL/Z.
Router2(config)#username remoteuser password remotepass
Router2(config)#username edt password edpass
Router2(config)#exit
```

Removing a user

To remove a user, you can use the standard `no` command and then specify the username in the same way that following the command removes the user named `remoteuser` from the local database.

```
Router2>enable
Password:
Router2#configure terminal
Enter configuration commands, one per line.  End with CNTL/Z.
Router2(config)#no username remoteuser
Router2(config)#exit
```

Enable user-level protection

Finally, you need to enable the `login local` setting on the interfaces you want to protect with this user-level protection, using a command similar to the following:

```
Router2>enable
Password:
Router2#configure terminal
Enter configuration commands, one per line.  End with CNTL/Z.
Router2(config)#line aux 0
Router2(config-line)#login local
Router2(config-line)#exit
Router2(config)#exit
```

Showing connected users

At times, you will want to find out who is connected to your router and performing management operations. You can easily do so using the `show users` command. Here is an example of the output:

```
Router2>enable
Password:
Router2#show users all
    Line       User        Host(s)           Idle       Location
*  0 con 0                 idle              00:00:00
  65 aux 0                                   00:00:00
  66 vty 0                 idle              00:02:01 192.168.1.3
  67 vty 1                                   00:00:00
  68 vty 2                                   00:00:00
  69 vty 3                                   00:00:00
  70 vty 4                                   00:00:00
  71 vty 5    remoteuser idle               00:01:05 192.168.1.137

  Interface   User             Mode        Idle     Peer Address
```

One line, listed with an asterisk, identifies the connection from which you ran the command. In addition, connections that do not show a user in the User column, such as vty 0, represent connections where a password was used for authentication, whereas the connection on vty 5 was made with user authentication. Forcing systems to use user-based authentication lets you see who is connected to the management interfaces.

Chapter 4: Setting Up Static Routes

In This Chapter

✔ **Examining how the routing process works**

✔ **Configuring routing using static route configuration**

Static routes are the basic routing form that you will use. For example, you will use them when your network is too small for other routing protocols, when you are setting up your router, prior to implementing your routing protocol, and when you want to have a backup routing plan in the event your routing protocol fails.

In this chapter, I present a small-scale sample network and show you exactly what you do to get routing tables up and going, and I identify issues arising from improper configuration. I walk you through the entire process of building static routing tables and show you what happens as you do so. The processes I describe in this chapter differ from those you see in Chapters 6 through 9 in this minibook where you use dynamic routing protocols to build routing tables.

In Chapters 6 though 9 of this minibook, you see the various dynamic routing protocols available for use on Cisco routers and become familiar with basic configuration and troubleshooting techniques for each of these protocols.

Knowing the Pros and Cons of Static Routing

Before I get into the nitty-gritty details of static routing, I want to discuss a few of the benefits and drawbacks of static routing, as compared to implementing dynamic routing protocols. On the benefit side, you have the following:

✦ **Predictability:** If you change your network design and layout and suffer from a device failure, static routes do not change. You always know the path your data will take.

✦ **Network bandwidth overhead:** Static routing has zero overhead, whereas all dynamic routing protocols have some degree of overhead. For example, on a network with 200 segments, the router will send updates from each interface every 30 seconds, and those updates are about 3KB of data. Over the course of a day, this traffic adds up.

✦ **Easy to configure:** This issue is relative, depending on the size of your network. Although small networks are easy to configure, as a network grows, applying changes to all the routers can become a big task.

The few drawbacks to static routing include the following:

✦ **Lack of scalability:** For the 200 segment network mentioned previously, which possibly contains 200 routers, you could be dealing with thousands of routing table entries. Manually calculating all those routes and keeping them up-to-date would be a Herculean task and very prone to error. Even if you implement a good network-addressing design that allows for route summarization, you are still left with an overwhelming number of routes to manage.

✦ **Large network implementation:** When working with a network of 200 routers, the task of updating one route can become a complex task, especially if you update the routes in the wrong order. In that case, you could lose access to a large section of the network until someone visits that router with a rollover cable or connects from another area of the network.

✦ **No redundancy:** Dynamic routing protocols can update routing tables in the event of device or interface failure, so if there are multiple possible paths, these protocols will continue to allow data flow. Static routes do not allow for this automatic failover or redundant paths, so if you have a failure, you must manually adjust routes to move data through an alternative path.

Building a Small Network with Static Routing

Now, I allow myself to create a small network for your amusement. This network has two routers and two workstations, with the workstations placed on the far ends of the network. Figure 4-1 illustrates this network. On it, the routers are configured so that the FastEthernet 0/0 (fa0/0) interfaces are for the computer side of the network and the FastEthernet 0/1 (fa0/1) interfaces are for the external side. Interface types are covered in Chapter 3 of this minibook.

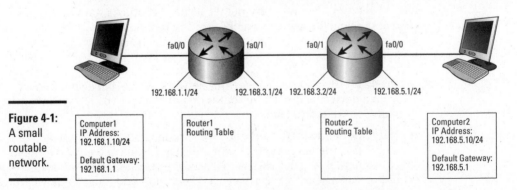

Figure 4-1: A small routable network.

fa0/0   fa0/1   fa0/1   fa0/0

192.168.1.1/24   192.168.3.1/24   192.168.3.2/24   192.168.5.1/24

Computer1
IP Address:
192.168.1.10/24

Default Gateway:
192.168.1.1

Router1
Routing Table

Router2
Routing Table

Computer2
IP Address:
192.168.5.10/24

Default Gateway:
192.168.5.1

Initially, if you sit at `Computer1` and attempt to contact `Computer2`, you cannot make the connection. If you use commands such as `ping` or `traceroute` (`tracert` on Windows) on `Computer2` to troubleshoot the connection, you receive the following results:

```
C:\>Ping 192.168.5.10
Pinging 192.168.5.10 with 32 bytes of data:

Reply from 192.168.1.1: Destination host unreachable.
Reply from 192.168.1.1: Destination host unreachable.
Reply from 192.168.1.1: Destination host unreachable.
Reply from 192.168.1.1: Destination host unreachable.
```

Getting network info from your router

If your network has only one router, what routing do you need to deal with? Other than enabling routing on the router, nothing needs to be done, because the router automatically adds routes in its routing table for all directly connected interfaces. So if you take a look at the interfaces on the router, you find a list of interfaces like the following:

```
Router1>enable
Password:
Router2#show ip interface brief
Interface          IP-Address      OK? Method Status      Protocol
FastEthernet0/0    192.168.1.240   YES NVRAM  up              up
FastEthernet0/1    192.168.5.1     YES manual up              up
Loopback0          192.168.255.254 YES manual up              up
```

Now, if you look at the routing table (using the `show ip route` command) and specify that it show the `connected` interfaces, you see two routes that allow data to be transferred between these two interfaces. When data arrives on one interface, if it is destined for the other network segment, it is passed through the other interface.

```
Router1>enable
Password:
Router1#show ip route connected
C    192.168.3.0/24 is directly connected, FastEthernet0/1
C    192.168.1.0/24 is directly connected, FastEthernet0/0
```

In addition to the routing table, you can also get data about your routes from the `show ip route summary` command, which shows a list of networks or subnets for your connected interfaces.

```
Router1>enable
Password:
Router1#show ip route summary
IP routing table name is Default-IP-Routing-Table(0)
IP routing table maximum-paths is 16
Route Source   Networks   Subnets   Overhead   Memory (bytes)
connected      2          0         144        272
static         0          0         0          0
Total          2          0         144        272
```

Configuring the second router

To make your sample network a little more realistic, a second router gives you a total of three network segments. You are not putting any computers on the middle segment; you would encounter this typical configuration if you were to lease a private link or virtual circuit from your telephone company or if you were routing over an internal backbone connection on your network.

In this case, the networks you want to route between (containing Computer1 and Computer2) are not directly connected to a single router; rather, one segment is directly connected to each router on your network. Note that you would normally configure each computer to use the local router as the default gateway, so this is expected in this scenario. When you issue a command such as ping to test the connection to the remote computer whose IP address is 192.168.5.10, the computer performs the logical AND process on your IP address and the remote IP address using the subnet mask. In this case, the AND process identifies the destination address as a remote address. In all cases where the address is remote, the computer consults its local routing table. In this case, nothing is in the local routing table other than the default routes and the route to the default gateway. Because no routes are closer, the computer uses the "catch all" route through the default gateway.

When the ping command goes through, the results resemble the following. The error may be that the destination host is unavailable. Or it may be that the entire destination network is unavailable because the router at 192.168.1.1 does not know how to get to the destination network segment.

```
C:\>ping 192.168.5.10

Pinging 192.168.5.10 with 32 bytes of data:

Reply from 192.168.1.1: Destination host unreachable.
Reply from 192.168.1.1: Destination host unreachable.
Reply from 192.168.1.1: Destination host unreachable.
Reply from 192.168.1.1: Destination host unreachable.

Ping statistics for 192.168.5.10:
    Packets: Sent = 4, Received = 0, Lost = 4 (100% loss),
Approximate round trip times in milli-seconds:
    Minimum = 0ms, Maximum = 1ms, Average = 0ms
```

The following code does two things. First, it enables routing on the router, which is necessary even to have routing on the two-segment network (this is not a default setting; you must instruct a router to route when there is more than one interface). Second, it adds a route to the 192.168.5.0 network segment (see Figure 4-2 for an illustration).

```
Router1>enable
Password:
Router1#configure terminal
Enter configuration commands, one per line.  End with CNTL/Z.
Router1(config)#ip routing
Router1(config)#ip route 192.168.5.0 255.255.255.0 192.168.3.2
Router1(config)#exit
```

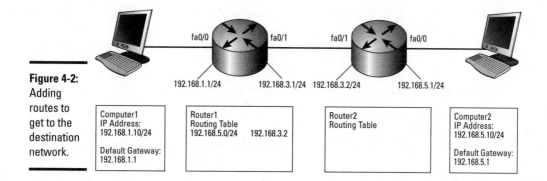

Figure 4-2:
Adding
routes to
get to the
destination
network.

Computer1
IP Address:
192.168.1.10/24

Default Gateway:
192.168.1.1

Router1
Routing Table
192.168.5.0/24   192.168.3.2

Router2
Routing Table

Computer2
IP Address:
192.168.5.10/24

Default Gateway:
192.168.5.1

fa0/0   fa0/1   fa0/1   fa0/0

192.168.1.1/24   192.168.3.1/24 192.168.3.2/24   192.168.5.1/24

When you use the `ping` command, the remote computer at 192.168.5.10,
you receive a slightly different error. The following error can have several
causes. In general, *Request timed out* error means that the routers know how
to get the data to its destination (otherwise you have the destination errors
from the previous use of `ping`), or at least they think they do.

```
C:\>ping 192.168.5.10

Pinging 192.168.5.10 with 32 bytes of data:

Request timed out.
Request timed out.
Request timed out.
Request timed out.

Ping statistics for 192.168.5.10:
    Packets: Sent = 4, Received = 0, Lost = 4 (100% loss),
Approximate round trip times in milli-seconds:
    Minimum = 0ms, Maximum = 1ms, Average = 0ms
```

If you have an issue with your routing tables, perhaps a router using the
default gateway rather than the static route you should have configured, you
might see the preceding error because the routers think they can route the
data through to its destination. You may also see this error if the routes to
the destination network are correct, but the routers on the reverse path are
not correctly configured. The `traceroute` command may give you a little
more information as to the nature of the error. In the following example, the
Windows version of `traceroute` (`tracert`) is configured to trace the route
for only four hops using the `-h 4` option to modify the command.

```
D:\utils>tracert -h 4 192.168.5.10

Tracing route to 192.168.3.1 over a maximum of 30 hops

  1    <1 ms    <1 ms    <1 ms   192.168.1.1
  2     *        *        *      Request timed out.
  3     *        *        *      Request timed out.
  4     *        *        *      Request timed out.

Trace complete.
```

**Book IV
Chapter 4**

**Setting Up
Static Routes**

This code indicates only that your computer's routing table is correct and that you passed the data on to your local router. Does your router know where to go from there? You still cannot be sure. You can connect to your router and verify the route, and then you can use ping to test the destination router and attempt to use traceroute to test the destination address, which shows you the router's route to the destination:

```
Router1>enable
Password:
Router1#show ip route static
S    192.168.5.0/24 [1/0] via 192.168.3.2

Router1#ping 192.168.3.2
Type escape sequence to abort.
Sending 5, 100-byte ICMP Echos to 192.168.3.2, timeout is 2 seconds:
!!!!!
Success rate is 100 percent (5/5), round-trip min/avg/max = 1/1/4 ms
Router1#traceroute 192.168.5.10

Type escape sequence to abort.
Tracing the route to 192.168.5.10

  1 192.168.3.2 0 msec 0 msec 4 msec
  2 192.168.5.10 0 msec 4 msec 0 msec
```

If you are using these commands at the router, in my case Router1, you can receive replies, but you cannot get replies from Computer1, which is behind Router1. Because the commands work from Router1, you can be pretty sure that Router1 has the proper routes.

Think about the difference between the source addresses used for Computer1 and Router1. To Router2 and Computer2, the source address of Computer1 is 192.168.1.10, and Router1 is 192.168.3.1. So the source address is the difference, because Router2 knows how to get to 192.168.3.1, but does not know how to get to 192.168.1.10.

The net result is that you cannot communicate from Computer1 to Computer2, but what is the real reason? With the testing that was done, the route to the 192.168.5.0/24 network, so the problem is with the return trip. Effectively, if you were to use the ping command on Computer2 to test the address of Computer1, you would see the same thing you saw when this exercise started — the results would be either *Destination net unreachable* or *Destination host unreachable*. The solution is to get the correct route in place for that data to get back to Computer1 and ensure that IP routing is enabled giving you a network that looks like Figure 4-3. Because the last test completed successfully, you are sure that the ip routing command had already been run in Global Configuration mode, since if it was not enabled you would not have received any results.

```
Router2>enable
Password:
Router2#configure terminal
Enter configuration commands, one per line.  End with CNTL/Z.
Router2(config)#ip routing
Router2(config)#ip route 192.168.1.0 255.255.255.0 192.168.3.1
Router2(config)#exit
```

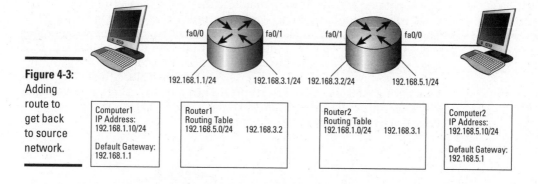

Figure 4-3:
Adding route to get back to source network.

Now to test the connection, go back to the original use of the ping command to test what was done at the very beginning. The result is now successful. You now have a valid route to and from the 192.168.5.0/24 network.

```
C:\ >ping 192.168.5.10

Pinging 192.168.5.10 with 32 bytes of data:

Reply from 192.168.5.10: bytes=32 time=1ms TTL=253
Reply from 192.168.5.10: bytes=32 time<1ms TTL=253
Reply from 192.168.5.10: bytes=32 time<1ms TTL=253
Reply from 192.168.5.10: bytes=32 time<1ms TTL=253

Ping statistics for 192.168.5.10:
    Packets: Sent = 4, Received = 4, Lost = 0 (0% loss),
Approximate round trip times in milli-seconds:
    Minimum = 0ms, Maximum = 1ms, Average = 0ms
```

When you examine the tracert again, success!

```
C:\>tracert -h 4 192.168.5.10

Tracing route to 192.168.5.10 over a maximum of 4 hops

  1    <1 ms     1 ms    <1 ms   192.168.1.1
  2    26 ms    17 ms    21 ms   192.168.3.2
  3     9 ms     9 ms    14 ms   192.168.5.10

Trace complete.
```

The routing is now set up for a small network.

As the network grows, it will be become more complex with more routes that need to be configured and maintained.

Adding a third router

The only thing you might want to add to this network is a third router that gives your network's users access to the Internet, as shown in Figure 4-4. To do so, you need to add additional routing entries on the new router, as well as configure the other routers to route Internet-destined traffic through Router3. The easy way to update your routes is to configure the gateway of last resort, which is used when you do not have a closer matching route. Configuring the gateway of last resort is equivalent to using the default gateway that you configure on your desktop computer. In fact, at the routing table level, these gateways are identical.

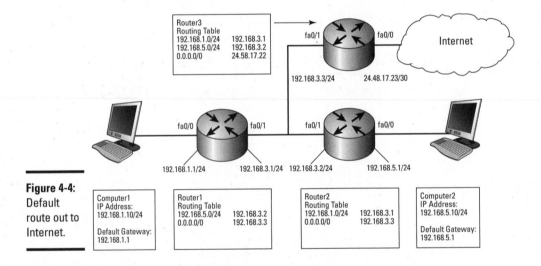

Figure 4-4: Default route out to Internet.

To apply this configuration change on Router1, you set the default route to point to 192.168.3.3 with the following command:

```
Router2>enable
Password:
Router1#configure terminal
Enter configuration commands, one per line.  End with CNTL/Z.
Router1(config)#ip routing
Router1(config)#ip route 0.0.0.0 0.0.0.0 192.168.3.3
Router1(config)#exit
```

This command tells the system to pass all data, going to any IP address with any subnet mask, over to the router at 192.168.3.3 on the directly connected network of 192.168.3.0/24. The destination always needs to be a device on a directly connected network segment. When scanning the routing table for a route to a destination address, the route closest to the destination address is used. However, if no other entry is found in the routing table, this route will be used.

Running around and around with routing loops

As your network grows, so does the chance to introduce loops into the routing tables. Figure 4-5 shows this issue in action. Note that the route on Router2 to get to 192.168.1.0/24 is removed, and a route on Router3 to send traffic for 192.168.1.0/24 to Router2 is added incorrectly. The net effect is that if you sit at Computer2 and attempt to use the ping command to test the IP address of Computer1, the data bounces endlessly between Router2 and Router3.

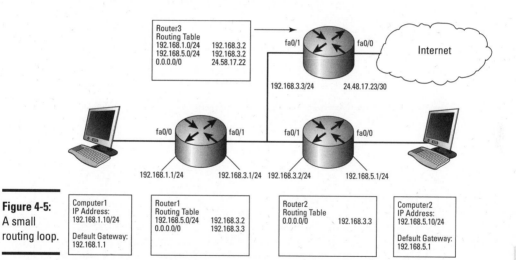

Figure 4-5: A small routing loop.

Computer1	Router1	Router2	Computer2
IP Address:	Routing Table	Routing Table	IP Address:
192.168.1.10/24	192.168.5.0/24 192.168.3.2	0.0.0.0/0 192.168.3.3	192.168.5.10/24
	0.0.0.0/0 192.168.3.3		
Default Gateway:			Default Gateway:
192.168.1.1			192.168.5.1

Well, endlessly is not quite correct. In Book I, Chapter 4, I discuss the structure of an IP packet and briefly introduced the Time to Live (TTL) in the packet header. This TTL is reduced by one every time a router processes an IP packet, and when the TTL is set to zero, it is removed from the network and an Internet Control Message Protocol (ICMP) message is sent to the source computer. Unlike the use of ICMP, when used with the ping command, ICMP sends status and control messages to IP hosts on the network. The message sent to the host is a *Packet Expired in Transit* message.

**Book IV
Chapter 4**

**Setting Up
Static Routes**

The following example shows a packet expiration message that was received when testing the connection to Computer1 from Computer2:

```
C:\>ping 192.168.1.10

Pinging 192.168.1.10 with 32 bytes of data:

Reply from 192.168.3.3: TTL expired in transit.
Reply from 192.168.3.3: TTL expired in transit.
Reply from 192.168.3.3: TTL expired in transit.
Reply from 192.168.3.3: TTL expired in transit.

Ping statistics for 192.168.1.10:
    Packets: Sent = 4, Received = 4, Lost = 0 (0% loss),
Approximate round trip times in milli-seconds:
    Minimum = 0ms, Maximum = 0ms, Average = 0ms
```

To further illustrate this issue of expired packets, here is a copy of the output of the traceroute command for the same message. You let it go for only 10 hops by using the −h modifier, but this is enough to see the pattern that has developed as the data bounces between Router2 and Router3.

```
D:\utils>tracert -h 10 192.168.1.10

Tracing route to 192.168.1.10 over a maximum of 10 hops

    1    <1 ms    <1 ms    <1 ms  192.168.5.1
    2    <1 ms    <1 ms    <1 ms  192.168.3.3
    3     1 ms     1 ms     1 ms  192.168.3.2
    4     1 ms     1 ms     1 ms  192.168.3.3
    5     1 ms     1 ms     1 ms  192.168.3.2
    6     2 ms     2 ms     2 ms  192.168.3.3
    7     2 ms     2 ms     2 ms  192.168.3.2
    8     3 ms     3 ms     3 ms  192.168.3.3
    9     3 ms     3 ms     3 ms  192.168.3.2
   10     4 ms     4 ms     4 ms  192.168.3.3

Trace complete.
```

This issue can be corrected by adjusting the route on Router3 to send data destined for the 192.168.1.0/24 network through Router1 rather than Router2. While this would get the data to the correct location, data for Computer1 would travel from Computer2 through both Router2 and Router3, and you should add a specific route on Router2 to directly route 192.168.1.0/24 data to Router1.

Most routing loops give you an expired packet, so by using the ping or traceroute commands, you can quickly identify the issue though output similar to what you see in this section. The lengthier task may be identifying the exact source of the problem, as it likely does with one routing table entry on one router. If you work sequentially through the routers on one end of the connection to the other end, you will find it.

Chapter 5: Configuring Serial Connections and WAN Links

In This Chapter

✔ Working with the telephone company's connection options

✔ Examining WAN technologies and connection options

✔ Setting up a basic serial connection to support a WAN connection

In Book IV, Chapter 1, I state that the key reason for using WANs is that you are using a network infrastructure you do not own. This chapter focuses on setting up Wide Area Network (WAN) links for your network. Many people use serial links to implement their WAN and Internet connections, but a moving trend is to implement fiber, Ethernet, or other connections directly at their routers. After discussing the types of links you can implement for WAN connections, I show you how to configure the serial connection.

After reading this chapter, you will appreciate the available WAN connection technologies, as well as how to configure them. I examine the role of the telephone company, and the general types of interfaces you can obtain from the telephone company. In each region, you are likely to find that the local telephone company has tried to implement newer and faster connection types, which, if you are in luck, means that just by plugging in a standard Ethernet-style connection, you can be up and running.

Finding Out Where the Telephone Company Fits In

You implement WAN links using whatever technologies your telephone company supports. You should be able to choose from many technologies. Although use of high-speed Internet connections and site-to-site VPN solutions is becoming popular, there are still many places outside major metropolitan areas where your choices will be quite limited.

Consider, for example, a connection between offices in New York to an office in Toronto: The traffic leaves the serial or WAN port on your router in Toronto and enters your service provider's network. The traffic then traverses your service provider's network — and possibly several service providers — until it arrives at the serial or WAN port on the New York router.

When the traffic is on the service provider's network, your traffic is isolated from other users' traffic, whereas your Internet traffic is mixed together with everyone else's traffic. Depending on the service provider, you can choose from various options or types of services.

Here are the three main options for connections offered by telephone companies:

✦ **Circuit switching:** A system that establishes a connection each time it has data to send, such as using a telephone.

✦ **Leased lines:** A system on which a connection that is always connected.

✦ **Packet switching:** A system on which the data on the service provider network may not always take the same path.

I discuss these options in the following sections.

Circuit switching

Circuit-switched solutions are characterized by connections that are established temporarily to send data. If you are using a circuit-switched solution, each time you send data to a location, you must establish the connection, send the data, and close the connection. This process is done automatically to addresses that are predefined by your telephone company and for which your router is configured. When you use circuit switching, your data always takes the same path and is guaranteed to arrive in order and intact. For these solutions, you contract the amount of bandwidth you require, and this bandwidth is yours, so you do not share it with other customers. Because you must pay for this bandwidth, this option may be appropriate for low-bandwidth solutions, but it becomes costly as bandwidth needs increase.

The main example of circuit-switched solutions is *Integrated Services Digital Networks (ISDN),* which is a solution that uses digital connections to carry either computer data or voice traffic. This solution uses two types of channels to carry data, B-channels and D-channels. A *B-channel* is capable of carrying data at a rate of 64 Kbps. A *D-channel* carries signaling data at a rate of 16 Kbps or 64 Kbps. Here are the main kinds of ISDN services In North America:

✦ **Basic Rate Interface (BRI):** The implementation of BRI supports two 64-Kbps B-channels to carry data at a combined rate of 128 Kbps. The signaling channel (D-channel) for BRI is 16 Kbps.

✦ **Primary Rate Interface (PRI):** The implementation of PRI supports up to 23 64-Kbps data channels (B-channels) to carry data at a combined rate up to 1.45 Mbps, while having one additional 64-Kbps D-channel carry the signaling information.

Leased lines

In a *leased line* solution, you purchase (or lease — surprise!) a permanent link while paying a monthly fee. In this case, you are not charged by the connection or the amount of data; instead, once you lease the line, you can send as much data over the link as the link will support. The permanent link is to your service provider's network, and it is sometimes referred to as a *point-to-point link*.

Leased lines tend to have more available bandwidth than circuit switch solutions. The main examples of these solutions in North America are T1 and T3 links.

✦ **T1 link:** These links are made up of 24 channels that carry data at 64 Kbps, yielding a total bandwidth of 1.544 Mbps. Unlike PRI lines, they do not require a signaling channel. As mentioned, you can have up to 24 channels. When installed, the link will have all 24 channels, but when you pay for your service, you can pay for, or use, only a portion of this link. This option lowers your monthly cost and is called a *fractional-T1 link*.

✦ **T3 link:** These links offer additional channels. This option uses 28 T1 lines that are combined and yields a total bandwidth of 44.736 Mbps.

Packet switching

Packet switching differs substantially from the previous two options in that circuit-switched and leased lines will have all your data following a single path between two destinations. With packet switching, each packet or piece of data can take a different path from source to destination, as shown in Figure 5-1. Switching in this example is similar to switching on your LAN, except it is implemented on a much larger scale. When implementing a packet-switched solution, you usually work with a *virtual circuit*, which, like a physical circuit, establishes a connection between two points, but in this case it is a temporary connection. From the point of view of the devices on either end of the connection, there is only one router hop from one end of the connection to the other, but in reality they go through a huge switched network, being handled by many devices.

Some examples of this type of connection include:

✦ **X.25:** This represents one of the oldest technologies in use. As a packet-switched solution, it makes use of a *packet assembler/disassembler* (PAD) (which prepares data packets for transmission and processes them after transmission) device that is connected to the router's serial port. Through this device, you are able to connect to the X.25 network and transfer your data at a rate of 2 Mbps.

**Book IV
Chapter 5**

Configuring Serial
Connections and
WAN Links

✦ **Frame relay:** This is the replacement for X.25 and implements the same basic solution, but in a purely digital format and allows for speeds as fast as 50 Mbps. This connection can give you the same speed as a T3connection.

✦ **Asynchronous Transfer Mode (ATM):** A packet-switched network environment that differs greatly from the previous solutions in that it uses a fixed-length packet size referred to as a *cell*. A cell is the standard 53 bytes in size. ATM is a WAN technology capable of sending large, low-delay types of data (such as video) and can sustain a transfer rate of 622 Mbps. The small packet sizes are not a disadvantage — because other solutions need to keep checking for the end of a packet, and ATM eliminates this need by using the standard-sized frames. However, partial frames or cells will be padded with empty data.

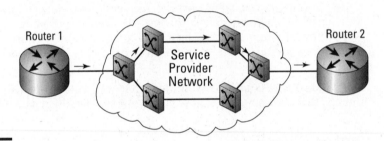

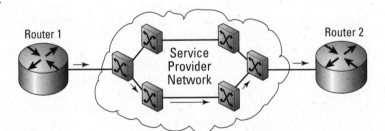

Figure 5-1:
With a packet-switched network, data may take different paths.

Connecting Your Devices

For any connection type that you may choose to use, you must establish a connection between the service provider and your router. How you do so will vary based on the type of connection. In general, you will use serial ports or ISDN ports or implement a Channel Service Unit/Data Service Unit (CSU/DSU).

Serial ports

One of the main methods of connecting the router to your service provider's network is via a serial port. Depending on your service provider connection, you may be provided with a CSU/DSU. The CSU/DSU serves the same purpose a modem (modulator/demodulator) in that it prepares your digital data to be sent over a telephone company network that may not be carrying a digital signal. These devices connect to the service provider connection, such as a T1 link, which is then connected to your router. Figure 5-2 illustrates this final link.

Figure 5-2: Implementing your WAN link using an external CSU/DSU.

This breaks the connection into two types of devices: Data Terminal Equipment (DTE) which end user devices, and Data Communications Equipment (DCE) which are telephone company devices. In the computer world, a computer represents the DTE and a modem represents the DCE, but when dealing with your service provider, your router is the DTE, and the service provider's communication devices are the DCE. So, the cable that connects to your router connects to the DTE, whereas the end of the cable that connects to the service provider's equipment connects to the DCE. If you want to simulate a router-to-router serial connection for testing before deploying your network equipment, you can use a special serial cable (back-to-back serial cable), as shown in Figure 5-3, which is defined with two specific ends, for DTE and DCE.

Integrated CSU/DSU

Over the years, to reduce cost or complexity, it has become common for people to integrate the CSU/DSU components into their routers. Rather than having another bulky device sitting in your communications room, you can have the functionality of the CSU/DSU integrated into the circuitry of your router. The drawback is that if you decide to change the type of connection you have, you may need to change your router. Consequently, Cisco came up with the WAN Interface Card (WIC) port, which allows you to change the type of service provider connection you use at a minimum cost, allowing you to reuse your existing router.

Figure 5-3:
A router-to-router back-to-back serial cable.

ISDN ports

With the prevalence of ISDN connections, Cisco has created and sold routers in a fixed configuration — rather than use WIC ports — that are preconfigured for ISDN environments. Your connectivity options are limited, but the price of these routers can represent an attractive price-point if you do not anticipate changing the connection types you use with your service provider.

Setting Up Your Serial Connection

Because I have discussed serial connections with some regularity, allow me to show you how to manage the connection from your Cisco device. For this example, you connect two routers by using a back-to-back cable or DTC-DTE cable, emulating a service provider connection between the two devices.

Configuring your serial connection

The basic configuration of a serial connection is no different than the other types of connections that are covered elsewhere in this book and covered in Book IV, Chapter 3. You enter Interface Configuration mode, set the IP address, and remove the `shutdown` command. Here is the code on `Router1` to setup the required connection.

```
Router1>enable
Password:
Router1#config terminal
Router1(config)#interface serial 0
Router1(config-if)#ip address 24.0.0.1 255.0.0.0
Router1(config-if)#no shutdown
Router1(config-if)#exit
Router1(config)#exit
```

Configuring serial link protocols

With the basic IP configuration out of the way, you are ready to implement the serial link protocol or encapsulation protocol. You can choose from either *High-Level Data Link Control* (HDLC) or *Point to Point Protocol* (PPP), which are encapsulation protocols used to format data to send across the wire. When you are sending data over a serial link, your data is encapsulated using a serial link protocol. Both ends of the connections *must* support and implement the same protocol.

HDLC does not support authentication. Because of this limitation and the compatibility issue, most people tend to implement PPP.

Working with HDLC

HDLC is an ISO standard, but that has not stopped vendors from putting their own spin on the implementation, which means that its implementation is somewhat vendor-specific.

HDLC is the default serial link protocol implemented on Cisco routers, so with no other changes, this is the protocol you are likely to find in use. To ensure that the HDLC protocol to be used, and for you to see the command, run the following command:

```
Router1>enable
Password:
Router1#config terminal
Router1(config)#interface serial 0
Router1(config-if)#encapsulation hdlc
Router1(config-if)#exit
Router1(config)#exit
```

Both ends of the serial link must use the same serial link protocol, so if one of your routers is using HDLC, it must be implemented on the other routers as well.

Working with PPP

PPP is an open standard supported by many vendors, and it tends to be compatible among the vendors. PPP is also link type independent, meaning it can run over many physical serial link types, and supports the following two types of authentication protocol:

✦ **PAP (Password Authentication Protocol):** An authentication protocol that provides security by a username and a password that are transmitted in plain text when a connection is established between two hosts. This option is not the most secure one because it allows the authentication information to be captured by someone who may be capable of capturing data in-between your routers.

✦ **CHAP (Challenge Handshake Authentication Protocol):** This protocol does not send the authentication information in plain text. When implementing CHAP, a secret password is configured on both routers, the same secret at both ends. This secret is then encoded by a mathematical function called a *hashing algorithm,* and the resulting value is called the *hash value.* This hash value is sent over the network rather than the secret. A hash value is a unique value that can be duplicated only if a user knows the original secret value.

```
Router1>enable
Password:
Router1#config terminal
Router1(config)#username Router2 password mypass
Router1(config)#interface serial 0
Router1(config-if)#encapsulation ppp
Router1(config-if)#ppp authentication chap
Router1(config-if)#exit
Router1(config)#exit
```

Make note of the username created in the preceding commands; this username matches the hostname of the router that will be connecting to `Router1`. The password assigned to this account is the secret that will be used. On `Router2`, you need to create a `Router1` account with a matching password.

Setting the clock rate

To finally get your system up and running, you need to set up the clock speed, which controls the speed at which data is sent over the connection in bits per second (bps). The DCE sets and controls the clock speed. So, in the case of a link from a service provider, the provider sets the clock speed, and when you connect to the external CSU/DSU, your serial port accepts the configuration. In the case of a back-to-back cable, one of the routers plays the role of the DCE, and that device sets the clock speed for the connection. If you are implementing the same type of layout in a lab, check the cable and identify the DCE side of the cable; then implement the clock speed with a command similar to the following:

```
Router1>enable
Password:
Router1#config terminal
Router1(config)#interface serial 0
Router1(config-if)#clock rate 64000
Router1(config-if)#exit
Router1(config)#exit
```

In this example, the clock rate is set at 64000 or 64 Kbps.

To find the clock rates that are available on your router, type `clock rate ?` when in Interface Configuration mode on your serial connection, as shown in this command example:

```
Router1>enable
Password:
Router1#config terminal
Router1(config)#interface serial 0
Router1(config-if)#clock rate ?
  1200
  2400
  4800
  9600
  19200
  38400
  56000
  64000
  72000
  125000
<300-125000>  Choose clockrate from list above
Router1(config-if)#end
```

Troubleshooting Serial Connections

As I repeat (repeatedly) in this book, to effectively identify and troubleshoot a problem, you must have the key information about the devices or services you are troubleshooting. Here, as in other chapters, I introduce some of the `show` and `debug` commands you can use to identify configuration or flow issues with serial connections.

Showing

The `show` command displays the configuration and status of your serial ports. In the following code, the items that stand out the most are the line protocols that are reported as down, meaning that the physical connection to the device at the other end of the connection is not established, as well as the encapsulation protocol that is in use, such as HDLC or PPP.

**Book IV
Chapter 5**

Configuring Serial
Connections and
WAN Links

```
Router1# show interfaces serial 0
Serial0 is up, line protocol is down
  Hardware is HD64570
  Internet address is 24.0.0.1/8
  MTU 1500 bytes, BW 1544 Kbit, DLY 20000 usec,
     reliability 255/255, txload 1/255, rxload 1/255
  Encapsulation HDLC, loopback not set
  Keepalive set (10 sec)
  Last input never, output 00:00:08, output hang never
  Last clearing of "show interface" counters never
  Input queue: 0/75/0/0 (size/max/drops/flushes); Total output drops: 0
  Queueing strategy: weighted fair
  Output queue: 0/1000/64/0 (size/max total/threshold/drops)
     Conversations  0/2/256 (active/max active/max total)
     Reserved Conversations 0/0 (allocated/max allocated)
     Available Bandwidth 1158 kilobits/sec
  5 minute input rate 0 bits/sec, 0 packets/sec
  5 minute output rate 0 bits/sec, 0 packets/sec
     0 packets input, 0 bytes, 0 no buffer
     Received 0 broadcasts, 0 runts, 0 giants, 0 throttles
     0 input errors, 0 CRC, 0 frame, 0 overrun, 0 ignored, 0 abort
     21 packets output, 714 bytes, 0 underruns
     0 output errors, 0 collisions, 12 interface resets
     0 output buffer failures, 0 output buffers swapped out
```

After correcting the preceding problem — in this case, the clock speed was not set on the DCE device — the line protocol is reported as being up:

```
Router1#show interfaces serial 0
Serial0 is up, line protocol is up
  Hardware is HD64570
  Internet address is 24.0.0.1/8
  MTU 1500 bytes, BW 1544 Kbit, DLY 20000 usec,
     reliability 255/255, txload 1/255, rxload 1/255
  Encapsulation HDLC, loopback not set
  Keepalive set (10 sec)
  Last input 00:00:09, output 00:00:08, output hang never
  Last clearing of "show interface" counters never
  Input queue: 0/75/0/0 (size/max/drops/flushes); Total output drops: 0
  Queueing strategy: weighted fair
  Output queue: 0/1000/64/0 (size/max total/threshold/drops)
     Conversations  0/2/256 (active/max active/max total)
     Reserved Conversations 0/0 (allocated/max allocated)
     Available Bandwidth 1158 kilobits/sec
  5 minute input rate 0 bits/sec, 0 packets/sec
  5 minute output rate 0 bits/sec, 0 packets/sec
     8 packets input, 1208 bytes, 0 no buffer
     Received 8 broadcasts, 0 runts, 0 giants, 0 throttles
     0 input errors, 0 CRC, 0 frame, 0 overrun, 0 ignored, 0 abort
     91 packets output, 3282 bytes, 0 underruns
     0 output errors, 0 collisions, 43 interface resets
     0 output buffer failures, 0 output buffers swapped out
     85 carrier transitions
     DCD=up  DSR=up  DTR=up  RTS=up  CTS=up
```

Debugging

After you know how to view current configuration information, take a look at the active connection and data going through the connection by using the debug command. You can choose from the following debug options. I focus on the interface option.

```
Router1#debug serial ?
  interface  Serial interface events
  m32_dma    Serial M32 DMA
  mueslix    Serial Mueslix
  packet     Serial network interface packets
  revive     Serial Revive
```

When you see the show command named Showing in the preceding section, you start with an issue with clock speed not being properly set on the DCE side of the connection. To see and diagnose a problem, I re-create the problem so that you can see what it would look like when troubleshooting with the debug command. When you have an issue with your connection, you can take a look at the information the debug command gives you about the serial interface. After the code example, I point out some information that you should be able to deduce.Router1#**debug serial interface**

```
Serial network interface debugging is on
Router1#
00:06:33: Serial0: HDLC myseq 32, mineseen 0, yourseen 0, line down
00:06:34: Serial0: attempting to restart
00:06:34: HD(0): Deasserting DSR, CTS and DCD
00:06:34: HD(0): Reset from 0x305CE4A
00:06:34: HD(0): Asserting DSR
00:06:34: HD(0): Asserting DCD and CTS
00:06:34: HD(0): Deasserting LTST
00:06:34: HD(0): Asserting DTR and RTS
00:06:43: Serial0: HDLC myseq 33, mineseen 0, yourseen 0, line down
00:06:45: HD(0): got an interrupt state = 0x8057
00:06:45: HD(0): New serial state = 0x0055

00:06:45: HD(0): DTR is up.
00:06:45: HD(1): New serial state = 0x0600

00:06:45: HD(1): Cable is unplugged.
00:06:45: HD(0): got an interrupt state = 0x805F
00:06:45: HD(0): New serial state = 0x005F

00:06:45: HD(0): DTR is up.
00:06:45: HD(1): New serial state = 0x0600

00:06:45: HD(1): Cable is unplugged.
```

Here are some key items to take note of in this output:

+ The connection is using HDLC. The HDLC connection is down.

+ There is an issue with communications, as shown by the asserting, deasserting, and reset commands. These are typically never good messages to see. Specifically, there is a problem in confirming serial communication commands, such as Ready to Send (RTS) and Clear to Send (CTS).

+ There is an issue with the HDLC communication, and after several attempts, it gives up, identified by the Cable is unplugged statement.

Another issue that shows up in the output is related to the lines that include the words mineseen and yourseen. They refer to the number of data control packets that have been sent over the connection, which are used only to monitor the connection. When the router sends data over an HDLC connection, it tracks a sequential number to ensure that all the data gets through. The number on Router1 is what Router1 calls mineseen, whereas Router1 call the sequence number reported by the other router yourseen.

Although HDLC is saying that the cable may be unplugged, you already know that the problem lies in the clock speed, which to Router1 looks the same because it cannot start the connection properly.

With the clock speed correctly set, the debug data looks like the following example. Notice the mineseen and yourseen data and that the line is up. The difference in the numbers occurs because Router2 has been sending data control packets that this router has never seen, because the interface was brought up later.

```
Router1#debug serial interface
Serial network interface debugging is on
Router1#
00:22:43: Serial0: HDLC myseq 10, mineseen 10*, yourseen 129, line up
00:22:53: Serial0: HDLC myseq 11, mineseen 11*, yourseen 130, line up
00:23:03: Serial0: HDLC myseq 12, mineseen 12*, yourseen 131, line up
```

Chapter 6: Meeting the Routing Protocols

In This Chapter

✔ Seeing how your router chooses between installed protocols

✔ Weighing benefits and drawbacks of distance-vector routing protocols

✔ Checking out the pros and cons of link-state routing protocols

*W*hen your network grows to the point where static routes are unmanageable, it is time to consider what routing protocol to use on your network. Unlike static routing table management, *dynamic routing table management* adjusts automatically for topology and traffic changes. In this process, the routers exchange information between devices, which allows the routers to build complex routing tables that span your network. These protocols include Interior Gateway Protocols (IGP), used inside your network, and Exterior Gateway Protocols (EGP), used to join your network to exterior or other networks.

Do not confuse *routing* protocols with *routed* protocols. The routed or routable protocols' list includes protocols, such as IPX/SPX and TCP/IP, and are able to move data between network segments by having the data pass through a router. In this chapter, I discuss *routing protocols*, which are protocols such as RIP, OSPF, EIGRP, and BGP, which I first mention in Book IV, Chapter 1. A *routing* protocol exchanges routing tables on routers, allowing global routing tables to be dynamically built, rather than your having to plan all your routing tables entries on all routers manually.

This chapter gives you a good idea about how these two classes of routing protocols function: IGP and EGP. The chapter also covers their strengths and weaknesses, as well as how your router decides which routing protocol to use when multiple protocols are installed on your router.

Checking Out Criteria for Routing Protocol Selection

People use two basic methods to classify protocols — by where they are used and by how they calculate routing. In this section, you see how to choose protocols based on where you plan to use them, the way the protocol manages data, and how your router chooses which protocol to use when more than one protocol is installed.

Classifying by where protocols are used

When classifying protocols by where they are used, you are talking about interior (IGP) versus exterior (EGP). In most cases, people are most concerned with the protocols that are running on the inside of their networks and maintaining their routing data because this is where most of their traffic is concentrated. In making your decisions about which protocol class you want to apply first to your network, it is likely the interior protocol because the exterior protocols typically pass information that was generated by the interior protocols. The two main breakdowns for protocols are

+ **Interior protocols** include RIP, EIGRP, OSPF, and ISIS.

+ **Exterior protocols** include BGP.

Classifying by how protocols calculate routing

In addition to classifying protocols by where they are used, you can also choose to classify protocols by how they calculate routing. When classifying them this way, you are talking about distance-vector protocols versus link-state protocols:

+ **Distance-vector protocols** include RIP, BGP, and EIGRP.

+ **Link-state protocols** include OSPF and IS-IS.

Distance-vector protocols

RIP, BGP, and EIGRP are in the distance-vector category. *Distance-vector protocols* base their routing choices on two things: the direction or vector they need to send the data, and the distance of the target network, which is calculated as hops or routers that the data needs to pass through.

Link-state protocols

Link-state protocols include OSPF and ISIS. Link-state protocols gather information about network connections known by all the routers in their group and build topology maps identifying how they see all the connections across the entire network or area in which they function. They then use this information to build their own routing table. In link-state routing, routing tables are not passed between routers; only the connection information is transferred between routers.

Other types of protocols

The exception to this grouping is EIGRP, which Cisco developed and calls an Advanced Distance Vector or *hybrid protocol*. EIGRP shares its routing table with its neighbors like a distance-vector protocol does. However, it sends the entire table only at startup; then it only sends updates like a link-state protocol does, so it has a bit of both sets of features. It is not uncommon to find that EIGRP has been added to either classification list, though in most cases you see it on the distance-vector protocol list when people have not separated EIGRP by itself.

Administrative distance

You can enable several routing protocols on your router at the same time, so you could be using EIGRP, OSPF, and RIP on your network simultaneously. If this is the case, your router will learn about routes to the same network through each of the available protocols, so it must choose the route to take to any given network. Because routers are not good at making these judgment calls, administrative distances are used. The administrative distance for a routing protocol is a numeric representation of how accurate the routing protocol is expected to be, where the lowest number is given to the most accurate protocol. This administrative distance is sometimes referred to as how *believable* a routing protocol or routing table entry is.

Each routing protocol is assigned a default administrative distance (see Table 6-1). Although these are default distances, you can change them on a per-router, per-protocol, or per-route basis using IOS commands. Typically, you do not need to change these default distances because they have been ordered so that the most believable routes are given the shortest distance. Given a route to a network, such as 192.0.2.0/24, if two routes in my routing table are networking, one is directly connected and one is retrieved by RIP. The route that says the router is directly connected to the network is likely to be the most believable or accurate route.

Table 6-1   Default Administrative Distances for Protocols

Route Source	Default Distance
Connected Network	0
Static Route	1
EIGRP	90
OSPF	110
RIPv2	120
External EIGRP	170
Unknown or unbelievable	255 (never used)

**Book IV
Chapter 6**

**Meeting the Routing
Protocols**

The routes that are expected to be the most reliable routes are given preference over other options for a network. The networks that your router is directly connected to are the most reliable choices, and static routes that you have put in are only slightly less reliable. If you have put in a static route, the router determines that you must want to use it. If you have a choice, the shortest distance is always preferable.

Introducing the Protocols

Table 6-2, which can be used as part of your evaluation criteria, has the most common protocols and a number of points of evaluation.

Table 6-2	Protocol Evaluation Criteria			
Protocol	*RIPv1*	*RIPv2*	*OSPF*	*EIGRP*
Type	Distance-vector	Distance-vector	Link-state	Distance-vector
Convergence Time	Slow	Slow	Fast	Fast
VLSM	No	Yes	Yes	Yes
Bandwidth Consumption	High	High	Low	Low
Resource Consumption	Low	Low	High	Low
Multi-path Support	No	Yes	Yes	Yes
Scales Well	No	No	Yes	Yes
Proprietary	No	No	No	Yes

✦ **Convergence Time:** Convergence time is the point at which all routers on your network know about all current routes for the network. When a router is added or removed from a network, a certain amount of time — convergence time — must pass before this change is propagated to all routers on the network.

✦ **Variable length subnet masks (VLSM):** This term refers to whether all routers on the network are required to use the same subnet mask. This requirement reduces your flexibility in assigning IP address network IDs to the network segments on your network.

✦ **Bandwidth Consumption:** This term refers to the amount of necessary network bandwidth to maintain and distribute routing table information on the network. To share and distribute routing table information, all routing protocols need to send an amount of data over the network, and some send more than others.

✦ **Resource Consumption:** In calculating and maintain routing table information on a router, a certain amount of processing power and memory is used.

+ **Multi-path Support:** When routes are discovered on the network that have loops in their paths, some segments have two possible routes, which represent multiple paths. Some routing protocols have support for multiple paths, by storing alternative paths in their routing information.

+ **Scales Well:** Some routing protocols operate well on small networks, but as the number of routers increases on the network, the routing protocol does not function as well. Routing protocols that can be used on small to very large networks scale well in size.

+ **Proprietary:** The routing protocol based on open standards or a proprietary protocol owned by one company can affect the level of support and the speed of changes.

Distance-Vector Routing

Distance-vector routing functions by passing routing tables between devices on the network. So the first router looks at its connected interfaces, builds a routing table, and passes that information to other routers on its connected interfaces. If the router receives routing tables from other routers, it updates any metrics used for choosing routes, such as RIP's hop count, and adds that information to its routing table. This information is then sent out with the routing table updates that are sent to neighboring routers.

Now, this process sounds really simple — the routers will just pass that information out and then everyone will know how to get to all other locations on the network — but there are some issues that affect most vector routing protocols. This section examines each of these problems.

Examining basic function of distance-vector routing

I said that these updates pass routing tables from router to router to get the information out to all routers, but what does this really look like? If you examine Figure 6-1, you see three routers with their interfaces configured according to the diagram, as well as the routing table on each router. In this instance, no routing protocol is running.

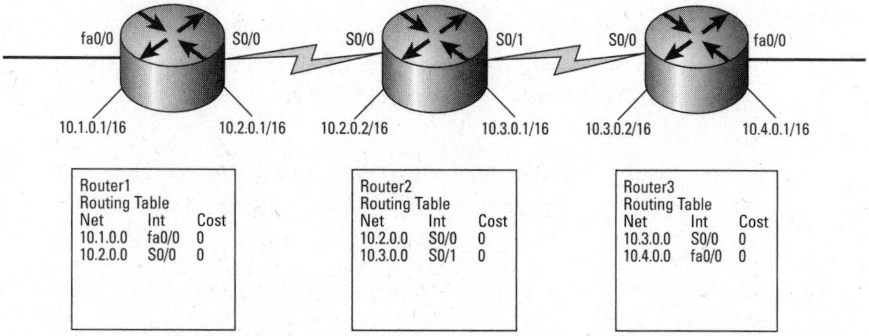

Figure 6-1:
A small routable network without a dynamic routing protocol.

| fa0/0 | S0/0 | S0/0 | S0/1 | S0/0 | fa0/0 |

10.1.0.1/16   10.2.0.1/16   10.2.0.2/16   10.3.0.1/16   10.3.0.2/16   10.4.0.1/16

```
Router1
Routing Table
Net        Int     Cost
10.1.0.0   fa0/0   0
10.2.0.0   S0/0    0
```

```
Router2
Routing Table
Net        Int     Cost
10.2.0.0   S0/0    0
10.3.0.0   S0/1    0
```

```
Router3
Routing Table
Net        Int     Cost
10.3.0.0   S0/0    0
10.4.0.0   fa0/0   0
```

If you now enable a dynamic routing protocol and give it some time to propagate changes to all areas of the network or converge, the routing information will look more like Figure 6-2. Note that the routers on each end of the network now know about the network segments at the other end of the network and have associated a hop count with the path to those networks.

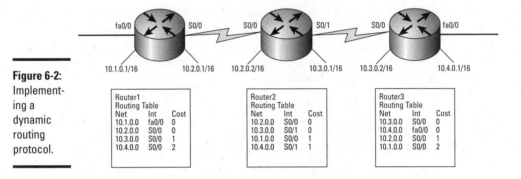

fa0/0   S0/0   S0/0   S0/1   S0/0   fa0/0

10.1.0.1/16   10.2.0.1/16   10.2.0.2/16   10.3.0.1/16   10.3.0.2/16   10.4.0.1/16

Figure 6-2:
Implementing a dynamic routing protocol.

Router1 Routing Table		
Net	Int	Cost
10.1.0.0	fa0/0	0
10.2.0.0	S0/0	0
10.3.0.0	S0/0	1
10.4.0.0	S0/0	2

Router2 Routing Table		
Net	Int	Cost
10.2.0.0	S0/0	0
10.3.0.0	S0/1	0
10.1.0.0	S0/0	1
10.4.0.0	S0/1	1

Router3 Routing Table		
Net	Int	Cost
10.3.0.0	S0/0	0
10.4.0.0	fa0/0	0
10.2.0.0	S0/0	1
10.1.0.0	S0/0	2

Setting up a routing protocol does not take much work; you need to give the routers only enough information to allow them to dynamically update their routing information between devices. Sharing of connection information or routing tables allows all routers in the routing group to know how to get to all the other network segments supported by the routing group.

Count to infinity and routing loops

In Figure 6-3, everything is working fine on the network, and the network is converged. Problems can happen with your routing protocol when a link or a router fails. In this figure, a failure happens on Router3 with interface fa0/0. When this link goes down, the route to 10.4.0.0/16 is no longer available; however, if you look at what follows, you can see the issue.

1. Router3 initially marks the route to 10.4.0.0 as a link down in its routing table.

2. Router2 sends out its routing table to each of its neighbors, which includes Router3, telling them that it has a path to 10.4.0.0 with a hop count of 1.

3. Router3 then updates its routing table with this new information, stating that the route to 10.4.0.0/16 is now 2 hops away, as shown in Figure 6-3.

4. Armed with the new information that 10.4.0.0/16 is available through another interface, Router3 sends out its routing table to its neighbors.

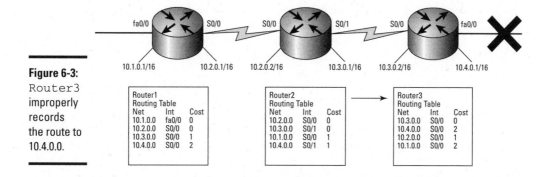

Figure 6-3:
`Router3` improperly records the route to 10.4.0.0.

5. `Router2` gets the update and identifies that the router that previously said it knew about 10.4.0.0/16 has updated the route from a hop count of 0 to 2, so `Router2` updates its own routing table. The old route may have been identified as an updated route, or it may have timed out of the routing table, depending on the routing protocol that is in use.

6. `Router2` then passes its own routing information out through its other interface (S0/0) to propagate the change to `Router1`, as illustrated in Figure 6-4.

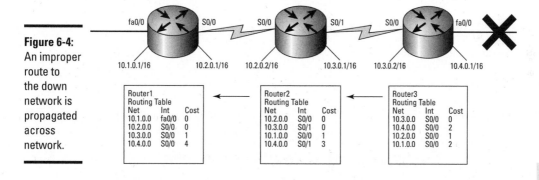

Figure 6-4:
An improper route to the down network is propagated across network.

7. `Router3` eventually receives the update from `Router2` telling it that the hop count to 10.4.0.0/16 has been updated to 3, and this process now continues.

This process continues to infinity because no mechanism is in place, in this case, to stop the process from continuing.

However, the RIP routing protocol has a built-in safety mechanism, to a degree. RIP has a maximum hop count of 16, and when the route to a network exceeds the 16-hop rule, the RIP protocol marks that network as unreachable so that it does not further propagate the route. This scenario does not change the information found in the router's routing table — it only limits how far the error is propagated.

When you send data to a host or device on the 10.4.0.0/16 network, it comes through the fa0/0 interface on Router1 and Router1 thinks that it can get to 10.4.0.0/16 within 4 hops by sending the data out through interface S0/0 based on Router1's routing table. Figure 6-5 shows what happens when the data is sent. As it arrives at Router3, Router3 determines that the route to 10.4.0.0/16 is back through Router2, which then causes the data to loop infinitely. There is a Time to Live (TTL) on IP packets (refer to Book II, Chapter 1 for more on TTL), which defines the maximum amount of time which an IP packet can remain on a network. After spending some time looping, the data will be dropped from the network and a message sent back to the sender of the data.

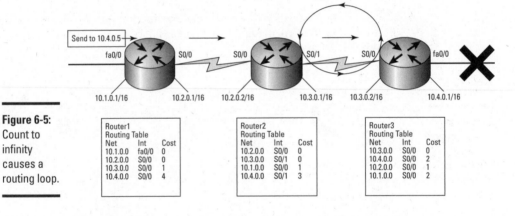

Figure 6-5:
Count to infinity causes a routing loop.

Preventing count to infinity issues

The following sections explore ways to prevent count to infinity and the resulting routing loops from happening on your network.

Split horizon

If you are using RIPv1, you have a solution in the form of a concept called *split horizon*. In this concept, if you receive routing on one interface, sending that information back out of that interface is not likely to be productive.

So, if you examine only the routing information for the network 10.4.0.0/16 in the routing process, the flow of the route information is passed as follows:

1. `Router2` learns of the route to 10.4.0.0/16 through interface S0/1 facing `Router3`.

2. `Router2` sends its routing table updates out through both of its interfaces, but filters the route to 10.4.0.0/16 out of the list when it sends the routes out through interface S0/1, as shown in Figure 6-6.

3. `Router1` receives the route to 10.4.0.0/16 from `Router2` on interface S0/0.

4. `Router1` sends its routing table updates out through both of its interfaces, but filters the route to 10.4.0.0/16 out of the list when it sends the routes out through S0/0, also as shown in Figure 6-6.

Figure 6-6: Routers do not send announcements on interfaces where they came from.

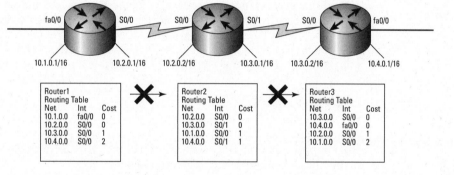

Route poisoning

Rather than using split horizon, RIPv2 implements a process called *route poisoning*. Following is the sequence for the route poisoning process:

1. `Router3` identifies that the link to 10.4.0.0/16 is down and immediately updates its metric for that network to infinity — or in the case of RIPv2, a hop count of 16 — and sends that routing table update out immediately, as illustrated in Figure 6-7.

2. `Router2` gets the update and then updates its own routing table by removing the route to 10.4.0.0/16, because it is no longer valid. After this update is complete, `Router2` sends its own update out through interface S0/0.

3. `Router1` gets the update, which no longer includes a route to 10.4.0.0/16, causing `Router1` to remove the route to that network.

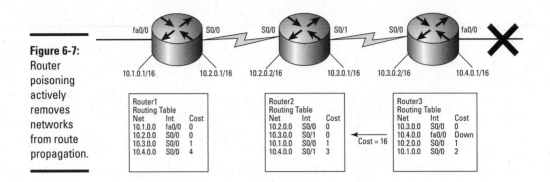

Figure 6-7:
Router
poisoning
actively
removes
networks
from route
propagation.

With router poisoning, the update process escalates so that improper route information is removed from the network in a timely manner. You can extend this system using a process called *poison reverse*. In this case, after Router2 sees the hop count or metric go to infinity, it also sends a routing table update back to Router3 with an infinite metric telling it that the route to 10.4.0.0/16 is no longer available. This process reduces the chance that an improper update will make it through to Router3 and cause a loop.

Hold-down timers

Hold-down timers are another solution to routing loops that some routing protocols implement. Hold-down timers prevent protocol update messages from improperly updating routes for links that are currently down. Following is the hold-down timers implementation sequence:

1. Router2 receives an update telling it that the link to 10.4.0.0/16 is down.

2. Router2 marks the route as possibly down and sets a hold-down timer.

3. Router2 waits for an update.

- If it gets an update with a metric better than the original one, Router2 records the route as up and accessible.

- If it does not get an update in the timer interval, Router2 removes the route from its routing table.

- Routes that Router2 receives with a metric worse than the original route are automatically removed.

During the hold-down period, if any data is being sent to the 10.4.0.0/16 network, the data is sent on as a delivery attempt. The delivery attempt is made in the event that the link to 10.4.0.0/16 is having an intermittent problem.

Triggered updates

Triggered updates deal with count to infinity issues by forcing an update as soon as the link changes.

So, going back to the network layout you have been using, when the link to network 10.4.0.0/16 goes down, Router3 sends an immediate update notifying its neighbors that the link is down. Router2 receives the update and immediately passes the update to its neighbors, such as Router1.

As part of its normal update schedule, Router2 might still receive another update from Router1 prior to getting the update to remove the route. The solution is to combine triggered updates with hold-down timers, which prevents routes with worse metrics from being added to a router's routing table.

Link-State Routing

Compared to distance-vector routing, *link-state routing* optimizes routing structures by performing calculations on the best routes instead of just passing full routing table information between routers. Link-state routing only sends interface information about the different interfaces existing on a router and the networks to which the router is connected. So, rather than send a 20-to-50–entry routing table, link-state updates send only the information about the router's four to six interfaces.

Understanding link-state protocol

Each router puts all the link-state information it receives in a *topological database,* which is a table that contains link information about all known routers. It does not define routes; instead, it records all the information required to get to every network segment connected to every router after the routing information is calculated.

There will probably be more than one route to each network, so it is important to evaluate each and every possible route to find the best route to each network segment. You can do so using the *Shortest Path First (SPF) algorithm,* which then builds the SFP tree. Since the router knows about all of the links on the network, it is able to evaluate all links from itself to determine the most efficient way to reach every other network segment on the network. This is referred to as the shortest path to each of those network segments. All of the shortest paths are stored in one location, which is referred to as the SFP tree.

After the SFP tree is built, the router reviews it to find the best possible route to each network. After the best routes are found, the router adds them to its own routing table. This routing table is built on each router, but it should be the same for all routers that receive the same updates, because they all use the same process to build the routing table.

When a router starts up and sends its initial link-state information to its neighbors, it reduces network overhead by only sending updates to its link information. These *Link State Advertisements (LSA)* are flooded out to all routers in their area or zone. LSAs are simply updates on their link status, so one is sent whenever a link is connected or disconnected.

Working with your strengths

This system of handling updates seems to be the key to the strength of link-state protocols. Although some variance occurs between the two protocols, in general, link-state protocols are different than distance-vector protocols in the following ways — you can decide if these differences represent benefits or drawbacks:

✦ Cost metrics are the main determining factor of route selection. These cost metrics are the point of evaluation to determine the best links, which may include the speed and capacity of the links.

✦ Less frequent routing updates.

✦ High degree of scalability to support much larger networks.

✦ Division of overall network into smaller segments to limit scope of routing changes.

✦ Only sends updates on link status and topology changes.

✦ Triggered updates can immediately notify systems of changes, reducing convergence times.

✦ Network design can reduce the size of the link-state database. When the network ID are laid out to support route summarization, then the reduce number of routes will reduce the size of the link-state database.

✦ Limited age of data, because LSA aging always keeps information current.

✦ Routing loops are almost eliminated because routers know what the entire network topology looks like.

✦ Large amounts of memory are required to support not only the routing table, but also the link-state database and adjacency database (which is table listing neighboring devices).

✦ Execution of the Dijkstra algorithm (the mathematical formula used to perform the shortest path calculation) requires the use of CPU cycles on the router, and for larger networks, this requirement means more CPU time spent on calculations.

✦ In large network implementations, link-state protocols can require a great deal of tuning to function properly. This necessity can present significant challenges to a network administrator.

If you have sufficient CPU and memory resources on your network routers and your network layout is not overly complicated, you should not suffer from the issues related to link-state protocols — but only reap the benefits. There is no reason that link-state protocols should not be used as primary routing protocol on your network.

Chapter 7: Checking Out RIP and EIGRP Characteristics and Design

In This Chapter

✔ Configuring common options for the RIP and EIGRP protocols

✔ Working with troubleshooting tools to manage the RIP and EIGRP protocols

As I discuss at length in Chapters 1 and 6 of this minibook, you can choose from various protocols to dynamically manage the routing tables on your network. In this chapter, you implement two of these protocols, RIP and EIGRP. You find out not only how to enable them, but also how to configure the main options you need to properly work with these protocols. You also examine the basic tools used in diagnosing issues that arise in their operation. After the protocols are up and running, you have the basic tools you need in order to manage the protocols. If you read this entire chapter, you will be able to work comfortably with the configuration and management processes for both RIP and EIGRP.

Working with Routing Information Protocol (RIP)

I first present RIP in Book IV, Chapter 1 with an introduction to the major routing protocols. RIP is designed to function on small to large networks but can suffer when a network is not designed to accommodate its eccentricities. This chapter focuses primarily on RIPv2, rather than on RIPv1, because with RIPv1, all systems must use class-based network masks or be subnetted exactly the same way. RIPv2, on the other hand, supports Variable Length Subnet Masks (VLSM). If you choose to deploy network IDs across your network you will likely want to deploy VSLM in order to conserve addresses on your network. So, if you plan to deploy RIP as a protocol, you will likely use version 2.

The biggest issue with RIPv1 is that all systems must use class-based network masks or be subnetted exactly the same way, whereas RIPv2 supports Variable Length Subnet Masks (VLSM). VLSM is covered in Book II, Chapter 1, if you want to find out more about it. The following sections cover the basic commands for setting up RIP and how to monitor or troubleshoot RIP on your network.

Understanding the RIP commands

To work with the RIP commands, you start by enabling the protocol. However, before enabling the routing protocol, you need to enable IP routing, if you have not already done so, which you can see in Chapter 3 of this minibook.

Enabling RIP

As with most routing protocols, when you enable the RIP protocol, you will be placed in Router Configuration mode (config-router), so take note of the change in the configuration prompt during the following example. The main configuration requirement is the list of networks for which RIP will be routing.

The following enables routing for two connected networks, 192.168.1.0/24 and 192.168.10.0/24, for a network that looks like Figure 7-1.

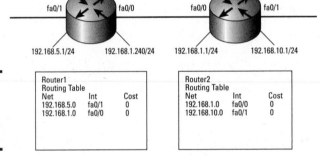

Figure 7-1:
A small network for RIP routing.

```
Router2>enable
Password:
Router2#configure terminal
Enter configuration commands, one per line.  End with CNTL/Z.
Router2(config)#ip routing
Router2(config)#router rip
Router2(config-router)#network 192.168.10.0
Router2(config-router)#network 192.168.1.0
Router2(config-router)#exit
Router2(config)#exit
```

Following this command, RIP automatically starts sending out copies of its routing information for the two identified networks through all of its network interfaces. RIPv1 sends the copies via a broadcast, whereas RIPv2 performs a multicast to 224.0.0.9. For Router2 to receive updates, you also must enable RIP on Router1 with the following commands:

```
Router1>enable
Password:
Router1#configure terminal
Enter configuration commands, one per line.  End with CNTL/Z.
Router1(config)#ip routing
```

```
Router1(config)#router rip
Router1(config-router)#network 192.168.5.0
Router1(config-router)#network 192.168.1.0
Router1(config-router)#exit
Router1(config)#exit
```

At the same time, RIP receives the data from neighboring RIP routers at 30-second intervals. After this data is received, `Router2` updates its routing table so that the new routing table looks like this:

```
Router2>enable
Password:
Router2#show ip route
Codes: C - connected, S - static, R - RIP, M - mobile, B - BGP
       D - EIGRP, EX - EIGRP external, O - OSPF, IA - OSPF inter area
       N1 - OSPF NSSA external type 1, N2 - OSPF NSSA external type 2
       E1 - OSPF external type 1, E2 - OSPF external type 2
       i - IS-IS, su - IS-IS summary, L1 - IS-IS level-1, L2 - IS-IS level-2
       ia - IS-IS inter area, * - candidate default, U - per-user static route
       o - ODR, P - periodic downloaded static route

Gateway of last resort is not set

R    192.168.10.0/24 [120/1] via 192.168.1.1, 00:00:07, FastEthernet0/0
C    192.168.5.0/24 is directly connected, FastEthernet0/1
C    192.168.1.0/24 is directly connected, FastEthernet0/0
S    192.168.3.0/24 [1/0] via 192.168.1.1
```

The last routing table has several routes. Notably, the first listed route has an R identifier, which denotes that this route was ascertained via RIP.

The C identifies directly connected network segments, and the S identifies static routes.

Showing routes coming from a specific routing protocol

To see only the routes that come from specific routing protocols, you modify the `show ip route` command in the following manner. Now, only the directly connected interfaces and the RIP-provided routes are shown.

```
Router>enable
Password:
Router2#show ip route connected
C    192.168.5.0/24 is directly connected, FastEthernet0/1
C    192.168.1.0/24 is directly connected, FastEthernet0/0
Router2#show ip route rip
R    192.168.10.0/24 [120/1] via 192.168.1.1, 00:00:15, FastEthernet0/0
```

Configuring your RIP version

The version of RIP that is currently enabled allows receipt of RIPv1 and RIPv2 data, but it sends out only RIPv1 data. To configure this version of RIP to support only the more modern and flexible version 2, use the following command. Note that this setting has a lot of flexibility, because you can configure RIP to send and receive any combination of RIPv1 and RIPv2 data.

```
Router2>enable
Password:
Router2#configure terminal
Enter configuration commands, one per line.  End with CNTL/Z.
Router2(config)#ip routing
Router2(config)#router rip
Router2(config-router)#version 2
Router2(config-router)#no auto-summary
Router2(config-router)#neighbor 192.168.1.1
Router2(config-router)#exit
Router2(config)#exit
```

The preceding command also includes two other commands within the router configuration prompt:

✦ `auto-summary`: RIPv2 supports the *auto-summary* feature, which automatically summarizes along classful boundaries. You can configure this behavior to use other network ranges in the interface configuration of your router, or you can completely disable auto-summary using the `no auto-summary` command in Router Configuration mode. In Interface Configuration mode, you can use the command `ip summary-address rip 10.1.0.0 255.255.0.0` to force the summarization to occur at a specific boundary rather than the Class A boundary. In this case, you would be forcing route summary to occur at the 10.1.0.0/16 boundary rather than the class boundary of 10.0.0.0/8.

✦ `neighbor`: RIP detects neighbor routers, but this process can take time because RIP has to wait for advertisements from neighboring routers. You can use the neighbor to specify on this router what the neighbor routers are. When you do this, rather than send a broadcast and multicast update, RIP sends unicast or directed RIP update messages. Configuring neighbors on each router takes a little more time, but reduces the network traffic associated with RIP by reducing the broadcast traffic.

Troubleshooting RIP

A major task in troubleshooting is gathering information to be used to identify the area where the source of your problem is. This section deals with commands that you can use to gather information about the RIP routing protocol in order to assist in your troubleshooting and problem resolution.

Getting network information

To start this process, look at the `ip route` command, which in addition to listing routes, can display summary information letting you know how many RIP-based networks exist in the routing table.

```
Router2>enable
Password:
Router2#show ip route summary
```

```
IP routing table name is Default-IP-Routing-Table(0)
IP routing table maximum-paths is 16
Route Source    Networks    Subnets     Overhead    Memory (bytes)
connected       2           0           144         272
static          1           0           72          136
rip             1           0           72          136
Total           4           0           288         544
```

To ensure that the routing protocol is up and functioning, use the `show ip protocols` command, which provides similar output to the following. However, first note some important things to look for in the output:

✦ Timers and when the next update will be sent to neighboring routers

✦ Version of RIP in use

✦ Interfaces in use for RIP

✦ Networks being routed by RIP

✦ Address from which you are receiving RIP information

```
Router2>enable
Password:
Router2#show ip protocols
Routing Protocol is "rip"
  Sending updates every 30 seconds, next due in 12 seconds
  Invalid after 180 seconds, hold down 180, flushed after 240
  Outgoing update filter list for all interfaces is not set
  Incoming update filter list for all interfaces is not set
  Redistributing: rip
  Default version control: send version 2, receive version 2
    Interface           Send  Recv  Triggered RIP  Key-chain
    FastEthernet0/0     2     2
    FastEthernet0/1     2     2
  Automatic network summarization is not in effect
  Maximum path: 4
  Routing for Networks:
    192.168.1.0
    192.168.5.0
  Routing Information Sources:
    Gateway         Distance    Last Update
    192.168.1.1     120         00:32:42
  Distance: (default is 120)
```

Note the last item, which lists the administrative distance. This point becomes important when using multiple routing protocols, because each protocol has a different default distance that determines which routing protocol is favored when a remote network is advertised on multiple routing protocols.

Seeing information RIP receives

You can view the contents of the RIP database to find out what information RIP has received. Doing so shows you the networks that are part of RIP, the summarization settings, and from which routers your router has learned routes.

```
Router2>enable
Password:
Router2#show ip rip database
192.168.1.0/24    auto-summary
192.168.1.0/24    directly connected, FastEthernet0/0
192.168.5.0/24    auto-summary
192.168.5.0/24    directly connected, FastEthernet0/1
192.168.10.0/24    auto-summary
192.168.10.0/24
    [1] via 192.168.1.1, 00:00:20, FastEthernet0/0
```

Debugging RIP

Finally, you have the system `debug` command. In regard to RIP, the `debug` command is limited to database changes. In the following output, you see the types of data you can get from `debug` command, which are also listed here:

✦ The RIP information your router is sending out and the networks included in the update

✦ The RIP version being used

✦ The RIP data being received, including the interface it arrived on, the router it came from, and the networks that are included

If you are using `debug` through a remote console, you use `terminal monitor` to see the debug information the remote console's screen.

```
Router2>enable
Password:
Router2#debug ip rip ?
  database  RIP database events
  events    RIP protocol events
  trigger   RIP trigger extension
  <cr>
Router2#debug ip rip
RIP protocol debugging is on
Router2#
*Mar 17 22:57:39.842: RIP: sending v1 update to 255.255.255.255 via
    FastEthernet0/1 (192.168.5.1)
*Mar 17 22:57:39.842: RIP: build update entries
*Mar 17 22:57:39.842:    network 192.168.1.0 metric 1
*Mar 17 22:57:39.842:    network 192.168.10.0 metric 2
*Mar 17 22:57:46.870: RIP: sending v1 update to 255.255.255.255 via
    FastEthernet0/0 (192.168.1.240)
*Mar 17 22:57:46.870: RIP: build update entries
*Mar 17 22:57:46.870:    network 192.168.5.0 metric 1
*Mar 17 22:57:53.654: RIP: received v1 update from 192.168.1.1 on FastEthernet0/0
*Mar 17 22:57:53.654:       192.168.10.0 in 1 hops
Router2#no debug ip rip
```

Working with Enhanced Interior Gateway Routing Protocol (EIGRP)

Because EIGRP has replaced IGRP in all ways, I do not cover IGRP except to say that, for legacy reasons, you may still see it on some routers.

Three main tables, which are stored in memory, support the EIGRP routing protocol:

✦ **Neighbor Table:** Information about all adjacent routers running EIGRP are stored here. This information includes sequence numbers and protocol timers.

✦ **Topology Table:** All destination networks that neighbor routers have reported knowing about are stored in this table. This table would include the metrics for every route reported, as some network ID may have multiple routes and the best route would be evaluated by the cost of the metrics.

✦ **Routing Table:** In addition to least cost routes, EIGRP evaluates secondary routes to each network and creates a list of feasible successors that are added to the routing table. A feasible successor is a route that would be used if the primary route to a network fails.

The information that EIGRP receives in its updates go into these three tables.

Using the EIGRP commands

The configuration of EIGRP is just about as easy as the configuration of RIP. One difference is the concept of an Autonomous System (AS), which defines a group of routers to which the EIGRP router belongs to. The AS number is exchanged as part of the routing protocol messages, and any message with a different AS number is ignored by your router. So, it is important that all routers in the same routing group share the same AS number.

Auto-summary

Just as you do when configuring RIP, you specify the connected networks that your routing protocols will be sending to other routers by using the network command. Also, as with RIP, there is an auto-summary option, which you can modify or disable.

```
Router2>enable
Password:
Router2#configure terminal
Enter configuration commands, one per line.  End with CNTL/Z.
Router2(config)#ip routing
```

```
Router2(config)#router eigrp 100
Router2(config-router)#network 192.168.1.0
Router2(config-router)#network 192.168.5.0
Router2(config-router)#no auto-summary
Router2(config-router)#exit
Router2(config)#exit
```

Auto-summary for EIGRP works similarly to the way it works for RIP. With auto-summary enabled, all routes are summarized as close to the classful boundaries. To change this feature, enter specific interfaces on your router and force summarization to occur at different boundaries — for example, `ip summary-address eigrp 100 10.0.0.0 255.255.0.0` for a router configured with networks of 10.0.1.0 and 10.0.100.0.

Reviewing the following routing table, you see the addition of D type routes. The D routers are routes that were learned through EIGRP, whereas EX identifies routes from EIGRP configured for external use.

```
Router2>enable
Password:
Router2#show ip route
Codes: C - connected, S - static, R - RIP, M - mobile, B - BGP
       D - EIGRP, EX - EIGRP external, O - OSPF, IA - OSPF inter area
       N1 - OSPF NSSA external type 1, N2 - OSPF NSSA external type 2
       E1 - OSPF external type 1, E2 - OSPF external type 2
       i - IS-IS, su - IS-IS summary, L1 - IS-IS level-1, L2 - IS-IS level-2
       ia - IS-IS inter area, * - candidate default, U - per-user static route
       o - ODR, P - periodic downloaded static route

Gateway of last resort is not set

D    192.168.10.0/24 [90/284160] via 192.168.1.1, 00:04:19, FastEthernet0/0
C    192.168.5.0/24 is directly connected, FastEthernet0/1
C    192.168.1.0/24 is directly connected, FastEthernet0/0
S    192.168.3.0/24 [1/0] via 192.168.1.1
```

Split horizon

EIGRP uses a behavior called *split horizon* (discussed in Chapter 6 of this minibook) to control routing updates. By default, this behavior is enabled on all interfaces on the router. You can disable split horizon on any or all interfaces.

Split horizon prevents route advertisements from going back out through the interface on which the route was originally learned.

```
Router2>enable
Password:
Router2#configure terminal
Enter configuration commands, one per line.  End with CNTL/Z.
Router2(config)#interface fastethernet0/0
Router2(config-if)#no ip split-horizon eigrp 100
Router2(config-if)#exit
Router2(config)#exit
```

Load balancing

EIGRP supports *load balancing*, which is sending data over multiple paths when they are available. There are two basic methods of load balancing with EIGRP, either based on equal costs or unequal costs. By default EIGRP will use equal cost load balancing. So if there are two or more paths to the same destination, they will be load balanced only if their total link costs are equal. Figure 7-2 shows a network with three paths and with total costs of 20, 25, and 45. In this case, the link with the cost of 20 is always used. If you want EIGRP to load balance over two links, the two links would require an equal cost. When the network does not naturally evaluate to equal costs, you can force it with the `variance` command, thereby making it unequal cost routing. In the sample network shown in Figure 7-2, the path through `Router3` has a cost of 25, by using the `variance` command, you can make it equal to the path through `Router4`, as shown here:

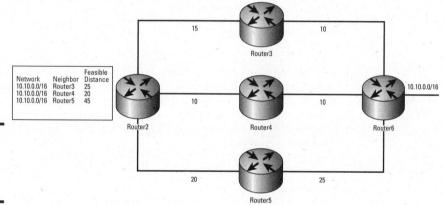

Figure 7-2:
An unequal cost network.

```
Router2>enable
Password:
Router2#configure terminal
Enter configuration commands, one per line.  End with CNTL/Z.
Router2(config)#ip routing
Router2(config)#router eigrp 100
Router2(config-router)#variance 2
Router2(config-router)#exit
Router2(config)#exit
```

The variance of 2 in the preceding output instructs EIGRP to take the least-cost route and multiply it by the variance. In this case, if you take the least-cost route of 20 and multiply it by 2, you end up with 40; so all routes with a cost less than 40 are considered to be equal. To route over all three links, use a variance of 3, making all routes less than 60 equivalent.

Some other methods for dealing with equal or unequal path routing involve changing the default system metric values. EIRGP uses the following calculation to generate a final metric, with lowest metrics being preferred:

```
metric = [K1*bandwidth + (K2*bandwidth)/(256 - load) + K3*delay] *
[K5/(reliability + K4)]
```

The default values for these settings are K1=1, K2=0, K3=1, K4=0, and K5=0, which means that the normal net metric is based on the bandwidth and delay of the links. If you use the same physical network infrastructure throughout your network, the metric is therefore based solely on the number of hops.

```
Router2>enable
Password:
Router2#configure terminal
Enter configuration commands, one per line.  End with CNTL/Z.
Router2(config)#ip routing
Router2(config)#router eigrp 100
Router2(config-router)#metric weights tos k1 k2 k3 k4 k5
Router2(config-router)#exit
Router2(config)#exit
```

Although these values can be changed, they can have a large negative impact on your network performance if they are set incorrectly. Rather than changing these values, you can modify the bandwidth and delay values on a link-by-link basis. To change both these values, use the following command:

```
Router2#configure terminal
Enter configuration commands, one per line.  End with CNTL/Z.
Router2(config)#interface FastEthernet 0/0
Router2(config-if)#bandwidth 1000
Router2(config-if)#delay 120
!--- Delay is entered in tens of microseconds.
Router2(config-if)#exit
Router2(config)#exit
```

Clearing your IP route

If you make frequent changes to routing protocol properties, be aware that you either have to wait for changes to propagate or wait for the relevant hold down timers to expire. You can override these delays by entering Privileged EXEC mode and using the clear ip route command.

Troubleshooting EIGRP

The basic command for checking the status of EIGRP and other routing protocols is show ip protocols. The following output shows the output related to EIGRP. However, first here are some key things to look for:

✦ No filters on interfaces, either incoming or outgoing

✦ Metric settings (automatically at the default settings)

✦ Maximum configured hop count

✦ AS number

✦ Summarization settings

✦ Networks this router is distributing

✦ Neighbors seen

✦ Administrative distance

```
Router2>enable
Password:
Router2#show ip protocols
Routing Protocol is "eigrp 100"
  Outgoing update filter list for all interfaces is not set
  Incoming update filter list for all interfaces is not set
  Default networks flagged in outgoing updates
  Default networks accepted from incoming updates
  EIGRP metric weight K1=1, K2=0, K3=1, K4=0, K5=0
  EIGRP maximum hopcount 100
  EIGRP maximum metric variance 1
  Redistributing: eigrp 100
  EIGRP NSF-aware route hold timer is 240s
  Automatic network summarization is not in effect
  Maximum path: 4
  Routing for Networks:
    192.168.1.0
    192.168.5.0
  Routing Information Sources:
    Gateway         Distance      Last Update
    192.168.1.1           90      00:03:43
  Distance: internal 90 external 170
```

In addition to the basics found in `show ip protocols`, a suite of commands is available through the `show ip eigrp` command. The following information shows the categories of information you can find by using the `show ip eigrp` command:

```
Router2>enable
Password:
Router2#show ip eigrp ?
  <1-65535>   Autonomous System
  interfaces  IP-EIGRP interfaces
  neighbors   IP-EIGRP neighbors
  topology    IP-EIGRP Topology Table
  traffic     IP-EIGRP Traffic Statistics
  vrf         Select a VPN Routing/Forwarding instance
```

The interfaces option

The `interfaces` option identifies which interfaces receive EIGRP messages, and how many possible unreliable and reliable routes exist.

```
Router2>enable
Password:
Router2#show ip eigrp interfaces
```

```
IP-EIGRP interfaces for process 100

                        Xmit Queue   Mean   Pacing Time   Multicast     Pending
Interface      Peers    Un/Reliable  SRTT   Un/Reliable   Flow Timer    Routes
Fa0/0          1        0/0          4      0/10          50            0
Fa0/1          0        0/0          0      0/10          0             0
```

The neighbors option

The EIGRP `neighbors` option gives you information about systems from which your router is receiving EIGRP packets and when that information is allowed to be modified.

```
Router2>enable
Password:
Router2#show ip eigrp neighbors detail
IP-EIGRP neighbors for process 100
H   Address               Interface       Hold Uptime    SRTT   RTO  Q   Seq
                                          (sec)          (ms)        Cnt Num
0   192.168.1.1           Fa0/0           11 00:02:02    4      200  0   10
    Version 12.0/1.0, Retrans: 1, Retries: 0
```

The topology option

The `topology` option displays information that goes into the topology table. In this case, you can see that the output includes a list of potential routes which can be used for the networks and on which interface the routes were learned. Notice that the listing includes successors, while if they were available, you would also see the feasible successors.

```
Router2>enable
Password:
Router2#show ip eigrp topology all
IP-EIGRP Topology Table for AS(100)/ID(192.168.5.1)

Codes: P - Passive, A - Active, U - Update, Q - Query, R - Reply,
       r - reply Status, s - sia Status

P 192.168.10.0/24, 1 successors, FD is 284160, serno 7
        via 192.168.1.1 (284160/281600), FastEthernet0/0
P 192.168.1.0/24, 1 successors, FD is 28160, serno 6
        via Connected, FastEthernet0/0
P 192.168.5.0/24, 1 successors, FD is 28160, serno 8
        via Connected, FastEthernet0/1
```

The traffic option

A `traffic` display provides the statistics on the EIGRP traffic that your router is seeing, the packets it has received, and the number to which it has responded. Notice that these statistics are for a specific AS identifier.

```
Router2>enable
Password:
Router2#show ip eigrp traffic
```

```
IP-EIGRP Traffic Statistics for AS 100
  Hellos sent/received: 272/109
  Updates sent/received: 13/13
  Queries sent/received: 0/0
  Replies sent/received: 0/0
  Acks sent/received: 5/7
  Input queue high water mark 1, 0 drops
  SIA-Queries sent/received: 0/0
  SIA-Replies sent/received: 0/0
  Hello Process ID: 167
  PDM Process ID: 166
```

The debug command

Finally, you come to the debug command. Be aware that enabling any debug command puts a load on your router. Notice that the following output gives you information on the neighbors, such as new adjacency (learning of a new *adjacent* or neighbor router), changes in link availability, and routing information.

```
Router2>enable
Password:
Router2#debug ip eigrp
IP-EIGRP Route Events debugging is on
*Mar 18 00:38:35.281: %DUAL-5-NBRCHANGE: IP-EIGRP(0) 100: Neighbor 192.168.1.1
    (FastEthernet0/0) is up: new adjacency
*Mar 18 00:38:49.569: %DUAL-5-NBRCHANGE: IP-EIGRP(0) 100: Neighbor 192.168.1.1
    (FastEthernet0/0) is down: peer restarted
*Mar 18 00:38:54.321: %DUAL-5-NBRCHANGE: IP-EIGRP(0) 100: Neighbor 192.168.1.1
    (FastEthernet0/0) is up: new adjacency
*Mar 18 00:38:58.913: %DUAL-5-NBRCHANGE: IP-EIGRP(0) 100: Neighbor 192.168.1.1
    (FastEthernet0/0) is down: peer restarted
*Mar 18 00:39:03.397: %DUAL-5-NBRCHANGE: IP-EIGRP(0) 100: Neighbor 192.168.1.1
    (FastEthernet0/0) is up: new adjacency
*Mar 18 00:45:05.109: %DUAL-5-NBRCHANGE: IP-EIGRP(0) 100: Neighbor 192.168.1.1
    (FastEthernet0/0) is up: new adjacency
*Mar 18 00:45:05.117: IP-EIGRP(Default-IP-Routing-Table:100): 192.168.1.0/24 - do
    advertise out FastEthernet0/0
*Mar 18 00:45:05.697: IP-EIGRP(Default-IP-Routing-Table:100): Processing incoming
    UPDATE packet
*Mar 18 00:45:05.697: IP-EIGRP(Default-IP-Routing-Table:100): Int 192.168.10.0/24
    M 284160 - 256000 28160 SM 281600 - 256000 25600
*Mar 18 00:45:05.713: %LINK-3-UPDOWN: Interface FastEthernet0/1, changed state to
    up
*Mar 18 00:45:05.717: IP-EIGRP(Default-IP-Routing-Table:100): Int 192.168.10.0/24
    metric 284160 - 256000 28160
*Mar 18 00:45:06.713: %LINEPROTO-5-UPDOWN: Line protocol on Interface
    FastEthernet0/1, changed state to up
*Mar 18 00:45:07.117: IP-EIGRP(Default-IP-Routing-Table:100): 192.168.1.0/24 - do
    advertise out FastEthernet0/0
*Mar 18 00:45:07.129: IP-EIGRP(Default-IP-Routing-Table:100): Int 192.168.10.0/24
    metric 284160 - 256000 28160
*Mar 18 00:45:07.141: IP-EIGRP(Default-IP-Routing-Table:100): 192.168.5.0/24 - do
    advertise out FastEthernet0/0
```

**Book IV
Chapter 7**

Checking Out RIP and EIGRP Character-istics and Design

```
*Mar 18 00:45:07.141: IP-EIGRP(Default-IP-Routing-Table:100): Int 192.168.5.0/24
    metric 28160 - 25600 2560
*Mar 18 00:45:07.161: IP-EIGRP(Default-IP-Routing-Table:100): Processing incoming
    UPDATE packet
*Mar 18 00:45:07.161: IP-EIGRP(Default-IP-Routing-Table:100): Int 192.168.5.0/24
    M 4294967295 - 256000 4294967295 SM 4294967295 - 256000 4294967295
Router2#no debug ip eigrp
```

If you have too many `debug` options enabled and the screen is overflowing with data, you can get the situation under control again by disabling all the options. Do this by typing `u all` to disable all possible debugging.

Chapter 8: Getting Comfortable with the OSPF and IS-IS Protocols

In This Chapter

✔ Configuring common options for the OSPF and IS-IS protocols

✔ Managing the OSPF and IS-IS protocols with troubleshooting tools

*I*n this chapter, you see a couple of link-state protocols: OSPF (Open Shortest Path First) and IS-IS, which I first discuss in Book IV, Chapter 1. Although in general, link-state protocols all work in the same manner, each is markedly unique to a degree in how they actually carry out their routing. IS-IS has found a home with service providers, and you will not likely implement it on your internal network, whereas OSPF is a popular Interior Gateway Protocol (IGP) that has been implemented on many internal networks. As with other protocols you may have looked at in this minibook in the IGP category, any of them will make a good choice. Using these protocols is easy and straightforward, so you may want to start considering them before your network grows to a point where static routing becomes cumbersome.

As you read this chapter, you will find out how to configure and implement the OSPF and IS-IS protocols, and you will see the main commands you will use to effectively troubleshoot these protocols.

Open Shortest Path First (OSPF)

Because OSPF is an open standard protocol, many people have contributed to its design and thousands upon thousands of people have reviewed it. In this section, I want to point out some functional components of this IGP and its use in your networks.

Getting comfortable with OSPF basics

Because every IGP behaves slightly differently from other IGPs, you should be familiar with a few OSPF terms that are used with the protocol before jumping into the configuration commands. This section attempts to clarify the major terms and concepts you should be familiar with.

OSPF as a link-state protocol

In link-state protocols, the *link* part of the protocol is the interface on the router, while the *state* is how it relates to its neighbors, which would include its address and network information. Before you get started, check out this short list of terms used in this section:

+ **Link State Advertisement (LSA):** A simple update on a router's link status, so one will be sent when a link is connected, disconnected, or otherwise changed

+ **Topological database:** A table in the router's memory that contains link information about all known routers (see Chapter 6 of this minibook)

+ **SPF algorithm:** A mathematical calculation that uses the Dijkstra algorithm (named after a Dutch mathematician) to determine the shortest path to destinations and that has been heavily applied to computer networks

+ **SPF tree:** A listing all of the routes to any destination with an order of preference

Each router that has been configured for an OSPF area sends out a Link State Advertisement (LSA) at regular intervals. All of this link-state information is stored in a topological database, after which an SPF algorithm is applied to the data in the database. (You find out how to retrieve information from these databases in the section "Troubleshooting OSPF," later in this chapter.) This process generates an SPF tree listing all of the routes to any destination with an order of preference. The preferred order is then stored in the routing table, giving the router the best routing choices to those destinations. Figure 8-1 illustrates this process:

1. Routers in exchange link-state data start the process.

2. Each router stores the link-state information in memory using a structure named the *topology table* or *topology database*.

3. The router processes all data in the topology table and makes use of the Dijkstra algorithm to determine all routes to all networks, as well as the least-cost routes.

4. All this information is stored in the SFP tree, identifying preferred and secondary routes.

5. The routing information is propagated to the routing table.

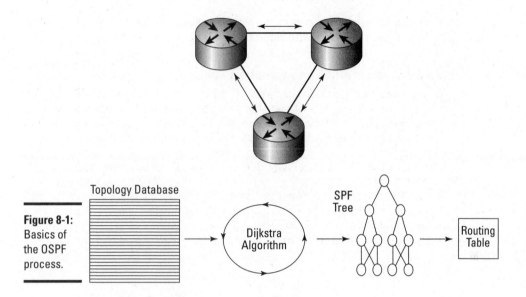

Figure 8-1:
Basics of
the OSPF
process.

Topology Database

Dijkstra
Algorithm

SPF
Tree

Routing
Table

OSPF packet types

OSPF works with a few different types of packets to convey information to
surrounding routers.

+ **Hello packet:** Exchanges information about neighbors with each other.

+ **Database Description packet:** Elects a version of the database to be used.

+ **Link-state request packet:** Requests a specific LSA from a neighbor.

+ **Link-state update packet:** Sends an entire LSA to a neighbor who has
requested an update.

+ **Link-state acknowledge packet:** Acknowledges the receipt of a link-state
update packet.

The default interval for sending LSA updates is 30 minutes, with a 4-minute
random offset to prevent all routers from sending at the same time. This
interval does not mean that when a change occurs on an interface, it takes
up to 30 minutes to start the replication process. Rather, changes in interface status or configuration are sent out immediately. The 30-minute interval
is used to refresh data that already exists on other routers. Because a router
expects to receive updates every 30 minutes, you may be wondering what
happens if an update does not show up on schedule. If an update is not
received within four intervals (120 minutes), the router is aged out of the
topology database. This might happen if something unexpected happens to
the router, such as a power supply failure or becoming unplugged.

All routers that share a common area identifier (or *area ID*) receive the LSA data, not just routers on the same data link.

Knowing areas and Autonomous Systems

When designing your OSPF network, the two main factors you work with are areas and how they fit within an AS. *Areas* are functional areas of your network, perhaps a building or the floor of a building, and *Autonomous Systems* are collections of areas, which typically are your entire network.

The overall OSPF network is divided into groups called areas, whereas all routers in an organization are probably part of a single AS, as shown in Figure 8-2. The *area* is defined as a logical division of the AS, broken up into contiguous sections of the IP network. In other words, you break the area along groups of subnets that can be grouped together with a single routing entry. In a typical large network, an area may consist of 30 to 40 routers.

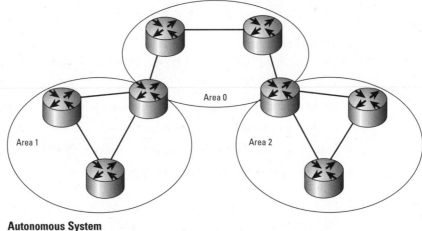

Figure 8-2: OSPF networks are Autonomous Systems that are broken into areas.

Area 0

Area 1

Area 2

Autonomous System

The Hello packet

The faster, more regular packet of OSPF management packets, is the multicast OSPF Hello packet, which goes to the address 224.0.0.5. The *Hello packet* is the mechanism that creates the neighbor relationships between routers. By default, these packets go out every ten seconds on broadcast media, alerting surrounding neighbors that the router is still up and running. The dead interval (the time when a neighbor is possibly down) for Hello information is four times the Hello interval, so if a router fails to send four sets of Hello packets, it will be flagged as unavailable and its routes will be suspect. It will later be removed when four update intervals have passed.

When OSPF Hello packets are sent out, they contain several pieces of information. Here is a list of the key items:

✦ **Router ID:** Found in the OSPF header, the Router ID is a 32-bit numeric identifier that, by default, is the highest IP address among all the available interfaces. By implementing a loopback interface, you can exercise some control over the Router ID. You can also use the `router-id` configuration parameter (discussed in the section "Keeping track of router IDs," later in this chapter) to set the Router ID to a preferred value.

✦ **Neighbors:** At the end of the Hello packet is a list of all known neighbor routers, which allows each neighbor to know about all other neighbors.

✦ **Area ID:** Neighbors must share a common segment, and their interfaces must belong to the same OSPF area on that segment. They must also share the same subnet and mask.

✦ **Router priority:** An 8-bit number for priority, used to select Designated Router (DR) and Backup Designated Router (BDR).

✦ **DR and BDR IP addresses:** The addresses of both the DR and BDR.

✦ **Authentication password:** The authentication password. Performing authentication is an optional security feature with the OSPF protocol.

✦ **Stub area flag:** Reduces updates by individually routing them with a default route.

Checking out the base cost

After the router gathers all the information, it calculates a base cost for each route. The cost is calculated with this formula:

```
Cost = reference bandwidth / interface bandwidth in bps
```

The *reference bandwidth* is the same as Fast Ethernet, which is 100,000,000. Fast Ethernet links always have a cost of 1. If you are calculating the cost of a Gigabit Ethernet link, you use 100,000,000/1,000,000,000, which gives you 0.1. The cost of an Ethernet link is 100,000,000/10,000,000, which gives you 10; the cost of a T1 link is 100,000,000/1,544,000, which gives you a cost of 64. The slower the link, the higher the cost, and the less it is preferred. The lowest cost link will always be preferred.

Configuring OSPF

Initially enabling OSPF requires only two commands:

✦ `router ospf process-id`: This command enables the OSPF process and then you will require a `network` command for each network for

**Book IV
Chapter 8**

**Getting Comfortable
with the OSPF and
IS-IS Protocols**

which you will be routing. The `router` command is the two-part command, where the *process-id* is a unique and arbitrary local ID for the OSPF process. OSPF is unlike other routing protocols that identify which routers belong to a group; here the router identifies the copy of OSPF that is running, because you can have more than one OSPF process running, allowing your router to participate in different AS groups.

✦ `network address wildcard-mask area area-id`: This command is similar to other network commands that identify the network by the IP address or the IP network appropriate for each interface for which you will be routing. With OSPF, the main difference is that you include both a wildcard mask to change the range of addresses you are working with and the area ID of the OSPF area to which the address belongs.

```
Router2>enable
Password:
Router2#configure terminal
Enter configuration commands, one per line.  End with CNTL/Z.
Router2(config)#router ospf 100
Router2(config-router)#network 192.168.1.240 0.0.0.0 area 0
Router2(config-router)#network 192.168.5.1 0.0.0.0 area 0
Router2(config-router)#exit
Router2(config)#exit
```

Working with wildcard masks

When working with wildcard masks (covered in detail in Book VI, Chapter 3), Cisco recommends sticking to the interface address with all zeros (0) in the mask. If you want to deviate from this method, breaking the mask at 8-bit boundaries is the next recommendation because it reduces the chance of making errors.

With the exception of the global wildcard mask of all zeros — which is special — there is the *matching rule*. With the matching rule, where there is a binary zero in the mask, the mask requires a match, but where there is a binary 1 in the mask, the mask does not care about the address. Figure 8-3 shows a sample on which I walk you through the use of wildcard masks which will be valid in different situations.

Wildcard masks work differently than subnet masks do. Subnet masks remove the host section of an address, leaving you with a network ID, whereas wildcard masks identify the portions of an address that need to match. If you reverse the bits and perform the logical AND process (the AND process is covered in Book II, Chapter 3), you end up matching the same network.

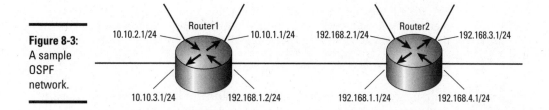

Figure 8-3:
A sample
OSPF
network.

If the figure matches the scope of your entire network, and `Router1` can use
these two network lines:

```
network 192.168.1.0 0.0.0.255 area 192
network 10.0.0.0 0.255.255.255 area 10
```

Whereas `Router2`, which has no 10.0.0.0/8 network segments, can use this
network command:

```
network 192.168.0.0 0.0.255.255 area 192
```

In this example, all networks in the 10.0.0.0/8 range can be routed through
`Router1`, and `Router2` can route all of the 192.168.0.0/16 networks. If you
add another router to the network and use an address from the 192.168.0.0/16
or 10.0.0.0/8 network blocks, you may encounter routing issues implementing these wildcard masks. Although you do less typing with the class-based
address masks (one network mask, rather than four, for all of `Router2`), you
must do more planning around the network addresses (which you should
be doing anyway). So, you can be more limiting in how you assign masks for
these network commands. `Router1`'s commands are as follows:

```
network 192.168.1.0 0.0.0.255 area 192
network 10.10.0.0 0.0.127.255 area 10
```

`Router2`'s network commands are as follows:

```
network 192.168.1.0 0.0.0.255 area 192
network 192.168.2.0 0.0.127.255 area 192
network 192.168.4.0 0.0.0.255 area 192
```

In this set of examples, you end up with two big differences. Based on the
mask now assigned to the 10.10.0.0/16 network block of `Router1`, your
router identifies itself as the router from all addresses from 10.10.0.0 through
10.10.3.255, which is fine as long as you do not plan to use 10.10.0.0/24
on another area of your network. On `Router2`, the router now routes for

**Book IV
Chapter 8**

**Getting Comfortable
with the OSPF and
IS-IS Protocols**

192.168.1.0 through 192.168.4.255. If you were not using the network segments on your network, you would identify it as the router for 192.168.0.0 through 192.168.7.255 with this single command:

```
Network 192.168.0.0 0.0.63.255 area 192
```

Although you can reduce your typing a little bit by using wildcard masks, doing so can cause a lot of confusion, so using the interface addresses will make life easier.

Keeping track of router IDs

When it comes to troubleshooting on your network, keeping track of the various Router IDs that show up in your raw network data can be confusing. Also, when an interface goes down, the Router's ID may change, further complicating matters.

You can assign a Router ID either by using the `router-id` command in Router Configuration mode or by assigning an address to a loopback interface that is higher than any other address on any other interface on your router. The loopback interface should never go down, so using it is a good choice and is the method that I will explain.

In the private address range, 192.168.255.0/24 represents the highest addresses you will likely ever use on your network. If you have fewer than 254 routers on your network, this range is ideal, but if you can, you should keep the 192.168.254.0/24 range available. By keeping the second range available, you will have another 254 addresses you will be able to assign as Router IDs. The following code enables a loopback interface numbered 0 and assigns an address to the interface.

```
Loopback
Router2>enable
Password:
Router2#configure terminal
Enter configuration commands, one per line.  End with CNTL/Z.
Router2(config)#interface loopback 0
Router2(config-if)#ip address 192.168.255.254 255.255.255.0
Router2(config-if)#exit
Router2(config)#router ospf 100
Router2(config-router)#network 192.168.255.254 0.0.0.0 area 0
Router2(config-router)#exit
Router2(config)#exit
```

The only item you might not know about in the preceding code snippet is advertising the network of your Router IDs in the OSPF routing interface. The command network `192.168.255.254 0.0.0.0 area 0` tells OSPF that the 192.168.255.0/24 network is a routable network ID on the network. This item is not required. By advertising the router to this network, you can use this address to connect to the router for remote administration. The drawback is that before advertising this network, you would have been able to also use this address block on your network.

Although I said that OSPF always uses the highest configured address of any interface as its Router ID, it actually always prefer a loopback interface over any other type of interface. With that said, when you configure multiple loopback interfaces, 192.168.254.0/24 still represents a good address block for assigning addresses.

When there are multiple paths to a destination, OSPF automatically performs equal cost-load balancing. It supports up to 16 paths to the destination, but by default only operates with four paths. You can change this behavior by using the `maximum-paths` command as follows:

```
Router2>enable
Password:
Router2#configure terminal
Enter configuration commands, one per line.  End with CNTL/Z.
Router2(config-router)#maximum-paths 10
Router2(config-router)#exit
Router2(config)#exit
```

Another way to influence the route selection is to manually adjust the cost of a link. In the earlier section "Checking out the base cost," you might have read that the cost of a link is based on the speed of the link, with FastEthernet being a 1 and faster or slower links being based off that link speed. To manually influence the cost, use Interface Configuration mode and the `ip ospf cost` command, as shown here (where the link cost is set to 5):

```
Router2>enable
Password:
Router2#configure terminal
Enter configuration commands, one per line.  End with CNTL/Z.
Router2(config-if)#ip ospf cost 5
Router2(config-if)#exit
Router2(config)#exit
```

Troubleshooting OSPF

As you probably realize by now, the best way to troubleshoot is to gather information. The first source of information is the `show` command. In this section, you will take a look at the most relevant options to be used with the `show` command to assist in your information gathering and troubleshooting of OSPF.

Viewing routes in the routing table

After OSPF is enabled, what do the routes look like in the routing table? You can use the show ip route command, which shows the standard internal OSPF routes listed with a letter O, inter-area routes listed with IA, and external routes listed with N1 or N2.

```
Router2>enable
Password:
Router2#show ip route
Codes: C - connected, S - static, R - RIP, M - mobile, B - BGP
       D - EIGRP, EX - EIGRP external, O - OSPF, IA - OSPF inter area
       N1 - OSPF NSSA external type 1, N2 - OSPF NSSA external type 2
       E1 - OSPF external type 1, E2 - OSPF external type 2
       i - IS-IS, su - IS-IS summary, L1 - IS-IS level-1, L2 - IS-IS level-2
       ia - IS-IS inter area, * - candidate default, U - per-user static route
       o - ODR, P - periodic downloaded static route

Gateway of last resort is not set

O    192.168.10.0/24 [110/11] via 192.168.1.1, 00:01:01, FastEthernet0/0
C    192.168.5.0/24 is directly connected, FastEthernet0/1
C    192.168.255.0/24 is directly connected, Loopback0
C    192.168.1.0/24 is directly connected, FastEthernet0/0
S    192.168.3.0/24 [1/0] via 192.168.1.1
```

To be more specific about the information you are requesting, you can request information for a specific route. The results show where you have read about the route and read exactly why this route is preferred over other routes that are similar to that destination.

```
Router2>enable
Password:
Router2#show ip route 192.168.10.0
Routing entry for 192.168.10.0/24
  Known via "ospf 100", distance 110, metric 11, type intra area
  Last update from 192.168.1.1 on FastEthernet0/0, 00:15:25 ago
  Routing Descriptor Blocks:
  * 192.168.1.1, from 192.168.10.1, 00:15:25 ago, via FastEthernet0/0
      Route metric is 11, traffic share count is 1
```

Viewing your IP protocols

The show ip protocols command (mentioned in the previous section "Viewing routes in the routing table"), will show you the OSPF process number and basic information about the OSPF protocol. The following list identifies the key pieces of information that you will see with the show ip protocols command:

✦ Filters you configured for the protocol

✦ The Router ID (note that in this case the Router ID is still set to the Fast Ethernet interface)

✦ Areas that the router routes

✦ Number of equal paths for which OSPF will load balance

✦ Local networks that OSPF has configured with areas

✦ Neighbors with their last update and administrative distance

The following output shows the particular settings for the OSPF protocol:

```
Router2>enable
Password:
Router2#show ip protocols
Routing Protocol is "ospf 100"
  Outgoing update filter list for all interfaces is not set
  Incoming update filter list for all interfaces is not set
  Router ID 192.168.5.1
  Number of areas in this router is 1. 1 normal 0 stub 0 nssa
  Maximum path: 4
  Routing for Networks:
    192.168.1.240 0.0.0.0 area 0
    192.168.255.254 0.0.0.0 area 0
  Routing Information Sources:
    Gateway         Distance      Last Update
    192.168.5.1        110        00:02:50
  Distance: (default is 110)
```

Viewing options for the show ip ospf command

Many options are available for the `show ip ospf` command. These options are listed in the following output, followed by a discussion of a few of the key ones. Bear in mind that the results for some commands may lead you to seek specific information in other areas. For example, if you do not see neighbors, you may want to investigate why they are not showing up.

```
Router2>enable
Password:
Router2#show ip ospf ?
  <1-65535>          Process ID number
  border-routers     Border and Boundary Router Information
  database           Database summary
  flood-list         Link state flood list
  interface          Interface information
  mpls               MPLS related information
  neighbor           Neighbor list
  request-list       Link state request list
  retransmission-list Link state retransmission list
  sham-links         Sham link information
  statistics         Various OSPF Statistics
  summary-address    Summary-address redistribution Information
  timers             OSPF timers information
  virtual-links      Virtual link information
  |                  Output modifiers
  <cr>
```

The first key command is show ip ospf, which shows basic configuration information related to the protocol and its operation. In this case, you see that the Process ID is 100, the router is only configured for one area, and the SPF algorithm has run twice on one LSA.

```
Router2>enable
Password:
Router2#show ip ospf
 Routing Process "ospf 100" with ID 192.168.5.1
 Supports only single TOS(TOS0) routes
 Supports opaque LSA
 Supports Link-local Signaling (LLS)
 Initial SPF schedule delay 5000 msecs
 Minimum hold time between two consecutive SPFs 10000 msecs
 Maximum wait time between two consecutive SPFs 10000 msecs
 Incremental-SPF disabled
 Minimum LSA interval 5 secs
 Minimum LSA arrival 1000 msecs
 LSA group pacing timer 240 secs
 Interface flood pacing timer 33 msecs
 Retransmission pacing timer 66 msecs
 Number of external LSA 0. Checksum Sum 0x000000
 Number of opaque AS LSA 0. Checksum Sum 0x000000
 Number of DCbitless external and opaque AS LSA 0
 Number of DoNotAge external and opaque AS LSA 0
 Number of areas in this router is 1. 1 normal 0 stub 0 nssa
 External flood list length 0
    Area BACKBONE(0) (Inactive)
        Number of interfaces in this area is 2 (1 loopback)
        Area has no authentication
        SPF algorithm last executed 00:06:37.652 ago
        SPF algorithm executed 2 times
        Area ranges are
        Number of LSA 1. Checksum Sum 0x006FFE
        Number of opaque link LSA 0. Checksum Sum 0x000000
        Number of DCbitless LSA 0
        Number of indication LSA 0
        Number of DoNotAge LSA 0
        Flood list length 0
```

Viewing information about interfaces

With show ip ospf interface, you can get more detail about the specific interfaces being used for OSPF. At this point, the loopback interface is configured, the timer intervals are still set to default values, a DR and BDR are selected, and 192.168.10.1 is the only neighbor.

```
Router2>enable
Password:
Router2#show ip ospf interface
Loopback0 is up, line protocol is up
   Internet Address 192.168.255.254/24, Area 0
   Process ID 100, Router ID 192.168.5.1, Network Type LOOPBACK, Cost: 1
   Loopback interface is treated as a stub Host
FastEthernet0/0 is up, line protocol is up
   Internet Address 192.168.1.240/24, Area 0
   Process ID 100, Router ID 192.168.5.1, Network Type BROADCAST, Cost: 1
   Transmit Delay is 1 sec, State DR, Priority 1
   Designated Router (ID) 192.168.5.1, Interface address 192.168.1.240
   Backup Designated router (ID) 192.168.10.1, Interface address 192.168.1.1
```

```
Timer intervals configured, Hello 10, Dead 40, Wait 40, Retransmit 5
  oob-resync timeout 40
  Hello due in 00:00:07
Index 1/1, flood queue length 0
Next 0x0(0)/0x0(0)
Last flood scan length is 1, maximum is 1
Last flood scan time is 0 msec, maximum is 0 msec
Neighbor Count is 1, Adjacent neighbor count is 1
  Adjacent with neighbor 192.168.10.1  (Backup Designated Router)
Suppress hello for 0 neighbor(s)
```

Viewing detailed info about neighbors

To view detailed information about the neighbors that are seen, you use the `neighbor` option. Here, you see that the neighbor is a Backup Designated Router (BDR) that has fully converged (believes that all routers know the current state of the network). Because the Neighbor ID does not match the neighbor's IP address, you can guess that it also routes for network 192.168.10.0/24 or that it has a loopback interface configured for that address. My guess is the former because 192.168.10.0/24 does not show up in the list of networks that it is a router for.

```
Router2>enable
Password:
Router2#show ip ospf neighbor

Neighbor ID     Pri  State      Dead Time   Address       Interface
192.168.10.1     1   FULL/BDR   00:00:32    192.168.1.1   FastEthernet0/0
```

You can explore more of the `show ip ospf` options on your own to become familiar with their output.

Debugging OSPF

Now, it is time to move on to the infamous `debug` commands that are available to OSPF. As with the `show` command, the `debug` command has many options. Because spreading the net too widely can cause a lot of information to sift through, you want to make the scope of the command as narrow as possible. Unlike other debugging commands, there is not a general `debug ip ospf`, so you are forced to be a little selective.

```
Router2>enable
Password:
Router2#debug ip ospf ?
  adj             OSPF adjacency events
  database-timer  OSPF database timer
  events          OSPF events
  flood           OSPF flooding
  hello           OSPF hello events
  lsa-generation  OSPF lsa generation
  mpls            OSPF MPLS
  nsf             OSPF non-stop forwarding events
  packet          OSPF packets
  retransmission  OSPF retransmission events
  spf             OSPF spf
  tree            OSPF database tree
```

Viewing events

The events option is just about the most general option among the available options. The output that follows shows these options:

✦ The router is sending Hello packets out to the multicast address on one of its network interfaces.

✦ The router is selected as the Designated Router.

✦ The router found a route to 192.168.10.0/24 from one of its neighbors.

```
Router2>enable
Password:
Router2#debug ip ospf events
OSPF events debugging is on

*Mar 18 02:58:36.069: OSPF: Interface FastEthernet0/0 going Up
*Mar 18 02:58:36.069: OSPF: Send hello to 224.0.0.5 area 0 on FastEthernet0/0
    from 192.168.1.240
*Mar 18 02:58:46.069: OSPF: Send hello to 224.0.0.5 area 0 on FastEthernet0/0
    from 192.168.1.240exit
*Mar 18 02:58:56.069: OSPF: Send hello to 224.0.0.5 area 0 on FastEthernet0/0
    from 192.168.1.240
*Mar 18 02:59:06.069: OSPF: Send hello to 224.0.0.5 area 0 on FastEthernet0/0
    from 192.168.1.240
*Mar 18 02:59:16.069: OSPF: end of Wait on interface FastEthernet0/0
*Mar 18 02:59:16.069: OSPF: DR/BDR election on FastEthernet0/0
*Mar 18 02:59:16.069: OSPF: Elect BDR 192.168.5.1
*Mar 18 02:59:16.069: OSPF: Elect DR 192.168.5.1
*Mar 18 02:59:16.069: OSPF: Elect BDR 0.0.0.0
*Mar 18 02:59:16.069: OSPF: Elect DR 192.168.5.1
*Mar 18 02:59:16.069:         DR: 192.168.5.1 (Id)    BDR: none
*Mar 18 02:59:16.069: OSPF: Send hello to 224.0.0.5 area 0 on FastEthernet0/0
    from 192.168.1.240
*Mar 18 03:25:46.084: %OSPF-5-ADJCHG: Process 100, Nbr 192.168.10.1 on
    FastEthernet0/0 from LOADING to FULL, Loading Done
Router2#no debug ip ospf events
```

You can discover a great deal from the various debug commands, but the scope of this book does not permit me to go into depth on all of them. However, if you plan to deploy OSPF, viewing information regarding the various commands will be a worthwhile investment.

Intermediate System to Intermediate System (IS-IS)

When comparing IS-IS to OSPF, you see some similarities. Both are link-state protocols and both use the Dijkstra algorithm to calculate the best route through a network. One major difference between the protocols relates to how they operate in the OSI model. IS-IS is a native Layer 3 (network layer) protocol, so it is capable of passing routing information for any routable protocol, and it is not restricted to IP like OSPF and many other routing protocols are. Most other routing protocols required modification in order to support IPv6, whereas because IS-IS is network-protocol neutral, it can support IPv6 right out of the gate.

Regarding the way it supports areas, IS-IS also differs from OSPF in that routers route as Level 1 or intra-area within an area, as Level 2 or inter-area between areas, or as Levels 1–2 when performing both types of routing.

Enabling IS-IS routing

The basic command to enable IS-IS routing is `router isis [area tag]`, where the area tag is either 1, 2, or 1–2. By default, if the area tag is omitted, the first instance of IS-IS uses Level 1–2 and Level 1 for later instances. After specifying the `router` command, you specify network entity titles on the `net` statements, which is like specifying the RouterID, the only requirement is that this value be unique across your network. In this case, you use `49.0001.0000.000a.00` as a base for the IDs and specify unique values for each router using `0a.00` and incrementing upward.

Unlike other protocols where you use the `network` command to identify networks that will be included in routing, with IS-IS, the `ip router isis` command is issued on each interface for which you want to route for `FastEthernet 0/0` and `FastEthernet 0/1`, as shown here:

```
Router2>enable
Password:
Router2#configure terminal
Enter configuration commands, one per line.  End with CNTL/Z.
Router2(config)#router isis
Router2(config-router)#net ?
  XX.XXXX. ... .XXX.XX  Network entity title (NET)

Router2(config-router)#net 49.0001.0000.0000.000a.00
Router2(config-router)#exit
Router2(config)#interface FastEthernet 0/0
Router2(config-if)#ip router isis
Router2(config-if)#exit
Router2(config)#interface FastEthernet 0/1
Router2(config-if)#ip router isis
Router2(config-if)#exit
Router2(config)#exit
```

When viewing the routing table, you see all the IS-IS routes listed with `i` and another identifier to show whether they are Level 1, Level 2, or inter-area (Level 1–2). You can see in the listing that the network of 192.168.6.0/24 is an IS-IS Level 1 network.

**Book IV
Chapter 8**

**Getting Comfortable
with the OSPF and
IS-IS Protocols**

```
Router2>enable
Password:
Router2#show ip route
Codes: C - connected, S - static, R - RIP, M - mobile, B - BGP
       D - EIGRP, EX - EIGRP external, O - OSPF, IA - OSPF inter area
       N1 - OSPF NSSA external type 1, N2 - OSPF NSSA external type 2
       E1 - OSPF external type 1, E2 - OSPF external type 2
       i - IS-IS, su - IS-IS summary, L1 - IS-IS level-1, L2 - IS-IS level-2
       ia - IS-IS inter area, * - candidate default, U - per-user static route
       o - ODR, P - periodic downloaded static route

Gateway of last resort is not set

C    192.168.5.0/24 is directly connected, FastEthernet0/1
i L1 192.168.6.0/24 [115/20] via 192.168.1.2, FastEthernet0/0
C    192.168.255.0/24 is directly connected, Loopback0
C    192.168.1.0/24 is directly connected, FastEthernet0/0
S    192.168.3.0/24 [1/0] via 192.168.1.1
```

Checking that IS-IS is running

To ensure that you have IS-IS running on your router, use the ever-popular
show ip protocols command. In the following listing, you see the
following:

✦ IS-IS is enabled on the router.

✦ Maximum equal cost load-balanced routing is 4.

✦ IS-IS is routing for two interfaces.

✦ There are two neighbor routes with an administrative distance of the
default 115.

```
Router2>enable
Password:
Router2#show ip protocols
Routing Protocol is "isis"
  Invalid after 0 seconds, hold down 0, flushed after 0
  Outgoing update filter list for all interfaces is not set
  Incoming update filter list for all interfaces is not set
  Redistributing: isis
  Address Summarization:
    None
  Maximum path: 4
  Routing for Networks:
    FastEthernet0/0
    FastEthernet0/1
  Routing Information Sources:
    Gateway         Distance      Last Update
    192.168.1.2         115       00:06:05
    192.168.5.2         115       00:05:46
  Distance: (default is 115)
```

Troubleshooting the IS-IS protocol

Once again, you investigate the show and debug commands to see how they can assist you in troubleshooting issues with the IS-IS protocol.

Viewing the show options

To start, here are the different options available in the show command:

```
Router2>enable
Password:
Router2#show isis ?
  *            All IS-IS address families
  database     IS-IS link state database
  hostname     IS-IS Dynamic hostname mapping
  ipv6         IS-IS IPv6
  lsp-log      IS-IS LSP log
  mesh-groups  IS-IS mesh groups
  mpls         IS-IS MPLS
  neighbors    IS-IS neighbors
  rib          ISIS local RIB information
  route        IS-IS level-1 routing table
  spf-log      IS-IS SPF log
  topology     IS-IS paths to Intermediate Systems
```

Among these options are several with useful information, most notably database, neighbors, route, and topology. Because you may have read about similar neighbor and route commands in Chapter 7 of this minibook, I now show you the output of the topology command. Notice that it includes both Level 1 and Level 2 routers, which both of the referenced routers are members of, because they were created with the default options on router isis. Router2 sees that the router Router1 is found on interface Fa0/0. So, with the topology command, you can see neighbors and further, whereas the neighbors command would only show adjacent routers.

```
Router2>enable
Password:
Router2#show isis topology

IS-IS paths to level-1 routers
System Id          Metric    Next-Hop      Interface    SNPA
Router2            --
Router1            10        Router1       Fa0/0        0017.e0c9.b7b0

IS-IS paths to level-2 routers
System Id          Metric    Next-Hop      Interface    SNPA
Router2            --
Router1            10        Router1       Fa0/0        0017.e0c9.b7b0
```

**Book IV
Chapter 8**

Getting Comfortable
with the OSPF and
IS-IS Protocols

Looking at debug options

Finally, you look at the debug options, which are similar to the OSPF debug commands shown earlier in this chapter. Depending on the types of problems you are experiencing, you may want to focus on different parts of the IS-IS protocol, such as adj-packets, protocol-errors, or spf-statistics.

```
Router2>enable
Password:
Router2#debug isis ?
  adj-packets       IS-IS Adjacency related packets
  authentication    IS-IS packet authentication
  checksum-errors   IS-IS LSP checksum errors
  local-updates     IS-IS local update packets
  mpls              IS-IS MPLS
  nsf               IS-IS Non-Stop Forwarding
  protocol-errors   IS-IS LSP protocol errors
  rib               IS-IS IP Routing Information Base
  snp-packets       IS-IS CSNP/PSNP packets
  spf-events        IS-IS Shortest Path First Events
  spf-statistics    IS-IS SPF Timing and Statistic Data
  spf-triggers      IS-IS SPF triggering events
  update-packets    IS-IS Update related packets
```

Chapter 9: Routing with BGP and IP Multicast

In This Chapter

✔ Configuring common options for BGP and multicast routing protocols

✔ Managing BGP and multicast routing protocols with troubleshooting tools

After the about Interior Gateway Protocols (IGP) in Chapters 7 and 8 of this minibook, this chapter takes a new tack by covering the only Exterior Gateway Protocol (EGP) discussed in this book: the Border Gateway Protocol (BGP).

Although you may or may not find it practical to implement BGP on your network, you are likely to receive some benefit from implementing multicast routing, particularly if you want multicast traffic to traverse your network without issue. In this chapter, you examine how to configure and troubleshoot the BGP protocol. In the multicast section, you see the main types of multicast routing, how to enable and configure a multicast router, and how to deal with troubleshooting information from the perspective of multicast routing.

Routing with Border Gateway Protocol (BGP)

As I mention in the introduction, BGP is an External Gateway Protocol (EGP), which means it is designed to act as a routing protocol on the edge of your network, passing routing information about the structure of your network behind your gateway router. This information can then be sent on to other BGP routers, informing them which networks are found behind the BGP router. A BGP router announces routes that they have learned and can also retransmit routes learned from the IGPs found on their networks, as illustrated in Figure 9-1.

BGP's purpose is not only to exchange its information, but also to exchange network reachability and availability information for the Autonomous Systems (AS) paths with other BGP systems on the network. This process allows all systems to construct topology graphs of the entire network infrastructure on both sides of the BGP link. This process also allows these systems to identify loops and other issues that may affect network performance and availability.

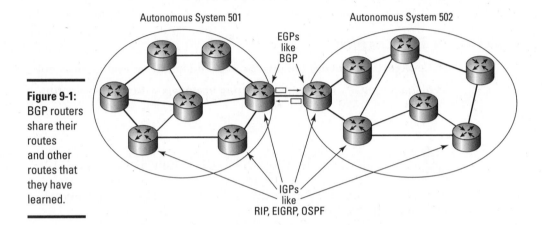

Autonomous System 501   Autonomous System 502

EGPs like BGP

IGPs like RIP, EIGRP, OSPF

Figure 9-1: BGP routers share their routes and other routes that they have learned.

BGP has several versions of BGP, and version 4 is the current one. When two BGP systems start communicating, they attempt to use version 4 of the protocol. If one system does not support version 4, they negotiate down to older versions of the protocol until they find a version they both can use.

Routing via weights

As with other routing protocols, BGP supports modification of the preferred route through modification of metric values. BGP does so with weights. A *weight* is the administrative value assigned to the local router. This value can be anything between 0 and 65,535 with a default value on Cisco routers of 32,768. To force traffic through a specific router, you can have its neighbors assign higher weights to routes than they have learned from that router. So, higher weights identify a preferred route, whereas with other routing protocols lower costs identify the preferred route.

Understanding BGP commands

The basic setup of a BGP system is straightforward, but its configuration is a little reverse to the way most protocols are configured. To set up, you use the `router` command as usual, but you want to assign an Autonomous System number to the router in the form of `router bgp` *as-number*. The AS number identifies the network that will exist behind the BGP router. Multiple routers for the same area must have the same AS number, and they are referred to as *internal neighbors,* whereas *external neighbors* have different AS numbers. To ensure that BGP operates efficiently, list a router's neighbors in Router Configuration mode, identifying each router's AS number using a command such as `neighbor {ip-address | peer-group-name} remote-as-a-number`.

In addition to these two configuration elements, you also list the network ranges that are inside your network with a command such as `network network-number [mask network-mask] [route-map route-map-name]`. The `network` command performs two tasks. It allows you to identify the network ranges you want to advertise to other routers, which may be subnetted or supernetted portions of your network, and via the `route-map` portion of the command, it lists where you want that information routed. Take a look at the following commands to set up one side of a BGP connection. These same steps would be executed on your other BGP router(s).

```
Router2>enable
Password:
Router2#configure terminal
Enter configuration commands, one per line.  End with CNTL/Z.
Router2(config)#router bgp 200
Router2(config-router)#network 192.168.5.0 mask 255.255.255.0
Router2(config-router)#neighbor 192.168.1.2 remote-as 100
Router2(config-router)#exit
Router2(config)#exit
```

Viewing routes in your routing table

Once you have BGP properly set up, you are able to see the routes listed in the routing table. The following shows the BGP routes in the routing table identified with a B. In addition to seeing where the route goes and how it gets there, you also see how long your router has known about that route, which is important, because if the link has been down or offline recently, this time will be very short.

```
Router2>enable
Password:
Router2#configure terminal
Enter configuration commands, one per line.  End with CNTL/Z.
Router2#show ip route
Codes: C - connected, S - static, R - RIP, M - mobile, B - BGP
       D - EIGRP, EX - EIGRP external, O - OSPF, IA - OSPF inter area
       N1 - OSPF NSSA external type 1, N2 - OSPF NSSA external type 2
       E1 - OSPF external type 1, E2 - OSPF external type 2
       i - IS-IS, su - IS-IS summary, L1 - IS-IS level-1, L2 - IS-IS level-2
       ia - IS-IS inter area, * - candidate default, U - per-user static route
       o - ODR, P - periodic downloaded static route

Gateway of last resort is not set

C    192.168.5.0/24 is directly connected, FastEthernet0/1
B    192.168.6.0/24 [20/0] via 192.168.1.2, 5d15h
C    192.168.255.0/24 is directly connected, Loopback0
C    192.168.1.0/24 is directly connected, FastEthernet0/0
S    192.168.3.0/24 [1/0] via 192.168.1.1
```

**Book IV
Chapter 9**

**Routing with BGP
and IP Multicast**

Viewing how the protocol is functioning

As with other protocols, the show ip protocols command shows you how the protocol is currently functioning. In the following output, you see these key pieces of information from the show ip protocols command:

✦ The BGP AS number

✦ Any filters set up for incoming and outgoing data

✦ Synchronization with IGPs that are currently running

✦ Visible neighbors

✦ Number of equal cost routing paths

✦ Routers that have provided routes to this instance of BGP, including their administrative distances

```
Router2>enable
Password:
Router2#configure terminal
Enter configuration commands, one per line.  End with CNTL/Z.
Router2#show ip protocols
Routing Protocol is "bgp 200"
  Outgoing update filter list for all interfaces is not set
  Incoming update filter list for all interfaces is not set
  IGP synchronization is disabled
  Automatic route summarization is disabled
  Neighbor(s):
    Address          FiltIn FiltOut DistIn DistOut Weight RouteMap
    192.168.1.2
  Maximum path: 1
  Routing Information Sources:
    Gateway         Distance      Last Update
    192.168.1.2        20         5d15h
  Distance: external 20 internal 200 local 200
```

If, as part of the configuration, you find you need to reset a part of the routing table, use the clear ip bgp command, which clear routes by neighbor-address, a peer-group name, or all connections. To reset a neighbor connection and then reset all other connections, use the following command:

```
Router2>enable
Password:
Router2#clear ip bgp 192.168.1.2
Router2#clear ip bgp *
```

Troubleshooting BGP

To troubleshoot with BGP, you must gather information about the protocol and how it is functioning. As with other protocols, the two main sources of information are the show command and the debug command, so the place to start is by reviewing the show commands that you can use with BGP.

BGP show commands

show ip bgp displays information about your router, including its Router ID and the networks that are visible with their metric, weight, and route flag. This command shows you whether the routes are internal (on the inside of your network) or stale (not updated recently and possibly down).

Notice that the RouterID is the address that was associated with the loopback interface, as with the OSPF protocol (covered in the previous chapter). Also as with the OSPF protocol, BGP uses the highest IP address of its connected interfaces as its RouterID, which you can force by using a loopback interface. To review both the OSPF protocol and how to configure the loopback interface, review the OSPF configuration in Book IV, Chapter 8.

```
Router2>enable
Password:
Router2#show ip bgp
BGP table version is 2, local router ID is 192.168.255.254
Status codes: s suppressed, d damped, h history, * valid, > best, i - internal,
              r RIB-failure, S Stale
Origin codes: i - IGP, e - EGP, ? - incomplete

   Network          Next Hop            Metric LocPrf Weight Path
*> 192.168.6.0      192.168.1.2              0             0 100 i
```

The show ip bgp command has many options for viewing additional information. One of these options is neighbors. Although it will serve you well to review most of these options, I will give you an idea as to what information can be found by reviewing the neighbors option. The command reveals the following information:

✦ BGP version that is in use.

✦ Neighbors that are visible. Although the command can be run with a neighbor specified.

✦ BGP messages that have been seen.

✦ BGP connections to other routers.

✦ Event timer summary.

```
Router2>enable
Password:
Router2#show ip bgp neighbors
BGP neighbor is 192.168.1.2,  remote AS 100, external link
  BGP version 4, remote router ID 192.168.6.2
  BGP state = Established, up for 00:11:11
  Last read 00:00:11, hold time is 180, keepalive interval is 60 seconds
```

Book IV Chapter 9

Routing with BGP and IP Multicast

```
Neighbor capabilities:
  Route refresh: advertised and received(old & new)
  Address family IPv4 Unicast: advertised and received
Message statistics:
  InQ depth is 0
  OutQ depth is 0
                        Sent        Rcvd
  Opens:                 1           1
  Notifications:         0           0
  Updates:               0           1
  Keepalives:           14          14
  Route Refresh:         0           0
  Total:                15          16
Default minimum time between advertisement runs is 30 seconds

For address family: IPv4 Unicast
 BGP table version 2, neighbor version 2
 Index 1, Offset 0, Mask 0x2
 1 update-group member
                        Sent        Rcvd
                        ----        ----
 Prefix activity:
   Prefixes Current:     0           1 (Consumes 48 bytes)
   Prefixes Total:       0           1
   Implicit Withdraw:    0           0
   Explicit Withdraw:    0           0
   Used as bestpath:    n/a          1
   Used as multipath:   n/a          0

                      Outbound    Inbound
 Local Policy Denied Prefixes:  --------    -------
   Bestpath from this peer:      1          n/a
   Total:                        1           0
 Number of NLRIs in the update sent: max 0, min 0

 Connections established 1; dropped 0
 Last reset never
Connection state is ESTAB, I/O status: 1, unread input bytes: 0
Local host: 192.168.1.240, Local port: 11001
Foreign host: 192.168.1.2, Foreign port: 179

Enqueued packets for retransmit: 0, input: 0  mis-ordered: 0 (0 bytes)

Event Timers (current time is 0x75ECBF0):
Timer        Starts    Wakeups         Next
Retrans        15         0            0x0
TimeWait        0         0            0x0
AckHold        14         8            0x0
SendWnd         0         0            0x0
KeepAlive       0         0            0x0
GiveUp          0         0            0x0
PmtuAger        0         0            0x0
DeadWait        0         0            0x0

iss: 2844915809  snduna: 2844916121  sndnxt: 2844916121    sndwnd:  16073
irs: 1529136828  rcvnxt: 1529137192  rcvwnd:      16021  delrcvwnd:    363

SRTT: 259 ms, RTTO: 579 ms, RTV: 320 ms, KRTT: 0 ms
minRTT: 0 ms, maxRTT: 300 ms, ACK hold: 200 ms
Flags: active open, nagle
IP Precedence value : 6

Datagrams (max data segment is 1460 bytes):
Rcvd: 20 (out of order: 0), with data: 14, total data bytes: 363
Sent: 25 (retransmit: 0, fastretransmit: 0), with data: 15, total data bytes: 311
```

Other show ip bgp options include the following:

```
Router2>enable
Password:
Router2#show ip bgp ?
  A.B.C.D          IP prefix <network>/<length>, e.g., 35.0.0.0/8
  A.B.C.D          Network in the BGP routing table to display
  all              All address families
  cidr-only        Display only routes with non-natural netmasks
  community        Display routes matching the communities
  community-list   Display routes matching the community-list
  dampening        Display detailed information about dampening
  filter-list      Display routes conforming to the filter-list
  inconsistent-as  Display only routes with inconsistent origin ASs
  injected-paths   Display all injected paths
  ipv4             Address family
  ipv6             Address family
  labels           Display Labels for IPv4 NLRI specific information
  neighbors        Detailed information on TCP and BGP neighbor connections
  nsap             Address family
  paths            Path information
  peer-group       Display information on peer-groups
  prefix-list      Display routes matching the prefix-list
  quote-regexp     Display routes matching the AS path "regular expression"
  regexp           Display routes matching the AS path regular expression
  replication      Display replication status of update-group(s)
  rib-failure      Display bgp routes that failed to install in the routing
                   table (RIB)
  route-map        Display routes matching the route-map
  summary          Summary of BGP neighbor status
  template         Display peer-policy/peer-session templates
  update-group     Display information on update-groups
  vpnv4            Address family
  |                Output modifiers
  <cr>
```

BGP debug commands

The list of debug commands is quite a bit shorter than the list of show options. The list of commands includes the following:

```
Router2>enable
Password:
Router2#debug bgp ?
  all    All address families
  ipv4   Address family
  ipv6   Address family
  nsap   Address family
  vpnv4  Address family
```

The output of the debug command includes key items such as these:

◆ Messages that are sent by this router

◆ Messages received by this router

◆ Items found in the received packets

**Book IV
Chapter 9**

**Routing with BGP
and IP Multicast**

```
Router2>enable
Password:
Router2#debug bgp all
BGP debugging is on for all address families

*Mar 18 09:22:00.327: BGP: 192.168.1.2 open active, local address 192.168.1.240
*Mar 18 09:22:00.331: BGP: 192.168.1.2 went from Active to OpenSent
*Mar 18 09:22:00.331: BGP: 192.168.1.2 sending OPEN, version 4, my as: 200
*Mar 18 09:22:00.331: BGP: 192.168.1.2 send message type 1, length (incl. header)
    45
*Mar 18 09:22:00.335: BGP: 192.168.1.2 rcv message type 1, length (excl. header)
    26
*Mar 18 09:22:00.335: BGP: 192.168.1.2 rcv OPEN, version 4
*Mar 18 09:22:00.335: BGP: 192.168.1.2 rcv OPEN w/ OPTION parameter len: 16
*Mar 18 09:22:00.335: BGP: 192.168.1.2 rcvd OPEN w/ optional parameter type 2
    (Capability) len 6
*Mar 18 09:22:00.335: BGP: 192.168.1.2 OPEN has CAPABILITY code: 1, length 4
*Mar 18 09:22:00.335: BGP: 192.168.1.2 OPEN has MP_EXT CAP for afi/safi: 1/1
*Mar 18 09:22:00.335: BGP: 192.168.1.2 rcvd OPEN w/ optional parameter type 2
    (Capability) len 2
*Mar 18 09:22:00.335: BGP: 192.168.1.2 OPEN has CAPABILITY code: 128, length 0
*Mar 18 09:22:00.335: BGP: 192.168.1.2 OPEN has ROUTE-REFRESH capability(old) for
    all address-families
*Mar 18 09:22:00.339: BGP: 192.168.1.2 rcvd OPEN w/ optional parameter type 2
    (Capability) len 2
*Mar 18 09:22:00.339: BGP: 192.168.1.2 OPEN has CAPABILITY code: 2, length 0
*Mar 18 09:22:00.339: BGP: 192.168.1.2 OPEN has ROUTE-REFRESH capability(new) for
    all address-families
*Mar 18 09:22:00.339: BGP: 192.168.1.2 went from OpenSent to OpenConfirm
*Mar 18 09:22:00.339: BGP: 192.168.1.2 went from OpenConfirm to Established
*Mar 18 09:22:00.339: %BGP-5-ADJCHANGE: neighbor 192.168.1.2 Up
```

Routing IP Multicast Traffic

IP Multicast Routing is a huge topic because several technologies are at use in IP Multicast Routing, which means that space permits me to give only a cursory explanation of how this technology works. All networks function fine without multicast routing, but you may find some benefit to enabling it on your network.

IP Multicast Data is data that is sent out to a large group of computers but travels over the network as a single network frame. It is typically managed at the data link layer as a broadcast, though it needs to reach only a subset of all computers on the network. *IP Multicast Routing* is the routing of the multicast traffic.

Knowing when to use multicast routing

Some situations that will benefit from enabling multicast routing include networks or companies that want to make use of the following:

✦ Multicast imaging solutions for desktop OS deployment implemented across routers. These solutions often work if the solution is limited to a single network segment.

✦ Music on Hold and some other features of IP-based phone systems. Although you may be able to implement this as a unicast solution, multicast will greatly reduce network utilization.

✦ Multimedia steaming solutions that allow for multicast transmission.

✦ With routing protocols that send data to systems in an area or AS via multicast. Typically, these messages only need to go as far as the local data link, so no routing will be required.

Getting to know the protocols

In this section, you examine three of four main protocols that are supported by the current Cisco IOS. Figure 9-2 shows you approximately where the protocols are used; the following is a list of the protocols:

✦ **Internet Group Message Protocol (IGMP):** Used to track devices on LANs that are members of multicast groups (or addresses). This protocol is used between the device and the network router.

✦ **Protocol Independent Multicast (PIM):** Used to track which multicast addresses or packets need to be sent to devices on the attached network segments or to other routers that are directly attached via network segments.

✦ **Distance Vector Multicast Routing Protocol (DVMRP):** Used to communicate with Internet-based devices on the Multicast Backbone (MBONE). Cisco supports communication between PIM and DVMRP. This protocol is the only one you will not see in this chapter, because it is used only with links to your service provider. At this time, most service providers do not support multicast traffic over their networks.

✦ **Cisco Group Management Protocol (CGMP):** A proprietary Cisco protocol used to communicate with Cisco Catalyst switches in operations that are similar to IGMP.

In Book II, Chapter 1, you may have read that multicast traffic is classed as a Class D network, with high order bits that are 1110. This yields addresses from 224.0.0.0 to 239.255.255.255 and can be written in CIDR notation as 224.0.0.0/4. The first block of these addresses, from 224.0.0.0 to 224.0.0.255, is reserved for use by routing protocols, which are covered throughout Book IV.

**Book IV
Chapter 9**

**Routing with BGP
and IP Multicast**

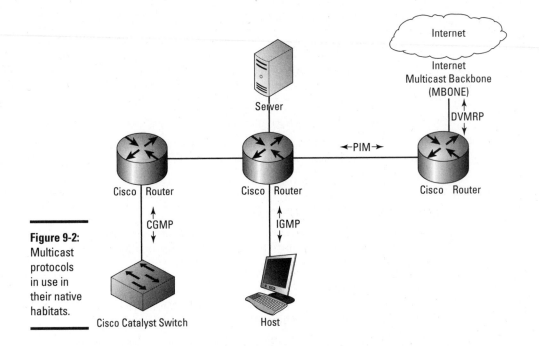

Figure 9-2:
Multicast
protocols
in use in
their native
habitats.

Working with IGMP

IGMP provides your routers with a method to join and leave multicast groups. Multicast groups and systems that have chosen to receive data being sent to a specific multicast address. Two types of devices, other than the originator of the multicast data, are on the network, as described in this list:

✦ **The Querier:** Sends out messages asking devices connected to its network segments which devices are members of specific multicast groups.

✦ **The Receiver:** Receives multicast traffic destined for a multicast address. This device may be a client device or a router, which then forwards the data on to other hosts and routers.

The querier may periodically send a request to find out what devices are in a specific group, because if all the client devices disappear, the router can stop forwarding data to some of the network segments.

IGMP packets are actually sent using multicast, where IGMP version 1 uses 224.0.0.1 as a general query address, and IGMP version 2 uses 224.0.0.2 as its general query address. IGMP group-specific queries are actually sent to the multicast group address that the router is currently querying.

IGMP has improved over the years:

✦ Version 1 was defined in RFC1112, and its main goal was to introduce a query-response system. This system would be used to specify which devices on a network segment were configured to receive data that was being sent to multicast groups.

✦ IGMP version 2 was defined in RFC2236 and greatly improved latency issues that existed in IGMP version 1. IGMP version 2 also implemented additional features, which include a leave process, group-specific queries, and an explicit maximum query response time.

✦ IGMP version 3 further extended the capabilities of the protocol by allowing source filtering, which means that the routers are actually informed as to which sources the traffic is expected from.

✦ IGMP version 4 offered further advancement to the protocol, but the biggest single enhancement to the protocol was the inclusion of IPv6 support.

Getting into PIM

PIM is a routing protocol like RIP or OSPF. It was designed to allow multicast routing without needing to rely on other specific unicast routing protocols. There are two main modes in which PIM will operate in two main modes: Dense mode and Sparse mode.

It is possible for a router to manage traffic for groups that are separately using either of these modes:

✦ When functioning in *Dense mode*, the router assumes that all other routers want to receive multicast data for a specific group. If a router receives these packets and does not need them because there are no clients that it is aware of, it sends a *prune message* (a message to remove a path) back to the originating router. In this Dense mode, the initial assumption of the protocol is that all routers want to get the messages or data, so more initial data is sent out over the network. This condition eventually creates a source-based multicast distribution tree. When running in Dense mode, the prune messages time out every three minutes, at which time group messages are flooded out of all interfaces again until new prune messages are received.

✦ *Sparse mode*, by contrast, involves the router assuming that no other routers want to get multicast traffic. In this case, the router closest to the host receives a multicast PIM join message from the receiver device. Directly connected routers send the PIM join message to upstream routers between themselves and the Rendezvous Point (RP), which is a router that is a designated meeting point. The RP's job is to keep track of all multicast groups in use on the network. The RP then sends join messages upstream toward the source host. In this case, the fewest possible routers are involved with seeing and handling multicast traffic, which makes them sparse or sparsely used. Figure 9-3 shows both these operational modes, which may give you an idea about how you might use them.

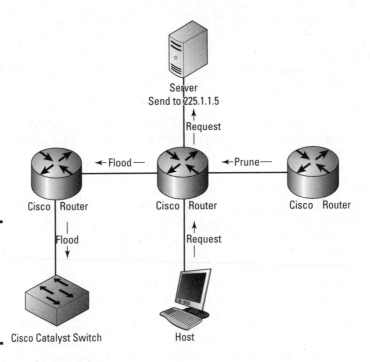

Figure 9-3:
How PIM could be implemented on your network.

Managing CGMP

CGMP is a Cisco implementation of an IGMP-like protocol designed specifically to interact with Cisco Catalyst switches in cases where the switch is not able to tell the difference between IP multicast data and IGMP report messages, as they are both sent to the same multicast group address when working at the MAC level. So CGMP is a helper protocol for the Catalyst switch.

Configuring multicast routing

Enabling basic multicast routing functionality on your network does not require a lot of work and can be implemented fairly quickly. Some configuration is done in Global Configuration mode and some configuration is done in Interface Configuration mode.

Enabling multicast routing

The first command that you perform in Global Configuration mode is the `ip multicast-routing` command, which enables multicast routing for the router. Enabling multicast routing initially does not route any data, due in fact that the default configuration leaves all router interfaces without multicast routing in their configuration.

To have multicast routing in a working configuration, you must enter each interface and configure the PIM on those interfaces. To enable PIM on an interface, you use the `ip pim` command, which accepts either a `dense-mode` or `sparse-mode` option. When you enable PIM on an interface, you automatically enable IGMP on those interfaces.

Supporting Sparse-Dense mode

Some groups may require Sparse mode or Dense mode in order to operate properly. Because you configure an interface for one mode or the other, you might find yourself in a catch-22 where you need both installed. To deal with this issue, Cisco supports all modes on its IOS routers, where the mode is applied to the multicast group on the router and not its interfaces. Because you may end up using Sparse mode for some groups, you require an RP to be configured. When using Sparse-Dense mode, you need to implement it throughout the network to avoid conflicts between Sparse mode and Dense mode interfaces. You implement the Sparse-Dense mode with the command `ip pim sparse-dense-mode`.

As just mentioned, an RP is a router on your network, so you need to assign this function to one or more routers on your network. Doing so does not require configuration on the RP router, but rather on the downstream router. The downstream router requires the address of an RP, which is accomplished by running the `ip pim rp-address` *rp-address* `[access-list]` `[override]` command using Global Configuration mode.

Sparse mode implementations require the RP to be specified, although Sparse-Dense mode it is an option as you can use Auto-RP.

Using Auto-RP rather than RPs

Rather than specifying specific RP routers, you can use Auto-RP to automate the selection and configuration of RP routers on your network. Auto-RP allows you to easily use multiple routers on your network because the RPs may be serving different groups or splitting the load over several routers. The routers could be based on the location of a multicast group's receivers and connectivity issues could be caused by inconsistent configuration across your network.

To configure Auto-RP mode, you need to make two configuration changes, one on the router you want to act as an RP and one on the router that will manage group mappings to RPs. The first command is issued in Global Configuration mode:

```
ip pim send-rp-announce type number scope ttl-value [group-list access-list]
    [interval seconds]
```

whereas the second command is

```
ip pim send-rp-discovery scope ttl-value
```

Testing connectivity

You can configure your router to be a member of a multicast group so that you can test connectivity. To add your router as a member, use the `ip igmp join-group group-address` command in Interface Configuration mode. By default, the router uses IGMP version 2, which maximizes functionality, because version 3 has some restrictions. To change versions, use Interface Configuration mode and enter this command: `ip igmp version {3 | 2 | 1`. All routers on the same network segment must use the same version of IGMP, but IGMP version 2 routers will work correctly if IGMP version 1 routers are on the network. So, given the network layout, `Router2` may have the following configuration commands to enable PIM routing — `Router1`'s setup commands then follow.

```
Router2>enable
Password:
Router2#configure terminal
Enter configuration commands, one per line.  End with CNTL/Z.
Router2(config)#ip multicast-routing
Router2(config)#ip pim rp-address 192.168.1.2
Router2(config)#interface FastEthernet 0/0
Router2(config-if)#ip address 192.168.1.240 255.255.255.0
Router2(config-if)#ip pim sparse-dense-mode
Router2(config-if)#exit
Router2(config)#ip pim send-rp-announce FastEthernet 0/0 scope 16 group-list 1
Router2(config)#access-list 1 permit 239.0.0.0 0.255.255.255
Router2(config)#exit
```

To set up Router 1, use these commands:

```
Router1>enable
Password:
Router1#configure terminal
Enter configuration commands, one per line.  End with CNTL/Z.
Router1(config)#ip multicast-routing
Router1(config)#ip pim rp-address 192.168.1.2
Router1(config)#interface FastEthernet 0/0
Router1(config-if)#ip address 192.168.1.2 255.255.255.0
Router1(config-if)#ip pim sparse-dense-mode
Router1(config-if)#exit
Router1(config)#ip pim send-rp-discovery scope 16
Router1(config)#exit
```

Troubleshooting multicast routing

Finally, from the "routing data book," you check out troubleshooting a routing protocol — in this case, the multicast routing protocol — so that you can effectively locate the source of issues that arise on your network. To start, you examine the options available through the `show` command and then move on to the options available through the `debug` command.

Getting information with show

When troubleshooting for information about the multicast routing protocol, first use the `show ip pim` command, which requires an additional option before providing information. The following shows the major options available, from interfaces to RPs to neighbors:

```
Router2>enable
Password:
Router2#show ip pim ?
  autorp     Global AutoRP information
  bsr-router Bootstrap router (v2)
  interface  PIM interface information
  mdt        Multicast tunnel information
  neighbor   PIM neighbor information
  rp         PIM Rendezvous Point (RP) information
  rp-hash    RP to be chosen based on group selected
  vrf        Select VPN Routing/Forwarding instance
```

Sparse mode PIM has several requirements for RPs on the network. So, if you are in Sparse mode, you want to take a close look at the several RP-based options. In addition, reviewing neighbors is always important, because if you do not see any neighbors, you probably have significant issues with the protocol implementation. Output about `neighbor` and `rp` look like the following; notice particularly the `version` and `rp` information:

```
Router2>enable
Password:
Router2#show ip pim neighbor
PIM Neighbor Table
Neighbor        Interface              Uptime/Expires    Ver  DR
Address                                                       Prio/Mode
192.168.1.2     FastEthernet0/0        00:02:16/00:01:26 v2   1 / S
Router2#show ip pim rp
Group: 224.1.0.1, RP: 192.168.1.2, v2, uptime 00:06:13, expires never
Group: 224.0.1.39, RP: 192.168.1.2, v2, uptime 00:05:58, expires never
Group: 224.0.1.40, RP: 192.168.1.2, v2, uptime 00:06:15, expires never
Group: 239.192.152.143, RP: 192.168.1.240, v2, v1, next RP-reachable in 00:00:31
Group: 239.255.255.250, RP: 192.168.1.240, v2, v1, next RP-reachable in 00:00:31
```

Also, much of the multicast routing involves requests from client devices via IGMP requests from the specific receiving devices that are connected to your network switches. To see that data, use one of the following commands:

```
Router2>enable
Password:
Router2#show ip igmp ?
  groups        IGMP group membership information
  interface     IGMP interface information
  membership    IGMP membership information for forwarding
  snooping      Snooping info on Catalyst Vlans
  ssm-mapping   Display IGMP SSM mapping info
  tracking      IGMP Explicit Tracking information
  udlr          IGMP undirectional link multicast routing information
  vrf           Select VPN Routing/Forwarding instance
```

Within the IGMP data are groups, interfaces, and membership, and although you may find that these options are the most important ones, I recommend testing all the options to see exactly what is going on.

In the following output, the groups option shows you the addresses for which the router is routing, as well as when the membership expires (because this is Sparse mode data), interface shows statistical information for the interface, and membership shows addresses or groups, who is subscribing to those addresses, and the interface on which they are working.

```
Router2>enable
Password:
Router2#show ip igmp groups
IGMP Connected Group Membership
Group Address    Interface         Uptime    Expires   Last Reporter
224.1.0.1        FastEthernet0/0   00:08:22  00:02:07  192.168.1.103
224.0.1.39       FastEthernet0/0   00:06:22  00:02:07  192.168.1.2
224.0.1.40       FastEthernet0/0   00:08:24  00:02:10  192.168.1.240
239.192.152.143  FastEthernet0/0   00:08:21  00:02:13  192.168.1.10
239.255.255.250  FastEthernet0/0   00:08:23  00:02:09  192.168.1.10
Router2#show ip igmp interface
FastEthernet0/0 is up, line protocol is up
  Internet address is 192.168.1.240/24
  IGMP is enabled on interface
  Current IGMP host version is 2
  Current IGMP router version is 2
  IGMP query interval is 60 seconds
  IGMP querier timeout is 120 seconds
  IGMP max query response time is 10 seconds
  Last member query count is 2
  Last member query response interval is 1000 ms
  Inbound IGMP access group is not set
  IGMP activity: 5 joins, 0 leaves
  Multicast routing is enabled on interface
  Multicast TTL threshold is 0
  Multicast designated router (DR) is 192.168.1.240 (this system)
  IGMP querying router is 192.168.1.2
  Multicast groups joined by this system (number of users):
      224.0.1.40(1)
Router2#show ip igmp membership
Flags: A  - aggregate, T - tracked
       L  - Local, S - static, V - virtual, R - Reported through v3
       I - v3lite, U - Urd, M - SSM (S,G) channel
       1,2,3 - The version of IGMP the group is in
```

```
Channel/Group-Flags:
    / - Filtering entry (Exclude mode (S,G), Include mode (*,G))
Reporter:
    <mac-or-ip-address> - last reporter if group is not explicitly tracked
    <n>/<m>        - <n> reporter in include mode, <m> reporter in exclude

Channel/Group            Reporter        Uptime   Exp.  Flags  Interface
*,224.1.0.1              192.168.1.103   00:09:40 02:52 1A     Fa0/0
*,224.0.1.39             192.168.1.2     00:07:41 02:53 2A     Fa0/0
*,224.0.1.40             192.168.1.103   00:09:42 02:54 1LA    Fa0/0
*,239.192.152.143        192.168.1.10    00:09:39 02:57 2A     Fa0/0
*,239.255.255.250        192.168.1.31    00:09:41 02:49 2A     Fa0/0
```

Debugging multicast routing

Debugging gives you detailed information about the PIM data that your router sees on the network. With PIM data, you can select the types of debug data you want to observe, or you can choose to see all of it by only using the command at debug ip pim.

```
Router2>enable
Password:
Router2#debug ip pim ?
  atm      PIM ATM signalling activity
  auto-rp  Auto-RP
  bsr      PIM Candidate-RP/BSR activity
  df       PIM RP designated forwarder election activity
  hello    PIM Hello packets
  tag      PIM multicast tagswitching activity
  vrf      Select VPN Routing/Forwarding instance
  <cr>
```

Here is a sample of the type of data you see with the debug command. In the output, notice the join messages, RP information, and protocol version.

```
Router2>enable
Password:
Router2#debug ip pim
PIM debugging is on
*Mar 26 08:42:40.040: PIM(0): Building Periodic Join/Prune message for 224.0.1.40
*Mar 26 08:42:40.040: PIM(0): Insert (*,224.0.1.40) join in nbr 192.168.1.2's
    queue
*Mar 26 08:42:40.040: PIM(0): Insert (192.168.1.2,224.0.1.40) sgr prune in nbr
    192.168.1.2's queue
*Mar 26 08:42:40.040: PIM(0): Building Join/Prune packet for nbr 192.168.1.2
*Mar 26 08:42:40.040: PIM(0): Adding v2 (192.168.1.2/32, 224.0.1.40), WC-bit,
    RPT-bit, S-bit Join
*Mar 26 08:42:40.040: PIM(0): Adding v2 (192.168.1.2/32, 224.0.1.40), RPT-bit,
    S-bit Prune
*Mar 26 08:42:40.040: PIM(0): Send v2 join/prune to 192.168.1.2 (FastEthernet0/0)
*Mar 26 08:42:45.292: PIM(0): Received RP-Reachable on FastEthernet0/0 from
    192.168.1.2
*Mar 26 08:42:45.292: PIM(0): Received RP-Reachable on FastEthernet0/0 from
    192.168.1.2
*Mar 26 08:42:45.296:         for group 224.0.1.40
*Mar 26 08:42:45.296: PIM(0): Update RP expiration timer (270 sec) for 224.0.1.40
```

```
*Mar 26 08:42:50.772: PIM(0): Send v2 Null Register to 192.168.1.2
*Mar 26 08:42:50.772: PIM(0): Received v2 Register-Stop on FastEthernet0/0 from
    192.168.1.2
*Mar 26 08:42:50.776: PIM(0):    for source 0.0.0.0, group 0.0.0.0
*Mar 26 08:42:50.972: PIM(0): Building Periodic Join/Prune message for
    239.192.152.143
*Mar 26 08:42:50.992: PIM(0): Received RP-Reachable on FastEthernet0/0 from
    192.168.1.2
*Mar 26 08:42:50.992: PIM(0): Received RP-Reachable on FastEthernet0/0 from
    192.168.1.2
*Mar 26 08:42:50.996:    for group 224.1.0.1
*Mar 26 08:42:53.776: PIM(0): Building Periodic Join/Prune message for
    239.255.255.250
*Mar 26 08:42:55.776: PIM(0): Send v2 Data-header Register to 192.168.1.2 for
    192.168.1.2, group 224.0.1.40
*Mar 26 08:42:55.780: PIM(0): Received v2 Register-Stop on FastEthernet0/0 from
    192.168.1.2
*Mar 26 08:42:55.780: PIM(0):    for source 192.168.1.2, group 224.0.1.40
*Mar 26 08:42:55.780: PIM(0): Clear register flag to 192.168.1.2 for
    (192.168.1.2/32, 224.0.1.40)
*Mar 26 08:42:59.492: PIM(0): Received RP-Reachable on FastEthernet0/0 from
    192.168.1.2
*Mar 26 08:42:59.492: PIM(0): Received RP-Reachable on FastEthernet0/0 from
    192.168.1.2
*Mar 26 08:42:59.496:    for group 224.0.1.39
*Mar 26 08:42:59.496: PIM(0): Update RP expiration timer (270 sec) for 224.0.1.39
Router2#u all
All possible debugging has been turned off
```

As with the PIM debugging, you can selectively enable IGMP for specific elements or for all IGMP debug data.

```
Router2>enable
Password:
Router2#debug ip igmp ?
  snooping  IGMP snooping activity
  vrf       Select VPN Routing/Forwarding instance
  <cr>
```

In the option for all debug information, notice that the type of information displayed includes protocol version, data requests received and from whom, and exclusion requests.

```
Router2>enable
Password:
Router2#debug ip igmp
IGMP debugging is on
*Mar 26 08:47:58.168: IGMP(0): Received v2 Query on FastEthernet0/0 from
    192.168.1.2
*Mar 26 08:47:58.168: IGMP(0): Set report delay time to 1.2 seconds for
    224.0.1.40 on FastEthernet0/0
*Mar 26 08:47:58.276: IGMP(0): Received v2 Report on FastEthernet0/0 from
    192.168.1.104 for 224.0.0.251
*Mar 26 08:47:58.276: IGMP(0): Report has illegal group address 224.0.0.251
*Mar 26 08:47:59.712: IGMP(0): Received v2 Report on FastEthernet0/0 from
    192.168.1.31 for 239.255.255.250
```

```
*Mar 26 08:47:59.712: IGMP(0): Received Group record for group 239.255.255.250,
    mode 2 from 192.168.1.31 for 0 sources
*Mar 26 08:47:59.712: IGMP(0): Updating EXCLUDE group timer for 239.255.255.250
*Mar 26 08:47:59.712: IGMP(0): MRT Add/Update FastEthernet0/0 for
    (*,239.255.255.250) by 0
*Mar 26 08:47:59.984: IGMP(0): Send v2 Report for 224.0.1.40 on FastEthernet0/0
*Mar 26 08:47:59.984: IGMP(0): Received v2 Report on FastEthernet0/0 from
    192.168.1.240 for 224.0.1.40
Router2#u all
All possible debugging has been turned off
```

Finally, for CGMP data, you only have the option to see all the `debug` information for the protocol.

```
Router2>enable
Password:
Router2#debug ip cgmp
```

Book V

Wireless

"Frankly, the idea of an entirely wireless future
scares me to death."

Contents at a Glance

Chapter 1: Getting Wise to Wireless LANs

In This Chapter

✔ **Checking out wireless technologies and standards**

✔ **Getting the skinny on frequencies and modulation techniques**

✔ **Comparing the different solutions on the 802.11 networking technologies**

Wireless technologies have been around for over a hundred years, with Nikola Tesla and Guglielmo Marconi making commercial use of wireless technologies from the beginning of the 20th century. With each major improvement in technology through the 20th century, there was an improvement in wireless communications. Just as people used early wireless to transmit traditional telegraph signals, people today use wireless to transmit traditional networking signals.

But mobile technology has gone way beyond the brick-like phones of the 1980s and has invaded all aspects of society. It would be rare for a networking specialist today to not have to work with wireless devices or wireless networking. This chapter reviews where this technology stands today and where it has come from and gives you a good overview of wireless technologies in general, as well as the specifics for wireless LAN technologies that you will likely encounter on the market. You look at the standards, basic types of wireless networking in use, the types of modulation used with WLANs, and the types of WLANs that are available for you in the 802.11 range.

As you progress through the rest of Book V, you see the basics of how to lay out your network (in Chapter 2), secure your network (in Chapter 3), and finish in Chapter 4 with an overview of the wireless solutions currently available from Cisco.

Understanding the Benefit of Wireless LANs

The main goal of wireless networking is to provide mobility to network users, regardless of where they and their network access devices may be. Within an office, this goal may be that moving users from one office to another should be easier, which with wired networking might require that you pay for the costly and manual job of running cables through the ceilings and walls. Outside of your office, wireless networks give you access to the Internet or even to corporate resources on an as-needed, where-needed basis.

A wide variety of networking devices exists in the world today, from smart-phones to netbooks to media players. People have developed a reliance on getting data directly from the Internet using high-speed connections. Because users have all sorts of wireless gadgets, they do not want to download and store information, but rather grab it from where it is and use it where they are. As a result, users have an ever-increasing desire to be able to access this information in more and more locations, wherever they may be.

Learning the Wireless Technologies

When wireless networks first emerged onto the market, the technologies were good only for limited distances. As the technologies have improved, so has the range of their usability. Four main classes of wireless networks exist based on range and geographical areas:

+ **Wireless personal-area network (WPAN):** The WPAN makes use of short-range wireless technologies, usually less than 10 meters, or 11 yards. These technologies include IrDA, Bluetooth, and ZigBee. Bluetooth has replaced IrDA as the main WPAN technology in use today, and ZigBee is an up-and-comer in that arena. Personal-area networks join devices such as cell-phones to computers to sync data and wireless earpieces to phones.

+ **Wireless local area network (WLAN):** WLANs make use of LAN technologies and cover a larger area than that of the WPAN. A WLAN typically provides network connectivity throughout an office, a building, or several buildings within a small geographical area, with all the networking components connected via LAN technologies. The technology used for a WLAN is short range and typically includes, but is not limited to, 802.11 networking components.

+ **Wireless metropolitan-area network (WMAN):** With another increase in the geographical area, you deal with the WMAN. The technologies used in a WMAN allow wireless connections over longer ranges than the WLAN, which are limited to several hundred meters or yards. The WMAN uses technologies such as WiMAX, which can cover several kilometers or miles. The distinction between the WLAN and WMAN is made primarily by the types of technology used.

✦ **Wireless wide-area network (WWAN):** The largest area covered is the WWAN, which uses public carriers rather than private equipment. The public carriers may make use of WiMAX but most often make use of other cellular network technologies (such as GPRS, HSDPA, and 3G) to communicate. When using a device on a WWAN, the user can connect to his office network via a secured connection or connect two offices within the area of the cellular network provider.

Following the Standards

When you move into a new neighborhood, sometimes you have good neighbors who respect your property boundaries, while other times, your neighbors encroach on your property and are a general nuisance; the same is true when your property is your wireless network. When working with wireless networks, your neighbors may interfere with your network by generating traffic on the same frequencies you are using, or by using devices that encroach on the frequencies that you are using. This issue is especially true when using unlicensed radio frequency (RF) bands, but it is easier to deal with when using the limited licensed radio bands. All commercial wireless networking solutions operate in the unlicensed RF bands, and the RF bands where wireless networks operate are full of noisy neighbors.

Licensed radio bands

When a national regulatory body (such as the FCC in the United States) allocates a frequency range to be used for a function, it can also specify how the frequency range can be used or shared.

What you do not need to know about RF bands

Radio frequencies (RF) are composed of a gradually changing wave oscillating at a rate that goes from 3 kHz (Kilohertz) up to 300 GHz (Gigahertz). Based on use, this full spectrum is broken up into smaller sections referred to as bands. One set of RF bands that you are likely familiar with is the FM (frequency modulation) band. This is where you listen to classical, rock, or pop music. The FM radio band operates at the frequencies between 87.5 to 108.0 MHz, with my favorite being 96.5 KOOL FM.

To use licensed radio bands, a license must be obtained from a government agency. This requirement is true of all users of these radio spectrums. A few of the uses of licensed radio bands are as follows:

✦ **AM broadcast** (short wave between 1.711 MHz–30.0 MHz, medium wave between 520 kHz–1,610 kHz, and long wave between 148.5 kHz–283.5 kHz)

✦ **FM broadcast** (87.5 to 108.0 MHz)

✦ **Cellular phones** (840 MHz)

In the larger electromagnetic spectrum, which includes the radio spectrum, the licensing of infrared and X-ray spectrums also exists.

Unlicensed radio bands

When hearing the term *unlicensed,* you may think there are no laws or that unlicensed radio bands are like the Wild West and people can do as they like. However, that is not completely the case: You must follow several regulations that cover the use of the unlicensed radio bands. The big differ-ence between licensed and unlicensed bands is that the licensed bands are allowed to be used only by the company that licensed them, whereas the unlicensed bands are used by anyone who wants to use them.

Unlicensed radio bands have been allocated to certain users by the govern-ment, but to be able to use and broadcast on these bands, you do not need to have a license; you only need to create compliant devices that are to be used. Regulations exist around these bands, so using unlicensed radio bands is not a free-for-all. In the United States, the FCC regulates all the electromag-netic spectrum, but it has set aside several ranges for public use.

Some of the types of unlicensed radio bands are as follows:

✦ **Industrial, Scientific, Medical (ISM):** This type includes several medical monitors and other devices that operate in the 900-MHZ, 2.4-GHz, and 5-GHz bands.

✦ **Unlicensed National Information Infrastructure (U-NII):** This type defines the specifications for the use of wireless devices such as WLAN access points and routers in the 5-GHz band.

✦ **Unlicensed Personal Communications Services (UPCS):** This type defines the specifications for devices operating in the 1.9-GHz band, where DECT6 cordless phones operate.

Wireless phone companies, such as Sprint and Rogers, have specific frequencies that only they are allowed to use by leasing them from the government. IEEE 802.11 networks have several choices of wireless bands that are available to them to use, without the requirement to lease the frequencies from the government.

The downside of the unlicensed frequencies or bands is that anyone else can use the same frequency ranges, which can cause interference for the signals you are trying to transmit.

So users of both licensed and unlicensed bands are required to follow a series of government regulations, but the unlicensed bands may be used by anyone who follows the guidelines and regulations. These guidelines cover issues like encroaching on neighboring frequencies and causing interference; so if everyone follows these rules, they will all be good neighbors, which is not always the case.

Some groups have helped to develop standards so that all users can be good neighbors with others who use those radio bands. These groups and standards bodies include the following:

+ **FCC (Federal Communications Commission):** Manages and sets standards with regard to the spectrum use

+ **IEEE (Institute of Electrical and Electronics Engineers):** A leading standards organization which publishes standards that are adopted across industries

+ **Wi-Fi Alliance:** An organization that attempts to create a single standard for WLANs, thereby ensuring interoperability

+ **ETSI (European Telecommunications Standards Institute):** Another standards organization that has contributed many worldwide standards

+ **ITU-R (International Telecommunication Union, Radiocommunication Sector):** With the FCC, defines how WLANs should operate from a regulatory perspective, such as operating frequencies, antenna gain, and transmission power

+ **WLANA (WLAN Association):** Provides information resources related to WLANs with regard to industry trends and usage. They are now defunct.

Sending Data Over the Airwaves

There is more than one way to skin a cat (not that I endorse cat skinning), and the same is true about sending data over the airwaves. As you read through this section, you discover the most common methods in use to send data over the air.

When sending data over radio frequencies (RF), remember these details:

✦ A lot of other traffic is out there, as well as natural phenomena such as atmospheric disturbances and electrical storms (you have to love a good lightening storm) that can cause interference with these signals. Either data sent on the same frequencies or blocked signals can interfere with your wireless communications.

✦ You need to modify a standard signal to transmit data. There are many standard methods to perform this task. (I show two common methods in the upcoming subsection "Modulating signals.")

✦ RF bands are only so wide and can therefore only handle so many *discrete sessions* or channels at a time. The entire FM radio spectrum has been broken up into 100kHz channels used to assign frequencies to radio stations. This means that there are only so many possible FM channels available for use.

It is not necessary that you understand all the details of signal processing to successfully manage your network, but you should know a few things about signals and their characteristics.

Understanding signals

When referring to a *signal* in relation to wireless communications, I am talking about an electromagnetic field with specific characteristics, being its oscillation frequency. If I were working with a different medium, the signal could be comprised of light (an optical signal), sound (an airwave signal), or electricity (an electrical signal).

When working with computer data, copper wires are used to send electrical signals; fiber-optic cables can send optical signals. If you want to send wireless signals, you use light waves for line-of-sight technologies (such as IrDA) or RF for non-line-of-sight technologies (such as Bluetooth).

When you listen to a radio station in your local area, this radio station broadcasts its content over a radio-wave signal that operates at a base waveform or wave of a specific set of dimensions consisting of an amplitude, period, and phase. This wave can be modified through one of the modulation techniques (discussed just a bit later in this chapter) to change its form, and thereby transmit information.

All signal waves have the same common characteristics, as shown in Figure 1-1. These are as follows:

+ **Amplitude:** The height of the wave
+ **Period:** The length of the wave to repeat one cycle
+ **Phase:** The offset of the wave from zero or how far a wave is through its cycle

You can measure the amplitude of the wave in many ways: From either peak (peak-to-peak) or from the center of the wave to the peak (peak or semi-amplitude). The *frequency* of the wave is the number of times it repeats over a given timeframe. There is a good chance you know more about frequencies than you give yourself credit for, because you likely tune your car stereo (or your stereo auto-tunes them for you) to your favorite frequencies on a daily basis to change channels. Those channels are just different spots on that frequency.

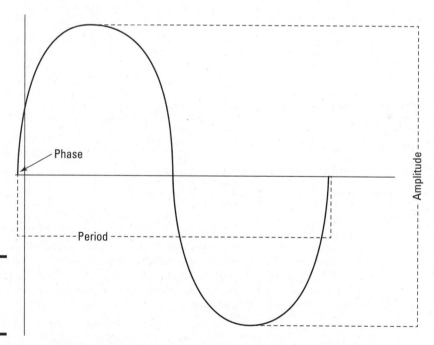

Figure 1-1:
Wave
character-
istics.

Modulating signals

You can now identify a waveform (refer to Figure 1-1) at a frequency. Modulation allows you to add data to that waveform by changing its basic form. The changes that you can make include the amplitude, the frequency, and the phase. In all cases, what you do to the wave prior to transmitting it (modulating) can then be undone by the receiver (demodulating) if the receiver knows what type of modification you are performing. When dealing with computers, which are composed of circuits that are either open or closed, you deal with only two states. As long as you can create two distinct states in the waveform, you can identify them as open or closed, on or off, or 0 or 1. Creating two distinct states then allows you to transmit binary data over RF. Figure 1-2 shows two basic types of modification of the initial carrier wave, which could be used to show binary number patterns.

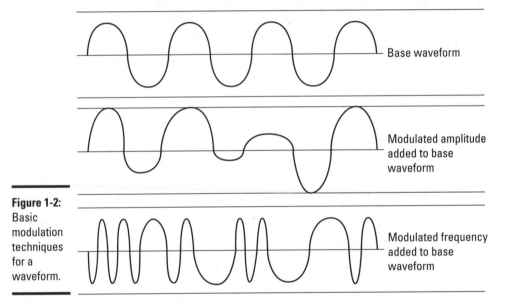

Base waveform

Modulated amplitude added to base waveform

Figure 1-2:
Basic
modulation
techniques
for a
waveform.

Modulated frequency added to base waveform

The two signal modulation techniques that you have likely heard the most about are amplitude modulation (AM) and frequency modulation (FM). The base waveform to which data will be added is referred to as the *carrier signal*. In the case of broadcasting a radio show, the added information is voices or music, whereas in the case of computer data, it is a series of 1s and 0s that represent binary data.

Introducing RF modulation techniques

In preparation for managing your wireless networks, you should know something about the different RF modulation techniques that are implemented in IEEE 802.11 networking.

You do not have to know everything about them; just be familiar with the terminology that is used in the following sections because it may be helpful when you are trying to find the source of interference or figure out how your network is being affected by interference.

Frequency-hopping spread spectrum (FHSS)

The FHSS modulation technique uses the available channels to transmit and receive data, but rather than staying on any one channel, it rapidly switches between channels using a pseudorandom pattern that is based on an initial key; this key is shared between the participants of the communication session. If interference affects only a few of the channels, this interference is minimized because each channel is used only briefly. If the interference is broad, it can still affect all the channels that are in use. This modulation technique requires that the initial seed or key be shared, but after that has happened, it is very difficult to eavesdrop on.

IEEE 802.11 wireless networks use this technique for modulation, while Bluetooth uses an adaptive version of this technique that stops using channels where interference or weak signals exist.

Direct-sequence spread spectrum (DSSS)

Rather than rapidly switching between several channels, DSSS spreads the carrier signal across the entire 22-MHz frequency range of its channel. For example, a device sending over channel 1 would spread the carrier signal across the 2.401- to 2.423-GHz frequencies (the full 22-MHz range of channel 1). At the same time it is transmitting the data over this channel, it also, at a faster rate, generates a noise signal in a pseudorandom pattern. This noise signal is known to the receiver, which can reverse or subtract the noise signal from the data signal. This process allows the carrier signal to be spread over the entire spectrum. With the entire spectrum being used, the effect of narrow-spectrum interference is reduced. Also, if the channel is being used by other devices, the effect of their signal is reduced because they are not using the same pseudorandom noise pattern.

DSSS has an advantage over FHSS in that it has better resistance to interference. It is used primarily by IEEE 802.11b networks and cordless phones operating in the 900-MHz, 2.4-GHz, and 5-GHz spectrums. IEEE 802.11g/n networks also sometimes use DSSS, but these newer networks tend to prefer orthogonal frequency division multiplexing (ODFM).

Orthogonal frequency division multiplexing (OFDM)

The slower that data is transmitted, the less likely that interference or line noise will cause a problem with the transmission. Multiplexing allows you to take several pieces of data and combine them into a single unit that can then be sent over the communication channel. In this case, OFDM takes the data that needs to be transmitted and breaks it into a large number of subcarrier streams (up to 52 subcarriers) that can then all be multiplexed into a single data stream. Because 52 subcarriers exist, the final data stream can be sent at a slower rate, while still delivering more data than other methods in the same time period.

This multiplexing process gives OFDM an advantage over DSSS because it allows higher throughput (54 Mbps instead of 11 Mbps), and it can be used both in the 2.4-GHz frequency range and in the 5-GHz frequency range. Multiplexing has many uses, and OFDM is used in any technology that needs to send large amounts of data over slower transmission lines or standards. OFDM is used with IEEE 802.11g/a/n networking as well as with ASDL and digital radio.

Multiple-in, multiple-out (MIMO)

MIMO allows multiple antennas to be used when sending and receiving data. The concept of spatial multiplexing allows these multiple signals to be multiplexed or aggregated, thereby increasing the throughput of data. To improve the reliability of the data stream, MIMO is usually combined with OFDM. When using multiple antennas, you can achieve higher transmission speeds — over 100 Mbps.

MIMO is used in both WiMAX and IEEE 802.11n networks and is the largest reason these networks achieve their high speeds.

Battle of the Bands

Early in WLAN development, many people were trying different technologies to achieve the goal of wireless LAN communication. As some clear winners started to emerge, a need existed for interoperation among these technologies. This desire for interoperation led to the development of standards around WLAN communications.

As with all other standards in communications, the WLAN standards allow all companies involved to build equipment to a level that allows their equipment to be used with (or to interoperate with) equipment made by other vendors. Interoperability was not necessarily true in the beginning, but by the time IEEE 802.11a and IEEE 802.11b emerged, the standards were set and all hardware vendors were able to build to a level that allowed interoperability.

Checkin' Out the 2.4-GHz band

Many of the wireless standards that have emerged were designed to operate in the already crowded 2.4-GHz band. Whether this was a good idea does not matter; it is what happened.

When working with the 2.4-GHz portion of the RF spectrum, the actual range that you are working with is 2.4000–2.4835 GHz. This range is broken up into 14 unique channels, with each one 22 MHz wide, but the center of each of these channels is only 5 MHz apart. Therefore an overlap exists between consecutive channels, which results in interference and prevents proper communication. In the United States, the FCC has allowed only 11 of these channels to be used, while countries like Japan have allowed all 13 channels to be used. Why? You would have to write to the FCC to find out.

Due to the overlapping of channels, if you are using multiple devices in a small geographical area where the devices' RF might come in contact with each other, you can choose from a maximum of four nonoverlapping channels — 1, 6, 11, and 14. Figure 1-3 shows how each of the 14 channels defined in the range overlap, while only channels 1–11 are used in the United States and many other countries, reducing those countries to only three nonoverlapping channels.

The 2.4-GHz RF band is used by IEEE 802.11 b/g/n networking, as well as Bluetooth and many cordless phones. This situation has caused issues because, in any given area, you can expect something to generate signal traffic in that frequency range. Poorly designed devices can bleed beyond their specified RF ranges and create additional interference for other devices. The 2.4-GHZ RF band is heavily congested with both properly and improperly designed devices.

The following sections take a closer look at the standards in this category.

IEEE 802.11

As with the early days of any technologies, a number of players in the industry were looking at different methods of transferring LAN data without wires from early on. As things moved along, a few groups emerged at the top of the pile. These groups used technologies that were not compatible with each other, and the most popular of these was collectively called 802.11-1997 or sometimes 802.11 Legacy. It is odd that this mash of wireless was associated under one name, because they were not compatible with each other. The common factors of this standard were the communication rates and base technology components that are common to all IEEE 802.11 networks.

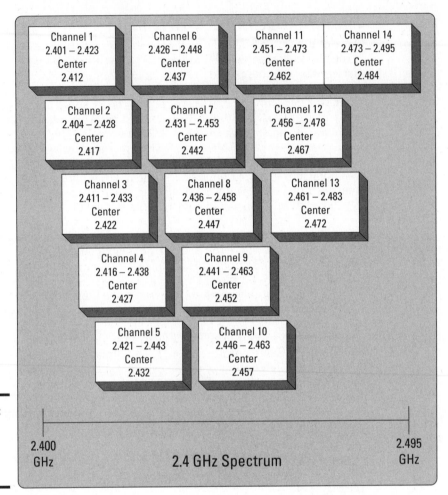

Figure 1-3:
IEEE
802.11b/g
channel
overlap.

Relevant jargon

Terminology that arose from this specification applies to all IEEE 802.11 networks. This terminology includes the following:

✦ **Access point (AP):** A device that allows wireless devices to access the physical network.

✦ **Basic Service Set (BSS):** A collection of a single AP and its associated client devices or stations (STA) form a BSS.

✦ **Distribution System (DS):** The interconnection of AP through wired media or wirelessly. When used wirelessly, this is called a Wireless Distribution System (WDS).

✦ **Extended Service Set (ESS):** One or more BSSs that are interconnected and appear as a single BSS.

✦ **Service set identifier (SSID):** An identifier for a BSS or ESS.

✦ **Distributed Coordination Function, which is carrier sense multiple access collision avoidance (CSMA/CA):** A method of sharing a single wireless channel by more than one STA.

✦ **Dynamic rate shifting (DRS):** Adjusts the transmission rate of a wireless channel based on the channel condition. The channel condition would be based on how strong or clear the wireless signal is.

✦ **Beacon frames:** A wireless management frame periodically sent over the wireless network.

✦ **Wired Equivalent Privacy (WEP):** Security and encryption standard for wireless networks.

✦ **Ad hoc networking:** A wireless network that does not have an AP.

✦ **Infrastructure networking:** A wireless network that has an AP.

These terms are fully described in the later chapters of this minibook, but I want to make you aware that they date back to the first IEEE 802.11 wireless networks.

How IEEE 802.11 works

While there is an alphabet soup of acronyms associated with 802.11 wireless networking, I want to start off by telling you about some of the specifications which define 802.11 networks. The specifications for IEEE 802.11 define three possible physical layer systems that could be used:

✦ Frequency-hopping spread spectrum (FHSS) in the 2.4-GHz band

✦ Direct sequence spread spectrum (DSSS) in the 2.4-GHz band

✦ InfraRed (which is in the specification but was not adopted by the industry)

In addition to defining the physical layer protocols, the specification defines the communication speed as 1or 2 Mbps.

The main benefit of IEEE 802.11 was that it offered RF wireless networks with greater range and throughput than other wireless technologies at the time, which were primarily infrared-based and thereby line-of-sight. Because this networking was based in the crowded 2.4-GHz spectrum, a great deal of interference existed, which was only partly minimized by FHSS and DSSS.

All the IEEE 802.11 networking standards use *carrier sense multiple access collision avoidance* (CSMA/CA). This collision mechanism is different from the Ethernet LAN standard, which uses *carrier sense multiple access collision detect* (CSMA/CD). In both cases, *carrier sense* means that all devices can sense or see other traffic that is transmitting, and *multiple access* means that multiple (or all) devices can access the media at the same time, but only one computer is allowed to send data at a time. (You can read more about both CSMA/CA and CSMA/CD in Book I, Chapter 4.)

Differences between LAN and WLAN technologies

The media over which data is sent is dramatically different between a wired LAN and a wireless LAN. Due to this difference in media, there is a difference between how the two types of LANs interact with the media. With wired LAN technologies, when a computer wants to send a frame out on the network, it does the following:

1. It uses its carrier sense to see whether anyone is using the network.

2. If not, it then sends a network frame out onto the wire and the signal goes to the end of the wire, where it bounces and returns to the sending computer. The maximum length of an Ethernet cable is set to require the bounce signal to return within a specified time limit.

3. When the computer sees what it sent, the computer knows that it was sent without a collision. But if what the computer sees is garbled, it knows that a collision occurred, and it then waits a random period of time and repeats the process.

This system of collision detection works because the physical media allows the sending computer to verify that its data was correctly sent on the media.

When working with WLAN technologies, here is what happens:

1. The frame is sent on the network, which has no mechanism to allow a signal to bounce, and as such, it relies on *collision avoidance*.

2. The method of sending data still starts with listening to the network to see whether anyone is using the media.

3. If no frames are detected for a specified period of time (known as the *distributed interframe space [DIFS]*), it is allowed to send its frame.

4. The receiving station performs the CRC (cyclic redundancy check) of the received packet and sends back an ACK (acknowledgment) frame when the media is free.

5. After the sending station receives its ACK frame, it knows that the data was sent correctly.

This collision-avoidance process generates more network frames to send data, but it follows a more orderly process than collision detection.

When the network is under high utilization, the collision detection process tends to move more data than collision avoidance; this is likely due to mandatory wait states that occur by devices honoring the DIFS.

Dynamic rate shifting (DRS) allows an AP to rate-shift to a lower bandwidth when the signal weakens. The signal becomes weaker proportionally to the distance between the AP and the target wireless device. In other words, the farther you go from the AP, the weaker the wireless signal becomes and the lower the transmission speed becomes because DRS automatically rate-shifts to a lower speed when the signal weakens.

IEEE 802.11b

In the 2.4-GHz spectrum, the first major upgrade to the WLAN specification is IEEE 802.11b, which raised the maximum bandwidth to 11 Mbps. This standard also relied primarily on Complementary Code Keying (CCK) as its modulation technique, which was a modified form of DSSS, while it would use DSSS when using slower connection speeds via DRS. The typical range for IEEE 802.11b is about 100 feet (30 meters) when operating at 11 Mbps.

The benefit of this standard over its predecessor is primarily in the maximum network speed, while IEEE 802.11b still suffered from interference on a crowded RF spectrum. The other drawback that the IEEE 802.11b standard suffered from was a slower transmission speed than the other standard at the time (IEEE 802.11a, which had a rated bandwidth of 54 Mbps). Even though IEEE 802.11a had higher throughput, IEEE 802.11b emerged as the dominant standard due to timing and market forces.

IEEE 802.11g

The next major improvement in WLAN networking in the 2.4-GHz band is IEEE 802.11g, which increases the maximum bandwidth to 54 Mbps and primarily makes use of the RF modulation technique of orthogonal frequency division multiplexing (OFDM) in addition to CCK and DSSS when speeds are reduced.

IEEE 802.11g offered an easy upgrade path for users of IEEE 802.11b as older devices were able to connect to newer radios, although this upgrade caused the radio to automatically fall back to the slower technology for all users. This issue was mitigated by many hardware vendors by including multiple radios in their APs, allowing one to be set to IEEE 802.11g only and one to be set to IEEE 802.11b. When using IEEE 802.11g transmission standards, a modified collision avoidance system is used, thereby reducing the delays and the wait states required for transmission.

Keep on Rockin' with the 5-GHz band

When working with the 5-GHz portion of the RF spectrum, you are primarily working with the range of 5.170–5.835 GHz. This range is broken up into 24 unique channels, with each one being 20 MHz wide and the center of each channel is at least 20 MHz apart. 5-GHz allows 24 unique conversations or communications to take place in that frequency range in the same physical area. If you are using IEEE 802.11a wireless networking, in a single room, you could operate 24 access points without interference between devices (not that you would likely want to do that).

In terms of wireless networking standards on the band, at the same time that IEEE 802.11b was being implemented in the 2.4-GHz RF band, IEEE 802.11a was being implemented in the 5-GHz band. IEEE 802.11a offered several advantages over IEEE 802.11b. It had a maximum transmission rate of 54 Mbps and operated in the less cluttered 5-GHz RF band. It uses OFDM as its RF modulation technique. Due to time to market and many other issues, this superior wireless technology took a backseat to IEEE 802.11b, which was vying for market position at the same time. (This situation seems to have been similar to the Beta-versus-VHS war that keeps repeating with new technology participants.)

The biggest drawback is that IEEE 802.11a is not compatible with devices that run in the 2.4-GHz spectrum, primarily IEEE 802.11b/g devices. The biggest benefits of the 5-GHz portion of the spectrum are the nonoverlapping channels and the lack of competition for channel space, as in addition to IEEE 802.11a/n networking, this RF band is primarily used only by cordless phones. Additionally, cordless phones in the 5-GHz spectrum honor the same non-overlapping channel designations as IEEE 802.11a, which causes less interference with the WLAN.

Most countries use 20-MHz wide channels but often authorize different frequencies to be used for the channels that could go as low as 4.905 GHz. For simplicity, I limit my discussion to the authorized channels in the United States.

For an IEEE 802.11a wireless network, the list of channels has been reduced by the FCC to 12, which are only channels 36, 40, 44, 48, 52, 56, 60, 64, 149, 153, 157, 161, and 165. Now following the standard gets more confusing when dealing with IEEE 802.11n, because the specifications for the standard allow the use of either 20-MHz channels or 40-MHz channels; the increase to 40-MHz channels allows for double the amount of data that can be sent over any one channel.

Technologies that support the 2.4-GHz and 5-GHz bands

The latest technologies for WLAN allow you to operate in both of the major RF frequencies. Being able to choose either frequency when operating the WLAN provides you with the best of both worlds and will likely be the trend moving forward. Right now the only relevant specification is IEEE 802.11n. In early versions of the draft specifications, this standard was only to use the 2.4-GHz RF spectrum. However, the final specification, ratified in September 2009, allowed operating in the 5-GHz RF spectrum as well. By allowing both of the previous RF spectrums to be used, it allows IEEE 802.11n devices to be backward compatible with both IEEE 802.11b/g and IEEE 802.11a devices and maximizes its possible acceptance in a network setting.

IEEE 802.11n uses both OFDM and MIMO RF modulation techniques. Although ranges are comparable with the IEEE 802.11 network specifications, it allows a maximum throughput of 600 Mbps when using four MIMO streams, or 150 Mbps for a single stream.

IEEE 802.11n offers many advantages over the previous IEEE 802.11 network specifications because it operates in both major RF bands, is backward compatible with other standards, and operates at higher data speeds.

Because it has only recently been ratified, many of the existing devices on the market conform to draft specifications, but you can expect that if you have any of these, a firmware-based upgrade to the final standard should be released soon.

Chapter 2: Planning Your WLAN

In This Chapter

✔ **Identifying the basic parameters to configure a wireless network**

✔ **Identifying common issues with implementing wireless networks**

✔ **Identifying and describing the purpose of the components in a small wireless network**

*W*hen working with wireless LANs, you need to know their operating modes as well as how to lay out access points (APs) to allow maximum coverage while reducing internal conflicts.

In this chapter, I show you how to set up your clients in either Ad Hoc or Infrastructure modes and the benefits of each mode, elements that make up a wireless network, and what configuration parameters you need to be aware of; you see the actual configuration in upcoming chapters. Finally, I show you how to design and lay out your access points on your network to provide ideal RF coverage. With this information, you will be well on your way to deploying a wireless network.

Setting Your Operation Mode

When you are working with a traditional wired network, you connect your computer to a network switch to interconnect all devices on your network; or you use crossover network cables to directly connect two computers. In the case of wireless networking, you still have two choices: You can connect two devices directly, or you can connect your devices using a central device, namely a wireless access point. These two methods are:

✦ **Ad Hoc mode** for when the devices connect without the aid of an AP. *Ad hoc* is Latin meaning "for this," and generally means "for this specific situation." The term ad hoc is regularly used to describe committees, organizations, or repairs that are thrown together quickly and for one single purpose. In the case of the wireless LAN, it is put together temporarily and without the aid of an AP. When the members of the ad hoc wireless LAN leave the area, the wireless LAN disappears.

✦ **Infrastructure mode** for when you use an AP to manage the connection of clients either between each other or with the wired LAN.

Ad Hoc mode

Back when floppy disks were the main method of transferring data between computers, I often encountered groups of users who took over a boardroom for a period of time to work on a project that required a good deal of sharing of documents with only a single printer for the room. Typically, the users did not need resources such as the Internet, because it was not nearly as pervasive then. Shuttling data back and forth on floppies was tedious and difficult (especially when the files exceeded the size of the disk). When the users came to my office and asked me for a better solution than those #@!#@ floppy disks, I would have one which only required a bit of extra work. As a provider of networking services for my users (unless I was one of those in that boardroom), I tossed them some cables and a hub (at the time) and said "Go to it!" because that equipment was enough at the time to put together a rag-tag network on a boardroom conference table. Wires were everywhere with one computer using the parallel port printer and all users sharing a folder from which they worked. This solution was not ideal, but it made the job of printing, sharing, and transferring files much easier and allowed them to complete their project in a shorter time period than if they used floppy disks.

Now fast-forward to today, and the floppies are now USB thumb drives, that boardroom hub is replaced with Ad Hoc mode wireless networks, and those guys do not even have to come in to see me.

Understanding Ad Hoc mode networking

When working with networking in Ad Hoc mode, you are connecting to another device that has the same wireless settings as the settings on your device. The benefit of ad hoc networking is that you do not need to preconfigure your network infrastructure to support a temporary group of users, while the users (or rather their devices) are able to share information among themselves. A sample ad hoc wireless network is shown in Figure 2-1, and it required very little configuration. The ad hoc wireless LAN is created by two or more computers that have configured their wireless LAN settings to be the same. This matching of wireless LAN settings allows the computer to form a direct network connection when they are close enough for the wireless signals to communicate.

In addition to device-to-device connections, you can also use ad hoc networking in *wireless mesh devices,* in which all devices (APs) connect to the *mesh* (that being a few devices that are clustered near each other, similar to the ad hoc network illustrated in Figure 2-1), and data will pass from AP to AP through the mesh until it reaches its final destination. The advantage of using this type of technology is that all APs can be provided with rudimentary routing information that allows the AP not only to handle routing changes as needed, but also to determine the best way to pass packets, or to be able to pass packets due to a hardware failure in one of the APs. After a hardware failure, all other APs update their paths for data so that they do not attempt to send data through the failed AP.

Figure 2-1:
A sample
wireless
ad hoc
network.

When dealing with Ad Hoc mode WLAN technology, focus on device-to-device connections. The wireless mesh combines ad hoc networking with an additional layer of software to support the mesh communication process.

Configuring an Ad Hoc mode WLAN

In most cases, when discussing Ad Hoc mode wireless networking, you are dealing with device-to-device connections. These connections are easy enough to set up in Windows with processes described in the following sections.

Configuring an Ad Hoc mode WLAN with Windows 7

If you have a Windows 7 computer (or a Windows Vista computer, which is very similar), you will use a process similar to the following to create and activate your ad hoc network.

1. **Click Start and choose Control Panel.**

This opens the Control Panel window.

2. **Select View Network Status and Tasks.**

This opens the Network and Sharing Center window.

3. **From the Network and Sharing Center window, select Set Up a New Connection or Network.**

The Set Up a Connection or Network dialog box appears.

4. **From the Set Up a Connection or Network dialog box, choose Set Up a Wireless Ad Hoc (Computer-to-Computer) Network and click Next; click Next again.**

The Set Up an Ad Hoc Network dialog box appears, as shown in Figure 2-2.

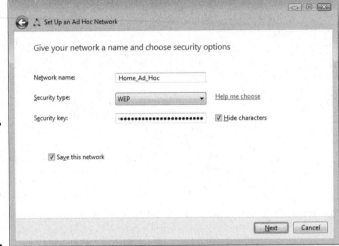

Figure 2-2:
Setting up
the ad hoc
network
configur-
ation in
Windows 7.

5. **In the Set Up an Ad Hoc Network dialog box, provide the following information:**

   a. *Add a network name for your wireless network.*

   b. *Indicate the security type as either WEP or No Authentication.*

   c. *If you chose WEP, provide the security key for the network and optionally select the Hide Characters box.*

   d. *Select Save This Network to keep this network for longer than one session.*

6. **Click Next to continue.**

   The confirmation dialog is displayed, showing you the information that you need to provide to other people who will want to connect to your ad hoc network.

7. **Click Close.**

   After the connection is set up, it initially becomes active and remains so until you connect to another network. If you did not choose to save the connection, it will be removed from your wireless configuration at that time and you will need to repeat this process to reactivate an ad hoc network connection.

Configuring an Ad Hoc mode WLAN with Windows XP

In Windows XP, follow these steps to configure an Ad Hoc mode WLAN:

1. **Click Start and choose Control Panel from the Start menu.**

   The Control Panel window opens.

2. **From the Control Panel window choose Network and Internet Connections.**

The Network and Internet Connections settings are displayed.

3. **From the Network and Internet Connections window, choose Network Connections.**

The Network Connection dialog box appears.

4. **Locate your wireless network card in the dialog box's list, right-click on it, and then click the Properties.**

The Properties dialog for that network card will be displayed.

5. **Click the Wireless Networks tab in the Wireless Network Connection Properties dialog box (shown in Figure 2-3) and click the Add button.**

The Wireless Network Properties dialog box opens.

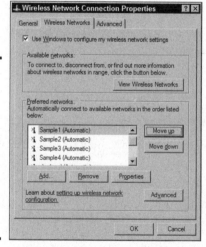

Figure 2-3: Wireless settings for each network connection are found in the network connection's Properties dialog box.

6. **Type a name for your new ad hoc network into the Network Name (SSID) text box or type the name of an existing network.**

7. **Select the This Is a Computer-to-Computer (Ad Hoc) Network check box at the bottom of the dialog box.**

8. **Use the Network Authentication and Data Encryption drop-down lists to select the settings that you would like to use.**

9. **If the WEP key is not provided for you automatically, deselect the The Key Is Provided for Me Automatically check box and type the WEP key into the Network Key and Confirm Network Key text boxes.**

A completed dialog box with these settings is shown in Figure 2-4.

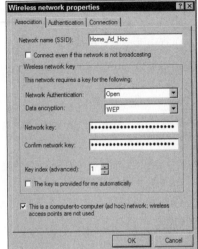

Figure 2-4:
Only a few
pieces of
information
are required
to set up
an ad hoc
network.

10. **Click the OK button to save your changes and close the Wireless Network Properties dialog box.**

11. **Click the OK button to close the Wireless Network Connection Properties dialog box.**

12. **If this is the first device that you have set up for this network, repeat the steps for your second device.**

The second computer sees the network show up in its list of available wireless networks.

By default, the TCP/IP settings for each network card will be set to use Automatic Private IP Addressing (APIPA), so because you will not have a DHCP server on your ad hoc network, both of your devices will choose a random address in the 169.254.0.0/16 network. This situation should be fine because you can then connect to the devices by either their computer name or IP address.

Activating your ad hoc network in Windows XP

If you have successfully created your ad hoc wireless network connection, then you are halfway on your journey to using the connection. The next step is to tell your computer that you want to use that new ad hoc wireless LAN. You tell your computer that you want to use the ad hoc network by following the appropriate steps for your operating system.

This process is only documented for Windows XP because Windows Vista and Windows 7 do not save these ad hoc connections. To activate a connection, you need to perform the setup again because when the connection becomes inactive, Windows 7 deletes the connection.

To active your new ad hoc network, you need to let Windows XP know that you want to use it. It is set up as an on-demand wireless connection. To do this, follow these steps:

1. **Click Start and choose Control Panel from the Start menu.**

   The Control Panel window opens on the screen.

2. **From the Control Panel window, choose Network and Internet Connections.**

   The Network and Internet Connections settings are displayed.

3. **From the Network and Internet Connections window, choose Network Connections.**

   The Network Connection window appears.

4. **Locate your wireless network card in the dialog box's list, right-click on it, and then click the Properties.**

   The Properties dialog box for that network card appears.

5. **Select the Wireless Networks tab.**

6. **Click the View Wireless Networks button.**

   The Choose a Wireless Network dialog box appears, as shown in Figure 2-5.

7. **Select your new ad hoc network connection and click the Connect button.**

   The connection changes to Automatic so that it can then automatically connect when within range.

This network now shows up in the list of available networks for the nearby users, who will see the network when examining the setting for infrastructure networks. (See the later section, "Connecting to a wireless network.")

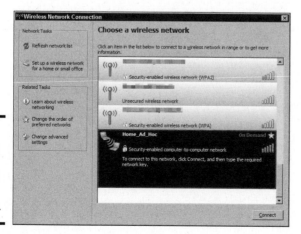

Figure 2-5:
Connecting
to an
on-demand
wireless
connection.

Taking your ad hoc configuration with you

You can make setting up your ad hoc networking easier for use by you and others by copying the configuration to a USB flash drive using the following process:

1. **Click Start and choose Control Panel.**

   The Control Panel window appears.

2. **From the Control Panel window, select View Network Status and Tasks.**

   This opens the Network and Sharing Center.

3. **Choose Manage Wireless Networks from the left menu.**

   The Manage Wireless Networks dialog box appears.

4. **Right-click your ad hoc network connection and choose Properties.**

   The wireless connections' Properties dialog box opens.

5. **Click the Copy This Network Profile to a USB Flash Drive link.**

   The Copy Network Settings dialog box appears, as shown in Figure 2-6.

6. **Insert a flash drive and click Next.**

   The configuration files for that wireless connection are copied to the USB flash drive, and the completion page is displayed, letting you know what to do next, as shown in Figure 2-7.

7. **Click Close.**

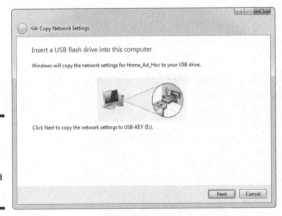

Figure 2-6:
Copying
your
settings to a
USB drive.

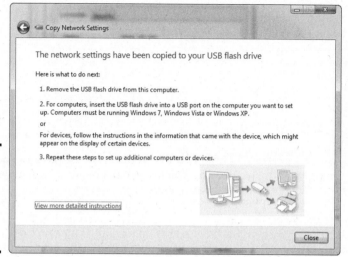

Figure 2-7:
Using your
settings
drive to set
up other
computers.

To make use of this USB drive, simply take to any computer running
Windows XP, Windows Vista, or Windows 7, and plug the USB drive into any
available USB connection. Autorun on the USB drive will take care of the rest
and set up your ad hoc network connection. You can repeat this process on
as many computers as you like.

You may be curious as to what is on this drive that allows for this magical
setup. The drive now contains these files (in addition to whatever you had
on the drive before):

✦ `Autorun.inf`

✦ `SetupSNK.exe`

✦ Smrtntky folder containing supporting files

The `Wsettings.txt` file in the Smrtntky folder contains your wireless
settings in an encrypted format. Here are the settings for my Home_Ad_Hoc
network:

```
Wireless Network Settings

Print this document and store it in a safe place for future reference.  You may
    need these settings to add additional computers and devices to your network.
Wireless Settings
```

```
Network Name (SSID): Home_Ad_Hoc
Network Key (WEP/WPA Key): 12345678901234567890123456
Key Provided Automatically (802.1x): 0
Network Authentication Type: open
Data Encryption Type: WEP
Connection Type: IBSS
Key Index:

To enable File and Printer Sharing on this computer, run the Network Setup Wizard.

To set up your Internet connection, follow the instructions from your Internet
    Service Provider (ISP).
```

These ad hoc networks are good to use when you are in a location where you have no infrastructure to which you can connect. Lack of infrastructure can be a problem in boardrooms or meeting spaces that have not been set up to support computers (either wired or wireless), or any other place where you need to connect a few computers. If someone has a small switch and cables, you can use those to set up a small, temporary network, but lacking a wire ad hoc solution, wireless ad hoc is the next best thing.

If you are using Windows to set up your ad hoc networking and you have a computer with a second network card that has an Internet connection, you can use Internet Connection Sharing to allow all the other computers on the ad hoc network to use your Internet connection.

Beware of the ad hoc networks that you do not know the source of. When making connections in public locations with public wireless access, such as airports and coffee houses, you should check these broadcasted networks prior to connecting to them. In Windows XP, any connection that is ad hoc, is shown as two computers rather than the wireless antenna (these two symbols can be seen in Figure 2-5), is likely not legitimate, and a person monitoring that network's traffic could attempt to gather information from your computer or from sites you are connecting to. In Windows 7, ad hoc networks look like three connected computers rather than a signal strength bar, both of which are shown in the upcoming Figure 2-10.

If you connect to a wireless network in Ad Hoc mode that also allows you to connect to the Internet, or any unknown network, you could be subject to a man in the middle attack using network-auditing software such as Cain and Able from Oxid.it. All your passwords could be exposed, including those for secured HTTPS Web sites. (The types of attacks your network may susceptible to are covered in Book VI, Chapter 1.)

Infrastructure mode

As opposed to Ad Hoc mode networks, which make wireless connections directly between computers, Infrastructure mode wireless networks use networking infrastructure. In this case, *infrastructure* refers to switches, routers, firewalls, and access points (APs). Infrastructure mode wireless networking is the mode that you most often encounter in your work as a networking professional supporting networks for clients or in a corporate environment.

At a minimum, the only network infrastructure component that is required for Infrastructure mode is an access point, but if an AP is all you have, you have no more than you would have had when using Ad Hoc mode. However, most Infrastructure mode implementations include other components from your traditional network infrastructure, as shown in Figure 2-8.

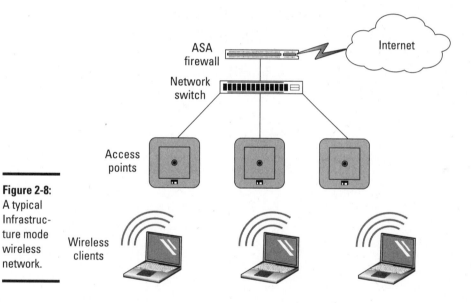

Figure 2-8:
A typical Infrastructure mode wireless network.

Connecting to a wireless network in Windows 7

If you are using Windows 7 (or Windows Vista, which is very similar), the process you use to connect to a wireless network is as follows:

1. **Click Start and choose Control Panel.**

   The Control Panel window appears.

2. **From the Control Panel window, select View Network Status and Tasks.**

   This opens the Network and Sharing Center window.

3. **From the Network and Sharing Center window, select Set Up a New Connection or Network.**

   The Set Up a Connection or Network dialog box appears.

4. **From the Set Up a New Connection or Network dialog box, select Connect to the Internet.**

   The Connect to the Internet dialog box appears.

5. **From the Connect to the Internet dialog box, select Wireless.**

   Your available Wireless Networks Connections window appears, as shown in Figure 2-9.

   You can also open this by clicking the wireless networks icon in your system tray.

Figure 2-9:
Viewing
nearby
wireless
networks
with
Windows 7.

6. **Right-click the wireless network to which you want to connect and then choose Connect.**

   Alternatively, click the wireless network, select the Connect Automatically check box for quick connecting in the future, and then click the Connect button.

The Connection dialog appears. If the network has no security, you get connected; but if the network is configured for security, then you are asked for credentials based on those security settings. In my case in Figure 2-10, I am asked for the network's WEP key.

7. **Provide the required information and click OK.**

When you are connected, you can tell by a lack of other icons associated with the Wireless Networks icon in your system tray.

Figure 2-10: Providing security credentials may be part of making the wireless connection.

After you set up the connection, it will initially become active and will automatically connect to this network whenever it is in range. If you did not choose to save the connection, it will be removed from your wireless configuration when the network is out of range.

Connecting to a wireless network in Windows XP

To connect to a wireless network that is broadcasting its SSID using Windows XP, follow these steps:

1. **Click Start and choose Control Panel.**

The Control Panel window opens.

2. **From the Control Panel window, choose Network and Internet Connections.**

The Network and Internet Connections settings appear.

3. **From the Network and Internet Connections window, choose Network Connections.**

The Network Connection window appears.

4. **Locate your wireless network card, right-click it, and choose View Wireless Networks.**

The Choose a Wireless Network dialog box appears, as shown in Figure 2-11.

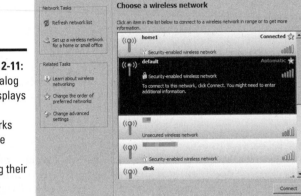

Figure 2-11:
This dialog box displays all the networks that are broadcasting their SSIDs.

5. **Select a wireless network from the list and click the Connect button.**

   If the network uses WEP or WPA (which are security features you will see in Chapter 3 of this minibook), you are prompted to enter the network key; then click the OK button. Otherwise, your connection is complete and you will be connected to the wireless network.

Enterprise infrastructure access point types

When working with APs in Cisco's enterprise infrastructure, you will encounter two modes of access points: Autonomous mode and Lightweight mode. If you use hardware from other vendors, their names may be different, but the function and operation will be similar.

Autonomous mode

When 802.11 networking began, all APs were Autonomous mode, which means that each AP worked as a standalone unit with no knowledge of or interaction among other APs. Autonomous mode was fine in the beginning when wireless networking was often limited to providing network access in common areas or boardrooms, and continuous roaming was not a requirement. Wireless networks tend to grow, and that means a typical network might deploy from one to ten access points across the network environment, and an environment of that size is still easily managed with Autonomous mode APs. Figure 2-8 shows an example of an Autonomous mode wireless network, where although these APs are connected to the same network, and may use the same SSID, they are all individually configured and separate from one another.

In most small networks, wireless still starts out as an idea to make life a little easier in conference rooms and boardrooms, so these networks tend to start with just one AP in those locations. If you are deploying only one AP on your network, then in all cases you will choose to deploy an Autonomous mode AP.

Unfortunately, after that first AP is deployed and users become used to the flexibility and functionality it offers, you will undoubtedly receive a request for another one.

If you are planning to deploy four or more APs on a new network, you should give thought to Lightweight mode APs because you will be close to the breakeven point in cost between purchasing autonomous APs, and going forward beyond that, you will have an easier infrastructure to manage using Lightweight mode APs.

Lightweight mode

Rather than using Autonomous mode APs, you can use Lightweight mode APs if you have a network component that offers Wireless LAN Controller services. Cisco offers the Lightweight mode option on most of its APs, so you can purchase them with either a controller-based IOS software image (using Lightweight Access Point Protocol, or LWAPP) or a standalone IOS software image (see Book I, Chapter 5 for general information about the IOS). A sample of how the controller and APs fits together in your network is shown in Figure 2-12. Some Wireless LAN Controllers have Power over Ethernet (POE) ports that allow you to connect APs to; you can also connect the AP to any other POE switch on your network. It does not matter where the AP is on your network, it will still get all of its management information from the Wireless LAN Controller.

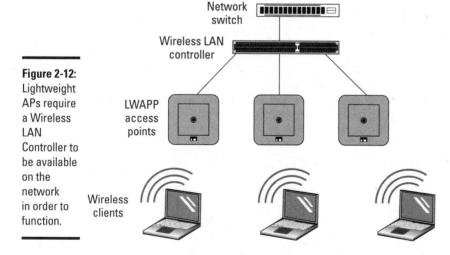

Figure 2-12: Lightweight APs require a Wireless LAN Controller to be available on the network in order to function.

To have Wireless LAN Controller (WLC) services on your network (which is the management device that manages your LWAPP devices), you can use any of the following:

+ Cisco 2100 series controller

+ Cisco 4400 series controller

+ Catalyst 6500 series Wireless Services Module (WiSM)

+ Cisco 7600 series Router Wireless Services Module (WiSM)

+ Cisco 28/37/38xx series Integrated Services Router with Controller Network Module

+ Catalyst 3750G Integrated Wireless LAN Controller Switch

In this scenario, the access points all have their configuration managed by the WLC. You can set a single policy on that WLC, and that configuration setting can be deployed to all managed access points, reducing the workload of managing hundreds of lightweight access points (when using the Cisco 7600 series Router Wireless Services Module). Also, in this configuration, some of the processing work that would normally be done at the AP can be offloaded to the WLC, leaving more CPU cycles available on the AP.

As mentioned earlier, if you are deploying four or more APs, you should get a quote on a solution that includes lightweight APs and a WLC because the price will likely be similar to the solution with autonomous APs. If you already have Autonomous mode APs, you can convert them to lightweight to blend them into your new managed network, or you can deploy them elsewhere in your organization where lightweight APs will not fit the requirements. Places that cannot use LWAPPs are locations that do not have direct and permanent network connectivity to the WLC, such as isolated segments of your network that have only periodic connections to where the WLC resides. Many of my clients run networks on ships or ocean platforms where there they would require autonomous APs.

Grouping Your Clients with SSID

After you get your hardware identified, mounted, and powered up, how do you get your clients to connect to and manage them? The following sections help you wrap your head around a few more concepts, which deal with grouping your wireless clients into manageable groups.

SSID basics

A *service set* refers to all the wireless devices that participate in a specific wireless LAN. This wireless LAN may be a local WLAN or an enterprise WLAN, spanning several buildings or areas. Each service set is identified by a *service set identifier* or SSID. The SSID should directly relate to the network that the WLAN or AP will connect the wireless device to:

✦ If you have multiple networks within an enterprise environment, multiple SSIDs can exist.

✦ If you only have one network, you should only have one SSID.

Figure 2-13 shows multiple access points hosting connections to multiple networks. This setup means that in a single area you will likely have multiple APs using the same SSID.

Figure 2-13:
Each SSID should identify a different or unique physical network that is allowing connections.

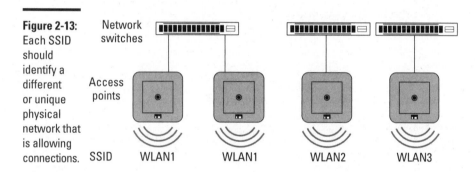

The SSID can be up to 32 characters long. It is usually made up of human-readable ASCII characters, but it could contain any of the possible 256 values in those 32 digits. When users connect to the WLAN identified by the SSID, they can make the connection automatically or manually, depending on how they have configured their network settings on their computers.

Using multiple SSIDs with a single AP

The SSID defines what is thought of as the wireless network, so my SSID is `Eds` and my neighbor is `Bobs`, so people can connect to my wireless network or `Bobs` wireless network. You would expect that my wireless network is not connected to the same wired network as `Bobs` wireless network is. So you think of those two SSIDs being associated with different physical networks.

In addition to multiple access points broadcasting or using the same SSID, a single access point can also use multiple SSIDs. Granted, using multiple SSIDs makes sense only if the AP allows you to map each one to a different network connection. This mapping would typically be accomplished through the use of VLAN tagging, as shown in Figure 2-14. If the user's device associates with a particular SSID, this traffic is then passed to the network switch destined for a specific VLAN. This switch allows each network to have a different set of security standards surrounding it. For example, you may have a wireless network, CorpSSID, which uses certificate-based authentication via WPA2 and AES encryption while using the same APs to provide a second wireless network, GuestSSID, which uses only WEP. Even though you are providing two wireless networks, you can isolate guest traffic from the rest of the corporate network and allow the guest devices to use only some services, such as allowing them through the firewall to get out to the Internet on ports 80 and 443.

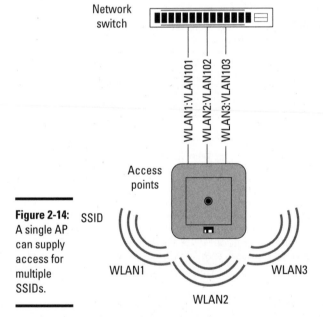

Figure 2-14: A single AP can supply access for multiple SSIDs.

Basic service set (BSS)

In simple terms, the BSS is one AP and its collection of clients. The AP is identified by a *basic service set identifier* (BSSID), which is a unique identifier for an AP and is usually a 48-bit MAC address of the AP. The MAC address allows each AP to be uniquely identified, even though they all may be providing service for the same SSID. The BSSID is used on beacon frame (a periodic broadcast on the wireless network announcing services and the SSID) as a means of identifying each AP.

Extended service set (ESS)

Extended service set (ESS) extends the BSS to more than one AP that shares the same logical link control layer. Effectively, if these APs share the same physical connection to the network or exist on the same physical segment, they can act as one unit with multiple radios, thereby increasing the possible throughput available on that AP. All the BSS units that make up the ESS would share the same SSID and would work on the same or different channels.

The benefit of the ESS is that it allows client roaming without interruption to network traffic or reconfiguration of the client.

Planning Around Interference

You have many factors to consider when planning a wireless network, from external sources of broad-spectrum interference to the characteristics of building materials to channel selection and range. Proper placement of your APs can make your network the talk of the company. Improper placement can make you the talk of the company in not-such-a-great way, with a lot of grumbling, cursing, gnashing of teeth, and with people calling you constantly to ask why they spent so much money on a product that does not seem to be working. (I try to avoid making people unhappy with IT purchasing decisions, preferring to have successful rollouts of new technologies with my users being happy.)

RF signal factors

Many factors influence radio frequency (RF) signals. You may get signal loss from building materials that usually comes from three main sources, which are based on the types of materials used. These three sources are as follows and are illustrated in Figure 2-15:

✦ **Absorption** occurs when RF waves are absorbed by the materials that they are attempting to pass through. Absorption typically occurs when the waves pass through walls or dense materials. Water and concrete have high RF absorption properties. If you need coverage in stairwells, remember that they are mostly concrete tubes with a bunch of diagonal concrete dividers.

✦ **Reflection** occurs when RF waves cannot penetrate a surface and are returned or bounced off the surface. Reflection is common with metal and glass surfaces. Reflection is the principle behind a *Faraday cage,* where the holes on the cage surface are smaller than the wavelength of the radiation or signal that they are attempting to block, thereby blocking the signal that is striking its surface. So even a thin layer of metal containing no holes can effectively block wireless signals from passing through it.

✦ **Scattering** occurs when the reflective surface is uneven, which causes many random bounces. A reflective signal may still have enough of its original properties to be used, but a scattered signal does not. In some cases where you cannot get a direct signal through to your location, you may be able to get a strong enough signal from a bounced RF wave, but only if that wave gets bounced off of a smooth surface; if the surface is uneven then the bounced signal will be useless.

The more issues you have with your signal between the client and the AP, the higher the noise level of the signal. Other sources of noise include other devices that operate in the same wireless band as your AP and devices that might cause broad-spectrum interference. Some level of noise always exists, but if the level is too high, the signal-to-noise ratio will be too low to sustain a proper connection.

Conducting a site survey

Just as a highway engineer will conduct a geographical survey of a location before planning and building a road, an IT professional should conduct a wireless survey before installing a wireless network. Factors such as absorptions, reflection, and scattering can cause degradation in the quality of a wireless signal. When conducting a site survey, you goal is to measure the quality of the signal as well as identify potential sources of interference. A site survey allows you to do the following:

◆ Identify other wireless networks in the area that might conflict with your network as well as other sources of interference.

◆ Place a temporary AP and measure the signal strength from different areas.

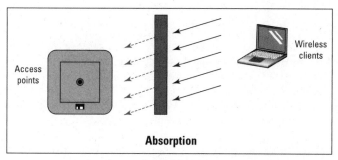

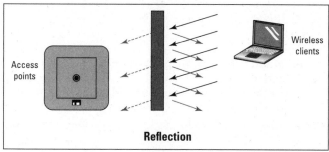

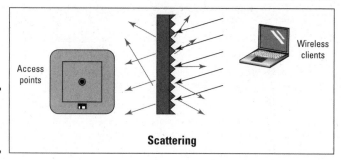

Figure 2-15:
Signal inter-
ference.

When planning your AP locations, remember to

+ Plan deployments in multiple floor buildings because signals will span floors. Remember that you are working in three dimensions.

+ Ensure that all areas where roaming is expected will be connected to a common Layer 2 data link.

Many methods of conducting a site survey and many tools are available for you to use. In most cases, people use 802.11 network devices and measure signal strength with some piece of software; but more expensive tools are available to measure signals across the RF spectrum, thereby showing you interference that may exist which is outside the 802.11 wireless network ranges. Because these tools are more expensive, most people who offer to do a site survey do not use this technology.

Because a site survey requires some networking hardware and software, I have several tools in my arsenal. Some of the software does a nice job of collecting data into a report, or I may have to take the collected data and make my own report.

You can use tools such as Network Stumbler (www.netstumbler.com) or MetaGeek's inSSIDer (www.metageek.net) for free to collect statistics or pay for a tool from a company such as AirMagnet (www.airmagnet.com). Figure 2-16 shows the interfaces for Network Stumbler. The AirMagnet toolsets are very nice and will make creating a polished report very easy.

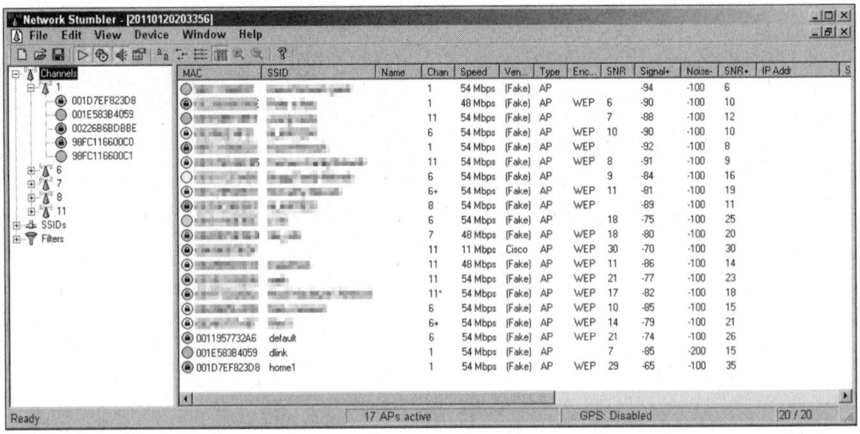

Figure 2-16: Network Stumbler has both text based and graphical interfaces.

Cisco recommends that, even after I conduct a site survey with these tools, I should then follow up with some pure performance testing using different devices, because I can get a wide range of performance differences based on the antenna gain and application limitations when switching between devices.

You can conduct the site survey using two methods:

✦ **Survey surround signals:** This method includes temporary APs that have been set up for your testing purpose. You place these test APs (often when testing you will have just one AP that you move around) close to your expected production locations. Then you test that signal from different locations to get a real-world rating for signal strength from various locations and to identify construction in areas that unexpectedly impact performance.

✦ **Performance testing:** This method is similar to the first method, but in addition to checking signal strength and sources of interference, you also do some performance testing. The closer to real world this test can be, the better. To perform this testing, you require another device connected to the AP, such as a laptop, running software. At a minimum, the device will be a Windows computer with a shared folder, with which you will copy files to and from (while documenting the transfer times). These times will be compared with results from other locations, providing you with not only signal strength, but also real-world performance.

I once deployed a wireless network for a hotel that was going to be using the wireless network for its 802.11 wireless phones, as well as its corporate and guest network access. These phones needed to work over the entire property, so I had to test signal strength in locations all sorts of areas, including walk-in freezers, stairwells, clock towers, and the parking garage. In many of these areas, I had no previous experience to draw on and had to perform a full suite of testing. Also, the situations for some of the areas were variable (for instance, the garage could be empty or full of reflective metal and glass cars and SUVs), complicating matters further. If you have done your homework, you should be able to get your initial placement of APs mostly correct, but you can expect to have to make some tweaks or moves based on unexpected situations that will arise.

Working with Multiple APs

A small wireless network composed of one AP connected to wired infra-structure makes it fairly easy to manage your wireless RF spectrum — you need to worry only about placement, channel selection, and the location of surrounding APs from your neighbors. This process gets somewhat more complicated when you are deploying multiple APs throughout a multi-story building, because in addition to your neighbors APs you need to worry about location, channel selection, and interference from your old APs with each other.

Selecting channels

I said in Chapter 1 of this minibook that you have only three channels to work with in North America when dealing with 2.4 GHz networking. Some people have suggested that you can get away setting up your channels in a four-channel manner by using channels 1, 4, 8, and 11. This setup would give you overlap in the shoulder area of the bands, but the overlap would be fairly small.

Cisco has done lab testing of the concept using four APs and four clients all transferring 50MB files to and from a server. Even with this limited overlap, data ends up being lost, and stations or computers wait their mandatory wait periods and retransmit data. These problems slow down the overall throughput. Table 2-1 shows the final results. So if you are told that you can use four channels when making your channel selections, this is not advisable and you should stick to the reliable and time tested three channel configuration.

Table 2-1	Comparing Three- and Four-Channel Systems
Channels	*Throughput (KB)*
1, 6, and 11	601.1
1, 4, 8, and 11	348.9

AP layout

I have already said that the simplest wireless network contains only one AP and that the issues that you need to deal with for one AP are generally place-ment and signal loss. Figure 2-17 shows a centrally located AP in an office with a few obstructions that may cause signal loss in the unshaded areas. In addition to the obstructions and construction material, there may be various sources of external interference that can reduce the size of the coverage area.

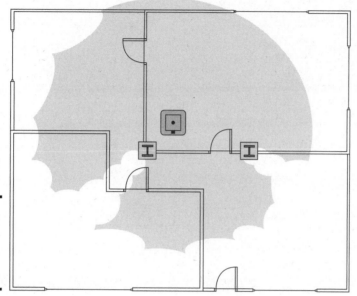

Figure 2-17:
Signal loss
in a single
AP WLAN
deployment.

Ignoring signal loss from building materials, if you have three APs in your layout and no outside interference, you should use all three of the non-overlapping channels (1, 6, and 11). The only exception to this would be if you had a more linear layout, where the APs at either end of the line were isolated by the middle AP. A typical pattern may give you a layout that resembles what is shown in Figure 2-18. Cisco recommends a 10–15 percent overlap between APs to allow complete coverage in the interim area, 15–20 percent for VOIP solutions.

This deployment would be more complex if you had to provide coverage using four APs. In that case, you would have to reuse at least one of the non-overlapping channels to complete the deployment. You can do that by isolating the AP with the reused channel from the other AP (which is using the same channel) by having stronger signals from the intermediary APs separate them. Staggering these AP channels allows you to provide coverage on all your network APs. An example of this is shown in Figure 2-19, where the two APs on channel 6 are separated by the combined signals from the APs on channels 1 and 11.

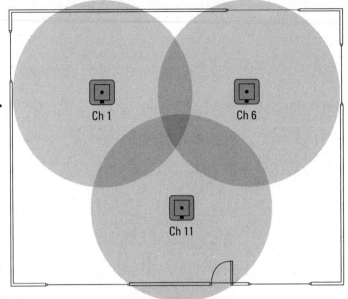

Figure 2-18:
Three APs
on your
wireless
network
usually
require
that all
three non-
overlapping
channels be
used.

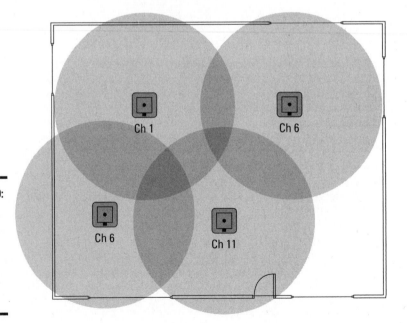

Figure 2-19:
Isolating
reused
channels
placing
other AP
signals in
between.

If the area gets even more crowded, in an attempt to provide better coverage or to support higher client density, you may need to take additional steps. In Figure 2-20, notice that

✦ An AP on channel 6 separates the two channel 1 APs, allowing that channel to be reused.

✦ All three channel 6 APs are primarily separated by the channel 11 AP.

✦ In addition to the physical placement, the power levels on the channel 6 APs have been reduced to provide a lower radius of coverage, thus preventing these APs from touching each other.

Having been involved in some large wireless rollouts, I can tell you that channel selection gets even more complicated when you have to do this type of RF management across a three-story building. In that case, you have to keep your channels separated not only per floor but also between floors.

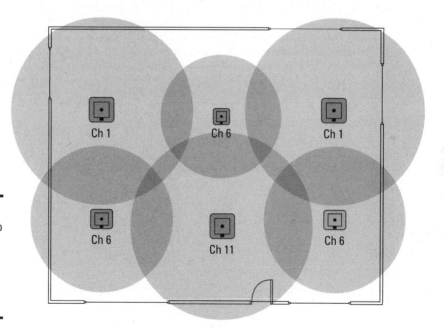

Figure 2-20:
Tuning radio strength or power can also isolate duplicate channels.

Automatic tuning

Some APs on the market support automatic tuning of channel numbers and signal strength, where the APs on the network identify each other and adjust their radio channels and signal strength to provide optimal coverage, even with APs from other organizations in close proximity. In challenging environments, you may need to actively manage your APs radio settings. Systems such as Cisco's Wireless LAN Controller, which knows about all internal network APs and can detect external APs, give you a good option for automatic tuning of channels and signal strength.

In automatic tuning, each AP goes off-channel for a short period of time to allow the AP to scan all channels to look for interference. Going off-channel means that there is a brief period when it ignores the wireless client devices that are connected to it, and does its scan of the other channels. This interruption is very brief, so the wireless clients will not be affected, other than a slight decrease in overall throughput. Because the Wireless LAN Controller also knows about all other APs that exist on the network, it can determine the strength and visibility of the surrounding APs. Knowing the strength and visibility of both its own APs and surrounding APs allows the WLC to recalculate the channel selection and radio strength of all APs on the network, thereby optimizing coverage over the whole network.

Chapter 3: Securing Your WLAN

In This Chapter

✓ **Finding out why using a secure WLAN is good practice**

✓ **Checking out various security risk mitigation methods**

✓ **Securing your management interface**

*T*o work with wireless networking, you need to know how to utilize the many options available to secure various aspects of your wireless network so that your data and private information remain private. Unlike wired networks, with wireless, you can never be sure where the users might be, which complicates network security. You can choose from many methods to secure wireless signals, such as Wi-Fi Protected Access (WPA) and WPA2; or to secure the entire wireless local area network (WLAN) or service set identifier (SSID), such as isolation via virtual local area networks (VLANs) or physical separation of the entire WLAN infrastructure.

In this chapter, I review some of the risks that you have to deal with and discuss the steps that you can take to reduce them.

Give the contents of this chapter a lot of thought prior to deploying your wireless network within your organization because wireless security is even more important than most other areas of network security because it is attacked from outside of your organization's premises.

This chapter helps you assess your own organization's security requirements and data risk levels that allow you to more easily develop a security model for your wireless implementation that is flexible for your users and secure for your data.

Understanding the Benefits of a Secure WLAN

The reason to secure your WLAN is pretty self-evident: To protect your data from prying eyes who may be a fair distance from your wired network connections.

Finding balance between functionality and security

Although inherent security risks are present with practically everything you do in life, steps can be taken to reduce them. If you are going for a walk in a strange town, you might stay on well-lit roads, carry only a limited amount of cash and credit cards, walk with other people, and stay aware of your surroundings. All these things may limit what might happen to you on your walk. Taken to more of an extreme, you can always choose to not go on the walk at all.

In the computer world, if you do not network your computers, you reduce, or all but eliminate, the risk of what can happen to your computer by undesirable elements, but you also reduce its functionality. So, security and functionality are tradeoffs for one another — at least to a degree. You can add a modem or a network card, attach your computer to other computers to share data, perform remote operations, and mitigate the risk of having these computers connected to each other and possibly the Internet by using antivirus software, software and hardware firewalls, intrusion-detection software and hardware, and other security and monitoring devices.

When you decide to add a wireless network to this mix, you have many of the same issues, but these issues are compounded because people can have local access to the network without actually being within physical access of your hardware (in your building or offices). Again, the added functionality of mobility needs to be weighed against the added risks of remote users exploiting security holes and getting to your private data.

Recognizing security risks

As with any wired network, any number of attacks can be perpetrated if an unauthorized computer is allowed to connect to your network. On secure networks, all unauthorized ports of network switches are disabled or disconnected; however, this is not possible when dealing with wireless networks in which the access point (AP) radio is either on or off.

✦ **Unauthorized access:** When a computer is on your network, it can sniff packets, perpetrate man-in-the-middle attacks, spoof valid network packets, capture passwords and other sensitive information, and cause a denial-of-service (DoS) attack. Controlling which computers are allowed to connect to your network can reduce your exposure to these security issues.

✦ **Insecure equipment:** Most networks have removed all their network hubs and replaced them with switches, which are more secure because switches treat each network switch port as a separate collision domain (in the carrier sense multiple access collision detect [CSMA/CD] sense), which means that when a device on port 1 sends frames to a device on port 2, and both MAC addresses are known to the switch, those frames only travel along the cables connected to port 1 and port 2. When a hub is used, however, the frame travels to every device connected to every port on the hub.

✦ **Insecure APs:** When dealing with wireless networks, an AP operates in the same manner as a hub, so all devices that are connected wirelessly to an AP radio can see all traffic that is sent on that radio. If a device is allowed to join a wireless network, it can perpetrate any number of attacks on the devices connected to the same AP as well as other attacks that only require it to be on the same network segment.

Some of the new standalone APs (such as the Cisco Aironet 3500 Series APs) and the Cisco Wireless LAN Controller (WLC) support the ability to isolate clients from each other. Although this is not truly isolation from the radio frequency (RF) perspective, it does allow for better security in situations when wireless security is your absolute highest priority. The cost of throughput on your network increases because it keeps wireless clients from talking to each other over the wireless network. This feature is useful in locations, such as coffee shops and common areas, where all wireless users want to get on the Internet but rarely need to transfer files between each other.

Checking Out Security Risk Mitigation Methods

When working with most wireless networking equipment, you have the following ways to protect your network data:

✦ Authentication and data encryption

✦ Media Access Control (MAC) address filtering

✦ Hiding the service set identifier (SSID)

✦ Intrusion detection and prevention

✦ User isolation using VLANs

The following sections examine these options in detail.

Authentication and data encryption

Authentication and data encryption comprise a large topic. Three main methods handle authentication and data encryption. I start with the oldest option, which everyone seems to have finally heard about, and then I move on to the newer options that provide substantially better security but are a little more work to set up, which is likely the reason adoption has been slow, but improving.

Reviewing WEP

One of the first major complaints that arose from wireless networking was from the security community. Quite rightly, the complaint was that with RF signals being broadcast over the air, nothing could stop someone from reaching out and grabbing them. At least with wired networking, a person had to be connected physically to the same hubs or switches to eavesdrop on a network conversation.

To deal with this issue, Wired Equivalent Privacy (WEP) was introduced. The goal of WEP is to provide the same level of privacy that you would have if you were still connected to a wired network. The goal was good; however, as with a better-built mousetrap, you end up with smarter mice.

The basis of WEP involves two sets of mechanisms:

+ **Authentication:** You need to prove your identity before participating in the network.

+ **Encryption:** Everything you send over the airwaves should be encrypted.

The basis of WEP encryption is tied to an encryption key, which is typically either 64-bit WEP or 128-bit WEP. With 64-bit WEP, you use a 40-bit key that is joined with a 24-bit initialization vector (IV) to generate an RC4 (Rivest Cipher 4) stream cipher. A 128-bit WEP uses a 104-bit encryption key, which is then joined with the 24-bit IV to create the RC4 cipher.

An *encryption key* is a string of text that is used in a *cipher* (or process) to encrypt data. Ciphers have been around for thousands of years and typically offer encryption strength though the strength of the key and the strength of the cipher process itself. If the cipher is strong enough, the only way you can read the data is to know the cipher and have the key. During WWII, the Germans created a cipher machine, dubbed the Enigma machine, with replaceable key wheels (or *rotors*). Allied forces captured several Enigma machines during WWII, but until they captured a book that listed which key wheels to use on which date, the machine was useless in directly reading German coded messages. In that situation, the encryption key is made up of the replaceable key wheels, and the cipher was the process that the machine used to internally code the messages based on the current key configuration.

Although WEP gives you a quick and efficient way to encrypt and decrypt traffic at high speed, it has some serious flaws. Even if you cannot read the data, you can still capture data packets off a wireless network because they travel over the air. One of the issues is that the IV must be unique for every packet that is sent over a time period, and because the IV is only 24 bits long, it can start repeating in as little as 5,000 packets, so it is not as random or secure as it could be. WEP has consistently been proven to be broken in as little as one minute and can be broken with readily available software. Given this, WEP is not considered to be reliably secure for networks. *Payment Card Industry (PCI),* which sets standards for credit and debit card transactions, prohibits the use of WEP in any part of a credit card transaction.

The WEP authentication can be configured as an open system that does not require authentication but rather starts a conversation with any device. That device is still required to know the WEP key if encryption is enabled.

If shared key authentication is used, all devices start their communication with the AP with a four-way handshake process, as shown in Figure 3-1:

1. The client sends an authentication request.

2. The AP sends a *challenge* (a random piece of data) to the client.

3. The client then encrypts the challenge by using the WEP key and returns it to the AP.

4. The AP decrypts the data it receives and compares it with the data it sent in the initial challenge. If the data matches, the device is sent an acknowledgment; if it does not match, it is sent a refusal.

   If the client is authenticated, it can start sending data to the AP, likely encrypting it using its WEP key.

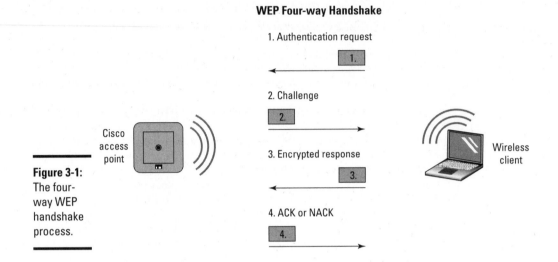

Figure 3-1:
The four-way WEP handshake process.

Looking at the big picture, when compared to a wireless network with no authentication or encryption services, WEP offers a great deal of protection. However, based on WEPs limitations, it should not be used for sensitive data or connected to networks that contain sensitive data. Here are the many places this light security option can be beneficial:

✦ **Low security environments:** For instance, you can use WEP on a system to stream music from your Apple iPod to your IEEE 802.11b wireless speakers. A system like that can be isolated from your home wireless network and does not contain much sensitive data (other than what is on your playlist).

✦ **Supporting legacy devices:** Another reason you may choose WEP over the other choices is the age of the wireless device you use, or what features it supports. I have many devices around ten years old that are still used on a wireless network. These old devices do not support the newer WPA and WPA2, so I am limited to WEP and managing what access that AP has to the rest of my network resources.

Getting serious with WPA

Due to the limitations of WEP, Wi-Fi Protected Access (WPA) was developed by the Wi-Fi Alliance. WPA makes use of most of the recommendations that are included in the IEEE 802.11i specification, which lays out security standards for wireless networks.

Rather than using a static encryption key like with WEP, WPA makes use of *Temporal Key Integrity Protocol (TKIP),* which can be implemented easily because it is a minor, but effective, upgrade. Rather than using a plain text IV to create the cipher key as WEP does, WPA combines the IV with a secret root key (which is a stronger encryption key); it also implements a sequence counter — all packets must arrive at the AP in the correct order, or they are rejected. Finally, WPA provides a rekeying function that updates the encryption key and neutralizes people who try to break the key because it changes at regular intervals.

Basically, TKIP manages the encryption process in a manner that is similar to WEP, but it adds an integrity check to verify all arriving packets. There are still many documented attacks that can be successfully carried out on a WPA network using TKIP, and as such, WPA required additional updating, which you see in the following section.

Getting even more serious with WPA2

WPA2 followed after WPA and implements all the IEEE 802.11i mandatory elements, which included making the encryption method stronger and introducing a new integrity check mechanism. WPA2 was developed by the Wi-Fi Alliance as a replacement for WPA.

The implementation of Advanced Encryption Standard (AES) increased the level of encryption to a place still considered the safest on the market. The initial key was set with either certificate-based authentication (using standard SSL public/private key pairs) or a *shared secret* (a string known by all parties in the encryption system). When security is initialized with a shared secret, entrance to the secured network provides a *breach point* (anyone who knows the key), whereas certificate-based authentication provides a less vulnerable option. Certificate-based authentication is available when using enterprise-mode authentication, whereas shared secret — also called a pre-shared key (PSK) — is used for personal-mode authentication.

The key difference between enterprise-mode and personal-mode authentication is that in the enterprise environment, the Remote Authentication Dial In User Service (RADIUS) services are provided to the network and available to be used with WPA2 authentication. A RADIUS server is an Authentication, Authorization, and Accounting server on your network. The RADIUS server works with an account database to validate user credentials for devices that support the RADIUS protocol in a secure and encrypted manner.

AES encryption can be managed with various key lengths from 128 bits to 256 bits.

As with most encryption methods, longer keys mean more security at the cost of some level of performance. Because the performance hit is minimal, the limiting factor is often devices that do not support the higher security levels. If that is the case for you, consider changing those devices or upgrading drivers.

To replace the TKIP integrity checks, WPA2 introduced Counter Mode with Cipher Block Chaining Message Authentication Code Protocol (CCMP) as the integrity-checking mechanism. Technically, CCMP performs all encryption and integrity checking, but I have broken it out here as the encryption mechanism for AES.

Although AES encryption is mandatory for WPA2, some WPA implementations allow it to be used as the encryption mechanism as well. You also sometimes see WPA2 with TKIP as an option; however, this does not replace AES for encryption but rather replaces CCMP as the integrity-checking mechanism. AES is then left as the encryption mechanism (as it is a mandatory component of WPA2). Regardless of the options you may be presented, always use the highest security possible on your network and replace devices that lower it.

If you care about your data on your network, always use encryption. If you are going to use encryption, always use the strongest encryption method that is available to you. If choosing WPA2 is not an option because of network devices not offering WPA2 support, consider replacing those devices if you consider your data more important than the functionality you get from the device.

Filtering the MAC address

When attempting to secure a wireless network, in addition to encryption and authentication of WEP and WPA, you can also keep users from connecting to your WLAN if they do not have a registered or authorized MAC address associated with their network card. In addition to adding a list of authorized MAC addresses to the individual APs that make up your wireless network, you can centrally maintain a list of authorized MAC addresses via a RADIUS server.

Because many operating systems allow you to locally set your MAC address on your network card, this security is only light security — like WEP. If an intruder knows a valid MAC address on your network, either by social engineering or by capturing wireless network frames, he can use that to gain

access to your network by manipulating his own MAC address. You will see a
noticeable issue only if the real computer is on the network at the same time.

I still know many home users who go through the extra work of authorizing
MAC addresses on their wireless network even after I suggest eliminating
that practice and instead using the more secure and easier to administer
WPA2. Some of these home users have not even implemented simple encryption like WEP and rely solely on the ability to block unauthorized MAC
addresses on their network. You may think this is even worse, as I sometimes have the conversation with IT staff in corporate environments as well.

Hiding the service set identifier (SSID)

Each WLAN AP sends regular broadcasts that include the name of the network, or SSID. Knowing the SSID of a network allows you to connect to the
network. Most APs allow you to disable the broadcasting of the SSID, which
prevents people from knowing your network name and makes it difficult
for them to connect to your network. Tools, such as Network Stumbler or
MetaGeek's inSSIDer (see Figure 3-2), monitor RF WLAN signals and can
easily identify whether WLAN networks exist in your area. Other tools,
such as Aircrack, can help you identify the SSID and even locate their WEP
encryption keys. inSSIDer in Figure 3-2 shows a Cisco Systems access point
with a hidden SSID, as opposed to the ones I hid in the image.

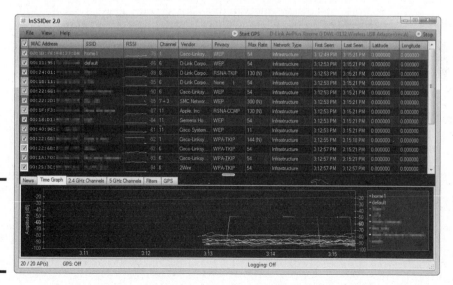

Figure 3-2:
inSSIDer
shows
your 802.11
neighbors.

As with MAC address filtering, disabling the SSID broadcast does not provide you with strong security; it only keeps the casual passerby from connecting to your WLAN. If they really want in, they likely already have the tools they need readily available.

Intrusion detection and prevention

An *intrusion detection system (IDS)* and an *intrusion prevention system (IPS)* monitor network traffic to and from the IDS or IPS systems to locate devices that attempt to infiltrate your network. When people attempt to gather information about your network, they run tools that leave a signature on your network or they send specific types of traffic to devices on your network. Having devices online for intrusion detection and prevention allows you to see who is scanning so that you can locate and block them.

When the IDS reacts to the intrusion and attempts to block the attempt automatically, the system is usually referred to as an IPS. The IDS detects only intrusion attempts, so think of it as an alarm, whereas IPS is an alarm and a security guard.

Most network providers, such as Cisco, have a full range of IDSs and IPSs that run either on a network gateway or inside the network, like the stand-alone appliance — Cisco IPS 4200 Series Sensor. These systems range in price based on the features they offer and how they integrate into the network. Cisco's products in this category are all IPS systems, and you can locate information about them through www.cisco.com by clicking the Security link and then clicking the IPS link.

Isolating users with VLANs

I discuss virtual local area networks (VLANs) in Book III, Chapter 5, but here I tell you even more about the wonders of this separation technology. You can implement VLANs in several ways when working with your wireless LAN (see Figure 3-3). VLANs allow you to

+ Separate different types of traffic based on the SSID to which they connect.

✦ Provide isolation between more secure and less secure clients when required to support clients that do not support the maximum security settings of the WLAN. A less secure SSID can be used only for the lower security clients; ACLs can then be used on the routers and firewalls to control their access.

✦ Provide guest Internet access out of your office while keeping these clients from accessing internal resources. These clients may get their access through a separate interface on your firewall, a separate firewall, or a secondary Internet service provider (ISP) connection rather than your main connection.

✦ Provide access to the management interfaces on network devices. Because most network devices allow for management to be conducted over a separate VLAN, thereby keep this traffic away from less secured VLANs.

If you follow the flow from the wireless clients at the bottom of Figure 3-3 to the Internet connections at the top, you can see that

✦ Each wireless computer has a connection to a different SSID.

✦ All SSIDs are hosted on the same LWAPP, but each SSID is associated with a different VLAN because the traffic on VLANs can be passed to the controller using a network connection.

✦ Traffic is passed in separate VLANs to the controller. The controller takes care of functions, such as decrypting WPA2 data and passing the data frames onto the wired network.

✦ Still on separate VLANs and using a single network connection, the traffic is passed onto a switch where VLAN traffic is separated into virtual networks, each with their own servers and network resources.

✦ All three of these virtual networks get their outside access through an ASA firewall, which can split the traffic from different VLANs through dual connections to two ISPs. This is done for load balancing for fault tolerant services.

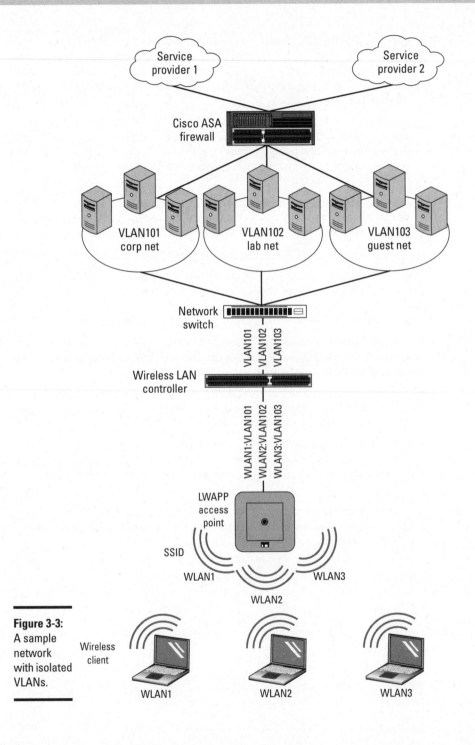

Figure 3-3:
A sample
network
with isolated
VLANs.

Securing the Management Interface

The management interface on APs is just as important, or even more important, than other networking devices that are secured behind locked doors. In this section, I introduce you to several things you can do to secure these interfaces.

Changing default passwords

All network devices — switches, routers, WLAN controllers, or access points — ship with a default system configuration that includes IP address configuration, SSID, users, and an administration password. Because this information is documented in the devices owner's manual and on the manufacturer's Web site, change these items prior to deploying these devices on your network; otherwise, unknown people can change your device configurations. Chapter 4 of this minibook takes you through the process of setting up a Cisco WLC, and during that process, you see how to change these required settings.

Years ago, default passwords were not a major concern. Many APs were deployed with default SSIDs, allowing the manufacturer of that AP to be identified and the default username and password to be known. However, this led to security breaches for those networks. Most manufacturers now promote that security is important and, in some cases, require all configurations to be manually set up before the AP or network devices can be used.

Some professionals deploy access points in areas where there is already a high concentration of wireless networks, and then connect to neighboring devices and configure them to cause less interference for the devices they deploy. How do they do this? Well, to put it simply the other devices are deployed with no WEP and have the default username and password. Although I do not agree with this behavior, if the other company has not taken basic steps to secure its network, the company is open to this behavior.

Even if you deploy WPA2 for your users, if you have not changed the default password for your devices, nothing stops your own users from connecting to your access point or WLC. After you connect to your wireless devices, your users may add a new SSID to your network; allow their unauthorized handheld devices onto the network; or reset the wireless device back to factory default settings. The actions of these users could be accidental or malicious, and thus, either disruptive or detrimental to the network operation and security.

Getting even more secure with SSH, SSL, TLS, HTTPS

Secure Shell (SSH), Secure Sockets Layer (SSL), Transport Layer Security (TLS), and HyperText Transfer Protocol over SSL/TLS (HTTPS) represent technologies that can be used to secure communication between a client and a server. Each has proven itself as a method of securing wired or wireless data and keeping it safe. When using wireless networking, use the following:

✦ **Secure Shell:** SSH is the secure replacement for Telnet. Unlike Telnet, which transmits its data in clear text over the network, SSH encrypts all data that it sends between clients and servers. SSH also allows you to authenticate with either a username and password, or by using certificate-based authentication. SSH has become the *de facto* standard when communicating with UNIX/Linux servers and network devices, such as routers and switches. In the WLC/AP environment, SSH can be used as a secure way to reach the management command-line interface for these devices. Always use SSH over Telnet for this type of access.

✦ **Secure Sockets Layer:** SSL was developed by Netscape and was established as a standard for HTTP traffic encryption. SSL has since been enhanced and replaced by TLS.

✦ **Transport Layer Security:** TLS is the standard method of encrypting client/server data that starts with a key exchange, authentication, and the implementation of standard ciphers. Many IP-based protocols, such as HTTP (HTTPS), Simple Mail Transfer Protocol (SMTP), Post Office Protocol version 3 (POP3), File Transfer Protocol (FTP), and Network News Transfer Protocol (NNTP), support TLS to encrypt data.

Because most major protocols support TLS, when using these protocols over wireless, use TLS if the server supports it. In many cases, the terms SSL and TLS are used interchangeably even if the technology in use is usually the newer TLS.

✦ **HyperText Transfer Protocol over SSL/TLS (HTTPS):** As the name suggests, HTTPS implements standard HTTP but encrypts all the data transfers with client devices. This is why your online banking websites all require you to use HTTPS when dealing with them. Your WLC and APs allow you to make configuration changes from your favorite web browser. Often by default, they have HTTP access enabled out of the box. Although HTTP access is available, when unencrypted, it allows for people with tools, such as *Wireshark* (a network packet capture tool introduced in Book I, Chapter 4), to capture your user credentials that you use to manage your WLC and APs. This is a serious security breach that is solved by enabling HTTPS. Most devices on the market that support HTTP access for management also support HTTPS access, and typically it is enabled with a simple click in a check box of the management web page.

Management access

When dealing with a residential-grade access point, you usually have only one networking interface and this interface is used for data access and management. When dealing with commercial- or enterprise-grade access points, they usually can support VLANs on the AP. Supporting VLANs at the AP allows you to support several service set identifiers over a single AP, which are then assigned to separate VLANs to isolate the traffic for each SSID. I discuss this earlier in this chapter in the "Isolating users with VLANs" section.

With VLAN support in your WLC and AP, you can assign the management network interface to a separate VLAN. If the management interface is on a separate VLAN, security can be assigned at routers or firewalls to restrict which network devices can connect to the management interface. Some wireless devices can also be set to prevent management access through their wireless interfaces so that a user on the wireless network cannot manage that AP.

Isolating the entire WLAN

Many companies operate a virtual private network (VPN) to allow their users to securely gain access to network resources when operating their mobile computers on a remote and unsecured network. This allows the IT department to isolate the remote computers from the unsecured network that they are on and to connect the remote computer to the corporate network.

With this same mentality, the IT department can operate its wireless network entirely outside of the corporate network, which lessens concerns about unknown wireless users accessing corporate information because the wireless network does not touch the corporate network. For a user to access corporate data, he would establish a VPN connection back to the corporate office through the wireless network. In this case, it is no different than if he was in a coffee shop using his unsecured wireless network. After the VPN connection is established, all network information from the mobile computer is encrypted and secured until it arrives back on the corporate network.

In this isolated WLAN scenario, security of the wireless signal is not as important because all corporate information is secured with the VPN connection. Therefore, if you have no encryption through to WPA2 on the wireless network, it is not a big deal, but I still recommend using the highest level of encryption because it never hurts to be too secure. If an unauthorized user gains access to the wireless network, she is very limited to the information she can do on that network. She can only access what is on the wireless network, which are other wireless clients and the firewall.

When corporate users are on the wireless network, they can either access the Internet or use their VPN solution to make a connection (via a VPN tunnel) back to their corporate network in a secure manner, as shown in Figure 3-4. This is not an uncommon scenario and is one that my company has implanted. So if I am at home, at a coffee shop, or on wireless in my own office and I want to access corporate resources, I just launch my VPN client and connect. Because of the mobility wireless gives me, even when I am at my desk in my office, I tend to connect wirelessly rather than through the available wired connection.

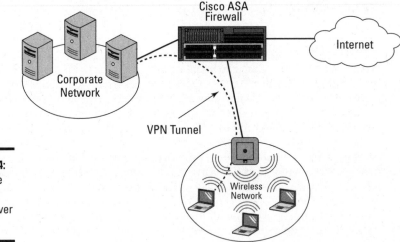

Figure 3-4:
Corporate wireless access over a VPN.

Chapter 4: Building a Cisco Wireless Network

In This Chapter

- Introducing a wireless local area network
- Simplifying with Wireless LAN Controllers
- Getting the lowdown on Lightweight Access Point Protocol
- Setting up a wireless LAN

As a network support professional, you need to understand which components make up a standard Cisco wireless network. Earlier chapters in this book show how to do some of the basic configurations for a wireless network. This chapter focuses on the management and configuration of a wireless network based on the Cisco Wireless LAN Controller. I show you how to deploy standalone or controller-based access points and what you need to do to deploy either wireless infrastructure. Along the way, I prepare you to make your deployment decisions by providing you with an overview of the components and letting you know how they work together. With this information, you can make informed choices for your network.

 Although this chapter just touches on the configuration for any of these solutions, you can go to Cisco's website and download the current Cisco xx00 Series Wireless Controller Installation Guide as well as the Cisco Wireless LAN Controller Configuration Guide. The installation guide walks you through the physical setup of the device, and the configuration guide primarily walks you through the software configuration of the device.

Introducing the Cisco Unified Wireless Networks Architecture (CUWN)

In today's technology market, the driving force behind mobile computing is actually mobile computer users. These users find it more and more convenient to be able to use their computing devices wherever they need to do a task. The more places that they can use their devices, the more places they want to be able to use them. The more they talk to other mobile users in their travels, the more ways they find out they can use their devices — as well as how they cannot use them. This push for more mobility while maintaining corporate accessibility gives corporate IT staff members a challenge in that they are typically concerned with the integrity, safety, and security of corporate data; allowing users in an ever-widening geographical area to have access to this data in ever-increasing new ways goes against the typical goals of corporate IT staff, which is to keep data as private as possible. To alleviate some of this concern, Cisco released information on the *Cisco Unified Wireless Network (CUWN),* which is less a product than it is a methodology and an integrated use of existing products. The unified part of this solution is that it incorporates a standard management methodology and goal across all the products that Cisco provides for both wired and wireless data communication, with data security in the front of all development thoughts.

So the CUWN takes data from a client through wireless access points and wired infrastructure to the servers or devices that will ultimately hold the data. As such, CUWN makes use of networking devices at all levels of the process, and Cisco offers tools to allow central management of all these devices through a series of management tools.

The Cisco Unified Wireless Network uses some or all the following components:

+ Cisco Wireless Control System (WCS)
+ Cisco WCS Navigator
+ Cisco Wireless LAN Controller (WLC)
+ Cisco Wireless LAN Controller Module (WLCM)
+ Cisco Wireless Services Module (WiSM)
+ Cisco Catalyst 3750G Integrated Wireless LAN Controller
+ Cisco Controller-Based or Lightweight Access Point (LWAP)
+ Cisco Aironet Wireless Bridge
+ Cisco Aironet 1500 Series Controller-Based or Lightweight Outdoor Mesh Access Points
+ Cisco Client Devices

The following sections look at some of these components in more detail.

Keeping it simple with Wireless LAN Controllers

Management of wireless local area networks (WLANs) can be challenging today with the widespread deployment of access points (APs). In networks where there is currently no wireless access, IT staff experience pressure to deploy a wireless solution; in established networks, the pressure is usually to increase coverage in the current solution. Cisco makes this easier for IT staff through the Cisco Unified Wireless Network, in which a wireless control module of some type is the central or key component. This control module can be a standalone component like the Cisco 2100 Series Wireless LAN Controller or could be integrated into another device like the Cisco Catalyst 3750G Integrated Wireless LAN Controller; in either case, the WLC components allow you to centrally manage and configure a number of access points (APs) in a simplified manner.

If you are going to deploy more than three APs on your network, either to start with or later on, seriously consider deploying a WLC-based solution.

WLC equipment

To have Wireless LAN Controller (WLC) services on your network, you can use any of the following:

✦ Cisco Small Business Pro Wireless Express 526 Mobility Controller with 521 Wireless Express Access Point (simplified management)

✦ Cisco 2100 series controller

✦ Cisco 4400 series controller

✦ Cisco 5500 series controller

✦ Catalyst 6500 Series Wireless Services Module (WiSM)

✦ Cisco 7600 Series Router Wireless Services Module (WiSM)

✦ Cisco 28/37/38xx Series Integrated Services Router with Controller Network Module

✦ Catalyst 3750G Integrated Wireless LAN Controller Switch

The Cisco Wireless LAN Controller is used to manage all aspects of multiple APs and can also take care of all your Radio Resource Management (RRM). RRM is the term given to managing your wireless radios, and it includes not only channel selection and signal power, but also deals with managing interference from unknown sources.

The two WLC devices that you will likely encounter most often are the Cisco 2100 series controller or the Cisco 5500 series controller.

✦ **The Cisco 2100 series controller:** This controller has eight network ports on it; two ports support POE to power APs, and the other ports can be assigned as management interfaces or assigned to support various VLAN and network connections that you may be using to isolate traffic for your SSIDs. This WLC system can manage up to 24 APs.

✦ **The Cisco 5500 series controller:** Depending on the model of the Cisco 5500 series controller you look at, you can manage up to 500 APs through up to eight network ports (transceiver slots), which are used as distribution system ports. This series of controller is typically connected to a network switch, which would provide network services for your APs.

WLC features

Most WLCs support the following features:

✦ **Distribution system ports:** These ports are used to connect the WLC to a network switch and act as a path for data.

✦ **Service port:** This port is used as a management or console port. This port is active during the boot mode of the WLC.

✦ **Management interface:** This interface is used for in-band management and provides connectivity to network devices (such as DHCP servers or Radius servers). If you want to connect to the controller's web management interface, it would be through this interface. The management interface is assigned an IP address and is the initial point of contact for Lightweight Access Point Protocol (LWAPP) communication and registration. (See the "Lightweight Access Point Protocol (LWAPP)" section a bit later in this chapter.)

✦ **AP-manager interface:** This interface is used to control and manage all Layer 3 communications between the WLC and lightweight APs.

For the best AP association results, the AP-manager interface should be assigned to the same IP subnet as the management interface.

✦ **Virtual interface:** This interface is used to support mobility management features, such as DHCP relay and Guest Web Authentication.

✦ **Service-port interface:** This interface is used to communicate to the service port and must have an IP address that belongs to a different IP subnet than that of the AP-manager interface and any other dynamic interface.

✦ **Dynamic interfaces:** These are VLAN interfaces created by you to allow for communication to various VLANs.

WLC features with LWAPP

When working with a WLC, you can manage autonomous-mode access points or lightweight-mode access points (LWAPs), both of which I discuss in Book V, Chapter 2. Supporting autonomous-mode access points allows you to introduce a WLC into an existing Cisco wireless environment, but saves the initial cost of replacing all the existing access points with LWAPs. Although you do not need to convert your existing APs to LWAPs, some features work only when you use Lightweight Access Point Protocol (LWAPP).

Some features that are available to you when working with the WLC and LWAPP include

✦ **Controller port mirroring:** Allows you to copy data on one port of your controller to another port for diagnostics.

✦ **Controller link aggregation (LAG):** Allows you to bond multiple ports together on your controller to allow multiple physical ports to be treated as a single logical port. With LAG enabled, you can support 100 APs on a single 4404 WLC, which still follows the recommendation of 48 APs per port. The 5508 WLC has no AP limit per port, but it does recommend using more than one gigabit port if supporting greater than 100 APs.

The more ports you load balance your traffic over, the fewer bottlenecks you will encounter from this link.

✦ **DHCP proxy** allows you to forward DHCP requests to the normal DHCP servers existing on your network.

✦ **Aggressive load balancing:** Distributes wireless clients between APs rather than waiting for clients to naturally migrate between APs. When a user travels through an office, her wireless signal on her connected AP reduces as she moves away from it. Typically, the wireless client remains associated with its current AP as long as it can, and when the signal is very weak, it re-associates with a closer AP. In an ideal world, the client would always immediately associate with the closest AP. Enabling Aggressive mode on the WLC causes the LWAP to force the client to a closer AP rather than waiting for the client to give up its existing AP, which ensures a stronger signal.

Aggressive load balancing provides better performance on the overall WLAN by ensuring that users are always on the closest AP.

✦ **Roaming support:** Client roaming support between AP on the same ESS, and also between controllers and subnets, as well as Voice over IP telephone roaming.

+ **Integrated security solutions:** Security solutions built around 802.1x and AAA or RADIUS servers.

+ **Cisco IDS and IPS support:** Cisco provides a full range of intrusion detection systems (IDSs) and intrusion prevention systems (IPSs). LWAPs can be an integrated component of either system.

+ **Internal DHCP server support:** WLC supports an integrated DHCP server, or you can use the DHCP server on your corporate network. In addition, WLC can ensure that all clients on the network have DHCP-assigned IP addresses for additional security. People with static addresses can attempt to be another computer that has specific access to secured network resources. Forcing DHCP addresses to be used prevents this type of intrusion.

+ **MAC filtering:** In Chapter 3 of this minibook, I discuss the purpose of MAC filtering to restrict WLAN access. Although MAC filtering is not a strong security feature, it does have features that many wireless network administrators demand. With WLC, you can specify that all MAC addresses be verified against registered addresses on AAA servers.

+ **Dynamic transmit power control:** Allows the radio strength to be tuned to allow for maximum coverage with minimal interference between APs.

+ **Dynamic channel assignment:** Allows for regular checks of RF channels in use in the area, and assigning channels that provide the least amount of interference or noise.

+ **Coverage hole detection and correction:** Allows for clients that are detected to be getting weak coverage to trigger a process that will re-evaluate the overall channel and signal strength on the network to correct the holes as part of an effective RRM strategy.

+ **Rogue AP detection and rogue device management:** Allows you to identify unmanaged APs in your area and determine whether they are actually on your local network. If they are on your local network, remedial action may be taken. When using rogue device management, unauthorized APs on your environment can have their wireless services interrupted.

Going mobile with Cisco WLAN access point (AP) devices

Cisco Aironet access points are designed to support a variety of environments from indoor to outdoor. The lightweight access points allow users to make use of all mobility features of Cisco's Unified Wireless Network and support all the standards of 802.11a/b/g/n. These devices offer reliable and secure communications using either single or double radios. The greatest advantage is with "zero-touch" configuration, which allows you to deploy APs right out of the box with no initial prep work.

Having a choice between two radios in an AP allows you to support twice as many wireless clients on one RF frequency (2.4 or 5 GHz) or to support clients on both frequencies at the same time. When using only one radio, you can support clients only on one of the two frequencies, and if you want to support clients on the other frequency, you must install a second AP. So having two radios in the same AP effectively gives you two APs in a single unit. Do not confuse this support for multiple service set identifiers (SSIDs), which I cover in Chapter 3 of this minibook, as even with a single radio, you can support multiple SSIDs.

Cisco's product line of APs include the following:

+ **Cisco Aironet 1040 Series** is designed as an entry-level device and includes integrated antennas.

+ **Cisco Aironet 1140 Series** is designed for indoor office environments and includes integrated antennas.

+ **Cisco Aironet 1260 Series** is designed for challenging RF indoor office environments and includes external antennas.

+ **Cisco Aironet 3500 Series** are for high-performance and mission-critical environments. They offer models with either internal or external antennas which would depend on the RF challenges in your environment.

These systems can be retrofit into 1130 and 1240 series mounting brackets for easy deployment.

+ **Cisco Aironet 1250 Series APs** are based on the IEEE 802.11n specifications and provide reliable coverage for all standards based on 802.11 a/b/g/n. This support allows for the use of high bandwidth applications, such as voice. These APs offer rugged metal cases with external antennas and are designed for factories and warehouses.

+ **Cisco Aironet 1500 Series lightweight outdoor mesh access points** are the ideal solution for outdoor areas.

Cisco Wireless Control System (WCS)

The Cisco *Wireless Control System (WCS)* is a software control system for a wireless network. This software is available from Cisco to allow you to design, plan, control, and troubleshoot a multi-controller wireless environment. Although you can deploy your controller-based wireless network, WCS provides you benefits when your network is supported by multiple WLC units.

Think of WCS as a controller for the WLC.

Unlike the other products listed previously in this chapter, WCS is primarily a software solution that runs on a server.

Lightweight Access Point Protocol (LWAPP)

The LWAPP runs on a WLAN controller and on lightweight access points (LWAPs) to route packets in and out of the WLAN on optimal routes. In other words, the WLAN controller is the gateway of the WLAN to the LAN. The key fact here is that if you do not have a functioning WLC running on your network, none of your lightweight APs will be able to function. So when your wireless network hits a level that is considered to be mission critical, it is imperative that you have more than one WLC to which your APs can connect. When you configure your APs on your network, you can assign primary, secondary, and tertiary controllers for your network. If the primary controller is unavailable, the backup controller will be used until the primary becomes available on the network again. And the tertiary controller allows your network when both the primary and backup controllers are unavailable.

Cisco has changed its terminology recently, and LWAPPs are now referred to as *controller-based* on Cisco parts lists, whereas non-LWAPP or autonomous APs are called *standalone*.

The controller and APs run protocols that route packets in and out of the WLAN and LAN, using the optimum path through the wireless mesh network and through the wired network linking the WLAN controller to other WLAN controllers. Communication between the LWAP and WLC works equally well at layer 2 with switches or at layer 3 with routers.

When working with the WLC and LWAPs, the LWAPP has a Split MAC function that determines which functions are performed by the LWAP and which functions are performed by the WLC.

The WLC usually performs these functions:

✦ 802.11 authentication

✦ 802.11 association

✦ 802.11 frame translation and bridging

✦ 802.1x/EAP/RADIUS processing

✦ Termination of 802.11 traffic on a wired interface

The LWAP usually performs time-sensitive operations, such as the following:

+ Frame exchange handshake between a client and AP

+ Transmission of beacon frames

+ Buffering and transmission of frames for clients in power-save mode

+ Response to probe request frames from clients

+ Provision of real-time signal quality information to the switch with every received frame

+ Monitoring each of the radio channels for noise, interference, and other WLANs

+ Monitoring for the presence of other APs

+ Encryption and decryption of 802.11 frames

If you have already purchased all your access points and they are autonomous, but you now want to roll out a WLC, then you can convert your APs to Lightweight mode by running a Cisco-supplied upgrade tool on your compatible Cisco AP. If you decide that you need to re-deploy some of these APs to locations where you are not using a WLC, you can reverse this process by reapplying the latest Cisco IOS for that Cisco AP.

Setting Up Your Wireless LAN

The following sections give you an overview of the basic process for setting up your wireless LAN. In this case, I focus on a WLAN that will be functioning with a Cisco Wireless LAN Controller (WLC).

Setting up and verifying the wired LAN to which the WLAN will connect

Although setting up a WLAN in your environment is not a huge undertaking, you need to plan and ensure you know a few things before starting the whole process. Nothing is worse than getting halfway through a deployment, only to find out you have to scrap the whole design and start again because part of the current infrastructure does not support a feature you wanted to use. This process assumes the following:

+ You have already planned the number and type of service set identifiers (SSIDs) that you will be supporting. SSIDs are defined in Chapter 1 of this minibook.

+ You have the VLANs that are required to support them. You will find out more about VLANs in Book III, Chapter 5.

+ You have security parameters around the VLANs.

+ You have conducted a site survey so that you know where each AP will be mounted. Your site survey knowledge can be located in Chapter 2 of this minibook.

Knowing all these items ahead of time can ease and speed the deployment of your wireless infrastructure.

Setting up the Cisco Wireless LAN Controller (s)

After unpacking your WLC, connect the console cable to the service port and set your computer's terminal settings to the following:

+ 9600 bps

+ 8 data bits

+ 1 stop bit

+ No parity

+ No hardware flow control

Mucking about with the Startup Wizard

When powering up your WLC, you need to perform some configuration. You are presented with the Startup Wizard, which does the following tasks:

+ Ensures that the controller has a system name of up to 32 characters.

+ Adds an administrative username and password, each up to 24 characters.

+ Ensures that the controller can communicate with the GUI, CLI, or Cisco WCS through the service port by accepting a valid Dynamic Host Configuration Protocol (DHCP) configuration or manual IP address and netmask.

Entering **0.0.0.0** for the IP address and netmask disables the service port.

+ Ensures that the controller can communicate with the network (802.11 distribution system) through the management interface, having you assign a static IP address, netmask, default router IP address, VLAN identifier, and physical port assignment.

+ Prompts for the IP address of the DHCP server used to supply IP addresses to clients and the controller management interface.

✦ Asks for the Lightweight Access Point Protocol (LWAPP) Transport mode.

✦ Collects the virtual gateway IP address — any fictitious, unassigned IP address (such as 1.1.1.1) to be used by Layer 3 security and mobility managers.

✦ Allows you to enter the mobility group (RF group) name, which is just a descriptive name for a group of APs.

✦ Collects the wireless LAN 802.11 SSID, or network name.

✦ Asks you to indicate whether clients can use static IP addresses. Allowing this option is more convenient for some users but offers less security. Disallowing this option requires that all devices get their IP configuration from a DHCP server.

✦ Asks whether you want to configure a Remote Authentication Dial-In User Service (RADIUS) server from the Startup Wizard. If you do want to use RADIUS, you are prompted for the server IP address, communication port, and shared secret (password).

✦ Collects the country code to ensure that it configures the radios for the local region.

✦ Enables or disables the 802.11a/n and 802.11b/g/n lightweight access point networks.

✦ Enables or disables Radio Resource Management (RRM).

Verifying connectivity to the wired LAN

If you have connected your management cable, proceeded through the Startup Wizard, and provided it all the information it required, you now have a running WLC supporting at least one SSID. If you choose to, you can perform any remaining configuration changes either from a remote terminal or via the web-based GUI. Throughout this chapter, I show you how to do your configuration from the command-line interface (CLI), but at the end of the chapter, I give you a quick tour of the web interface. The following sections allow you to configure additional SSIDs.

Enabling the 802.11 bands

Using the command-line interface (CLI), you can enable or disable the supported radios with the following commands:

```
config 802.11a disable network
config 802.11b disable network
config 802.11a enable network
config 802.11b enable network
config {802.11a | 802.11b} 11nsupport {enable | disable}
```

To save and view your configuration changes, use the following commands:

```
save config
show {802.11a | 802.11b}
```

You then see output that looks something like this:

```
802.11a Network.............................. Enabled
11nSupport................................... Enabled
802.11a Low Band......................... Enabled
802.11a Mid Band......................... Enabled
802.11a High Band........................ Enabled
802.11a Operational Rates
802.11a 6M Rate............................ Mandatory
802.11a 9M Rate............................ Supported
802.11a 12M Rate........................... Mandatory
802.11a 18M Rate........................... Supported
802.11a 24M Rate........................... Mandatory
802.11a 36M Rate........................... Supported
802.11a 48M Rate........................... Supported
802.11a 54M Rate........................... Supported
...
```

Configuring the SSID

In the case of Cisco Wireless LAN Controllers, an SSID is configured as part of a WLAN so that each WLAN maps to an SSID. Within the WLAN settings, you can configure security, quality of service (QoS), radio policies, and other wireless network settings. Each controller supports up to 16 WLANs.

The following commands allow you to configure an additional SSID:

```
show wlan summary
config wlan create wlan_id profile_name ssid
```

When the WLAN is created, it is automatically disabled for security. After you have completed all your security settings, you can enable the WLAN with the following commands:

```
config wlan enable wlan_id
save config
```

Configuring WLAN security

Configuring security settings on WLAN sets is for all your associated access points. You can configure either static WEP or WPA for wireless security.

Configuring WEP keys

To configure static WEP keys, follow these steps based on a specific WLAN ID:

1. **Disable 802.1x encryption:**

```
config wlan security 802.1X disable wlan_id
```

2. **Configure the WEP key as 40/64-, 104/128-, or 128/152-bit:**

```
config wlan security static-wep-key encryption wlan_id {40 | 104 | 128}
    {hex | ascii} key key_index
```

The default key level is 104, which requires you to enter 26 hexadecimal or 13 ASCII characters for the key.

3. **To configure WPA1 or WPA2, use the following commands:**

```
config wlan disable wlan_id
config wlan security wpa {enable | disable} wlan_id
config wlan security wpa wpa1 {enable | disable} wlan_id
```

4. **To enable WPA2, use the following command:**

```
config wlan security wpa wpa2 {enable | disable} wlan_id
```

5. **Choose Advanced Encryption Standard (AES) or Temporal Key Integrity Protocol (TKIP) for data encryption:**

```
config wlan security wpa wpa1 ciphers {aes | tkip} {enable | disable}
    wlan_id
config wlan security wpa wpa2 ciphers {aes | tkip} {enable | disable}
    wlan_id
```

The default values are TKIP for WPA1 and AES for WPA2.

6. **Choose a system for authenticated key management, which would be 802.1X, Pre-Shared Key (PSK), or Cisco Centralized Key Management (CCKM):**

```
config wlan security wpa akm {802.1X | psk | cckm} {enable | disable}
    wlan_id
```

The default value is 802.1X.

7. **When using PSK, set a preshared key:**

```
config wlan security wpa akm psk set-key {ascii | hex} psk-key wlan_id
```

WPA preshared keys must be 8 to 63 ASCII text characters or 64 hexadecimal characters long.

8. **Enable the WLAN:**

```
config wlan enable wlan_id
```

9. **Save your settings:**

```
save config
```

Setting up Cisco access points

When using a Cisco lightweight APs, you need to set up the WLC to accept registration of APs. This set up is all part of the controller discovery process.

As previously mentioned, Cisco's lightweight access points (LWAPs) use the Lightweight Access Point Protocol (LWAPP) to communicate between the components of the wireless network infrastructure. In this environment, your access point needs to be associated or linked with a controller to properly function. The *discovery process* is the system that allows this association to occur. After an access point is associated with a WLC, its full potential can be reached.

1. The LWAP sends a join request to the controller.

2. The controller acknowledges this request by sending a join response to the lightweight access point.

3. The LWAP has permission to become associated with the controller and stores the controller connection information locally.

After the discovery process is complete, the controller can manage all aspects of the lightweight access point, such as its configuration, firmware, control transactions, and data transactions.

Methods for discovering an AP

A lightweight access point can be discovered in the following ways:

✦ **Layer 3 LWAPP discovery:** This discovery occurs when the LWAP is on a different subnet from the WLC and the AP uses the IP address rather than the Layer 2 MAC address.

✦ **Layer 2 LWAPP discovery:** This discovery occurs when the LWAP and WLC are on the same subnet and the discovery data is placed in Ethernet frames that contain the MAC addresses of the two devices.

Layer 2 LWAPP discovery cannot be used in Layer 3 environments.

✦ **Over-the-air provisioning (OTAP):** This option is supported only by Cisco 5500, Cisco 4400, and Cisco 2100 series WLCs. If the option is enabled, all associated access points send neighbor messages. These neighbor messages allow new LWAP devices to receive the WLC's IP address, where they can conduct the rest of the discovery process. After this process has been completed, the option on the controller should be disabled.

✦ **Locally stored controller IP address discovery:** After a discovery has been completed, the AP stores the addresses for its controllers in non-volatile memory so that, for later deployment, it has all the necessary controller information. This process is called *priming the access point*.

✦ **DHCP server discovery:** This option allows the DHCP option 43 to provide controller IP addresses to the access points.

✦ **DNS discovery:** Domain Name System (DNS) information for the controller can be stored in your DNS zone. The record should be called `CISCO-LWAPP-CONTROLLER.localdomain`, where `localdomain` is the access point domain name. After the AP knows the IP address of the controller, it can connect to the controller to complete the registration process.

Locating a specific LWAP

From time to time, you may need to locate a specific lightweight access point on your network. The easiest way to do this is to configure the access point to flash its LEDs. This feature is supported on any controller software release 4.0 or later and all lightweight access points. To flash an access point's LEDs, issue the following command:

```
debug ap enable Cisco_AP
```

To cause a specific access point to flash its LEDs for a specified number of seconds, issue this command:

```
debug ap command "led flash seconds" Cisco_AP
```

You can enter a value between 1 and 3600 for the `seconds` parameter. To disable LED flashing for a specific access point, use the following command:

```
debug ap command "led flash disable" Cisco_AP
```

Configuring backup controllers

Due to the importance of having an active controller on your network to support your wireless network, you should not rely on only having a single controller on your network. Controllers may be distributed between a central site and regional sites and still manage all APs anywhere on the network. Controllers at the central site and regional sites do not need to be in the same mobility group, and using the CLI on the controller you can specify a primary, secondary, and tertiary controller for your lightweight access points.

Starting with controller software release 5.0, you can configure timers for the primary and secondary controllers so that the time taken to discover a failed primary controller is reduced. If, during that timed interval, a controller has not received any data packets from the other controller, it then sends an `echo` request to the controller. If there are no results from the `echo`, the controller considers the other controller to be failed. From the lightweight access point's perspective, if a controller fails two consecutive discovery requests, it is considered to be failed.

In all failure cases, the secondary and then the tertiary controllers are attempted to be contacted. When the primary controller comes back on line, the access points automatically fail back over to the primary controller. To configure backup controllers, follow these steps:

1. **Configure a primary controller for a specific access point:**

   ```
   config ap primary-base controller_name Cisco_AP [controller_ip_address]
   ```

2. **Configure a secondary controller for a specific access point:**

   ```
   config ap secondary-base controller_name Cisco_AP [controller_ip_address]
   ```

3. **Configure a tertiary controller for a specific access point:**

   ```
   config ap tertiary-base controller_name Cisco_AP [controller_ip_address]
   ```

4. **Configure a primary backup controller for a specific controller:**

   ```
   config advanced backup-controller primary backup_controller_name backup_
       controller_ip_address
   ```

5. **Configure a secondary backup controller for a specific controller:**

   ```
   config advanced backup-controller secondary backup_controller_name
   backup_controller_ip_address
   ```

6. **Configure the fast heartbeat timer for local, hybrid-REAP, or all access points:**

   ```
   config advanced timers ap-fast-heartbeat {local | hreap | all} {enable |
       disable} interval
   ```

7. **Configure the access point primary discovery request timer:**

   ```
   config advanced timers ap-primary-discovery-timeout interval
   ```

8. **Save your changes:**

   ```
   save config
   ```

9. **Verify the configuration changes that you made by using these commands:**

   ```
   show ap config general Cisco_AP
   show advanced backup-controller
   show advanced timers
   ```

Web authentication process

The web authentication process is a Layer 3 security function that allows the controller to block all client IP traffic with the exception of DHCP traffic. After the client has obtained an IP address, the only action that is open to the user is to attempt to connect to a website. Any HTTP-related traffic is then captured. The user's web browser session is redirected to a default or custom login page, where the user is prompted for authentication information in the form of a username and password.

Because this system includes a self-signed certification, the first time that this process takes place the user is prompted with a security alert that should be accepted.

You have a few options for the login page: The basic controller administration page allows some simple modification of the page text and the presentation of the Cisco logo. The following options are available as login pages:

✦ The default login page

✦ A modified version of the default login page (as shown in Figure 4-1), directs users to the receptionist for login credentials. This allows you to provide additional directions for new users, but limits the level of customization.

✦ A customized login page that you configure on an external web server

✦ A customized login page that you download to the controller

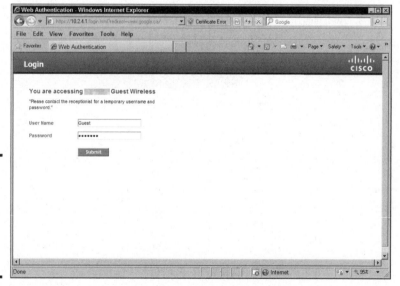

Figure 4-1:
Modified version of default web authentication page.

After the user successfully logs in, he is presented with a successful login page and then automatically redirected to the originally requested URL.

Using the Cisco graphical user interface (GUI)

For both the Wireless LAN Controller and autonomous APs, you also have an option of using the GUI to perform your configuration. This GUI is web-based and can be configured to operate over HTTP or HTTPS. Because the WLC module may be embedded in a switch, firewall, or router, you may find that some WLC management is performed through one of Cisco's other management interfaces, such as Cisco's Security Device Manager (SDM) or Adaptive Security Device Manager (ASDM). The SDM can be launched from the web management interface of Cisco's Integrated Services Router (ISR). The ASDM is the main management interface for Cisco's Adaptive Security Appliance (ASA) firewalls and is also launched through the web management interface.

Figure 4-2 shows a sample of the web interface used for managing the Cisco 2106 WLC; the interface for the 4400 series WLC and 5500 series WLC is similar.

Figure 4-2: The administration GUI on the Cisco 2106 WLC.

Figure 4-3 shows the management interface for the Autonomous mode Cisco 1250 Series Access Point. Note that its interface appears quite different from that of the WLC you saw in Figure 4-2. In this case, the SSID management is found in the SSID Manager on the Security menu (located in the left menu), whereas the WLC has SSID settings on the WLAN menu.

The other interface that is quite different is that of the Cisco ASA firewalls using the ASDM, which is shown in Figure 4-4. This interface is shown only to illustrate the differences in Cisco's management tools, because the company has a wide set of tools for its appliances. In the case of the ASDM, Cisco uses the web interface on the ASA firewall to launch a Java applet which is the ASDM. By using a Java applet, Cisco has more options available to manage windows and controls (such as radio buttons and check boxes) that can be limiting in a web interface.

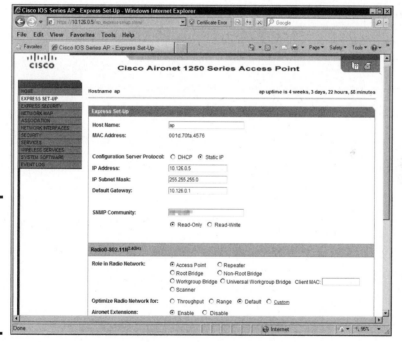

Figure 4-3:
The administration GUI on the Cisco 1250 Series Access Point.

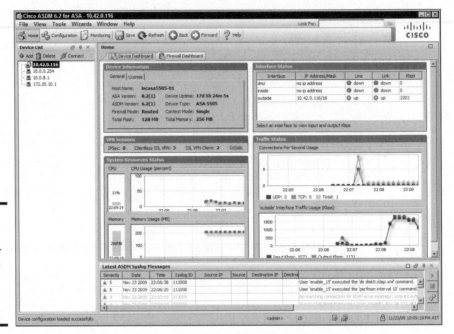

Figure 4-4:
The administration GUI on the Cisco ASA 5505 firewall.

Book VI

Security

"We found where the security breach in the WLAN was originating. It was coming in through another rogue robot-vac. This is the third one this month. Must have gotten away from its owner, like all the rest."

Contents at a Glance

Chapter 1: Defending against Common Attacks with Basic Security Tools

In This Chapter

✔ Reviewing internal network attacks

✔ Identifying external attack methods

✔ Implementing firewall rules to protect your network

✔ Working with other protection tools

*W*hen dealing with security on your Cisco network, you can focus on a number of areas. In this chapter, you look at high-level devices in the form of firewall devices and proxies. In many cases, your firewall device may have proxy components built into it, or the proxy components will operate on a separate device or host. In my discussion on firewalls, I focus on the features found in the Cisco Adaptive Security Appliance (ASA) because they are fairly common when compared with the other devices on the market. (You find out how to manage and configure the ASA in Chapter 2 of this minibook.) You also look at the types of attacks to which you may be susceptible on your network. (For the specific functions of Network Address Translation [NAT] and Access Control Lists [ACLs], see Chapter 3 in this minibook.)

So sit back and review the types of attacks that the bad guys will likely attempt on your network. I follow that up with steps and tools you can use to prevent these attacks or to remediate the damage caused by such attacks. Remember, although these tools and attacks may be carried out by others with the intent to steal information or harm your network, you may also want to use the same tools and attacks as part of a network audit.

Knowing Your Enemy

In *The Art of War,* Sun Tzu said that "if you know your enemies and know yourself, you will not be imperiled in a hundred battles." By this, he means that the more you know about your enemies and how they will operate, the better you can avoid being drawn into unwanted battles. Knowing what your enemy is going to try provides you the opportunity to protect yourself. So in these sections, I show you some of the things that crafty (or sometimes not-so-crafty) enemies may try.

Two main types of attacks take place on a network: those that are run from inside the network and those that try to make their way in from the network's perimeter. I start by going through the most common internal attacks, and then I move on to describe common external attacks.

Handling attacks from within

Although everyone wants to trust the people that they work with, a large number of attacks occur from within your network. These attacks may be from employees or from non-employees who are in your building, and on your network. Although much of the focus on security deals with the perimeter of your network and the access points, you must not forget about the inside of your network and what you can do to defend yourself after the attacker is inside. The most common types of internal attacks are packet sniffing, man in the middle, cached credentials, masquerade, and network scanning. The following sections look at each of these attacks and what you can do to defend yourself.

Packet sniffing

Packet sniffing captures network traffic at the Ethernet frame level. After capture, this data can be analyzed and sensitive information can be retrieved. Such an attack starts with a tool such as Wireshark (described in Book I, Chapter 4). Wireshark allows you to capture and examine data that is flowing across your network. Any data that is not encrypted is readable, and unfortunately, many types of traffic on your network are passed as unencrypted data — even passwords and other sensitive data. Obviously, this situation represents a danger to your corporate data. Many applications that house corporate data (even those with slick Windows-based GUIs) still use Telnet as the data transfer mechanism. *Telnet* is a clear text, unencrypted data transfer mechanism. A person with a packet sniffer can view this data as it crosses your network. Figure 1-1 shows FTP logon data captured behind the FTP window, showing the user's password. Having your FTP password known allows the attacker to have your level of access to your FTP site, and any secret data that may be there; on top of that, many users who use the same password for all systems on the network. Now the attacker may have access to several of your corporate systems.

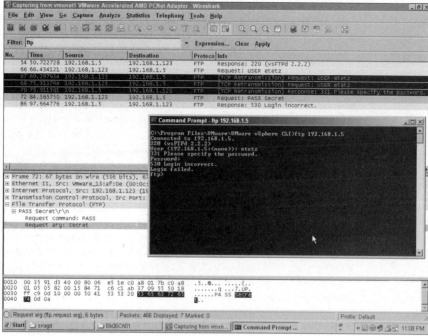

Figure 1-1:
FTP logon
data in a
packet
capture.

In addition to capturing cleartext sessions, such as login traffic, an attacker can have an application that captures only specific data from a network, such as network authentication packets, which she then reviews to crack network passwords.

If you are using switch-based network, you make packet sniffing a little tougher. On a switch-based network, the sniffer will see only data going to and from the sniffer's own network device or broadcast traffic, unless the attacker uses a monitoring port on a switch. If you have not secured your switches and your switch configuration documentation with a strong password, you are leaving yourself open to a packet-sniffing attack.

A packet-sniffing attack on a switch-based network happens like this: The attacker connects to a switch and uses information from that switch to locate his own MAC address. The attacker locates his MAC address via show address-database, which lets him know what port the address is seen on. The attacker can follow the path until he finds the switch to which he is connected. From there, the attacker can enable a monitor port as the port to which he connected. Now he can see all the traffic on that switch and can start a packet capture of data.

Switch security is the first line of your network security from internal hacking. Switch security is the path attackers must go through to get to the rest of your network. If you can keep attackers from connecting or restrict their ability to gain sensitive information, you beat them.

Man in the middle

Man in the middle is a type of masquerade attack. A man-in-the-middle attack works like this: If the attacker places herself between you and the server to which you are talking, the attacker can see all the data (encrypted or not) that you are sending to the server. This particular attack is very disconcerting because they can easily see the data that you expect is 100-percent secure, even your HTTPS dealings with your bank.

In this attack, the attacker takes over the role of a device between you and the system you are talking to. This device could be a router, where the attacker confuses the switch ARP table and has data destined for the router to be sent to her. Then she relays the data to the router. In this way, the attacker can still deal with the router and the server on the other side of the router, but the attacker sees all the traffic. This setup allows an attacker to capture passwords, even for secure sites, such as banking.

Tools that can conduct this type of attack are freely available. One such tool is Cain & Abel from www.oxid.it.

Man in the middle is one of the most insidious attacks, because you may not even know it is happening. For this reason, any unsecured network should be considered hostile or even broken.

Cracking cached credentials

Another source for attackers to gain access to system passwords and sensitive data is right on your workstations. Many users leave their computers unattended for periods of time. Even if the computer is powered off, an attacker can boot from a USB device and access your entire hard drive, or if left on and unlocked, he can do whatever he wants. One set of files attackers are often after hold the credential cache. That file contains all the passwords you have told Windows to save on the system.

Cain & Able has the unique ability to extract data from your system, such as passwords that are stored in a variety of password caches. Figure 1-2 shows a list of server passwords that have been cached on the local workstation. Attackers accomplish this type of data retrieval by reversing the hashing (or encrypting) process that hid the password in the first place.

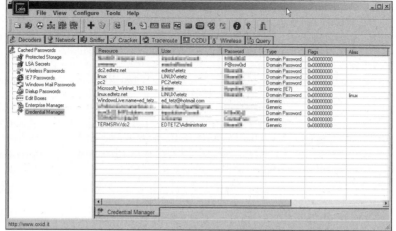

Figure 1-2:
A list of
passwords
retrieved
from the
local system
by Cain.

Masquerade

A *masquerade attack* is a type spoofing attack where the attacker pretends to be someone or some device which he is not. (The man-in-the-middle attack can be considered a masquerade attack because the man in the middle pretends to be a router or some other type of middle device.) E-mail addresses, URLs, and network devices such as routers can all be spoofed. Masquerade attacks often succeed because people see what they expect to see.

One effective masquerade is to create a fake Windows server. Clients on that network automatically attempt to authenticate to this fake Windows server with their current logon credentials. A client does this authentication by accepting a random challenge word from the server, encrypting it using her password as the encryption key, and sending that newly encrypted string to the server. The attacker running the masquerade server knows what word was originally sent as the challenge, so he can compare that encrypted string with the string he gets from a series of password attempts. When the attacker finds a matching string, he knows the password.

Network scanning

Network scanning allows you to find out what systems are on your network, what services they may be offering, and sometimes a fair bit more than that, such as services with known vulnerabilities or systems that the IT staff thought were removed from the network years ago. One of the most common general purpose network scanners is Nmap, or network map, with its Windows-based Zenmap, available from `http://nmap.org`. From the attack perspective, this tool is part of most attacker's information-gathering arsenal. With a list of systems, operating systems, and running services, she can pick the weakest members of your network herd.

As an internal auditing tool, I regularly use Zenmap to verify available IP addresses on a network. By providing Zenmap a network ID and few seconds, it can provide you with a list of used IP addresses, matching MAC addresses, DNS names for those systems, open ports on those systems, and even the OS type for the hosts that it has found. The following code is an example of the type of information you can see from a Zenmap or an Nmap scan of a system. It discovered the following:

- ✦ This is an Ubuntu Linux computer.
- ✦ This machine shares files out to Windows-based computers.
- ✦ This machine hosts a website.
- ✦ This machine is running VMware Server.
- ✦ This host supports SSH and VNC as remote access methods.
- ✦ This host is running a mail server and an FTP server.

```
Starting Nmap 5.21 ( http://nmap.org ) at 2011-04-15 02:01 Atlantic Daylight Time
NSE: Loaded 36 scripts for scanning.
Initiating ARP Ping Scan at 02:01
Scanning 192.168.1.5 [1 port]
Completed ARP Ping Scan at 02:01, 0.30s elapsed (1 total hosts)
Initiating Parallel DNS resolution of 1 host. at 02:01
Completed Parallel DNS resolution of 1 host. at 02:01, 0.00s elapsed
Initiating SYN Stealth Scan at 02:01
Scanning 192.168.1.5 [1000 ports]
Discovered open port 445/tcp on 192.168.1.5
Discovered open port 111/tcp on 192.168.1.5
Discovered open port 5900/tcp on 192.168.1.5
Discovered open port 53/tcp on 192.168.1.5
Discovered open port 21/tcp on 192.168.1.5
Discovered open port 80/tcp on 192.168.1.5
Discovered open port 22/tcp on 192.168.1.5
Discovered open port 25/tcp on 192.168.1.5
Discovered open port 443/tcp on 192.168.1.5
Discovered open port 139/tcp on 192.168.1.5
Discovered open port 8222/tcp on 192.168.1.5
Discovered open port 902/tcp on 192.168.1.5
Discovered open port 8009/tcp on 192.168.1.5
Discovered open port 8333/tcp on 192.168.1.5
Discovered open port 1984/tcp on 192.168.1.5
Discovered open port 2049/tcp on 192.168.1.5
Completed SYN Stealth Scan at 02:01, 1.53s elapsed (1000 total ports)
Initiating Service scan at 02:01
Scanning 16 services on 192.168.1.5
Completed Service scan at 02:03, 116.14s elapsed (16 services on 1 host)
Initiating RPCGrind Scan against 192.168.1.5 at 02:03
Completed RPCGrind Scan against 192.168.1.5 at 02:03, 0.03s elapsed (2 ports)
Initiating OS detection (try #1) against 192.168.1.5
NSE: Script scanning 192.168.1.5.
```

```
NSE: Starting runlevel 1 (of 1) scan.
Initiating NSE at 02:03
Completed NSE at 02:03, 25.06s elapsed
NSE: Script Scanning completed.
Nmap scan report for 192.168.1.5
Host is up (0.0014s latency).
Not shown: 984 closed ports
PORT      STATE SERVICE        VERSION
21/tcp    open  ftp            vsftpd 2.2.2
22/tcp    open  ssh            OpenSSH 5.3p1 Debian 3ubuntu4 (protocol 2.0)
| ssh-hostkey: 1024 5b:6d:35:57:65:42:7f:8a:73:7e:00:e3:89:f9:15:bf (DSA)
|_2048 4d:6e:be:c4:3b:0c:55:f5:46:dd:b8:05:05:1c:94:ea (RSA)
25/tcp    open  smtp           Exim smtpd 4.71
| smtp-commands: EHLO linux Hello isc-10065.local [192.168.1.137], SIZE 52428800,
     PIPELINING, HELP
|_HELP Commands supported: AUTH HELO EHLO MAIL RCPT DATA NOOP QUIT RSET HELP
53/tcp    open  tcpwrapped
80/tcp    open  http           Apache httpd 2.2.14 ((Ubuntu))
|_html-title: Ed's Web Page Test Zone
111/tcp   open  rpcbind        2 (rpc #100000)
| rpcinfo:
| 100000  2         111/udp  rpcbind
| 100003  2,3,4     2049/udp nfs
| 100005  1,2,3     43439/udp mountd
| 100021  1,3,4     52866/udp nlockmgr
| 100024  1         57570/udp status
| 100000  2         111/tcp  rpcbind
| 100003  2,3,4     2049/tcp nfs
| 100024  1         35177/tcp status
| 100005  1,2,3     41859/tcp mountd
|_100021  1,3,4     41980/tcp nlockmgr
139/tcp   open  netbios-ssn    Samba smbd 3.X (workgroup: NET)
443/tcp   open  ssl/http       Apache httpd 2.2.14 ((Ubuntu))
|_html-title: Ed's Web Page Test Zone
445/tcp   open  netbios-ssn    Samba smbd 3.X (workgroup: NET)
902/tcp   open  ssl/vmware-auth VMware Authentication Daemon 1.10 (Uses VNC, SOAP)
1984/tcp  open  bigbrother?
2049/tcp open  nfs            2-4 (rpc #100003)
5900/tcp open  vnc            VNC (protocol 3.7)
8009/tcp open  ajp13          Apache Jserv (Protocol v1.3)
8222/tcp open  http           VMware Server 2 http config
|_html-title: VMware Server 2
8333/tcp open  ssl/http       VMware Server 2 http config
|_html-title: VMware Server 2
MAC Address: 00:22:15:BA:93:1C (Asustek Computer)
Device type: general purpose
Running: Linux 2.6.X
OS details: Linux 2.6.19 - 2.6.31
Uptime guess: 11.438 days (since Sun Apr 03 15:32:20 2011)
Network Distance: 1 hop
TCP Sequence Prediction: Difficulty=203 (Good luck!)
IP ID Sequence Generation: All zeros
Service Info: Host: linux; OSs: Unix, Linux

Host script results:
| nbstat:
|   NetBIOS name: LINUX, NetBIOS user: <unknown>, NetBIOS MAC: <unknown>
|   Names
|     LINUX<00>              Flags: <unique><active>
|     LINUX<03>              Flags: <unique><active>
|     LINUX<20>              Flags: <unique><active>
|     \x01\x02__MSBROWSE__\x02<01> Flags: <group><active>
```

```
|     EDTETZ.NET<1d>       Flags: <unique><active>
|     EDTETZ.NET<1e>       Flags: <group><active>
|_    EDTETZ.NET<00>       Flags: <group><active>
|_smbv2-enabled: Server doesn't support SMBv2 protocol
| smb-os-discovery:
|   OS: Unix (Samba 3.4.7)
|   Name: Unknown\Unknown
|_  System time: 2011-04-15 01:59:48 UTC-3

HOP RTT     ADDRESS
1   1.41 ms 192.168.1.5

Read data files from: C:\Program Files\Nmap
OS and Service detection performed. Please report any incorrect results at
     http://nmap.org/submit/ .
Nmap done: 1 IP address (1 host up) scanned in 147.66 seconds
          Raw packets sent: 1021 (45.684KB) | Rcvd: 1016 (41.416KB)
```

What does this information allow an attacker to do? Well, it gives an attacker a fairly complete list of services that are offered by this network device, and if he wants to find a way onto a network, he can examine this list of services offered for a service that is known to be weak and use that as a method or path to gain access to the system. For example, if an attacker has found a Windows computer telling him that TCP port 3389 is available, he can run Remote Desktop Connection (`mstsc.exe`) to connect to that computer and try a number of common passwords for the Administrator account, or he can run some tools or exploit some known weaknesses in the Windows OS.

Dealing with external attacks

Attacks that start from outside a network fall into a couple of categories: They tend to be either denial of services (DoS) or attempts to gain access and exploit a system. In many cases, these are both one and the same. When your devices are running correctly, they have space to log data and access attempts, and applications — especially the security applications — all have enough memory to operate. Many of the attacks in the DoS category flood the systems with so much data that these data logs overflow (so you cannot see what the attacker is attempting), and security applications or processes run out of memory and possibly shut down or malfunction. When your system has nonfunctioning security applications and a lack of logging, the attacker can take control of that system to further her access on your network. The following sections describe common external attacks you need to be aware of and prepared for.

SYN flooding

In Book II, Chapter 2, I describe what a three-way handshake looks like. What would happen if I did not complete the process? The situation would be like getting a phone call at home, but when you answer the call and say "Hello" (the second step in the process), the person on the other end does not respond or tells you to hang up. In this case, you stay on the phone for some period of time, during which you cannot take any more calls.

In the TCP world, your network devices are capable of handling a limited number of connections. It is a high number, but it is limited based on the device and its configuration. Figure 1-3 shows what happens in a *SYN flood,* an attack where the attacking device sends a series of SYN requests with the goal of overwhelming the system. What the attacking system does not do is respond to any of those returned SYN-ACK packets. Because you have a limited number of listening connections on your system, for a relatively short period of time, you cannot accept a new connection because all the lines are busy waiting for ACK packets from the person who opened all the connections.

Figure 1-3:
When all the Listening connections are consumed, legitimate users are prevented from connecting.

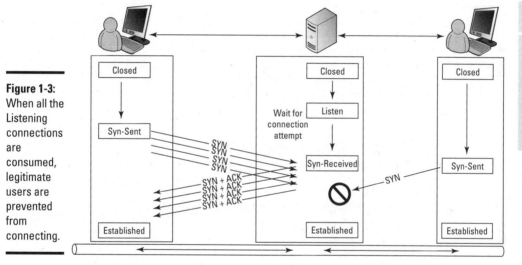

SYN flooding is a denial-of-service attack because legitimate users of the system cannot connect and do what they would typically be able to. This attack may interrupt services, or it may be an attempt to fill log files so that the actual attack does not leave any trances. After one of your systems has been targeted by a SYN flood, you may be able to connect to the flooded system and clear these half-opened connections rather than waiting for the system to time them out and clear them on its own schedule. Although SYN flooding is an old attack, it is still an effective attack on many systems.

Cisco devices allow you to do a few things to reduce the effectiveness of these attacks:

✦ Increasing the TCP backlog

✦ Reducing the SYN-RECEIVED timer

✦ Implementing a SYN cache

✦ Implementing SYN cookies

Smurf attacks

Smurf attacks are popular DoS attacks, likely named because of its use of a large number of small ICMP packets. The goal of this attack is to create a crushing amount of traffic. This attack came about as a function of ICMP and the network broadcast address. If an attacker has a large network segment that he is aware of, he can send a ping or an ICMP Echo Request to that broadcast address. Each host on that network should take that because the broadcast address was used, though the Echo Request is actually destined for itself. What it should then do is generate an Echo Reply back to the attacker's computer. This Echo Reply could cause a full Class B address block to generate up to 65,000 replies for one request packet.

This Echo Reply floods the attacker's computer with replies that could then cripple his computer with only a few Echo Requests being sent out. Now, what if the attacker modifies that Echo Request when it goes out, and instead of specifying his address as the source of the packet, he specifies another address? This trick allows an attacker to cause that crippling number of replies to be sent to an innocent third party, who would be the actual target of the Smurf attack.

Distributed denial of service (DDoS)

In a *distributed denial-of-service (DDoS)* attack, the attacker takes the same basic process as with any denial of service attack: He generates a sufficient amount of traffic to overwhelm the targeted device. The method may be a SYN flood attack or other attack, but what makes a DDoS attack unique is that the attack comes from more than just one device.

A virus may turn your computer into a robot waiting for commands to be run from a controlling server or device. This allows your computer to play a small role in a DDoS attack on some poor unlucky server or network. This way, if your defense to the DoS attack was to identify and block offenders, you can no longer defend your system because the attack comes from many places at the same time.

So if an attacker has an army of robot computers to generate SYN flood or Smurf attacks, she can wield a crippling level of power. (Insert maniacal laughter.)

Password attacks

Sometimes people attempt password attacks on a running system; but with passwords that lock accounts out after a few failed logon attempts, this attack is not very productive. More typically, password attacks capture RAW logon traffic from the network or break into a backup of a domain controller or workstation on the network. If an attacker reboots a workstation on a network from a CD or USB key, he can quickly grab a copy of the Windows SAM and security files from the Windows directory.

With these files in hand, the attacker can spend as much time as he wants trying to guess the passwords that are found in these files. In the case of the workstation, these security files give an attacker the local passwords on a computer, such as the local Administrator account; which he can then use to get a hold of network passwords which will provide more access to the network.

From the SAM file, an attacker can attempt to use two methods to crack these passwords:

✦ **Brute force attack:** With this attack or password-guessing technique, the cracking software goes through every password possibility from *a* through to *zzzzzzzzzz*, including all possible numbers or punctuation characters. This process of finding a password can take a very long time, longer for every extra character put into the password.

✦ **Dictionary attack:** This password-guessing technique can be done much faster, and it makes use of dictionary or word list files. These files are readily available on the Internet and include dictionaries such as the standard Oxford dictionary, every word found in the works of William Shakespeare, and even obscure or made-up language dictionaries such as Klingon. With these word lists in hand, the attacker can quickly compare these words to the hash values for the Windows passwords found in the SAM file. To speed things up even more, he can have his computer go through the dictionary files and create a password hash for every word, and then he just needs to compare the pregenerated hash values with those found in the SAM file. This process can give the attacker even more speed in finding these passwords. Despite warnings not to, many people still use standard dictionary words for their passwords.

To protect your network from these possibilities, you need to provide some level of protection to the local OS installations, especially for workstations that are in the public or in areas of high public access. Workstations that must be in those areas should have physical security preventing them from being rebooted from custom media. Passwords used on these systems should be different from main domain client systems. Finally, use a strong password policy, which includes regular changes to the passwords and a requirement that the passwords should not be dictionary words.

Implementing Firewalls

A strong perimeter security helps to protect your network from external attacks. The main element on the perimeter security front is a firewall.

Types of firewalls

You can deploy several types of firewalls and other security options. The different types of firewalls include the following:

✦ **Packet filtering:** These firewalls use ACLs to inspect the data that they forward down to the IP layer. This inspection allows them to classify data based on the TCP or UDP ports, as well as the source and destination IP addresses. This filtering allows you to make forwarding decisions. Some organizations use packet filtering to allow only traffic that meets approved criteria to pass out of the firewall.

✦ **Stateful inspection:** Also known as Stateful Packet Inspection (SPI) firewalls, these firewalls not only allow packet filtering, but it pays attention to the flow of the packets. Rather than evaluating each packet as a separate entity, it looks at the flow of the traffic and identifies packets that are replies to others. SPI can evaluate packets that are suspicious and part of an attack profile.

✦ **Application layer firewall:** This firewall can be a specific firewall, but it tends to fall in the category of proxy and reverse proxy servers. In this case, there can be a deep packet inspection into the data to validate that it is not only allowed, but also not part of an attack on the systems that make up your network. These firewalls tend to be specific for the application layer protocol that they are protecting. Common choices here are HTTP, FTP, and SMTP.

Ingress and egress filtering

Most firewalls act as gatekeepers for networks or network segments and exist in a position where a router would exist. In fact, if the feature set has been enabled, your Cisco router can easily be called a firewall if it does any filtering of the traffic on your network. As a gatekeeper for your network, this device carefully filters out undesirable traffic that attempts to enter your network.

Although most people think of firewalls as protecting the network from incoming traffic, they can also prevent traffic from leaving your network. You can restrict your internal users from getting off of your network and going anywhere they would like. That is part of the egress filtering, which can be just as important as the ingress filtering.

I know some very paranoid people that use deny Access Control Lists (ACLs) as their basic network access rule on all firewalls in both directions, so all network traffic incoming or outgoing needs approval. I cover ACLs in Chapter 3 of this minibook. This method does take some commitment, but it ends up being very secure, if you manage to still keep it functional.

Defending data with the DMZ

A *demilitarized zone (DMZ)* is an area two opposing military forces have declared as a buffer zone between each other. Both sides agree that they will stay out of that area. For computer networks, the DMZ is an area where you have placed servers that the public at large — or at least people outside your network — need access to. These are placed outside your network and may have the ability to talk to your internal server. Although the servers are placed outside your network, they are not totally unprotected; they are still behind a firewall in a configuration similar to one of the options shown in Figure 1-4. The DMZ segment may be installed next to your current firewall or may be an actual zone between your network and the public network. Either is a valid DMZ option, each offering a benefit tradeoff between ease of configuration and security.

Finding holes in your firewall

You can run Nmap internally on your network to identify devices, but you can also run it from outside your firewall to identify holes in the firewall. Steve Gibson of Gibson Research Group (www.grc.com) offers a test for open ports from outside your network through his Shields Up! tool. The following figure shows what the results look like. This tool shows you what type information you are allowing to pass from your workstation to outside your firewall. Kind of spooky.

In the figure, the results show what I expected: No proof of a firewall existing on most ports, except for the ports on which I actually host services.

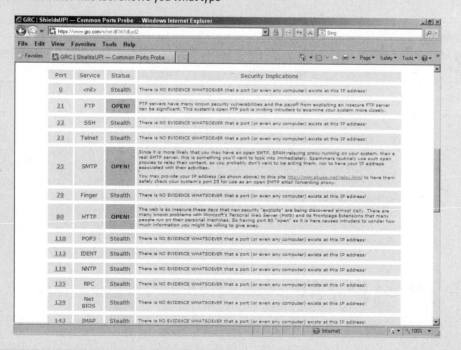

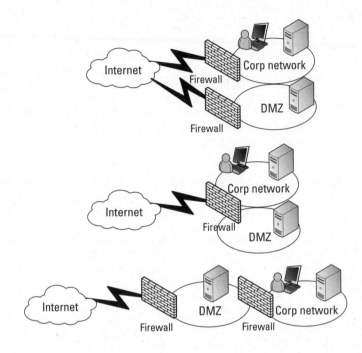

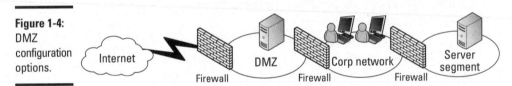

Figure 1-4:
DMZ
configuration
options.

In the same manner as creating a DMZ, I have some clients who have isolated their servers on a separate network segment, with a firewall defend-
ing that segment. In this scenario, they have a DMZ protecting their public
facing servers, their users behind the DMZ with protection from another
firewall, and then their servers protected from their users behind yet
another firewall. This scenario means that if an attack or a virus gains access
to the user network, it will not get immediate access to the servers as well.
Although this setup may seem a bit paranoid, it *is* very secure.

Defending Your Network against Attacks

As I mention earlier in this chapter, perimeter defense is one level of defend-
ing your network from attacks, and it works wonderfully to protect from
external attacks. Perimeter defense is just part of the protection suite. I am
a strong believer in defense in depth. *Defense in depth* means that several
layers of security protect your network and its data, like Russian nesting
dolls.

Perimeter defense

The job of perimeter defense basically falls to your firewall devices. Short of unplugging your network from the rest of the world, this perimeter defense seems to be a necessary evil. Now in some cases, people have gone with the unplugged solutions. (For example, the following scenario is not uncommon in the military: Several levels of networks operate, each with a specific protection level, the highest of which says you are not connected to any outside networks and no extra devices are allowed to be connected to this secured network.) This unplugged solution, however, does not work for most businesses.

So, as a necessary evil, you need to deal with a perimeter that you will attempt to defend. Limiting the number of connections from other networks, such as the Internet, to the network helps a lot because you have fewer connections for which you need to manage protection. Ideally, from the security perspective, you have only one connection to the Internet; whereas sometimes within a company, operation requirements mean that some groups within the organization require additional connections.

Active tools

In addition to managing your perimeter, you should implement intrusion detection systems (IDS) and intrusion prevention systems (IPS), which both offer a similar suite of options. In fact, you can think of IPS as an extension of IDS because an IPS system actively disconnects devices or connections that are deemed as being used for an intrusion.

IDS devices can be network-based devices, running as appliances or separate servers running software, which is performing the IDS role, but they can also be installed on client or network computers. The later is often referred to as host-based intrusion detection system (HIDS). These devices can reside inside your network, behind your firewall, detecting abnormalities there, and/or they can be placed outside your firewall. When they are outside your firewall, they are typically targeted for the same attacks that run against the firewall, thereby alerting you to attacks being run against your firewall.

Cisco offers several options for IDS and IPS systems and offers these as standalone systems or add-ons for your existing security products. The following are two such options:

✦ Cisco ASA Advanced Inspection and Prevention Security Services Module

✦ Cisco Catalyst 6500 Series Intrusion Detection System (IDSM-2) Module

IDS and IPS have several methods for working with detection. Similar to viruses on your network, intrusions and attacks have features that are recorded as a signature or behavior. So when the IPS system sees this type of data or behavior, the IPS system can swing into action. Suspicious behavior can also trigger these systems. This behavior can include a remote system attempting to ping every address on your subnet in sequential order, and other activity that is considered to be abnormal. When the IPS system sees this activity, the IPS can be configured to blacklist or block the source device, either indefinitely or for a period of time.

The other way these systems can identify suspicious traffic on your network is to have them run in a Learning mode for a period of time. Over the course of weeks, they can classify regular traffic patterns on your network and then limit traffic to those established patterns. If you introduce new software to your network, you may need to manually add appropriate rules or run a learning period and then put the system back into Prevention mode. This necessity is even true of the host-based systems because they update their rules from the management or policy server that is running on the network.

These systems help prevent the spread of *Day Zero attacks,* which are new viruses or network attacks that are different from all the previous network intrusions. Because these Day Zero attacks are new, you do not have a specific signature for the attack; but the attack still needs to perform the same suspicious behaviors, which can be detected and blocked. So even if I have never seen the attack profile in the past because it is new, I can still block it because it will do things that I have chosen not to allow.

Defense in depth

The best defense is a multilayered defense *(defense in depth).* If you review information about historic battles, in many cases, one side made a break through the front lines (the perimeter) and was able to move though a huge area because nothing was there to stop them. Other more defended areas had reserve troops behind the front lines that were able to quash the breakthrough.

So history shows time and time again that defense in depth is better than only perimeter defenses. The downside is that defense in depth tends to have higher costs. I had one client wonder whether he really needed to continue to pay to have his antivirus from one company scanning incoming e-mail on the outside of the firewall, then scan it again with a product on another the internal mail server, and then scan on the clients with a third product? Well right after pondering this, he was hit with a new Day Zero virus, which made it through the first two scans before being picked up at his client machines. The company is still running three layers of scanning.

So your cost for depth of defense may be a direct financial cost or may be in the time you spend to configure and manage it. However, because attacks can start from inside or outside your perimeter, you need to defend all areas of your network. And many of these attacks can start, willfully or accidentally, from inside your perimeter defenses.

Security Tools

You should use many different tools in your security arsenal. (My, more military metaphors!) Starting at your perimeter is your firewall. Other products you can consider in your defense toolkit are antivirus software, anti-malware software, spam filters, intrusion detection software, and vulnerability scanners. And, of course, you need to work with your network's users to make sure they understand and follow basic safe practices.

Personal firewalls

Just like your network firewalls, you can run internal firewalls on your network, even firewalls on your network devices. Microsoft has been nice enough to provide OS-based firewalls for all operating systems since Windows XP. So the cost of using this firewall is very reasonable, and it gives you a layer of protection right at each of your servers and client computers.

Although you get a free firewall with your operating system, some people choose to purchase a third-party firewall (such as Symantec Endpoint Protection) to give them enterprise network configuration and monitoring tools that will be used with the firewall. In many cases, the extra cost is worth the investment because you get easy-to-use management tools. The cost is outweighed by the cost of your time.

Antivirus software

Antivirus software keeps growing to defend against new threats. Rather than get into every type of anti software available, I focus on the three most common categories of threats that antivirus software protects against:

+ **Viruses** are small, malicious programs that get installed without your knowledge, and they have specific goals, such as remote management of your computer or forwarding sensitive data from your device to another system over the network.

✦ **Worms** are small programs that tend to replicate over the network without much help from people to move them. Their goal is twofold: to spread and to accomplish whatever nasty business the worm writer intends.

✦ **Trojans** are small programs that need the computer operator's help to infect the computer or device. (The name is tied to the Trojan Horse of Greek legend, which would not have succeeded for the Greeks inside the horse, if not for people of Troy bringing the horse into the city.) Trojans are applications that are not what they claim to be. A common one is that pesky Windows Security Center Trojan that tells you that your computer is heavily infected, and you should install the software to fix it. Of course, installing the software infects your computer with the Trojan. Trojans also get packaged into other applications, so that when users install that application, they release the Trojans on their poor computers.

The first worm on the Internet was the Morris Worm back in 1988. It was claimed to have been a mistake and was supposed to help gauge the size of the Internet. It *infected* a system and started a task on that system to locate and infect other systems. Unfortunately, it would infect the same systems again and again, which eventually used up all CPU cycles on the infected servers, bringing them to a halt. The spread of this worm made use of known exploits on the servers and the fact that people tend to use common and weak passwords. These same principles are in use by virus writers today.

Because antivirus applications prevent the spread of viruses, many viruses these days make their first task disabling your antivirus software so they have free access to the system.

Anti-malware

Malware is software, hardware, or firmware that is malformed or malwritten such that it causes problems on computers or network devices. Malware are not viruses per se, but they are definitely undesirable and unwanted on any computing device. There is a bit of an overlap between anti-malware applications and antivirus applications, with antivirus applications typically ignoring code in the unwanted category and leaving that to the anti-malware applications.

Malware can slow a computer, give you unwanted pop-up ads, report Internet usage in the form of tracking cookies and other techniques, and do things that the world at large thinks is dodgy. Some applications make agreements to bundle malware with their products, and removing the malware could prevent the application from working. Some may say that is the price you pay for "free" software. (I wholeheartedly disagree!)

A variety of applications can help defend against malware and the sites that may try to push it. A few that I use regularly are Spyware Blaster (shown in Figure 1-5) and Spybot – Search & Destroy. I like these two tools because they both offer the ability to immunize your web browser against a huge number of infections. Spybot – Search & Destroy is also capable of scanning your system for files and registry entries that you want to have removed from your computer. I regularly install these tools on systems that I am called to clean or on systems that are going out to certain groups of users.

Spyware Blaster is free if you do not mind doing your updates manually. To update your system, click Update in the Updates window and then go to the Protection Status window and click the Enable All Protection link.

Malwarebytes, shown in Figure 1-6, is another tool that makes quick work of infections on your computer. The purchased version has auto updating and active protection against new infections Malwarebytes can run a scan of your entire computer and remove infections. I have found that multiple scans with all the tools, starting in Safe Mode booting and moving to Normal booting, typically gets rid of the most invasive programs. Do not forget your antivirus scans as well.

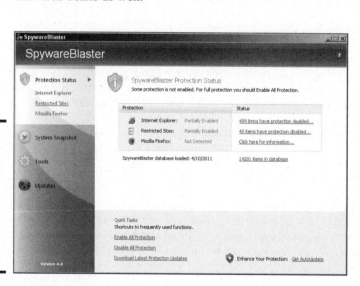

Figure 1-5: Spyware Blaster has an easy configuration; just click Enable All Protection.

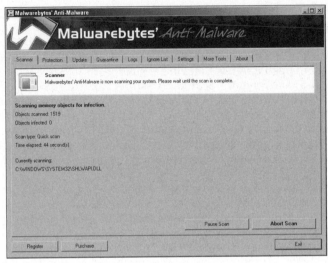

Figure 1-6:
Malware-
bytes runs
full or quick
scans
of your
computer
for files or
settings you
may want to
remove.

All these tools have been created with a lot of common sense, and it takes only a few mouse clicks to enable protection. Also with a few mouse clicks and several minutes of waiting, you can have the tools scan your system and then delete or fix any problems.

Spam filters

E-mail *spam* is all that gunk in your inbox that you did not ask for, which can include product promotions, viruses and exploits, and scams trying to get you to pay for a free trip to Italy. Spam e-mail is unsolicited, unlike e-mail from mailing lists that honor a request to unsubscribe.

E-mail spam (not the canned meat called SPAM) is a global problem. Most experts agree that well over 90 percent of all of the e-mail sent these days is spam. A recent Microsoft report claims that 97 percent of all e-mail is unwanted.

Without any spam filters, spammers would dump a tremendous amount of e-mail in users' mailboxes. The cost of spam is that to prevent it from filling users' inboxes, you need a frontend server to receive e-mail and filter out the spam. If you want people to be able to retrieve *false positive messages* (legitimate e-mail that was accidentally caught by the spam filter), you also need to store that spam for a period of time. So you have now paid for a server, hard drive capacity, power, cooling, and time — all to handle something that you do not want.

You can place spam filters on a filtering server outside the network or on a server inside the network. Personally, I like to keep this data outside my firewall. I can even have filtering on my local computer where I read my mail, but this is the last place where I typically want this job if I can avoid it.

Intrusion detection

Both intrusion detection systems (IDS) and intrusion prevention systems (IPS) have a place in my protection toolkit. These tools are like burglar alarms for a network or network devices. They can be installed outside the network, on the interior of the network, or even on specific hosts or computers on the network. This may well be a distant early warning (DEW) system for a network. When things start going down, these systems may prevent an attack from becoming a problem or at least let you know that it is happening before it has a chance to really take hold.

Vulnerability scanners

You can find several tools to scan your network for security holes. The premiere scanner is Nessus, which can perform a wide variety of scans and knows of many security holes in major products. It can generate detailed lists of items that you should check. Nessus is now distributed by www. tenable.com, and you can download and try it before purchasing it. Nessus used to be a free product but is now capable of doing approved audits for a variety of organizations, whose authorizations like to carry a licensing fee. In addition to Nessus, you can find a variety of other scanning tools listed at http://sectools.org.

User common sense

Making sure users follow basic, common-sense guidelines can really be one of the toughest security tools to properly implement. Even smart people can get duped into clicking that link, entering a credit card number, or believing the Nigerian royal family will give them money. (It makes me think of a line used in the BBC television series *Hustle:* "Everybody wants something for nothing, and we give them nothing for something.")

Phishing for information

Remember: Legitimate companies *never* ask for personal data via unencrypted e-mail. If you receive such an e-mail, it is likely a *phishing scam*— a message from a scammer that looks like it comes from a legitimate company, such as a bank. These phishing e-mails, and the scam websites they link to, can look very convincing and may even include logos from the companies they purport to be. Do not click a link in an e-mail, or worse, enter any information on that linked website, because that is a favorite trick of the weasely people to get gullible folks to divulge personal information such as usernames, passwords, or credit card numbers.

If you need to update your personal information with a company, always be sure to go to the company's (secure) website by using your web browser.

Make sure users understand that if something does not seem right, or perhaps is too good to be true, very likely they should avoid it. Ask users to always be cautious and get the possible scammer's phone number and call him back, Google the name (or the Subject line of the e-mail), or just take a minute and think about it.

Do an Internet search for *Internet scams* to get a list of things you should avoid and then share the list with your network's users. If your search phrase includes a few details about a specific scam, you will likely find the one that you are concerned about. (I do have to hand it to some of these e-mails or websites trying to get your money. Some of them look pretty legit.)

Chapter 2: Securing Networks with Cisco's Adaptive Security Appliance

In This Chapter

✔ Locating firewalls in the OSI network model

✔ Getting a grasp on the IOS

✔ Connecting to the ASA

✔ Setting up your firewall and user accounts

✔ Applying a base configuration to the ASA

✔ Setting up a DHCP server

✔ Viewing licensing information

In this chapter, I introduce you to the world of firewalls via Cisco's Adaptive Security Appliance (ASA). Specifically, I show the configuration of the Cisco ASA 5505, but this configuration could easily apply to any of the ASA products in Cisco's product line. I show you how to configure the ASA using either the command line or the Adaptive Security Device Manager (ASDM). You see how to run a basic setup of this device and how to change many of the settings after setup is complete.

Locating Firewalls in the OSI Model

Unlike routers and switches, firewalls can technically operate at just about any level of the Open System Interconnection (OSI) network model, depending on their functions. So an application layer firewall could be used to block HTTP traffic to and from your network. If you think that sounds like a proxy or reverse proxy server, well, yes it is.

In most cases, when you think of a firewall, you think of a network layer, or layer 3, firewall. The network layer firewall takes the place of a router on your network and filters traffic based primarily by IP address header information. In this chapter, I show you how to configure and use your Cisco Adaptive Security Appliance (ASA), which is just that type of firewall.

Getting to Know the Internetwork Operating System

The Internetwork Operating System (IOS) that is in use with the ASA has most of the same features as the IOS for other devices. The IOS used for the ASA has a few specific commands, but in general, you follow the same process for entering User EXEC mode, Privileged EXEC mode, and Global Configuration mode.

Getting help in the IOS is quite easy. Type a question mark (?) at any point on the command line to see what commands are available to you or to find out how to complete a command that you are working on. In addition to tab completion, you can usually quickly figure out most commands.

If you are completely new to IOS configuration, a complete command reference guide for each IOS routing component can be downloaded from Cisco at `www.cisco.com/cisco/web/psa/reference.html` in the Product/ Technology Support section. Select your IOS version from the Products list.

Making Connections

In Book I, Chapter 5, I introduce how to connect to your device to make configuration changes. The three basic methods of making configuration changes to a router are

+ **Console connection:** This involves having direct access to the router. The changes are made through your computer's serial port and a roll-over cable. This is command line access to a router.

+ **Telnet or SSH:** These options give you remote command-line access to the router to make configuration changes. However, because Telnet sends all data in unencrypted text over the network, SSH should be used in its place.

+ **Adaptive Security Device Manager (ASDM):** Represents the most popular graphical configuration interface for your ASA devices.

You can always make a console connection to your ASA, so take a few minutes to locate a rollover cable for your ASA and the console port on the ASA. If you do not have serial port on your computer, get a USB to serial port adapter for your computer and test it with your Cisco ASA. Testing the adaptor is best to do before you need to make an emergency connection to your ASA.

If you have already enabled SSH access to your ASA, ensure that you have also disabled Telnet access. SSH is as easy to use and is the only secure remote access option to the command line interface.

Running the ASA Setup Wizard

When you first unpack a new ASA or if you erase the configuration, when the ASA boots for the first time, it automatically enters setup. If your ASA does not, you can set up from Privileged EXEC mode. The following code shows the basic setup process, with responses you need to add in bold. Within just a few minutes, you can have your ASA up and running.

```
Pre-configure Firewall now through interactive prompts [yes]?
Firewall Mode [Routed]:
Enable password [<use current password>]: enable
Allow password recovery [yes]?
Clock (UTC):
  Year [2011]:
  Month [Apr]:
  Day [16]:
  Time [13:16:14]:
Inside IP address: 192.168.1.12
Inside network mask: 255.255.255.0
Host name: ASAFirewall1
Domain name: edtetz.net
IP address of host running Device Manager: 192.168.1.123

The following configuration will be used:
Enable password: enable
Allow password recovery: yes
Clock (UTC): 13:16:14 Apr 16 2011
Firewall Mode: Routed
Inside IP address: 192.168.1.12
Inside network mask: 255.255.255.0
Host name: ASAFirewall1
Domain name: edtetz.net
IP address of host running Device Manager: 192.168.1.123

Use this configuration and write to flash? yes
INFO: Security level for "inside" set to 100 by default.
WARNING: http server is not yet enabled to allow ASDM access.
Cryptochecksum: 23d86fb3 f78f728a cd7f48cd 9faf22c0

1417 bytes copied in 2.40 secs (708 bytes/sec)

Type help or '?' for a list of available commands.
```

Notice how little information you need to enter to get basic management access to your ASA over the network (well, almost). The setup process has set up the internal IP address and configured an Access Control List (ACL) entry to allow only the IP address of the computer that ran the setup to manage the ASA from one host on your network, but it has not actually enabled access. The message in setup actually tells you that the HTTP server has not been enabled. So prior to closing out this connection, you want to enable the HTTP server using the following commands:

```
ASAFirewall1> enable
Password: ******
ASAFirewall1# configure terminal
ASAFirewall1(config)# http server enable
ASAFirewall1(config)# copy running-config startup-config

Source filename [running-config]?
Cryptochecksum: 6431b60b a26d0b05 941fa189 e3edf475

1913 bytes copied in 1.740 secs (1913 bytes/sec)
ASAFirewall1(config)# end
```

From this point, you can connect your ASA to a switch and manage it from a device with the IP address you specified in the initial set up of the device.

The ASA 5505 places all switch ports into VLAN 1 (your Inside VLAN) by default, whereas the large ASA devices have a dedicated management interface or port. The management function can be configured to operate over the other interfaces on the ASA.

After you have the management interface up for the ASDM, you can run the Startup Wizard through the ASDM (even if you already set up the ASA on the command line). The benefit to running the Startup Wizard is that you can go to the computer you identified as your management computer and point your web browser to the interface address of your ASA. (*Note:* You need to have Java installed on this computer.) Unless you install a valid certificate that matches the name of the ASA, you are presented with a certificate error, as shown in Figure 2-1.

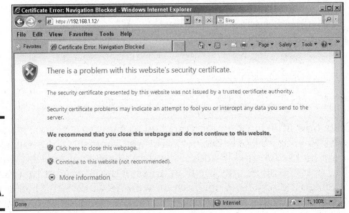

Figure 2-1: Certificate error on connection to your ASA.

After you are connected to your ASA, the introduction page appears, as shown in Figure 2-2. This page allows you to make a decision. Because you need to have Java installed on your computer, you have three choices here:

✦ **Install ASDM Launcher and Run ASDM:** Installs the ASDM on your computer. If this is the computer you will always use to perform your management, this method makes the most sense.

✦ **Run ASDM:** This option uses Java Web Start to launch the ASDM tool directly from the copy installed on the ASA. This is beneficial if you are not at your normal computer because you do not install any software.

✦ **Run Startup Wizard:** This option also uses Java Web Start to launch ASDM, with one exception; after the ASDM has launched, the Startup Wizard runs automatically.

To perform the network configuration of the ASA, the following process walks you through the Startup Wizard:

1. **Click the Run Startup Wizard button on the introduction page.**

You receive a warning related to the security settings on Java.

Book VI Chapter 2

Securing Networks with Cisco's Adaptive Security Appliance

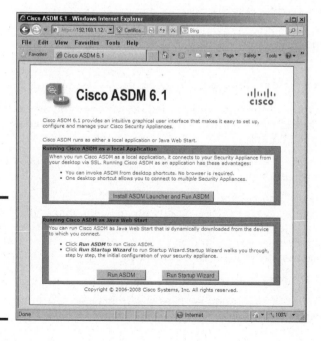

Figure 2-2: Launching the ASDM provides you with three options.

2. **If you are sure that you are connected to the correct device on the network and not some fake device trying to collect your credentials, dismiss the warning message.**

   Because you expect this message from the ASDM, continue to the website.

   The Cisco ASDM Launcher dialog box, as shown in Figure 2-3, appears.

3. **If you have an enable password, but no actual users, skip the Username field, fill in the enable password in the Password field, and click OK.**

   If you have already created an administrative user, provide the username and password in the appropriate fields.

Figure 2-3:
Authenticate
with your
username
and
password or
the enable
password.

The Starting Point page, as shown in Figure 2-4, appears.

4. **Select one of the following, based on whether you are setting up the ASA initially or whether you are using setup to change an existing ASA installation:**

   • *Modify Existing Configuration:* You can choose to modify the existing configuration.

   • *Reset Configuration to Factory Defaults:* With the exception of the management interface, modify the default configuration. As it turns out, a lot of small networks out there require only simple changes to their configuration, and as such, re-running the Startup Wizard is the easiest way to make these changes.

5. **Click the Next button.**

   The Basic Configuration page, as shown in Figure 2-5, appears with two optional items which you can choose to do.

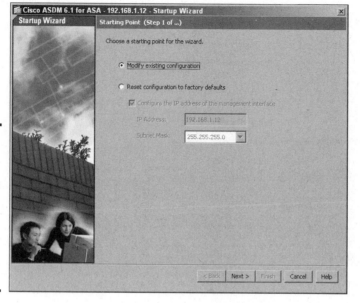

**Book VI
Chapter 2**

Securing Networks
with Cisco's Adaptive
Security Appliance

Figure 2-4:
Step 1 of
the Startup
Wizard asks
whether
you want
to modify
the current
configura-
tion.

6. **(Optional) Select from the following items:**

- *Configure the Device for Teleworker Usage:* This option supports teleworkers or remote workers via a virtual private network (VPN). If you select this option, you are presented with an extra page of questions for the Easy VPN Remote Configuration near the end of the Startup Wizard. On this page, you can also tell the Startup Wizard the name of the firewall device, such as ASAFirewall1, and the domain name to which the device belongs, such as edtetz.net.

- *Change Privileged Mode (Enable) Password:* If you are not happy with your current enable password, change it here before you complete this step of the Startup Wizard.

7. **Click the Next button.**

Depending on the number of interfaces you are licensed for (which you can find out by checking out the "Examining Your License" section, later in this chapter), you can configure up to three interfaces. The basic license for the ASA allows you to have only two interfaces. The Interface Selection page of the Startup Wizard, as shown in Figure 2-6, appears.

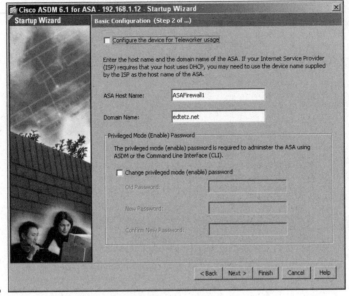

Figure 2-5:
Step 2 of
the Startup
Wizard
allows for
device
naming and
password
configura-
tion.

8. **Choose virtual local area networks (VLANs) for the Outside, Inside, and optionally, DMZ interfaces.**

   - The *Outside VLAN* faces the Internet.

   - The *Inside VLAN* faces your corporate network.

   - The *DMZ VLAN* operates parallel to your corporate network. The *Demilitarized Zone (DMZ)* is an area where you can place servers, such as mail, web, or ftp servers, that the public at large — or at least people outside your network — need access to.

   For each of these interfaces, you assign a VLAN to the segment or choose not to use the interface at all. By default, the Inside interface is configured for VLAN 1, which you can change if you want; however, because this is the default VLAN on your switches, you may not want to change it. For your Outside interface and DMZ interface, you can choose another VLAN or go with the ones chosen by default.

   Enabling the inside VLAN, outside VLAN, and DMZ VLAN interfaces does not actually associate any particular switch ports to those interfaces. The interfaces are virtual and need to be associated to physical inter-faces on the switch. This means that any number of ports can be associ-ated to any of these interfaces.

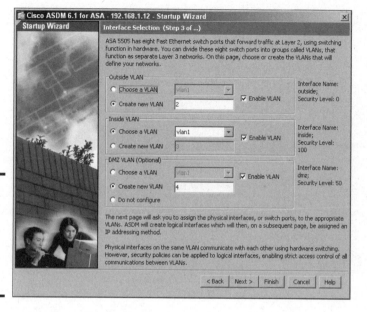

Figure 2-6:
Enable and
set VLANs
to be used
for each
type of
interface.

9. **Click the Next button.**

The Switch Port Allocation page, as shown in Figure 2-7, appears.

10. **Assign the ASA switch ports to the three VLANs by selecting the port in the Available Ports or Allocated Ports panes and clicking the Add or Remove buttons.**

Initially, all your ports are associated with the inside VLAN. In most cases, associate the lowest interface, or Ethernet 0/0 of an ASA 5505, with the outside VLAN because you will likely want to use the additional ports on the inside of your network. Also, on the ASA 5505, the last two ports supply Power over Ethernet (POE) to power up devices, such as phones or access points (APs), which is yet another reason you want the upper ports to be associated with the inside network.

As you choose a switch port and associate it with a VLAN or interface, you are prompted with a message telling you that it may be removed from an existing VLAN. Because all ports start out associated with the Inside interface, you see this message for all your port reassignments.

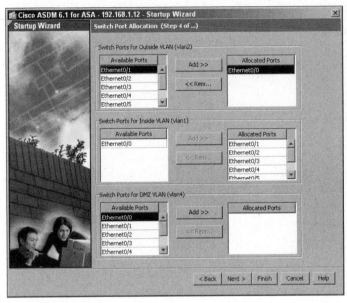

Figure 2-7:
Assign ports
to network
interfaces
on the
Switch Port
Allocation
page.

11. **Click the Next button.**

The Interface IP Address Configuration page, as shown in Figure 2-8, appears.

12. **Assign IP configuration for each of your IP addresses.**

For your outside address, you can manually assign an address, which is not uncommon for business Internet connections. If your Internet connection supports either Dynamic Host Configuration Protocol (DHCP) or Point-to-Point Protocol over Ethernet (PPPOE), select the appropriate option. If you use DHCP, tell your ASA to use the default gateway it receives from DHCP as the system-wide default gateway for this device. If you choose not to use the system-wide default gateway option, you need to configure a manual route through ASDM or the `route outside 0 0 <IP address of gateway>` at the command-line interface (CLI).

13. **Click the Next button.**

The DHCP Server page, as shown in Figure 2-9, appears. For small businesses or regional offices, the ASA may represent the only real device on the network other than printers and computers. You may have these locations set up without any local servers onsite.

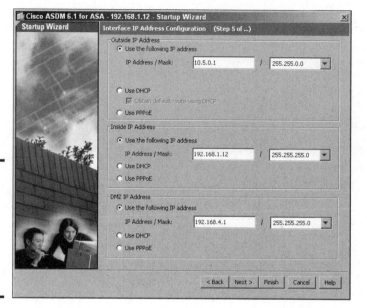

Book VI
Chapter 2

Securing Networks
with Cisco's Adaptive
Security Appliance

Figure 2-8:
Specify IP
addresses
from the
Interface
IP Address
Configura-
tion page.

14. **(Optional) Select the Enable DHCP Server on the Inside Interface check box to have the ASA act as a DHCP server for this network segment.**

15. **(Optional) Select the Enable Auto-Configuration from Interface check box so that you can copy most of these settings from an existing interface.**

    Enabling the Auto-Configuration check box is very useful for Domain Name System (DNS) and Windows Internet Name Service (WINS) server addresses that are constantly being used on all network segments and may all be the same for the organization.

16. **Configure or change any of the missing information in the following:**

    • *Starting IP Address:* The first address to be handed out in the DHCP range.

    • *Ending IP Address:* The last address to be handed out in the DHCP range.

    • *DNS servers 1 and 2:* The DNS servers that are handed out to DHCP clients.

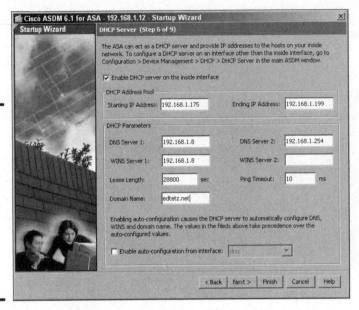

Figure 2-9:
The ASA
supports
a built-in
DHCP
server,
which
can be
configured
during the
Startup
Wizard.

- *WINS servers 1 and 2:* The WINS servers that are handed out to DHCP clients.

- *Lease Length:* The lease length determines when DHCP clients are required to renew their leases on the DHCP supplied addresses.

- *Ping Timeout:* The Ping Timeout setting is used by the DHCP server because it pings each address that it is ready to give, prior to assigning the address, to verify that the address is not in use. This reduces the chance of duplicate IP addresses being created on the network.

- *Domain Name:* The domain name of the DHCP client belongs to.

17. **Click the Next button.**

The Address Translation (NAT/PAT) page, as shown in Figure 2-10, appears.

18. **Set up Network Address Translation or Port Address Translation.**

Choose from the available address translation methods:

- *Use Port Address Translation (PAT):* Most small offices, which use only one public IP address on their Internet connection, use PAT on their connection. PAT can use a specific address or the main address from their outside VLAN interfaces. PAT allows an entire office to share (or translate to) a single external IP address for Internet access.

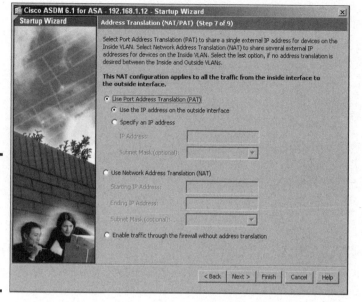

**Book VI
Chapter 2**

Securing Networks
with Cisco's Adaptive
Security Appliance

Figure 2-10:
NAT
and PAT
translate
internal
addresses
to external
addresses.

- *Use Network Address Translation (NAT):* Selecting NAT puts one-to-one mapping (or translation) between internal and external IP addresses, so you can specify a range of addresses to use on the outside VLAN interface. If you use ASA internally on your network (for example, to protect a server subnet), you may want to select the Enable Traffic through the Firewall Without Address Translation radio button if you use public addresses on your internal network (not likely) or if you use the ASA as firewall on the interior of your network.

For more about NAT, turn to Chapter 3 of this minibook.

19. Click the Next button.

The Administrative Access page, as shown in Figure 2-11, appears.

20. Set what systems on your network can connect to your ASA to perform management or configuration changes.

Use the following process to add new management interfaces. If you want to use ASDM, you need to select the Enable HTTP Server for HTTPS/ASDM Access check box, whereas the Enable ASDM History Metrics check box saves usage data regarding accessing the ASDM interface.

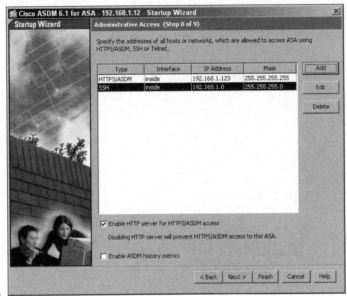

Figure 2-11:
Configure
the methods
of remote
adminis-
tration on
the Adminis-
trative
Access
page.

In the command line setup, you only have the option to ASDM connections to be made from a single computer. This page allows you to specify additional systems that can perform management of your ASA and the type of connection they make to perform that configuration.

If you add a new management option, the Add Administrative Access Entry dialog box, as shown in Figure 2-12, appears. Select your desired options to create the new Administrative Access entry:

a. *Choose HTTP (ASDM), SSH, or Telnet from the Access Type drop-down list.*

b. *Choose Inside from the Interface Name drop-down list.*

   Inside is typically the most secure interface option, but in some cases, such as if you need to be able to conduct remote administration over the Outside interface, you should be very restrictive in the address from which the administration is performed.

c. *Specify either a specific address from which administration is performed in the IP Address text box or give a network range defined by either an IP address or a Network ID from the Subnet Mask drop-down list.*

   Remember, the more restrictive you can be with this configuration, the more secure your ASA is.

d. *Click OK.*

   You return to the Administrative Access page.

Figure 2-12:
Adding
another
management
connection.

Book VI
Chapter 2

Securing Networks
with Cisco's Adaptive
Security Appliance

If you allow your firewall to be administered from the outside interface, you leave yourself open to potentially being compromised by someone you do not know.

21. Click the Next button.

The summary page of the configuration Startup Wizard appears, providing a summary of the configuration that you have applied to the system. All these configuration changes are written into the running configuration on the ASA. After the configuration changes are made, you see the standard ASA ASDM management screen, as shown in Figure 2-13. From this interface you can

- Perform any other configuration changes.

- Relaunch the Startup Wizard or other wizards.

- Perform basic monitoring of the ASA via the home page.

- Perform more detailed monitoring of the ASA and connections that it hosts through the Monitoring pages.

- Run additional management and troubleshooting tools.

- Save the current configuration to flash memory.

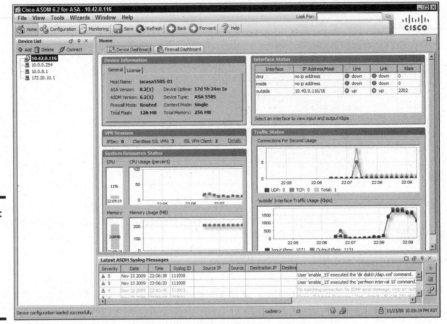

Figure 2-13:
The ASDM configuration and management interface.

Performing a Basic Configuration

Through the rest of this chapter, I walk you through some of the common configuration items that you will likely want to configure on the ASA. Although I give examples from the ASA 5505, if you are working on any other member of the ASA family, your configuration is performed in much the same manner. For most of the options, I show both the command line method of applying the configuration and the ASDM.

You have only a few things to worry about to get a basic routing configuration on your ASA. This section takes a look at each of these configuration items.

Device name

Setting a name for your ASA does not impact the function of the unit, but it does make it a little easier when you connect to the device to make configuration changes or if you are using a remote monitoring tool that can identify the device by name. In general, you do not want to apply the incorrect configuration to a device, possibly opening your entire network to the Internet or disabling your remote access to the device. The following code allows you to use the Cisco CLI to set a new device name on the Cisco ASA.

```
ciscoasa> enable
Password: ******
ciscoasa# configure terminal
ciscoasa(config)# hostname ASAFirewall1
ASAFirewall1(config)# end
```

Standard firewall ports

As with all the Cisco networking devices that this book examines, you can connect a number of ports to cables on the ASA. The ASA's ports, as shown in Figure 2-14, are

✦ **Console:** Serial configuration port for command line access to ASA management and configuration.

✦ **Ethernet/Fast Ethernet/Gigabit:** Standard network interfaces that are used to connect different network segments. Depending on the ASA model you have, you have a mixture of Fast Ethernet and Gigabit ports, which will be copper RJ45 connections or small form-factor pluggable (SFP) modules. Also, depending on your device, you may have Power over Ethernet (POE) ports.

✦ **USB ports:** Currently not used on the ASA series, the USB ports are there for future features that may be implemented in the series.

✦ **Expansion port:** If your ASA model has an expansion module, it will be either the Security Services Card (SSC) or Security Services Module (SSM) connection for an appropriate expansion card model. These cards offload VPN encryption or implement additional feature sets, such as e-mail antivirus scanning.

Figure 2-14:
Standard
ports on
ASA 5505.

Interfaces

In this section, I describe the basics of configuring Fast Ethernet and Gigabit Ethernet connections.

To start your configuration, connect to your ASA and get into Global Configuration mode using this set command:

```
ASAFirewall1>enable
Password:
ASAFirewall1#configure terminal
```

The next step is to choose your interface by number. You can choose from Ethernet (which actually means Fast Ethernet on the ASA) or Gigabit interfaces. After choosing Ethernet or Gigabit, specify the port number. All devices in current IOS versions are numbered starting at the motherboard in one of these formats: network-module-slot/port, 0/interface-card-slot/port, or network-module-slot/interface-card-slot/port. Effectively, all modules are connected to the motherboard slot on the ASA, which is always slot 0 (this is the first zero in the interface name):

```
ASAFirewall1(config)#interface Ethernet 0/0
```

Now you can set the specifics of the network connection or use the Auto settings for Duplex and Speed modes. Duplex modes include Full- or Half-Duplex, whereas speeds are typically from 10 Mbps up to the speed of the interface:

```
ASAFirewall1(config-if)#duplex auto
ASAFirewall1(config-if)#speed auto
```

For switches, you might not want to use the description option to name interfaces, but it is a good idea on your ASA to give yourself a description to help prevent you from changing the configuration on the wrong interface. (It can be a career-limiting move to shut down the wrong interface at a critical time in your business!) The description does nothing to assist with the configuration; it only prevents some level of human error:

```
ASAFirewall1(config-if)#description Internal Interface
```

This may seem a little strange. You have done all this work, so there is a good chance that you want to use this interface now. But exit out of the configuration and check your running configuration; you notice one configuration item that is a little strange:

```
ASAFirewall1#show running-config interface Ethernet 0/0
!
interface Ethernet0/0
switchport access vlan 2
```

So there is one important item that is missing, or actually, is present. Unlike routers, all the interfaces on your ASA are enabled by default, but they are all put into the default inside VLAN. As with your switch interfaces, the `no shutdown` command gets rid of the `shutdown` command. Complete the configuration of your ASA interface with the following command:

```
ASAFirewall1(config-if)#no shutdown
```

If you are working on the console or have `terminal monitor` enabled, you receive a status message telling you that the interface has been enabled. This message is similar to the following:

```
%LINK-5-CHANGED: Interface Ethernet0/0, changed state to up
```

That is everything that is required (and then some) for you to configure an ASA interface. If you trust the Auto settings for Speed and Duplex modes, you likely just need to assign an IP address to the VLAN interfaces and associate one or more ports to that VLAN interface. A description is nice to have and other configuration options are required based on configuration of other parts of your network, such as VLAN configuration.

After you have the interface up and running, if you are using auto for your speed and duplex settings, examine the interface to ensure that it has detected settings that you are happy with. Do this with the `show interface` command:

```
ASAFirewall1# show interface Ethernet 0/0
Interface Ethernet0/0 "", is up, line protocol is up
  Hardware is 88E6095, BW 100 Mbps, DLY 100 usec
        Auto-Duplex(Full-duplex), Auto-Speed(100 Mbps)
        Available but not configured via nameif
        MAC address 001f.ca8c.93d2, MTU not set
        IP address unassigned
        13666 packets input, 1134634 bytes, 0 no buffer
        Received 0 broadcasts, 0 runts, 0 giants
        0 input errors, 0 CRC, 0 frame, 0 overrun, 0 ignored, 0 abort
        0 L2 decode drops
        13660 switch ingress policy drops
        142 packets output, 13321 bytes, 0 underruns
        0 output errors, 0 collisions, 0 interface resets
        0 babbles, 0 late collisions, 0 deferred
        0 lost carrier, 0 no carrier
        0 rate limit drops
        0 switch egress policy drops
```

In all that information, notice that the interface and line protocols should both be *up,* or properly connected to the network and communicating with other devices. In the preceding example, the interface detected Full-Duplex as well as a speed of 100 Mbps. Incorrect Duplex settings between ends of a connection can cause packet errors.

IP addresses

Because you plan to route from this interface, you need to give your client devices an IP address it can connect to. This is done in the VLAN interfaces with the following command:

```
ASAFirewall1(config-if)#ip address 192.168.1.240 255.255.255.0
```

You can configure your ASA to use DHCP using the command `ip address dhcp`, but this would not typically be used for a static network device, such as a router. If you connect this ASA as a NAT device to your Internet service provider (ISP), it would represent the only case where this would likely be used. (You can find out more about NAT in Chapter 3 of this minibook.)

Security zones

Your Cisco ASA works with three default security zones, which it assigns the values of Inside (100), Outside (0), and DMZ (50). By default, any device at a higher security zone level can communicate with devices at a lower security zone, but devices at a lower security zone cannot initiate connections to devices at the higher zone level.

By default, devices on the Inside and DMZ interfaces can both establish connections to devices on the Internet; as well, devices on the Inside interface can establish connections to devices on the DMZ interface.

You set these security levels using the ASDM when you configure your VLAN interfaces, as shown in Figure 2-15.

Passwords

Although it is not actually necessary to have a password on your ASA, it is a very good idea. If you do not configure any passwords and enable Telnet, anyone can connect to your ASA from any interface, and reconfigure your ASA to their hearts' desire, giving themselves access to your entire internal network.

Aside from creating a user accounts, the only password used on the ASA for authentication is the enable password.

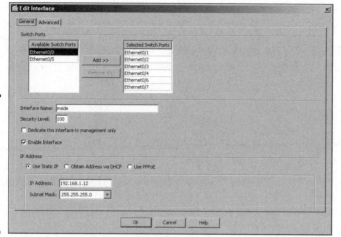

Figure 2-15:
Editing
your VLAN
interfaces
allows you
to adjust
the security
level.

Setting the enable password

The enable password is used every time you move from User EXEC mode
to Privileged EXEC mode. This gives you security on your ASA because
Privileged EXEC mode is where all the dangerous commands are, including
Global Configuration mode. To set an enable password, use the following
command:

```
ASAFirewall1>enable
ASAFirewall1#configure terminal
ASAFirewall1(config)#enable password mypass
```

This creates an enable password for you that is stored in your Configuration
file. To view this password, you can show your running configuration using
the following command:

```
ASAFirewall1>enable
Password:
ASAFirewall1#show running-config | include enable password
enable password VpEu/DBiUqr.VhG7 encrypted
```

When you configure your ASA, set the enable password.

Setting the Telnet password

If you need to remotely manage your ASA, you can choose between Telnet
and SSH. Telnet is less secure than SSH because it sends data over the network in clear text. However, some people justify using Telnet because if they
are running it only on a secured management network, some of the risks are
mitigated.

So, in spite of risks, it is good to know how Telnet works and how to administer it. I show you how to perform the setup to allow Telnet access to the ASA. You need to worry only about two commands: One to enable Telnet, and one to set the inactivity timeout. The default timeout is five minutes, which closes the connection after five minutes of inactivity. (I would not want Telnet to time out much longer or shorter.)

```
ASAFirewall1>enable
Password:
ASAFirewall1#configure terminal
ASAFirewall1(config)# telnet 192.168.1.0 255.255.255.0 inside
ASAFirewall1(config)# telnet timeout 5
```

These commands order access to the system through Telnet and require a Telnet password to be set. If you look at the running configuration, this is identified with the `passwd` command. (Notice that by default the command is stored in an encrypted format, such as the enable password.)

```
ASAFirewall1>enable
ASAFirewall1# show running-config | include passwd
passwd 2KFQnbNIdI.2KYOU encrypted
```

The default Telnet password is *cisco;* it is a *really* good idea to change it from the default.

To set the password for Telnet, use the following commands:

```
ASAFirewall1>enable
Password:
ASAFirewall1#configure terminal
ASAFirewall1(config)#passwd telnetpass
ASAFirewall1(config)#end
```

To have access to the ASA for Telnet, you need to have both an enable password and the Telnet password specified in your configuration.

Setting the SSH password

To set up access to the ASA for SSH, you have a few additional steps to perform to allow access. SSH access is not possible with only a password — you need to have a user account created on your ASA. (I show you how to create user accounts later in this chapter in the "Working Users" section, but for now I assume that you have a user named *remote* with a password named *remote.* (Please do not use such an easily guessed username and password on your production network!)

To set up SSH access, you need to ensure the following commands have
been issued:

```
ASAFirewall1>enable
Password:
ASAFirewall1#configure terminal
ASAFirewall1(config)#domain-name edtetz.net
ASAFirewall1(config)#crypto key generate rsa
INFO: The name for the keys will be: <Default-RSA-Key>
Keypair generation process begin. Please wait...
ASAFirewall1(config)#ssh 192.168.1.0 255.255.255.0 inside
ASAFirewall1(config)#ssh timeout 5
ASAFirewall1(config)#exit
```

You see the SSH commands in your running configuration. To ensure that
you have created a Rivest Shamir Adleman (RSA) authentication key, use the
following command:

```
ASAFirewall1>enable
Password:
ASAFirewall1# show crypto key mypubkey rsa
Key pair was generated at: 08:36:47 UTC Apr 17 2011
Key name: <Default-RSA-Key>
 Usage: General Purpose Key
 Modulus Size (bits): 1024
 Key Data:

  30819f30 0d06092a 864886f7 0d010101 05000381 8d003081 89028181 00a42987
  298d346b 9594ac23 4c00a9a6 934da77d baed3666 11a72016 71d7014e 5df955f2
  d5cdf615 9ea0e89d da3b79a1 97b70df7 8ad508e7 0ef74c66 ec6c39e6 8663f363
  3a0ff4c4 02c66bf8 3190a053 1b9f3bd7 b92f24bd 523c608c da6da849 1fbe5706
  1169c73a 57437e16 cdff6f38 35f08075 c6449a6f 142d0bc0 7d8d361a 63020301 0001
Key pair was generated at: 08:46:56 UTC Apr 17 2011
Key name: <Default-RSA-Key>.server
 Usage: Encryption Key
 Modulus Size (bits): 768
 Key Data:

  307c300d 06092a86 4886f70d 01010105 00036b00 30680261 00a5bd13 6d1cc29a
  86af47cd a340fd67 2b5ee15d 6babb483 f096d6af e69ebad5 0701cc69 5318718d
  873fa38e 4a7cb828 36e157d0 0c85dba0 fcb4b276 2a130446 d54ac52a 0c64df36
  4879d6d7 0d7d5329 ddb6c046 95ac1abd 50c04275 fc88d5fd 6b020301 0001
```

So the `crypto key generate rsa` command has successfully created a
set of RSA encryption keys, and the rest of the command sequence enabled
SSH, and only allowed SSH on the internal interface. The `crypto key` command needs to be issued only once on the ASA. With this done, you can now
use a program, such as PuTTY, to connect to this ASA on TCP port 22.

By default, the SSH version is set to 1 and 2. If you want to use only version 1
or only version 2, use the `ssh version` command, which is followed by the
version you want.

If you want to change the SSH version through the ASDM:

1. **Launch ASDM and click the Configuration link at the top of the page.**

   The Configuration page appears.

2. **Choose Device Management in the bottom of the left navigation pane.**

3. **In the Device Management navigation pane, click the + sign next to Management Access, click the + sign next to Command Line (CLI), and then click Secure Shell (SSH), as shown in Figure 2-16.**

   From here, you can add an authorized address from which to allow SSH traffic and set the interface to be used for that traffic. To add or edit an entry, use the appropriate button to the right of the screen.

If you try to connect to the ASA, you may still see that you cannot use SSH to connect to the ASA. If you attempt to connect, you see that the SSH service is running on TCP port 22. You are given the prompt regarding the server certificate that is used and are asked to verify and store the key. After you do this, you are asked to provide a login name, which you have not yet created.

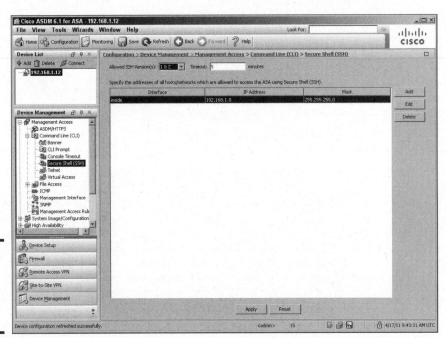

Figure 2-16: You can configure SSH in ASDM.

To create a user that can log in via SSH or the CLI, use these commands at the command line:

```
ASAFirewall1>enable
Password:
ASAFirewall1#configure terminal
ASAFirewall1(config)#username RemoteAdmin password AdminPass privilege 15
ASAFirewall1(config)#aaa authentication ssh console LOCAL
```

The last line of the preceding command set tells the ASA to use the local ASA user database as the Remote Authentication Dial In User Service (RADIUS) or Authentication, Authorization, and Accounting (AAA) server. This again needs to be done only once. The user account that was created has the highest level of privilege and can be used to access not only SSH, but also the ASDM console. There are lower privilege settings that can be applied to the user, but that would restrict what commands are available to them in Privileged EXEC mode.

Creating users in the ASDM

To create the user in ASDM:

1. **Click the Configuration button and then click the Device Management tab on the bottom of the left navigation panel.**

2. **Click the + sign next to Users/AAA and then click User Accounts.**

   You can then click the Add, Edit, and Delete buttons on the right of the screen to add, change, or remove users, respectively. Figure 2-17 shows you the User Account screen.

To set up the local account database to be used for SSH access:

1. **Click the + sign next to Users/AAA and then click AAA Access.**

2. **Select the SSH check box.**

If you want to use your newly created account for ASDM as well, in the Device Management pane, click the + sign next to Users/AAA and then click AAA Access; select the HTTP/ASDM check box. Alternatively, you can specify aaa authentication http console LOCAL in your configuration.

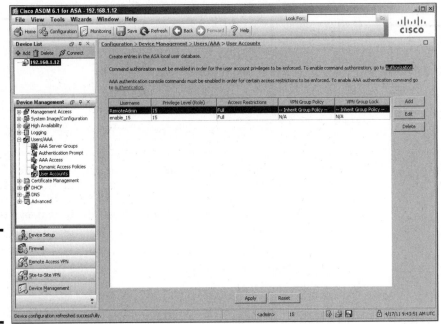

Figure 2-17:
Creating
a user
account in
ASDM.

Banners

A *banner* is a message that is presented to a user that is using the ASA. When this message is shown to the user depends on the type of banner you have configured for use. You can configure four main types of banners on your Cisco ASA. These banners are

✦ **Message of the Day (MOTD):** This type of logon message has been around for a very long time on Unix and mainframe systems. The idea of the message is to display a temporary notice to users, such as issues with system availability; but because it is displayed when you connect to the device prior to login, most network administrators use it to display legal notices regarding access to the ASA, such as Unauthorized access to this device is prohibited, and violators will be prosecuted to the full extent of the law.

✦ **Login:** This banner is displayed before login to the system but after the MOTD banner is displayed, unless an EXEC banner has been configured. This is typically used to display a permanent message to the users.

✦ **Exec:** This banner is displayed after the MOTD and after login. This is the notice for users prior to entering Privileged EXEC mode. This can be used to post reminders to your network administrators.

✦ **ASDM:** This banner is displayed after authenticating to the ASDM interface, but prior to displaying the ASDM interface.

To configure each of these banners, examine the following commands, which set up all four banners on your ASA:

```
ASAFirewall1(config)#banner motd This device is for authorized personnel only.
ASAFirewall1(config)#banner motd If you have not been provided with permission
ASAFirewall1(config)#banner motd to access this device - disconnect at once.
ASAFirewall1(config)#banner login *** Login Required. Unauthorized use is
    prohibited ***
ASAFirewall1(config)#banner exec *** Ensure that you update the system
    configuration ***
ASAFirewall1(config)#banner exec *** documentation after making system changes.
    ***
ASAFirewall1(config)#banner asdm *** Login Required to access $(hostname).
    Unauthorized use is prohibited ***
ASAFirewall1(config)#exit
```

Unlike banners on switches and routers, you do not use a delimiter character to end the message, but rather add a line at a time to the banner message. You can use two tokens that are replaced when the message is displayed: $(hostname) and $(domain).

All these banners can be configured easily using ASDM by clicking the Configuration link at the top of the page, and then clicking the Device Management button in the bottom of the left navigation pane; next, click the + signs next to Management Access and Command Line (CLI), and then click Banner, as shown in Figure 2-18.

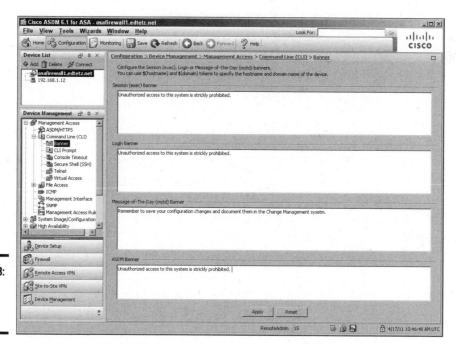

Figure 2-18: Banner settings in ASDM.

Setting Up User Accounts

In the "Passwords" section earlier in this chapter, I mention that SSH requires user accounts to allow login for SSH. These accounts can be stored in a local database on the ASA or can be stored on a central access server — *Terminal Access Controller Access-Control System (TACACS)*. TACACS is an industry standard authentication server similar to that of RADIUS, but not compatible with RADIUS. Most small organizations, and even some larger ones, rely on the local database for user authentication because of the amount of work required to set up RADIUS. However, if you already have RADIUS set up, you would use the following configuration to enable it. Many RADIUS servers are available, including Cisco's Secure Access Control Server (ACS) for Windows or Microsoft's Internet Authentication Service (IAS).

```
ASAFirewall1>enable
Password:
ASAFirewall1#configure terminal
ASAFirewall1(config)# aaa-server RADIUS_SERVER_GROUP protocol RADIUS
ASAFirewall1(config)# aaa-server RADIUS_SERVER_GROUP (inside) host 192.168.1.2
ASAFirewall1(config-aaa-server-host)# key secretkey
ASAFirewall1(config-aaa-server-host)#exit
ASAFirewall1(config)#exit
```

To use the local database for authentication, do two things:

1. Create at least one user account.

2. Configure your ASA to use the local database rather than a password on an interface basis.

To create a user in the account database, use a command like the following to specify the username and password:

```
ASAFirewall1>enable
Password:
ASAFirewall1#configure terminal
ASAFirewall1(config)#username RemoteAdmin password AdminPass privilege 15
ASAFirewall1(config)#username remoteuser password remotepass
ASAFirewall1(config)#aaa authentication ssh console LOCAL
ASAFirewall1(config)#exit
```

If you do not specify a privilege level, the level defaults to 2. This is enough for VPN users but not administrative users, who are normally set to privilege level 15.

To remove a user, use the standard `no` command. You need only to specify the username in the same way that following command removes the `remoteuser` account from the local database:

```
ASAFirewall1>enable
Password:
ASAFirewall1#configure terminal
ASAFirewall1(config)#no username remoteuser
ASAFirewall1(config)#exit
```

You can also manage users with the ASDM interface, as I describe in the earlier section, "Creating users in the ASDM," in this chapter.

Configuring Dynamic Host Configuration Protocol

If you have not read it yet, you may want to review the DHCP process I describe in Book IV, Chapter 2. After you have determined your address ranges, configure your DHCP settings with this short list of commands:

```
ASAFirewall1>enable
Password:
ASAFirewall1#configure terminal
ASAFirewall1(config)#dhcpd address 192.168.1.175-192.168.1.199 inside
ASAFirewall1(config)#dhcpd dns 192.168.1.8 192.168.1.254 interface inside
ASAFirewall1(config)#dhcpd wins 192.168.1.8 interface inside
ASAFirewall1(config)#dhcpd lease 28800 interface inside
ASAFirewall1(config)#dhcpd ping_timeout 10 interface inside
ASAFirewall1(config)#dhcpd domain edtetz.net interface inside
ASAFirewall1(config)#dhcpd enable inside
ASAFirewall1(config)#exit
```

To view your current settings, use the following command to extract all DHCP-related items out of your `running-config`:

```
ASAFirewall1>enable
Password:
ASAFirewall1# show running-config | include dhcp
dhcpd address 192.168.1.175-192.168.1.199 inside
dhcpd dns 192.168.1.8 192.168.1.254 interface inside
dhcpd wins 192.168.1.8 interface inside
dhcpd lease 28800 interface inside
dhcpd ping_timeout 10 interface inside
dhcpd domain edtetz.net interface inside
dhcpd enable inside
```

Other items can be configured for DHCP, including Global DHCP options and a *DHCP relay,* which forwards DHCP requests onto another DHCP server to get address information for clients on a network. (This is beyond the scope of this book, but if you want to find out more, review the Configuring DHCP in the Cisco ASA 5500 Series Configuration Guide www.cisco.com/en/US/docs/security/asa/asa84/configuration/guide/asa_84_cli_cfg.pdf.)

If you want to use ASDM to manage your DHCP settings, click the Configuration button, and then click the Device Management tab in the left navigation pane. Click the + sign next to DHCP and then click DHCP Server, as shown in Figure 2-19. You may find that managing your settings this way is easier.

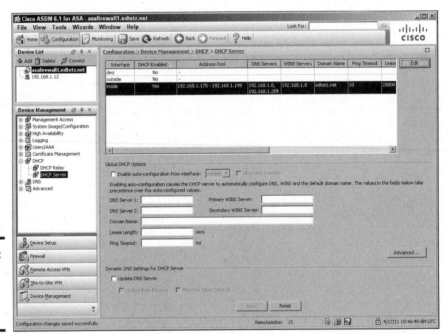

Figure 2-19: DHCP Server settings in ASDM.

Examining Your License

If you want to know what you are licensed for by way of your ASA, you can find out in two places. If you reboot your ASA, licensing information is shown during the boot process. You likely will not want to reboot your ASA just to see the licensing information though, so you can also view it through the ASDM. Launch the ASDM, and on the Home screen, click the License tab in the Device Information section. I show an excerpt of the boot process in the following code so you can see the licensing that is presented during the boot process:

```
CISCO SYSTEMS
Embedded BIOS Version 1.0(12)6 08/21/06 17:26:53.43

Low Memory: 632 KB
High Memory: 251 MB
PCI Device Table.
Bus Dev Func VendID DevID Class               Irq
 00  01  00   1022   2080  Host Bridge
 00  01  02   1022   2082  Chipset En/Decrypt  11
 00  0C  00   1148   4320  Ethernet            11
 00  0D  00   177D   0003  Network En/Decrypt  10
 00  0F  00   1022   2090  ISA Bridge
 00  0F  02   1022   2092  IDE Controller
 00  0F  03   1022   2093  Audio               10
 00  0F  04   1022   2094  Serial Bus          9
 00  0F  05   1022   2095  Serial Bus          9

Evaluating BIOS Options ...
Launch BIOS Extension to setup ROMMON

Cisco Systems ROMMON Version (1.0(12)6) #0: Mon Aug 21 19:34:06 PDT 2006

Platform ASA5505

Use BREAK or ESC to interrupt boot.
Use SPACE to begin boot immediately.

Launching BootLoader...
Default configuration file contains 1 entry.

Searching / for images to boot.

Loading /asa803-k8.bin... Booting...
Loading...
```

```
Processor memory 188010496, Reserved memory: 20971520 (DSOs: 0 + kernel:
    20971520)
Guest RAM start: 0xd3800080
Guest RAM   end: 0xdd400000
Guest RAM   brk: 0xd3801000

IO memory 39403520 bytes
IO memory start: 0xd0fff000
IO memory   end: 0xd3593000

Total SSMs found: 0

Total NICs found: 10
88E6095 rev 2 Gigabit Ethernet @ index 09 MAC: 0000.0003.0002
88E6095 rev 2 Ethernet @ index 08 MAC: 001f.ca8c.93d9
88E6095 rev 2 Ethernet @ index 07 MAC: 001f.ca8c.93d8
88E6095 rev 2 Ethernet @ index 06 MAC: 001f.ca8c.93d7
88E6095 rev 2 Ethernet @ index 05 MAC: 001f.ca8c.93d6
88E6095 rev 2 Ethernet @ index 04 MAC: 001f.ca8c.93d5
88E6095 rev 2 Ethernet @ index 03 MAC: 001f.ca8c.93d4
88E6095 rev 2 Ethernet @ index 02 MAC: 001f.ca8c.93d3
88E6095 rev 2 Ethernet @ index 01 MAC: 001f.ca8c.93d2
y88acs06 rev16 Gigabit Ethernet @ index 00 MAC: 001f.ca8c.93da

Licensed features for this platform:
Maximum Physical Interfaces : 8
VLANs                       : 20, DMZ Unrestricted
Inside Hosts                : Unlimited
Failover                    : Active/Standby
VPN-DES                     : Enabled
VPN-3DES-AES                : Enabled
VPN Peers                   : 25
webVPN Peers                : 2
Dual ISPs                   : Enabled
VLAN Trunk Ports            : 8
AnyConnect for Mobile       : Disabled
AnyConnect for Linksys phone : Disabled
Advanced Endpoint Assessment : Disabled

This platform has an ASA 5505 Security Plus license.

Encryption hardware device : Cisco ASA-5505 on-board accelerator (revision 0x0)
                             Boot microcode   : CN1000-MC-BOOT-2.00
                             SSL/IKE microcode: CNLite-MC-SSLm-PLUS-2.01
                             IPSec microcode  : CNlite-MC-IPSECm-MAIN-2.04
```

Chapter 3: Securing Networks with ACLs and NAT

In This Chapter

✓ **Working with Access Control Lists (ACLs) to restrict traffic flow**

✓ **Creating ACLs**

✓ **Detecting viruses with ACLs**

✓ **Configuring NAT**

I could cover Access Control Lists (ACLs) along with switches, routers, or firewalls because most Cisco products use ACLs in one manner or another. As such, I cover them all in one place. Although the syntax may vary slightly from platform to platform, the principles and application of ACLs remain fairly consistent.

ACLs are actually required as part of implementing Network Address Translation (NAT) on your network, so I discuss both ACLs and NAT within this chapter. Additionally, I show you how easy it is to restrict traffic with just a few key strokes (and therefore, how easy it is to mess up traffic flow on your network with just a few key strokes).

Securing Networks with ACLs

ACL stands for Access Control List. An ACL has a list of entries, which are called Access Control Entries (ACEs). The entries that make up the list affects the access that one network device has to another network device. ACEs are not necessarily a negative restriction; in some cases, an ACE is a method of granting a person or device access to something. Therefore, an ACE's two big roles are in the Deny category and the Permit category.

To work with ACLs properly, you should know where to apply them on your network. You can apply ACLs in two areas, either near the source of the traffic or close to the destination. If you put an entry close to the source or the destination, then you can likely take care of your control needs by needing to touch only that one device.

If you can place your rules near the source of the traffic, then you have a benefit of stopping the traffic at that point. If you have the rules placed near the destination of the traffic flow, the traffic actually goes almost all the way to the destination before being told that it is not allowed. For example, Canadians have something called *preclearance* for travelling into the United States. This is like placing ACLs near the source because, before you board your plane in Canada, you go through all the U.S. Customs processing. This means that you know if you are allowed in the United States before you get to the plane. Likewise, putting your ACLs near the source cuts down on the traffic crossing your network.

In some cases, you do not have control over the source location or locations. If you have a very large WAN, traffic could enter the network from the Internet in several locations. This means you need to put matching ACLs on several devices across the WAN so, rather than putting those rules on all the other devices, you can put the ACLs or rules in one or two devices near the destination of the traffic. This means that traffic crosses the network, only to be rejected as the traffic approaches the goal. Although this strategy increases traffic on the network, it gives you an implementation that is easier to maintain because you now have to worry about only one device.

Creating ACLs

You will work with two types of ACLs:

+ **Standard ACLs,** which have fewer options for classifying data and controlling traffic flow

+ **Extended ACLs,** which offer the ability to filter or control traffic based on a variety of criteria

This section delves into these ACLs, including creating and managing your network's traffic flow with them.

Standard ACLs

Standard ACLs are easier and simpler to use than extended ACLs. However, in their simplicity, you lose some functionality, such as managing access based on Transmission Control Protocol (TCP) or User Datagram Protocol (UDP) ports. Standard ACLs are numbered from 1–99 and from 1300–1999 (expanded range). They only permit or deny access based on the source IP addresses.

Wildcard masks

When you create a standard ACL or an extended ACL, you use a wildcard mask to identify the devices or addresses that will be affected by the ACL.

In a subnet mask, the bit pattern has ones separated from zeros with the ones on the left of the number and the zeros on the right. This scenario is more concerned with the network that devices are on and less concerned with the actual hosts on that network. Therefore, the focus on the number is where the ones are, not where the zeros are located. The same is true of the wildcard mask, where you are dealing with the access of hosts to a resource. Because you are now concerned with the hosts, the focus is reversed; therefore, the bits are reversed. In the wildcard mask, you are less concerned with the networks and more concerned with the hosts on that network. Therefore, the wildcard mask still has zeros and ones separated, but now the ones are on the right and the zeros are on the left.

With that said, for a Class C network block, such as 192.168.5.0/24, where you are looking at the subnet mask of 255.255.255.0, for a wildcard mask you would be looking at 0.0.0.255 (which would still focus on the network address and the hosts found on that network block). Table 3-1 shows a breakdown of comparable subnet masks and wildcard masks. Although you use CIDR notation to simplify writing subnet masks (with 255.0.0.0 becoming /8), this notation does not apply to wildcard masks.

Table 3-1	Wildcard Masks by the Bit	
CIDR Notation	*Subnet Mask*	*Wildcard Mask*
/8	255.0.0.0	0.255.255.255
/9	255.128.0.0	0.127.255.255
/10	255.192.0.0	0.63.255.255
/11	255.224.0.0	0.31.255.255
/12	255.240.0.0	0.15.255.255
/13	255.248.0.0	0.7.255.255
/14	255.252.0.0	0.3.255.255
/15	255.254.0.0	0.1.255.255
/16	255.255.0.0	0.0.255.255
/17	255.255.128.0	0.0.127.255
/18	255.255.192.0	0.0.63.255
/19	255.255.224.0	0.0.31.255
/20	255.255.240.0	0.0.15.255
/21	255.255.248.0	0.0.7.255
/22	255.255.252.0	0.0.3.255
/23	255.255.254.0	0.0.1.255
/24	255.255.255.0	0.0.0.255
/25	255.255.255.128	0.0.0.127
/26	255.255.255.192	0.0.0.63

(continued)

Table 3-1 *(continued)*

CIDR Notation	Subnet Mask	Wildcard Mask
/27	255.255.255.224	0.0.0.31
/28	255.255.255.240	0.0.0.15
/29	255.255.255.248	0.0.0.7
/30	255.255.255.252	0.0.0.3
/31	255.255.255.254	0.0.0.1
/32	255.255.255.255	0.0.0.0

Access Control Entries

The Access Control List is made up of a series of entries. Each ACL is numbered, and all entries in the same list are equally numbered. By default, when you add entries to the list, the new entries appear at the bottom. The only exception is the implicit entry at the bottom of every list, which is a deny all. Each Access Control Entry (ACE) has the following structure in your configuration:

```
access-list <number> <access> <source network or host ID> <wildcard mask>
```

If you create a single entry ACL permitting all hosts on the Class C network of 192.168.8.0, then the complete ACL would be:

```
access-list 10 permit 192.168.8.0 0.0.0.255
access-list 10 deny any
```

In the previous ACL, however, the last line would not actually appear in the ACL. If you used the show command to view this ACL you would actually see:

```
Switch1>enable
Password:
Switch1#configure terminal
Enter configuration commands, one per line.  End with CNTL/Z.
Switch1(config)#access-list 50 permit 192.168.8.0 0.0.0.255
Switch1(config)#end
Switch1#show access-list 50
Standard IP access list 50
    permit 192.168.8.0, wildcard bits 0.0.0.255
```

So what happens if you want to add another entry to your list? You would use the same command. The following code shows how to add the 192.168.9.0/24 block to ACL with a permit:

```
Switch1>enable
Password:
Switch1#configure terminal
```

```
Enter configuration commands, one per line.  End with CNTL/Z.
Switch1(config)#access-list 50 permit 192.168.9.0 0.0.0.255
Switch1(config)#end
Switch1#show access-list 50
Standard IP access list 50
    permit 192.168.8.0, wildcard bits 0.0.0.255
    permit 192.168.9.0, wildcard bits 0.0.0.255
```

Modifying ACLs

Notice that each new entry you add to the ACL appears at the bottom of the list, which in this case, does not make a difference. Unlike the routing table, which looks for the closest match in the list when processing an ACL entry that will be used as the first matching entry. If, for instance, you want to have one host on the 192.168.8.0/24 blocked on your ACL, then there would be a difference. You need to add deny for 192.168.8.200 to your ACL:

**Book VI
Chapter 3**

**Securing Networks
with ACLs and NAT**

```
Switch1>enable
Password:
Switch1#configure terminal
Enter configuration commands, one per line.  End with CNTL/Z.
Switch1(config)#access-list 50 deny 192.168.8.200 0.0.0.0
Switch1(config)#end
Switch1#show access-list 50
Standard IP access list 50
    deny    192.168.8.200
    permit 192.168.8.0, wildcard bits 0.0.0.255
    permit 192.168.9.0, wildcard bits 0.0.0.255
```

Notice deny was added to the top of the list, whereas the additional permit was added to the bottom of the list. Additionally, this entry does not include the wildcard bits. The ordering behavior is by design, with any entry for a single host being more important and therefore filtered to the top of the list. The reduction of the ACE for the single host is also expected. You could add the single host this way, instead of writing out all the zeros in the wildcard mask.

```
Switch1(config)#access-list 50 deny host 192.168.8.200
```

You can make a new ACL that will deny the same two Class C address blocks, but permit the first four addresses in the 192.168.8.0/24 range (192.168.8.0-192.168.8.3). Here is the result if you build the ACL in this order.

```
Switch1#configure terminal
Enter configuration commands, one per line.  End with CNTL/Z.
Switch1(config)#access-list 60 deny 192.168.8.0 0.0.0.255
Switch1(config)#access-list 60 deny 192.168.9.0 0.0.0.255
Switch1(config)#access-list 60 permit 192.168.8.0 0.0.0.3
Switch1(config)#end
Switch1#show access-list 60
Standard IP access list 60
    deny    192.168.8.0, wildcard bits 0.0.0.255
    deny    192.168.9.0, wildcard bits 0.0.0.255
    permit 192.168.8.0, wildcard bits 0.0.0.3
```

Because the entries are added to the ACL in the order that you type them, the permit ends up at the bottom of the list. If you test this ACL, an address like 192.168.8.2 would be picked up by the first ACE and would not receive the permit from the third ACE. How do you fix this? Well, you have a few choices:

✦ You can remove the ACL from where it is being used, delete the ACL, create a new one in the correct order, and add it back to where it is being used. This lengthy process actually leaves the system open from the time you remove the ACL from where it is being used, until it is added back. This has been the standard method of managing ACLs. When working with ACLs this way, you would copy all the steps required into notepad.exe. This includes the steps to remove the old ACL and add the new ACL. After the entire process is staged in notepad.exe, use the copy command to copy and paste into your CLI management application, such as putty.exe.

✦ If your device supports it, you can edit the ACL by using the IP command in the following code. This allows you to put line numbers into your ACL, an option that you do not have when editing the ACL from Global Configuration mode. This makes use of ACL Configuration mode. When putting your line numbers in, you want to leave a gap between the entries in the ACL.

```
Router1(config)#ip access-list standard 60
Router1(config-ext-nacl)#10 deny 192.168.8.0 0.0.0.255
Router1(config-ext-nacl)#20 deny 192.168.9.0 0.0.0.255
Router1(config-ext-nacl)#30 permit 192.168.8.0 0.0.0.3
```

With this pre-planning done, you can then add a new ACL entry at the top of the ACL by choosing a number that is less than 10, similar to the following:

```
Router1>enable
Password:
Router1#configure terminal
Router1(config)# ip access-list standard 60
Router1(config-ext-nacl)#5 permit 192.168.8.0 0.0.0.3
Router1(config-ext-nacl)#end
Router1#show access-list 60
Standard IP access list 60
    5 permit 192.168.9.0, wildcard bits 0.0.0.3
    10 deny   192.168.9.0, wildcard bits 0.0.0.255
    20 deny   192.168.9.0, wildcard bits 0.0.0.255
    30 permit 192.168.8.0, wildcard bits 0.0.0.3
```

This allows you to edit the ACL on the fly (that is, without removing it from the interfaces where it is used) without removing the ACL and recreating it, saving you a lot of time and effort, as long as there is a gap in the numbering where you can add your new entry.

Depending on the IOS version and device, you may have other options. If you look at the Adaptive Security Appliance (ASA), you do not have to preplan.

So review the following code, where the ASA automatically numbers the lines for you:

```
ASAFirewall1>enable
Password:
ASAFirewall1#configure terminal
ASAFirewall1(config)# access-list 60 deny 192.168.8.0 255.255.255.0
ASAFirewall1(config)# access-list 60 deny 192.168.9.0 255.255.255.0
ASAFirewall1(config)# exit
ASAFirewall1# show access-list 60
access-list 60; 2 elements
access-list 60 line 1 standard deny 192.168.8.0 255.255.255.0 (hitcnt=0)
    0x318d5521
access-list 60 line 2 standard deny 192.168.9.0 255.255.255.0 (hitcnt=0)
    0xba5e90e1
ASAFirewall1#configure terminal
ASAFirewall1(config)# access-list 60 line 1 permit 192.168.9.0 255.255.255.248
ASAFirewall1(config)# exit
ASAFirewall1# show access-list 60
access-list 60; 3 elements
access-list 60 line 1 standard permit 192.168.9.0 255.255.255.248 (hitcnt=0)
    0x451bbe48
access-list 60 line 2 standard deny 192.168.8.0 255.255.255.0 (hitcnt=0)
    0x318d5521
access-list 60 line 3 standard deny 192.168.9.0 255.255.255.0 (hitcnt=0)
    0xba5e90e1
```

By using the ASA, you can still add lines on the fly or manually number ACL entries. If you want to use the same line again, the ASA will renumber your entire list if it needs to. This is truly the best of both worlds.

Adding remarks

When you look at your running-config to view the ACLs, it can become somewhat confusing because the ACLs will all run together, as shown here:

```
Switch1#show running-config | include access-list
access-list 50 deny    192.168.8.200
access-list 50 deny    192.168.8.201
access-list 50 permit 192.168.8.0 0.0.0.255
access-list 50 permit 192.168.9.0 0.0.0.255
access-list 60 permit 192.168.8.0 0.0.0.3
access-list 60 deny    192.168.8.0 0.0.0.255
access-list 60 deny    192.168.9.0 0.0.0.255
```

To make this easier to read, you should start each ACL with a remark line. This does not show up when using the show command; but is in your running-config. This is what it would look like:

```
Switch1#show running-config | include access-list
access-list 50 deny    192.168.8.200
access-list 50 deny    192.168.8.201
access-list 50 permit 192.168.8.0 0.0.0.255
access-list 50 permit 192.168.9.0 0.0.0.255
access-list 60 remark This ACL is to control the outbound router traffic.
access-list 60 permit 192.168.8.0 0.0.0.3
access-list 60 deny    192.168.8.0 0.0.0.255
access-list 60 deny    192.168.9.0 0.0.0.255
```

Book VI
Chapter 3

Securing Networks
with ACLs and NAT

So far, I have shown you how to work the ACLs on a switch or router, but syntactically it is a little different on the ASA. For starters, the ASA does not make use of the wildcard mask, but rather uses the less confusing (unless you are expecting it) subnet mask. In the following code, I paused to get the help information on a switch and on an ASA while adding the access list. Notice in the help information it actually tells me if it wants a subnet mask or a wildcard mask.

```
Switch1(config)#access-list 50 permit 192.168.8.0 ?
  A.B.C.D  Wildcard bits
  log      Log matches against this entry
  <cr>
ASAFirewall1(config)# access-list 50 permit 192.168.8.0 ?
configure mode commands/options:
  A.B.C.D  Netmask for the IP address
```

Otherwise, the creation and management of the ACLs is the same across most of the Cisco product line.

Extended ACLs

The previous sections describe Standard ACLs, but there is another type, Extended ACLs. Here is a summary of what extended ACLs support:

✦ Numbered from 100–199 and from 2000–2699 (expanded range)

✦ Permit or deny based on source or destination IP addresses

✦ Permit or deny based on protocol, such as ICMP, GRE, TCP, UDP, and so on

In this section, I describe a router that is connected to the 192.168.8.0/24 segment on an internal interface (FastEthernet 0/0) using address 192.168.8.1/24, and to the 10.0.2.0/24 segment on an external interface (FastEthernet 0/1) using address 10.0.2.1/24. In this case, you would manage the 192.168.8.0/24 network and some unknown and untrusted group manages the rest of the network, as shown in Figure 3-1. On this network, you want to allow users to access only web servers outside the network. In order to support this, you need to create two ACLs, 101 and 102.

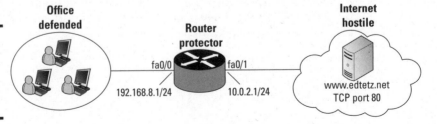

Figure 3-1: A sample network to implement ACLs.

You use `access-list 101` (see Listing 3-1) to manage the traffic leaving the office and `access-list 102` (see Listing 3-2) to manage traffic coming from the untrusted network into the office.

Listing 3-1: Creating ACL 101

```
Router1>enable
Password:
Router1#configure terminal
Enter configuration commands, one per line.  End with CNTL/Z.
Router1(config)#access-list 101 remark This ACL is to control the outbound router
    traffic.
Router1(config)#access-list 101 permit tcp 192.168.8.0 0.0.0.255 any eq 80
Router1(config)#access-list 101 permit tcp 192.168.8.0 0.0.0.255 any eq 443
Router1(config)#end
```

Listing 3-2: Creating ACL 102

```
Router1>enable
Password:
Router1#configure terminal
Enter configuration commands, one per line.  End with CNTL/Z.
Router1(config)#access-list 102 remark This ACL is to control the inbound router
    traffic.
Router1(config)#access-list 102 permit tcp any 192.168.8.0 0.0.0.255 established
Router1(config)#end
```

If you examine ACL 101 in Listing 3-1, the breakdown on the format of the command is as follows:

✦ The ACL is number 101

✦ It permits traffic

✦ It allows TCP traffic

✦ The source that it is allowed from is defined by 192.168.8.0 with a wild-card mask of 0.0.0.255

✦ The destination host is `any` host

✦ The TCP traffic that is allowed is on port 80

✦ The second line is the same, but it allows traffic on TCP port 443

If you do the same examination of the second ACL, ACL 102 in Listing 3-2, you should end up with the following:

✦ The ACL is number 102

✦ It permits traffic

✦ It allows TCP traffic

✦ The source that it is allowed from is `any` host

✦ The destination host is defined by 192.168.8.0 with a wildcard mask of 0.0.0.255

✦ The TCP traffic that is allowed is any traffic on an established session

The last item on ACL 102 is something to look at a bit more. In Figure 3-2, a client computer on the 192.168.8.0/24 network has created a TCP session with a remote server. This TCP session had a handshaking process that established what ports were going to be used, which was a randomly chosen port on the client and port 80 on the server. The port that is used in the ACE is dependent on the destination address, and in this case, the destination port is a randomly chosen port on the client. Rather than specifying that every possible port is open, which would not be secure, the option is to say that any established session on the client is allowed. Therefore, if the client opens the connection, this ACL will allow the traffic to come back in.

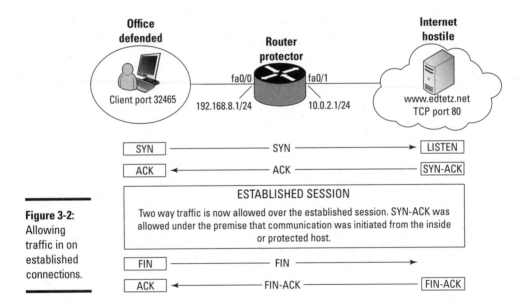

Figure 3-2:
Allowing
traffic in on
established
connections.

Applying an ACL

After you create an ACL, it would be good to use it. Your router has two interfaces and each has a direction of traffic travel where you can apply an ACL. In this case, you apply the ACLs only to the outside interface.

Applying an ACL or modifying an ACL on the fly can give you a lot of grief if you do it remotely across the network, even more so if that device is in a locked room a continent away. Schedule a reboot to deal with mistakes or errors. There is nothing more annoying than applying an ACL, only to lose your SSH or Telnet access to the device because you did not include those ports (TCP 22 and 23) in your ACL. So, before you apply the ACL, use a command such as `reload in 10` that will cause the router to reboot in 10 minutes. If you lose access to the router in those 10 minutes, you will have it back after the reboot. If you do not make any mistakes or need to reboot, then you can abort the reboot with `reload cancel` and then save your changes with `copy running-config startup-config`. Here is a copy of the whole process:

```
Router1#reload in 10 *ACL Change Recovery*

System configuration has been modified. Save? [yes/no]: yes
Building configuration...
[OK]
Reload scheduled in 10 minutes by console
Reload reason: *ACL Change Recovery*
Proceed with reload? [confirm]
Router1#
*Apr 19 13:46:45.637: %SYS-5-SCHEDULED_RELOAD: Reload requested for 13:56:26 UTC
     Tue Apr 19 2011 at 13:46:26 UTC Tue Apr 19 2011 by console. Reload Reason:
     *ACL Change Recovery*.
Router1#reload cancel
Router1#


***
*** --- SHUTDOWN ABORTED ---
***

*Apr 19 13:46:57.557: %SYS-5-SCHEDULED_RELOAD_CANCELLED:  Scheduled reload
     cancelled at 13:46:57 UTC Tue Apr 19 2011
```

This can sometimes be confusing if you think of *out* as *out of your network*. Instead, think of *out* as *out of the network device*. Picture the router as a bucket with two hoses for each interface; two hoses carry water into the bucket, and two carry water out of the bucket. If you want to, you can use a stopper (an ACL) to restrict the flow of water into or out of the bucket.

In most cases, you want to apply both of your ACLs to the same interface, and typically to what I call the most hostile interface. Using only one interface will help in your frame of reference, `FastEthernet0/1`. (I discuss why you use `FastEthernet0/1` shortly.)

```
Router1>enable
Password:
Router1#configure terminal
Enter configuration commands, one per line.  End with CNTL/Z.
```

```
Router1(config)#interface fastEthernet0/1
Router1(config-if)#ip access-group 101 out
Router1(config-if)#ip access-group 102 in
Router1(config-if)#end
```

If you use an older IOS or a different type of device, you may find that while in Interface Configuration mode that the `access-group` command is the root command, and not found in the `ip` command. Do not worry, that is just how it is. So do not be afraid to use `access-group 101 out` instead of `ip access-group 101 out`.

You can only apply one ACL, on each interface, in each direction. That is your limitation.

Although I applied the configuration to the outside interface, I could have applied the configuration to different interfaces, in different directions; but that affects what traffic crosses the inside boundaries in the router or network device. The same ACLs could have been applied like this:

```
Router1>enable
Password:
Router1#configure terminal
Enter configuration commands, one per line.  End with CNTL/Z.
Router1(config)#interface fastEthernet0/1
Router1(config-if)#ip access-group 101 out
Router1(config-if)#exit
Router1(config)#interface fastEthernet0/0
Router1(config-if)#ip access-group 102 out
```

In this case, all the traffic crosses the inside boundary in the router. Another example could be blocking ICMP traffic using the example in Figure 3-3. If you block ICMP traffic, you prevent people from pinging addresses in the range. In this case, the range is 192.168.8.0/24. By applying that ACL to the exterior interface (`FastEthernet0/1`) in the inbound direction, you prevent devices from pinging any addresses in that range, including the address associated with `FastEthernet0/0`. Interior users can still ping the 192.168.8.1 of the router. Now, if you move that ACL to the interior interface, in the outbound direction, you still prevent that traffic from reaching the hosts on the 192.168.8.0/24 network segment, but you see these side effects:

✦ Hosts on the network cannot ping the router.

✦ Hosts outside of the network cannot ping hosts on the network.

✦ Hosts outside the network can ping the internal address of the router.

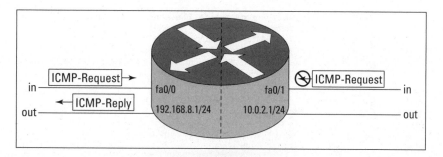

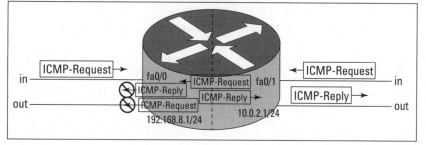

Figure 3-3:
Applying
ACLs to
interfaces.

Why is that, you may wonder. Well, the rule now applies to traffic that is leaving the interior interface of the router. The interface of the router that has 192.168.8.1 address associated with it is actually inside the router, and the ACL only applies to traffic that is leaving the router, not to traffic that is inside of the router. Keep this in mind as you decide which interfaces to apply the ACLs to. As I said earlier, typically, it will be applied for In and Out on your hostile interface. (*Hostile* is a relative term; think of it as more protected/secured interface and less protected/secured interface, with the lesser interface being the hostile interface.)

Using ACLs as a Virus Detection Tool

You can do a few things with your ACLs related to viruses. If you know a virus that has a certain type of traffic, perhaps on TCP port 1090, you can create an ACL that makes use of the log option. This allows information about these packets to be recorded in the system log, which could go to a centralized Syslog server. I tell you more about Syslog servers right after you look at this code example showing you the little change you need to make to your ACEs to enable logging. Simply by adding log to the end of the ACE, any traffic that matches the ACE will be logged.

```
ASAFirewall1(config)# access-list 103 deny tcp any any eq 1090 ?
configure mode commands/options:
  inactive    Keyword for disabling an ACL element
  log         Keyword for enabling log option on this ACL element
  time-range  Keyword for attaching time-range option to this ACL element
  <cr>

Router1(config)#access-list 103 deny tcp any any eq 1090 ?
  dscp        Match packets with given dscp value
  fragments   Check non-initial fragments
  log         Log matches against this entry
  log-input   Log matches against this entry, including input interface
  precedence  Match packets with given precedence value
  time-range  Specify a time-range
  tos         Match packets with given TOS value
  <cr>
```

Cisco IOS devices have a small log configured on them. When you consider that your router may have as little as 64MB of memory, this does not leave very much space to maintain log information for very long. The alternative to using the router's memory for logging is to have your log information sent to a server on the network. *Syslog* is an industry standard format for accepting and storing these log messages. Many Syslog servers are available for different operating systems, including Kiwi Syslog Server for Windows from www.kiwisyslog.com. Kiwi Syslog Server is available as a free version and is often suitable enough for many people. To enable your device to send messages to a Syslog server, use this command on your IOS device (192.168.1.5 is the IP address of my Syslog server):

```
Router1>enable
Password:
Router1#configure terminal
Enter configuration commands, one per line.  End with CNTL/Z.
Router1(config)#logging 192.168.1.5
```

Rather than logging the data, you can view it in real time on the device using the debug command, such as debug ip packet 103 detail, on the device where you expect to see that type of data. The following is debug showing a denied access attempt for a device with the 10.0.2.25 IP address:

```
Router1>enable
Router1#terminal monitor
Router1#debug ip packet 103 detail
IP packet debugging is on (detailed) for access list 103
Router1#
00:11:55: %SEC-6-IPACCESSLOGP: list 103 denied tcp 10.0.2.25(3541) ->
    192.168.8.10(1090), 1 packet
Router1#no debug all
All possible debugging has been turned off
```

Where You Can Use ACLs

Although the focus of ACLs seems to be about controlling traffic flow, the ACL can be used as a tool in other areas as well. Here is just a short list:

+ **Control the propagation of routing information:** You can use an ACL to manage a distribute list for where your routing table updates will be sent.

+ **Control debug output:** You can use an ACL to permit a type of traffic with the sole intention of using the `log` option to be able to track when that traffic occurs. (See the previous section for an example.)

+ **Router management:** By implementing an ACL, you can control which devices can access your virtual terminal (vty) connections.

+ **Encryption management:** ACLs can manage which data you want to encrypt between two points or routers, as well as what traffic you want to leave unencrypted or drop.

Setting Up Network Address Translation

You cannot use private address spaces on a network and have those devices communicate with Internet devices without doing some type of translation to convert addresses of one type to addresses of another type. Think about a large company with a large building and many offices. Mail comes to the mailroom and someone in that mailroom has the job of translating addresses from John Smith, Big Company, 123 Some Street, Thistown, Thatstate to Office 212. To translate the address, the mail clerk looks up John Smith's office address in a table. People outside the company do not need to worry about the fact that John's office is 212.

Network Address Translation (NAT), as defined in RFC1631, works on a similar principle. All your devices have internal addresses that are used, and you have a pool of external of public addresses that you can use. When an internal device talks to an external device, then a mapping is placed in a table between those two addresses. This mapping can be done manually or automatically. Devices outside of the network will see only the external address, and when they send data back, it is matched on the mapping table and redirected to the correct internal address. The actual device inside the network using that outside address can change over time. For example, you may see 192.168.8.50 using the public address of 192.0.2.100, but tomorrow you may have 192.168.8.58 using the address of 192.0.2.100 and 192.168.8.50

using the address of 192.0.2.101. This would be the same as moving John Smith to office 503 and placing another person in office 212; the mailroom will still deliver the mail to the correct person. Figure 3-4 illustrates NAT.

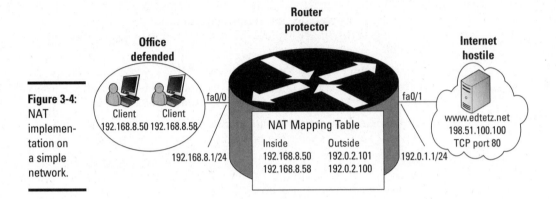

Figure 3-4: NAT implementation on a simple network.

Requirements for NAT

NAT resolves a few problems for the world at large:

✦ **Shortage of IPv4 addresses:** NAT allows everyone to use a functionally unlimited number of addresses inside of their network, while only needing a handful of public addresses; thereby reducing the number of public addresses in use.

✦ **Security:** NAT adds a layer of obfuscation to your network by providing different addressing to your public connections.

✦ **Administration:** NAT allows you to restrict outside access to only those devices or addresses that you have manually configured, rather than allowing the Internet free access to your network.

Types of NAT

NAT can be configured to work on your network a few different ways. How you choose to implement NAT depends on what your goals are for NAT and your public address management. NAT methods include

✦ **Static NAT:** Puts a permanent mapping between an internal private address and a public address. In this scenario, 192.168.8.50 will always map out to 192.0.2.75. This type of NAT may be used for allowing traffic into a mail server or web server.

✦ **Dynamic NAT:** Puts a dynamic mapping between an internal private address and a public address. This also creates a one-to-one relationship on a first-come-first-served basis. The public address that is used by private devices can change over time and cannot be trusted. This would allow systems out, when you are not concerned with outside devices trying to connect in, as with the previous web server example.

✦ **Overloading:** This is also known as Port Address Translation (PAT). In this case, multiple internal devices are able to share one public address, as mappings are placed into the mappings table based on the source and destination ports that are used. As long as ports are available to be remapped, then any number of devices can share a very small pool of public addresses or just one public address.

✦ **Overlapping:** NAT can be used when public or registered addresses are used inside your network. In this case, you may use a public address block on multiple internal networks. NAT allows you to translate those "internal" addresses to other publicly accessible addresses when you connect to the "public" side of the router.

Many people quickly become lost understanding local, global, inside, and outside addresses. The following list describes the different types of addresses:

✦ **Local:** This refers to what happens on the inside of your network.

✦ **Global:** This refers to what happens on the outside of your network.

✦ **Inside Local Address:** This is an address of a host on your internal network, for example, 192.168.8.25.

✦ **Inside Global Address:** This is the mapped address that people on the Internet would see, which represents the inside host.

✦ **Outside Global Address:** The IP address of a remote Internet-based host as assigned by the owner that can communicate with an inside host, for example, 192.0.2.100.

✦ **Outside Local Address:** This is the address that the inside hosts use to reference an outside host. The outside local address may be the outside host's actual address or another translated private address from a different private address block. Therefore, the router could translate that address to 192.168.10.50, or it could be the public address of the external host. The internal hosts would contact this address to deal with the external host.

The following list summarizes the basic process that NAT follows (see Figure 3-5):

1. An internal host (HostA) sends an IP packet to an external host (HostB).

2. When the packet arrives at the router, the router examines the packet and sees whether the NAT configuration is supposed to apply to it.

3. The source IP address and port are recorded in the mapping table and matched to an external address and port on the router. This may be in the external range of addresses or be the actual router's address, based on the NAT configuration.

4. The data is sent to HostB referencing the mapped address information as the source of the new IP packet.

5. When HostB sends data back to HostA, HostB references the known source address (192.0.2.100) in the IP packet that it received.

6. When the router receives the IP packet, it examines its mapping table and finds the referenced destination IP address information and the internal it maps to. When the mapping is found in the table, it re-addresses the destination address in the IP packet and sends it onto the new destination.

7. The IP packet arrives at HostA using its internal network address.

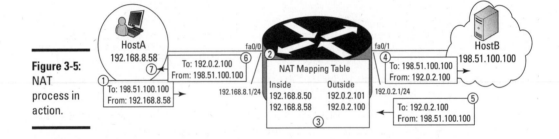

Figure 3-5:
NAT
process in
action.

A timer is set when dynamic entries are added to the mapping table. Every time that mapping is used, the timer is reset. If the mapping is not used before the timer expires, then that mapping is removed from the mapping table.

Setting up NAT

NAT is very easy to set up. For these examples, I use the network shown in Figure 3-6.

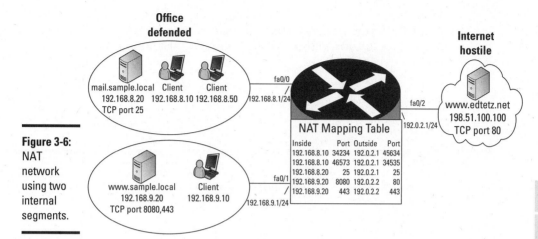

Figure 3-6: NAT network using two internal segments.

This example sets up NAT on the router, but implements a one-to-one dynamic mapping. This allows dynamic assignment of the actual addresses, but you have the same number of inside and outside addresses so that every device receives an address. Without overloading, this is critical. Here are the commands that you need to issue to configure NAT on the router:

```
interface FastEthernet 0/0
description Inside Interface
ip address 192.168.8.1 255.255.255.0
ip nat inside
exit
interface FastEthernet 0/1
description Inside Interface
ip address 192.168.9.1 255.255.255.0
ip nat inside
exit
interface FastEthernet 0/2
description Outside Interface
ip address 192.0.2.1 255.255.255.0
ip nat outside
exit
access-list 10 permit 192.168.8.8 0.0.0.7
access-list 10 permit 192.168.9.8 0.0.0.7
!--- Access list only allows hosts 192.168.8.8 to
!--- 192.168.8.15 and 192.168.9.8 to 192.168.9.15
!--- out through NAT.
ip nat pool no-overload 192.0.2.10 192.0.2.25 prefix 24
ip nat inside source list 10 pool no-overload
```

For this example, say you only have one outside address assigned to you by your ISP. All your traffic must go through this one address. This is the PAT example, as the one address will be translated on a port basis.

```
interface FastEthernet 0/0
description Inside Interface
ip address 192.168.8.1 255.255.255.0
ip nat inside
exit
interface FastEthernet 0/1
description Inside Interface
ip address 192.168.9.1 255.255.255.0
ip nat inside
exit
interface FastEthernet 0/2
description Outside Interface
ip address 192.0.2.1 255.255.255.252
ip nat outside
exit
access-list 10 permit 192.168.8.8 0.0.0.7
access-list 10 permit 192.168.9.8 0.0.0.7
!--- Access list only allows hosts 192.168.8.8 to
!--- 192.168.8.15 and 192.168.9.8 to 192.168.9.15
!--- out through NAT.
ip nat pool ovrld 192.0.2.1 192.0.2.1 prefix 30
ip nat inside source list 10 pool ovrld
```

Finally, you have two servers on the inside of the network that have internal addresses of 192.168.8.20 and 192.168.9.20. The first server is used for e-mail and the second server is a web server. The web server has the site running on the less standard TCP port 8080, but you want outside users to use TCP port 80.

```
interface FastEthernet 0/0
description Inside Interface
ip address 192.168.8.1 255.255.255.0
ip nat inside
exit
interface FastEthernet 0/1
description Inside Interface
ip address 192.168.9.1 255.255.255.0
ip nat inside
exit
interface FastEthernet 0/2
description Outside Interface
ip address 192.0.2.1 255.255.255.252
ip nat outside
exit
```

```
access-list 10 permit 192.168.8.8 0.0.0.7
access-list 10 permit 192.168.9.8 0.0.0.7
!--- Access list only allows hosts 192.168.8.8 to
!--- 192.168.8.15 and 192.168.9.8 to 192.168.9.15
!--- out through NAT.
ip nat pool ovrld 192.0.2.1 192.0.2.1 prefix 30
ip nat inside source list 10 pool ovrld
ip nat inside source static tcp 192.168.9.20 8080 192.0.2.2 80
!--- This uses the second available address on external
!--- interface, while it could have used the configured
!--- address on FastEthernet0/2. It could have also been
!--- configured for the Interface address using this command.
ip nat inside source static tcp 192.168.8.20 25 interface FastEthernet0/2
```

Use your ports when you create static mappings to allow inside resources to publish out through the external interface of your router or firewall. Avoid using commands such as `ip nat inside source static 192.168.1.50 192.0.2.50`, which effectively places your entire host 192.168.1.50 outside of your router or firewall. This is much more exposure than you need for that host.

Making use of the `interface` command is useful when your ISP assigns your outside address through either DHCP or PPPoE dynamically. The `interface` command allows your configuration to use whatever address happens to be assigned to your router or firewall.

Using the later scenario, if you are required to change the IP address of the web server (perhaps moving from the 192.168.9.0/24 network to the 192.168.8.0/24 network, or changing the port number back to the standard port 80), then these changes can be made at the router with no impact to users outside of the network. The DNS entry pointing to the outside address will remain the same and their lives will continue as normal. Often, people are amazed by how easy managing this exterior/interior mapping of their network is.

Viewing translations

If you want to see the IP NAT mappings or translations, you can use the `show` and `debug` commands. Table 3-2 summarizes some of the commands that give you information about the translations running on your Cisco device.

Table 3-2	Commands to Manage and View NAT Status
Command	*Description*
clear ip nat translation	Removes a dynamic NAT translation from the mapping or translation table
debug ip nat	Displays information about IP packets that are being translated by NAT
ip nat	Defines that data on the selected interface is subject to NAT translation rules
ip nat inside source	Configures NAT to use an inside destination address
ip nat outside source	Configures NAT to use an outside source address
ip nat pool	Configures pool of addresses to be used as outside source addresses
show ip nat translations	Shows a list of active NAT translations

Chapter 4: Cisco Security Best Practices

In This Chapter

✔ Looking into the areas of management

✔ Delving into Authentication, Authorization, and Accounting

✔ Collecting and monitoring logs

✔ Securing protocols

✔ Managing the network's configuration

✔ Implementing physical security

Security is often the elephant in the room. Security is there, and obvious, but nobody wants to be the one who brings it up or acknowledges it. I know a company that is absolutely paranoid about security and has hoops upon hoops for people to jump through to get new equipment added to the network, but it also has remote computers that have almost no security on them that have access to the entire network with no network Access Control Lists (ACLs). Why? Because a common misconception is that if you manage ACLs on remote devices, you can get yourself in a bind by doing things wrong.

Security should never be skipped because it is too difficult or too scary. There is always some uncertainty by implementing new systems, but there is also uncertainty about the safety of your data by not implementing security systems. Given a choice, I would rather explain difficulties with a new, safer system, or even data loss by implementing a new system, rather than explain why everything was lost due to inaction.

Now, I am not saying to implement new and difficult systems for the sake of having the newest systems. This whole process of data and network security should start with an audit, followed by an evaluation of business goals and risks, and finally a review and alignment of the two. This should give you a list of deficiencies that the business determines to be actionable risks, which can then be rolled into a deployment plan. Security and data safety may involve implementing new systems that require a capital outlay for the organization, or the safety may simply be a change in business process or software and configuration changes, which has a cost in staff time or possibly consultant compensation. <Shameless plug> Remember, it is often well worth hiring a consultant, like Ed Tetz, to come to your network and implement a solution in a fraction of the time that it may take you to implement it yourself. </Shameless plug>

In this chapter, I introduce you to many of the security tools that you need to be familiar with and use to protect your network, including Authentication, Authorization, and Accounting (AAA), log collection and monitoring, secure protocols, configuration management, monitoring traffic, securing traffic with ACLs, and physical security.

Management Areas

According to Cisco, three main areas of network management play a role in your device and data security. The following are the areas of the devices that need protection through your security measures; these all relate to soft security features (as opposed to hard security features like locked doors and alarm systems) and are the

+ **Management plane:** This is the area that is responsible for communication with the management interfaces of your devices. The management interfaces include applications and protocols, such as Secure Shell (SSH), Simple Network Management Protocol (SNMP), and Telnet.

+ **Control plane:** This is the area that is responsible for infrastructure. The infrastructure includes applications and protocols that deal with maintaining network infrastructure between devices. Control applications and protocols include routing protocols like Enhanced Interior Gateway Routing Protocol (EIRGP), Open Shortest Path First (OSPF), and Routing Information Protocol (RIP).

+ **Data plane:** This is the area that is directly responsible for the movement of data through the network and networking devices.

This chapter gives you guidance in how to implement security on your network, but I do not provide all the details related to implementing all these features.

Finding Out About Known Issues with Cisco Devices

The best way to find out about issues with your Cisco devices and their Internetwork Operating System (IOS) is to stay updated on Cisco advisories, which are posted to Cisco's support website by the Product Security Incident Response Team (PSIRT). To read more about the latest advisories, visit www.cisco.com/go/psirt.

If you do not know that you have issues with your devices, it makes it hard to keep them secured. When the advisories are posted, they detail what the issues are and the steps that need to be taken to mitigate or eliminate the risks from the issue.

Leveraging Authentication, Authorization, and Accounting

Authentication, Authorization, and Accounting (AAA) services play a critical role in securing your network resources because they offer a secure method of maintaining a central database of users and passwords. Depending on the server that you use (Remote Authentication Dial In User Service [RADIUS] or Terminal Access Controller Access-Control System [TACACS]) and the AAA servers your devices support, you cannot only authenticate users and devices, but you can also push out configuration settings to those users or devices. An example of pushing out configuration information is the association of virtual local area networks (VLANs) with users; when a user authenticates at a switch, the port they are connected to dynamically joins the VLAN that the user is supposed to be a member of. Within the Cisco ISO, AAA authentication can be used to limit the commands that are available to a user and to log the commands that a user issues.

Authentication fallback

One issue that can befall you when you implement AAA is what happens when AAA is unavailable. Your Cisco devices support a secondary authentication method for just that case arising. As secondary authentication methods, you can use the enable password, local user accounts on the device, or line authentication. In Book III, Chapter 3 and Book IV, Chapter 3, you see how to configure line passwords on the console port, AUX port, and Virtual Terminal (vty) sessions.

The preferred secondary authentication method is actually the enable password because the other types of passwords use Type 7 passwords (which I complain about shortly). The enable password can use the secret option that implements a one-way hashing algorithm, which is a more secure option. Because you need to configure the enable password, you need to protect your systems by overriding it with `enable secret`. Although doing so is required only as a backdoor security option when AAA authentication is unavailable, if you are using it, you have the extra work required to support local passwords or user account on your devices.

Some versions of the Cisco IOS support using the same password hashing algorithm for user passwords as you use with the secret password. If this option is available to you for your local user accounts, your local user accounts are preferred over the enable/secret password.

Avoiding Type 7 passwords

Type 7 passwords were created to obscure the passwords found in the configuration files, but they were designed to support fast decryption during authentication. To support this speed, they implemented the Vigenère cipher. Unfortunately, the process for decrypting passwords are well-known; as such many tools, such as Cain & Abel, can quickly decrypt Type 7 passwords by using the toolbar tool button identified in Figure 4-1.

Cisco Type-7 Password Decoder button

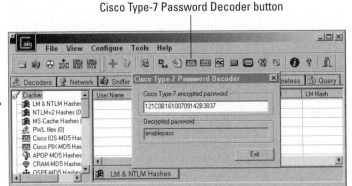

Figure 4-1: Using Cain & Abel to read a Type 7 password.

Even Message-Digest version 5 (MD5) and Advanced Encryption Standard (AES) hashed passwords can be cracked, but they take substantially more time because every possible password needs to be hashed and compared to the version that is hashed in the configuration files. Figure 4-2 shows Cain & Abel completing a crack on my secret password. (Keep in mind though that the password was between only five and six characters, and I gave Cain & Abel a list of the necessary letters.) If the password was between 1 and 16 characters and made up of standard letters and numbers, the brute force guessing would take upward of $9x10^{13}$ years — processing 3,000 passwords a second — on the computer that I used. Using a more powerful computer would have resulted in faster times; but really, what difference would a few thousand years make in cracking the password?

Use AAA for authentication, avoid local usernames and passwords, and if you are using locally stored passwords, make sure that passwords you care about are not stored as Type 7 passwords.

The secret password is a more secure option because of encryption than most of the other password options. If you do not set your secret password but you do configure a cleartext (unencrypted) password on your console port, you grant anyone who gains console or vty access privileged access to your system. After a user can enter Privileged EXEC mode, he can do whatever he wants in the device IOS, including taking a copy of all the device's usernames and password.

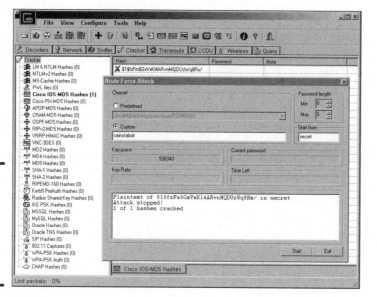

Figure 4-2:
Using Cain
& Abel to
eventually
crack
an MD5
password.

To grant you a higher level of security, you can specify `service password-encryption`, which encrypts future passwords in your configuration file. The `service password-encryption` command is how you configure your system to use the low security Type 7 passwords. To work with the `service password-encryption` command, you simply enable password encryption, and any passwords in your configuration file are encrypted (or encoded) automatically with Type 7 hashing. The `service password-encryption` process is not reversed with the `no service password-encryption` command because the passwords remain encrypted until you reset them. The following code shows how to set up `service password-encryption`:

```
Router1#enable
Password:
Router1#configure terminal
Enter configuration commands, one per line.  End with CNTL/Z.
Router1#show running-config | include enable password
enable password enablepass
Router1#configure terminal
Enter configuration commands, one per line.  End with CNTL/Z.
Router1(config)#service password-encryption
Router1(config)#enable password enablepass
Router1(config)#exit
Router1#
Router1#show running-config | include enable password
enable password 7 121C0B16100709142B3837
Router1#show running-config
<content delete for brevity>
!
line con 0
 exec-timeout 0 0
 password 7 070C2E425E080A16
 login
```

```
line aux 0
 password 7 104F1C0115160118
 login
line vty 0 4
 privilege level 15
 password 7 1311121E0509106A
 login local
 transport input telnet ssh
!
<content delete for brevity>
```

Type 7 passwords can be read easily with any number of tools on the Internet, so they must be treated almost the same as cleartext passwords. `service password-encryption` is different from the secret password: The secret password is a one-way MD5 hash, whereas `service password-encryption` uses the Type 7 or Vigenère hash.

When dealing with usernames in your configuration file, the `username secret` command may be issued in Global Configuration mode to configure your local users to have their passwords encrypted with MD5 hashing. In the following example, I created two user accounts — one with Type 7 hashing and one with MD5 hashing. Look at how they appear in the configuration file with `service password-encryption` disabled initially.

```
Router1#enable
Password:
Router1#configure terminal
Enter configuration commands, one per line.  End with CNTL/Z.
Router1(config)#username etetz password 0 type7pass
Router1(config)#username etetzs secret 0 md5pass
Router1(config)#exit
Router1#show running-config | include etetz
username etetz password 0 type7pass
username etetzs secret 5 $1$hbNJ$QbM1G5AjnbiKVYgNFL4DN/
Router1#configure terminal
Enter configuration commands, one per line.  End with CNTL/Z.
Router1(config)#service password-encryption
Router1(config)#exit
Router1#show running-config | include etetz
*Apr 22 14:38:30.867: %SYS-5-CONFIG_I: Configured from console by console
username etetz password 7 02121D4B0E511F205F5D
username etetzs secret 5 $1$hbNJ$QbM1G5AjnbiKVYgNFL4DN/
```

Notice the difference in the preceding code example as to the appearance of the three types of passwords and how they are identified in the file, `password 0` (no encrytion), `password 7` (Vigenère hash), and `secret 5` (MD5 hash). The encrypted passwords for the user accounts identify the hashing algorithm that was used (by the 5 or 7 preceding the password), and the passwords are displayed in encrypted text.

Centralizing Log Collection and Monitoring

George Santayana once wrote, "Those who cannot remember the past are condemned to repeat it." This is as true today as it was over 100 years ago when he wrote it. How can you know the history of your network? By logging.

Logging allows you to see what happened to your network in the past. Regular reviewing of your logs can also identify issues before they become problems. Cisco devices, however, have limited buffer space to store logs, and when you reboot the device, you lose them.

Collecting logs in one location

The solve Cisco devices' limited buffer space, use a Syslog server. You can find a Syslog server for Windows from Kiwi Software (now part of SolarWinds) at www.kiwisyslog.com. You can choose from many other Syslog servers, all at different price points, ranging from free to thousands of dollars. The purpose of a Syslog server, regardless of the cost, is to collect log data from a variety of devices and consolidate it in one place where it can easily be monitored, searched, and analyzed. If you use Linux or Unix, you have a huge selection of free Syslog servers.

The *Syslog server* acts as a collection point for your logging activities, allowing all your network logs to be stored in one place so that you can search it easily. The Syslog server is a must for network security because without a Syslog server, your logs will remain on scattered devices and will never be reviewed or archived.

The downside is that Syslog can send a lot of small pieces of data very fast, so it uses User Datagram Protocol (UDP) and cleartext to prevent overloading the network. To prevent unauthorized users from reading those cleartext packets and to isolate your Syslog traffic, you need to use a separate management VLAN. This management VLAN should be in place already because that is where you isolate all your switch and router management traffic. Another option, in place of the management network, is to enable network layer security for all this traffic through IPSec or another type of encryption mechanism.

You can easily enable logging from the Cisco side of the equation. (The more difficult part is the configuration of the Syslog server.) Use code similar to the following example, which needs only to specify the IP address of the log server:

```
Router1#enable
Password:
Router1#configure terminal
Enter configuration commands, one per line.  End with CNTL/Z.
Router1(config)#logging host 192.168.8.20
Router1(config)#exit
```

Choosing a logging level

With almost all Cisco's Enterprise-level devices are eight default logging levels that range from zero to seven. Each of these logging levels is tied to a detail in the data logging, as I specify in Table 4-1. These levels allow you to easily choose a block of data that you wish to have logged into the system logs, and then actually sends the log info via SNMP or to Syslog destinations. Take care as you increase the levels because you increase the load on your device CPU. This is especially true of level 7.

Table 4-1	Cisco System Logging Levels	
Level	Title	Description
0	Emergencies	System is unusable
1	Alerts	Immediate action needed
2	Critical	Critical conditions
3	Errors	Error conditions
4	Warnings	Warning conditions
5	Notifications	Informational messages
6	Informational	Normal, but significant, conditions
7	Debugging	Debugging messages

As with most things with the Cisco IOS, this is not very difficult to set up or configure. In Global Configuration mode, use two commands. `logging trap` specifies which logging level should be sent to your Syslog server; `logging buffered` configures the logging level that displays in the temporary buffer.

```
Router1#enable
Password:
Router1#configure terminal
Enter configuration commands, one per line.  End with CNTL/Z.
Router1(config)#logging trap 6
Router1(config)#logging buffered 6
Router1(config)#end
```

Dealing with logging in the console, monitor, and buffer

Cisco makes it possible to send logging data to the console session or to the remote vty terminals that have specified that they want to see logging data by issuing the EXEC command `terminal monitor`. However, if logging is also sent to the console, this command places a high load on the CPU. To control whether logging displays in the console session or the monitor sessions, use the commands `no logging console` or `no logging monitor`, respectively. If you want to see the log buffer, you can use the `show log` command at any time while in User EXEC mode or Privileged EXEC mode.

When logging to any display, such as the console or monitor sessions, you have overhead on your Cisco device. Console logging causes overhead even if you view the console at the time but disconnect with the console left open. The recommendation is to log data only to the buffer. You can configure the buffer with the size of the buffer with the `logging buffered` command. The buffer size varies with your device, but in the following example, the size is set to 32KB and with logging at level 6, or the information level:

```
Router1#enable
Password:
Router1#configure terminal
Enter configuration commands, one per line.  End with CNTL/Z.
Router1(config)#logging buffered 32768 6
Router1(config)#end
```

When collecting logging data in a Syslog server, the device's interface IP address is used — and included in the data — to send logging data to the server. When the IP address changes, it can cause a lot of confusion when reviewing the logs. To keep consistency in your logs, you can configure the loopback interface with an address and then configure that interface address to be used as the logging source interface. Here is the command to configure logging to use the loopback interface address:

```
Router1#enable
Password:
Router1#configure terminal
Enter configuration commands, one per line.  End with CNTL/Z.
Router1(config)#logging source-interface Loopback 0
Router1(config)#end
```

When reviewing your logs and piecing together a timeline for a major network issue, your times and time reference need to all make sense. Network Time Protocol (NTP) servers for centralized time management helps keep times synchronized, and placing a time level attached to your log entries helps as well. The following command configures your logging to include date and time, down to milliseconds, and includes the time zone:

```
service timestamps log datetime msec show-timezone
```

By default, the system clock is configured for Coordinated Universal Time (UTC). However, if you prefer to use a local time zone for your devices (say, to avoid the question, "Why was that going on at that time of night?"), try using this set of commands:

```
Router1#enable
Password:
Router1#configure terminal
Enter configuration commands, one per line.  End with CNTL/Z.
Router1(config)#clock timezone AST -4
Router1(config)#service timestamps log datetime msec localtime show-timezone
Router1(config)#end
```

Implementing Secure Protocols

Use secured protocols wherever they make enough sense to implement. By default and historically, many unsecured protocols have been implemented to support your Cisco devices. This is not Cisco's fault — when Cisco implemented the protocols, no secured options were available. Over the years, as newer secured options became available, many people did not adopt them because they were comfortable with what they knew. I still have to work hard to convince some clients that SSH is not really any more complicated or difficult to implement than Telnet is.

The following table gives common unsecured protocols and the better, more secure protocol choices.

Instead Of . . .	*. . . Use This Secure Protocol*
Telnet	Secure Shell (SSH)
Trivial File Transfer Protocol (TFTP)	Secure Copy Protocol (SCP)
File Transfer Protocol (FTP)	SCP, SSH, or Secure File Transfer Protocol (SFTP)

Managing Configurations

How do you manage configuration of your devices? Do you just read about the change, connect to the device, type in the change, use the `write memory` command, and exit? If so, I have bad news for you; this is not the way you should do manage configuration.

The concept of change management needs to be followed rigorously for very important devices. Cisco IOS devices allow you to store configurations in text files and then apply them a section at a time. Ideally, you have a duplicate of important equipment in a networking lab, but that is a luxury few people can afford. Lacking a lab, pre-record the configuration changes you will make, including a back-out plan, such as scheduling a reboot to roll back configuration changes. If possible, have some sort of review and approval process to better track configuration changes. If your organization is large enough to have different groups within the IT department, that review and approval process needs to include people from the other IT groups, such as desktop support, because the changes you make on the network may impact user connectivity to network devices. Having the other groups aware of what is going on allows them to respond better to issues that arise as a result of the networking changes.

Simple change management processes are easy to set up. The key components of any change management system revolve around documentation, recovery processes, and communication. These key elements can typically be implemented with a few small changes in your processes.

Storage of your configuration files is important because they contain passwords that could give unauthorized access to your network devices. These should be stored with an appropriate level of security because poor storage can undermine your security goals.

Password management

I discuss two key features when dealing with passwords and users within your Cisco devices. If you are using local accounts, you can enable two features for password management:

**Book VI
Chapter 4**

**Cisco Security
Best Practices**

✦ Password Retry Lockout

✦ Service Password Recovery

Password Retry Lockout

When users attempt to authenticate, there is no limit to how long they can try incorrectly. If you want to put a limit on the system, you need to enable a failed login lockout system. This system is built into the current Cisco IOS.

A failed login lockout is important because any users that have been granted privilege level 15 (the highest set of security rights) are not typically locked out. After enabling this feature, even these privileged user accounts are locked out if they exceed their login attempts. The number of privileged users you have should always be kept to a minimum. After locked out, these accounts are locked until you manually unlock them. To enable this, you simply need to change the AAA authentication process to use the new version AAA authentication (which supports account lockout) that Cisco cleverly calls `new-model`. Do not worry, even though you change AAA authentication process, you can still specify that users will be authenticated locally and not via the AAA server, as I have in the following set of commands:

```
Router1#enable
Password:
Router1#configure terminal
Enter configuration commands, one per line.  End with CNTL/Z.
Router1(config)#aaa new-model
Router1(config)#aaa local authentication attempts max-fail 5
Router1(config)#aaa authentication login default local
Router1(config)#end
```

If an account is locked out, you can use the following command in Privileged EXEC mode to unlock an account, as in the following example. This command can apply a specific user or `all`.

```
clear aaa local user lockout username etetz
```

The counter is never reset, so if you have several failed logins over a few days, reset the counter with a command specifying all accounts, or just yours. Here is the command to issue in Privileged EXEC mode:

```
clear aaa local user fail-attempts username etetz
```

Service Password Recovery

The current Cisco IOS supports a fairly new command: `service password-recovery`, or perhaps more specifically, `no service password-recovery`. This is a Global Configuration mode command that modifies the behavior of your password recovery process.

Anyone with console access and the ability to reboot the Cisco device can set her own enable or secret password on the device. (I cover this process in Book I, Chapter 5.) *Recovery* is more about being able to recover a device that has a password you have forgotten or lost by setting a new password, rather than actually recovering the password. This poses a bit of a security risk, especially because you may not notice the password has been changed. You may notice the reboots of the device, but that is all.

By adding the `no service password-recovery` to your configuration, the password recovery process does not allow you to recover the password without erasing the entire configuration. If your device configuration is erased, someone has likely been messing around with your equipment. The other advantage of `no service password-recovery` is that it offers you the advantage of not having your configuration fall into the wrong hands for devices you have removed from the network and prevents the password from being reset for devices that are still on the network. When the device is recovered, with the configuration lost, you know something is up with the device.

If you plan to enable this feature for security, make sure that you maintain configuration backups of your device.

Here is the code example to enable this feature on your Cisco device:

```
Router1#enable
Password:
Router1#configure terminal
Enter configuration commands, one per line.  End with CNTL/Z.
Router1(config)#no service password-recovery
Router1(config)#end
```

Managing services

Many services run in the background on Cisco devices. These services are often unused for your network, but unfortunately leave holes in your system that allow attackers to gain access to it. If you are not using these services, consider disabling them on your devices.

The following small services can easily be disabled with a pair of commands, `no service tcp-small-servers` and `no service udp-small-servers`:

✦ `echo` (port number 7)

✦ `discard` (port number 9)

✦ `daytime` (port number 13)

✦ `chargen` (port number 19)

In addition, the following list of commands disables other common services that you likely do not need to have running on your system. Most of these commands are issued in Global Configuration mode:

✦ `no ip finger`

✦ `no ip bootp server`

✦ `no ip dhcp boot ignore`

✦ `no service dhcp`

✦ `no mop enabled`

✦ `no ip domain-lookup`

✦ `no service pad`

✦ `no ip http server`

✦ `no ip http secure-server`

✦ `no service config`

✦ `no cdp enable`

✦ `no cdp run`

✦ `no lldp transmit`

✦ `no lldp receive`

✦ `no lldp run global`

Setting up timeouts

Without setting up timeout settings for Privileged EXEC Mode, your sessions stay open indefinitely. This is especially true of the console port. I have plugged in to console ports of clients' devices, only to find out that I am in Privileged EXEC mode or Global Configuration mode from their last session, which may have been months ago. Because they did not log out and I had access to the console port, I had no problem getting elevated permissions.

To avoid this potentially dangerous situation, you need only type a command in each of your configuration line interfaces. The command's format is exec-timeout <minutes> [seconds]. The default setting disables sessions after ten minutes; exec-timeout 0 disables the timeout altogether.

```
Router1#enable
Password:
Router1#configure terminal
Enter configuration commands, one per line.  End with CNTL/Z.
Router1(config)#line con 0
Router1(config)# exec-timeout 5
Router1(config)#line vty 0 4
Router1(config)# exec-timeout 5
Router1(config)#end
```

In addition to setting a timeout on these settings, you can force vty sessions to be encrypted via SSH. This is easy to implement with the following code example:

```
Router1#enable
Password:
Router1#configure terminal
Enter configuration commands, one per line.  End with CNTL/Z.
Router1(config)#line vty 0 4
Router1(config)# transport input ssh
Router1(config)#end
```

However, if you do not need to have remote terminal access to these devices, the better option is transport input none, which disables all vty access. In addition to this inbound access, you can create management SSH sessions from one device to another. So by connecting to one device, you can then launch a connection from that device to connect to another device. Limiting this connection may be accomplished with transport output ssh, which limits you to an outgoing SSH session, whereas transport output none can prevent all outbound connections.

Keeping alive TCP

Transmission Control Protocol (TCP) sessions eventually timeout, whereas the TCP keepalive command sends periodic packets to keep these sessions alive and available. Another benefit of this command is that half-opened or orphaned connections are also dropped.

The TCP sessions that are monitored can be inbound or outbound. You can specify which direction you want these keepalive commands to operate. The following set of commands run them in both directions:

```
Router1#enable
Password:
Router1#configure terminal
Enter configuration commands, one per line.   End with CNTL/Z.
Router1(config)#service tcp-keepalive-in
Router1(config)#service tcp-keepalive-out
Router1(config)#end
```

Leaving room for management

With recent versions of the Cisco IOS, you can reserve memory space for access to the console. When your device is under attack, the typical attack profile attempts to overflow the available memory on the device to exploit weaknesses. The side effect of this is that when you attempt to connect to the console to see what is happening to the device, you find that you cannot get access because there is no memory for even the console session to operate.

Cisco provides a method to reserve a block of memory for the console. This means that when you need to launch the console session, memory is always available. In this example, I reserve 4MB of space for the console session:

```
Router1#enable
Password:
Router1#configure terminal
Enter configuration commands, one per line.   End with CNTL/Z.
Router1(config)#memory reserve console 4096
Router1(config)#end
```

Securing SNMP

Simple Network Management Protocol (SNMP) is one of the small IP-based services that runs on your Cisco devices. If you use SNMP on your network, you can increase your security by using strong community names (which are like passwords) or by disabling the services if you are not using them. In the following example, I set the community names to understandable names; however, in production, community names are treated like strong alphanumeric passwords.

```
Router1#enable
Password:
Router1#configure terminal
Enter configuration commands, one per line.   End with CNTL/Z.
Router1(config)#snmp-server community READONLYPW RO
Router1(config)#snmp-server community READWRITEPW RW
Router1(config)#end
```

To then properly secure this traffic further, you can implement an ACL such as the following two ACLs, which restrict access to the ReadOnly connections to one segment of the network (192.168.8.0/24) and access to the ReadWrite connections to a single host (192.168.8.10).

```
Router1#enable
Password:
Router1#configure terminal
Enter configuration commands, one per line.  End with CNTL/Z.
Router1(config)#access-list 90 permit 192.168.8.0 0.0.0.255
Router1(config)#access-list 91 permit 192.168.8.10
Router1(config)#
Router1(config)#snmp-server community READONLY RO 90
Router1(config)#snmp-server community READWRITE RW 91
Router1(config)#end
```

Replacing and rolling back

Current Cisco IOS versions allow you a few new commands to manage your configuration backups and archiving. Backup and archiving give you an easier recovery process for configuration errors. Remember, a good configuration management process (such as the IT Infrastructure Library (ITIL) configuration) helps, but backup and archiving are tools to help you as well.

If you have archived a configuration, you can replace the current running configuration with an archived copy manually or automatically. The manual process makes use of the `configure replace` command issued in Privileged EXEC mode. This command replaces the running configuration with the contents of the file. If you use the command `copy <filename> running-config`, you actually merge the two files.

To enable the archiving feature, which is strongly recommended by Cisco for all supported devices, you need only issue five easy commands. The following command set saves the archives to the specified path, automatically creates a new archive every 1,440 minutes (once a day), saves the last 14 files, and takes an extra archive when you issue the `write memory` command:

```
Router1#enable
Password:
Router1#configure terminal
Enter configuration commands, one per line.  End with CNTL/Z.
Router1(config)#archive
Router1(config-archive)# path flash:archived-config
Router1(config-archive)# maximum 14
Router1(config-archive)# time-period 1440
Router1(config-archive)# write-memory
Router1(config-archive)#end
```

If you are low on space on your devices, you may want to reduce the number of archives you save on your device.

After the archiving system is configured, you can force an archive to be generated with `archive config` command and see the list of archives using the `show archive` command. Both of these commands are executed in Privileged EXEC mode. Here is what the commands looks like:

```
Router1#archive config

Router1#show archive
There are currently 5 archive configurations saved.
The next archive file will be named flash:archived-config-5
  Archive #  Name
    0
    1        flash:archived-config-1
    2        flash:archived-config-2
    3        flash:archived-config-3
    4        flash:archived-config-4 <- Most Recent
    5
    6
    7
    8
    9
    10
    11
    12
    13
    14
```

Taking the talking stick with terminal lock

In larger IT shops, having several people who make configuration changes on your network devices is common. One thing that can happen is that they start tripping over each other in making the changes. Nothing can be more annoying than starting to make a configuration change that someone else is in middle of making. This can lead to a lot of confusion, and worse, corrupt the configuration. To avoid this problem, Cisco provides an exclusive editing option so that only one user or session can make configuration changes on a device at a time, by implementing configuration mode exclusive.

The configuration mode exclusive system operates in either Manual or Automatic mode. In Automatic mode, exclusive access is granted automatically to the first user who enters Configuration mode using the configure terminal command. In Manual mode, the user needs to issue the command configure terminal lock. To enable Automatic mode, use these commands:

```
Router1#enable
Password:
Router1#configure terminal
Enter configuration commands, one per line.  End with CNTL/Z.
Router1(config)#configuration mode exclusive auto
Router1(config)#end
Router1#configure terminal
Enter configuration commands, one per line.  End with CNTL/Z.
Router1(config)#
*Apr 22 19:31:44.825:  Configuration mode locked exclusively. The lock will be
    cleared once you exit out of configuration mode using end/exit
Router1(config)#exit
Router1#
*Apr 22 19:32:09.617: %SYS-5-CONFIG_I: Configured from console by console
```

In the following code, notice that after enabling the Manual mode, you can still enter Configuration mode without engaging the lock. Enable the Manual mode as follows:

```
Router1#enable
Password:
Router1#configure terminal
Enter configuration commands, one per line.  End with CNTL/Z.
Router1(config)#configuration mode exclusive manual
Router1(config)#end
Router1#configure terminal
Enter configuration commands, one per line.  End with CNTL/Z.
Router1 (config)#hostname NewRouter1
NewRouter1(config)#exit
NewRouter1#
*Jun 24 20:20:44.079: %SYS-5-CONFIG_I: Configured from console by console
NewRouter1#configure terminal lock
Enter configuration commands, one per line.  End with CNTL/Z.
NewRouter1(config)#
*Jun 24 20:21:04.051:  Configuration mode locked exclusively. The lock will be
    cleared once you exit out of configuration mode using end/exit
NewRouter1(config)#hostname Router1
Router1(config)#exit
Router1#
*Jun 24 20:21:31.567: %SYS-5-CONFIG_I: Configured from console by console
```

Using logs to tell you what is going on

Cisco allows newer IOS versions to log configuration changes that have been made on your Cisco devices. Many of the configuration management changes that have been incorporated into the IOS make it easier for IT departments to be ITIL-oriented and compliant. ITIL places a heavy focus on configuration management and change management on all your IT resources.

The hidekeys and logging size commands can improve the default settings by removing password data from the logs and increasing the size of the change log. Additionally, you can have this change information sent to your Syslog server. Doing so is all recommended by Cisco as part of configuration management.

```
Router1#enable
Password:
Router1#configure terminal
Enter configuration commands, one per line.  End with CNTL/Z.
Router1(config)#archive
Router1(config-archive)# log config
Router1(config-archive-log-cfg)#  logging enable
Router1(config-archive-log-cfg)#  logging size 200
Router1(config-archive-log-cfg)#  hidekeys
Router1(config-archive-log-cfg)#  notify syslog
Router1(config-archive)#end
```

To view your current configuration for logging, use the following command in Privileged EXEC mode:

```
Router1#show archive log config all
  idx   sess         user@line       Logged command
    1    1       console@console  |  logging enable
    2    1       console@console  |  configure terminal
    3    1       console@console  |  archive
    4    1       console@console  | log config
    5    1       console@console  |  logging enable
    6    1       console@console  |  logging size 200
    7    1       console@console  |  hidekeys
    8    1       console@console  |  notify syslog
```

Managing network features

Many default network features are not typically necessary and can be exploited by unnamed people who attack your network. Here are some commands you need to consider running to secure your devices:

+ `Router1(config)#no ip source-routing`

+ `Router1(config-if)#no ip redirects`

+ `Router1(config)#ip dhcp snooping`

+ `Router1(config)#ip dhcp snooping vlan <vlan-range>`

+ `Router1(config-if)#ip verify source`

In addition to these useful commands, consider enabling some of the port security features available on your Cisco devices. These are particularly good for your switches to prevent users from doing things they should not be doing.

Port security

Port security allows you to enable several security options related to the ports on your switch. This includes settings like the number of devices that are connected to each switch port, which can prevent users from connecting unauthorized network switches or access points. The following code example performs several actions, which include:

+ Configuring ports for connecting to access devices rather than switches

+ Having the device remember devices connected by a Media Access Control (MAC) address

+ Setting a maximum number of possible devices

+ Setting an action for violation of the restrictions, such as protect, restrict, shutdown, and shutdown VLAN

```
Switch1#enable
Password:
Switch1#configure terminal
Enter configuration commands, one per line.  End with CNTL/Z.
Switch1(config)#interface fastEthernet 0/1
Switch1(config-if)#  switchport
Switch1(config-if)#  switchport mode access
Switch1(config-if)#  switchport port-security
Switch1(config-if)#  switchport port-security mac-address sticky
Switch1(config-if)#  switchport port-security maximum 2
Switch1(config-if)#  switchport port-security violation shutdown
Switch1(config-if)#end
```

When the port has been shutdown or disabled, you can re-enable the port or interface by issuing the `shutdown` and `no shutdown` commands in succession.

Anti-spoofing ACLs

Some attempted break-ins to your network are done by spoofing an IP address so that the attacker attempts to make his own outside address look like an address in your network. To deal with this issue, you can configure your router to drop or discard packets that come in from outside interfaces with purported internal addresses. This can be done with the following commands in which the external interface of the router is `FastEthernet0/1`, and the internal addresses encompass the 192.168.0.0/24 and 10.0.0.0/8 networks.

```
Router1#enable
Password:
Router1#configure terminal
Enter configuration commands, one per line.  End with CNTL/Z.
Router1(config)#ip access-list extended ACL-ANTISPOOF-IN
Router1(config-ext-nacl)# deny    ip 10.0.0.0 0.255.255.255 any
Router1(config-ext-nacl)# deny    ip 192.168.0.0 0.0.255.255 any
Router1(config-ext-nacl)# exit
Router1(config)#interface fastEthernet0/1
Router1(config-if)# ip access-group ACL-ANTISPOOF-IN in
Router1(config-if)#end
```

Getting Physical with Security

Obvious, but often disregarded, advice is to always secure the physical access to your network infrastructure. There are uncounted methods of disrupting your network if an attacker gains physical access to your switches and routers. Many companies either do not realize their risk or choose to ignore it by inadequate physical security.

Physical security need not be complex: Simply installing locks on doors is the key to physical security. An inexpensive lock from the hardware store is an easy start to this security process. Figure 4-3 shows a more complex (and more secure) lock that uses proximity cards.

As your security needs increase, systems, such as the one shown in Figure 4-3, allow you to control access to all areas of your building and offer logging of who opens which doors and when.

If your networking equipment needs to be out in the open (not in a dedicated room with a secure lock), make sure you have the equipment secured in a lockable communications rack that is mounted to a wall. These are standard 19-inch racks about 2 feet in height that are mounted to a wall but come with a locking door on the front of the unit, such as the APC NetShelter WX 13U Wall Mounted Rack (AR100HD) available from www.apc.com.

Figure 4-3:
A standard
proximity
card and
card reader.

Index

• *U* •

• X •

Notes

Notes

Notes

Apple & Macs

iPad For Dummies
978-0-470-58027-1

iPhone For Dummies,
4th Edition
978-0-470-87870-5

MacBook For Dummies, 3rd
Edition
978-0-470-76918-8

Mac OS X Snow Leopard For
Dummies
978-0-470-43543-4

Business

Bookkeeping For Dummies
978-0-7645-9848-7

Job Interviews
For Dummies,
3rd Edition
978-0-470-17748-8

Resumes For Dummies,
5th Edition
978-0-470-08037-5

Starting an
Online Business
For Dummies,
6th Edition
978-0-470-60210-2

Stock Investing
For Dummies,
3rd Edition
978-0-470-40114-9

Successful
Time Management
For Dummies
978-0-470-29034-7

Computer Hardware

BlackBerry
For Dummies,
4th Edition
978-0-470-60700-8

Computers For Seniors
For Dummies,
2nd Edition
978-0-470-53483-0

PCs For Dummies,
Windows
7 Edition
978-0-470-46542-4

Laptops For Dummies,
4th Edition
978-0-470-57829-2

Cooking & Entertaining

Cooking Basics
For Dummies,
3rd Edition
978-0-7645-7206-7

Wine For Dummies,
4th Edition
978-0-470-04579-4

Diet & Nutrition

Dieting For Dummies,
2nd Edition
978-0-7645-4149-0

Nutrition For Dummies,
4th Edition
978-0-471-79868-2

Weight Training
For Dummies,
3rd Edition
978-0-471-76845-6

Digital Photography

Digital SLR Cameras &
Photography For Dummies,
3rd Edition
978-0-470-46606-3

Photoshop Elements 8
For Dummies
978-0-470-52967-6

Gardening

Gardening Basics
For Dummies
978-0-470-03749-2

Organic Gardening
For Dummies,
2nd Edition
978-0-470-43067-5

Green/Sustainable

Raising Chickens
For Dummies
978-0-470-46544-8

Green Cleaning
For Dummies
978-0-470-39106-8

Health

Diabetes For Dummies,
3rd Edition
978-0-470-27086-8

Food Allergies
For Dummies
978-0-470-09584-3

Living Gluten-Free
For Dummies,
2nd Edition
978-0-470-58589-4

Hobbies/General

Chess For Dummies,
2nd Edition
978-0-7645-8404-6

Drawing
Cartoons & Comics
For Dummies
978-0-470-42683-8

Knitting For Dummies,
2nd Edition
978-0-470-28747-7

Organizing
For Dummies
978-0-7645-5300-4

Su Doku For Dummies
978-0-470-01892-7

Home Improvement

Home Maintenance
For Dummies,
2nd Edition
978-0-470-43063-7

Home Theater
For Dummies,
3rd Edition
978-0-470-41189-6

Living the
Country Lifestyle
All-in-One
For Dummies
978-0-470-43061-3

Solar Power Your Home
For Dummies,
2nd Edition
978-0-470-59678-4

Internet

Blogging For Dummies,
3rd Edition
978-0-470-61996-4

eBay For Dummies,
6th Edition
978-0-470-49741-8

Facebook For Dummies,
3rd Edition
978-0-470-87804-0

Web Marketing
For Dummies,
2nd Edition
978-0-470-37181-7

WordPress
For Dummies,
3rd Edition
978-0-470-59274-8

Language & Foreign Language

French For Dummies
978-0-7645-5193-2

Italian Phrases
For Dummies
978-0-7645-7203-6

Spanish For Dummies,
2nd Edition
978-0-470-87855-2

Spanish
For Dummies,
Audio Set
978-0-470-09585-0

Math & Science

Algebra I
For Dummies,
2nd Edition
978-0-470-55964-2

Biology For Dummies,
2nd Edition
978-0-470-59875-7

Calculus For Dummies
978-0-7645-2498-1

Chemistry For Dummies
978-0-7645-5430-8

Microsoft Office

Excel 2010 For Dummies
978-0-470-48953-6

Office 2010 All-in-One
For Dummies
978-0-470-49748-7

Office 2010 For Dummies,
Book + DVD Bundle
978-0-470-62698-6

Word 2010 For Dummies
978-0-470-48772-3

Music

Guitar For Dummies,
2nd Edition
978-0-7645-9904-0

iPod & iTunes For
Dummies, 8th Edition
978-0-470-87871-2

Piano Exercises
For Dummies
978-0-470-38765-8

Parenting & Education

Parenting For Dummies,
2nd Edition
978-0-7645-5418-6

Type 1 Diabetes
For Dummies
978-0-470-17811-9

Pets

Cats For Dummies,
2nd Edition
978-0-7645-5275-5

Dog Training For Dummies,
3rd Edition
978-0-470-60029-0

Puppies For Dummies,
2nd Edition
978-0-470-03717-1

Religion & Inspiration

The Bible For Dummies
978-0-7645-5296-0

Catholicism For Dummies
978-0-7645-5391-2

Women in the Bible
For Dummies
978-0-7645-8475-6

Self-Help & Relationship

Anger Management
For Dummies
978-0-470-03715-7

Overcoming Anxiety
For Dummies,
2nd Edition
978-0-470-57441-6

Sports

Baseball
For Dummies,
3rd Edition
978-0-7645-7537-2

Basketball
For Dummies,
2nd Edition
978-0-7645-5248-9

Golf For Dummies,
3rd Edition
978-0-471-76871-5

Web Development

Web Design
All-in-One
For Dummies
978-0-470-41796-6

Web Sites
Do-It-Yourself
For Dummies,
2nd Edition
978-0-470-56520-9

Windows 7

Windows 7
For Dummies
978-0-470-49743-2

Windows 7
For Dummies,
Book + DVD Bundle
978-0-470-52398-8

Windows 7 All-in-One
For Dummies
978-0-470-48763-1

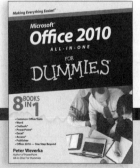

Available wherever books are sold. For more information or to order direct: U.S. customers visit www.dummies.com or call 1-877-762-29
U.K. customers visit www.wileyeurope.com or call (0) 1243 843291. Canadian customers visit www.wiley.ca or call 1-800-567-4797.

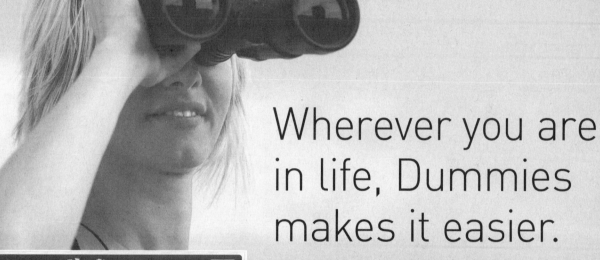

Wherever you are in life, Dummies makes it easier.

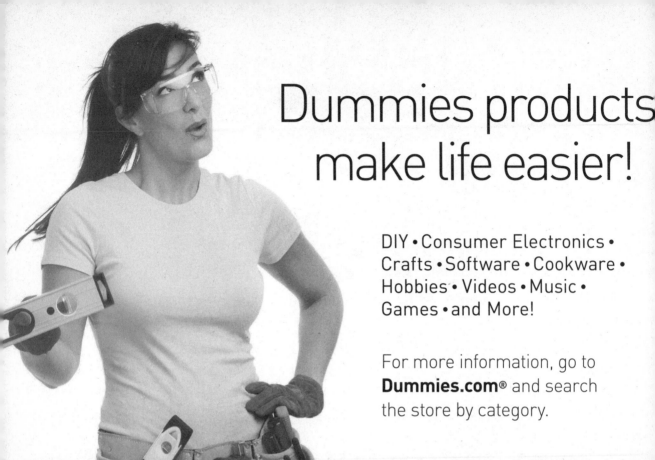

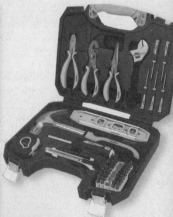